45.00

✔ 70335

Hollywood's Overseas Campaign: The North Atlantic Movie Trade, 1920–1950 examines how Hollywood movies became one of the most successful U.S. exports, a phenomenon that began during World War I. Focusing on Canada, the market closest to the United States, on Great Britain, the biggest market, and on the U.S. movie industry itself, Ian Jarvie documents how the fear of this mass medium's impact and covetousness toward its profits motivated many nations to resist the cultural invasion and economic drain that Hollywood movies represented. The national sentiments used to justify resistance to Hollywood imports are shown to be essentially disingenuous, in that they were motivated by special-interest groups that felt their power threatened by U.S. movies or considered themselves entitled to some of the profits. The efforts of various Canadian and British interest groups to limit film imports and foster domestic production failed because of lack of capital, mismanaged propaganda campaigns, and audience resistance. Indeed, as Ian Jarvie argues, Hollywood's ability to exploit their weaknesses derived, to a great extent, from its mastery of supply, distribution, and the coherent orchestration of the component parts of the industry through the Motion Picture Producers and Distributors of America.

"Ian Jarvie has dug up a mountain of primary documents and if by no other criterion *Hollywood's Overseas Campaign* stands as a major book in the history of the cinema as a world institution."

    – Douglas Gomery, University of Maryland, College Park

	Canada	Great Britain	United States
1920			
1921			
1922			Fordney–McCumber tariffs MPPDA formed
1923			
1924			
1925	MPDEC formed		
1926	⊢——— Imperial Economic Conference ———⊣		Canty appointed
1927		Cinematograph Films Act	
1928	⊢——————— Motion picture industry converts to sound ———————⊣		
1929			Hawley–Smoot tariffs
1930			
1931	White Report		
1932	Trial of Famous Players		
	⊢——— Ottawa Imperial Conference imposes Imperial Preference Tariffs ———⊣		
1933			
1934	Ontario Film Bureau wound up		
1935			NRA Code for motion picture industry
1936		Moyne Report	
1937			
1938	National Film Board founded	Cinematograph Films Act renewed	Antitrust suit launched against U.S. major producers
1939		⊢—— Anglo–American Film Agreement signed ——⊣	
1940			
1941			
1942		⊢—————Lend–Lease begins—————⊣	
1943			
1944		Palache Report	Berle memorandum
1945		⊢—————Lend–Lease canceled—————⊣	Johnston succeeds Hays MPEA formed
1946		⊢————U.S. loans G.B. $3.75 billion————⊣	
1947		⊢—— MPEA boycott of British market begins ——⊣	
1948		⊢——— Boycott ends with agreement ———⊣	
		Cinematograph Films Act renewed	
	⊢——————— GATT finalized ———————⊣		
			Antitrust suit settled by consent decrees HUAC investigates the movies
1949	Canadian Cooperation Project launched	NFFC started	
1950			

Hollywood's Overseas Campaign
The North Atlantic Movie Trade, 1920–1950

Cambridge Studies in the History of Mass Communications

General Editors:

Garth S. Jowett and Kenneth R. M. Short, University of Houston

Advisory Board:

Erik Barnouw, Columbia University, Emeritus
Lord Asa Briggs, Worcester College, Oxford University
Jean-Noël Jeanney, University of Paris
Frederick Kahlenberg, University of Mannheim
Everette Dennis, Gannett Center for Media Studies, Columbia University
Thomas Cripps, Morgan State Univeristy

Cinema and Soviet Society, 1917–1953, Peter Kenez, University of California, Santa Cruz

Hollywood's Overseas Campaign: The North Atlantic Movie Trade, 1920–1950, Ian Jarvie, York University, Toronto

Hollywood's Overseas Campaign
The North Atlantic Movie Trade, 1920–1950

Ian Jarvie
York University, Toronto

CAMBRIDGE
UNIVERSITY PRESS

Published by the Press Syndicate of the University of Cambridge
The Pitt Building, Trumpington Street, Cambridge CB2 1RP
40 West 20th Street, New York, NY 10011-4211, USA
10 Stamford Road, Oakleigh, Victoria 3166, Australia

First published 1992

Printed in the United States of America

Library of Congress Cataloging-in-Publication Data

Jarvie, I. C. (Ian Charles). 1937–
Hollywood's Overseas Campaign: The North Atlantic Movie Trade, 1920–1950 /
Ian Jarvie.
    p.   cm. – (Cambridge studies in the history of mass communications)
Includes bibliographical references (p.   ) and indexes.
ISBN 0–521–41566–7 (hc)
1. Motion pictures, American – Marketing.   2. Motion picture industry – United
States – History.   3. Motion pictures – Canada.   4. Motion pictures – Great
Britian.   I. Title.   II. Series.
PN1993.5.U6J3   1992
384'.8'0973–dc20   92–7723

A catalog record for this book is available from the British Library.

ISBN 0-521-41566-7   hardback

Passages from archives in the Public Records Office (Kew, Richmond,
Surrey) are reproduced with the permission of the Controller of Her
Majesty's Stationery Office.

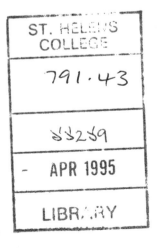

To the memory of
Brian Sanders
(1937–1987)

The act of perceiving or conceiving the past can be undertaken in many different ways, few of which can legitimately be described as historical. The behaviour and goals of the public prosecutor are not to be confused with those of the historian, no matter what parallels can be found between the investigatory methods of the historian and those of the professional detective. The discovery of guilt and the rebuking of sin are exercised in criminology and theology not historiography. The historian who chooses to indulge in these activities is stepping aside from or outside the responsibilities, duties and obligations of his craft.

– D. C. Watt, *Personalities and Politics*

To an extraordinary but understandable extent, the history of inter-war imperial economic policy is the history of negotiations with respect to objectively insignificant goods.

– Ian N. Drummond, *British Economic Policy and the Empire, 1919–1939*

Contents

Tables and Figures

Tables

Preface

This is a study of the growth, structure, and direction of trade in motion pictures between Canada, the United Kingdom, and the United States over the period 1920–50. It is largely based on official documents; press reports and other secondary materials have been used sparingly. A few remarks about the spirit in which the research was undertaken may be helpful.

At the time covered by this book, British and American film critics and historians displayed ambivalence when writing about Hollywood and its works. They admitted that in the silent-film era much interesting entertainment and film art was created but claimed that after the arrival of sound, creative directors were constrained and even sometimes silenced by commercial considerations. (The unsatisfactory careers of Stroheim, Von Sternberg, and Welles were frequently cited.) These critics and historians loved art and distrusted commerce, so the public's manifest liking for Hollywood commercial films needed explanation. Condemning public taste was an option to be used with caution. It was preferable to condemn commerce for minimizing the art available to the public, while lavishing praise upon enclaves where art was said to flourish, such as documentary or avant-garde films. A similar ambivalence toward American films lives on in some present-day film scholars. The devotions of the screening room and the keyboard yield exposés of American commercial films as oppressive and reactionary.

By contrast with this ambivalence, I share the positive attitude of the public toward American films. Whether Hollywood produced art or commercial products, its dominance of world film trade was a fact – a fact deserving historical explanation. One advantage of this point of view is some detachment from cultural and nationalist concerns. The philosopher R. G. Collingwood argued that the point of view of the losers in history is almost impossible to retrieve (1939, p. 70). That is not my experience of studying the film trade across the North Atlantic. Canada and Britain were the losers, and their film-historian scribes have blamed lack of national will, philistinism, fifth columnists, various stabs in the back, and the like, assuming that some strategy existed that, had it been adopted, would have stemmed American film exports and neutralized their effects. This is a fond illusion. Different strategies could at most have delayed the outcome. The structural, entrepreneurial, and financial advantages of the U.S. firms, combined with the experience gained from catering to a diverse domestic audience, sanction a compelling explanation of the domination of world screens by the United States.

Distrust of commerce has often gone together, in writing about the national cinemas of Britain and Canada, with nationalist indignation about the dominant influence of American films. Such indignation is foreign to me. Born in the United Kingdom, a Canadian by naturalization, I have since school days shared with my friends an interest in and attraction to the United States and its civilization. Our primary means of contact was, of course, the movies (which, I would insist, we always knew romanticized, rather than accurately depicted, American society). It seemed to us odd that the films we liked and the civilization they depicted (which we also liked) were so regularly denigrated, and even denounced, by elites among our compatriots. Still, that raised an interesting question: Why were children growing up in the mother country of a great empire extensively exposed to American films? An obvious answer was that non-Americans like ourselves enjoyed them. A follow-up question then was, Why did we enjoy American films more than we enjoyed British films?

This book concentrates on the first problem. It gives relatively short shrift to the films themselves, being mainly concerned with the industrial strategies used to market U.S. films and the complementary national policies Canada and Britain developed to resist them. Although there is some discussion of the nature of overseas demand for the American film product, this is not the main emphasis. We, the overseas audience, preferred U.S. films to our own and readily cooperated with whatever schemes Hollywood devised.

I find nothing to apologize for and nothing incorrect about my youthful (and to some extent continuing) preference for American films over all others, including British. Similarly, trying to explain the course of the trade struggle, I see no reason to pretend that U.S. dominance owed much to British and Canadian mistakes. The United States did indeed have a fifth column in Britain and Canada – namely, the strong demand for American movies among overseas audiences. In the course of the book I venture some ideas on the source and strength of this demand. But American success still needs explanation. After all, the U.S. film industry could have blundered and failed to exploit the demand for its products. From time to time there were episodes of bungling, but none so serious that American dominance was jeopardized. How is that dominance to be explained?

Studying these matters through the medium of official documents disclosed a multiplicity of viewpoints. This posed problems for the book's structure. Events and processes were viewed differently by observers in each country.

The Imperial Conference of 1926, for example, looked different to each participating country: To the Dominions (of which Canada was one) it appeared an occasion to affirm Empire loyalty but also an opportunity to lobby, and perhaps even to assert some independence of, the mother country. To the United Kingdom it appeared an occasion to rally Empire support of the mother country and to further policies aimed at maximizing British influence. To the United States, which was of course an outsider country looking on, it appeared to be an episode of conspiracy to, among other things, discriminate against American exports. These differing appearances impaired the attempts of official and other elites in each country to grasp how the conference was viewed in the other two. Thus the important statement of policy regarding the desirability of British motion picture production made at the conference (reproduced as Figure 2.A.) was variously interpreted.

The historian with access to at least some documents from all three countries, and some inclination to find a coherent explanation of events, tries to put together a big picture that makes sense of all the partial views: why they were held, why they were partial, and how action based upon incomplete assessments fell out in practice. Able to read both sides of all the bilateral exchanges, we can try to assess whether one or the other side saw matters more clearly or whether both were mistaken. Yet it is also important to try to see matters as they seemed to participants, with the partial information available to them and the interpretations they chose to put upon it. How the actors view the situation they are in is vital to grasping its logic (Jarvie 1972, Chap. 1).

The structural narrative problem presented to the historian by this multiplicity of viewpoints is the question of how to sustain narrative momentum and coherence while also giving voice to the many, overlapping views of the participants. A strictly chronological structure would move intolerably slowly, since each event or process would have to be rotated through all points of view. It would also require constant digression, to draw out from the detail the overall historical interpretation of the successive views the different countries were taking. My first thought was to try crosscutting, that venerable editing device perfected in two classic films of D. W. Griffith. At the end of *Birth of a Nation* (1915), he cut back and forth between scenes showing marauding soldiers closing in on helpless people and others showing the hooded KKK riding to the rescue. He modified this pattern in his next film, *Intolerance*, where four stories of intolerance from different periods of history were set up in parallel and then intercut at an increasing pace as they reached their denouements. What Griffith could do with fictional narrative where form and content were one did not suit the historical purpose of doing justice to real events. These real events have some shape to them, perhaps, but certainly not that of narrative closure.

It was in Christopher Thorne's magisterial work *Allies of a Kind* (1978) that I found a model for the present topic. That book is a study in Anglo–American relations as refracted through the war against Japan (1941–5). The book's four main parts are chronological divisions. Thorne covers each period by giving first an overview, then an account of the events in the war, then American and British views on China, on empire in Southeast Asia, on India, and on Australia and the southwestern Pacific. Of course, his model needed modification for my purposes. Although my time span – 1920–50 – is longer, both the subject and the events and processes are far less portentous. Therefore I could afford to organize by country first, then by period. In lieu of three overviews, I have one – the General Introduction – and I commence the study of Canada (Part I) with a close examination of a single episode of 1930–2, the investigation of Famous Players Canadian Corporation for monopolistic practices, their trial and acquittal, an episode that contains within it the central problems of the international film trade as they affected and were affected by Canada (Chapter 1). Having thus plunged into the problems, I subsequently present a chronological narrative of film-trade matters in Canada, splitting it into a flashback to events before the emblematic episode of the antitrust trial (Chapter 2), followed by an account of subsequent events (Chapter 3).

The British and American parts (Parts II and III) follow a more orthodox temporal organization. The three countries are arranged in the book in ascending order of economic importance and also, not incidentally, ascending order of volume of official documentation. Thus events and processes covered sketchily at first in Part I are returned to with more detail and, I hope, more complete explanations, in Parts II and III. The American part specifically revisits some earlier matters to broaden the perspective. This is because I believe that a full grasp of American actions is the key to explaining much that went before. Although Canada and Britain were responding to U.S. actions as they understood them, the Americans, by contrast, were initiating events for reasons that need to be worked out and with successes and failures that need to be assessed carefully. Such working out and assessment are woven into the narrative of the American part, a narrative that is, of course, without closure.

My structure, then, reveals a thesis: Studies of the Canadian film industry such as those by Peter Morris and Pierre Berton, studies of the British film industry such as those by Rachel Low, Michael Chanan, Margaret Dickinson and Sarah Street, and the contributors to Curran and Porter (1983), lack a crucial explanatory dimension. Many events in the history of the film industry in those countries were driven by real or anticipated American actions. But those American actions cannot be explained using only the point of view of officials, journalists, and historians working within their own country. With the exception of Dickinson and Street, none of the histories just mentioned saw fit to examine the U.S. materials. Dickinson and Street used them selectively, and their controlling interpretations were entirely

British-centered. At the risk of my interpretations striking the reader as American-centered, I shall argue that a broader explanatory framework is possible when one takes into account materials from all three countries. Only then can one venture to suggest that there is a difference between how things seemed in the three countries and how they were, and it is this methodologically crucial discrepancy between the views in the materials and the viewpoint of the book that warrants hope that it is a contribution to history.

This book has been in the making for almost ten years, ensuring that my list of debts is long. A great deal of travel and study away from my home university was necessary and was made possible by Canada's Social Science and Humanities Research Council (Grants 410-85-0209, 410-86-0548, 451-86-288), York University's internal research funds, and St. John's College, Cambridge, which granted me two terms in residence as a Visiting Overseas Student in 1987. To each of these, my thanks. I made use of the facilities of numerous libraries and public archives, most of which are included in the list of sources in the References. Over this long haul I have benefited from discussions with, among others, Robert Allen, Gregory Black, Marybelle Burch, Noel Carroll, Richard Collins, Thomas Cripps, David Culbert, Charles Harpole, Florence Jacobowitz, Richard Jewell, Garth Jowett, Richard Kozarski, D. L. LeMahieu, Robert Macmillan, John O'Connor, Nicholas Pronay, K. R. M. Short, Peter Stead, Sari Thomas, William Ulriccio, and the anonymous readers for Cambridge University Press. Beatrice Rehl, Michael Gnat, and Christie Lerch did wonders in the final stages. Although I thank them all, it is important to be clear that the responsibility for what is herein claimed and argued is mine. It remains to note the dedication to the memory of my oldest and dearest friend, Brian Sanders. Brian was a diplomatic historian, and he and I often talked out historical matters and ideas. He lived in Washington, DC, and I enjoyed his hospitality on many research trips to the National Archives. It grieves me deeply that because he was the victim of a senseless and unsolved street murder he will not see this book, and it and I will not have had the benefit of his keen and good-humored criticism.

General introduction

A. The problem and its context

Why were American films the dominant cinema fare of Canada and Great Britain after World War I? The answer proposed in this book is that the American film industry, exploiting the lessons learned in the competitive domestic market, was able to take advantage of the disruption of film production in belligerent countries caused by World War I. Production capacity in the United States was raised to the limit and exports cultivated assiduously. Integrated corporations oligopolistically dominated supply at home and abroad. Advantage having been gained, product development and distribution policies were tailored to maintain that market share wherever legally permitted; where there were legal impediments they were disputed.

Overseas trade in American films brought up most of the issues attendant on the global spread of the artifacts of American popular culture in general, and of American mass media materials in particular. Those artifacts include films, popular literary forms (comics, paperbacks), popular music, popular dances, soft drinks, candy and fast food, modes of dress, and – latterly, and most prominent of all – television shows.[1] Not only American artifacts have spread. Jeremy Tunstall has argued that American influence reaches deeper still: The very forms in which mass media communications are delivered worldwide are struck from American templates. Newspapers, magazines, films, radio, and television in every language are modeled on American forms.[2]

The global spread of American popular culture was a cultural matter and a commercial matter at the same time (Ninkovich 1981). Free trade in culture is usually taken for granted; free trade in commerce, by contrast, is seldom taken for granted, and few countries ever strictly implement it. Free trade in popular culture is controversial both culturally and commercially. The performances of the Toronto Symphony are not monitored for Canadian content by a government agency, but popular music on Canada's radio stations is. There was no British Act of Parliament mandating a quota on the nationality of the novels in bookstores; but there was a Cinematograph

1

Films Act of 1927, twice renewed, that required the showing of a percentage of British films in British cinemas. Since the artifacts of popular culture were treated differently from those of traditional or "high" culture, they must have been conceived of as different sorts of things. Films were not in the same trade or cultural category as symphonies or novels.

Consider some ways in which traditional (high) and popular (mass) culture were different. Before the twentieth century, most traditional or high cultural goods traded freely but, it must be admitted, on quite a small scale. Music, opera, dance, the plastic arts were the pleasures of an elite, one that frequently adopted an internationalist outlook on culture. Mass culture, by contrast, was the pleasure not of these internationalized elites but of the inchoate masses of late industrial society, masses with purchasing power and electoral votes. Mass culture, unlike traditional or high culture, was not the unique product of artisans or of a cottage industry; its items were industrially produced on a large scale, part of a consumption-oriented economic system driven to expand its markets and its controls over markets, regardless of national boundaries. Mass culture did not claim to offer disembodied and timeless aesthetic experience, but rather delivered concrete pleasure to suit the quotidien life and fantasies of ordinary people. Such materials responded to, and reflected, the expectations of their audiences. Thus mass cultural commodities contained popular self-presentation of the originating society.

Motion pictures were an early focus of the arguments about whether free trade in popular culture was a Good Thing or a Bad Thing.[3] Motion pictures were a new commodity, of a kind not seen before. Their physical bulk as exports involved at most a few hundred items per year (cases containing film cans). Yet they were reusable and reproducible and could generate revenue greatly in excess of that produced by some raw material or manufactured good of comparable bulk. Unlike a piece of machinery or a ton of ore, though, motion pictures as cultural artifacts were taken to be the product of *mentalités,* capable in turn of influencing mentalities. In the post-Hegelian era, which took seriously a newly parochial view of culture, trade in those commodities thought to have cultural significance was singled out for a type of attention not granted other commodities. This attention was directed at both imports and exports of such goods. The import of cultural goods was the import of alien mentalities; the export of cultural goods offered foreigners a glimpse of the exporter's mentality, some but not all aspects of which might be suitable for broadcast.

The development of these lines of thought about popular culture was not without its analogs in debates about traditional or high culture. Members of the intellectual and cultural elites were capable of characterizing foreign music, writing, and opera as expressing the ethos of the countries where they were produced – as "Germanic" or "Italianate," for example – but this seldom led to the demand for direct curbs on cultural free trade (the exceptions are important ones). Such demands were likely to be met with the argument that traditional or high culture delivered a timeless and universal aesthetic pleasure that posed no threat to a nation, especially as its rewards were not accessible to the masses.[4] The small scale of the commerce involved in traditional or high culture was also a factor. Trade unions sometimes objected to foreigners being allowed to perform, but this was an issue of economic rather than cultural nationalism.

The period 1920–50 is simply a specific research period, by no means the whole of the matter. The problem of the rise of the American film industry to domestic and international dominance before 1920 is one that has been ably tackled by other historians. The work of Garth Jowett, Douglas Gomery, Lary May, Kristin Thompson, and Richard Kozarski is notable. By 1920 new historical realities were in place. After 1950 movies declined in relative commercial and cultural importance in comparison with television and popular music, but the lineaments of debate about American dominance continued, and the debate continues to this day. The shape of the problem, the parameters of debate about it, and the explanations offered in the case of films are much the same as those offered now that attention focuses more on television and music. Thus our research into the film situation and the many attempts to explain it will have a certain air of déjà vu, reminding us of arguments heard just yesterday, in discussions of the trade in television programs, cable systems, and satellite transmission.

B. Outline history of discussion of the problem

During and after the 1914–1918 war Hollywood films achieved world dominance with a completeness which astonished people in many countries and which has still not been fully explained.
— Jeremy Tunstall, *The Media Are American*

In seeking out why it was that American films dominated the cinema screens of Canada and Great Britain in the period under study, various possible lines of inquiry suggest themselves. Market domination could be explained by the product (films), by the consumers (audience), or by the suppliers. Breaking these possibilities down, we could look to:

(a) qualities of the American films themselves;
(b) absence of qualities in competing films;
(c) audience taste in Canada and Great Britain;
(d) audience distaste for competing films;
(e) the operations of the American industry that manufactured, distributed, and marketed the films; and
(f) the operations of American economic imperialism in general and media imperialism in particular.

All these lines of inquiry are fruitful and have been pursued at various times. The organized American motion picture industry itself thought that

(a) and (b) explained its domination. Contemporary British and Canadian observers of the situation feared that (c) and (d) were the explanation. Factors (a)–(d) all focus on the demand side of the issue. By contrast, factor (e), which I favor, concentrates on supply. Factor (f), a Marxian thesis, bypasses the classical economic analysis of supply and demand for an explanation in which both demand and supply are managed or manufactured by larger historical and political forces.

History, I take it, is the search for explanations of past events that puzzle us. The search has to be disciplined by primary evidence. The relevant evidence extends beyond the films. The political, social, and economic history of films cannot be separated from the general political, social, and economic history of the times. A general view of history that appeals to many writers about films is Marxism. Marxism reveals the plot of history, and the task of the historian is to work out the details. Thus the question of why it was that American films dominated the cinema screens of Canada and Great Britain between roughly 1920 and 1950 has been explained by the "media imperialism" thesis, the view that American domination of the mass media was part of the apparatus inevitably required to sustain the exploitation of the rest of the world by American capital. Dating back in film studies at least to the communist writers F. D. Klingender and Stuart Legg's *Money behind the screen,* in 1937,[5] this thesis was recycled by Guback in 1969 and has become a received view.

Such non-Marxist literature as there is on our question divides, as noted, between those who seek explanation in the films and the audiences and those who seek explanation in the industry. A rough differentiation would call the first "explanations from demand" and the second "explanations from supply." One of the earliest and best explanations from demand was penned by John Grierson, later famous in the documentary movement in Britain and Canada. Grierson had traveled in the United States in the 1920s and familiarized himself with sociological thinking, so that when he was asked to prepare an analysis of the domination of British screens by American films in the 1920s and also to seek out opportunities where Britain's film industry might compete, he produced in 1928 a penetrating document.[6] Treating films as a social institution, Grierson fastened on the audience satisfactions American films delivered. American films were, he held, optimistic in outlook, full of practical example and vitality. British films, by contrast, lacked encouragement and did not make you feel good. Grierson commended the production values of American films, their blending together of sex, adventure, and violence. The star system was peculiarly apposite to individualistic cultures. He thought the opportunity for British producers lay in epic films, films about the Empire, and short, semieducational films.

Jeffrey Richards (1984) and Peter Stead (1981, 1982, 1989) have taken Grierson-type ideas a good deal farther, offering evidence that class and regional divisions in Great Britain made the West End odor of so many British films unacceptable to large numbers of cinemagoers, who much preferred the exotic but not totally strange idiom of American films.[7] (Although there are only hints of evidence, a similar line of thought applied to Canada, at least to its English-speaking population.)[8] A limited audience loyalty to the local film product, and favorable attitudes to the American product, are certainly part of the answer to our question. Audience resistance is not something readily overcome, nor is a partiality for the competition. Nevertheless, demand does not invariably conjure up appropriate supply, and satisfying foreign demand was never at the top of the American film industry's agenda.

What is the explanatory value of supply? As all commentators note and emphasize, the American film industry primarily catered to the U.S. domestic market.[9] That domestic market happened to be quite large, virtually as many seats as the rest of the world's cinemas put together. Considerable entrepreneurial and organizational skills were required to market and distribute commodities throughout the length and breadth of that vast country. There was regional diversity as well as ethnic complexity, and in our period rapid urbanization was under way (see §D). Thus, American film entrepreneurs faced domestic challenges in supply and demand. Their success helped prepare them for the international market.

A number of writers – the anonymous authors of *The British Film Industry* (1952); Douglas Gomery (1979) and those influenced by him; and, most notably, Kristin Thompson (1985) – have concentrated on the advantages of the industrial organization of the American film industry. The industrial policies honed in the United States domestic film market were applicable abroad; they consisted primarily of division of labor, economies of scale, vertical integration, and substantial expenditure on publicity. Concentration on the strategic function of distribution, and the vertical integration of firms upward or downward from that middle position, were also lessons applied both at home and abroad. The U.S. companies that operated abroad were distributors, not producers. They followed a policy of wholly controlling distribution through foreign subsidiaries rather than operating through local agents. Since American films were in heavy demand, the distributor's position was one of considerable power over foreign exhibitors. It was also, of course, lucrative. The lucre so generated was used to buy into whatever local film industry there was – studios, production companies, chains of cinemas – or was loaned out to make films. Common to all of this was a longer-term vision in which these companies saw themselves trading overseas year after year. Thus they thought strategically as well as tactically. If trading conditions were difficult, negotiation, compromise, pressure, even boycott were options to choose in light of possible payoffs in the future.

C. The approach of this book

This book describes a struggle for market control. The commodity traded was motion picture films. The issue was free trade in this commodity. The aim of the United States after 1917 was to consolidate its dominance of the international trade in films and to defeat foreign attempts at protection; Canada had no clear aims and merely patrolled the edges of the trading floor, making faces. A glare from the American side was usually sufficient. Great Britain was divided against itself. Powerful elements of its elites (for cultural and political reasons), as well as certain production and union elements in the film industry (for commercial reasons), favored strong protective barriers, support of a local production industry, and an aggressive export policy to pay for all this. Other elements of the film industry were against such protection (for commercial reasons) and, had they been asked, many cinemagoers would have agreed (for cultural reasons). A series of lulls, truces, and phoney wars preceded the gradual ebbing of hostilities in the 1950s. The action shifted to other commodities.

The issue of free trade in commercial goods was doubly complicated when the goods in question were motion picture films. These mass cultural artifacts challenged the power of ruling elites in Canada and Great Britain and undermined their cultural self-confidence. Resistance to the domination of American films between 1920 and 1950 reveals much more than do divisions over free trade in general. It also reveals the strain and tension caused by the emergence of the mass society and mass culture of a mass democracy.

Just after the end of World War I, when our study begins, the U.S. motion picture industry totally dominated the screens of Canada and Britain, which showed most of what the United States produced, made little of their own, and exported still less of that. A potent medium of mass culture in Canada and Britain was thus supplied by and dependent upon a foreign power. The mass culture of the United States was a particular challenge to Canada and to the United Kingdom. The United States had its origins in a group of rebellious British colonies, which, having gained independence by force of arms, proceeded to found a nation and a political culture explicitly antithetical to much that was held dear in European countries, including Britain. More directly challenging, the United States developed an expansive and universalist political ideology, which in effect invited the masses of the world to admire it, look to it, and either come to or copy the American model.[10] But before the era of mass media, the United States had remained apart, admired from a distance by the British Left (Pelling 1956). When American mass media exports arrived, they contained subversive democratic and social ideas (Hollins 1981).

The subversion was felt more palpably in Canada, which had from time to time staved off armed American attempts to fulfill its manifest destiny as the successor state to all of British North America (and indeed of French, Spanish, and Russian North America).[11] That separateness had been sustained in Canada's English-speaking parts by cleaving to a loyalty to the mother country and to a vision of Canada as those British North American colonies that did not rebel. (The minority French-speaking population of Canada presents a complication best left to the detailed discussion in Part I.) During the period we shall be examining, a transition was taking place as Canada moved away from the United Kingdom toward political and economic independence. This transition was being negotiated while Canada tried to maintain distance from the United States. The intrusion of American mass culture in vast quantity was (and is) considered by some to be a threat to this project.[12]

All of Britain and much of Canada shared a language with the United States, so after the arrival of sound at the end of the 1920s there was no "natural" communication barrier around their cultures. Thus the United Kingdom and Canada saw American motion pictures as a cultural and even a political threat to their continued distinctness and viability.[13] The very fact that their own internal masses were attracted to and patronized American films presented the possibility of the insidious growth of a rootless and disloyal body of opinion.

American films, developed and usually paid for in a domestic market of great size and affluence, were an attractive commodity to export. The end product was compact, easily shipped, reusable within limits, and self-promoting (movies sell moviegoing). Copyright was retained, so that as long as the film drew audiences, its owners drew revenue. During the time when films were silent, there was nothing foreordained about the American film industry's domination of world trade in films. The disruption of European film industries by the World War I, however, offered the American film industry a window of opportunity.

Sound films were a great challenge to American hegemony because English, unlike pantomime, had no claims to be a universally understood language. However, by that point (1926) the American film industry was strategically placed and sufficiently well financed to exploit sound technology, to buy up some of the patents, to battle foreign patent holders, to standardize the systems, and, to entrench English as the sole acceptable medium of the American mass media. The ready implementation of sound had the consequence of closing for a time the American domestic film market to non–English-speaking countries. By the time the European countries converted to sound (several years after the United States) the costs of challenging America's by now well-established dominance ensured that they were never able to regain their pre–World War I position on American screens.

Of all the foreign markets that the American film industry penetrated and dominated, the largest, by any calculation, was the United Kingdom; the closest was Canada. What was the view of these overseas developments within the United States?

The policy of "liberal developmentalism" (as Rosenberg 1982 calls it) in the United States eventually led to strong support from government agencies for American exporters, including film exporters. There was no specific policy to promote films, although viewed from abroad it seemed there was. On the contrary, there was some unease among ruling elites about just what the United States was selling when it sold films abroad. These doubts scarcely inhibited the promotional effort. Canada followed the lead of Britain, which endeavored to create a national policy, in the form of public legislation, with the dual aims of curbing and reducing the American market share and fostering a home industry that could penetrate the American market. At times British efforts were partially successful; at no time were Canadian efforts successful. At all times the Americans publicly protested that Britain and Canada were not playing fair.

These were the background differences of interest that led to the trade struggle. One party being found in possession of the field, and in over-whelming strength, the outcome was perhaps foregone. In Canada there was a relatively rapid coming to terms with this appraisal of the situation, and a subsequent maneuvering that had mainly to do with obtaining fa-vorable terms for surrender. In the United Kingdom there was a protracted struggle that at one point seemed to be pushing back, but overconfidence led to overextension. In the end Britain lost interest in the struggle, and it is doubtful if British officials ever achieved a realistic appreciation of the situation. Historians in the United Kingdom reproduce some of the self-deception to be found in the official documents.

Given the strength of the enemy, why did the British choose to fight? Both sides misappreciated the situation. The apparently breezily confident U.S. motion picture industry was far from confident and had a poor grasp of the relevant economic strengths and weaknesses of its major opponent, Britain. Hence it continued to act aggressively even when rounds were won. Similarly, the British appreciation of their situation was faulty. The fun-damental secrets of the success of the Americans were opaque to them. They put it down to chicanery rather than strategy. The result was the wasting of millions of British investors' pounds in a quite futile attempt to take victory away from the United States.

Previous accounts of this trade war have undervalued the explanatory power of mutual misappreciation of the situation. They have also focused on the tactics of specific rounds and thereby missed the grand strategy of the struggle. This book attempts to get at the grand strategy, for I believe it is at that level that we can best explain the victory of the U.S. motion picture industry and its realization of its fundamental aim of maintaining its domination of the world trade in motion pictures in each and every significant market. There are a number of more specific contributions that this book makes to the history. Aiming to get at grand strategy, it is assumed that the organized industry and its interactions with government are the sites, and the sources, that need study. Hence documentation is largely drawn from the extensive files to be found in the public archives of the three countries concerned. Secondary sources have been used sparingly, and press sources scarcely at all.

To get up to the heights of grand strategy, I shall proceed slowly by examining first the faint traces the struggle has left in the National Archives of Canada and elsewhere (Part I, "A small market – Canada"). Why begin there? We could compare this expository technique to a movie that begins, not with a long or establishing shot, but with a close-up of an intriguing detail. The relatively small size of the Canadian market, the easy victory of the Americans, help explain why we find so little archival material in Canada. Nevertheless, events and actions there are special cases of the issues later to be found in the British evidence, which help explain them, but which also direct us on toward the American evidence.

The next stage is an examination of the substantial evidence of struggle left in the papers at the Public Record Office in London (Part II, "America's biggest foreign market: The United Kingdom"). The exposition at this point could be compared to a film's opening close-up being followed, not by a long or establishing shot, but by the camera gradually pulling back to a medium shot. The detail begins to make sense, but, manifestly, there is more to come. For the entire thirty years covered by this book, British officials and businessmen clung to the fond hope that some strategy or other would create a second Hollywood on the Thames. They could acknowledge no inherent advantages lying with the Americans (except the size of their market); they discounted the burgeoning economic strength of the American industry; and they had only a glimmer of the effective strategy that was producing the American success. Not that a better grasp would have enabled them to win; rather, it might have made them reassess their aims.

After scrutinizing in this way two of the film markets that were dominated by American films from roughly 1920 to 1950, we turn to the extensive public records about films available across the United States: central government files in Washington, DC, and in the various Presidential libraries; studio files available at several universities and other locations; and personal papers of important figures (Part III, "The U.S. motion picture industry and its overseas system"). At last the exposition pulls back to a long shot that enables us to correct our first efforts to understand the Canadian and British situation, to try to integrate it with the view from the United States, and to begin to construct the omniscient point of view of the historian. It transpires that although market dominance was not gained by strategy, it was held by strategy, and challenges were beaten off by strategy. Some of that strategy was conscious, some was not; some was hit upon by happenstance and even over resistance. Nevertheless, "strategy" is the best name for it.

D. Historiographical, methodological, and background matters

"What actually happened" is, of course, a loaded phrase. Many things actually happened, and only some are selected for attention here. "Explaining what actually happened" is also a loaded phrase, because what constitutes a satisfactory explanation is hotly disputed. My principles of selection are fairly orthodox, fastening on governments, major firms and trade organizations, and the actions of strategically positioned individuals in both, as the locus of action and of explanation. My view of a satisfactory explanation is one that accounts for most of the well-known facts, is testable, and follows the model of the logic of the situation (see Jarvie 1972, chap. 1).

This study straddles economic history and diplomatic history, two subjects with very different approaches, and covers three countries, so something needs to be said about the overall picture of these three societies that is built into this study of the film trade between them. The economic history is institutional and driven by the idea of corporatism; the diplomatic history rests on the idea that the key players are certain strategic elites and organized public opinion. Beyond this, each country works differently. The relevant variables are, first, the size, concentration, and distribution of the population of potential moviegoers and the infrastructure of cinemas to serve them; second, the governance of the country, with respect to the locus of jurisdiction for films, the relevant organs of government, and the formation of opinion in governing elites; and third, the level of economic development in general and of the film industry in particular.

To begin with, Canada. This sprawling country, with its population strung out just north of the border with the United States, had until the late 1920s a predominantly rural population (Intro Table). Yet, despite that, its urban areas generated greater box-office revenue than its scattered rural areas. A large percentage of the total national box-office revenue was generated in the two biggest centers of population, Toronto and Montréal.[14] These two cities were also the centers of finance and business. However, the locus of national political power was not to be found there. The Federal government, Parliament, party headquarters (Liberal, Tory, CCF), and the associated bureaucracy were located in Ottawa, an artificially designated capital city some distance from either large city and not itself a major cinemagoing center.[15] Import tariffs and direct taxation were then Federal matters, but otherwise films were adjudged a Provincial responsibility. Provincial political power was scattered among the regional centers of Halifax, Charlottetown, Fredericton, Québec City, Toronto, Winnipeg, Regina, Ed-

Intro Table. *Urbanization in Canada, Great Britain, and the United States*

| | Population (in millions) | | | | | | | | |
| | Canada | | | Great Britain[a] | | | United States[b] | | |
Year	Total	Urban	Rural	Total	Urban	Rural	Total	Urban	Rural
1900							75.9	30.1	45.8
1911	7.2	3	4.2	42	31.8	10.2	—	—	—
1920							105.6	54.1	51.5
1921	8.7	4.12	4.58	44	34	10			
1930							122.7	68.9	53.8
1931	10.3	5.40	4.9	46	36	10			
1939				47.8	38.4	9.4			
1940							131.6	74.4	57.2
1941	11.5	6.4	5.1	—	—	—			
1950		•					151.2	96.8	54.4
1951	14	8.73	5.27	50.2	39.6	10.6			

[a]There was no U.K. census in 1941.
[b]There was no U.S. census in 1910.
Sources: Canada, *The Canadian Encyclopaedia*; Great Britain, *Annual Abstract of Statistics 1954* (rounded off); United States, Bureau of the Census figures.

monton, and Victoria. (Newfoundland, anomalously, remained a British colony until 1949.) This dispersion of power away from the large financial and business centers made public opinion harder to organize and to discern. There was, for example, no national press: Each major city had regional newspapers. The dispersal of the population was matched by a diffusion of power.

Public opinion, as a consequence, was to be found in a dispersed political, business, professional, and media elite. The nationalisms of this elite were complex. In Ontario, the Maritimes, and the West, loyalty to Britain and the British Empire was constantly invoked as synonymous with Canadian patriotism. Canadian nationalism was frequently expressed by a contrast between Canadian mores and values and those attributed to the United States (some might argue that this was less pronounced in the Prairie Provinces). These sentiments were no doubt sincerely held, but it is hard to separate them from the clear interest all the members of these elites had in the continued existence and difference of Canada. Fowke argued in 1952 that the National Policy that undergirded Canadian history from even before Confederation down to about 1930 was pursued to serve "the commercial, financial, and manufacturing interests of the central provinces" (Fowke 1952, p. 245). Since Canadian film production never even aspired to the hundreds of films needed to supply the cinemas each year, the Canadian industry consisted mainly of exhibition and distribution. Since the cinemas wanted to exhibit American films, it was easy for American firms to exercise power through distribution. Since Canadian audiences showed no consistent desire to see British films, and since, again, the supply of British films always fell far short of what was required to program the nation's cinemas, there was little chance of dislodging the Americans.

By contrast with Canada, Great Britain was a small, densely populated country, the bulk of the population of which had long lived in cities (see Intro Table). It was a unified state in which some censorship and licensing powers were local, but most of the powers affecting the film business resided in the central government, especially the Board of Trade. Furthermore, national government, politics (Liberal, Conservative, Labour), finance, business, and public opinion were all orchestrated from the single metropolitan center of London. Watt specified British public opinion as consisting of:

opinion within Parliament, Whitehall, the press (the "quality" press being given more weight than the "quantity" press), in constituency parties, trade unions, professional associations and grass roots opinion whenever that seems to be crystallising. (Watt 1965, p. 55)

London was also the largest market for motion pictures; hence a large segment of potential moviegoers, of public opinion, and all of the relevant elites were concentrated in one place.

The British market was large: The cinemagoing habit was intense, and some cinemas showed three programs a week. As in Canada, there is evidence of audience preference for American films, particularly in working-class districts and in Scotland. There was a steady demand for British films. Local production simply never reached the numbers to challenge American domination – even had the films been popular.

Whereas the populism and egalitarianism of the United States made it a natural incubator for the development of mass culture, Britain was a traditional European society, with entrenched institutions and practices of hierarchy and deference. In voting, the extension of the franchise was not complete until 1928. In addition to being construed as a foreign invasion, the dominance of American motion pictures on British screens was also seen as a threatening eruption from below of the tastes and values of the industrial masses. There is little work on British mass cultural history comparable to that of Jowett and Sklar on the United States; recently, however, LeMahieu has written a superb portrait of the various reactions to the growth of the mass culture of press, films, and radio in Britain, especially among those of "cultivated mind." Above all, he writes, there was the struggle to reassert cultural hierarchy:

Commercial culture...sought to maximize its audience by collapsing cultural distances. Through a complex and constantly evolving identification between producer and consumer, it eroded the cultural boundaries between, say, a popular newspaper and its female readership. The new technologies of communication directly contributed to this process by preserving, replicating, and distributing messages, which, at low cost to the consumer, brought Hollywood to Birmingham and Harlem to Hartlepool. In its restless search for profitability, commercial culture diminished the distance between producer and consumer. Elite culture, on the other hand, measured itself by the distances it constantly affirmed. (LeMahieu 1988, p. 104)

The main result of the emergence of commercial popular culture, according to LeMahieu, was convergence on a newly synthesized common culture of films, radio programs, and newspapers that was broadly popular and accepted (though not without vigorous elite dissent).

The United States, not unlike Canada, but with a more widely dispersed population, had no metropole. Although relatively thinly populated, the country was in our period larger in population than Canada and the United Kingdom put together. It underwent the transition from a rural to a predominantly urban population about fifteen years earlier than Canada (see Intro Table). Its most lucrative movie markets were the various large cities, especially New York, Chicago, Detroit, Boston, Philadelphia, San Francisco, and Los Angeles. Its various elites were dispersed, much like Canada's. Finance and business were headquartered in many cities, especially New York and Chicago. Federal government elites of politicians (Republican and Democrat) and bureaucrats were concentrated in Washington, although there was a good deal of circulation to and from business, finance, and the law. Watt (1965) summarizes U.S. public opinion as

opinion within the Administration, within Congress, within the organised pressure groups to whose representatives both Administration and Congress feel obliged at least to give an attentive hearing, and opinion in the press generally and among the corps of syndicated commentators especially, as well as grass-roots opinion. (Watt 1965, p. 55)

State politicians and bureaucrats were localized in forty-eight state capitals. And there was similarly no national daily press, although national weekly magazines flourished and these gave extensive coverage to movies. An added complication was that the business elite that owned and ran the movie companies was headquartered in New York. The managerial and creative elites that made the movies were, after about 1920, overwhelmingly to be found on the opposite coast, in Los Angeles. Jurisdiction over films, in the absence of federal legislation, lay almost entirely with the states. Washington, DC, was the main locus for government assistance to exporters.

The emergence of popular and mass culture in the United States is the topic of a large and constantly growing literature that, in the 1970s, began to include serious sociohistorical study of the films. It is crucial to a grasp of film as a commodity in international trade that we set it in its home context as present historians see it, as well as how contemporaries saw it. "What actually happens" is, after all, the product of how people act and how things actually are, as opposed to how people see them.[16] Writing as recently as 1976, Jowett, in *The Democratic Art*, concentrated on the efforts of various groups to understand and control the sudden eruption of the movies into American society. He found it hard to tell what the overall impact of movies on America had been. In the same year Sklar, in *Movie-Made America*, found the movies' influence everywhere. These two theses are not, of course, contradictory. Only four years later Lary May attempted an overall interpretation of the role of films in the birth of mass culture in the United States, connecting them to profound "alterations in work, leisure and family that characterised the modern era" (May 1980, p. xi).[17] Beginning as a marvel of nineteenth-century technological magic, the movies had sunk, by 1908, to the status of a cause for alarm.

Why was it that "good" men and women now appeared threatened by the immigrants' forms and places of entertainment? And how did the pariah institution of the movies manage to overcome this opposition to become a legitimate form of mass entertainment? (p. 45)

May's answer is that the political elite wanted to conserve the family as the controlling force over society by meliorating the dangers of class mingling and new status for women. Reformers put the blame on industry and cities running wild in the pursuit of pleasure and consumption rather than supporting the work ethic and the family. Industrial and commercial jobs were routinized, but they made leisure and surplus income possible. However, any suggestion of immorality in cinemas or on the screens found the movie business disrupted by protests and threats of legislation. The answer, self-regulation, embodied the goals of Anglo–Saxon reformism, thus bringing movies into the political mainstream.

May stresses the importance of movie stars and the movie capital, Hollywood, in the social impact of this emerging component of mass culture. Between 1908 and 1929 the moviegoing experience itself was elevating its public with the provision of picture palaces, "the cathedrals of the motion pictures" that "democratized the styles of elite estates or hotels" (p. 147). These buildings help us to understand why the masses could identify with the stars. One way to make respectable the disreputable amusement where classes and sexes mixed was by providing sumptuous buildings in better neighborhoods, with "an atmosphere that made no distinction between public and private values. Like libraries, state houses and public buildings, the movie house would educate as it entertained" (p. 150). Fusing low life and high life, they became a tame form of night life.

Most western European nations industrialized within a more aristocratic, hierarchical tradition. Consequently, the movies did not become identified with the perpetuation of egalitarianism. Nor were they part of a moral revolution that was eroding Victorian behavioral codes. In twentieth century America, however, movies and mass culture were key elements in the transition from nineteenth century values of strict behavior toward a greater moral experimentation. (p. 165)

Hollywood's role was crucial: It was the happy ending at the end of the frontier.

Other countries also centralized studios; but in America the production site was surrounded by a community where the stars really lived the happy endings, in full view of the nation. Here moviedom became much more than something seen on the screen, or touched in the theater. At a time when the birth of a modern family and consumption ideals might have remained just a cinematic fantasy, Hollywood showed how it could be achieved in real life. Out in California, stars participated in an exciting existence, free from the former confinements of work and Victorianism. (p. 167)

Hollywood was the creation of lower-class immigrant Jews, who were outsiders, commercially opportunistic, sensitive to current styles, and able to suspend their own tastes and calculate the desires of others. They came from a festive and expressive culture, mixing moralism, humor, and sensuality. In movies they could build a business that would open up a new class order in which they would be integrated, not excluded (pp. 174–5; cf. Gabler 1988).

The screen star was a model for the consumer economy, which wanted to induce demand for the current and new.

New players and fresh stars arose to satisfy each generation's tastes. Every major production portrayed the hero and heroine breaking from the past, symbolized by the latest outfits and hairdos, and more opulent surroundings. (p. 232)

Hollywood itself stood for a private ideal of passion, fun, and pleasure.

Rarely was a star portrayed as born into this status and wealth. Rather, he was an average, unknown American who used his talent for expressing charisma, charm, and sex appeal. Rising from anonymity, he acquired fame, which rested not on domination of others, but on the ability to entertain and make people happy.... Yet at all times, the stars were ordinary folks whose lavish lifestyles could be democratized. Thus they were the models, not the enemies, of the middle class. (p. 233)

Indeed, they offered the ultimate solace of escape:

Neither sex could use the quest for expressiveness to challenge economic inequalities, routinized work, or the continuing separation of sexual roles in public life.... Instead, by constantly changing clothes, manners, and styles, adults in leisure could avoid facing their half-hearted rebellions from the sexual roles of the past. (p. 237)

Shortly after May's book on the movies in American society appeared, the diplomatic historian Emily Rosenberg synthesized a bold interpretation of American economic and cultural expansion in the first half of the twentieth century, along with which movie exports flowed.

[The] American dream of high technology and mass consumption was both promoted and accompanied by an ideology that I shall call liberal-developmentalism. . . . Liberal-developmentalism merged nineteenth-century liberal tenets with the historical experience of America's own development, elevating the beliefs and experiences of America's unique historical time and circumstance into developmental laws thought to be applicable everywhere.

The ideology of liberal-developmentalism can be broken into five major features: (1) belief that other nations could and should replicate America's own developmental experience; (2) faith in private free enterprise; (3) support for free or open access for trade and investment; (4) promotion of free flow of information and culture; and (5) growing acceptance of governmental activity to protect private enterprise and to stimulate and regulate American participation in international economic and cultural exchange.

To many Americans, their country's economic and social history became a universal model. In order to become a modern society, a nation needed extensive capital investment generated by foreign borrowing and by exports; development of educational, transportation, communication, and banking institutions; a steady supply of cheap labor; maximization of individual initiative for people deemed most efficient; wide-open land use and freewheeling environmental practices; and a robust private business sector solidly linked to capital-intensive, labor-saving technology. This blueprint, drawn from America's own experience, became the creed of most Americans who dealt with foreign nations.[18]

Rosenberg describes the establishment in 1912 of the U.S. Department of Commerce and its important Bureau of Foreign and Domestic Commerce; the latter's enlargement under Woodrow Wilson's secretary of commerce William C. Redfield; and the starting of *Commerce Reports,* "government sponsored market research" that "amounted to a substantial subsidy for businesses engaged in foreign commerce" (p. 66). From 1917, consuls were given broad instructions on the gathering of economic intelligence of interest to American business. She stresses the global influence that flowed from American dominance in international communications over the period 1912–32 in cable, wireless, news services, films, and airlines (see also Denny 1930, pp. 68–9 and 369–402). Films, in particular, were designed for a diverse, multiethnic patronage at home and hence were perfectly suited to the world market. They did not stem from the traditions of elite art.

American filmmakers liked to think they were producing a universal, nonpolitical art form that was democratic in its impulses; in fact, they largely peddled formula art based on a distorted view of American tastes and manners. The American cinema was also touted as a vehicle for world peace. Will Hays . . . declared that film was promoting peace by destroying barriers between nations. A French critic accused Hays of assuming that "the only way to assure peace is to Americanize the thoughts, the language, and the souls of foreigners." But if Hays did, indeed, confuse international harmony with Americanization, he was articulating a view shared by most American politicians and businessmen. (p. 101; cf. Jarvie 1988a)

Rosenberg stressed that the rhetoric veiled what was in effect American government attempts to protect and sustain the effective domination of the international trade in films by privately owned American firms. This was part of a general policy to use the economic power and influence of the United States to force countries to accept the policies of liberal developmentalism: equal and open access for trade and investment and an emphasis on private, rather than public, ownership.

> The American dream as represented in the ideal of liberal-developmentalism differed from the reality of America's expanding cultural and economic influence. Americans involved in international affairs could preach and even believe in the basic tenets of free enterprise, open access, and free flow, while they themselves applied them selectively and ignored their contradictions. (p. 234)

Even if overdrawn, and unfair to American officials (cf. Part III), this is a pithy, direct, and challenging interpretation of events.

The one specifically revisionist idea about the U.S. economy used here is that of "corporatism."[19] I find persuasive the view that a new social form, also called "cooperative neocapitalism," emerged after World War I, promoted, if in somewhat different ways, by Herbert Hoover as secretary of commerce and by the New Deal. Hoover's version, "associationalism," according to Michael Hogan,

> envisaged an organic political economy in which public and private elites cooperated in the job of economic management... accepted the economic collectivism and interdependence that come out of industrialization, the rise of organized and bureaucratized concentrations of private economic power, the concomitant decline of market forces, and the consequent need to supplement these forces with institutional regulating and coordinating devices. (Hogan 1987, p. 4)

The brunt of those devices was to be borne by the private sector, especially in the form of trade organizations, although it was government's role to facilitate their creation. The hope was that

> enlightened functional elites, rather than public authorities, were to act as agents of economic rationalization by working within and between groups to eliminate waste, allocate resources efficiently, tame the business cycle, and optimize output. (ibid., p. 75)

This common thread of ideas, which Hogan traces through the New Deal to the Marshall Plan, makes more sense of the behavior of the American film industry and of American government officials than any other I have come across.

To a considerable extent, much of the story told here is new – or at least new in its specificity and detail, which deviates from and corrects previous, less fully researched accounts. This, however, is not its only claim on the reader. There is a more general significance both to its narrow topic and to its more general framework. The narrow topic is the economic history of the movies and of the film export trade. Here the general significance is that this book contributes new material about the movies as a business, including as an important foreign business. Movies are not just a commodity like any other, but they are a commodity, they were traded, and U.S. firms managed to dominate and hold onto the world market. Market domination and profitability in turn permitted many things characteristic of U.S. films – their stars, their music, their high professional gloss, their impersonality (in the sociological sense), their tightly structured narratives, their formal and expressive conventions – to become the norm or standard against which virtually all publics measured films, and against which all foreign industries measured themselves.

Events involving the international trade in films were a precursor of what we now call the international market in mass communications software. There is a close connection between the film and television program industries of the United States, and the latter has been to a remarkable extent able to duplicate the international trading feats of the former. Some television markets have been at least as dominated by American products as ever was achieved by motion pictures, and, even in those markets where there is a strong indigenous television industry, constant campaigns of resistance against American material are necessary. A 1990 book depicts the situation in the international trade in television at a trade fair in Miami as follows:

AMIP's [American Market for International Programs] purpose was to enable the broadcasters from [foreign] countries to sell their programmes to the far-from-eager buyers from the USA. All over the world, it seems, television producers are prey to a perennial pipe-dream: that somehow the very best of their output – prize-winning dramatizations of literary classics, ground-breaking documentaries, acclaimed recordings of ballets and opera, folk dance and song – will find an audience in the vast, rich and fragmented American market. It doesn't happen. Foreign produced programmes account for less than 2 per cent of American viewing time, most of it on the non-profit Public Broadcasting Service (PBS). (Eberts and Illott 1990, pp. 1–2)

This book tells how that pipe dream was originally dreamed by foreign filmmakers, especially those of Great Britain, about the U.S. market. For them, too, it did not happen. My suggestion is that television followed the same path as film: The fundamental strategies that U.S. firms developed for marketing their films abroad were readily adapted to the marketing of television programs, with comparable success. Thus, for those interested in continuing the trade war against American materials, rather than simply leaving it to the market, there may also be lessons as to just what will not work, and perhaps also about ensuring that one fights on the basis of realistic expectations.

In the face of American dominance, two kinds of argument, broadly speaking, have been used to justify government intervention in the film industry: one cultural, the other commercial. The cultural arguments have always been to the effect that locals should see local material, their own culture represented on the screen. A corollary was that local material would exclude or minimize foreign material. The commercial arguments were to the effect that employment of local resources, labor, and capital was preferable to importing products made by foreigners. (There were also political arguments, which have been alluded to already, and, although they were seldom explicitly set down, we shall find clear evidence of them.)

Both arguments took for granted the conservationist role of the nation-state in culture and commerce. Both kinds of argument assumed that film was a homogeneous product for which there was no differential demand. These assumptions are open to question. When nation-states protect culture by banning jeans or rock and roll, ridiculing chewing gum and Coca-Cola®, they do not necessarily carry their citizens with them. When they extol the virtues of the local product, they face a public with tastes of its own.

Much needs to be written on all this, especially regarding the worldwide unease created in the period 1915–55 by the aggressive export of American films and the relative readiness of audiences everywhere to patronize them. Of all the countries in the world, this unease was perhaps most poignant in Great Britain, coproprietor of the language of American films, largest source of foreign earnings for American films, and sensitive both culturally and industrially to American film imports. Almost as poignant was the predicament of Canada, which shared a 3,000-mile border with the United States, had a population two-thirds of which shared the use of English with the United States, and was in its very origins an alternative form of nation building in North America.

A final word on the concepts used in this book. Commerce and culture are sharply distinguished. "Commerce" names an arena of practice: the exchange of goods and services for money. "Culture" refers to the abstract and rather foggy notions of ways of life and national identity. This distinction is rarely observed in the evidence we shall be examining. The officials and businessmen of the countries that struggled with the United States over motion pictures had a tendency to fuse these two matters, sometimes confusedly, sometimes deliberately. That tendency strengthened the conviction of American officials that all parties were concerned about commerce but that foreign countries sometimes talked about it in the deceptive and mystifying rhetoric of culture.[20] Thus could the ordinary business of trade in a commodity be described as a "cultural invasion." Thus could censorship bodies that directed much energy against American imports be seen as instruments in restraint of trade. Time and again we shall see how officials in Britain concocted position statements that spoke of a determination to defend British culture and ways of life, while behind the scenes discussing why businessmen of British nationality were entitled to a share of the considerable profits being made out of films.

Neither commerce nor culture was a concept readily used by film historians in the past. Even today, writing about film as a commercial commodity, a trade good, grates on the amateurs and aesthetes who think of film as art.[21] Culture is a concept that hardly appears at all in the evidence we shall be examining, and then only in the form "cultural." In the period under study, "culture" nearly always carried a real or implied capital C: That is, it referred to what I have called "traditional or high cultural" activities. "Film culture" would have seemed a contradiction in terms. Changes in usage have now made culture an all-embracing term, a use pioneered in anthropology and sociology. Culture in this all-embracing sense is easily mistaken for an independent, rather than a dependent, variable. Thought of as an independent variable, it can be reified, which encourages a mystifying way of talking, one that blurs issues of social cause and effect. Whenever there was a respite in the struggle over movie markets, it was because the American side had finally extracted from their Canadian or British opponents' cultural talk some practical and straightforward commercial position to negotiate and settle. Thus, when general wartime conditions led Britain in 1939 to seek drastic reductions in the dollar remittances for films, Joseph Kennedy was able to negotiate a deal that held until Lend–Lease eased the situation. Yet when, after 1945, British cultural protectionism got mixed up with British industrial and labor protectionism and with the ambitions of British filmmakers for a Hollywood on the Thames that would make significant inroads into the American domestic market, there resulted ten years of basically fruitless attrition warfare, which the Americans, never blinded by cultural claims, won.

National identity, national character, national culture, ways of life, and outlook (anachronistically to mix terms we use today with terms used in the past) are vague and intangible entities that the social sciences teach us to treat gingerly. They all involve indefensibly broad generalizations about populations that just happen to be within a national boundary. Although such notions are deployed in the evidence to be examined, I find little of explanatory value in them. It is belief in them and action predicated on this belief that is concrete and real.

Notes

1 A study of Americanization in general would also have to include the spread of American slang and argot and American social institutions. It could be held that mass production of automobiles and labor-saving devices altered social patterns, and that American media materials and modes of speech affected social relations between persons, especially within the family.

2 "The Americans have largely managed to 'fix' the basic format of each medium – as a consequence of being early with the technology, having an affluent enough audience to reach a large scale quickly and having a federal government favorably disposed to encouraging commercial media expansion. Thus the pattern of American

newspapers around 1900, of Hollywood films around 1920 and American television around 1950, were widely copied by other countries looking for a model of what the new medium was" (Tunstall 1977, p. 77).

3 The categories of *1066 and All That* seem unavoidable here. See Sellar and Yeatman 1931.

4 Although we shall not find examples of it in the chapters to come, it would be disingenuous not to acknowledge that the likes of Goebbels, Stalin, and Khomeini found this line of argument self-condemnatory.

5 LeMahieu (1988, p. 13n) wisely comments that the work of Klingender and Legg "should be used with care."

6 Reprinted in full in Jarvie and Macmillan 1989.

7 Not to be overlooked as a piece of ethnography is Leslie Halliwell 1985, which describes North of England lower-middle-class cinemagoing in the second half of our period.

8 Characteristically, Francophone Canadians disliked British films but accepted American ones. This has as much to do with politics as with language.

9 An authoritative early analysis of this topic is Lewis 1933 (esp. chap. 13).

10 Well summarized in Lipset 1990, chap. 2.

11 Most notably the War of 1812 and the Fenian Raids.

12 A recent survey focusing on film is Magder 1989.

13 A recent example by the nationalist film writer Harcourt (1989) is riddled with unacknowledged elitist assumptions.

14 City by city box-office figures were compiled by the Dominion Bureau of Statistics in the 1930s.

15 A useful background book on Federal civil servants is Granatstein 1982.

16 I tried to argue this point in Jarvie 1981b.

17 May's ideas about the United States parallel LeMahieu's idea of the convergence on a common culture in Great Britain. Page numbers hereafter are given in parentheses in text.

18 Rosenberg 1982, pp. 7–8. (Page numbers are given hereafter in parentheses in text.) Her interpretation utilized and extended some twenty-five years of revisionist scholarship (see Hawley ed. 1981).

19 For an elegant summary of revisionist trends, see Hawley 1981, Introduction.

20 "Whatever the alleged grounds for foreign objections or opposition, our negotiations usually discovered a perfectly natural economic rivalry at the bottom of them. This fear of competition from the United States increased as our hold on the screens of the world assumed larger proportions"; Hays 1955, p. 507.

21 In Canada, however, journalists and politicians have latterly taken to referring to broadcasting, films, journalism, writing, music, dance, and education as "the cultural industries."

PART I
A small market – Canada

CHAPTER I

The White Report and the trial of Famous Players, 1932

In his authoritative history of films in Canada, Peter Morris (1978) dated their first exhibition to Ottawa in 1896. Exhibition outlets spread rapidly across the country, in big cities and small towns. Intermittent forays into production occurred in various centers, but only Provincial and Federal government agencies sustained production. Government films were distributed alongside and outside the regular commercial channels and were often shown in nontheatrical outlets such as schools, churches, and union or benevolent-society halls. Commercial distribution was gradually gathered into the hands of subsidiaries of the major American companies, which handled not only American films but also some of the films imported from other countries. Such indigenous commercial production as existed was not undertaken by these American subsidiaries, although they had considerable say in the fate of those films.

Morris, in common with most historians of Canadian film, treated American domination as an unfortunate fact, because the Americans had nothing to gain from fostering creative film production activity in Canada. If we exclude the government agencies, little was produced in Canada, and therefore few films were exported – so few, in fact, that I propose not to discuss this limited commerce. In the film trade of the North Atlantic triangle, the film industry in Canada was primarily an importer. As a matter of fact, those imports were overwhelmingly American; as a matter of aspiration, there were people in Canada that wished to break American domination and to bring in British (and perhaps more French) films. The major episode in which these issues came to the fore was the investigation of Famous Players Canadian Corporation (FPCC) in 1930.

1.1. A shaggy-dog story

In no foreign country did the U.S. film industry achieve more complete commercial and cultural domination and penetration than it did in Canada. Indigenous film production in Canada was nugatory.[1] By 1925, one source claims, some 98.7 percent of the films shown on Canadian screens were

25

made in the United States and distributed in Canada by American-controlled firms.[2] Cultural patriots and commercial patriots complained that this was unsatisfactory. Between 1930 and 1932, the Federal government and some Provincial governments seemed to be positioning themselves to remedy the situation. But their efforts proved half-hearted and were abandoned without explanation, leaving American control virtually intact.

In outline, what happened in those two years was this. Ruling elites of the British Empire, including those in the "White Dominions" (Canada, Australia, New Zealand, and South Africa), had agitated against the dominance of American films throughout the 1920s. The issue was on the agenda of the Imperial Conference of 1926, as we shall see. In Canada, matters came to a head in 1930. Following formal complaints – which may or may not have been stage-managed – the principal American film companies operating in Canada as distributors were the subject of an inquiry by a Federal commission, held under the provisions of the Combines Investigation Act of 1923. In his 1931 report, Peter White, the commissioner, found that American-controlled firms were operating an illegal combine, or trust, against the public interest (Canada, Ministry of Labour, and Combines Investigation Branch 1931 [the White Report]). Although the act was administered by the Canadian Department of Labour (in one of those balancings of jurisdictions in which Canada specializes), prosecutions were undertaken at the level of Provincial attorneys general. Prosecution on one civil and two criminal counts was launched in the Supreme Court of the Province of Ontario at Toronto, the city where the companies charged had their national headquarters. The accused were acquitted; the Crown did not appeal, and no steps were taken to implement the advice of counsel and of the trial judge that special legislation covering the film industry be enacted. Why, after such expenditure of effort, was the issue dropped at both levels of government? Why did Canada decide not to prosecute the trade war any further?

The issue of American control of a (or perhaps at the time the)[3] major mass medium had been raised and seriously investigated. Trading practices thus disclosed had been tested against existing law. American control was found to be exploited in a legal manner. For reasons yet to be discovered, this episode was to be the end of the matter. What might have been an opportunity for further action was not taken up, and it was business as usual for the American-controlled firms that had been vindicated. This is what I mean by calling the narrative a "shaggy-dog story": It has no punch line, so we have to puzzle over its meaning. Before revisiting it in detail, let me summarize what I think can to be learned from it.

(1) The entire episode crystallizes the cultural and commercial problems posed by the foreign success of American movies and the business practices used by Paramount Publix and their subsidiaries to promote their product. By displacing locally owned production, distribution, and exhibition inter-

ests, Hollywood secured its market, reduced its risk, and created powerful enemies. These enemies were its local business rivals in theaters and distribution. The business they were all in was highly visible, and the locals usually had good connections to the press and the political elite. This and other elites were deprived, by Hollywood's strategy, of an effective role in the movie business. This was an unstable feature of an otherwise successful Hollywood forward policy in foreign countries, and one upon the resolution of which the consolidation and maintenance of Hollywood's dominance was to turn.

(2) Both locally owned competitors of American firms and self-appointed cultural critics viewed Hollywood's foreign success as a "problem": a state of affairs commercially and culturally improper. Both groups argued for altering that state of affairs, if necessary by deploying the power of the national government. Business rivals such as independent theater owners and distributors of British films, who sought economic gain, looked to state action as the last resort. Negotiation was to be preferred. Here the cultural critics thought differently. Transborder business that affects the demand schedule of a mass electorate presents a threat to conventional notions of sovereignty. Sovereignty is nonnegotiable. Thus, otherwise progressive and even radical cultural elites become etatist when the issue is foreign domination of the industries of mass culture. Business groups are relatively easy to identify, and their interests are manifest. The makeup of cultural elites, the constituencies for whom they speak and with what authority, and their interests, are much more difficult to identify. Like politicians and others, their rhetoric often suggests that they speak for the inarticulate masses. However, when the music of the box-office turnstiles also speaks for the masses, and speaks differently from the elite, we may be alerted to an undemocratic and paternalistic undertow.

(3) By the time White began his investigation, Hollywood's overseas business practices had been institutionalized for some time, and this enabled him to compile a coherent account of their development and current functioning. Canada is an entirely typical case study in Hollywood business methods, generalizable not only to Britain but to much of the rest of the world. The detail of White's findings may have only local significance; the broad picture they present, however, was much the same elsewhere.

(4) Although White had found there was a combine against the public interest, the court found only that Hollywood's business practices were unsentimentally ruthless but by no means unequivocally illegal. Famous Players, and the other companies charged in the indictment, owned or controlled all the major distributing firms in Canada and the great bulk of the strategically important theaters. Hence they were firms whose position made it "natural" for them to get special treatment in the market – however unfair that looked to their competitors, however culturally intrusive it seemed to the cultural elite.

(5) All of this helps us to understand why White's conclusion that an illegal combine existed was convincing to the grand jury, but unconvincing to the trial judge. State power is sometimes a blunt instrument. Short of forbidding American firms to do business in Canada, an inconceivable option, laws simply presented a challenge to the ingenuity of businessmen with a product to sell for which there was proven, strong demand.

(6) Although there was pressure to "do something" about American domination – both for cultural and for commercial reasons – it was not at all clear what should be done. Such suggestions as were made faced obvious difficulties, and that, in the absence of other evidence, may be all we can say to explain why they were never tried.

To pursue the White matter further will take us into two separate scenarios: first, the story of the White Report in more detail, as a kind of turning point (or, in film parlance, key sequence) in the story of Hollywood in Canada. After that we can turn to another story, in which the White Report was simply a chapter or sequence *simpliciter:* namely, the years before and after the court case. This should enable us to run twice more through the points just listed, once with closer attention to detail, and again with a better grasp of the broad background. Both reruns will help us to deepen our grasp of what happened in this small, contiguous market for Hollywood films.

1.2. The lead-in to the White Report

Canada's Combines Investigation Act was passed in 1923 (Ball 1934; Bladen 1932). It provided for a registry presided over by a registrar, who, at the time in question, was F. A. MacGregor. Members of the public who believed that they were the victims of a combine (trust) could request the registrar to investigate their complaints.

All through the 1920s, the growth in power and influence of the FPCC had raised accusations of monopoly and of unfair pressure on those who did not wish to cooperate with it or sell out. The FPCC owned or controlled some 207 cinemas, most of them showing first-run movies, and, through leasing and other arrangements, effectively influenced the behavior of its rivals. The FPCC was controlled by Paramount Publix of the United States, the head of which was Adolph Zukor (Fig. 1.1). Zukor's strategy, in Canada as in the United States, had been to seek strategic, rather than total, control of the market for films. He acted so as to get power over those cinemas that generated the greatest percentage of total revenues. These "first-run" houses were so called because their size and splendor, and/or their central location, made them the logical choice as the first theater in which to show a new film in their locality. First-run houses accounted for some 50 percent of the revenues a film would eventually generate (see Huettig 1944, p. 78).

Besides being centrally situated and lavishly appointed, first-run theaters

Figure 1.1. The Paramount brass at a railway station in the 1920s. *Left to right*: Sidney Kent, Adolph Zukor, Jesse Lasky, and Cecil B. De Mille. (British Film Institute–Stills, Posters and Designs.)

charged top admission prices. In order to milk these situations to the maximum, provision was made to prevent first-run theaters located near one another from showing the same film at the same time (zoning), and to ensure a separation in time between a film's first run and its reappearance at a second-run theater that charged lower admission (clearance).

Armed with the strategic power base of first-run theaters, defended by zones and clearances, Zukor could use that power to extract favorable terms from other (American-controlled) distributors (who coveted the exposure their films would get in his outlets) and to reward those firms that imposed severe conditions on his competitors. The FPCC was a ruthless, prosperous, and American Goliath, almost naturally pitted against the would-be Canadian Davids in the small-business field of independent cinemas. So dominant was the FPCC that in Canada the very term "independent theater" came to mean a theater in which the FPCC had no direct or indirect financial interest, and a "closed town" meant one in which the only theater or theaters were operated by the FPCC or one of its subsidiaries or affiliates (Greenwald 1950, p. 49).

Formal moves to put the machinery of the Combines Investigation Act in motion began with a document dated 28 June 1929, signed by six independent exhibitors and their counsel, J. Earl Lawson, which alleged that "the Famous Players Canadian Corporation and the ten film distributing companies were using unfair coercion and discrimination against independent exhibitors and that the Canadian public was being detrimentally affected thereby." They applied to the registrar for an investigation.

The registrar conducted a preliminary investigation, with the assistance of Professor K. W. Taylor. In November 1929, the registrar's report was submitted to the minister of labor, Peter Heenan, recommending a full-scale investigation, because they had found prima facie evidence of a combine. Heenan declined to initiate an investigation, explaining,

I am of the opinion that, owing to this industry being of such a nationwide character, to launch a public investigation by a Commissioner during election time might be liable to misconstruction so on the whole I thought it would be better to leave further procedure until after the election.[4]

To what "misconstruction" a full-scale investigation of a nationwide industry might be open is unspecified. Prime Minister Mackenzie King's administration was not given to attacks on American business in Canada. To take on a business so much in the public eye might have been seen as publicity seeking, much as American congressional committees later gained attention by subpoenaing film stars. In Canada, assertive nationalism independent of the mother country (the United Kingdom) was a feature of Liberal politics of the time, and an investigation of the influence of American business, one charge against which was the lack of distribution of British films in Canada, might need careful timing.

At all events, the national election did not occur until the summer of 1930, when R. B. Bennett's Tories were returned to power, taking over on 7 August. Shortly afterward, on 23 September 1930, Peter White was appointed commissioner, and on 4 October Angus Heighington was made government counsel. Since Heighington's brother was related by marriage to Strachan Johnson, counsel for Famous Players, this led to some protest about a possible conflict of interest. Although Prime Minister Bennett was told that "if the inquiry is abortive, it will be blamed on the influence of the New York interest," the new minister of labor, G. D. Robertson, stood firm on his selection.

Commission hearings began in November 1930 and concluded in March

1931. Both Ray Lewis, the eccentric editor of the trade paper *Canadian Moving Picture Digest,* and Col. John A. Cooper, head of the major film-trade organization, the Motion Picture Distributors and Exhibitors of Canada (MPDEC), complained about the conduct of the inquiry. Lewis argued that some evidence was being ignored; that no testimony was being taken from the Province of British Columbia; and that the connection between the FPCC and the Paramount Publix Company of New York was not being looked into. Bennett was friendly, but noncommittal, in his reply to her.

To Cooper, he was positively hostile. Reports were reaching Bennett that Cooper served the American interests who were the principals behind his ostensibly Canadian firms well. In a 2 June 1931 cable to Bennett, F. S. Ravell, Canadian representative of British International Pictures, had said,

Had interview with Col. Cooper...who informed me that...Robertson Minister of Labour was his personal friend and would pull the necessary strings to prevent any adverse legislation concerning Paramount Publix or other American film interests in Canada under recent government investigation.

This sort of information led to reproofs to Cooper, such as "I frankly cannot but think the activities of the interests you represent have not been beneficial to Canada."[5] So Cooper's fulminations on behalf of his organization's members were to no avail.

Although the stenographic transcript of the investigation ran to 7,882 pages, a preliminary report was rapidly prepared. On 6 May 1931, Johnson, the counsel for Famous Players, telegraphed Prime Minister Bennett to argue that the preliminary report should not be published but should simply be made available to the FPCC so that they could negotiate with the minister. The reason for his proposal was that once the report was finalized and published, if illegal activities were found, it would have to be forwarded to the Provincial attorneys general for possible prosecution.[6]

Close friend of Cooper's or not, Robertson proceeded to have the preliminary report declared the final report, to publish it in July, and (on 14 July 1931) to write to Lt. Col. W. H. Price, attorney general for Ontario, that he was forwarding a copy of it and the evidence, "for such action as you may be pleased to institute because of the conditions appearing."[7]

Before turning to the Ontario prosecution, it will assist matters if we closely analyze the contents of the report.

1.3. White's findings

The White Report (Canada, Ministry of Labour, and Combines Investigation Branch 1931) is a mine of information on film distribution and exhibition in Canada at the end of the 1920s. White was able to calculate, for example, that of 548 films released in the season 1928–9, only some 73, or 7.69 percent, were British. (We shall come to the full significance of this

Table 1.1. *Canadian distribution territories*

| Territory | Headquarters | Theaters | |
		Indep.	Chain
Ontario	Toronto	258	117
Québec	Montréal	146	53
Winnipeg	Winnipeg	124	24
Calgary	Calgary	144	30
B. C.	Vancouver	41	30
Maritimes	Halifax	96	45
Totals		809	299

Source: White Report (1931), p. 14.

in a later Chapter 10.) White makes the point that if British pictures were distributed in Canada in the same manner as American pictures, much could be done to place before the public British manners, British English, and British ideals (p. 158).

For distribution purposes, Canada was divided into six "territories" (Table 1.1). White identified ten distributors in the country, all of them American subsidiaries. Of the 1,108 theaters in the country, 809 were "independent" (i.e., of the FPCC), whereas 299 were organized into chains of three or more. Of these 299, no less than 207 were controlled by the FPCC. Film rentals were fixed by Famous Players, although some bargaining was done. The large number of independent theaters had no effective trade organization.

Large blocks of FPCC shares were held by two other companies: Paramount Publix, of New York City, and the Montreal Trust Company. The Paramount shares were voted by N. L. Nathanson, Adolph Zukor, and I. W. Killam. One of the major assets of the FPCC was a franchise agreement of 3 February 1920 giving it exclusive first-run rights to all Famous Players–Lasky motion pictures. Thus this largest chain had a lock on the largest supply of premium pictures.

In addition to investigating the American distributing firms, led by the FPCC, White considered the role of the Canadian trade organization known as the Motion Picture Distributors and Exhibitors of Canada (MPDEC), whose head was a Canadian veteran of World War I, the previously mentioned Col. John A. Cooper.[8] Colonel Cooper admitted to the commission that all the exhibitor members of his organization were Famous Players employees and that their inclusion as members was window dressing. The MPDEC was in effect an organization of distributors, not exhibitors; the latter term had been added to the name to make it appear a broader-based group when lobbying the Canadian government. White intimated that the

MPDEC in fact did little for exhibitors (p. 167). But a more important question was the relation of this supposedly "Canadian" trade organization to its sister organization in the United States, the Motion Picture Producers and Distributors of America (MPPDA), nicknamed the "Hays Organization" after its permanent head (between 1922 and 1945), Will H. Hays, of whom we shall hear much more. White's finding on this relation between the Canadian and American trade organizations was unequivocal: The MPDEC, the report states, "is financed by U.S. producers" (p. 29); it is "a mere offshoot of the corresponding organization in the United States, presided over by Mr. Will Hays," on which it "was patterned and from which it originated, and from which it derived its inspiration, and with which it has kept in close touch throughout, which collects . . . the bulk of its funds, and which in fact dictates its policies and controls its activities" (p. 30). Although Colonel Cooper was said, in the report, to be personally pro-British, he was described as a captive of his organization and criticized for having made discouraging public statements about the prospects for British films (p. 159).

Treating of the MPDEC's liaison activities with women's organizations and other pressure groups seeking to curb immorality in the movies, White was as harsh as Prime Minister Bennett had been:

It is almost amusing, if it were not pathetic, to learn that Col. Cooper has succeeded in convincing [Mrs. H. L. Lovering of the Local Council of Women for Saskatchewan] that he, employed and paid as he is by the United States producers, is standing between them and the public in the matter of censorship, when as a matter of fact his activities in regard to censorship . . . have been directed towards a relaxation and criticism of the standard set up by the various Censor Boards in Canada. (p. 211)

As in the United States, the so-called Film Boards of Trade, set up to arbitrate contract disputes between distributors and exhibitors, were under direct control of the distributors' trade organization, the MPDEC.

White detailed case after case of theater acquisition in Canada by the FPCC. Such an acquisition invariably began with a direct offer to purchase or take over a property, but rarely at a price high enough to tempt the owners readily to agree. The direct offer would be followed up by pressure tactics: using influence to make film bookings difficult to obtain; assisting competitors; cutting admission prices at competing theaters; or even threatening to build a competing theater on a neighboring site. As can be seen from Table 1.1, the prime market within Canada was the Province of Ontario and, within that, Toronto. The end result of FPCC acquisition tactics in that city was that of the ninety-two theaters, more than one-third, or thirty-seven, were owned, controlled, or operated by the FPCC. Those thirty-seven were not a random set but included most of the large, luxurious, strategically located first-run theaters, which among them accounted for 45,763 of the 70,743 total seats in the city – that is, 64 percent. This Famous

Players domination of the Toronto market, the report said, was typical of their positioning of themselves in the country generally: "Taking Canada as a whole, Famous Players occupy either an exclusive or a dominant position in all towns and cities having a population of 10,000 or more," except for ten locations (p. 101).

The influence of the FPCC's domination of Canadian outlets on other American-owned companies operating in Canada was shown by letters from Carl Laemmle, of Universal Pictures, and J. P. O'Loghlin of Fox Film Corporation, who both averred that for access to first-run movies they were completely at Nathanson's mercy.

In addition to theater acquisition, White looked into the practices of clearances, block booking, and blind booking. A *clearance* was an agreement to give an exhibitor exclusive right to show a film in his "zone" for a specified period. Typically, a film could not be rebooked into a zone until twenty-eight days after its first run was completed. (This was the "protection" period). The report admitted that some limited protection of this sort was justified but went on to argue that the FPCC used its power to ensure that the competition, though it earned a living, did not get rich. The FPCC

has demanded and obtained... protection for periods longer than is necessary for the proper conduct of the business of these theatres, by reason of which Famous Players has been able to lessen, by reason of actual or tacit agreements or arrangements, and has lessened competition in many areas and districts, and generally in Canada, in the supply of motion picture films to the independent theatres and... this has been detrimental to the public in that:

1. It has cost the public more money
2. It has prevented large sections of the public from seeing pictures while they are still fairly new
3. It has given Famous Players and its affiliates an undue advantage over its competitive exhibitors, and over the public generally in Canada. I consider that this advantage is not one which one might expect to legitimately flow from the large purchasing power which Famous Players has. (p. 144)

Block booking meant that distributors could not book pictures singly but only in groups, or "blocks." In *blind booking,* distributors insisted that exhibitors take some films in the block "blind," or sight-unseen – usually because the films had not yet been made.[9] White was equally clear about the effects of the practices:

Block booking and blind booking prevail generally in the sale of pictures by distributors in Canada, and... by reason of the consequent over-buying on the part of the exhibitor [to ensure that he had secured sufficient product], and the showing of inferior pictures, the system of distribution by block booking and blind booking is decidedly detrimental to the public. (p. 157)

Specifically, the system intimidated independents and prevented theaters from individualizing their booking policy.

White's conclusions were, as a result of all the practices detailed, un-sparing:

I find as a fact that Famous Players has in many important locations a monopoly of the moving picture business; in others, such a position as enables them to dominate the business, and this applies to practically all the towns and cities in Canada of 10,000 or more population where they or their affiliates have theaters, and almost with equal force this finding applies to practically all towns and cities where they are operating theatres. (p. 106)

1.4. The prosecution of Famous Players

When the White Report appeared in July 1931, the American embassy at Ottawa summed it up as having found that 95 percent of Canadian film distribution was controlled by the Famous Players combine, which acted against the public interest, threatened independents, and denigrated British films. There was, the dispatch surmised, the possibility of prosecution in Provincial court.

Sure enough, a week later, on 14 July, as we saw, Minister of Labour Robertson wrote to attorney general Price of Ontario. He sent Price the White Report; a transcript of the evidence; the exhibits; and a card index to the evidence, with a hint that prosecution was in order.[10] Perhaps because he knew what was coming, Price acted promptly and, on 16 July, wrote to R. H. Greer, a prominent barrister, to retain him as counsel for the Crown, "with a view to arriving at a conclusion as to whether information [the legal name for an accusation] should be laid and if so, against whom."[11]

A nice technical problem tickled the lawyers for a while. White had found a national combine operating across Canada. Action against it could, there-fore, have been initiated in every Province. Such actions would have du-plicated one another, since some of the same evidence would have been used, and there was an obvious danger of delay and inconsistency. On 31 July, the attorney general of British Columbia wrote to Price, "It occurs to me that if proceedings are to be taken, such a step should be general and that the Provinces should act in unison if the proceedings are to be effec-tive."[12] By 8 August, Price confirmed that there probably would be a pros-ecution and said that Ontario was the appropriate venue, because the Canadian offices of the accused companies were all in Toronto. He, too, wondered about some sort of collaboration. British Columbia was joined, on 12 August, by the Saskatchewan acting deputy attorney general, inquiring about joint prosecution and agreeing to cooperate with Ontario.[13] On 29 August, the attorney general of British Columbia telegraphed that he was contacting all the Provincial attorneys general: "How about one central proceeding at place where most evidence available and all share in expense if fine imposed pro rata expense to be taken therefrom."[14] This neat cost-

and risk-sharing idea was quashed by the attorney general of Ontario, who noted, on 17 September, that all fines would have to go to the municipality where trial was held and so could not be shared. Also, there was little evidence that needed to be taken from other Provinces, so perhaps it would be sufficient were all to declare that they were cooperating in the prosecution. In a separate letter on 18 September, he asked the attorney general of British Columbia to cover the expenses of witnesses who had to be brought from there.[15]

Meanwhile, Greer had taken the massive transcript up to his summer cottage to read. From there he sent a letter asking for a junior counsel to assist him, as well as for one of the attorneys who had worked for the White Commission. His cogitations gave birth to a long letter, dated 14 September 1931, in which he analyzed the legal issues raised by the report. He argued that Famous Players' demands for lengthy "protection" periods were extortionate and violated section 498 of the Criminal Code, as well as the Combines Investigation Act. Some of the evidence made him indignant:

It seems scarcely credible that in these days men would act as these men [agents of the FPCC] are sworn to have done and their conduct seems to us reprehensible to the extreme and without justification from any standard of fair competition in business and to come directly within the mischief [harms] of both the Combines Investigation Act and the Code.[16]

His letter did not directly say whether he considered prosecution advisable. Indeed, he went on to say that the business practices of the industry were such that only a statutory body like a commission, modeled on that for a public utility, would achieve a satisfactory result. Similarly, when it came to ensuring the showing of more British pictures in Canada, a statutory quota was indicated, since Famous Players had no commitment to show British films.

The United States production interests are extremely powerful and appear to have unlimited resources and . . . so far as it is possible for them to do so they do and will prevent the showing of British pictures in their theatres as a regular part of their show, except for an isolated picture of outstanding merits which appeals to them only by reason of its box-office drawing power.[17]

Later, as we shall see, Greer claimed he had fully advised the government of the difficulties that the prosecution would face. Given what seemed the overwhelming evidence collected by White, and his quite unequivocal findings, together with the readiness of other Provincial attorneys general to share in prosecution, the weight of official legal opinion was clearly that prosecution was unavoidable, even if tricky. The decision to prosecute was announced on 22 September, and the very next day the offices of Famous Players were raided and their files seized. The case was taken to the grand jury on 19 October, where, despite predictions that as much as a week would be needed, a bill of indictment was returned after only two days of hearings.

The particulars of the charges were that in 1924–30 Famous Players, by its theater ownership and contracts,

compelled the public to pay higher prices;

enforced "protection";

threatened to put independents out of existence;

restricted proper supply of films to others;

enforced "one theatre one contract" on everyone but itself;

discouraged theater building by others;

did not themselves sign the Standard Exhibition Contract [an effort to set uniform business terms] but enforced it, through the MPDEC, on others;

dictated the conditions for independents;

imposed severe credit terms;

indulged in block booking and blind booking;

enforced deposit and arbitration awards, but not against itself; and

spent money lobbying against motion picture legislation favoring the showing of Empire films in British Columbia.

Moreover, the Standard Exhibition Contract was illegal, the MPDEC was under the control of MPPDA, and the MPDEC was formed to raise prices.[18]

Trial began on Monday, 25 January 1932, before Justice Charles Garrow and lasted three weeks, until Saturday, 13 February. Thirty witnesses were called by the Crown. There was a delay of twenty-two days before the verdict was announced on 7 March: The accused were acquitted of all charges.[19] Before we can conclude and reflect on this shaggy-dog story, we need to analyze the trial as seen through the eyes of the judge.

1.5. The judgment of the court

Justice Charles Garrow, of the High Court of Justice for Ontario, filed his judgment in Rex *v*. Famous Players on 18 March 1932.[20] The case had been brought under the Combines Investigation Act, (Revised Statutes of Canada, chapter 26) and under section 498 of the Criminal Code. The indictment charged fifteen corporations and three individuals, but one corporation (the Tiffany Company), though named, was never served or proceeded against. After first objecting, the accused had agreed to be tried by judge without jury. Four of the companies charged were exhibitors, the rest distributors, except for the trade organization MPDEC. The three individuals charged were N. L. Nathanson, formerly managing director of the FPCC; S. Bloom; and I. S. Fine, of B&F Theatres. The defense's attempt to argue that supplying film for a limited time is not a "dealing in an article or commodity that may be the subject of trade or commerce" as defined in the act was dismissed on the grounds that precedent held that supply might relate to anything whatever. Justice Garrow wrote in his opinion:

[The] question I think, so far as the Combines Act is concerned, is this. Has the evidence established that there existed during the years mentioned between the accused, or some of them, an actual or tacit agreement entered into within this Province which had or was designed to have the effect of preventing or lessening competition in or substantially controlling within Ontario or generally the purchase, barter, sale or supply of film? (p. 312)

In answering this question, Garrow summarized the notes he had taken on the testimony. One witness, Arthur Cohen (managing director of Famous Players), had explained "protection" as

the amount of time which the parties agree shall elapse between the end of the run of a specified picture in a first-run theatre, and the beginning of the run of the same picture in the same district or locality in a subsequent run theatre. This time is arrived at by contract between the parties, and the Crown asserts that the exercise of this right of protection which is almost universally conceded as being proper in itself, has been so extended as to operate detrimentally to many of the independent theatre owners. It may be explained that independent theatre owners are all those who are not members of or affiliated with Famous Players. (p. 313)

There was a great oversupply of pictures in Canada. "I think it must be taken as established upon the evidence," Garrow wrote, "that there is competition for business between all distributors" (p. 315). In 1931, there had been 48 million admissions to Famous Players theaters; in 1930, 55 million. Colonel Cooper had testified that 20–25 percent of the films brought into the country were not brought in by MPDEC members. He defended the Standard Exhibition Contract, saying it had been fully discussed beforehand with the companies and had been adopted only gradually.

J. P. O'Loghlin, chief officer of the Fox Film Corporation, testified that until sound arrived films were sold by a flat rental fee; afterward they were sold by percentage of the take. Sixty percent of Fox's revenue came from Famous Players, and in Toronto 55–60 percent of their revenue was derived from Famous Players theaters. He said that he had had many differences of opinion with Nathanson and certainly had never tried to lessen competition or agree on a fixed length for the protection period.

Witness C. O. Burnett, of the Canadian Film Board of Trade, testified that arbitration had to do with collecting debts and did not put anyone out of business.

Garrow commented that these witnesses "gave their evidence fairly and frankly with no attempt to conceal or distort the facts, and apparently willing to lay all the information in their possession before the court" (p. 322).

Witness Bert Wainwright stated that Nathanson had told him that if he built a theater on Danforth Avenue (in Toronto) he would not find it as easy to get pictures as it had been in the past. Yet he did build, and he did get pictures, even though his theater was not wired for sound. Other witnesses (for the prosecution) did not seem to provide evidence of an actual shortage of films. The same went for witness B. Friedman, who said the films available to him were not the right kind of films; the same also for witness James. A couple of witnesses asserted that a two-week protection period was sufficient. There were two witnesses from Ottawa. Time and again an amicable buying out or standoff was arranged with B&F. Garrow dismissed the evidence of H. Redway of Toronto and of one Starkman.

It was obvious, Garrow concluded, that there was no price fixing.

The Government's counsel had made the argument that Famous Players

through its control of so many theatres was able to create and did create an unfair situation favourable to itself and disadvantageous to all others in imposing terms as to protection unfair to its rivals in that those terms prevented them from getting film as soon as otherwise they might. (p. 343)

In the judge's view, the standard contract was a scheme in furtherance of this and constituted a conspiracy. But the Canadian statute requires that the combine be shown to operate to the detriment of the public, whether consumers, producers, or others. "There is nothing to indicate that Famous Players were or are responsible for the existence of the Cooper organisation, or that they dominated or controlled its operations" (p. 345). It had many exhibitor matters to deal with, and the Famous Players members rarely attended. Famous Players was quite a dictatorial company, but the exhibitors rose in revolt. Famous Players was a big customer, and so got a good deal of consideration. But the standard contract specifically left prices, protections, and other matters for negotiation. Conspiracy to put good customers (i.e., the independents) out of business would not make business sense.

Threats by B&F to build competitive theaters were not of themselves unlawful. "That there was any general discrimination against the independent theatre proprietors has not in my opinion been made out [proved]" (p. 347). "All this and much besides to the same effect negatives the suggestion that the independents as a class were the victims of a conspiracy designed to cut off or limit their supply of film" (p. 348).

It is essential that one is able to gather from all the evidence that the combine or conspiracy actually did in fact exist between at least some two or more of the accused; that there was a common design or plan to do the thing forbidden by the statute not resting on intention merely but reduced to a common undertaking to carry that intention into effect.... I have not been able to gather from the material before me that the existence of such a combination between the parties has been made out. (p. 349)

So, in declaring that the prosecution had failed to prove its case and discharging all of the accused, Justice Garrow had held, inter alia, the following:

1. On the facts the Crown had not made out the cases.
2. The U.S. cases cited were not applicable, owing to the form and wording of the (Canadian) act.
3. Threats made had been to do something lawful and so were not impeachable.
4. Seized documents were not evidence of the truth of their contents against the accused without (further) proof of adoption or recognition of them or that they had been acted upon.

1.6. The upshot

Professor Taylor, White, the minister of labor, the Provincial attorneys general, and Counsel Greer notwithstanding, the court had found that the practices objected to were lawful and the advantage accruing to Famous Players could be harmlessly attributed to their purchasing power as the largest firm in the business. In a letter accompanying his bill for services, Greer reminded Price, that Greer had said at the beginning that the problem might need the establishment of a regulatory commission, along the lines of the board that regulated the railroads. This was a body set up to regulate an industry when it was thought that the unregulated market would not deliver appropriate service, at an appropriate price, to the consumer.

It would be helpful if we could know the content of the postmortem on the case conducted within the office of the Ontario attorney general: what options were considered and why they were not pursued. Neither those records nor whatever the attorney general may have said to the Provincial cabinet is to be found in the surviving documents. At all events, no commission or similar body was ever proposed, and no new legislation was introduced. In the period before the case, the Ontario legislature had amended the Theatre and Cinematograph Act to give the government power to impose a quota favoring British films. In speaking during debate on the Second Reading of the bill, the provincial treasurer, Edward A. Dunlop, disclosed that in 1930 two thousand films had been censored, of which a mere seventeen were British.[21] These powers taken were never, in fact, used.[22]

Before we analyze such interaction, we may ask whether the entire investigation of Famous Players was economically motivated. Was the concern a general one about an alleged combine, or was it a specific one that the combine was American and that it was favoring American cultural materials? These things can never be conclusively settled, but this one is about as clear-cut as they ever are. Since there was no indigenous film production industry in need of protection, the questions related to ownership and control of distribution and exhibition. And since the large American firms mostly operated through wholly owned subsidiaries, the only Canadians threatened economically were a handful of independent theater owners. The legal juggernaut was not, I think, wheeled into place for their benefit. Business interests at best might have hoped for opportunity if American domination could be lessened. Underlying the prosecution and the amended Theatre and Cinematograph Act of the preceding year was, I would claim, cultural concern with the influence of American forms of popular culture on Canadians. Magazines, radio, sports, and movies flowed up from the south and found a receptive Canadian audience. Ontario, bastion of the United Empire Loyalists (descendants of Americans who sided with the British in the War of Independence) where the Union Jack floated over the Provincial legislative assembly building, was ruled by an elite that defined its identity as British. (Colonel Cooper was a member of this elite.) To the extent possible, they wanted British popular culture to be available as an alternative, indeed as a counterweight, to American.[23]

If this is so, then it is puzzling that nothing more was done after 1932. The quota powers were not utilized, and the Federal Parliament made no attempt to regulate the film industry by means of a commission, as it would with radio and, later, television. Subsequently other measures, such as the creation of the National Film Board, were undertaken, but that still leaves us unable to explain the interval. My best guess is this:

Ontario concluded it could not act alone but that a quota had to be national.

In the midst of a depression, such adventures as investing government money in promoting filmmaking in Ontario were not viable.

British film production was in a fairly sorry state.

Public preference in Canada was clearly for American films and stars.

Thus, although encouragement for British films was in order, realistically it was accepted that American dominance was virtually complete and, for the moment, unshakable.

But to go farther than this, it will be best, I think, to try to get a longer-term picture of the film industry in Canada before the White Report and only then move on to recount the subsequent attempts to regulate trade in movies within the Dominion.

The White Report case neatly illustrates the economic foreign policy of the U.S. film industry. The strategy was, simply, to dominate the market and then to utilize the leverage of domination to prevent the emergence of rival centers of power, while permitting those exhibitors not under control some sort of livelihood. The small number of American distributors and their direct links with the principal theaters and sources of revenue enabled them judiciously to buy up or indirectly control the strategic centers of exhibition. Once secured, the system was maintained by zoning; clearances; first, second, and subsequent runs; and by blind and block booking. None of these would have worked if there had not been a strong demand and serious lack of competitive product. Talk in the report and elsewhere of a serious oversupply of films in Canada was quite ill informed: The presence of lots of films that no one wanted to see did not constitute an oversupply. The fact was that the major American firms had little difficulty in disposing of their entire product line, despite the inferiority of some of it, precisely because of the strong demand for some of it.

Notes

1 Despite the claims of Morris (1978).

2 This is an American figure; see Table 2.2 of the present volume.

3 I have tried to make the case for movies as the major mass medium in this period (its rivals were the press and radio) in two earlier essays (1982, 1986).

4 Quoted from the R. B. Bennett Papers, PA MG 26 K, vols. 452–3, as copied in the *Dreamland* materials, File 59, Canadian Film Archives (hereafter CFA. A list of abbreviations of archives where primary materials used in the present volume were found is given in the References).

5 Ibid.

6 Ibid.

7 Ibid.

8 John Alexander Cooper (1868–1956); born Clinton, Ontario; attended the University of Toronto, took B.A. in political science (1892), L.L.B. (1893). Before World War I editor of *Canadian Magazine* and *Canadian Courier;* after war established Canadian Government Bureau of Information in New York; he returned to Canada (1921), entered advertising and part-time work as secretary of the MPDEC (full-time 1925); stayed in post until 1944, although after 1939 concentrated on war relief; temporary commissioner of the National Film Board (1939–40) (see Evans 1984, pp. 72–6); throughout life was associated with patriotic organizations (e.g., Canadian League, Association of Canadian Clubs), wrote and lectured on Canadian nationalism and British patriotism.

9 Jesse Lasky gives a hair-raising account of "blind selling" in his autobiography (1957, pp. 197–202). Lasky was for many years in charge of production on the West Coast for Paramount.

10 Robertson to Price, 14 July 1931, AO, RG 4, Series a–32, 1931, File 1900.

11 Price to Greer, 16 July 1931, ibid.

12 [?] to Price, 31 July 1931, ibid.

13 [?] to Price, 12 August 1931, ibid.

14 Telegram [?] to Price, 29 August 1931, ibid.

15 Price to [?], 19 September 1931 and 18 September 1931, ibid.

16 Greer to Price, 14 September 1931, ibid.

17 Ibid.

18 Particulars of 23 November 1931, AO, RG 22, Series 391, Supreme Court of Ontario – Assize Indictment Clerk – Report, York, 1932, "The King vs. Famous Players et al."

19 There was rather full coverage of the trial in the *Toronto Daily Mail and Empire,* 26 January 1932–15 February 1932.

20 This section is entirely based on two sources: AO, RG 22, Series 391, Supreme Court of Ontario – Assize Indictment Clerk – Report, York, 1932, "The King vs. Famous Players et al."; and Rex *v*. Famous Players 21 1932 O.R. 307–49. Page references are to *Ontario Reports*. A great deal of documentation concerning the trial appears to have been discarded in the era before the Ontario Archives were properly organized.

21 *Globe and Mail*, 27 March 1931.

22 Pendakur (1990, pp. 91–4) offers a Marxist explanation of the inaction, premised on Canada's cultural dependency on Britain and on Britain's economic dependency on international (i.e., U.S.) capitalism. He holds the anticombine legislation to have been a sham.

23 This was forcefully put in a memorandum of 9 May 1930 by the chairman of the Board of Censors of Moving Pictures, J. C. Boylen, to George Patton of the Motion Picture Bureau. AO, RG 56, Series A–1, Box 5, File 5.3, Correspondence on Moving Pictures 1913–1934.

CHAPTER 2

Before the White Report, 1920–1930

To place the White Report and the trial of Famous Players in context, we look first at the structure of the Canadian film industry; then at the domination of it by the United States. Attempts to cope with this domination began at the Imperial Conference of 1926 and came to a head with the passage of legislation in Britain to foster British production by guaranteeing it a market share. Once quality British films were available, it was hoped that other parts of the Empire would act to foster their consumption.

2.1. The structure of the Canadian film market

The picture that has already partly emerged from our study looks something like this. Canada was an enormous land, thinly populated on the average, but containing several large cities and hundreds of small towns. English-language film distribution was organized from Toronto. The country was subdivided into territories, some, but not all, of which corresponded to the Provinces that constitute the Canadian federation. The *exchange* (or distribution headquarters) for each territory was in a large city. The communications link used for moving films was the railroad. Of the approximately 1,100 theaters, fewer than one-quarter were consolidated into chains and centrally booked by their owners. The remainder were technically independent, although complex arrangements and understandings seem to have existed with the distributors and the chains.

As in the United States, theater chains were originally regionally based, successful theater owners expanding to control more theaters in areas they knew. Growth, consolidation, and rationalization in the United States eventually led to much more extensive chaining, covering, for example, much of the South, or the Northeast, or California. The situation was similar in Canada, where economic logic tended to dictate national chains, able to open new films in all the principal markets at one time. No proper studies yet exist of the relation of all this to advertising. So long as advertising was local, local control was sufficient to recoup whatever was spent on it. But with the wider circulation of big-city newspapers, and then of national magazines, and the use of these as outlets for advertisement and movie publicity materials, an ever-larger reach was the economic logic of theater ownership. When national radio networks (and later, of course, television) offered a coast-to-coast advertising medium, only coast-to-coast ownership of theaters would ensure that publicity was not being given away.

Canada's thin ribbon of population made its market a peculiar one – like a midwestern state, on a hugely magnified scale. There were a few relatively sophisticated large cities, able to support premium theaters and to generate the bulk of film revenue. There were also many small towns with only one theater. These yielded modest revenue and could not be relied upon to reflect the same taste in movies as the big cities. This was a structure familiar to American distributing and exhibiting firms. Moreover, in much of Canada the language and culture were such that advertising materials and campaigns planned for the United States could be used unaltered in Canada. It is no wonder that this other dollar-land to the north should have been treated as simply a segment of the overall "domestic market" for films (Jarvie 1991).

In making this judgment, I am siding with the implicit assumptions of the U.S. motion picture companies. For their purposes, Canada behaved much like a part of the United States. Perhaps we can learn something from this. Although Canada was a political alternative to the United States, economically and in certain cultural respects it resembled the United States far more than the United Kingdom. Not all British films were bad, but when they were good their success in Canada may have had more to do with nostalgia, guilt, and a lost aspiration than with current loyalties.

Some estimate of the maturity of the Canadian film industry can be gauged from its various attempts to form a trade association. According to a document in Colonel Cooper's papers,[1] a first organization, the Motion Picture Distributors Association, was formed 8 January 1920 in a meeting at the King Edward Hotel in Toronto. A Mr. Hague was elected secretary and a Mr. O'Loghlin secretary-treasurer. Also present were various industry figures, including Messrs. Ouimet, Kauffman, Rosenfeld, Barrett, Allan, Weeks, Bach, McCabe, and Soskin. In March of the following year the group was reorganized by Arthur Cohen, who became president, with Rosenfeld vice-president, Cooper secretary, and Drummond treasurer. Aiming to combat unjust legislation and unjust propaganda, this organization also debated the merits of acetate versus nitrate film; the need for fireproof exchange buildings; the establishment of central screening rooms in branch centers; improved methods for revising positive films; and express rates, amusement taxes, and censorship fees. More important was the struggle to get exhibitors to pay cash in advance, or C.O.D., and the principle of "One town, one contract" to displace contracts each covering several theaters.

In 1924, Will Hays, who interested himself in the situation in Canada, suggested a new group, the Chartered Association, which was duly formed on 17 November 1924, with Cooper as president, Cohen as secretary, and as directors Hague, Philip Riesman, Ira H. Cohen, O. R. Hanson, and J. W. Berman. "The chief difference between this association and the other, was the addition of 'exhibitor membership.' This feature never was a great success and was abandoned in 1931."[2] The fees paid by the members of the association were collected by the Hays Organization office in New York City and remitted to Canada. Monthly statements were sent from the Toronto office to the New York office. "In the Minutes of the meeting on March 12th, 1925, it is reported that Mr. Pettijohn of the Hays Office had visited Canada in January and organized Film Boards of Trade in Toronto and Montreal."[3]

Riesman and Cohen resigned as directors, and J. P. O'Loghlin, M. A. Milligan, Thomas W. Brady, Clarence Robson, and B. F. Lyon were elected.

A new Standard Exhibition Contract had been approved in the United States and a Canadian edition of it has been prepared and was adopted early in 1926. It came into force in Canada on May 1st, 1926. This brought arbitration [by the Boards of Trade, to settle contract disputes] into being under all Canadian contracts for the first time.

In 1928, there were 369 arbitration cases, involving $111,000. The following year (the first in which sound appeared), there were 523 cases, with claims amounting to $223,000. Other matters in which the association involved itself were lobbying against a 12.5-percent Federal tax on film remittances sent abroad, proposed in 1933 (finally imposed in 1935, at 5%); reducing the number of films condemned by the eight Provincial censor boards; lobbying for reducing the duty on imported printed advertisements; and fighting a Nova Scotian proposal to put the whole industry under government control. By 1938, box-office receipts had reached $33,625,000.

For reasons unexplained in the history, an unincorporated association was formed in September 1940, with Cooper as chairman of the Board of Directors, O'Loghlin as president, and E. H. Wells as secretary-treasurer. No successor organization presently exists, and it is unknown whether the records of all these years survive somewhere. Thus the full history cannot be pursued. It is worth noting that the ill will remaining from the Famous Players trial was declared gone by 1933. We await a proper history of motion picture pioneering in Canada – the opening up of theaters, the building of chains, and the arrival of sound. Historians have concentrated on the making of films, which means either laboriously researched attention to the passingly interesting or total concentration on the National Film Board. Neither gives us a context of the distribution and exhibition of films in general, and hence some sense of the audience in the context of Canada as a whole.

One other feature of the structure of the industry as importer needs to be made. As a small market, Canada did not always constitute sufficient marketing bait for exporters. The United States, as we have seen, treated the Canadian market as another territory of the U.S. domestic market. In the case of imports from the United Kingdom, this posed a problem. When U.S. firms sought out films to import, they also sought Canadian exhibition rights. British firms, far more interested in U.S. exhibition rights than Canadian rights, were inclined to yield them. Thus Canadian importers competed not just against each other but also against U.S. importers. Oscar Hanson, of Canadian Educational Pictures, reported to the Motion Picture Distributors and Exhibitors of Canada (MPDEC) that British producers had refused to make separate Canadian contracts with him until they had made arrangements in the United States and that when a separate deal was offered it was at an unrealistic price.

During all of our conversations, I did not meet one British Producer who intimated that he would be willing to send a representative to Canada to study conditions so that he would be in a position to cooperate with us in an intelligent manner.

In search of forty pictures, Hanson found himself offered only nine, at exorbitant prices.

After I returned, I got in touch with an American producer, and in a few days I was able to make a contract for seventy Feature Pictures to be delivered during the next two years on much more favourable terms than the best offered me in England.[4]

The problem created by having Canadian exhibition rights to some British films in the hands of U.S. firms is insufficiently remarked by historians, for it continued well into the 1950s. Justice Garrow had found that Famous Players was such a large force in the Canadian market that they were able to bargain for exceptional treatment. Similarly, American firms in the market for British films were in a powerful position. Firms refusing them Canadian rights were dissipating goodwill, as well as, perhaps, good deals. Only when the British motion picture industry began to develop its own overseas distribution branches was it possible to get around the problem.

2.2. American domination of the Canadian film market

Two facts are sufficient to explain the world dominance of the motion-picture industry by the United States by the early 1920s. One is the contingent fact that during the period when the movie business was consolidating itself, developing the vertically integrated and oligopolistic structure that is now so familiar to historians, all major Western film-producing nations, except the United States, were fighting World War I. There were big audiences for movies in belligerent countries, but labor and capital to produce and means to transport exports were constrained. For one thing, the major trading partners and their overseas territories were on opposite sides. For another, physical interdiction of shipping was practiced, greatly restricting free movement of what product there was. For three years, from 1914 to 1917, the United States was neutral and far less subject to these constraints, which were more effective than any protective tariff.

But, as Rachel Low argues, in her authoritative *History of the British Film, 1918–1929* (1971), the deeper cause, which may merely have been strengthened by the war, was the structural advantage of the large domestic U.S. market (p. 300). This thesis is a trifle oversimplified, because there were other large domestic markets in the world, far from the combat zone – India and China, for example – that were unable to exploit this competitive advantage. The large U.S. domestic market was able to capitalize on its advantage as part of a general process of industrialization and capital formation that had already made the United States the largest industrialized power in the world. Thus, presented with the drying up of foreign competition for its home screens, discovering the immense latent demand for its product both at home and abroad, the entrepreneurs of the U.S. film industry, most of whom came from the exhibiting and distributing side of things, were able to put to profitable use all the capital they could lay hands on.

U.S. entrepreneurs seem rapidly to have come to terms with the idea that spending copious sums of money on the production of films was a risk that could pay high dividends. Thus costly and spectacular films were made. Even more important, the leading personnel – the star attractions – were an investment. Whether because their cost accounting told them that the more they spent, the better the public liked it, or because they knew their competition could not match their rate of spending, by the mid-1920s the top Hollywood studios were spending at levels that precluded their making a profit in the domestic market, thus fostering an aggressive cultivation of overseas sales.[5]

The situation as it developed in Canada was typical of the other White Dominions and even of Britain. A considerable amount of cinema building had taken place in Canada in all urban centers, and a strong cinemagoing habit had developed among the population. What the population saw was overwhelmingly American. This is testified to, not only by figures compiled by nationalists and business rivals, but by figures the Americans compiled – and were pleased about.

The figures shown in Table 2.1, taken from parliamentary documents, are clearly from Canadian Customs sources, since that was the only body that counted film imports by feet. The duty on film was calculated by the linear foot, and hence the "value" given is a customs value, related solely to length and gauge, disregarding earning value at the box office. This technical point – that customs duties on movies normally have to be assessed at the national border, prior to any assessment of a film's value in earnings – persistently troubled those countries that sought to use tariffs to counter American dominance, as we shall see.

Table 2.1. *Film Imports to Canada, 1922–6*

	1922	1923	1924	1925	1926
UK					
Feet	452,546	296,241	924,495	309,150	286,158
Value (Can$)	29,640	21,463	72,293	23,870	23,069
France					
Feet	118,287	53,513	16,948	69,445	14,764
Value (Can$)	8,384	4,210	1,317	5,551	1,061
USA					
Feet	20,382,417	18,875,452	19,858,022	22,291,820	23,593,221
Value (Can$)	1,716,161	1,524,069	1,626,644	1,797,689	1,898,698

Source: Ottawa Consul to State Department, 16 March 1927, NA, RG 59 1912–1929 842.4061, Motion Pictures–Canada, Microfilm M 1435, Roll 19.

The figures in Table 2.1 reveal clearly that American domination in the Canadian market was established by 1922, although, since they are among the earliest official figures I have come across, we may surmise that the state of affairs had come about earlier. Using the Canadian dollar-value figures, we can calculate that British films amounted to 1.68 percent of imports in 1922, French films to 0.48 percent, and U.S. films to 97.82 percent. The amounts fluctuate over the five years shown, but by 1926, when agitation about the situation had risen to a peak, from the American point of view things were better, from the nationalist point of view worse. In 1926, only 1.19 percent (by value) of film imports were British, 0.08 percent were French, whereas 98.70 percent were American. For all intents and purposes, American domination of the film trade in Canada was total. Perhaps in no other commodity was the American export drive more successful than this one, and although, on the scale of major industries, films were small, it is not surprising that there were vigorous attempts to conserve the advantage.

As already noted, Canada was never a center of film production, never registered significantly in the world trade in commercial films. Hence in looking at its relations to the United States and the United Kingdom in these matters, we must always remember that Canada is a client, not a competitor. It is true that from time to time schemes were devised and hopes expressed that this situation would change: It never did.

Throughout our study of the Canadian and British ends of the triangular trade, we shall also need to attend to two seemingly separate issues that might better be fused: Let me call these the "economic" and the "cultural" dimensions. On the surface we are here dealing with trade in a commodity – films. If there is an indigenous industry producing that commodity, there will always be forces at work seeking to disadvantage the foreign competition and advantage the domestic producers. To the extent that indigenous businesses handle and profit from the imports, there will be countervailing forces seeking to conserve that source. Given the virtual absence of domestic film production in Canada, the business forces seeking to disadvantage American imports were weak. Virtually all the entrepreneurs who made a profit from the film trade owed their livelihood to American imports. Some of those men were themselves American imports: for example, N. L. Nathanson, who had emigrated to Canada from Minneapolis, took citizenship, and built up a theater chain that was eventually part of Famous Players. The Allen brothers, Jules and Jay, were also Americans; they built up a powerful chain, which they sold to Nathanson in 1922. Others – many others – were as Canadian as they come, as patriotic as they come – yet were making a good living from commodities imported from Hollywood. A good example would be Ernest Ouimet (see Morris 1978, pp. 23–5). We have already noted that the trade organization the Motion Picture Distributors and Exhibitors of Canada (MPDEC) was headed by Colonel Cooper, a decorated veteran of World War I and a stalwart patriot.[6]

Business interest, then, cut neatly across issues of nationality and, derivatively, culture. Many loyal Canadians had a strong interest in defending the unimpeded importation of Hollywood films. Nevertheless, cultural and nationalistic arguments need not be taken at their face value. Some may have come from those trying to make a livelihood from domestic films or, more likely in the Canadian case, from imported British films. Had the balance of advantage been adjusted to favor the commodity in which they traded, then we would be inclined to assess their arguments as having as much to do with economic self-interest as with national and cultural attitudes. Just because their campaign failed, we do not have to take their cultural rhetoric about the importance of British culture to Canadian nationhood at face value.

It is not my intention to reduce nationalistic and cultural concerns to economic ones. To show this, here are some incidents revealing unalloyedly patriotic motives. From about 1911 on, there is evidence of unhappiness in the Province of Ontario with American films that literally "waved the flag." Showing the Stars and Stripes on the screen could have had dramatic point in patriotic or historical subjects, but the evidence suggests that it was indulged in a good deal more than that, partly because producers found that it got a positive audience response back home. Soon after Ontario established a Provincial censor board on 1 July 1911, the censors began snipping at what they considered excessive displays of the Stars and Stripes, to the annoyance of production companies.[7] A Canadian agent reported, "At first they confined themselves solely to condemning pictures of the 'Revolutionary War' showing the downfall of the British flag, however, it has got so now they will not permit the American flag to be shown at all."[8]

The U.S. State Department was in a difficult situation. Their only proper channel of contact was Ottawa, but, as they well knew and Ottawa reminded them, censorship was under Provincial, not Federal, jurisdiction.[9] The U.S. consul general at Montréal reported that there was considerable anti-American feeling "worked up in every way among the English element of the Provinces of Ontario and Québec," although "I must say that I have heard of no feeling against American products where needed or where money can be made from them."[10] Note the intrusion of an economic reduction, followed by the comment that "some managers of American firms see in the action of the Board of Censors a move for the protection of Canadian film manufacturers."[11] It is a running theme of the evidence that when cultural objections were raised against American films, American business-men and officials interpreted the move as one of commercial discrimination in rhetorical disguise. In this case they were, I think, mistaken. George B. Armstrong, chairman of the Ontario censor board, claimed that showing the Stars and Stripes on the screen had provoked disturbances in theaters, in the inflamed atmosphere aroused by American politicians who talked of annexing Canada.

Two years later, the topic continued to crop up in State Department files. In writing to Secretary of State William Jennings Bryan, J. G. Graham, general manager of the Universal Company of New York, illustrated how heavily involved American interests already were:

This Company has a contract with the Canadian Film Exchange, headquarters, Calgary, Alberta, Canada, operating offices at Calgary, Vancouver, Toronto and Montreal.... [They release film] each week for use throughout the United States and Canada.... We are only one of fifteen or twenty various manufacturers in the United States who are each week shipping film to their respective Agents in Canada.[12]

Whether or not Ontario had eased up on the flag censorship is unclear, but in 1913 the trouble complained of was coming from censors in British Columbia, although Canadian authorities wrote to the Americans that the problem had been exaggerated: Sometimes the Stars and Stripes was let through and was greeted in Canadian theaters by applause. These showings were confirmed by the attorney general of British Columbia, who said that sometimes there had also been hissing and altercations. His letter on the topic seems to me to be free of commercial motivation:

As to the policy of this Department in connection with cutting out the display of United States flags in films which are censured [sic] by this Department, I may say that where a picture is thrown on a screen, which is the exact representation of a scene which has taken place in the United States, such as a procession, there is no attempt to cut out the flags themselves, but where flags are very conspicuous and so interwoven in the thread of the story that it is impossible to cut them out without destroying the scene of the narrative, then we have no alternative but to reject the reels in their entirety.

We have had some instances of a suggested story of the Civil War in the United

States, manufactured by American Film Companies, who have pieced together some semblance of a plot, where the "filling-in" is done with United States flags. These scenes do not possess any historical worth, they are merely skeletons around which the flag is draped, the purpose, of course, being to educate reverence for the flag amongst the children of residents of the United States with which we do not complain, but if there is to be any extra display of flags in the scenes depicted in this Province we, of course, prefer our own Union Jack.[13]

Here we have two jingoisms in collision with one another: the jingoism of American motion picture companies, who were prepared to paper together films with shots of the flag; and the jingoism of a Canadian Provincial politician in an era when assertions of Canadian identity were made in the rhetoric of the British Empire. The American complaints, of course, were that such censorship spoiled their films commercially – not artistically. Nevertheless, both sides were displaying cultural and nationalist sentiments that seem not to derive from concern with commercial advantage.

The flag saga continued after the United States entered World War I and began to take it as a subject for films. Predictably, in those films, the American role was played up, and the role of the other Allies was played down, if noticed at all. Like excessive displays of the flag, such underrepresentation of the role of Canadian and British troops aggravated feelings in Ontario, where the Provincial treasurer, as the minister responsible for censorship, threatened that

hereafter unless more films depicting the part played by Great Britain and Canada in this war are shown on the screen...I will be obliged to instruct the censors to cut out much of the material....I do not see why the Film Exchanges cannot obtain such material as I have indicated, and certainly our Canadian citizens will not much longer stand for the exaltation of an army of another nation and forgetfulness of our own.[14]

Without yet venturing an opinion as to just how many Canadians this voice from the political elite represented, I reiterate my point that we have here genuine concerns deriving from culture and nationality. The answer made by the industry, in this case, however, drives us back to commerce and prepares us for it to utilize the rhetoric of culture and nation. George Kleine, a founder of the Kalem Company and the Motion Picture Patents Company, wrote to the State Department from Chicago, pointing out that Canadian and British troops were not available to American producers and that there were few British or Canadian firms to make their films. As to preparing special versions for Canada, a commercial fact had to be faced:

The making of feature motion pictures involves large sums of money and owing to the limited population of Canada, it is commercially difficult to localize subjects, unless they are of such a character as to have a world market.[15]

No doubt Kleine was being disingenuous when citing a lack of British and Canadian troops as a reason for not showing the Canadian and British part

Table 2.2. *U.S. percentage of film imports to Canada, 1923–6*

1923	98.3%	1925	98.7%
1924	95.3%	1926	99.1%

Source: U.S. Consul General, Ottawa, to State Department, 11 March 1926, NA, RG 59 842.4061, Motion Pictures–Canada 1912–1929, Microfilm 1435, Roll 19.

in the war. Lack of French Foreign Legionnaires never stopped American companies from filming stories involving them. The straightforward explanation of the emphasis on U.S. troops was obvious: In developing stories for the domestic market, Hollywood emphasized and celebrated the exploits of America's own fighting men, and such films went into the maw of exports in the normal way. This is a pattern that was to be repeated time and again, and it is perhaps Hollywood's most persistent form of blundering. Either stories exaggerated the role of the United States, or what was taken for granted in America was, to one degree or another, offensive abroad. Patriotic stories of the triumph of the Colonials in the Revolutionary War were bound to offend people of United Empire Loyalist sympathies in Ontario and elsewhere in Canada. Similarly, villainous or ludicrous characterizations of the British could scarcely be expected to sit well with audiences in Britain. The blundering invariably consisted of such films being sucked into the export pipeline, arousing protest or censorship and forcing American production companies hastily to engage in damage control.

In 1919 in Ontario, we begin to see more clearly the intertwining of cultural and national concerns with commercial interests. That year it was decided that licenses to distribute or exhibit motion pictures would be granted only to British citizens. Since the motion picture business in Ontario was largely American owned, this had to do with power and money, not with culture and nation. After the Provincial election, the Province backed away and decided that licenses would also be issued to aliens (except enemy aliens). This was, after all, Ontario, where the censors would not allow any German film to be shown until 1927, a decision several times confirmed by the Provincial cabinet.

It is my contention that by the time agitation about American films in general began (as opposed to specific objections about flags or troops), in the twenties, culturalist and nationalist arguments must be treated with circumspection. A good deal of money was clearly at stake, and nativists wondered why foreigners should get it.[16] To the British or Empire patriot, the situation as it shows up in the American-reported figures was about as dismal as could be. Their calculations, based on Canadian customs records of film imports and their country of origin, gave the results shown in Table 2.2. Another set of figures, compiled by the U.S. Department of Commerce in 1927, are of interest (Table 2.3). The figures in the first four rows of

Table 2.3. *Canadian film imports from the United States 1913–27*

Year	Feet	Value ($)
1913	9,000,000	71,000
1923	19,500,000	850,000
1924	19,700,000	850,000
1925	23,000,000	915,000
1926	20,985,072	731,604
1927[a]	8,432,301	302,180

[a]First nine months only.
Source: North to Poole, 27 October 1927, NA, RG 151, BF&DC 281, Motion Pictures–Canada.

Table 2.3 are suspiciously rounded, suggesting that they are estimates, if not guesstimates. The source gives no information as to how these figures were compiled or what data base was used. They must be looked on, therefore, as at best a guide, rather than an authoritative source.

Two external facts are important here. The British film industry was in a (worsening) slump. Second, as Rachel Low candidly acknowledges, British films were, by and large, abysmally bad (Low 1971, p. 298). Not surprising, then, that a campaign was afoot to boost them in Ontario, when, by 1930, as we have seen, seventeen British films were censored, against one thousand American. In 1924, the U.S. consul at Montréal reported several press items directed against the alleged "propaganda" of American films. From elsewhere in the Empire came Australian press comment deploring the U.S. domination of their screens and urging government assistance to the U.K. film industry, in the name of welding the Empire more closely together and broadening the national mind. The *Montreal Star* advocated a discriminatory duty.[17] Two years later the *Ottawa Citizen* editorialized on British moves toward quota legislation, writing that "through the films, the radio, the cheap magazines and the Sunday newspapers, Canadians are being made more and more to think, talk and act like Americans. This is not good for the national spirit. It is a problem."[18]

For those looking for a fifth column, one was at hand in the Canadian Government Motion Picture Bureau (Backhouse 1974), whose head seemed to look favorably on U.S. films and unfavorably on British and who talked freely to the U.S. consul. In a 1926 dispatch to the State Department, consular officers at Ottawa were reassuring that a quota system in Canada along the lines then being discussed in Great Britain was unlikely. In the following quotation from the dispatch, it is reasonable to surmise that the person referred to as "one well conversant with the motion picture business in Canada" was Raymond Peck, director of the bureau.[19]

It has been said, by one well conversant with the motion picture business in Canada, that when British motion picture producers "learn how to tell a story in film" and improve their technique to a degree comparable to that of American motion picture films, no *quota system* will be necessary to enable them to compete in Canada; and that, until the British pictures meet such requirements, the Canadian public is not interested in their productions. This, it is believed, is fairly typical of the Canadian attitude on the subject.[20]

Perhaps the Ottawa consulate was going beyond its evidence, since Peck was by no stretch of the imagination "typical." As remarked earlier, ruling elites were strenuously arguing the contrary position: namely, that there was a strong, latent demand for British pictures in the Dominion. It was because of this belief that quota legislation was eventually passed in Ontario, British Columbia, and Alberta (Morris 1978, p. 312, note 10).

The question remains, who was right? As for Peck's assertion that British films of the time were poor, especially when compared with the American product, he was undoubtedly correct. Rachel Low, the scrupulously fair and judicious "official" historian of British films, makes no bones about it. She even quotes sources who said that advertising a film as British even in Britain itself was a way of driving audiences away (Low 1971, pp. 298–311). Despite these deficiencies, were the U.S. consular officials mistaken in their belief that there was no demand for British films in Canada? Again, although they may not have had the evidence, I fear their conclusion was correct. There is plenty of evidence that the ruling elites were living under an illusion: that Britain and things British were by no means universally loved by most Canadians.[21] The combination of a general view among Canadian cinemagoers that British films were poor entertainment, together with a distaste among certain groups in Canada for things British, is powerful but not clinching evidence. No direct evidence from official documents for 1926 is available, but in the ensuing years various efforts were made to promote British films, and individual successes often raised hopes. But the distributors invariably reported that, in the long run, British films were not as profitable, not as well marketed, and not as reliably supplied as they needed to be to compete with Hollywood.

In a 1926 letter to W. H. Price, Provincial treasurer of Ontario, Colonel Cooper recapitulated a correspondence that they had had two years before on the subject of British films.[22] The treasurer had remarked that American dominance was unfortunate and

that there would be an advantage in showing Old Country pictures because we should get away from American patriotic ideals, American historical reflections and antipathies.[23]

In his reply, Cooper had brought up the case of the British film *Woman to Woman,* which censorship had not deemed fit to show in either Ontario or Québec. He noted that on 19 June 1926 the treasurer had asked whether it would be possible to start an industry in Canada, "providing Ontario insisted on a quota of Canadian pictures, say 25%." Cooper had responded that the Allens had made a specialty of showing British films, without any great success. He also noted that the Regal Film Company maintained an agent in London to seek out likely product. The problem was one of supply of quality pictures. He noted that British exhibitors had recently voted down a proposal to allocate 10 percent of screen time (a quota) to British films. Although "they would use all the good British pictures they could get and be glad to get them, they declined to be forced to use inferior British pictures, because of the financial loss involved." For his part, Cooper offered the following reassurance:

We have honestly tried to make certain that every British film suitable for this market was brought out here and distributed. Moreover, all these films are brought to us direct and do not come through American sources. I mention this because a *Telegram* correspondent recently intimated that the opposite was done.[24]

Cooper's letter had been provoked by a quota motion proposed to the Provincial legislature by one of their members, Russell Nesbitt, asserting

that in the opinion of this House it is expedient for the encouragement of British industry and for national and education purposes that persons licensed to exhibit moving pictures in Ontario should be restrained from confining such exhibitions to pictures produced elsewhere than in the British Empire and that to this end regulations should be made restricting the exhibition in Ontario of pictures of non-British origin to a percentage diminishing with each year until not more than twenty-five per centum of the pictures exhibited in any one year shall be pictures produced elsewhere than in the British Empire and that the Board of Censors be instructed to report on the practicability and extent of such restrictions.[25]

Cooper had good reason to react. The poor audience response to British films, the limited supply of them, their censorship troubles, and the ready profits to hand from American films scarcely made the prospect of a 25-percent cap on U.S. motion pictures palatable. Of course, Nesbitt's ideas were quite impracticable as well. Even Great Britain never got to the stage of reserving 75 percent of screen time for British pictures. Still, we can read into Nesbitt's proposal the aggressive seriousness with which some patriots viewed the U.S. domination of Canadian and Empire screens. The gravamen of Cooper's letter is that these questions had been previously and seriously gone into and that unless there was an improvement in the objective problems of supply, quality, and censorship, such sentiments could be satisfied only to a limited extent.

Price may not have trusted Cooper in this, for he was simultaneously told, by George Patton, head of the Ontario Motion Picture Bureau, that Patton was "daily receiving more and more requests for British pictures, especially since the showing of the tour of the Prince of Wales."[26] The bureau made what we now call documentary and promotional pictures on behalf of the Ontario government and distributed them to nontheatrical outlets at home and abroad. Eccentrically, the films were 28-millimeter width and so could not be shown in commercial theaters. At all events, Patton's enthusiasm for British pictures and their potential was not based on a close working understanding of the theatrical audience; Cooper's was.

My own inclination is to go against the sneers at Cooper delivered by Prime Minister Bennett and others and take at face value his assurance that nothing would have pleased him more than to have successfully distributed lots of British pictures. That attitude is consistent with the other known facets of Colonel Cooper's public life. We need not impugn his sincerity or his patriotism because he argued that the film industry was not interested in unprofitable British films. Some patriots outside the business (such as the British Empire Film Institute) were prepared to say they wanted to promote British films, even at a loss. In a way, their wish was granted by the various government filmmaking organizations that developed in Canada and Britain. Yet the history of the distribution of the films of those government branches provides a decisive argument on Cooper's side. An infinitesimal number of people saw these nonfictional films, compared to the large number that saw the average Hollywood film. It was not only financially unsound to distribute unpopular British pictures; it was also a waste of time. Cinemagoing is a voluntary activity, and if the public will not come to see or stay all the way through a film, then neither commercial aims nor cultural aims can be realized.

2.3. The Imperial Conference of 1926

Imperial conferences were periodically convened to bring together senior officials of all the self-governing territories of the British Empire for an exchange of views. (Later they became biennial meetings of heads of government at the Commonwealth Conferences.) If we envisage the Imperial Conference of 1926, held in London, as a scene in the script that is being realized in this book, then it is the first of several scenes of which we shall shoot three separate sets of takes. Our first set of takes will concentrate on showing how the conference was viewed by Canada and Canadians, at least as they have left traces in documents, and what aims Canada pursued at that conference. The second set of takes (Part II, §4.2) will be shot from a different angle: that of the British organizers and hosts of the conference, who displayed quite different aims and interests. Our third set of takes (Part III, §10.3) will be different again, since we shall look at the conference as it was viewed from a distance by the Americans, who were uninvited outsiders, suspicious that the Empire was a trading bloc aimed at thwarting U.S. business interests (Betts 1985).

In considering the 1920s, we have already had to negotiate our way through Canadian culturalist and nationalist concerns about American domination, expressed in a vocabulary that is no longer current. Canadians do not now identify themselves as British, no longer affirm that it is British voices, values, and ideals that they want put into the movies. Nationalists who wish now to contrast Canada with the United States and to decry the influence of American mass culture are endeavoring to develop a vocabulary that refers to a distinctly Canadian identity, separate from both the British and the U.S. Nevertheless, for purposes of historical fidelity, we must look closely at how our ancestors actually spoke and thought. One major expression of a universalized British cultural sentiment as applied to films centered on the Imperial Conference of 1926. This was some years before the "Imperial preference" policy was promulgated at the Imperial Economic Conference at Ottawa in 1932, a trade policy giving preferential treatment to a wide range of goods from the Empire. Contrary to the Marxist model of an empire as a vast store of labor and natural resources to be exploited and grow fat on, the British Empire seems to have become a drain on the mother country. At the conference of 1926, Britain was clearly looking for means to make a little money out of the Empire. An economically small item, no. 5 on the agenda, received greater attention than it might seem to have deserved; its importance was magnified by the idea that culture rather than force would hold together the White Dominions.[27]

Nothing will permit us to disentangle patriotic and commercial issues here. The British film industry was, as noted, in a parlous state by the mid-1920s. Naturally, interest groups were looking for ways to revive it. The American market was large but, after all, under the control of the U.S. film industry. The British Empire market looked almost as large, and hence rather attractive. But the Americans had more than 90 percent of the market in Britain, and the same went for the Empire as a whole. In fact, films were one of the few U.S. industrial products that had successfully penetrated and dominated the British Empire market, a fact that was evaluated quite differently on the two sides of the Atlantic. Britain's view was, positively, that the Empire was its natural arena of operations and should be more vigorously exploited. Negatively it was argued that U.S. dominance in films was harmful not just economically but culturally. American films did not preach the kinds of messages Britain thought desirable for its colonial subjects. In so arguing, it found an eager and accepting audience among segments of the Canadian elite – the politicians, the bureaucrats, and the "guardians of culture," as Sklar (1976) called them.

During the early 1920s, there seems to have developed among the network of Empire patriots a view that a greater flow of British popular culture was a vital means of enlightening Empire peoples and sustaining the cohesion of the Empire around a set of British ideals and values. In a speech to the British Empire Film Institute, this was forcefully expressed in a manner that signals the conceptual shift that was going on, from an Empire built up (and hence originally held together) by military force to one held together by "family ties," not only to the motherland but also among the component parts.

> When I think of Empire I never think of Great Britain and Empire, I think of Empire with Great Britain in it, therefore, when I think of films of the Empire, I do not merely conceive our going round the Empire showing people things we do here, but I conceive of films of Imperial character, showing the people of Canada what is being done in Australia, and the people in New Zealand what is being done in India; what I call really representing in the film the whole activities of that enormous territory and diversified in people, in race, in religion, which makes a great complex under the British flag.[28]

In preparation for the Imperial Conference of 1926, the British circulated a paper entitled "Exhibition within the Empire of Empire Films."[29] This is quite a revealing document, and I reproduce it as Figure 2.A in the appendix to this chapter. It states that American domination of film markets is the problem, and that U.S. domination extends throughout the Empire. Neither advantages of climate nor of national character, it is said, explain the American success, which was due to the gains the U.S. industry had made during World War I; the size of the American market, which permits recouping of the cost of even the most expensive films, thus making low overseas prices possible; and the resultant capacity of the U.S. companies to spend lavishly on the superproductions that their clientele demands and to obtain which exhibitors must accept block booking and blind booking. Almost lost among these reasons is the demand the "clientele" makes for American super-productions. And although climate and national character are dismissed, they are dismissed without argument. Varied climate and scenery are, in fact, often cited by historians as part of the natural advantages of the Southern California country where American film production eventually was centered. When Canadians try to make the case for more Canadian production, either indigenous or in the form of Hollywood subsidiaries, they invariably refer to the diversity of scenery and climate available in Canada. And John Grierson, later the planner behind and first boss of the Canadian National Film Board, in a 1928 paper for the Empire Marketing Board about why Hollywood films were successful (Jarvie and Macmillan 1989), pointed specifically to aspects of the American national character and ethos as infusing U.S. films with a spirit of optimism, egalitarianism, and energy that was a great part of their appeal.

Since the British paper prepared for the Imperial Conference of 1926 was the first full-scale official attempt to explain American dominance of the international trade in films, it deserves the closest scrutiny. But first a point about audiences. The "great United States home market" was then a population of approximately 120 million. One figure for the size of the population of the British Empire at the time is 460 million.[30] On the face of it, the British backyard should have been more than a sufficient base from which to challenge Hollywood. But this view does not stand up to analysis. The U.S. domestic market was a strength to Hollywood, not merely because of its size, but because of its purchasing power and the rate of moviegoing. A large, wealthy population is of no value to the movie business if moviegoing is not one of its habits. Great interest in and desire for movies is of no value if the infrastructure of cinemas is not in place or if the potential customers cannot find the wherewithal to make the cinemas an attractive investment prospect. The impoverished millions of Asia and Africa who were within the British Empire did not constitute much of a market for either British or American films, but the British home market, where there was a high rate of participation and a reasonably high purchasing power, was attractive both to Hollywood and to British film producers. It was, however, only one-third the size of the U.S. market, and its price levels were somewhat lower. There were thus elements of self-deception in the idea that Britain and the Empire could constitute an alternative base for erecting a stable movie industry. As we shall see in Part II, after World War II it became painfully apparent to the British that the key to a stable and prosperous industry was sales, not to the British Empire, but to and within the dreaded U.S. domestic market itself.

The British position paper, having made economic points about Hollywood's quasi-monopoly, switched to an analysis of cultural consequences:

A position in which so powerful an influence as that of the Cinema, reaching as it does all classes and all ages of the community, is exercised throughout the Empire almost wholly by non-British producers is obviously a dangerous one. . . . The influence exercised is indirect. . . . It is clearly undesirable that so very large a proportion of the films shown throughout the Empire should present modes of life and forms of conduct which are not typically British, and, so far as setting is concerned, tend to leave on the minds of untutored spectators the impression that there are no British settings, whether scenic or social, which are worth presentation. . . . It is from this point of view that the need for some action directed towards the revival and expansion of the film producing industry in this country has been urged upon His Majesty's Government by those concerned in the development of the Empire and the spread of the ideas of which that Empire is an expression, and also by interests concerned with education, art, literature, and drama.

Only at this point, after these cultural ruminations, was it conceded that the industry and its ancillaries offered employment, and that film production was a technology in which Britain wanted to participate. Nonfiction (or "interest") films were not widely popular, because the public objected to instruction as such. So the focus of the discussion was to be entertainment films. The paper mentioned that proposals to legislate a British films quota had been postponed, for the time being, in order to see if a voluntary arrangement could be worked out. And the document concluded by disclaiming any hostility to U.S. interests; indeed, the authors stated that they "would welcome any action which American producers may take, by the production of films in this country or by cooperation with producers here or in any other way, to assist in the development of the industry in this country."[31]

Since U.S. films dominated the Canadian market to at least the same extent they did the U.K. market, and since the United States's contiguity to Canada meant that there were transborder flows of all other forms of American mass culture, Ray Peck argued, in a memorandum to his deputy minister, that Canada was perhaps more vitally interested in these questions than any other portion of the Empire except Britain. Peck said that the conference preparatory paper created an ideal opportunity for the creation of a U.S. subsidiary movie industry in Canada, along the lines of the automobile industry. The last phrases that I quoted from the document certainly must have encouraged him in this. Essential to such a scheme, however, was the definition of the term "British film." If it meant a film made in Britain, by Britons and with British money, no advantage would accrue to Canada. But if the British could be persuaded to class as British those films made in the Empire with the participation of U.S. interests, Canada would be the obvious place to invite Hollywood to operate.[32] It may be hindsight, but I find this argument hard to swallow. Facilities, labor, and capital on the necessary scale were all unavailable in Canada and would have had to be imported from the United States. The film market, despite grandiose claims, was not on the scale of the automobile market. And if the British wanted scenes and ideals of their own, Britain, its writers, and its actors would seem to be where production would need to concentrate. Of course, both the British and the Canadians did not notice a third alternative that Hollywood in fact pursued, although not perhaps consciously, to placate Imperial sentiment. This was the importation of British writers, directors, and actors to Hollywood itself, sometimes to integrate them into films set just about anywhere, at other times specifically using them in British settings reconstructed in the California studios. In my view this is the most obvious explanation of what Jeffrey Richards calls the "first cycle" of Hollywood Imperial films in the 1930s. What is astonishing is how these films presented the Empire in a sympathetic light that ran counter to the tradition of anti-Imperialism in the United States and specifically counter to the hostility to the British Empire of the Roosevelt administration (Richards 1973, p. 4).[33]

In his remarks about motion pictures to the Imperial Conference on 21 October 1926, Sir Philip Cunfliffe-Lister, president of Britain's Board of Trade, spoke less of cultural matters than of commercial ones. Cunliffe-Lister cited testimony given to a Congressional committee in the United States by Julius Klein, head of the Bureau of Foreign and Domestic Commerce in the Commerce Department under Secretary of Commerce Herbert

Hoover, in which Klein stated that South America, originally a market for British goods, had now become a market for American goods primarily because of the influence of American films.

This stands to reason. Millions are spent on newspaper advertisements which comparatively few readers will do more than glance at; but this publicity pays. The Cinema presents day by day to countless spectators an alluring advertisement of foreign goods.

Cunliffe-Lister then went on to mention block booking, blind booking, and the quota as matters for technical discussion. Only at the end did he turn to cultural matters. He spoke of the desire that people throughout the Empire had to get to know the Empire better.

The strongest bonds are the least definable – a common outlook, common ideals, a common atmosphere exemplified, for instance, in our common literature. If this be so, can we be content that the cinema, this new and all-pervading influence, should appeal to the most impressionable of our people (for cinema audiences are for the most part young) always in a foreign setting and a foreign atmosphere.[34]

The next day, the prime minister of Canada, Mackenzie King, made some guarded comments about films, remarks almost entirely of a cultural character, even to suggesting that the cultural advantage came from trade in films and predicting that the American advantage would lessen with time, "as has been the case with other industries in older lands." Having mentioned the slight problem of Federal versus Provincial jurisdictions in Canada, he ended by making the point Peck wanted: "I need only add that I assume that, in any discussion or policy as to production of British films, we mean films produced in any part of the British Commonwealth."[35]

The technical subcommittee at the conference, which had to examine a mass of material assembled by Britain's Board of Trade, was not, apparently, able to come up with any clear policy on films to be commended to the Empire. The final resolution on films endorsed by the conference went as follows:

The Imperial Conference, recognizing that it is of the greatest importance that a larger and increasing proportion of the films exhibited throughout the Empire should be of Empire production, commends the matter and the remedial measures proposed to the consideration of the Governments of the various parts of the Empire with a view to such early and effective action to deal with the serious situation now existing that they may severally find possible.[36]

This resolution could be taken as the departure point for many subsequent events, including the White Report, the Ontario quota legislation, the trial of Famous Players, the later quarrel between Canada and Britain over "quota quickies" (cheap "British" films made solely to satisfy the quota), the revisions to the definition of "British films" in 1938, the founding of the National Film Board, and the Canadian Cooperation Project. To the rest of these we shall come in due course. First, and above all, the Empire had to wait for the British government to act: Unless and until the British film industry could be revived and set on a steady and predictable course, it could not provide an anchor for Imperial film aspirations. Other countries in the Empire could not promote British films until there were enough British films to promote. As he had signaled in his remarks to the Imperial Conference, Cunliffe-Lister[37] was persuaded of the necessity of quota legislation to reserve some British screen time for British films as an incentive to British and foreign investors. He did not want taxpayers' money to plug the gap.

2.4. Britain legislates a quota

A full account of the origin and nature of the British quota legislation will be offered in Part II. Here our interest is in how events in London appeared to Canadian observers to affect Canadian interests. As we have already seen, Prime Minister Mackenzie King had followed his officials' suggestions in arguing that for quota purposes "British films" should be defined to mean all films made within the Empire, rather than simply those flowing from the mother country. The proposal was aimed partly at ensuring classification as British for those documentary, travel, and interest films that some Imperial governments were manufacturing – in Canada at both the Provincial and the Federal levels. But these were a minor item in the film trade and, as factual films, could probably have been exempted anyway without altering the definition of "British." Peck, in urging his deputy minister, F. D. O'Hara, to seek an Imperial definition, had a bolder scheme in mind, one scarcely relevant to Australia, New Zealand, South Africa, and other parts of the Empire. This was the hope to persuade Hollywood to set up a subsidiary movie industry in Canada.

In treating of this, Morris, writing in the 1970s, after "branch-plant" (subsidiary) had become a negative epithet in Canadian nationalist political discourse, displayed a fierce and slightly anachronistic nationalism when he offered to "excuse" Peck for espousing these views (Morris 1978, p. 163). Peck's thinking was that Hollywood could be persuaded to see Canada as the gateway to the Empire. By making a certain number of films in Canadian centers the Americans would gain access to the Empire market for these films as "British." The U.S. producers would bring know-how and capital to Canada, where it would be blended with Canadian capital and personnel (much stress was laid on the number of Canadians who were doing well in Hollywood), thus permitting the development of some indigenous film making capacity. If we try to take off the nationalist blinkers, this was not a discreditable dream. But it was a dream, because Hollywood was consolidating, not looking to let others in on its prosperity, and because British protectionism was only one of a whole series of fronts on which Hollywood's dominance was being challenged. Two other major European markets –

Germany and France – were in the throes of protecting their domestic industry and, unlike Canada, Britain, Germany, and France, already had production facilities. It was thus much more important for Hollywood to deal with these major markets than to look to Canada for a keyhole solution to one of them.

What unsettled Morris was, of course, the "forgetting the meaning" that Peck's ideas involved (Morris 1978, p. 159). Peck was thinking of economic matters: the flow of money, know-how, and employment to Canada. He lauded Canada's landscape and variety as backgrounds for films but made no attempt to suggest that a Canadian ethos would find its way into Hollywood films made in Canada. For those convinced that such a Canadian ethos exists and deserves to be fostered in mass cultural productions such as films, Peck's proposals missed the point. Yet we would also do well to remember that many of the cultural arguments supporting British films came from the Empire, not from Britain – at least at first. At first the problem in Britain was the collapse of the British film industry in the face of American competition, and what is agreed in retrospect to be the inferior quality of the product of the collapsed industry. Without, I hope, being unduly cynical, it is hard not to conclude that the people who were alarmed about this collapse were those who had been, or hoped to be, making money from the film industry and who now were not. Money was being made, but it was being made by the Americans and those who worked with them in Britain.[38] Businessmen, like trade unionists, very naturally shift to a nationalist register when their competition is foreign. We might therefore construe the "cultural" campaign for more British films to serve Imperial ideological purposes as a coded front for a campaign to seize back economic advantage from the Americans.

In offering Imperial-content arguments for more British films, Canadian and British spokesmen were innocently offering to save British businessmen, whose primary interest was money. If Mackenzie King's words were inspired by material sent up through bureaucratic channels by Peck, then King was fronting for a position that was unambiguously interested in the commercial value to Canada of the U.S. subsidiary loophole, not at all to the serving of Imperial ideology. The British government was doing much the same. It had postponed passing a quota law in 1926 in order to try to force the British film industry to come up with a rescue scheme of its own. As mentioned, the British exhibitors had been reluctant to join in, for the simple and obvious reason that their part of the business was doing fine with Hollywood films. In coming forward with a bill in 1927, the British government partly relied on the nationalist arguments cooked up by the ailing industry as a way of gaining respectable support. In Canada, Deputy Minister of Trade and Commerce F. D. O'Hara wrote to Under Secretary O. D. Skelton, in External Affairs, that he was skeptical of the British government's love of the quota. He stressed that British films were not of real and competitive value, that their producers lacked the necessary enterprise, resources, and adaptability, as well as the technical knowledge of the business. "The . . . result has been that their films have been devoid of those ingredients necessary to real competitive film values. This, perhaps, has been one of the main causes for the failure of British films." He also suggested that the quota might give an opportunity to Canadian fly-by-night artists.

In his reply, Skelton conceded that O'Hara's views were to the point. However, the British government was under a good deal of pressure to do something, "and it might be easier to pass a law than to develop the enterprise, resources and technical knowledge required to enable the industry to succeed by its own efforts."[39]

A summary (issued by the Board of Trade) of Cunliffe-Lister's testimony to the British Parliament in support of the quota of the bill (the Cinematograph Films Act of 1927) reveals that there he reversed the order of priorities he had used at the Imperial Conference. In 1926 he had started with commerce and buttressed it with cultural and nationalist arguments. In the House of Commons in 1927, he began with cultural considerations.

The motion picture was the most universal medium by which national ideas and national atmosphere could be spread.

The country [Britain] would be very concerned if it were depending on a foreign literature and a foreign press — or if the press were foreign in the same proportion as films were.

Millions of people throughout the Empire were being unconsciously influenced in their ideals and outlook by films, yet only 5% of the films shown in the British Empire at present were of British origin.[40]

Students of the media will no doubt be struck by the comparison of films to the press. Implicit in the argument is the idea that in some way it is a function of the press to spread national ideals and national atmosphere. Also implicit is a parallel between a nation — with its literature, films, and press — and the Empire. The Empire was being positioned as a vast, abstract nation — multicultural, diversely governed, yet giving formative allegiance to common national ideals and national atmosphere, what earlier we have seen referred to as a common outlook, common ideals. However delusory this sounds now, the documents attest to what those of us old enough to remember Empire Day can confirm, that some ideologues held that the British Empire was not a vulgar residue of conquest and rapacity, but vast numbers of peoples voluntarily subscribing to common values derived from British tradition.

The rest of Cunliffe-Lister's remarks were about commerce. He again quoted Dr. Julius Klein's thesis that films had helped to advertise American products. All the rest of Cunliffe-Lister's remarks were an elaboration on this.[41] Thus he made a tactical decision not to invoke the interests of British businessmen (necessary, really, because some British businessmen were doing very well out of American films and had no complaints); not to overtly attack the Americans (since that had been declared not to be the intention); but instead to accentuate the positive. What was sought was power over, and input to, a nation-forming institution and an advertising institution.

In an analysis of the quota law as finally passed, F. C. Badgley, who had succeeded Peck as director of the Canadian Government Motion Picture Bureau, stressed that the definition of "British" was satisfactory to Canada.

This change, in my opinion, is distinctly favorable to Canada, as it will permit of outside capital being used for the production of "British films." In other words, it means that the big American producing companies can finance Canadian companies and make pictures in Canada that will be "British films" in every sense. This should prove a boon to production activities in Canada and I look forward to considerable development along this line.[42]

As passed in 1927, the Cinematograph Films Act provided for a modest 5 percent quota of British films for films shown in the United Kingdom in 1928, which was to rise over the ten years of the act until it reached 20 percent in 1936–8. A complication was that distribution (film wholesaling, called in Britain "renting") and exhibition were separate businesses that lacked an identity of interests, so it was necessary to mandate separate quotas. The renter's quota was 7.5 percent for the year ending 31 March 1929, rising to 20 percent for 1936–9. The renter's quota exceeded the exhibitors', in an attempt to force renters to provide more "British" films for exhibition than was mandated, in order to give the exhibitors some choice. If the percentages required look low, one must remember the American dominance (shown in Table 2.2) and the often-made argument that the British industry might not be able to fulfill the demands that the legislation placed upon it. And indeed, from time to time, easements were required.

With the British industry in deep trouble, the act, despite the broad Imperial definition of "British," was not drafted to favor Peck's dream. Britain was the big market, and hence Hollywood's first priority in complying with the act was to encourage the revival of the British domestic industry by judicious infusions of money, thereby ensuring a flow of product to their subsidiary renting companies in London. The effect of the act was that if, say, MGM's London division wanted to release all of MGM's Hollywood output in Britain, they had to ensure that they also handled the required proportion of British product. To ensure enough British films, the manufacture of mainstream Hollywood films north of the Canadian border was one possibility, but so was the making of Hollywood films in London and the financing of inexpensive British films for quota purposes, not to mention the input of Hollywood money and advice into films that were British according to the letter of the legislation but that would nevertheless play in Peoria. All of these latter schemes took precedence over the former

Canadian one. As we now know, only a couple of small operations were ever set up in Canada to make quota-acceptable movies there.

So, even with full implementation, the British quota act was not especially favorable to Canadian hopes, and the modest goals it set were going to take some time to produce films that would please the distributors represented by Colonel Cooper, who were said to be eager to handle any British pictures that would attract audiences.

If we take events at face value, we could argue that the quota act was the British response to the resolution passed by the Imperial Conference of 1926. There remained the question of the responses of other Empire governments. Quota legislation was a possibility, but, until British product existed, scarcely a practicable one, and one complicated in Canada by the division of responsibility between Federal and Provincial governments. Some kind of ingenious quota amendment to the tariff structure (Annett 1948), for example, might be desirable but could be seen as interfering with Provincial jurisdiction. The British Cinematograph Films Act had important clauses designed to inhibit block booking and blind booking. It is perhaps in these that we may find the intermediate stage between the Imperial Conference resolution and the investigation of Famous Players in Canada under the Combines Act. In anticipation of British films that were commercially viable beginning to flow, Canada needed to know whether Colonel Cooper's protestations that his organization wholeheartedly supported British films could be trusted. Thus, not only was Famous Players on the investigator's agenda, but also the MPDEC, as at worst a tool of Zukor, at best an organization likely to favor American films.

Appendix: "Exhibition within the Empire of Empire Films"

"Exhibition within the Empire of Empire Films," a discussion document prepared for the Imperial Conference of 1926, signaled the beginning of a twenty-five-year effort to make London an alternative pole of film making for the British Commonwealth and Empire. The document is reproduced in its entirety as Figure 2.A. (pp. 68–74).

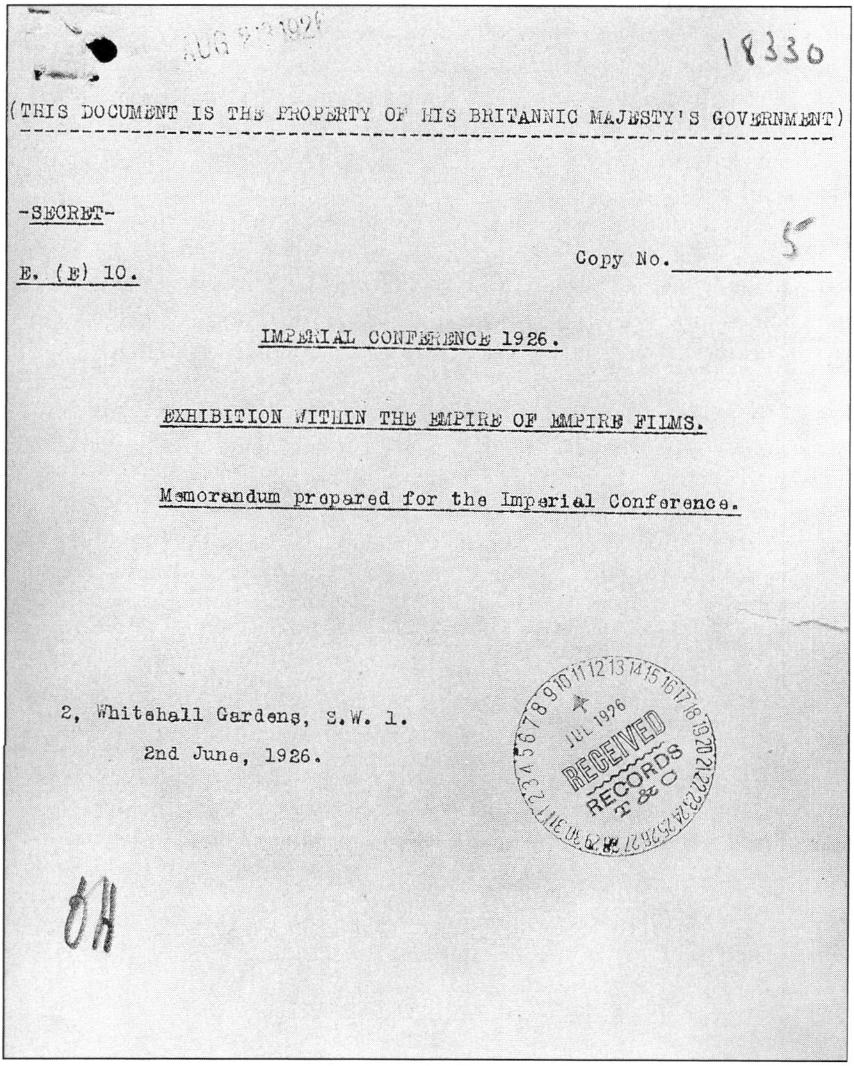

18330

(THIS DOCUMENT IS THE PROPERTY OF HIS BRITANNIC MAJESTY'S GOVERNMENT)

-SECRET-

E. (E) 10.

Copy No. 5

IMPERIAL CONFERENCE 1926.

EXHIBITION WITHIN THE EMPIRE OF EMPIRE FILMS.

Memorandum prepared for the Imperial Conference.

2, Whitehall Gardens, S.W. 1.

2nd June, 1926.

RECEIVED JUL 1926 RECORDS T & C

Figure 2.A. "Exhibition within the Empire of Empire Films," a discussion document prepared for the Imperial Conference of 1926. (PA, RG 20, Trade and Industry, vol. 45, file 18830, Imperial Economic Conference 1926.)

(1) His Majesty's Government have recently had under serious
consideration the problem presented by the fact that the Moving
Pictures exhibited at the Cinema Houses throughout the Empire
are almost wholly the product of foreign countries, particularly
the United States of America. The proportion of British films,
that is films produced within the Empire by British companies
employing British artists, to the total number shown in the
United Kingdom has been rapidly declining, and at present
amounts to scarcely 5 per cent. It is understood that a similar
position prevails throughout the Empire generally, and that in
some parts practically none but foreign films are shown.

(2) The quasi-monopolistic control of the market by the
United States film producing companies is not due to any special
advantages of climate or of national character. It is to be
ascribed to:-

    (a) The position which the American producers occupied
as almost the only suppliers during the war period, the
greater experience so gained and the progress made in
technique, and the marketing organisation then developed and
the resultant goodwill acquired.

    (b) The great United States home market, combined
with the fact that the chief producers there own or control
large numbers of Cinema Houses; this makes it possible for
the cost of even the most expensive films to be recovered,
and usually more than recovered, in the home market, so
that the exhibition rights of the films can be sold or
rented abroad at very low prices which nevertheless
represent almost entirely additional profit and with which
producers in this country cannot compete, since their home

Figure 2.A. (*cont.*)

market is probably not one-sixth of the American, and they have no 'tied' houses.

(c) The resultant fact that the American concerns are able to spend more lavishly on production than producers here can do, and so to produce 'super' films which most exhibitors must take to maintain their clientèle and which they can generally get only on condition of taking a number of other films, of the ordinary 'programme' type, which they may not have seen and which may not have been produced at the time the rental contracts are made. The result of this system of 'block' and 'blind' booking is that even when a satisfactory British film is made the producer may have great difficulty in finding a remunerative market, since exhibitors may be, and often are, booked up for many months ahead.

(3) A position in which so powerful an influence as that of the Cinema, reaching as it does all classes and all ages of the community, is exercised throughout the Empire almost wholly by non-British producers is obviously a dangerous one. It is not suggested that foreign films are the medium of intentional anti-British propaganda, or that, except in a very small proportion of cases, they are open to positive objection; the influence exercised is indirect and for that reason more difficult to deal with. It is clearly undesirable that so very large a proportion of the films shown throughout the Empire should present modes of life and forms of conduct which are not typically British, and, so far as setting is concerned, tend to leave on the minds of untutored spectators the impression that there are no British settings, whether scenic or social, which are worth presentation. However, good the foreign films may be in

Figure 2.A. (*cont.*)

70

themselves, there is still a need for the shewing of
more home-produced films; however good foreign education may
be, we should still feel that if we sent our children to
be educated exclusively in foreign countries they would
miss something important in their education.

(4) It is from this point of view that the need for
some action directed towards the revival and expansion
of the film producing industry in this country has been
urged upon His Majesty's Government by those concerned in
the development of the Empire and the spread of the ideas
of which that Empire is the expression, and also by
interests concerned with education, art, literature, and
drama. The object aimed at is of importance also,
not only because of the amount of employment which the
industry affords both in itself and in the other industries,
often highly skilled, which are ancillary to it, but also
because the technical applications of the cinematograph are
as yet only beginning to be realised, and it is highly desirable that the British Empire should take its part in the
development of this, as in all other scientific industries.

(5) Whilst the cinematograph can to some extent be
used advantageously for direct or indirect official or
semi-official propaganda (as has been done for example
at the Wembley Exhibition by the Governments of the United
Kingdom and other parts of the Empire and more generally
by some of the Dominion Governments and occasionally by
Government Departments here and industrial undertakings
or groups of undertakings), and the possibility of cooperation between the Governments of the Empire in this
respect might be explored with advantage, such action does
not deal adequately with the position outlined above.

'Interest' films (to use the ordinary trade term)

Figure 2.A. (*cont.*)

71

of the kinds to which such action has hitherto been restricted are not widely popular with the general public, which objects to instruction as such, and consequently there is no particular inducement to exhibitors to rent them; the average rentals paid for ordinary 'programme' films under the conditions described in 2(c) above, are such that even the offer of 'interest' films at only nominal prices presents small inducement to the 'renters' (the distributing trade) to take them or to exhibitors to show them.

The problem, then, so far as the United Kingdom as a supplier is concerned, is to develop the industry in this country, on a sound economic basis, and this can only be by the production of films which shall be British in character and atmosphere and also be of such entertainment value as will enable them to obtain a remunerative market. The solution of this problem is primarily a task for those directly concerned, but there is room for State action to encourage and facilitate their efforts.

(6) A number of proposals directed towards this end have been under the consideration of His Majesty's Government, and numerous conferences have been held with representatives of the three branches of the trade - the producers, the renters and the exhibitors - and with others interested from the various points of view set out above. A particular proposal which has been specially urged is that there should be obligation upon the renters to take a fixed proportion of British films and that there should be a corresponding obligation upon every exhibitor to show a fixed proportion of British films, such proportion being small at first and gradually increasing. But whilst there is believed to be a desire on the part of the majority of exhibitors, and possibly of renters also, to give a preference to British films, they are necessarily governed

Figure 2.A. (*cont.*)

72

largely by commercial considerations and must have some security that in the event of a quota system being imposed an adequate supply of British films of suitable quality and 'drawing' power would in fact be forthcoming, and in the existing state of the industry here such a guarantee is not at present possible.

(7) The President of the Board of Trade accordingly announced in March of this year, that whilst His Majesty's Government would be prepared in the last resort to seek from Parliament power to impose a quota system on either renters or exhibitors or both, as may appear on full consideration to be most effective and equitable, they hoped that all the trade interests concerned would endeavour to reach a voluntary arrangement to co-operate in the production of films in this country, and that if there were indications that such an arrangement could be made they would be willing, in order to give it a fair test, to defer action in respect of a quota for one year from an agreed date. The President of the Board of Trade also announced that if the problem of 'block' booking – as to the objectionable character of which representations have been made by all branches of the trade – cannot be dealt with effectively by agreement within the trade itself His Majesty's Government would be prepared to introduce legislation at an early date.

In the statements made from time to time on this subject the President of the Board of Trade has emphasised the fact that the growing feeling in the United Kingdom and any measures contemplated by His Majesty's Government are not inspired by any hostility to United States interests but solely by the larger considerations set out above; and that His Majesty's Government would welcome any action which American producers may take, by the production of films in this country or by co-operation with producers here or in any other way, to assist in the development of the industry in this country.

Figure 2.A. (*cont.*)

73

(8) It is not yet possible to indicate the effect of the wide-spread public discussion of the position of the United Kingdom film industry or of the official pronouncements as to the Government's attitude. By the time that the Imperial Conference meets, however, it will be possible for the position to be fully reviewed, and it is suggested that the whole subject is one which then might be usefully considered at the Conference.

Figure 2.A. (*cont.*)

Notes

1 NYPL, Cooper Papers, "History of the Motion Picture Association," 6 April 1944.

2 Ibid.

3 Ibid.

4 Hanson's letter is quoted in Cooper to Monteith, 4 February 1928, AO, RG 56, Theatres Branch A-1, Box 1, British Films 1926–1932.

5 This strategy of cost–push competition is more familiar today in television, where prime-time series are sometimes budgeted at a level beyond the maximum they can earn during their first season. Only overseas sales, reruns and syndication can roll them over into profit. Naturally, the risk is that shows that flop on the first run may never garner these sheaves.

6 See note 8 to Chapter 1.

7 Motion Picture Distribution and Sales Co. to Secretary of State, 20 October 1911, NA, RG 59 842.4061, Motion Pictures Canada 1912–1929, Microfilm M1435, Roll 19.

8 Canadian Film Exchange to Motion Picture Distribution and Sales Company, 24 October 1911, ibid.

9 U.S. Consulate, Ottawa, to State Department, 14 November 1911, ibid.

10 Harrison Bradley, Consul General, Montréal, to State Department, 4 November 1911, ibid.

11 Bradley to State Department, 4 November 1911, ibid.

12 Graham to Bryan, 13 June 1913, ibid.

13 Attorney General of British Columbia to U.S. Consul General, Vancouver, 24 September 1913, ibid.

14 Circular letter by Ontario Provincial Treasurer, 3 December 1918, ibid.

15 George Kleine to State Department, 12 December 1918, ibid.

16 This view was articulated by Ray Lewis, editor of the *Canadian Moving Picture Digest*, in a letter to Premier Ferguson of Ontario, 11 June 1930, AO, RG 3, Prime Minister's Office, Ferguson Papers, Box 107, File Moving Pictures 1930. The figure she gives is $28 million.

17 U.S. Consul General, Montréal, to State Department, 20 May 1924, NA, RG 59 842.4061, Motion Pictures Canada 1912–1929, Microfilm 1435, Roll 19.

18 U.S. Consul General, Ottawa, to State Department, 30 March 1926, ibid.

19 This surmise stems from the arguments made by Peter Morris (1978), from my own examination of letters by Peck in Canadian and U.S. archives, and from the report of Peck's address to the Ottawa Lions Club reported in the *Canadian Moving Picture Digest* 18 (15 January 1927).

20 U.S. Consul General, Ottawa, to State Department, 11 March 1926, NA, RG 59 842.4061, Motion Pictures Canada 1912–1929, Microfilm 1435, Roll 19. Emphasis in original.

21 Evidence for this view also comes from the following paragraph by the chief Canadian trade commissioner in London, which includes a positive evaluation of American films: "It is appreciated that the present United States control of the film industry results from praiseworthy enterprise and far-reaching organisation, and that it presents a monopoly with which it is difficult to compete. Many of the American films also provide distinct and good entertainment. Upon the other hand, I have frequently

heard in Canada, as elsewhere, that there are many people who resent the way in which this monopoly is exercised to the practical exclusion of United Kingdom and other Empire films. Indeed, our own department is a considerable producer and distributor of films and would doubtless like to see the outlet broadened." Harrison Watson to W. McL. Clark, 23 April 1926, PA, RG 20, vol. 31; File 16613, vol. 1.

22 The original correspondence, summarized in Cooper's letter, appears not to have survived.

23 Cooper to Price, 17 March 1926, AO, RG 56, Series A-1, Box 1, Film 1.1, Theatres Branch.

24 Ibid.

25 Ibid.

26 Patton to Price, 16 March 1926, AO, RG 56, Series A-1, Box 1, British Films 1926–1932.

27 It would be a distraction, at this point, to go into the racism and anti-Semitism that complicated the issue in some minds, but these should not be forgotten. A forceful expression of the benevolent paternalism of white toward black and of the worry that American films undermined that position is to be found in the remarks of Senator J. F. Guthrie of Australia, quoted in Australian *Parliamentary Debates,* 11 August 1926. (Cf. also Chapter 5, note 17, in the present volume.)

28 Speech by Sir Alfred Mond to·the British Empire Film Institute, 21 April 1926, PA, RG 20, vol. 31, File 16613, vol. 1. This pamphlet on the inaugural dinner also contains a number of examples of the paternalistic racism mentioned in note 21.

29 PA, RG 20, Trade and Industry, vol. 45, File 18830, Imperial Economic [*sic*] Conference 1926.

30 Figure given by Lord Gainford to the British Empire Film Institute, 21 April 1926, PA, RG 20, vol. 31, File 16613, vol. 1.

31 Ibid., note 29.

32 Peck to O'Hara, 22 September 1926, PA, RG 20; vol. 45, File 18330.

33 In his 1986 article, Richards attributes an approximation to this explanation to Margaret Farrand Thorp (p. 158).

34 PA, RG 20, vol. 31, File 16613, vol. 1.

35 Ibid.

36 PRO, CAB 32 115.

37 For a biographical footnote on Sir Philip, see Chapter 4, note 15.

38 As we shall see in Part II, there was, as might be expected, more than a whiff of anti-Semitism in the way American interests and their British agents were thought about.

39 Both quotations from an exchange between Skelton and O'Hara, 24 January and 1 February 1927, PA, RG 20, vol. 31; File 16613, vol. 1.

40 "Statement of Sir P. Cunliffe-Lister in moving the second reading of the Cinematograph Films Bill," PA, RG 20, vol. 31; File 16613, vol. 1. The document is undated, but the debate referred to took place in the House of Commons on 22 March 1927.

41 Ibid.

42 Badgley to O'Hara, 14 December 1927, PA, RG 20, vol. 31; File 16613, vol. 2.

CHAPTER 3

After the White Report, 1932–1950

3.1. Hollywood's backyard: Benefits and drawbacks

Having begun with the shaggy-dog story of the White Report and Rex *v.* Famous Players, we went on to a flashback review of the events that preceded that failure to curb American domination of motion picture distribution and exhibition in Canada. To complete our coverage of the Canadian point of the "North Atlantic triangle" trade in motion pictures, we shall now look at the aftermath of the White Report. That story is almost entirely one of Hollywood's success in dominating and exploiting this convenient backyard known as Canada. Since nationalists have much on their side when they claim that Hollywood's influence was baneful, note a few ways in which Canada benefited. Canada did get all of Hollywood's film output, since Canada was treated like another state or territory of the United States. Furthermore, Canada was sent the original American versions, not something doctored for abroad. Any changes that were made came from the local censors.

In most cases it is the "domestic" editions of films that are sent to Canada as well as advertising which is also primarily designed for use in the home market. The editions for Britain and Australia are seldom sent here.[1]

And, finally, Canadians saw the films early, sometimes before residents of the United States. Indeed, Montréal and, especially, Toronto, as large midwestern cities with a high rate of cinemagoing, were sites to preview or test-market new American films. And even where such advance screening was not undertaken, release patterns developed in which Toronto and Montréal often joined New York, Chicago, and Los Angeles as locations to showcase new movies in advance of general release. This was not only because they were lucrative markets but also because centers of communication were good sites to begin word of mouth (the most important element in film promotion).

The shaggy-dog story of the investigation, trial, and exoneration of Famous Players Canadian Corporation epitomizes the Canadian role in the film trade in the North Atlantic triangle. At various times there were different ways of construing the problem, different hopes for the future, different schemes, but the outcome was always the same: American domination remained intact, Canadian film consumers were apparently getting what they wanted, and the nationalists and imperialists were frustrated.

Three major events stand out in the remaining twenty years of our study: the process of renewal of the British Cinematograph Films Act of 1927, during 1936–8; the formation of the National Film Board, in 1939; and the Canadian Cooperation Project, 1948–56. The renewal of British legislation was finalized in 1938, only months before formation of the National Film Board was considered. And we cannot overlook the role of film in World War II. Film's importance in the war derived primarily from its perceived value for propaganda and morale purposes; nevertheless, as a result there was improved film commerce between Britain and Canada, an improvement that once again raised the hope of reducing American domination.

3.2. Through to the Imperial Economic Conference, Ottawa, 1932

In 1927, F. L. Herron, foreign manager of the Motion Picture Producers and Distributors of America (MPPDA, or the Hays Organization for short), had warned the U.S. consul in Vancouver that the effect of the quota legislation going through the British Parliament would be that British producers would make low-cost, hastily produced films to fulfill quota requirements. He also said that only the uninitiated could imagine that production could be shifted out of Hollywood for other than location shooting.[2] Both predictions were correct. The rise of the "quota quickie" industry in the United Kingdom was a notorious consequence of the 1927 act. And Canada suffered both ways: Only one small studio was opened to produce "British" films on Canadian soil under Hollywood auspices: Central Films, of Victoria, BC, and what this company produced was precisely "quota quickies."

Herron was not all-seeing, though, and the 1927 act was not a total failure. It was structured intelligently enough to attract some British and American money to the making of British films, so that the British film industry slowly began to recover from its slump of the mid-1920s. Besides money, of course, the British needed to raise the general standard of their films. That was harder to do. Given the role he was to play in Canadian film, consider these ideas of John Grierson in 1932:

The Imperial Conferences of 1926 and 1930 called easily for "more British films." The amateurs of the breakfast-table have been calling ever since. They either complain wildly of the cheapness and vulgarity of all things American, or they say again, and yet again, that English cinema has only to go to English literature and English scenery to conquer the world. Actually the path of cinematic conquest is a little more difficult. The Americans are entrenched, with a production system and a far-flung distribution system which represents the concentrated building of more than a decade. They have already in that time caught the eye and ear of the world; they have even set the movie standards of the world. Ordinary sense might warn us that there is a colossal job of work to be done in creation and commerce, if we are to make up the leeway.

I think we rather foolishly underestimate this task when we decry the quality of American films. They represent a command of invention, a mastery of technique and a courage of dramatic effect which our own films only rarely approach. The United States itself, by its very medley of strange races and swift happenings, is almost bound to prosper the more inventive aspect of story-telling. And there has been wealth enough behind the picture business to add almost every possible talent to the team-work of the studios. The larger imaginative qualities have been lacking, but their achievement is none the less solid and impressive....

Cinema, to be of real influence, must command its audience, and command it on a world-wide scale. It is doubtful if English cinema at its present stage of development can meet that condition.

That we have not yet begun ... is, I think, largely due to the weird parochialism of our production system.... We face it with a cinema which is so circumscribed in its material that it cannot even be called a cinema of England. It is London cinema, and West End London at that.

It is not satisfactory to face the world with British films, which are, in fact, the provincial charades of one single-square mile within the Empire. They neither project England nor project that very much larger world in the Dominions and Colonies. There is an unknown England beyond the West End, one of industry and commerce and the drama of English life within it, which is barely touched.[3]

Translated into simple terms, American standard-setting meant that audiences expected those qualities of entertainment that were routinely provided by American movies. The key ingredient not mentioned by Grierson was stars. The American motion picture industry had taught audiences to like stars, to follow stars, and to expect stars. Most of the world-class stars belonged to Hollywood.

The effect of this British legislation on Canadian filmgoers was modest. Gradually, through the 1930s, the number of British films released in Canada increased, even though there was no quota to favor them. Sometimes, as when *The Private Life of Henry VIII* was a sensational success, there were overoptimistic claims that the millennium had arrived. Still, the trend was upward, and there can be little doubt that the protection and the incentives that the quota system gave the British industry were among the causes of its revival and its beginning to learn how to take on Hollywood. A home-grown British filmmaker such as Alfred Hitchcock extended his range well beyond the West End and was, by the end of the decade, sufficiently free of parochialism to be wooed and won by Hollywood. American money and talent were imported to the United Kingdom, so that by the end of the period covered in this book Britain was poised to become a capital for the production of international style films and remains so to this day. The impact of documentary films and the war ended the hegemony of the West End of which Grierson complained, although the extent of it before the war should not be exaggerated by overlooking, for example, the 1930s films of Sir Carol Reed, particularly *Bank Holiday.*

But we must not focus solely on developments in Britain as they impacted on Canada, without considering the Hollywood response and also the overall changes in the motion picture industry. As already noted, Hollywood produced in the 1930s quite a few literary adaptations, films set in Britain (viz. *A Yank at Oxford* and *Goodbye Mr. Chips*), and a whole subgenre of Imperialist films (see Richards 1973, pt. 1). These functioned to demonstrate both the larger imaginative grasp Grierson thought Hollywood was lacking and to placate those who thought Hollywood taught only Americanization. More important, perhaps, were economic changes. The increased cost of making sound films and the huge investment in wiring every theater for sound were correlated with the production of somewhat fewer pictures, which were slightly longer. From a norm of around sixty to seventy minutes in the silent period, feature pictures in the sound era gravitated toward a norm of ninety minutes. This virtually ensured that fewer films were produced and that, as British films made a comeback, their rising percentage of the market looked healthy.

For all these reasons, then, the situation that had caused such an alarm to be raised at the Imperial Conference of 1926 and that had brought about the 1927 British Cinematograph Films Act was easing. The government of Canada chose not to revise the Combines legislation, while the government of Ontario did pass legislation permitting but not imposing a quota in 1931. No quota ever was proclaimed. One can speculate on the reason, but the only evidence I have come across is from O. J. Silverthorne, long-time chief censor of Ontario, who in 1949 remarked that the quota powers were never used because it was thought to be a Federal matter, and because there was a fear that foreigners might import mediocre British films to satisfy the quota but discredit the British product. He had been invited to comment because of new calls for a quota.[4] Silverthorne partly articulated a demonic view of the American interests that comes through the files, centered especially on Colonel Cooper. Accused in the White Report of having spoken against a resolution encouraging British pictures, at a meeting of the Federation of Chambers of Commerce of the British Empire in London in 1930, Cooper vociferously protested, pointing out that he had merely cited the difficulties involved but had endorsed an amended resolution.[5] Two years later Cooper was happy to deliver the news that in the first seven months of 1933 some forty-nine British pictures had been released in Ontario. In the first nine months, sixty-five had been released, double the amount for the whole of 1932.[6] Conveniently ignoring the possible impact of the British

Table 3.1. *Motion picture imports to Canada, 1931–2*

	Length (ft)	Value (Can$)
From the U.K.	1,316,449	104,306
From the U.S.	8,315,774	706,918
Total[a]	10,477,240	877,981

[a]Includes imports, from other countries.
Source: Ottawa to State Department, 13 April 1933, NA, RG 59 1930–1939 842.4061, Motion Picture–Canada.

quota on the health of its industry, Cooper argued that he had always maintained that

when British pictures improved they would find a good market in Canada. The fairness of this statement is being fully supported by the result. I am not saying that all theatre owners are using twenty per cent British pictures. There are quite a number of small theatre owners in various places throughout the Province who have not yet convinced themselves that their customers like British pictures.[7]

Cooper's figures were consistent with those being reported to Washington by the consulate at Ottawa, which, for the year ending 31 March 1932, were as shown in Table 3.1. The percentages place British films at about 12.6 percent of the total by footage. This is a considerable improvement on the figures from the 1920s shown in Table 2.1.

Cooper's eagerness to reassure the authorities in Ontario, that center of United Empire Loyalist sentiment, is understandable in the commercial climate of the time. Relations between the United States and Britain were strained over the payment of war debts, over the passage of the Hawley–Smoot tariffs by Congress (which had also hit Canada particularly hard), and by the aggressively protectionist response of the Empire at the Imperial Economic Conference of 1932 in Ottawa, where a structure of duties that became known as "Imperial preference," or the "Ottawa duties," was adopted. The basic idea of Imperial preference was to minimize duties on intra-Empire trade and to discriminate against all other nations (although Britain did negotiate bilateral most-favored-nation agreements with Scandinavia and Argentina). There was clear sentiment to include film in these arrangements, but the fact of American dominance of the motion picture trade, the fact that the revival of the British film industry was just under way, and the seemingly insatiable demands of the audience meant that in practice Imperial preference could not be applied to films. Most Empire countries charged a small duty per foot on imported positive film – a duty unrelated to box-office value – with a reduction for Empire product. This discrimination was so marginal that American representatives scarcely ever protested it. Their monies were largely derived from film rentals, and these were in turn partly a function of box-office take.

The editor of the *Canadian Moving Picture Digest*, Ray Lewis, estimated that in 1930 Canada remitted to the United States some $28 million per annum in rentals.[8] This payments situation for films was similar throughout the Empire. At Ottawa, a new government strategy was promulgated to supplement physical quotas: the idea of taxing the rental revenues. At the Imperial Conference of 1932, the subcommittee on film and radio of the Committee on Methods of Economic Cooperation reported as follows:

It has been suggested that aid might be given to the distribution of Commonwealth films and at the same time revenue might be derived from the imposition, in addition to the footage customs duties now in force, of a special levy upon the value of all foreign films displayed, this levy being based on the value of such films for rental purposes, while Commonwealth films are exempted from the levy. We appreciate that in practice the collection of the levy could not be made at the moment of entry because the actual value on which it should be assessed might not be ascertainable until rental contracts are made.[9]

This notion of an ad valorem duty was attractive but apparently presented grave technical problems of implementation. A similar duty was finally imposed in Britain in 1947, with disastrous consequences that I shall outline later (Part II, Chapter 7). Meanwhile, the Canadian move was of course an obvious attack on American interests and likely therefore to provoke tremendous resistance. In effect the tax would penalize the successful businessman, whereas the footage tariff was the same for all. But just as Canada never managed to bite the quota bullet, so the country also never managed to venture into an ad valorem duty. Instead, Canada looked to the Income Tax Act provision for taxes on companies and proposed a tax at 13 percent of the gross rentals for foreign films. Because this was a tax on gross, not net profit, it was much more severe than it looked. Some estimates were that as much as 80 percent of the box-office dollar was spent in Canada, only the remainder accruing to the American principals. So the income tax proposal looked like an attempt to tax away about two-thirds of Hollywood's remittances. Naturally there was intense lobbying against it, and eventually it was dropped. In 1939, with war in the offing, it was reintroduced at 5 percent and accepted with nominal protest.

3.3. The renewal of the British film legislation

The British Cinematograph Films Act of 1927 had made provision for ten years of rising quotas. In 1936, preparatory to its renewal, a commission under Lord Moyne was set up to assess its successes and failures and to recommend any necessary changes. From Canada's point of view, we have seen that a small amount of quota quickie production had started; that more British films were available, of better quality; but that the American domination of the market was still overwhelming. (A full account of the act from the British point of view is reserved for Part II of this book.) What the British were aware of, however, was that Canada had taken no measures at either the Federal or the Provincial level to discriminate in favor of British films. There was slight preference in the footage duty, but otherwise in Canada British films competed in the same market on the same terms as American films, sometimes even being in the hands of American distributors who had bought the North American rights, consistent with the treatment of Canada as part of the U.S. domestic market. Meanwhile, Canada had been host to a quota quickie operation and, with all the eager talk of subsidiaries, seemed to see Canada as a potential production center.

From behind the sentiments and the talk, a genuine conflict of interest began to emerge. The British utilized Imperial sentiment as an argument for promoting their film industry and favoring its films. The Canadians tried to cash the Imperial talk into a commercial opportunity for themselves, under the umbrella definition of "British." It is perhaps not surprising that the Cinematograph Films Act of 1938 revised the definition of "British films" specifically to exclude films made in the Empire by Hollywood. This was not accomplished without hesitation, protest, and argument, which we shall look at briefly. But it is yet another of the many events over the years that gave the lie to the attempt to argue that Imperial sentiments could harmonize intra-Empire interests.

The criteria for a "British" film, under the 1927 act, were these:

made by a British subject or subjects, or by a British company;

photographed in a studio in the British Empire;

scenario author a British subject;

75 percent of monies paid for wages and salaries to British subjects or those domiciled in the British Empire.

A "British company" was one incorporated anywhere in the British Empire, the majority of the directors of which were British subjects. Neither the Moyne Committee Report, which preceded the revised legislation, nor the White Paper [legislative proposals] introducing the bill suggested revision of these criteria. Canada's deputy minister of trade and commerce, J. G. Parmelee, asked F. C. Badgley, director of the Canadian Government Motion Picture Bureau, for an analysis of the legislation and whether Canada should present any arguments to the British government. Finding nothing to object to, Badgley counseled that this was unnecessary.[10]

The very day that Badgley was offering these assurances (meanwhile noting that he had no up-to-date information), the chief Canadian trade commissioner in London cabled Parmelee the news that Geoffrey Mander, a British Liberal M.P., has proposed an amendment that would have substituted "Great Britain and Colonies" in appropriate places, thus rendering Canadian-produced films "foreign." Although the president of Britain's

Board of Trade (Oliver Stanley) had rejected the amendment on behalf of the government, he did not do so categorically. On the assurance that the matter was important and would be looked into, the amendment was withdrawn. Before the report stage was reached on 3 February 1938, the commissioner sought instructions as to what arguments, if any, should be made.

Subsequently (in a long memorandum to the Canadian assistant deputy minister of trade and commerce), Badgley gave a gloomy analysis of the arguments Canada could make. The amendment, he noted, was specifically directed "to prevent the Dominions, especially Canada, being used as a base of operations by U.S. film producers for the purpose of defeating the intention of both the current Films Act and the new bill."[11] Canada was "going to have a very difficult time making out a good case for Canadian films because of the fact that the only company now actively producing films in Canada is pretty obviously producing 'quota' films." These "assist in the establishment and development of a film industry in Canada" and bring in jobs and money. This hardly benefited the U.K. film industry, and "after all, the whole purpose of the present Films Act and the new Films Bill is to protect and make possible the greater development of the film industry of the United Kingdom, rather than that of the whole Empire."

As a result, only limited arguments were available to Canada, namely, that a production industry in each part of the Empire was desirable, to facilitate better understanding and closer relations; that the British quota advantages were essential to the survival of Canadian (quota quickie) film companies; and that the latter involved jobs and money.

We may point, perhaps, to the large increase in the number of British films that have been exhibited in this country and to steadily increasing revenue being derived by the producers of British films from the Canadian market but we can hardly attribute that to any reciprocal efforts on the part of the Dominion. It may be attributed more readily to the fact that British films have improved to such an extent as to find steadily increasing favour among Canadian "movie" patrons and to propaganda on behalf of British films and film stars that has been carried on by the British film industry and the distributors of British films in this country that has had [the] effect of making British films and British film stars better known to Canadians.

Badgley went on to suggest that a much fuller account of the business dealings and amounts involved with Central Films was required if a plausible case for it was to be made. Meanwhile Skelton had inquired of Parmelee how important the Canadian interests involved were and whether Parmelee would prepare a memorandum for External Affairs.[12] The memorandum that External Affairs sent to the London High Commission followed Badgley's recipe. Central Films was declared small and no threat to British production; "British preference" was declared essential for the survival of Canadian films; and British pictures were selling well in Canada (see the figures in Table 3.2).

Canada had marshaled her guns, but they were not big ones. Before we

Table 3.2. *Number of U.K. films as a percentage of*
U.S. films imported into Canada, 1932–7

1932	U.K. films numbered 7.5% of U.S. films
1933	10%
1934	12%
1935	15%
1936	16.5%
1937	17–20% est.

Source: Skelton to Parmalee, 13 January 1938, PA, RG 20, vol. 31; File 16613, vol. 2.

look at the British reply, it is interesting that Badgley, who had been around a long time, had come to the conclusion that the British legislation was intended only to assist the U.K. film industry. Gone are the references to intra-Empire exchanges of film; gone are the appeals to Empire sentiment. Canadian quota quickies were seen as jobs and money taken away from British film workers and so not eligible for protection.

In response the British offered a compromise: Empire films would count for the exhibitors' quota but not for the renters'. Although noting the Canadian preferred customs duty of 1.50¢ per linear foot on British films, the British argued that they in turn extended a "very substantial preference" to Dominion negatives. Although heartened by the greater success of U.K. films, it was pointed out that these still did not represent more than 10 percent of the total Canadian film business and that less than £100,000 accrued to Britain. Such progress as had been made "in the face of what must obviously be a very severe competition from the United States, must therefore be attributed mainly to the quality of the films themselves." As for Central Films, either they were making quota quickies, which "cannot be regarded as the type of Empire production which the Imperial Conference Resolution of 1926 was intended to encourage," or they would seem to be in a favorable position to secure a share of the Canadian market. So long as their films counted as British, they displaced British films, studios, and labor.

The situation would be altered were effective Dominion-wide reciprocity offered to British films, the way the 1927 act offered it to Empire films.[13] Since it was mentioned neither in these official papers nor in all the histories of the National Film Board, I note also that the new bill being contemplated in the United Kingdom imposed for the first time a quota on "short" (that is, documentary) films. The British short film industry had declined during the life of the 1927 act, and the Moyne Committee had accepted the idea of some protection. Since Canada's principal production had been of short films, this was something of a blow. However, "nonstandard" films (i.e., those of gauges other than 35mm, such as 16mm) were excluded from the quota, and we may see there an incentive for the ("substandard") distribution of many a National Film Board movie on 16mm film.

Parmelee noted that "in actual practice the advantages are not likely to prove of any value to Canadian-made films except in exceptional cases.... The ability of Canadian-made films to qualify for Renter's Quota under the present Act has been the one thing, above all others, that has made possible the disposal of Canadian product to renters in the United Kingdom, and has been the greatest single factor in the development of the Canadian film producing industry, such as it is."[14] He concluded that the amendments to the quota act would destroy the Canadian feature industry. He was correct in this, and, by March–April it was clear that the British government felt unable to resist the pressure to plug this loophole in the quota. The dream of Canada as headquarters of Hollywood subsidiaries for the British Empire was ended.

3.4. The National Film Board

All accounts of the origins of the National Film Board of Canada suggest that far-sighted public servants, observing the success of the documentary film movement in Great Britain,[15] conceived the idea of revamping the Canadian Government Film Bureau to fulfill a broader mission of communication and nation building within Canada and promoting the country abroad. Nothing in the files connects the defeat of the Canadian arguments concerning the 1938 Cinematograph Films Act in February with the invitation to John Grierson to come to Canada and advise, which he did in May. Yet Ontario had wound up its Motion Picture Bureau in 1934, Central Films would have to close, and if there was to be any coherent film policy and production organization in Canada it looked as though the Federal government would have to define it. In inviting Grierson to do the honors, Canada made a more decisive move than perhaps could have been realized. From the time of his visit to Hollywood in the 1920s, Grierson had been a keen and appreciative observer of the U.S. industry, one firmly convinced that its international success turned on its having special qualities to offer that could not be matched in, say, Great Britain.[16] Coming to Canada, where the Norris, Peck, Badgley line had long turned on the hope of subsidiary plants and where nonfictional filmmaking had been relatively unadventurous, Grierson was only being consistent when he offered no support for that kind of thought. His shrewd proposal was to let Hollywood be Hollywood in its proper sphere of influence, and concentrate Canadian effort in a sphere where it had not developed strength. Making documentaries, which might also be called public service filmmaking, was not a field into which Hollywood had much ventured. Thus, without undermining or competing with Hollywood's success, without challenging the public's taste for its product, there was filmmaking space into which Canada could move, especially for national purposes.

Grierson is the most written-about figure in Canadian film studies, so all the details need not be rehashed here. Suffice it to say that he proposed a strengthened and reorganized film bureau, with an expanded mission to be a service department within the government and to make films on its own part. This was adopted in short order, and the National Film Board (NFB) was put into operation in October 1939. As its first commissioner, Grierson was again consistent in cultivating good relations with Hollywood, especially during the war, when NFB films were widely circulated on the commercial distribution networks in the United States[17] – a period of unrivaled opportunity for the documentary film to achieve exposure in the commercial film trade. Grierson may even have dreamed of becoming the head of an American version of the NFB that would be an arm of Hollywood.[18]

3.5. The impact of World War II

The entire period of World War II fell under the ten-year life of Britain's revised Cinematograph Films Act, with its quotas and its exclusion of Dominion films from the "British" category. Hollywood's position remained stable, since no further moves had been made in Canada against U.S. interests through either tariff or tax. The war made first two and then all three of the North Atlantic triangle countries into close allies. British films (e.g., *The 49th Parallel*) and American films (*Corvette K-225*) were shot on location in Canada. In Britain the documentary movement was revitalized by the new mission provided by the war, and in Canada the National Film Board grew rapidly under similar imperatives. The British acknowledged that their film production had to be limited by shortages of labor, buildings, materials, and money; hence the enforcement of the quotas was less rigid than envisaged under the legislation. The principal way in which the war had negative impact on the international film trade was that both Britain and Canada wished to buy a great deal of war matériel from the United States (before the latter country entered the war in December 1941), which had, under U.S. law, to be paid for in cash. This meant that both countries queried all nonessential expenditures of their U.S. dollars, and the question was whether films were essential or not.

In Canada's National Archives there is little information on the film trade during the war. Most of the information in what follows derives from American sources. American consuls general in certain countries were required to send reports to the State Department at least once a year on the motion picture situation. The report submitted from Ottawa early in 1940 began by noting that exchange control[19] had been imposed on 15 September 1939, although regular commercial transactions were unimpeded. The Canadian preferential tariff for British films continued, and there were no quotas. Under the revised trade agreement that came into effect on 1 January 1939, film imports from the United States paid a duty of 2.75¢ per linear foot, whereas British, French, and Polish films paid only 1.5¢. Distributors paid an 18-percent income tax, share dividends that went abroad were taxed at 5 percent at source, and there was a special income tax of 5 percent on remittances of motion picture payments to nonresidents. "Protests made by motion picture interests at the time Parliament increased the tax on film remittances indicated that remittances to film producers in England, France and the United States approximated $4 million annually." Gross rentals were $10,315,500; recalculating on the basis of film exchange receipts gave estimated figures of $4.5 million in 1937, $5 million in 1938 and 1939 (these strike me as more reliable than Lewis's $28 million, mentioned earlier).

As of May 1939, Canada had 1,251 theaters, with 663,887 seats. Of the theaters, 375 were served by the Toronto exchange, 110 in Toronto alone; 203 were served by the Montréal exchange, 62 in Montréal alone. (Dominion Bureau of Statistics figures were noted to be slightly lower.) There were 57 large theaters, with annual receipts in excess of $100,000; these theaters accounted for 22 percent of admissions, 29 percent of receipts. Centers of population tended to have more double-feature programs.

Ontario and New Brunswick required, as a censorship rule rather than a law, that newsreels contain 50 percent British and Canadian content. The U.S. consul noted that American films were having less trouble with censorship in Ontario than ten years before. In 1929 there had been 219 rejections, whereas in 1938 there were 26, in 1939, 19. The explanation was "internal regulation and censorship within the United States' film industry." Censors usually cut for moral and political reasons:

Particular attention in recent years has been devoted to the attempted use of film for propaganda contrary to the democratic outlook of the Canadian people. This has been emphasized since Canada declared a state of war with Germany.... As a war measure all foreign language films except French talking pictures have been banned from showing in Ontario.[20]

Such a ban tells us much about the continuing xenophobia in Ontario and also reveals its selective but convenient indulgence toward American films, which were foreign but did not use a foreign language. Meanwhile,

British films have shown a further marked improvement and the record runs and increased attendance enjoyed by them served to demonstrate that the public appreciated British productions.

Canada, as a contiguous export market for United States films and motion picture equipment, probably has more in common with the domestic film market than with the foreign market which the American industry serves. Geographical propinquity, similarity of living standards, style preferences, and social organization, plus the extensive infiltration of motion picture publicity and music via radio and magazines,

Table 3.3. *Canadian box-office receipts (in millions), 1939–41*

1939	(Can$) 34
1940	37.8
1941	41.5

Source: WNRC, RG 84 Post Records, Ottawa, 840.6 Motion Pictures, "Motion Pictures in Canada–1942," 17 August 1943.

as well as identical commercial practices in distribution of films, serve to emphasize the similarity between the Canadian and the domestic American market for the motion picture industry.[21]

Noting that America's chief competition in Canada was British films, the report gave the rather illogical figures of 75 percent of features as American, 20 percent French, and 7 percent British. But of the total box-office receipts, 90 percent were for American films, and only 5 percent each went to British and French films. Finally, this American summary of the situation mentioned that there were no Canadian facilities for feature film production, "but such production is economically impossible in the case of feature pictures and there is not a national impulse to produce pictures in Canada, such as is found in some countries."[22]

By and large we can trust these facts and figures as general guides. The mission of the consulates was to feed accurate information home to assist marketing and planning strategy. Whether Canada lacked the impulse to make feature films was arguable; what was unarguable was that money and resources were not forthcoming. That Canadian censorship showed a trend to accept American self-censorship, that tastes and standards were similar to American, all indicated a shrewd analysis of the relatively trouble-free passage that Hollywood films were having in Canada at this point. It is perhaps surprising that the consulate expressed no opinion on whether the rising popularity of British films posed any threat to American interests.

In an update of the report six months later, it was noted that exchange control had stabilized the value of the Canadian dollar. Box-office receipts were up 11 percent compared to 1939, attendance up 9 percent. The average admission price was 24.9¢. A new war exchange tax of 10 percent had been applied to all imports from outside the sterling area, computed on fair market value. Of imported films, 455 were U.S. films, 42 British, and 56 French.[23]

The American archives suffer from gaps and lacunae, and the next surviving report is from 1943. Most notable are several sets of figures about expenditure on films by the Canadian public, which show that box-office receipts had been steadily climbing during the war (Table 3.3). This growth

Table 3.4. *Per capita expenditure on motion pictures in Canada, 1930–41*

1930	(Can) $3.77
1939	3.03
1940	3.35
1941	3.63

Source: WNRC, RG 84 Post Records, Ottawa, 840.6 Motion Pictures, "Motion Pictures in Canada–1942," 17 August 1943.

was far greater than the rate of inflation and paralleled trends observed in the United States and the United Kingdom in wartime. Per capita expenditure on motion pictures in Canada did not show the same growth (Table 3.4); these, of course, are population averages in which both the infantile and the senile are included. Since the usual admission price was (as earlier stated) about 25¢, the 1930 figure amounts to just over fifteen admissions per head per year, or slightly over one a month. By 1941 movie expenditure had almost recouped its position of 1930, that is, before the Depression really hit.

It was calculated that 85¢ of every box-office dollar was spent within Canada.

Canada is one of the smaller markets for the products of Hollywood, contributing from four to five per cent of the total revenue of United States producers. The British film industry has been unable to compete successfully with the United States in providing Canada with films since the days of the first World War. Proximity, cultural and economic ties, and voice preference all help to account for Hollywood's predominance, which has also been strengthened and protected by financial links between the two countries.

Consequently, United States influence is predominant among Canadian film distributors. It is similarly predominant among exhibitors who own and operate the theaters.[24]

Similar remarks regarding the popularity of American motion pictures in Canada were made by the American consul at Winnipeg in a dispatch to the State Department. He wrote that American pictures were more popular than British pictures with prairie people because prairie people "are like Americans in their taste, ideas, and mode of life, and what the Americans like they like." Such differences as there were between Americans and prairie people boiled down to the latter being more conservative and less impulsive. This fragment is worth our attention because it provides a clue to the advantage Hollywood enjoyed. If it was true that what Americans liked prairie people liked – in motion pictures, of course – then Hollywood's job was that much easier. What suited the domestic audience suited some

Canadians; no special adaptation and no special line of product were required.[25]

Could this evaluation from a Prairie Province be untrue elsewhere? On the contrary:

The testimony of those connected with the motion picture trade in Toronto is in agreement that American films enjoy an overwhelming popularity and preference with audiences in this city. Toronto is noted for its strong imperial loyalty and local newspaper reviewers are generally biased in favor of British films. However, these factors do not seem to affect the tastes of the public.[26]

This comment alerts us to the problems of using newspaper evidence to estimate the popularity of the dominant American product. (Newspaper reviewers and commentators were the embryo of a media elite that consistently expressed nationalist and anti-American sentiments.[27]) The only qualification offered concerning American films was a patriotic one, with echoes of 1911:

Too much flag-waving in American films and too little attention shown in them to the efforts of the Canadian and British forces, especially American news reels, are particularly resented by Canadians.[28]

In a fascinating confidential annex to his 3 November 1944 dispatch, the Toronto consul reported that J. J. Fitzgibbons, the American-born manager of Famous Players, believed that the Nathanson–Odeon/Empire–Universal theater group was agitating through Grierson (now head of the National Film Board and described as "extremely pro-British") to get a quota law. An attempt had been made to get the lieutenant governor of Ontario to proclaim a quota but without success. The State Department was advised that Canada wanted to be advertised and that publicity for Canadian institutions, culture, social problems, people, and political and commercial status, as well as ideas for movie stories and locations, might lessen the friction. We have here an early indication of the thinking behind the Canadian Cooperation Project (CCP), the subject of the next section. Since the source of the speculation about quotas was named, and since Fitzgibbons was deeply involved in the CCP, someone may have been using the consulate to float a trial balloon. The deal was to be this: more Canadian content in American pictures, in return for no trade discrimination against them. The description of Grierson as "extremely pro-British" is a puzzle. Grierson was, and remained, British. But we know from his writings and from his policies that he appreciated Hollywood for what it did, considering it peerless, from which I think it follows that he was never a believer in the "Hollywood on the Thames" theory, nor would he have been a believer in the mini-Hollywood at Trenton (see Morris 1986; Jarvie and Macmillan 1989). If he was engaged in lobbying for a quota, it would be most surprisingly inconsistent with all this.

Table 3.5. *Canadian box-office hits of 1943–4*

FPCC, 1943–4	All studios, 1943
This Is the Army	*Yankee Doodle Dandy*
Lassie Come Home	*Random Harvest*
[As] Thousands Cheer	*My Friend Flicka*
Sweet Rosie O'Grady	*Casablanca*
Madame Curie	*Coney Island*
Standing Room Only	*Hello Frisco, Hello*
Heaven Can Wait	*This Is the Army*
The Uninvited	*Stage Door Canteen*
Claudia	*In Which We Serve*
No Time for Love	*Hitler's Children*

Sources: FPCC information from Toronto Consul to State Department 3 November 1944; all studios information from U.S. Consulate General, Ottawa, Supplemental Report 24 November 1944, both in WNRC RG Post Records, Ottawa, 840.6 Motion Pictures, 1936–1954.

Later in November 1944, the American consulate at Ottawa had to file a special report in response to a questionnaire sent out under the signature of A. A. Berle, assistant secretary of state, on the topic of the prospects for American motion pictures in the postwar world. The position of this document in the evolving American commercial strategy must await analysis at the proper place (see §12.2). Apart from noting the continued stringency of Québec's censorship, which criticized American movies for (among other things) teaching English, a supplement noted that 39–42 percent of Hollywood's Canadian revenues derived from Ontario, whereas the more populous Québec generated only 15–19 percent. It was also reported that people thought the greatest weakness of British films was their lack of stars.[29] We might also contrast the list of box-office winners from Famous Players in the 1943–4 season with that from a broad cross section of exhibitors (Table 3.5).

Such material as survives in the various U.S. archives for the years after this period is rather scrappy and inconclusive. There continued to be complaint about even the Canadian editions of American newsreels: "The commentary which accompanies the war films in the newsreel gives the impression that American troops are winning the war. This seems to be so to an American seated in a Canadian motion picture theater. Certainly it must seem so to a Canadian."[30] The Americans gained the impression that the National Film Board was inhibiting the distribution of American-made documentaries.[31] And finally, there was information that the Queensway film studios in Toronto had a connection with the J. Arthur Rank Organisation in Britain and that Renaissance films in Québec was an offshoot of the French film industry. These last items were the kind of follow-up commercial intelligence requested in Berle's circular and show a continuing alertness to the possibility of strategic attack on American interests in the Canadian film market.

The suspicions were mostly web spinning, weaving patterns from separate and isolated events that were not coordinated by some overall plan. As mentioned, British films had experienced something of a renaissance during the war, when they found subjects and audiences hitherto denied to them, both at home and abroad. It was to be expected that in the Dominion of Canada, which had in 1939 declared war on Germany out of loyalty to the Commonwealth, there should have been a heightened interest in, and appreciation of, British mass cultural products. With so many Canadians stationed in the United Kingdom, there was much curiosity about life there, and of course a great thirst to have the British side of the war dramatized.[32]

Whether there really was improved contact between British filmmakers and the popular audience; whether the better box-office business was more than temporary: These questions were hard to resolve. A cold look at the natural advantages enjoyed by the United States, with its large and prosperous domestic market, its obvious determination to defend that by all means and the manifest demand for its product, should have made all but the most naïvely optimistic hesitate. Short of a collapse of the U.S. industry, the prospects for its potential rivals were poor. The layman tends to see this as having to do with the organization of production. In fact it has to do with distribution. It is much easier to assemble money and talent to make a picture than to promote, advertise, and sell it and to circulate the prints efficiently. The barrier is not the arcane quality of distribution; it is that distribution is a continuous activity, based upon steady and reliable flow. Movie theaters at the period we are studying ran each movie for a short time, usually a week or less. This meant that an exhibitor was persuaded to buy, not picture by picture, which would give him fifty-two decision headaches per year, but in bundles or "blocks," among which there would be attractive pictures he had heard about but also a strong second string of product that would permit program change and that would turn a modest but satisfying profit. To break into that system, a newcomer would get nowhere with one film, however good. The newcomer would have to sell to an existing distributor, who would take his product and blend it with others into a saleable block. Only distributors who could not find enough pictures would be interested; others would have commitments to their continuing suppliers. My contention throughout this book has been that U.S. dominance flowed from such command of distribution.

3.6. The Canadian Cooperation Project

Few people outside of Canada have ever heard of the Canadian Cooperation Project (CCP). Indeed, inside Canada only a few film historians know about

it. Those who do present it as everything from a farce to a sellout, and
perhaps both. In his entertaining but heavily slanted book *Hollywood's
Canada* (1975), the nationalist journalist Pierre Berton presents the problem
as being that, at a time when Canada's supply of U.S. dollars was short
and restrictions were placed on remitting them abroad, Hollywood had
"taken 17 million dollars out of Canada" (p. 169). We do well to remember,
reading Berton, that Hollywood films earned dollars because millions of
Canadians wanted to see American motion pictures. Berton treats the entire
scheme as one intended to "stifle any nationalistic outcries" (p. 172). "From
start to finish, the Canadian Cooperation Project was a public relations
man's boondoggle." Berton's entire theme is that the Canadian public, and
indeed the more gullible of Canadian public officials, were hoodwinked by
the clever snake-oil salesmen of Hollywood into accepting the CCP as a
substitute for a quota against American pictures and legislation to force
Hollywood to invest in production in Canada.

But basically the idea was simple and not absurd at all, although its
results were indeed. An important context that Berton overlooks is this.
Almost from the moment they were liberated by Allied armies, a number
of European countries had made it clear that they intended to revive their
own film industries, to discriminate strictly against Hollywood, and to freeze
the earnings of American films until dollars were no longer short. There
were episodes of this kind in France and the Low Countries in 1944–5, and
more were to come in Central and Southern Europe. Hollywood was embattled by these restrictions and by the frustration of being unable to receive
the money that Hollywood films did earn. This meant more borrowing to
finance production. The most bitter and protracted experience was in the
largest overseas market, the United Kingdom, where the imposition of a 75
percent ad valorem tax was met by a U.S. boycott.

It is, then, no wonder that Hollywood pulled out all the stops in an effort
to have Canada not join this pattern of European behavior, which the
Americans were bound to see as an attempt to have the same number of
Hollywood films but to pay less for them. Perhaps forewarned by the events
in Europe, they acted to preempt Canadian legislative measures. As early
as 1927, American officials had seen a connection between Canadian film
content and increased sales in Canada:

American producers should include in their pictures whenever possible some favorable references to Canada. All of this helps to maintain the present interest in
American films. "The Canadian" was a great success likewise other pictures partially
filmed in this country. The Canadian National Railways and Canadian Pacific Railway Company are among our friends because they realize that the more we mention
Canada in our pictures the more Americans will want to visit the Dominion. Naturally the greater the rail tourists traffic the greater the revenue for them.[33]

In 1948 it was proposed more formally that Hollywood spend additional
dollars in Canada by shooting films or parts of films there; that, in these

films and others, Hollywood endeavor to publicize Canada's problems, virtues, and trade and tourism opportunities. In return, Canada would ignore the European pattern and not control the remittance of the dollars that movies earned.

Different Canadians wanted different things. Minimizing expenditure of U.S. dollars was a general government objective. Ross McLean, who had succeeded Grierson as head of the National Film Board, wanted to find ways to use the earnings of Hollywood films to finance the film industry in Canada. And still others wanted redress for American films' flag waving, slighting of Canada's role in the war, and general tendency to caricature, as well as relief from expending dollars on third-rate Hollywood B pictures. This was a rich and unrealistic bill of fare. Had the Canadians stuck to the first point – namely, a temporary dollar shortage that required a partial freeze on remittances – they might have found Hollywood more receptive than expected. Joseph Kennedy had negotiated such a freeze in Britain in 1939, which continued until the dollar problem was eased by Lend–Lease. After the war, new British freeze arrangements preceded and succeeded the boycott.

Not surprisingly, the Hollywood opening position was no freeze on remittances. Where perhaps the Canadians made a tactical mistake was in being distracted by the essentially frivolous items on the list, thus giving Hollywood an opening to address those concerns. A freeze was a temporary solution to a temporary problem. Canadian complaints about slights and self-esteem, the low quality of some Hollywood pictures, and the diversion of Hollywood money into Canadian production were neither temporary nor amenable to direct practical action. So, although we cannot gainsay the ludicrous aspects of what follows, we should lampoon neither side. Hollywood was a group of anxious businessmen aiming to defend their interests, not to trick the Canadians. And perhaps more important, the Canadians were not gullible fools, dazzled and seduced by Hollywood glamour. They again were men with, alas, a different set of interests, trying to accomplish it without setting up a coherent strategy.

Berton rightly points out that the gist of the Hollywood plan was to divert more dollars into Canada, rather than prevent the remittance of Canadian earnings.[34] Basically, the idea was that if American motion pictures could promote Canada, then tourism and trade with the Dominion might increase and compensate for the drain of dollars through movie rentals. Seven points seem to have been agreed on at the January 1948 meetings in Ottawa between Canadian government officials and representatives of the Motion Picture Association of America (MPAA) – successor in 1945 to the Motion Picture Producers and Distributors of America (MPPDA) and, from that year, headed by Eric Johnston:

1. The production of a film about Canada's trade problem;
2. More complete newsreel coverage of Canadian events;

3. Production of short films about Canada;
4. Release of more National Film Board films in the United States;
5. The interpolation of Canadian sequences in U.S. feature films;
6. Promotional radio records by Hollywood stars; and
7. Selective export of films to Canada "to avoid dollar expenditures by Canada for gangster films or other pictures of a low-toned nature."[35]

In the Canadian files we have one other theme, the opportunity for Canadian capital to participate in American production and marketing. This is a puzzle. Canada wanted to conserve dollars, not spend them in the United States. I take it that what was meant was that Canadian capital was to be permitted to participate in American film production in Canada, thus gaining a share of the return when those films were shown in the United States and elsewhere. Donald Gordon, deputy governor of the Bank of Canada, drew the attention of Minister of Trade and Commerce C. D. Howe to the risky nature of film financing. But Gordon's most important contribution to the discussion was to argue that advertising Canadian tourism and informing Americans about Canada were far and away the most important objectives of the CCP. He foresaw $3–6 million flowing, over twelve to eighteen months, from the effort. And he concluded that the project should not be coordinated through the NFB, because "views expressed on its behalf to the Industry do not seem calculated to contribute to results"; he also noted the "divergence of view among agencies of government as to the aims that should be pursued."[36]

I do not find here evidence of gullible Canadians. What I find is subscription to the theory that "the tremendous power of the motion picture medium to influence public attitudes needs no elaboration." I find a calculated decision not to have an economic fight with the American motion picture industry, but rather to accept eagerly their agreement to promote Canada. The naïveté of Berton and other nationalist analyses of the CCP episode shows in their failure to appreciate the power of the American motion picture industry. That industry had built close and cooperative relations with the U.S. Congress and with well-placed officials in the Departments of State and of Commerce. The British were well aware of this. What the Canadian files do not reveal is whether Canadian officials were fully apprised. Britain was the U.S. film industry's biggest overseas market; Britain was also one of the Big Three and a Great Power. Technically, Britain could resist the motion picture industry, but in practice the cost of such resistance was not worth it. As the British also found after World War II, geopolitical dependence on the United States was the overriding priority. No evidence has come to hand indicating whether Canadian officials reached the same conclusion. Let us assume they had. Then it made sense to accept Hollywood's public relations efforts on Canada's behalf, rather than have a confrontation over a small amount of dollars (compared to the scale of needed economies).

Having hit hard at the nationalist analysis of this episode, I do not want to conceal the ludicrousness of the idea of inserting Canadian references into the dialogue of Hollywood films, setting stories in a synthetic Canada, or some of the public relations efforts published in annual reports of the CCP (a sample of which I reproduce in Fig. 3.1). There does, however, remain the question of explaining the episode, if one is not to dismiss it as a boondoggle or worse. What made Canadian government officials accept the CCP as a substitute for exchange controls on film remittances? Although attempts were made by film men to place a dollar value on the efforts of the CCP, I do not think we need assume Canadian politicians and officials took them seriously. If the CCP was a bilateral deal, then one must concede that one side certainly did not know the value of what it was getting. It might be more appropriate to remember what it is we are dealing with.

Movies were a major, if not the major, mass medium of entertainment at the time. As all the evidence discussed in Part I shows, American movies were immensely popular with Canadians. Whether because British movies were substandard, because no one was quite sure if Provinces or the Federal government had responsibility, because nation building required documentaries rather than features, or because Hollywood could show Canada favorably, the fact is that no drastic action against American movie interests has ever been successfully carried through in Canada. The Rex *v.* Famous Players prosecution failed, and from that point on there had been talk, and even threats, but no action. Canadian governments showed an admirable grasp of the political realities. An anti-American rhetoric might sound fine to selected groups and elites, many of whom, one suspects, did not go to the movies much, if at all. Conversely, such public rhetoric, by making the movies sound a bit raffish, may have enhanced their pleasurable appeal to other, less privileged, groups. When it came down to it, a lot of voters enjoyed American movies, regarded their pleasure in them as something of a right, and might have understood neither United Empire Loyalist nor balance of payments arguments for any curtailment. The best policy seemed to be, talk big and *say* you carry a big stick, but in fact carry no weapon at all.

In concluding Part I, I need to reiterate that the U.S. motion picture industry was forceful in pursuit of its interests and resourceful in the production of arguments, pressures, and schemes to defend its position in Canada. That position was immeasurably strengthened by the lack of strong or credible competition. It was also assisted by the tacit cooperation of the public, which never showed any sign of serious discontent with the product – if anything, quite the contrary. Resisting the influence of an American mass medium for commercial reasons was not a serious matter in Canada. Resisting that influence for cultural and nationalist reasons was more serious but bedeviled by the confusion of aims. Vocal Canadian elites proclaimed a British nationalism when the box office and American consuls were noting

newsreels

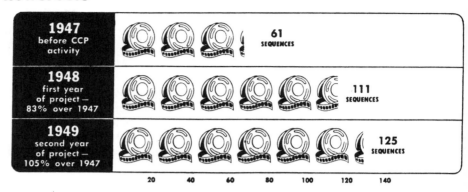

short subjects

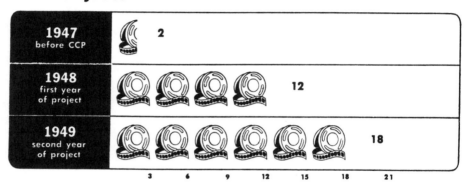

features

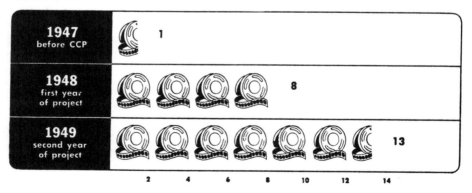

Figure 3.1. Report of Canadian subjects produced and/or released by U.S. motion picture companies in the interest of the Canadian Cooperation Project. (NAO, RG 20, Trade and Industry, vol. 575, file A338, Canadian Cooperation Project of the Motion Picture Association of America, General.)

how similar Canadians were in taste and outlook to Americans and how cordially they consumed the films. A variant of this situation prevails today. Vocal political and cultural elites proclaim a national identity different from both Britain and the United States and in the name of it impose controls on the mass media that are similarly incongruent to the box office and other measures of mass taste and preference (Collins 1990). Clearly, willful elites can get away with policies that ignore popular sentiment, provided they do not seriously deprive the Canadian public of the bulk of its American mass media fare. Much the same is true of Canadian relations with the United States generally: A degree of independent action is permitted, provided there is no serious encroachment on major U.S. interests. Prime Minister Pierre Trudeau's now somewhat hackneyed image of the perils of living next to an elephant apply in the movie business as to much else in Canadian cross-border policy.

Notes

1 Boylen to Monteith, 12 May 1928, AO, RG 56, Series A-1, Box 1, Censor File 1922–1926. This is confirmed by a letter from F. L. Herron, foreign manager of the Motion Picture Producers and Distributors of America, of 29 May 1928. He ventures "that there are very few, if any, of the films going into Canada that are not of the same edition as those issued in the United States. It is very seldom that the edition of the film shown in the domestic market is changed before it is distributed in Canada, England or the Continent. There are a few cases such as *Peter Pan* where changes have been made, as in the domestic edition an American flag was used, while in the edition that went outside of the United States a British flag was used." AO, RG 56, Series A-1, Box 1, File 1.7.

2 Herron to Vancouver Consul, 1 August 1927, NA, RG 59 842.4061 Motion Pictures – Canada 1912–1929, Microfilm 1435, Roll 19.

3 John Grierson, "The Future for British Films," *Spectator,* 14 May 1932, quoted in Cooper to Henry, 20 June 1932, AO, RG 3, Box 153, Henry Papers, Motion Picture Bureau 1932.

4 Silverthorne memo, 11 February 1949, AO, RG 6, Series I-2, Box 49, Motion Picture Censorship and Theatres Inspection Branch 1948–1951.

5 Cooper to Henry, 14 July 1931, AO, RG 3, Box 142, Henry Papers, Motion Picture Bureau 1931.

6 Cooper to Dunlop, 1 September and 4 October 1933, AO, RG 56, Series A-1, Box 2, File 2.2.

7 Ibid.

8 Lewis to Ferguson, AO, RG 3, Box 107, Ferguson Papers, General Correspondence 1930. The figure seems very high. At the time of the Canadian Cooperation Project nearly twenty years later, the figure was put at $15 million. See Appendix A to Report on West Coast Meeting and Studio Visits of Messrs. Fitzgibbons, Mills and Owensmith, attached to Fitzgibbons to Howe, 16 July 1951, PA, RG 2 18, vol. 170; File M-27, vol. 2.

9 Ottawa Consulate to State Department, 13 April 1933, NA, RG 59, 842.4061, Canada 1930–1939.

10 Badgley to Parmelee, 16 December 1937, PA, RG 20, vol. 31; File 16613, vol. 2.

11 Badgley to Chamberlain, 22 January 1938, ibid. All of the quotations from the Badgley memo are from this source.

12 Skelton to Parmelee, 13 January 1938, PA, RG 20, vol. 31; File 16613, vol. 2.

13 All quotations from Colonial Secretary to Canadian High Commissioner, 18 February 1938, PA, RG 20, vol. 31; File 16613, vol. 3.

14 Parmelee to Skelton, 22 February 1938, PA, RG 20, vol. 31; File 16613, vol. 2.

15 For which see Sussex 1975, Low 1979, and Swann 1989.

16 See Jarvie and Macmillan 1989 and the other pieces in that special issue of the *HJFRTV:* Pronay 1989, Aitken 1989, and Morris 1989.

17 See Evans 1984.

18 See the papers on Grierson in PA, RG 25 A–12, vol. 2120, file 1062 / 1.

19 The control by the state, through the banking system, of dealings in gold and in foreign currencies.

20 Ottawa Consulate General, "Required Report on Motion Pictures," 1 February 1940, WNRC, RG 84 Post Records, Ottawa, 840.6 Motion Pictures, 1936–54 (these records hereafter cited as "Motion Pictures, 1936–54").

21 Ibid.

22 Ibid.

23 Ottawa Consulate General, "Required Report on the Canadian Motion Picture Market," 10 August 1940, "Motion Pictures, 1936–54."

24 "Motion Pictures in Canada – 1942," 17 August 1943, in ibid.

25 Winnipeg Consul to State Department, 5 October 1944, in ibid.

26 Toronto Consul to State Department, 3 November 1944, in ibid.

27 For the useful phrase "media elite" and an excoriation of the views of its members, see Brimelow 1986.

28 Toronto Consul to State Department, 3 November 1944, "Motion Pictures, 1936–54."

29 "American Motion Pictures in the Post-War World," 7 November 1944 and 24 November 1944, in ibid.

30 Atherton to State Department, 28 February 1945, "Motion Pictures, 1936–54."

31 Parsons to Dickey, 15 October 1945, in ibid.

32 Canada was not monolithic, of course. There were elements that dissented from the declaration of war and from conscription. These were especially noticeable in Québec.

33 North to Herron, 22 March 1927, NA, RG 151 281, Canada Motion Pictures, Box 1555.

34 In this its concept compares with the Empire Marketing Board, which Constantine (1986, p. 198) interprets as a surprising by-product of unsuccessful tariff reform.

35 WNRC, RG 84, Post Files Ottawa 840.6, Motion Pictures Confidential Files 1948.

36 Gordon to Howe, 24 June 1948, PA, RG 20, vol. 575, File 338.

PART II

America's biggest foreign market: The United Kingdom

CHAPTER 4

The road to a British quota system, 1920–1927

Unlike Canada, where the commercial film industry consisted mainly of exhibition and distribution, Britain had a tripartite industry. There was exhibition, a very profitable sector; distribution, which was partly American owned and controlled; and a continuous flow of commercial production – although aggregate output fluctuated widely. These three sectors seldom found their interests in harmony. Exhibitors wanted a guaranteed flow of product at reasonable prices that would draw audiences. Producers wanted a guaranteed market for their films in preference to those of foreigners. Distributors were a house divided against itself, some acting for their principals, exhibition interests; others for their principals, American interests; still a third group attempting to achieve a kind of independence by handling either British or foreign films. The position of Britain in the film trade in the North Atlantic triangle was thus a tangled one, reflecting both foreign and domestic rivalry with the United States compounded by the direct intervention of legislation and regulation.

4.1. Fears of U.S. influence on the mass electorate

Among many developments of concern to British ruling elites between the wars,[1] I single out two that seem especially important to policy on motion pictures. They were the extension of the franchise in Britain, and the changing commercial and geopolitical position of the United States. One was a domestic development, the other foreign. The domestic concern was the emergence of the politics of mass culture; the foreign matter concerned the changing place of Britain in world trade and the international security system.

The United Kingdom extended the franchise to all adult males in 1918 and to females in 1928. This created a vast new common electorate, the political inclinations of which were uncertain (see Hollins 1981). Among the fears that preyed upon ruling elites was that of an inchoate mass electorate, subject to manipulation by the mass media, especially the popular press. The evident popularity of the new medium of the movies with the

103

mass was a further cause of concern and one to which several historians have paid close attention. The use of the movies as an instrument of propaganda for keeping the new electorate entertained and also for shaping opinions lurks behind elite dealings with the movies in the interwar period in Britain. The anxiety of British ruling elites was shared by parallel elites in Canada and the United States.

My phrase "lurks behind" is carefully chosen. The anxiety was seldom confessed to or named. For example, in the debates in Parliament concerning the Cinematograph Films Act of 1927, commercial and cultural considerations were brought up, but not political ones, still less political propaganda. Yet here and there the files yield evidence that officials were thinking about these matters. There was, for example, the establishment of a new position for a "cinematograph adviser" within the Stationery Office, to advise and coordinate departmental film activities within the government. The appointment of Col. Foxen Cooper to the job may be some indication of what was intended, whether or not it was achieved.[2] Other countries were thought to have stocks of propaganda films.[3] The Foreign Office actively involved itself in the censoring of both British and foreign films on sensitive subjects – indeed was shocked to find that the British Board of Film Censors was a private body, not a government department.[4] Some Foreign Office correspondence with the British Embassy at Rome in 1928 reveals that the U.S. Embassy assiduously pressed the case of the American film interests in Italy; that American films implying Canada was being Americanized were made; that American commercial films got the cooperation of the armed services; and that films about the war showed

America's share in the war magnified out of all recognition in graphic scenes on the western front, either military forces of the other Allies do not figure at all or only do so in order to be rescued from defeat by the heroism of American troops.[5]

The argument went on to claim that to the average cinema audience, even more than to the average newspaper reader, the enormous majority of lying statements or implications were quite indistinguishable from the truth, and the writer believed that this fact must be taken as a point of departure in dealing with the new problems raised by the development of the cinematograph as a means of influencing world public opinion.[6]

The other, foreign, development was the astonishingly rapid rise of the United States from reluctant minor actor in the world drama to leading player. The symbolism of President Wilson's powerful presence at the Versailles Conference was backed by the realities of American military and economic power. Having emerged, before World War I, from its long-time debtor status to creditor status (with fluctuations), the United States also began to pursue a much more forward and active trading and export policy throughout the world (Costigliola 1977). British ruling elites, anxious to hang on to such power as they could, conceived of the idea of cultivating a special relationship with the United States in which they could play Greece to America's Rome. Present-day British historians are inclined to stress the self-deception of this end, both the belief that the Americans could be bamboozled and the reluctance to accept the fact of diminishing British significance – a certain blindness to manifest differences between the national interests and policies of the two nations.[7]

Films were, it is true, a mere detail on this larger canvas. They had, however, a certain visibility and prominence because they were so popular with the newly enfranchised masses. Thus, in facing the fact of U.S. dominance in the international trade in motion pictures, the British elites were torn. Although there were sympathetic mandarins in America who also despised Hollywood and distrusted its effect on the masses, the industry was a powerful lobby and one not to be alienated by the elites of a country that wished to curry favor and cultivate formal and informal policy alignments with the United States. Similarly, although British businessmen might demand a share of the money to be made from films by passing legislation, it was impolitic either to inflame influential groups in the United States or to deprive the British masses of their foreign-made pleasures.

Whereas the story to be told of Canada in the international trade in films is a shaggy-dog story lacking narrative punch, by contrast the story of Great Britain's involvement in that trade involves drama and excitement, dreams and hopes, failures and disappointments. It is not exactly a sob story, but there certainly is only a limited sort of happy ending. In presenting this story I shall once again resort to the flashback technique, plunging immediately into an emblematic episode (§§4.2–4) and then shifting back to an explanatory historical narrative (§4.5). Chapters 5–8 take the story to the end of our period.

Which past episode would be most emblematic of the forces at work on the British point of the triangle? I have chosen the momentous decision of 1927 to enact quota legislation giving protection to an almost moribund British film industry. This legislation profoundly affected the future development of the British film industry and its economic foreign policy, and so was also relevant to what happened in Canada.

The Cinematograph Films Act of 1927 was, to spell it out, "an Act to restrict blind booking and advance booking of cinematograph films, and to secure the renting and exhibition of a certain proportion of British films."[8] Requiring that all films shown in Britain be registered with the Board of Trade made it possible to enforce trade previewing of films instead of blind booking and made it easier to determine whether, for purposes of the act, a film was British. A percentage (quota) of British films was required to be shown in all cinemas, and a somewhat higher percentage of British films was required to be handled by the "renters," or distributors, to ensure some choice for the exhibitors. Over the ten years of the act (1927–37), the required percentages were to be raised in annual increments. The act itself did not work perfectly and so was modified at each of its renewals in 1938 and 1948. Nevertheless, the 1927 act did make a substantial difference and provided the frame within which the British film industry operated for nearly fifty years: a frame, that is, of protectionism and state oversight.

4.2. A letter to the *Morning Post*

The British tradition of ventilating issues in the correspondence columns of the *Times* is known far beyond Britain's shores.[9] But the *Times* was not the only powerful organ of opinion; several other reputable metropolitan dailies were also effective outlets. The *Morning Post* was known to be influential in Conservative Party circles and was hence a sure bet to bring an issue to the attention of the party, which was then in power under Prime Minister Stanley Baldwin. An impressive array of cultural leaders and other dignatories signed a letter of 20 June 1925 to the *Morning Post* on the subject of films.[10]

Sir:

The present position and future prospects of the film industry in this country have become matters of grave national concern, and we venture to think that the importance of the issues involved is not yet clearly realised, either by the general public or in official quarters.

The production of films occupies an important place in the industrial life of several other countries and gives employment to large numbers of people.

We have in Great Britain approximately 4,000 cinema theatres and halls where pictures are shown, and it is estimated that twenty millions attend "the pictures" each week, while the yearly receipts amount to about thirty millions sterling. Yet it is a humiliating fact that of the pictures exhibited not 5 per cent. are British productions, all others having their origin abroad, mainly in the United States, although quite recently Germany has come forward as a serious competitor with the Americans in the production of what are known as super-films.

Important as is the commercial aspect of this problem, high national and patriotic interests are involved. No one who has followed the development of this new form of popular entertainment can be in any doubt as to the immense importance of films as a subtle means of propaganda, none the less powerful because it is indirect. Films have an atmosphere of their own. The bulk of the films shown in this country have, to say the least of it, a non-British atmosphere. These films are shown in our Dominions, Colonies, and Dependencies, and in all the countries of the world outside the British Commonwealth of nations. Many of them are inferior productions, neither healthy nor patriotic in tone, while the psychological influences which they convey may have far-reaching consequences.

What is the explanation of this state of things, which we venture to describe as deplorable? It is precisely because there is as yet no authoritative reply to this question that we are venturing to address you and make a public appeal to the Prime Minister to institute an inquiry and, at the same time, permit a judgment to be formed as to the measures which should be taken to establish a film industry in this country on a sound foundation.

In making this appeal for an authoritative inquiry, we purposely refrain from discussing the many explanations and suggestions which have been canvassed; but, in our judgment, the very variety of these suggestions implies an unanswerable argument for an impartial examination of the whole of the facts affecting the present state and future of the film industry in this country.[11]

Lena Ashwell[12]	Thomas Hardy	Robert Bridges
Cecil Harmsworth	Lord Burnham	Sidney Lee
Lord Carson	Charles McLeod	J. R. Clynes
Martin Conway	Charles W. C. Oman	Lord Dawson of Penn
Lord Riddell	Robert Donald	Gordon Selfridge
Edward Elgar	Ethel Snowden	

Although of varied interests – the arts (Ashwell, Bridges, Conway, Elgar, Hardy, Lee, Oman); politics (Carson, Clynes, Snowden); and business (especially newspaper magnates, viz., Donald, Harmsworth, Riddell, and Burnham) – and of diverse political coloration, the signatories all belonged to one or more of the British ruling elites – what was later called the "establishment." Their letter, by being printed in a respected metropolitan daily rather than in one of the mass-circulation newspapers, addressed itself to other members of those elites. Possibly several of the signatories had a financial interest in the industry. The distinguished cultural figures (Hardy, Elgar, and Bridges) most likely did not. We have here the intersection of several interest groups that could agree, at least, that they deplored American domination of the British film market and that some sort of government inquiry and, possibly, intervention was required. The presence of a former Home Secretary, a Lord Justice of appeal; the man who devised the Ministry of Information (if his *DNB* entry is to be believed[13]), and of various experts in propaganda who ran newspapers is not to be overlooked, given the close connection historians have found between the British Board of Film Censors and the intelligence community (Pronay 1982). In all this, the voice of the cinemagoing masses was not heard.

The text of this letter deserves scrutiny. These prominent persons refer to a "grave national concern," one apparently hidden from "the general public" and "official quarters." Members of the patrician / guardian elite identify themselves with the national interest, properly construed. Thus they can write of U.S. domination being "a humiliating fact" when that would scarcely seem coherent with the mass popularity of the American product.

Movies involve "high national and patriotic interests"; "no one ... can be in any doubt" about their "immense importance" as "a subtle means of propaganda," propaganda that is "neither healthy nor patriotic" and that has "far-reaching" psychological "consequences." These sentiments were typically and frequently invoked in the period covered by this book but never subjected to scrutiny. Consider a parallel case: the Americanization of the English language. There have been no debates in the House of Lords suggesting a government inquiry into the pervasive influence of American

English on the English language. True, some schoolteachers and other guardians of culture deplored and discouraged that influence, but official and legislative action has not been suggested, and British elites are inclined to mock the French Academy's attempt to defend the purity of French by inventing alternatives to words and expressions it considers foreign.

An argument sometimes made about films is that Britain and the British Empire are linked to British ideals, values, and outlook and that these should be present in a proportion of the popular culture. These Hegelian sentiments are perhaps a way of ignoring other forces that shaped Britain and the Empire during this period, not to mention the quite problematic matter of whether films were indeed the subtle means of propaganda claimed. Political historians of this period argue that the interest of the British ruling elites in mass communication stemmed from the recentness of the creation of a mass electorate by the extension of the franchise to all adults (see Taylor 1988; Stead 1981). How was this new, mass electorate to be orchestrated by the extant political parties? Mass-circulation newspapers, films, and radio were all thought to be means of molding public opinion on political matters and deserved therefore to be carefully watched, and possibly even controlled, by the political elites. It is certainly striking to contemporary observers to note how film censorship in Britain maintained a strict political control[14] (as we have seen was also the case in Canada).

To come back to U.S. influence, it remains to ask in what ways U.S. ideals, values, and outlook might be thought prejudicial to high national and patriotic interests in Britain and the Empire. No evidence was offered that U.S. films assaulted Britain or the British political system. The letter to the *Morning Post* said American films had "to say the least of it, a non-British atmosphere," one "neither healthy nor patriotic in tone." What was it referring to? Here is a guess that may be far-fetched yet agrees well with the arguments of film historians such as Jeffrey Richards (1984). What was being referred to as the neither healthy nor patriotic, non-British atmosphere of U.S. films was their promotion of an ideology different from the paternalistic form of democracy developed in Britain. At the risk of overgeneralizing, here are some prominent features of U.S. films en masse that may have discomfited the British (and Canadian) political elites. Slapstick comedy ridiculed authority figures, from policemen to the clergy; business and political elites were frequently portrayed as unscrupulous and corrupt; an atmosphere of egalitarianism and opportunity for all was pervasive; and narratives often achieved closure only by the efforts of an individual hero, acting in the spirit but not the letter of the law. There was no place for deference and respect to those set over us; no natural social station where ordinary people would find unambitious contentment. Those in the British ruling elites who believed in the propaganda power of films were correct to fear the American product, because it portrayed a successful society that rejected deference. From this point of view, American films were radical and possibly inflammatory social documents, both in the United Kingdom and in the Dominions and Colonies. Russian films, which were more overtly preaching against the ancien régime, were, it should be remembered, almost totally excluded from commercial exhibition in Britain, Canada, and the United States during the interwar period. One might, then, see the apprehensions of the political and cultural elites about U.S. films as similar in kind to the attitude to Soviet films – a less immediate danger, perhaps, and certainly demanding a more delicate means of restriction than outright banning – this being a period when Britain was coming to terms with the reality of American economic power.

The editorial comment on the letter, printed in the same day's issue of the *Morning Post,* harped on block booking and the "strong backing of the American Government" for the export of U.S. films, "The Americans took advantage of our absorption in the war," and they now "dump into our country films at prices with which our own producers could not possibly compete." Such cheap pictures were described as "positively harmful to the children who see them" (again, harm not specified). British films had not had a fair chance, for "there has never been any question of the ability of British film producers to present pictures just as artistic as the best films of America." As we have already seen in studying Canada, the latter assertion goes against the evidence. British films were on the whole cheap and inept; few met the standards of international trade (albeit set by American films, yet endorsed by the public at the box office); and the capacity to make films in sufficient numbers was simply not there. British filmgoers voted with their ticket purchases. Although an exceptional British film would draw a large audience, the routine U.S. film would outdraw the routine British film. Public preference was overlooked by both the letter writers and the newspaper, as so often also by those who wrote and spoke on the subject.

This letter and the editorial showed that a powerful axis had formed between cultural figures and the arguments they could muster, and business figures and the arguments they could muster. Neither, necessarily, were regular consumers of films. Rather the contrary: The suspicion is inescapable that members of the ruling elites seldom attended the cinema. They were therefore operating in the pure atmosphere of paternalism: deciding what was best for the general public in whose name they sometimes presumed to speak. In addition to wishing to maintain the power and position of people of their own background, they also defended particular dispositions of power: The culturalists were mounting a defense of the British Empire; the business spokesmen were trying to defend British profit. Since both groups interlocked with "official circles," they were heard and attended to. Thus it was that until film legislation was abandoned by the Thatcher government, commercial film affairs were subject to successive British acts of Parliament. And whereas Canadian efforts to resist U.S. domination were a flop, British efforts had some limited success, by various measures of success. Certainly the minute percentage of British screen time devoted to British films in the 1920s was decisively changed.

This letter to the press did not come out of the blue. One of its signatories, and possibly its drafter, Lord Burnham, had spoken on the subject in a debate in the House of Lords in May 1925. Dickinson and Street present a fairly full account of the background, drawing on the trade press, parliamentary debates, and official papers (1985, chap. 1). But they make little attempt to exercise historical sympathy with the U.S. point of view. (The House of Lords debate was more balanced.) The authors also display a parochial bias favoring Britain and, within Britain, favoring a cultural rather than commercial emphasis in policy. Thus they look askance at the Board of Trade for always treating films as just another industry. Yet they never subject their culturalist presupposition to close analysis. Indeed, they sympathize with the film trade unions and their socialist proposals for nationalizing the industry, invariably backed by culturalist arguments. More skepticism toward the self-servingness of union proposals might have been salutary.

Dickinson and Street report that 1925 saw agitation from a number of quarters about film matters. The Federation of British Industries (FBI), devout believers in the Prince of Wales's dictum that "trade follows the film," wanted a film industry that would help British exports, especially to the Empire. The near-defunct status of the British film industry was therefore a problem for the FBI. The film trade itself was divided: Distributors and exhibitors who were doing well from American films saw no problem; owners of moribund or struggling production companies and persons aspiring to make British films were loud in their complaints. Both arguments from commerce and arguments from culture were paraded, but the former were the stronger. Indeed it was only at the Imperial Conference the following year that a coherent cultural argument was finally formulated. The summer of 1925 was a key moment. The FBI held a conference on film production in early May. The Lords debate was in mid-May, and in June and July both the FBI group and the Cinema Exhibitors Association (CEA) met with the president of the Board of Trade and drew up proposals. A Joint Trade Committee produced a proposal for film quotas in November that was defeated in a vote by the exhibitors, clear evidence of the divided interests of the trade, even though, in his remarks to the Imperial Conference in the summer of 1926, the president of the Board of Trade, Sir Philip Cunliffe-Lister (whom we have met earlier),[15] was still holding out hope that a voluntary scheme would obviate legislation.

Working from the film trade press, Dickinson and Street detail the activities of the FBI and the CEA as they conferred and tried to devise schemes. It may be worthwhile to look at the House of Lords debate. On 14 May 1925, Lord Newton[16] rose to call attention to the present position of the British film industry and to ask the government to appoint a departmental committee to inquire into the sources of its economic depression and to recommend measures to reestablish this industry, "having regard to the industrial, commercial, educational, and Imperial interests involved."[17] He declared himself without any personal financial interest in the industry. There were, he said, four thousand cinemas in Britain, taking around 20 million admissions per week (over 1 billion a year); the takings amounted to £30 million per annum, on which £3 million in entertainments tax was levied. None of these figures, of course, was from the production sector, which, he declared, was dying. He deplored the tendency of "highbrows" to attribute the failure of British films to the "incapacity of the people who are engaged in the business."

Lord Newton stated that the Americans had taken advantage of World War I to seize their market share, which was at 95 percent in Britain and 99 percent in the Colonies and Dominions. Working from a base of twenty thousand cinemas, the U.S. producers could outspend their competition and yet charge less for their export products than a British company would need to get a fair price. He granted that the Americans had shown initiative:

The fact is, the Americans realised almost instantaneously that the cinema was a heaven-sent method for advertising themselves, their country, their methods, their wares, their ideas, and even their language, and they have seized upon it as a method of persuading the whole world, civilised and uncivilised, into the belief that America is really the only country which counts.

Newton said he was not ashamed to admit that he frequented cinemas to a certain extent, for he found there theatrical action, the portrayal of the remotest parts of the world, entertainment, and an absence of that "drivel masquerading as humour" that was to be found on the stage – all this at about one-fifth of what it cost to attend the theater. Although he had castigated highbrows, he revealed himself to be something of one, deploring that there was little demand for high-class productions, just as there was little demand for The *Times Literary Supplement* compared to the comic magazines *Tit Bits* and *Comic Cuts*. Unfortunately, what the public wanted was rubbish:

If our people are content to witness perpetual rubbish, let it, at any rate, be English rubbish in preference to American rubbish, because in producing English rubbish the money will at least be spent in this country.

He grieved that colored people saw in these American films white people presented under most unfavorable conditions, and he called the effect on British people "denationalising." The effect of films on business he illustrated by saying that they had created a demand for American fashions that had caused British clothing and boot manufacturers to alter their machinery. More than this, U.S. films distorted history, as in their portrayal of the War of Independence.[18] But only the particularly patriotic exhibitor would care what he exhibited, provided it made money.

Lord Gainford,[19] for the FBI, said an official inquiry was premature, since the FBI's own scheme was in development and would make the inquiry unnecessary.

Viscount Burnham (later, as we noted, a signatory to the letter to the *Morning Post*) was less optimistic. He praised the patriotism of the leaders of the U.S. industry for extending its efforts all over the world and said that they would spare no effort to keep their hold on "this great trade" and its influence. He argued that the scale of production favored the wealth and numbers in America and that, in the judgment of experts, "it will be very difficult, it may be impossible, to oust America from the virtual monopoly she now enjoys." Whether from confusion or different sources of information, Viscount Burnham stated that there were three thousand cinemas in Britain and fifteen thousand in the United States.[20]

Responding for the government, Viscount Peel[21] noted that in 1914 25 percent of the films shown in Britain were British, whereas by 1923 only 10 percent were, and that the percentage was presently lower. Similarly, there were twenty (production?) firms in 1923 but only four or five active in 1925. He offered additional confusing figures, suggesting seventeen to twenty thousand cinemas in America compared to three thousand in Britain. Vertical integration, he argued, was what closed the American market. Talented people in Britain could be lured away to America with vast salaries. He thought that nothing short of the prohibition of U.S. films would be necessary to give an opportunity to British film exhibitors.[22] He had

heard the criticism rather freely expressed that the public in this country deliberately prefer these American films to our own. Whether that is a criticism of our own films I do not know, but I think that, if you talk to the exhibitors, they will tell you that, for some reason or other, these American films, whether owing to their good qualities or their bad qualities – I do not dogmatise on that point – for the moment seem to attract audiences far more magnetically than British films.

Claiming that the causes of the depression in British film production were thus pretty well understood, Viscount Peel declined (on behalf of the government) to agree to an inquiry but rather urged Lord Newton to undertake a public campaign to alert the "cinema haunters of this country" to the "tremendous advantages of the British film."[23]

Lord Gorell[24] drew attention to the powerful trade organization (the Motion Picture Producers and Distributors of America) that had been formed, headed by "an American ex-Cabinet Minister." This reference to Will Hays and the MPPDA was not developed with reference to U.S. export success but rather to the claim that the U.S. motion picture industry was not internally split as was the British. That conclusion was not accurate. The American industry was split, but not so neatly along the two lines dividing producers from distributors, and distributors from exhibitors, as in Britain. Because of vertical integration, all the major American production companies were distributors as well, and because some chains were owned by distributors the split was around the edges of the MPPDA: smaller and independent production companies, unaffiliated chains and theaters, served by residual states rights distributors.[25] Had there been government intervention in the U.S. film industry, these particular lines of division might have caused problems, but not to the extent of the total divergence of interest that characterized the situation in the British industry, two parts of which (distribution and exhibition) were prosperous, while the third part (production) languished.

When Viscount Peel's radical solution of prohibition was eventually tried in 1947, the relative power of these divided sectors was sharply highlighted. Meanwhile, the Lords debate aired nearly everything not stated in the letter to the *Morning Post,* allowing us to see the policy questions that confronted Britain. Neither the enigma of the public attitude nor the general shortage of cash made the situation amenable to a simple solution. Furthermore, as was twice noted, not only were U.S. motion picture interests entrenched in Britain: They were in an almost unassailable position and seemed to have the resources and the will to act to maintain that position. Indeed, the only point missing from this Lords debate was any sense that the Americans could, did they so wish, buy up the whole British film industry, not just individual personnel. The role of large capital and the scale of its power was not, I think, in focus, although it did come up in the House of Commons debate (§4.3). Lords and Commons did not know it at the time, but within two years the introduction of sound to motion pictures would sharply focus attention on the need for large amounts of capital. This one technological change rendered at a stroke all cinemas, all studios, all the stock of recyclable hit films, and even some of the human capital in the form of stars, obsolete. Massive infusions of new capital were required to reequip and to renew the business.

Many ideas were being canvased in 1925 beyond making block booking illegal and devising a quota on British films. The small domestic market and the few sources of risk capital turned attention toward the idea of a government-backed "film bank" to make production loans and of a subsidy for centralized studio facilities with state-of-the-art equipment. The impression given is of a penurious production sector looking to the taxpayer for support and generating arguments beyond merely those of jobs to make the case plausible. Recall that the perception in Canada was that Britain needed facilities and that Trenton, in Ontario, would serve, with no apparent sense that the British saw themselves as hard up, not as world travellers able to consider spending in Canada. And of course British business and unions were not much interested in creating an industry and jobs where they would be to someone else's advantage. Canadians seem to have been all too ready to take appeals to Imperial solidarity literally and to construe the British as ready to transfer an entire industry abroad. In fact, the ruling Conservative government also felt financially strapped and was not willing to subscribe to any scheme that required taxpayer's money to assist the production of films. What it wanted was to create – by legislation only if unavoidable – the conditions in which a prosperous private-sector production industry could develop.

In the papers prepared for the Imperial Conference of 1926 (as we have seen in §2.3), the British concentrated almost entirely on the cultural argument at a time when Empire patriotism was expressed, in the White Dominions and elsewhere, as loyalty to things British. It followed that British films were preferable to non-British. As a courtesy (but, I suspect, no more), Canadian films, Australian films, and other rare creatures were commended and seen as part of an intra-Empire cultural flow. Apparently the British took it for granted that London would be the base for the Imperial film industry.

Dickinson and Street claim that a secret draft of a quota bill was shown to the Economic Subcommittee of the Imperial Conference. They do not cite their evidence, and there is no trace or mention of this in the extant Canadian papers. It seems a somewhat unlikely development, quite apart from the impropriety of showing draft legislation to strangers before showing it to Parliament. In his remarks to the conference, the minutes of which are marked "Secret," Cunliffe-Lister said that if voluntary efforts failed he inclined to a quota but that he was unclear as yet as to whom it would affect and how it would be enforced. He did not, in other words, speak like a man floating a specific proposal to see what the reaction would be.

Given that his primary concern was commercial, a more plausible reading of his use of the Imperial Conference is this. In a framework of Empire solidarity and a perceived threat from U.S. films, could a scheme be devised that would utilize the Empire market as a means of giving British production a large enough "domestic" (or captive) base to permit a profitable industry to develop? It is not clear if he expected the Dominions to offer quota schemes. It is clear that any straightforward discrimination against U.S. films would conflict with commercial treaties and with Prime Minister Baldwin's pledges to maintain free trade. It was also clear that an ad valorem duty on imported films was a technically difficult alternative, because there was no sure way to estimate a film's value – what it would earn.

By the end of 1925, Dickinson and Street contend, the split interests of the British film industry had scuttled any hope of a voluntary scheme. Sporadic efforts seem to have continued well into 1926, so that Cunliffe-Lister could tell the Imperial Conference that he hoped not to have to legislate, but that if necessary he would. By January 1927 he told the cabinet that the film trade could not agree, and on 10 March 1927 the Cinematograph Films Bill received its First Reading. The debate on principles (the Second Reading) deserves close attention. It ran mostly on party lines, but not entirely. Some Conservatives were far from happy with its protectionism, and some Liberals and Labourites were unhappy about its elitism. Let us scrutinize it.

4.3. The debate on the Second Reading

On the success or failure of the British film industry much more depends than its own future. It inevitably involves great interests, national and imperial, and the anxiety which was exhibited at the Imperial Conference and the determination registered there to remedy an intolerable position are shared, I believe by the majority of British people throughout the whole Empire, that that determination must be translated into action.

– Sir Philip Cunliffe-Lister

Cunliffe-Lister began the debate by invoking the resolution passed by the Imperial Conference the preceding year in which Britain was seen as necessarily taking a leading role.[26] The cultural importance of motion pictures, he said, was generally recognized in the House, the country, and throughout the Empire.

The cinema is today the most universal means through which national ideas and national atmosphere can be spread, and, even if those be intangible things, surely they are among the most important influences in civilization. (col. 2049)

He rhetorically appealed to how "we" should feel about foreigners dominating British literature or the press. Then he switched to arguments from commerce, emphasizing the value of films as a form of advertising for national products. He quoted Dr. Julius Klein's Congressional testimony stating that South America's switch from being a market for British goods to one for American goods was due to the selling power of American films,[27] but he made no mention of the possible impact of World War I on Britain's grip on this market. He quoted the British trade commissioner in Canada:

The cinema film has also operated against British trade. The production, distribution and exhibition of films in Canada is almost entirely controlled by foreign interests. The effect of the constant exhibition of foreign films on the sentiment, habits and thought of the people is obvious. The picture[s] show the foreign flag, styles, standards, habits, advertisements, etc. (cols. 2041–2)

After reviewing the history of attempts to get effective voluntary arrangements, Sir Philip ran through the bill clause by clause and ended on a cultural high note: "On the success or failure of the British film industry much more depends than its own future. It inevitably involves great interests, national and Imperial" (col. 2049).

First on his feet to oppose was Ramsay MacDonald, leader of the Labour Opposition, asking the House to refuse to agree to a bill that "compels British traders to supply goods irrespective of their comparative merits and the demands of their customers" (col. 2050). He seized on an inconsistency in Sir Philip's commercial arguments, for there had been appeal to the advertising power of films for British goods, yet nothing in the bill's definition of British films prevented the display in them of foreign goods. He rested his own case on cultural considerations. The only serious argument for British films, MacDonald held, was that they "should uphold to foreign nations a better conception of the moral conduct and social habits of people who profess to belong to the leading nations of the world than, unfortunately, is the case with so many films that are being exported, for instance, to China" (col. 2051).

MacDonald asked rhetorically if music should have a quota, or tobacco. He insisted that the bill was a party bill, emanating from one special section of the producers. He also pointed to another inconsistency. Sir Philip had refused to admit that Britain could not produce films that would attract audiences; MacDonald held that the whole bill rested on such an admission. On the principle of assisting an ailing or infant industry, MacDonald granted that intervention was justified, but only if it was for a limited time, not a permanent quota, which would give British producers a guaranteed monopoly with no regulation of their prices and profits and would force exhibitors to show films their customers might not care for.

MacDonald claimed the exhibitors were being victimized:

There is not a single exhibitor in this country but will now find his programmes interfered with and find himself compelled to put films upon the screen that, if he were a free man, he would not think of putting on the screen. (col. 2057)

Pressing this argument home, MacDonald made what in retrospect was a vital point: that what was lacking was not just any old British films, but quality British films, British films audiences would go to, but the bill had only a quantity quota and not a quality test. He concluded that the bill did little to encourage the use of British scenery, history, and folklore as subject matter for films. All the ideological intricacies of Labour's attitude to the legislation, and the internal divisions it revealed, are nicely brought out by Jones (1987, pp. 49–52, 93–8).

Walter Runciman,[28] speaking against the bill, also tried to speak up for the public, who, he declared, were entitled "to the best films that the world can produce, no matter from where they come." As would others, he made comparisons with the theater and the opera and asked rhetorically what the effect of quotas there would be.

The truth is, that this Bill has been devised by those who have a commercial interest in the British film industry, and have no consideration whatever for those who get either enjoyment or education out of attendance at the picture palaces. (col. 2062)

It was curious for an Opposition member to argue in this way. Cultural and educational arguments were precisely those that had been orchestrated through the Imperial Conference, and these arguments were specific to this mass medium that was relatively new and were not applicable to traditional, minority art forms such as the theater and opera. Far greater government powers had been taken over radio.[29] Reaching for an even more far-fetched parallel, he asked whether there should be a quota on art exhibits such as the current show of Flemish art at the Royal Academy. An interlocutor from the floor asked whether these paintings degraded the white race in Asiatic countries, to which Runciman retorted that the bill offered no remedy for such a problem and that the government should reconsider it.

Sir Charles Oman (a signatory to the letter to the *Morning Post*) rebuked the Leader of the Opposition for lack of constructive criticism and stressed the importance of the bill to the "moral advantages" of the Empire. He argued that present conditions in the British film industry were deplorable; that enough films could be produced in England; and that the exhibitors did not necessarily know what the public wanted. "I have the greatest distrust of the judgment of exhibitors as well as a distrust of the judgment of managers" (cols. 2067–8).

Col. Harry Day[30] confessed to a connection with the cinema industry. He argued that the bill was solely to protect the producer – not the exhibitor, the renter, or the public. He offered the thought that lack of sunshine, and fog – even inside studios – inhibited the scale of production in Britain. He further suggested that of British films made, not 1 percent was "what one would call good films worth showing" (col. 2070). People intending to go to the cinema avoided houses playing a British film. He stressed that the small base of cinemas did not permit the financing of superproductions, given that the American and Continental markets were closed. Contesting Cunliffe-Lister's figures, he suggested America had five times as many cinemas as Britain (the earlier estimates were four times), and he also expressed skepticism that before the war cinemas had shown 25 percent British films. (He seems to have been correct about this; see §4.5.)

As his speech went on, it became ever-clearer that Colonel Day spoke for the exhibitors, or at least for a certain segment of them. He argued that American materials were popular and cited the excellent runs of American stage shows in the West End. He declared the bill iniquitous for trying to control the exhibitor's business, for trying to compel the public "to witness films in which they have no interest" (col. 2072).

Finally Colonel Day came up with an argument that was forceful and novel in that it showed the economic logic of blind booking and the difficulty of "building up the business without it." Having devised an idea for a film and a cast, an American producer gets bookings from one hundred or two hundred theaters. With those promises he can then secure a line of credit from his banker to make the film. British banking laws and practices being entirely different, British producers will not take such risks. The colonel wandered away from this argument but eventually returned to it when considering clause 1 of the bill. Its force was this. Filmmaking was highly risky because returns from a film could range from almost zero to multiples of the initial investment, with no certain way to tell which it would be. Whatever return there was came from distribution to theaters; hence to prearrange some minimal distribution guarantee was a way to ensure that returns would not be zero. But this arrangement could not but be "blind," because we are talking of financing a film not yet made. Colonel Day went on to say that show business generally had been built up by contracts made in advance. If one wanted to stretch things a bit, one could argue that the bill was itself a form of blind booking in disguise, because it provided that a percentage of British films would be rented and shown when nothing was known of those films except that they were British; furthermore, this was an intrinsic provision of the bill. Unless there was a guaranteed or reserved market for British films, producers would not be able to get lines of credit. Blind booking made films a plausible investment.

Colonel Day also insisted:

There can be no question that, if this Bill becomes law, the majority of exhibitors in this country will be compelled to force upon the public a lot of absolutely futile and rubbishy films. (col. 2082)

At the time, this probably seemed a terrible exaggeration. As it turned out, it was a correct prediction of the flood of "quota quickies" – films made quickly, and on small budgets, strictly to the requirements of being "British" under the act, which to some measure further contributed to public hostility to the generic category of British films. Those who worried at the lack of quality control and those who understood the financing of the business foresaw this consequence, one that was remedied in 1938 when the act was renewed. Day's only false prediction was that British producers, because they had a guaranteed market, would use it to drive up their prices unreasonably. The competition between firms trying to fill the output of quota films seems to have been sufficient to curb any such tendency.

Herbert G. Williams[31] rose to deplore the nature of many of the entertainment offered in cinemas. He spoke of

the evil of showing to coloured races and to, shall we say, less educated people than the average inhabitant of this country, representations of the lives of white people which are completely contrary to the life the bulk of us live. (col. 2088)

He thought a British film industry needed to be built up before such evils could be driven out of the British Empire.

This argument, that American films hampered colonial rule because they debunked the image of whites on which colonial rule depended, is one of the hardest to see the force of today. British colonial rule having ended long ago, the romantic and benevolent picture of it erased, we no longer assume that the image of whites in films had much bearing on how easily that rule was maintained. Our difficulties are compounded because, time and again, speakers failed to specify particular films that offended, yet their Commons audience seemed to be in the know, for they uttered murmurs of assent. It is interesting that during the heyday of the act under debate, Alexander Korda and Michael Balcon produced historical adventure films about the British Empire that gave solace to the vision of it behind comments such as those of Williams. In a discussion of these films, Richards (1973, pp. 1–220) treats them as part of a romantic mystification of the Empire, overlooking the apparent function of countering or offsetting subversive images of whites attributed to Hollywood. Richards is probably correct to argue that their principal function was a domestic one for the United Kingdom, because such films were not in fact at all popular outside the White Dominions.[32]

Sir Alfred Butt[33] made a new point worth notice. If the public had the cinema habit, then they were effectively "compelled to witness films produced largely by those having a foreign nationality." This was charmingly put but is nonetheless a non sequitur. It assumed that the cinema habit was formed regardless of what was playing at the cinema. Thus overlooked was the strong possibility that the habit developed from a taste for what was regularly shown and that therefore the claim of being "compelled" was specious. Sir Alfred took it for granted that, "from a national point of view, it is not good that Britishers should be compelled to imbibe the ideas which are put into those productions by foreigners" (col. 2089). This conclusion is far from obvious. Everything turns on what one means by "a national point of view." To take an example raised during the debate, the British were presented as the wicked enemy in some U.S. films about the various wars between America and Britain.[34] A perfectly good argument can be made that seeing British actions from an alternative point of view is an excellent educational experience, encouraging skepticism toward sentiments such as "My country, right or wrong." However, if "the national point of view" *means* "My country, right or wrong," then skepticism is a Bad Thing (see Jarvie 1976).

Andrew MacLaren[35] also raised a new point, but one of questionable clarity and relevance. His concern was the development of film art, not the development of the film industry. Producers in Britain who were artistically deficient, he felt, would get a guarantee and protection from the bill.

Artists in this country have more than once stated to me openly that the film, as produced in Great Britain, is inartistic, lacking in vision and shows no great conception, and that that is the handicap and nothing else. (col. 2094)

Instead of industrial protection, perhaps the minister of education should ask for money to set up schools for the development of the art of the cinema. British film productions were laughed at in Germany and in Sweden, he said. There was no need for this, although some in the industry would not know how to take advantage of the opportunity from an artistic point of view, due to inexperience and a tendency to deal in maudlin sentiment.

Viscount Sandon[36] offered the thought that the bill had nothing to do with business but was to be compared to the government making a grant toward repairs to Westminster Abbey. He expanded by telling the House that the bill was "necessary for social domestic and Imperial reasons and for trade as a whole as opposed to the Film Trade" and called it unfortunate that the bill was misleadingly sponsored by the Board of Trade (col. 2096). The bill could not be directed against the exhibitors, because, if they were ruined, what would the producers do with their films? The domestic social aspect was that films were not, as they had been called, "the cleanest recreation of the present age." Rather they were American productions, and English and American tastes, he quoted the *Times* as saying, were irreconcilably different.

This high-flown defense was immediately countered by Percy A. Harris,[37] who jibed that Cunliffe-Lister should change his title to Minister of Customs, since he found so many ingenious methods of protecting industry while serving in a free trade administration. As for the Empire, "The Empire must be in a very bad way if it wants legislation of this character to bolster it up" (col. 2101). Furthermore, despite denials, the proposed machinery would involve a considerable bureaucracy. And, in the end, "You can exhibit these films, but you cannot make the public sit them out" (col. 2101). He sarcastically suggested that a clause might be added to the bill imposing a penalty on those who leave their seats during a British film and a register of those attending. The bill was "monstrous and absurd."

The success of the American films is largely due to the skill of the actors, the Charles Chaplins, the Mary Pickfords and the dozens of well-known actors. It would be much better, if the Minister wants to help the industry, to subsidise, or even start an institution to train actors so that they can learn the art and acquire equal skill with some of their foreign competitors.[38] (col. 2103)

Harris concluded by calling the bill protectionist and to be resisted in the name of freedom.

Thomas Johnston[39] excoriated the level of British films and pointed out that it was easy and cheap for any foreign film producer to get a naturalization certificate and hence become "British." He argued that many dramatic works might come from foreign originals. And he continued, up to the cutoff of debate, to hammer home the point that the bill was patronage for films that might well be rubbish.

This point, where the debate in the Commons was held over for conclusion on another day, is a good place to stress the function of studying it at length. There was unusual interest in the bill among backbenchers, and virtual silence from ministers and shadow ministers. (This level of interest and of fractious debate was to result in one of the longest and most intensely struggled committee stages in the history of modern Parliaments.) Strong opinions were expressed about the degree of real impact films had. The general public was to a great extent mute on the matter, and the writings of the elite tend to be those of a subgroup of intellectuals rather than of the governing classes. We gained some access to those views in the letter to the *Morning Post*. The Lords debate was an airing of the issues by an elevated body not charged to govern. In this Commons debate, we get some insight into the thinking of the British political elite about films and their impact, especially because the composition of the Commons and its rather relaxed rules meant that the speakers spoke more informally than one might expect in such august surroundings.

Both opponents and proponents were split on the question of whether to rely on the argument from culture or the argument from commerce. In the case of the latter, some disdained commercial aspects, others spoke of them frankly, and the same applies to the former. Only when the argument from culture could be turned away from art and from education onto the political dimension of the Empire and its preservation did the argument become wholehearted. On the whole one is struck by the mixed level of the debate. Some of the arguments were clear but specious; others vague; and relatively few spoke to the point or offered testable predictions of the consequences of the bill. Let us now turn back to the debate's resumption, on 22 March 1927, when the bill was carried through to a decisive vote.

Opposition Leader Ramsay MacDonald took the position that his party was to welcome proposals to deal with blind and block booking but otherwise rejected the bill. Not all speakers on his side maintained consistency with this position. At the resumption the first speaker was Philip Snowden, from the Labour Party, whose wife had signed the letter to the *Morning Post* and who vigorously opposed the bill as a creation of the Federation of British Industries. Surprisingly for a Labour leader, he concentrated on the argument from commerce, of which he was skeptical. Neglected, he maintained, were the interests of the 30 million people who depended on the cinema for their entertainment and of the exhibitors who arranged it. The Americans and their product were successful because they had gone into the business with the enterprise and acumen so characteristic of them. This, plus good climatic conditions, and no sparing of expense, explained their success. He reminded the House that the Americans bought talent wherever it appeared and that they alone provided sufficient films to supply British cinemas, so that "America has made the cinema industry in this country."[40] In regard to block and blind booking, Snowden made the ingenious argument that a commission from a publisher to a writer was a form of buying blind, since the book was yet to be written. He did not see how business could be done without blind booking. This argument of Snowden's was not consistent with the position he was supporting.

The finale of his speech expatiated on the problems of the exhibitor and his public. Since cinemagoing was an optional luxury and not a necessity, exhibitors had to provide what the public wanted or have it stay away. There seemed to him no realistic prospect that British producers could come up with the quantity of good films the quota law required. The result would be bad and indifferent films (col. 243). He made fun of "the party opposite" because, although the party of private enterprise, they were creating a guaranteed market and an absence of competition. He reiterated MacDonald's point that some quality test, not just a nationality test, was required. In other words, the bill provided for more British films, but the public would want only good British films. Thus small-town cinemas would have to show inferior product, and competing cinemas might have to show the same films in second and third runs to make up their quota responsibilities. He pointed to looseness in the definition of "British" that would permit naturalized foreigners, whose films had the atmosphere of their origins, to qualify for "British" status. Concluding, Snowden argued that films should give the international point of view and that members opposite would have rejected the bill were it not for party discipline.

For the government side, Lt. Col. Moore-Brabazon[41] expressed surprise that the Labour speakers had not called for nationalization and had defended private enterprise. He was the first speaker to refer to radio broadcasting, noting that from radio's early days, "the Government thought it right that broadcasting should be controlled," to prevent propaganda from foreign countries (col. 248). The cinema started as a showman's business and remained in such hands, but now needed to be in new hands. Praising American films for their mechanical perfection, their scale and effects, he noted that "the American film has never exploited the propaganda position as it could have done if it had meant to" (cols. 249–50). Yet their films are produced for the United States and for nobody else. The future lies with them only if the British abandon it to them, ignoring the possibilities for films of their three hundred–year history and leaving filmmaking in its present hands. (One wonders whether his references to "showmen" [and Wardour Street] were for some M.P.'s coded allusions to Jews.)

Rhys Morris[42] fleshed out Moore-Brabazon's allusions to showmen by referring to unpatriotic exhibitors. Claiming that the bill created thirteen new offences, Morris went through several clauses and queried the wisdom of this. Col. R. V. K. Applin[43] drew a distinction between "superfilms" that were expensive to make (over £100,000) and ordinary films costing £10,000. Only the Americans could afford to make the first, but there was no reason why Britain should not make more of the second kind. He followed this point with a rambling discussion of censorship and of whether the German *Konqtingent* scheme was effective.[44] He offered to refute those who said there were no good British films with a list: *Hindle Wakes, The Flag Lieutenant, The Triumph of the Rat, Mademoiselle from Armentières, Mons, Palaver, The Lodger, The Chinese Bungalow,* and *Second to None.*[45] He proceeded to list the film studios operating or being built in Britain and concluded that by 1936 it was possible that British films would have regained 50 percent of the market.

For Labour, John Beckett[46] returned to the way the bill would create a monopoly for certain businessmen, whose claim to make superior pictures was doubtful, given *The Cabinet*,[47] which was lower and more objectionable than any American film he had seen. In a forceful speech he addressed the question of artistic quality and noted that Douglas Fairbanks (Sr.) had said that in order of artistic merit Russian films came first, American second, and British at the bottom. He also noted that

The Government have actually refused to allow some of the very best Russian pictures to be exhibited in this country because they are afraid they will not square with their own political opinions; as if art had ever known any frontiers or limitations of country and nationality. (col. 263)

Rejecting quotas as an attempt to govern international art, he appealed to the government to listen to the dissidents within its own ranks.

Sir Frank Meyer,[48] who spoke next, declared his long connection with the exhibition business and proceeded to attack a bill he found undesirable. First he spoke to the "subsidiary objects" of the bill. One was to use British films to sell British goods. He found this unsound. Another was to prevent lowering the standard of British taste and even of British morals. He found this implausible, since the small quotas envisaged would seem an insult if that was the problem. Still another was to get British films shown abroad. This required good films. As an exhibitor he affirmed that he was more than delighted to take any British film of quality. He argued that the quota would stimulate production, but not production of good quality. The Americans spent a considerable amount of money on their productions and imported foreign talent. Their costs were so high that they relied on foreign sales for profit. Their systematic use of forward financing (raising production money in advance) ensured a continuous supply of films, and he suggested that the FBI should turn its attention to obtaining such a financially sound system for British production. He said he could not support the bill.

In a sarcastic mode, Col. J. C. Wedgwood[49] commented that the president of the Board of Trade gave the impression of never having sunk so low as to go to the pictures himself; hence there was not one word in his speech about the common people who did. Admitting that he himself was a film fan, Wedgwood castigated the government as a lot of highbrows. First, he noted, the price of the pictures would go up because of the machinery the bill required. Second, the lack of competition would enable prices to be forced up farther. Third, people who wanted to see Leatrice Joy and Laura La Plante could not be made to see Sybil Thorndike. Fourth, American films were more amusing. Fifth, films show us the unfamiliar and even exotic. British films were not as funny, and they were more sloppily sentimental.

The people who go to see the pictures are thoroughly satisfied with what they are seeing today, and I think it is for the Government to make out a case to show us why we should perforce change the minds and tastes of people who go to see the pictures. (col. 274)

Declaring the bill to be an import from Germany, Wedgwood argued that British capital not invested in films would be invested in something else and that British people, unlike Germans, have not been trained to do and think as the state thinks they ought to do and think.

Lt. Col. Charles Howard-Bury[50] accused the Opposition of denigrating British films and playing into the hands of American capital:

You have these great American financial interests whose object is to prevent the industry from starting, and they are using all their endeavours to decry our films and to say they are bad and are not worth showing. The Americans were the earliest to realise that it is no longer a question of trade following the flag but of trade following the film. In Canada 95 per cent of the films shown are American. We want to show our ideals and our life as it is and not American ideals and American life as portrayed by American films. (cols. 277–8)

This strong statement of an argument from culture was long overdue in the debate, which constantly got mired in technical discussions of the commercial effects of the bill's provisions.

G. R. Hall Caine[51] spoke next, noting that only Colonel Day and Sir Frank Meyer had spoken from technical knowledge of the industry. He noted that distributors agreed to share risk on the basis of their estimate of the attractiveness of a project and that this system of forward financing was essential if the British industry was to function. Any such films would need to penetrate the American market if they were to be profitable, and so perhaps American participation needed to be cultivated.

Neville Smith-Carington[52] described the American hold on the industry as a "tied-house system," or ring of trusts (cartels), that owned not only distribution firms but also publicity agencies and trade journals, all of which assisted in securing the interests of the trust. He envisaged filmmaking throughout the Empire as a new employer giving opportunity to British migrants. He echoed speakers who had sung the praises of British history, British pageantry, and British scenery as suitable film content. The association, in the minds of so many speakers, of films with sensational visual spectacle shows more of a Cecil B. De Mille than a highbrow approach.

Our own Empire is most eager to see films depicting scenes in the mother land, and it would be a great thing if we could see their scenes on our films. (col. 287)

Arthur Greenwood,[53] winding up for the Opposition, pressed the issue of how more British films would ensure better British films. But his main cultural argument was the deplorable effect of films, both British and American, on the peoples of the East:

This Bill cannot touch that great question which may prove to be one of the most important questions of our day, namely, that question of the exhibition in the East and elsewhere of undesirable films, giving impressions of the life of white people which can only disgust and revolt the people of the East. That may prove to be an important factor in determining our relations with the people of the East in future.[54] (col. 298)

He finished by declaring the bill a kind of caricature of the "slave state" of socialism, with its licenses, its registration, its records, its books, its inspections, and its penalties. "To anybody who has read its provisions, the Bill is the wildest farrago of administrative nonsense that was ever contained in the pages of a Measure submitted to this House" (col. 297).

The solicitor general, Sir Thomas Inskip,[55] winding up for the government, answered none of the questions put but contented himself with reiterating the bill's aim of rescuing an industry that had been submerged by the Americans. He accused the Opposition of employing false analogies and said the competitive element would be introduced by the staggering of the renters' and exhibitors quotas, the former raised one year ahead of the latter. He said whatever influence films had on trade had better be for British rather than American goods, and he added up film production figures for New Zealand, Australia, and South Africa to claim that the sixty films needed for quota purposes in 1928 would be more than sufficiently provided.

Lt. Cdr. Joseph Kenworthy[56] ended the debate with the claim that the bill was his child, but that he now opposed it. It did not solve the problem of finance, which in America was of international outlook.

The great superfilm from Hollywood is not an American film but an international film. The industry is in the hands of an international race, the Jews. It is none the worse for that. (col. 309)

And he drove home perhaps the second most crucial point concerning commerce (the first being the absence of quality incentives): "There is no guarantee that American capital will not come here and control firms established in this country. That is what has been done in Germany" (col. 310).

This debate took more than eight hours of House of Commons time and trod the same ground over and over. A Conservative and free trade government proposing an industrial measure to build up a relatively minor industry tickled the Opposition. That the Labour Opposition should largely frame its objections in terms of the sovereignty of the consumer in a free market tickled the government benches. The Opposition went so far as to grant the so-called infant-industry argument, one of the handful of exceptions to free trade allowed by Adam Smith. There was a division within government ranks on this, some thinking protection should be temporary, others unsure.

Where there was uncertainty, cultural considerations seem to have been uppermost. Curiously, the cultural arguments did not polarize along party lines. Most speakers deplored poor pictures, fretted about U.S. influence, and said that by virtue of talent and tradition Britain ought to be able to make decent pictures. The Opposition, however, had constantly to argue for leaving the emergence in British pictures of these talents to the free enterprise system. The government presented a bill that did not in fact address how talent and tradition would be translated into pictures of merit.

Perhaps most germane to present purposes were those concerns about Empire and the East, where the commercial trade in films was seen as having ineluctable cultural effects over which it was desired to exercise some control. Yet although this point was brought up, and although it clearly concerned many speakers, neither the bill itself nor, as amended the act, succeeded in addressing the matter.

4.4. The act as amended

The Bill passed Second Reading handily by a vote of 243 for and 135 against. In August it moved into committee, the reports on which take up hundreds of pages of Hansard. Here is how it was reported back to Washington by the U.S. Embassy in London:

The Committee's action on the Bill was extraordinary in the intensity of feeling which characterised it. The Committee sat for a longer number of hours than any other in the history of Parliament. There were 300 divisions (formal taking of votes) during the 25 days sitting, 52 of them during the final day.

Despite this, the bill was essentially unchanged, even though both the *Times* and the *Daily Telegraph* had signified intense disapproval of the clause that allowed quotas to be disregarded if they were not commercially practicable.

The Board of Trade, the report went on, had supported the bill with all its force and

prevailed upon the Government to override in a ruthless manner all opposition offered. . . . Thinking opinion in England is in apparent agreement on the necessity of a development of British film policy whether by the control of foreign films (particularly those of American origin), the encouragement of British production, the education of the film public, the control of exhibitors, renters, et al, or by the combination of these or similar measures. The existence of opinion as to the desirability of a national film policy is evident. What is lacking is agreement as to the means by which the desiratum may be attained.[57]

The act made blind booking and block booking illegal by making registration compulsory and contingent on previous showing to the trade. Advance booking was restricted to six months in advance. For films over 3,000 feet in length, a renter had to fulfill a quota of 7.5 percent British films of the total length of film he rented in the year beginning 1 April 1928. The exhibitor's year began on 1 October 1928 and was set at 5 percent of the footage of the film, multiplied by its number of showings. Both quotas rose incrementally to 20 percent in 1936, where they held until the expiration of the act in 1938. An advisory committee to the Board of Trade on the administration of the act was set up under the chairmanship of Sir A. F. Whyte, with two representatives of producers, two of renters, four of exhibitors, and four nontrade members (Mrs. Philip Snowden, Sir Hall Caine, Sir Robert Blair, and St. John Ervine).

4.5. The situation the act sought to correct

Before we study the effect of this major element of British film policy on the international trade in films, we need to look back to the events that preceded it. Why was it, basically, that the British industry needed this massive legislative intervention? What had brought about the 95-percent U.S. dominance that created such commercial and cultural anxieties? Only the most general and sketchy remarks were made in the Commons debate, but we can now, thanks to historians such as Low, try to piece together a more convincing account. Before doing that, there are some general theoretical and methodological questions about the issues to be addressed. For, what we are trying to understand is the development and then the capturing of a film market. Both for historical purposes and for the purpose of assessing whether the commercial and cultural anxiety was proportional to the threat, we need to spell out how we understand the market. In the debate just summarized, one of the major problems was apparent: There were no wholly reliable figures. The count of cinemas, number of films or cinemagoers, size of the industry, capitalization of the industry, and number employed in it, both in Britain and in the United States, were all disputable.

To take only the most glaring example: From time to time the U.S. film industry was described as its fourth-largest industry in the United States. When subjected to the scrutiny of a professional economist, this ranking turned out to be totally mythical (see Huettig 1944, chap. 2). The same, I fear, would be true of Captain Garro-Jones's[58] claim that three hundred thousand people were employed in the American film industry (col. 2107). Nowhere near that number was employed in production in Hollywood, but likely considerably more were employed if one counted all the people who worked in the twenty thousand cinemas. Let us examine the problems generally.

In looking at any territory as a market for films, a number of simple statistical measures have to be established:

1. the number of cinemas in the territory, a raw figure that needs refinement; hence,
2. the total number of seats in those cinemas;
3. both the cinemas and their seating, broken down into showcase, first-run, second-run, and so on;
4. the population of the territory and the ratio of cinemas, seats, and seats of various types to that population as a whole;

5. a participation rate of cinemagoing – that is, a number indicating how many times per week, month, and year a person goes to the cinema (calculated from the gross admission figures and population);
6. the average price of a cinema ticket;
7. the sort of returns that are possible in the market – its maxima, so to speak – which will be important for purposes of assessing the attractiveness of the market to the supplier.

None of these figures is more than a guideline, because rates and tendencies change: A best-selling film may reach more of the population than usually goes to the cinema, and an economic slump may depress cinema generally.

As noted earlier, the U.S. domestic market was not merely large. True, the population of the United States was bigger than that of any European, African, or South American country. Furthermore, there were more cinemas in the United States absolutely than in any other country. But this was not the sole strength of the market. There was also a high rate of cinemagoing by the population and considerable specialization of the leisure dollar. This contrasts with Canada, where there were proportionately fewer cinemas, a lower rate of participation, and hence lower per capita expenditure. The key to the U.S. filmmakers' interest in and exploitation of the British do-mestic market is that, after the United States, the British market was second to none by these other measures. The density of cinema building, the number of seats, the rate of participation were all high. Only the relative lowness of the admission price, which reflected the lower cost of living in Europe generally vis-à-vis the United States in this era, meant that, with between one-quarter and one-third as many cinema seats as the United States, the British market could yield not quite one-quarter to one-third of the revenue.

The paucity of figures is a problem. Low, for example, admits the dif-ficulty of even estimating the number of cinemas in Britain in 1920 because of the unknown numbers closed by the war and never reopened. Unfortu-nately, it was only after the 1927 act that reliable statistics began to be generated, for it was only then that the civil service had the power to gather data from an industry not exactly forthcoming about its workings. So, although it would be nice to be able to study the road to 1927 in the same detail in which we can study events from 1927 onward, the data are just not there. The best we have is the account that Kristin Thompson (1985) generated from a close scrutiny of the U.S. film trade press, supplemented by meager amounts of official statistics.

The most important point she makes is that American domination of the British market was established well before the outbreak of World War I – *pace* those members of Parliament and others who would continue to blame what they thought of as this British misfortune on war conditions rather than on British lack of business savvy. Britain was a major site of trans-shipment, and this seems to have attracted U.S. motion picture firms to use it as a distribution center for their European business. But the British market offered other attractions. Before 1915 there was no tariff on film imports, the country was small, densely populated, yet with a population almost one-half the size of the United States. A particular opportunity presented to U.S. firms was the free market conditions in the film trade. Whereas U.S. theaters had standing orders or exclusive contracts with film suppliers, in Britain renters sold and hired prints to any theater, and there was an over-supply that kept prices down. Thus U.S. firms could readily enter the market and adopt whatever strategies they found paid. Thompson argues that the profitability of film trading on an international basis was such that British firms increasingly concentrated on renting, to the neglect of production. This, she goes on, opened the field to foreign firms and, perhaps more pertinently, made British production less attractive to investors.

The upshot was that by 1911 *Daily Consular and Trade Reports* stated that U.S. films made up 60–70 percent of the films imported into Britain, and Thompson reprints a table from *Bioscope* showing the U.S. share of the films released in sample weeks to have reached just under one-half by mid–1911. She allows that there may have been a slight decline in 1913–14. But meanwhile the American firms utilized British agents to handle sales to much of the rest of the world. It was only when the British distribution became manifestly less profitable than the system of tying producers, distributors, and theaters together evolved in the United States (sometime late in the war) that U.S. firms began to set up their own offices abroad and started to introduce the standing order and tied systems that served them so well domestically.

Thompson's view is that once the uncertainties of the first months of the war were over – uncertainties about shipping, and hence supply – there was little change. The rapid increase in American exports began in the second half of 1915 and especially in early 1916. And there began at the same time the new marketing strategy of opening offices abroad and cutting out London intermediaries, thus depriving London of its control of many film markets and, permitting U.S. control, which was exercised solely for profit maximization and not in the interests of an entrepôt. It was changes of trading structure that positioned New York as the new center controlling the world trade in U.S. films, so that after the war, when the European industry revived somewhat, it faced a formidably well-organized U.S. industry in a dominant position. New overseas branch offices permitted U.S. firms to enter close relations with local firms, to acquire knowledge of and to place investments in the local markets. U.S. firms thus, according to Thompson, built up an unrivaled expertise as exporters that owed nothing to their European competitors.

One further matter overlooked by Thompson that needs to be considered is product differentiation. Firms attempt to convince the public that their product is different from and, of course, superior to that of other firms. In early film trading, where many of the figures were expressed in footage, it seems to have been an axiom that one foot of film was equivalent to any other foot of film as product. This was not to be so for long, as genres, stars, films of different lengths, and spectacles introduced differentiation. In the pre–World War I period, much of film trading could be expressed in footage. My guess is that during the rapid changes of the war the U.S. product came to be differentiated *as such,* in addition to the differentiations *within* the American product. Certain qualities came to be offered by and expected from U.S. films, qualities that were highly salable in much of the world. Most notable of these qualities was that the films contained the work of popular stars, stars never remotely matched in numbers and drawing power by any other producing country. So the U.S. firms, with their new commercial strategy, were offering a product attractive enough for them to squeeze previous practices out and to impose their own; to utilize their own profits and the goodwill generated among their customers by the latters' profits to strengthen the American export situation in local markets worldwide.

These were the conditions that led to the 1927 Cinematograph Films Act. U.S. firms developed both a set of product lines and a business organization to market them that already showed signs before World War I of being a formidable presence in the export trade. The fortuitous coincidence of that war with the flowering of these developments enabled the American industry to take a commanding position. It is central to my argument, however, that its position was maintained to some extent because there was more demand for its differentiated product than there was for that of any of its rivals. Even were French films more popular in France than American, or British more popular in Britain than American, which was far from the case, there still remained the fact that there was more British demand for American films than for French or Italian films. U.S. films could have dominated world trade even had they not dominated in any single market, because they dominated each rival in each market. However, as it happened, they dominated both foreign rivals and the domestic industry in quite a few places.

Thompson's interesting suggestion that there was a switch away from production in Britain around 1911 (Thompson 1985, p. 29) is underdeveloped and needs more evidence than she provides. But at least it is a beginning toward understanding why the financing of film production became far better organized and more forthcoming in the United States than in Britain – which in 1911 was equal to or ahead of New York as a world financial center and capital market.

Notes

1 On the idea of ruling elites, see the Introduction to this volume.
2 Treasury letter, 5 January 1924, PRO, FO 395 400 P21.

3 PRO, FO 395 410 P1499 1926.

4 P1207 and many others in PRO, FO 395 410.

5 Graham (Rome) to Foreign Office, 27 March 1928, PRO, FO 395 431 P580.

6 Ibid. Another powerful paragraph reads: "But the question I would submit for consideration is, whether Great Britain can afford to deny herself the assistance of the film, with its immense future possibilities, as a defensive weapon or as a simple means of assertion and explanation? Must we continue to allow the masses abroad to see every aspect of life outside their country through highly-coloured American spectacles? If, as I believe will sooner or later be the case, we decide that we cannot ignore the film, we shall be obliged not only to encourage British production but also to find some means of securing publicity in foreign countries."

7 See, e.g., Gardner 1956; Kottman 1968; Costigliola 1977; Hogan 1977; Louis 1977; Thorne 1978; Reynolds 1982; McKercher 1984; Watt 1984b.

8 Wording from the short description of the act itself.

9 The practice is theorized in Watt 1965, chap. 1, who describes it as one of the "semi-private organs of communication" (p. 2) used by elite ruling groups.

10 Dickinson and Street (1985, p. 19) misattribute the letter to the *Daily Telegraph*, a paper with which the *Morning Post* later merged.

11 Quoted from U.S. Consulate General, London, to State Department, 23 June 1925, NA, RG 59, State Department Decimal File 1910–1929, 841.4061 / 47, Microfilm 580, Roll 98.

12 Lena Ashwell (1872–1957), actress-manager who shifted her attention from West End theater to bringing theater to the working class. Edmund Cecil Harmsworth (later Viscount Rothermere) (1898–1978), son of Lord Northcliffe and himself a newspaper proprietor, eventually of *Daily Mail*; at the time, Unionist M.P. for Isle of Thanet. Sir Edward Carson (1854–1935), distinguished barrister; Ulster leader, war cabinet member; Lord Justice of Appeal (1921–9). Sir (William) Martin Conway (1856–1937), art critic; professor; explorer and mountain climber; M.P.; Director General of Imperial War Museum from 1917. Lord Riddell (1865–1934), presided over newspaper empire that included *News of the World*. Sir Edward Elgar, O.M. (1857–1934), composer of distinction; also wrote patriotic music and served as Master of the King's Musicke. Thomas Hardy, O.M. (1840–1928), novelist and poet. Lord Burnham (1862–1943), owner of *Daily Telegraph*. Sir Charles McLeod (1858–1936), East India merchant with a special interest in tea. Professor Charles Oman (1860–1946), held Chichele Chair of Modern History, Oxford. Sir Robert Donald (1861–1933), journalist and editor; claimed to have thought up Ministry of Information; directed it during World War I; served on committees on the British Empire Exhibition and for Imperial Wireless Telegraphy; had interests in several newspapers. Ethel Snowden (1881–1957), suffragette; temperance campaigner; author; wife of Philip (later Viscount) Snowden, Labour leader and Ramsay Macdonald's Chancellor of the Exchequer in the first Labour government. (In noting her appointment as a Governor of the BBC, the judicious and low-key Asa Briggs [1961, p. 194] implies she was a busybody.) Robert Bridges (1844–1930), poet and essayist; Poet Laureate. Sir Sidney Lee (1859–1926), biographer; editor of *DNB*. J. R. Clynes (1869–1949), trade unionist, successively Lord Privy Seal, Leader of the House of Commons, and Home Secretary in Labour governments of the 1920s. Lord Dawson of Penn (1864–1945), physician to the royal family; ideas of 1920 on the nation's health and its problems prefigured the organization of the National Health Service

twenty-five years later. Gordon Selfridge (1864–1947), American-born proprietor of Selfridge's department store; pioneer of visually sophisticated newspaper advertising.

13 Reeves 1986, pp. 21–2, offers a balanced account.

14 See especially Richards 1981, 1982, and Pronay 1982.

15 Philip Lloyd-Graeme (1884–1972), name changed to Cunliffe-Lister when wife inherited that estate in 1924; became Viscount Swinton, (1936); educated at Winchester and Oxford; Conservative M.P. for Hendon (1918–35); held many ministerial posts; autobiography (Swinton 1948) fails to mention films policy at all.

16 Thomas Wodehouse Legh (1857–1942); educated at Eton and Oxford; former diplomat, soldier, and Conservative M.P.

17 All of his remarks are quoted from *Parliamentary Debates (Lords)*, 14 May 1925, vol. 61, cols. 273–6.

18 No one, so far as I know, ever made this argument against the way in which French films, for example, quite routinely portrayed Napoleon as a hero.

19 Joseph Albert Pease (1860–1943), educated at Cambridge; coal and electricity magnate; Liberal M.P.; Chairman of Board of Governors of BBC (1922–6); Vice Chairman (1926–32).

20 *Parliamentary Debates (Lords)*, 14 May 1925, vol. 61, col. 283.

21 William Robert Wellesley (1867–1937), Viscount Peel, later Earl Peel; educated at Harrow and Oxford; former Unionist M.P.; had held several ministerial posts.

22 *Parliamentary Debates (Lords)*, 14 May 1925, vol. 61, col. 288. Viscount Peel misspoke when he said "exhibitors": His intention was clearly to say "producers."

23 Ibid., cols. 288–9.

24 Reginald Gorell Barnes (1884–1963), lawyer, journalist, soldier; active in teachers' professional organizations.

25 The "states' rights" system of distribution antedated the system of national distribution developed in the 1920s. In the states rights system, a film was leased to independent exchanges in each territory of the United States, with the territory usually being a state. The exchange had exclusive rights to the film in the territory and in turn rented it to exhibitors in that area, while taking care of the practical matters of booking dates; shipping prints; retrieving, cleaning and repairing them; and collecting monies owed. (See Lewis 1933, p. 11; Slide 1986, p. 326.)

26 *Parliamentary Debates (Commons)*, 16 March 1927, vol. 203, col. 2039. Hereafter cited, by column number, in parentheses in text.

27 *New York Times*, 27 February 1926.

28 Walter Runciman (1870–1949). Later First Viscount Runciman. Member of shipping family. President of Board of Trade (1914–16). Was Liberal M.P. for Swansea.

29 The Wireless Telegraphy Act of 1904 subjected all broadcast and receiving sets to licensing; the Wireless Telegraphy (Explanation) Act of 1925 made the license fee unequivocal; and the BBC operated under a monopoly granted by Royal Charter in 1926.

30 Col. Harry Day (1880–1939), director of insurance companies; Labour M.P. for Southwark Central.

31 (Later Sir) Herbert G. Williams (1884–1954); marine engineer; headed Empire Industries Association; Conservative M.P. for Reading; Parliamentary Secretary to the Board of Trade (1928–9).

32 An unstudied topic is the censorship trouble that self-representations of the Empire caused in its outposts. A sticky matter was the reception of the film *India Speaks* in India. See PRO, FO 371 18769 1935.

33 (Sir) Alfred Butt (1878–1962), self-described breeder of bloodstock; chairman and managing director of the Theatre Royal, Drury Lane; other theatrical enterprises; Unionist M.P. for Balham and Tooting.

34 Writing about his schooldays, the American philosopher Sidney Hook recalled, "It is hard for people today to understand that before World War I it was the English [*sic*] who were the national enemy – especially of children – not Germany or Japan or Russia, because our greatest foreign wars had been with England. The Irish boys hated the English for additional reasons" (Hook 1987, p. 13).

35 Andrew MacLaren (1883–1975); educated at Technical College and Glasgow School of Art; Labour M.P. for Stoke-on-Trent (off and on between 1922 and 1945).

36 Dudley Ryder (1892–1987), Viscount Sandon; later sixth Earl of Harrowby; was then Conservative M.P. for Shrewsbury.

37 (Later Sir) Percy Alfred Harris (1876–1952), active in London County Council; Liberal M.P. for Bethnal Green.

38 It is ironic that Harris named a man trained on the English stage and an actress from Canada as examples of the foreign competition Britain needed a school to compete with.

39 Thomas Johnston (1881–1965), founded and edited *Forward* magazine; called for greater public control of broadcasting in debate on Wireless Telegraphy Act of 1925; Labour M.P. for Dundee.

40 *Parliamentary Debates (Commons)*, 22 March 1927, vol. 204, col. 239. Hereafter cited by column number in parentheses in text.

41 John Theodore Cuthbert Moore-Brabazon (1884–1964), Conservative M.P. for Chatham; pioneer aviator; a director of The Kodak Company; later created Lord Brabazon of Tara (after the family seat in Ireland, not *Gone with the Wind*).

42 (Sir) Rhys Hopkin Morris (1888–1956), lawyer; Independent Labour M.P. for Cardiganshire.

43 Col. R. V. K. Applin (1869–1957), Conservative M.P. for Enfield.

44 "The German 'kontingent' law required that foreign pictures could be imported only through the purchase by a foreign producer or distributor of a permit or kontingent which was issued to the domestic producer on the completion of a picture" (Lewis 1933, p. 399).

45 It is interesting to note the mixed reception given these films by Low (1971).

46 John Warburton Beckett (1894–1964), journalist; company director; Labour M.P. for Gateshead.

47 No film of this name is listed in Low 1971. It may be a reference to *The Cabinet of Dr. Caligari*.

48 (Sir) Frank Meyer (1886–1935), Conservative M.P. for Great Yarmouth.

49 Col. J. C. Wedgwood (1872–1943), Labour M.P. for Newcastle-under-Lyme.

50 Lt. Col. Charles Kenneth Howard Bury (1883–1963), educated at Eton and Sandhurst; soldier; Conservative M.P. for Chelmsford (1922–4, 1926–31).

51 G. R. Hall Caine (1894–1962), son of novelist Sir (Thomas Henry) Hall Caine; specialist in paper; Conservative M.P. for East Dorset.

52 Neville Woodford Smith-Carington (1878–1933), Conservative M.P. for Rutland.

53 Arthur Greenwood (1880–1954), a lifelong Labour activist; held high positions in the party; Labour M.P. for Nelson and Colne.

54 He had earlier remarked that "there is another side – the question of propaganda. I am no lover of the straw-hatted, gum-chewing American, and I am not at all excited at the prospect of witnessing many American films, but it is true that there is a certain subtle propaganda influence in the films of every nation, and that the very atmosphere of the cinema does make the mind more receptive of the influence of the film itself" (col. 296).

55 Sir Thomas Inskip (1876–1947), served in naval intelligence; high law officer.

56 Lt. Cdr. Joseph Montague Kenworthy, R.N. (1886–1953), first Liberal, then Labour M.P. for Central Hull; subsequently became tenth Baron Strabolgi and Opposition Chief Whip in House of Lords; Autobiography, *Sailors, Statesmen – and Others* (1933).

57 London Embassy dispatch of 29 August 1927, "Modification of the Film Bill in Parliamentary Committee," NA, RG 59 1910–1929, 841.4061, Microfilm 580, Roll 98.

58 Capt. G. M. Garro-Jones (1894–1960), later Baron Trefgarne; barrister; company director; Liberal, then Labour M.P.

CHAPTER 5

Trade policy, politics, and the 1938 act, 1928–1938

The British film industry, as both importer and exporter, was governed through the decade 1928–38 by the 1927 legislation. Early in the period the American, British, Canadian, and European industries converted to sound. The process of chaining theaters and assembling vertically integrated companies consolidated industry power in fewer hands. (See Table 5.1 regarding distributor consolidation.) American-financed production in Britain began, and some British films had success in the United States. Powerful elements in the British political and cultural elites were dissatisfied with the legislation and worked hard to alter its terms when renewal was being considered between 1936 and 1938. In the final legislative stages, American and other interests made a concerted effort to ease its terms.

5.1. British and U.S. reaction to the situation created by the 1927 act

Rachel Low, the preeminent historian of the British film, was unequivocal:

> The 1927 quota legislation had a profound and damaging effect on the structure of the British film industry. Discussion of it continued throughout the early and middle 1930s in Parliament and in the trade, and when the Act expired in 1938 it was replaced by one with very different terms. (Low 1985, p. 33)

The damaging effect Low referred to was that the act promoted the growth of British film production on the cheap. A short boom in production, once its enactment seemed likely, was followed, in 1936–7, by a collapse. Low believed that the flaw in the act was that it concentrated on what got shown, on measures concerning exhibition and distribution, while making inadequate provision for production, that is, for what was available to be shown. Her judgment that the 1938 act had very different terms needs testing.

Low's view was colored, it is apparent, by the culturalist presupposition that the film is an art and that what should have been taking up quota space on distributors' shelves, and quota time on British cinema screens, was high-quality British films.[1] It is far from clear that this was Parliament's intention

135

Table 5.1. *Leading British distributors in 1920, 1926, and 1929*

Year and distributor	Total films offered for hire (Amer. & Brit.)	Brit. films offered for hire
1920		
Famous-Lasky (Paramount)	89	3
Jury's Imperial (MGM)	77	11
Fox (20th C.–Fox)	67	1
Western Import	62	0
Vitagraph (Warner Bros.)	51	0
Walterdaw	50	8
Film Booking Offices	40	1
Gaumont	37	7
London Indep. Film Trading Co.	30	2
Goldwyn (MGM)	26	0
Pathé	24	1
Butchers'	23	18
Stoll	22	13
General Film Renting	19	8
1926		
Famous–Lasky (Paramount)	64	0
European (Universal)	55	1
Fox (20th C.–Fox)	49	0
Gaumont	48	5
First National (Warner Bros.)	47	1
Wardour	43	1
W&F	35	3
Jury–Goldwyn (MGM)	33	0
Pathé	33	0
Ideal	29	0
PDC	29	0
Film Booking Offices	26	0
Stoll	25	6
Butchers'	24	1
Western Import	22	0
Warner Bros. (Late Vitagraph)	18	0
1929 (American "majors" capitalized)		
Gaumont–British	102	18
Maxwell Group (later ABPC)	87	15
PARAMOUNT	62	4
FOX	59	4
UNIVERSAL	52	3
JURY–METRO–GOLDWYN (MGM)	37	1
WARNER BROS.	36	2
PDC	33	2
Tiffany	19	1
UNITED ARTISTS	17	2

in legislating. Cultural arguments had, it is true, been voiced in the debates over the 1927 act, but, as we saw, those arguments had less to do with art, more to do with nation building.

The commercial arguments, by contrast, shaped the act. Given that many British citizens were eager to expend their shillings and pence at the cinema box office, should not some of that bounty accrue to British entrepreneurs? Here Low's point about inadequate provision for production cuts deep. When a cinema showed a film, a third or less of the box-office gross went to the renter (Low 1985, p. 3). By the time the renter had deducted costs, seldom more than 10 percent of that initial cinema gross found its way to the producer. It was this bare 10 percent of that the act aimed partially to reserve for British business, although it is quite unclear that Parliament understood how little of the gross box-office takings in fact left the United Kingdom.

The logic of the situation created by the 1927 act for the U.S. distributors was clear to another secondary source, seemingly just as authoritative as Low.

> The primary purpose of an American renting company in this country was, and is, to sell the product of its own studio. Any investment in British production constitutes direct competition with Hollywood output, because an American renter can only get screen-space for a British film at the expense of an American one. (*The British Film Industry* 1952, p. 50)

This is not quite right. It confuses screen space with renting, forgetting that renters were competitive and that their statutory obligation was to carry a percentage of British films, not to get them shown. Screen space (calculated as footage shown) was the exhibitor's problem. Another error in the assessment is that it portrays Hollywood's overseas production as competitive with its domestic production. This assumes that Hollywood was disinclined or unable to transfer some of its scheduled production abroad. No evidence is presented for this point. From the late 1930s Hollywood made movies abroad on a considerable scale, a policy that was expanded still further

Notes to Table 5.1

Source: *The British Film Industry* (1952), p. 40–1, 52; compiled from the *Kinematograph Year Book* (1921, 1927, 1930). The actual periods covered are Dec. 1919–Nov. 1920, Dec. 1925–Nov. 1926, and Dec. 1928–Nov. 1929.

after World War II. Such overseas production was not a case of Hollywood competing with itself but rather of the substitution of an overseas production venue for a domestic one.

Thus the analyses of Low and *The British Film Industry* laid stress on American complicity in "quota quickies" and missed the incentive presented to Hollywood to shift major work overseas. Naturally, having built their factories on the West Coast of the United States and then having recently equipped them for sound, there was incentive already for U.S. firms to utilize plant and personnel fully. But there was also flexibility in the system, especially as no studio ever produced enough films for the full line of its product to satisfy the needs of the distributing arm of the vertically integrated company. As labor and other costs rose on the West Coast, as foreign countries created incentives to shoot there, economic logic indicated that Hollywood take a financial interest in primary foreign work and transfer some of its production abroad.

Economic nationalists have their criticism of all this as "the branch-plant (subsidiary) syndrome." My point is to stress that quota quickies were a wise expenditure of money only for a short period and so long as the other factors mentioned stayed comparatively small. Once convinced that the situation created by foreign governments was reasonably stable, Hollywood had an incentive to look at the allocation of screen time as a matter of where, how, and at what cost film production could most profitably be carried out. If the West Coast factories were, for all practical purposes, fully occupied, and if part-ownership of foreign-based enterprises was permitted, there was no obstacle in principle to what came to be called "runaway" production, which, since it was under the auspices of production arms of the main distributors, created an equal incentive to distribute those films.

The analytic errors of Low and *The British Film Industry* must not distract us from the main task of discerning the effect on the international film trade of the 1927 act. On the debit side, poor "British" pictures made by or for London offices of American distributors and the boom-and-bust conditions in British production were attributed to the legislation. It happens, however, that the period of the act coincided with major structural changes in the film industry that seem unconnected with the legislation and that certainly contributed to its problems. One has already been mentioned: the conversion to sound. The U.S. industry began that conversion in 1926–7, and well before the end of the decade the silent film was a dead letter. Sound required extensive rebuilding of studios, the creation and equipping of whole new technical departments, considerable disruption among personnel, both behind and in front of the camera, as well as costly equipping and refurbishing of the twenty thousand cinemas across the country. Film production was rendered more expensive, and a greater amount of fixed capital was invested in the industry; these developments more or less doomed the private-company model of Hollywood industrial organization. The major producers all had to approach the New York capital market, which naturally in return wanted to extend its control, and in order to have their shares traded the major companies had to comply with the requirements of the New York Stock Exchange and the Securities and Exchange Commission.

On a reduced scale, much the same was true of the United Kingdom, where the conversion to sound followed hard on the heels of America, if only because there was public interest; and of course there was business interest, since Hollywood would shortly no longer be supplying silent films. (The photograph in Fig. 5.1 was taken at that time.)

An important consequence of the changeover to sound was that it contracted the overseas market for U.S. films in their original versions. Subtitled or even dubbed, they became identifiably foreign to all non–English speakers, and even to English speakers in the United Kingdom and the Empire. More pointedly, and overlooked by many commentators, they were harder to understand. Some of the continuity of silent films had been provided by intertitles, which were easily and cheaply supplied in any local language. Yet we should remember that the vast popularity of American films around the world involved audiences some substantial percentage of which could not read. But because the films were acted in pantomime style, this was seldom a barrier to their being understood. Indeed some categories of films, especially action and comedy films, could be understood even without reading the intertitles. Sound not only brought a specific tongue to the screen; it also brought a new style of acting and narrative that relied on the spoken word and dispensed with the broad gestures of pantomime.

Hollywood thus faced a momentous fallout from the introduction of sound. The California industry was creating a new film culture, more naturalistically acted and hence tending toward a theatrical sophistication considerably less universalized than pantomime; it was employing music that was culturally specific too. That new culture had to be sold to overseas audiences used to something different, and sold over the barrier of the spoken word. The technical solutions to the latter problem – namely, dubbing in another language or printing so-called subtitles on the film itself – took time to perfect and always remained something of an obstacle. The new stars of sound pictures were notable for their voices – think of the loss entailed by dubbing Al Jolson, Eddie Cantor, or Groucho Marx – yet only quick readers ever found subtitles acceptable.

These matters may help explain why the British and Empire markets took on an enhanced significance for Hollywood during the life of the 1927 act. In developing the new sound-film culture, it was obvious that other English-speaking countries had the fewest barriers to the understanding and hence enjoyment of it. That Britain and the Empire represented the largest concentrated bloc of film-purchasing power outside the United States was also

Figure 5.1. British film legislation created a boom. Shown here, British International Pictures talent and executives at the time it was expanding Elstree Studios. *From left*: Alfred Hitchcock, Joe Grossman (studio manager, behind Hitchcock); Betty Balfour; three unidentified individuals; John Maxwell; unidentified; Monty Banks; E. A. Dupont. Probably at the time of *Champagne*, 1928. (British Film Institute–Stills, Posters and Designs.)

an attraction. Remembering that some parts of the world were not fully wired for sound before the mid 1930s,[2] we can see that consolidating the British and Empire markets was an astute, risk-reducing strategy. (For the world market in 1931, see Fig. 5.2.) Those markets presented the fewest natural obstacles to the new Hollywood product, and to the degree that they were secured they provided a basis for the experiments and time needed to devise suitable adaptations for foreign-language markets.

The other major structural development during the life of the 1927 act

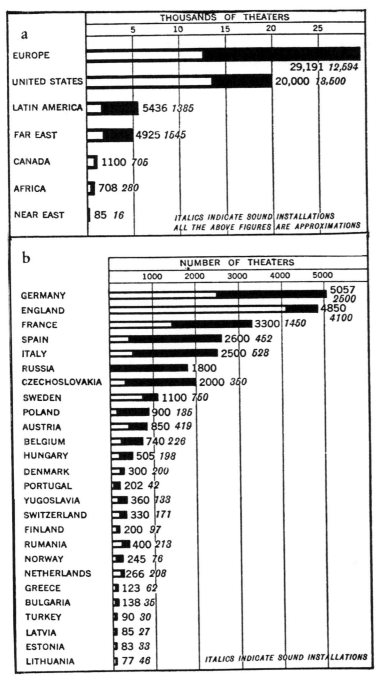

Figure 5.2. Motion picture theaters in 1931: (a) worldwide, (b) Europe (Howard T. Lewis, *The Motion Picture Industry* [New York: Van Nostrand, 1933]. Data compiled by M. P. Dennis, Bureau of Foreign and Domestic Commerce.)

exposed a lag between British and U.S. vertical integration of production, distribution, and exhibition. Vertical integration was economically advantageous because of the specialized, purpose-built nature of the retail outlet, the cinema or movie house.[3] Because this retail outlet did not have to offer a wide and competitive range of merchandise at one time, it was to the mutual interest of retailer and supplier to work together, through agreement, contract, or direct ownership. Such connections minimized the supplier's marketing problems and permitted the retailer to develop among its patrons an association with the particular products of the supplier. Just as consumers shop to a certain extent by brand name, so cinemagoers partly chose by the near-equivalents in the film business – stars, filmmakers and, perhaps, studios. There is little doubt that studios tried to build brand-name images for themselves, and to film specialists each Hollywood studio of the golden era (and several British firms also, viz., Gainsborough, Ealing, and Hammer), had a distinctive style. Examples would be the image of an MGM musical or a Warner Bros. gangster film.[4]

Be that as it may, the limited uses to which cinema buildings could be put and their dependence on the variety and guaranteed supply of one kind of product made the economic logic of combination inescapable. *The British Film Industry* (1952) pointed out that substantial vertical integration was in place in the U.S. film industry by 1923. Nothing similar was true of the British film industry by the time the act of 1927 was passed. No British production company had hitherto been large or stable enough to initiate such a process of integration. Several of the major distributors were primarily agents or subsidiaries of American corporations and would undertake such a process only on instructions from their principals. Most significant, if we judge by what happened in the United States, exhibition was still dispersed and small-scale. Horizontally integrated holdings of cinemas are known as "chains" in the United States and in Britain as "circuits."[5] Some small circuits existed in Britain in 1927, but major capital and imaginative entrepreneurs had not moved wholeheartedly into the business as they would in the subsequent period. Shortly after the passage of the act, the first two major circuits, Associated British Picture Corporation (ABPC) and the Gaumont–British Picture Corporation, had been formed. Films shown on a circuit were booked centrally, in London. Thus a small staff in the metropolitan capital did the programing for cinemas in all sorts of communities around the country. This is to be contrasted with the small proprietor, who would book from the films available those that, in his best business judgment, he thought would go down well with local audiences.

Gradually, both ambitious British entrepreneurs and American firms discerned a situation of which they could take advantage. First there was the clustering together of cinemas into centrally run circuits. Once these circuits were in place, they became both models for the organization of the cinema business and targets for takeover and merger. The mergers that produced

ABPC and Gaumont–British were from within the industry, distributors taking on circuits, then more circuits. American firms saw the possibility of participatory links through their base in distribution. But the possibilities were apparent even, it seems, to a complete outsider, the flour-milling magnate J. Arthur Rank. Since the U.S. distributors were forced by the 1927 act to distribute some British pictures in Britain, an incentive was created for them to acquire production interests in British films, so that they could profit even from unprofitable ones. Similarly, if cinemas were to be compelled to show British pictures, American participation in the exhibition side of the industry would ensure that, were these quota films successful, American firms would be among the beneficiaries.

All these factors, then – the provisions of the 1927 act, the arrival of sound, and the newly emerging opportunities for profit on a large scale – had transformed the cottage-scale British film industry into a sophisticated corporate structure by the time the act was due for renewal. Oscar Deutsch had brought brand names to cinemas by building up his spectacular Odeon circuit (see Sharp 1969). This, plus a complex pattern of mergers (described in *The British Film Industry* 1952) gave the impression that the business was a prosperous one.

In fact there had been not just expansion but overexpansion, both in buildings (supercinemas and studios) and in production. Some expansion of production was to be expected, in order to fill the guaranteed market segment created by the 1927 act, a segment that grew over the ten-year life of the act. It was perhaps a natural feature of the free market that rather more companies should have been floated in 1928–9 than could survive in that market. But this early expansion was on a small scale. The later and more disastrous expansion had much to do with the entrepreneur Alexander Korda,[6] and, in particular, his foreign success with *The Private Life of Henry VIII* (London Films 1933). Costing between £50,000 and £80,000, not a huge amount but certainly a large one, the film was distributed in the United States by United Artists and made money there. This seemed to prove that the British film industry could make films acceptable to U.S. audiences. *The British Film Industry* (1952) argued that this single example created an overeagerness to invest in production, which led rapidly to business failure. By 1937 several companies were failing, including Gaumont–British and Gainsborough, and many investors had been burned, especially the Prudential Assurance Company.[7]

Various reasons can be given for the electric effect on the British trade of the success of *The Private Life of Henry VIII* in the American market. The U.S. film business was, on the world scale, the biggest game in town. The fifteen thousand or more cinemas constituted the largest concentration of box-office power in the world.[8] But the major reason was this: Besides dominating the world trade in films, Hollywood and its pictures also set the standard for what was required to make really big money. Hollywood pictures were, by world standards, very costly. Much of the cost – in stars, sets, locations, and polish – was visible on the screen. This high average standard of work was a minimum that foreign films had to match if they wanted to compete. And, since Hollywood dominated international trade, "compete" here included the American market and much of the world market, the expectations of which had been raised by U.S. films.

The problem for British film producers was that with a small domestic market, even one with a reserved sector created by legislation, the costs of matching the standard set by Hollywood went far beyond what could be earned at home. This had been true enough in the silent-film period; it was still more disproportionately true under the regime of sound. The negative cost of *All Quiet on the Western Front* (Universal 1931), for example, was said to be $1,456,776, of which slightly less than $242,791 was general studio overhead and $104,258 was scenario cost. Up to mid–1933, the most expensive British film ever made was said to be Gaumont's *Rome Express*, the total cost of which had been just under $250,000.[9] The competitive costs were beyond what the capital markets of those countries were willing and able to supply. Hence the promise of being able to make films that would thrive at the American box office was crucial to filmmaking decisions, and their costing, in lands far from Hollywood.

As we saw in our analysis of the parliamentary debates on the 1927 act, earnest hope and belief was expressed in some quarters that there were no intrinsic (filmmaking) obstacles to the domestic and overseas success of British films. As we also saw in the Canadian discussions, it was believed by elites in Canada, the United States, and even in some quarters in Britain that Britain could not match the filmmaking skills of Hollywood, could not therefore please the audience, and thus was not a serious player in the international market. Among those in Britain who did not accept this, various excuses were devised. Suggestions were made that the U.S. domestic market was oligopolistically closed; that structure or showmanship was lacking in Britain; that investors were timorous.

The Private Life of Henry VIII seemed to show that Britain could manage the professional standard necessary to please the public and that the right film could then do well both at home and in the United States. The success of the film showed that the U.S. market was not totally closed, which, some thought, should have reassured British investors. But because the film was partly American-financed, its U.S. distributor had a stake in handling it properly. The film's fame should be distinguished from its profit. Racy subject matter made it something of a succès de scandale. Close analysis of the career of the film in the United States would, I believe, show that it had in fact a limited release, confined to major cities, and that it gained, by Hollywood standards, a modest return. This lack of penetration indicates a feature of the American market of concern to U.S. showmen: There were sectors of the U.S. public that resisted British films. Earlier complaints of lack of quality were overcome; political objections (in Irish-American areas, for example) were perhaps exaggerated; but a recurring problem was audience complaints that they could not understand British accents. Comments to this effect are in American files to be discussed later.[10] They are difficult to assess, simply because of the success of so many British thespians in Hollywood, few of whom developed transatlantic accents.

Assessing the state of the British film industry under the 1927 act is, then, obviously a difficult task. I intend to make critical use of the work of Simon Rowson, an entrepreneur with Ideal Films and a director of ABPC, who held an M.S. degree and who published a number of essays in the mid-1930s trying to assess the state of affairs as the time for the 1927 act to expire grew closer.[11] He took a rather different view from Low and *The British Film Industry*. The first of his essays is especially pertinent here. In 1934 Rowson read a paper to the Royal Statistical Society in which he sought to calculate by indirect means the sum of money remitted annually to New York for the showing of U.S. films in Great Britain. Using entertainments tax figures to arrive at a box-office net of £35 million for Great Britain and Eire, with an average of 33.7 percent going to the renter, and deducting all the costs, taxes, and profits retained in the United Kingdom, Rowson arrived at a figure of £5.5 million ($24.75 million, at the prevailing exchange rate) for remittances to the principals in New York (Rowson 1934, p. 640).[12] In the course of his calculations Rowson noted the value of British film production in 1933 to have been £2.9 million. One begins to see from these figures, which were informed estimates, how dollar signs danced before so many eyes, and why these "overseas remittances" looked like such a tempting target for diversion into British production.

Some time before the success of *The Private Life of Henry VIII,* official files yield evidence that British attention was on both the American market and the "tribute" America was receiving from film exports to Britain and the Empire. In 1931 the Federation of British Industries, which had a Film Producers' Group, tried to recruit Foreign Office help for an ambitious scheme. Their principal contacts were the high officials Sir Robert Vansittart and Sir Arthur Willert.[13] They based their positive case on "the importance of films as a means of reaching and influencing vast audiences" and "the value of the film industry from a national point of view" and their negative case on the

point that the populations of all countries in the Empire are gradually – almost imperceptibly – becoming Americanised in manners and customs, habits and methods, speech and idiom through constant familiarity with American films. This applies more particularly to the younger generations and to native populations.[14]

The argument was that "it becomes a national question if there is danger of the most universally popular form of educative entertainment becoming wholly dependent on foreign control."[15] Complaining that British films were shut out of the large American market (for understandable reasons), and noting that "it is becoming increasingly evident that the secret of success in the film trade is the control of means of exhibition,"[16] the scheme floated was to create a large financial institution capable of buying American cinema chains and financing British productions on a suitable scale. The term "film bank" was not used, but the idea seems to be similar. However, at this point there was no mention of government financial backing; the stress was laid on bringing into the industry "influential persons of the right type," "serious people," to displace the present regime of "persons of no particular repute."[17] A spectacular start to the scheme, it was thought, would be the production of a film that clearly met professional standards and had appeal at the American box office. A scenario about the first governor of Virginia and Pocohontas was mooted, and the idea was to try to persuade someone of the filmmaking eminence of Charles Chaplin to provide the professional input.

In writing to the ambassador to France, where Chaplin was believed to be, Willert mentioned the desire to "induce respectable capital to launch a company of which the Chaplin-produced film would be the first output" and the willingness of Van (sc. Sir Robert Vansittart) to lunch with Chaplin to discuss the scheme.[18] Nothing seems to have come of this particular initiative, but the parameters of concern are clear for us, and they reach far beyond what the 1927 act had contemplated.

Given that virtually no Board of Trade records about films from the early and mid-1930s have been preserved at the Public Record Office, we can perhaps glean some further information from the work of Rowson, as a supplement to the trade press, union records, and the views of Klingender and Legg (on which Dickinson and Street relied so heavily).

Rowson reverted to the problems of the industry twice in 1935. The first was an address to the annual conference of the Cinema Exhibitors Association (CEA) at Cardiff in June, and again in December, in another paper that he read to the Royal Statistical Society, published in their journal the following year. In the address to the CEA, he argued that the film trade should be united rather than divided, and that in the long run the only stable foundation for British exhibitors was British films.[19] To substantiate this second "principle," he made the argument that Hollywood productions of British subjects – *Cavalcade* (Twentieth Century–Fox 1932), *David Copperfield* (MGM 1934), *Bengal Lancer* (sc. *The Lives of a Bengal Lancer,* Paramount 1934), and *Clive of India* (Twentieth Century–Fox 1934) were instanced – "could have been produced [in Britain] at much less cost and ... even greater attractiveness than they actually enjoyed" and with fewer "mistakes." Alas, no evidence was offered to back up this extraordinary claim.

Rowson then offered a speculative argument: To depend on a foreign supply of a commodity was to render oneself vulnerable to boycott, a device already in use "in certain Continental markets a few years ago to coerce the trade in those countries to accept the terms dictated by the American companies" (p. 3). He accurately predicted how short a time it would take such a boycott to bring British exhibitors to their knees (see Chapter 7 of the present volume). The 1927 act, he maintained, was primarily responsible for this not having happened – he nicknamed it the Exhibitor's Defence Act. Rowson's logic was faulty. Foreign supply creates a dependence only if there is a monopoly. Incidentally, although export cartels were illegal under U.S. antitrust legislation, obtaining a "determination" (i.e., an authoritative ruling) to that effect could easily take long enough for a boycott to work. Alternatively, depending on the advice of the State Department, the Justice Department could simply decide to do nothing. Both scenarios were to be played out in the 1947–8 boycott of the British market.

In reviewing the period before the 1927 act, Rowson argued that in 1919 the British film industry had just been poised to expand when a wave of "unnatural" foreign competition (p. 7) drove prices down, flooded the market, and extended advance booking to as much as 1½–2 years ahead.

In 1923 the British National Film Week, under the patronage of the Prince of Wales, sponsored British Film Weeks throughout the country. Yet it failed in its promotional aims, because renters and producers overlooked their dependence on poor product:

Exhibitors showed considerable willingness to co-operate in the campaign. Renters tried to cash in on their failures. They brought down films from the shelves, dusty with age, outmoded and forgotten, expecting to reap a harvest with product that neither the exhibitor nor the public had any use for. I have no doubt myself that the failure of the well-meaning campaign was largely attributable to the short-sighted policy of the producers and renters of those days. (p. 8)

Otherwise, Rowson argued that the British film industry at his time of writing owed its existence principally to the 1927 act. Although rationalization, integration, and mergers had reduced the number of renters and exhibitors, the main objects of the act had been "triumphantly" (p. 16) achieved, namely:

A substantial British film industry had been established.

Films worthy of screening at home and throughout the Empire were made.

A larger proportion of British films was shown on British screens.

Renters' quota liabilities had been exceeded by between two and three times. Exhibitors had about doubled their liability. This took up the slack caused by having eighty to ninety fewer foreign films available because talkies and the Depression had lowered Hollywood's production.

In places like Glasgow, Newcastle, Manchester, Birmingham, Bristol, London and elsewhere, where the number of concurrent first-runs is above the average, and where therefore the absorption capacity for new films makes exceptional demands on the available supply, it often happens that important houses are compelled to screen films which, by no stretch of imagination, can be regarded as acceptable. (p. 19)

According to exhibitor reports, there were fewer good British films and more bad ones than among foreign films. The solution seemed to Rowson to be a minimum cost test for production. The figure he suggested was £10,000–12,000, excluding story cost. Rowson decried the idea of a quality assessment board (p. 24).

Rowson insisted that the 1927 act should be renewed, because under it:

A whole trade practice of immense advantage had developed.

An industry employing considerable capital and labor had developed.

Exhibitors had enjoyed immunity from attack by foreign monopolists.

The public had learned to appreciate the high-grade entertainment that could be supplied by good British films.

"[T]he Government has found that their purpose of creating and developing British cultural values in and through film has been thoroughly realised." (p. 26)

"[A]n expert trade of appreciable magnitude has grown up, which shows signs of steady expansion in the proximate future." (p. 26)

Rowson concluded with the suggestion that the advisory committee created under the act become a trade tribunal for handling the internecine disputes between sectors of the industry.

In a second article in the *Journal of the Royal Statistical Society,* published in 1936, Rowson attempted a statistical portrait of the cinema industry in the United Kingdom in 1934 (the year for which he had obtained figures). For the economic historian, this established a valuable mid-Depression benchmark of the size of the U.K. film market in relation to the U.S. and Canadian markets.

Rowson calculated that admissions to cinemas in the United Kingdom ran at about 18.5 million per week, which came out to about thirty visits per year for every person over the age of fifteen.

In endeavoring to compile figures for the number of cinemas, their seating, and their regional distribution, Rowson came up with those displayed in Table 5.2. He commented,

It appears from the foregoing table that there were, at the end of 1934, about 4,305 cinemas in Great Britain containing 3,872,000 seats, or an average of 900 seats each. Adopting an estimated total population of 45.5 millions in 1934 there was a cinema for every 10,600 persons (men, women and children) and one cinema seat to every 12 persons. If, as before, the children of less than 15 years are excluded, these figures become 7,940 and 9 respectively. (Rowson, 1936, p. 76)

This led to the question of whether the cinema market was saturated and further building unwise. Yet 70 percent of cinemas were small (that is,

Table 5.2. *Number of cinemas and seats in various areas of Great Britain at end of 1934*

District	No. of cinemas	No. of seats (000's)
1. London (postal area)	401	462
2. Home counties	343	295
3. Eastern counties	227	171
4. West of England	369	268
5. Midlands	585	501
6. Yorkshire and district	534	475
7. Lancashire and district	699	684
8. North of England	304	262
9. North Wales	62	42
10. South Wales	259	201
11. Scotland	522	511
Total: Great Britain	4,305	3,872

Source: Rowson (1936), p. 76.

contained fewer than 1,000 seats), and their seating amounted to 52.5 percent of the total. Smaller cinemas were on the whole older, cheaper, less well-adapted to sound, and less prosperous than the new supercinemas. He also found that there were more cinemas per person in remote areas than there were in London. But he showed that size, opening hours, and frequency of programing change would have to be factored in before any conclusions could be drawn regarding saturation (or indeed, he might have added, comparative rates of attendance). By elaborate extrapolation from the recorded number of feet of film going through the projectors, Rowson showed that cinemas were on average one-third full.

Turning to the United States:

So large a part of the import trade...is made up of goods consigned to agents in this country for what is in effect realization at the best prices they can make, that it is not surprising that valuation at the port is unsatisfactory and almost impossible. Of two films produced in Hollywood costing, perhaps, £100,000 each, one may gross £60,000 to the agent in this country, and the other not more than £10,000. After payment of all costs and expenses in this country, the former might leave a surplus of £40,000 and the latter nothing at all for remittance to the producers. Not even the most expert trade valuers could make a worthwhile estimate of the value of any film on its first arrival at a British port. It follows, therefore, that accurate declaration of value on importation is in such cases impossible. (Rowson, 1936, p. 99)

Table 5.3. *Long (3,000 + ft) films registered for renters' quota, 1929–35*

Year ending March 31	British	Foreign	Total
1929	128	550	678
1930	96	506	602
1931	122	556	678
1932	153	464	617
1933	159	481	640
1934	190	484	674
1935	189	477	666

Source: Rowson (1936), p.1.

Because production of long films (3,000 feet or longer) in Britain by then exceeded quota requirements (Table 5.3), Rowson felt justified in declaring the 1927 act a success (Rowson 1936, p. 108). He showed that this result was due to the activities of British companies. American-controlled companies (with the exception of United Artists) did no more than cover their quota requirements.

American reactions to the 1927 act are more fully discussed in Chapter 10 (§10.3). Suffice it to say here that they consisted largely in the expression of considerable displeasure with it, refusal to acknowledge the legitimacy of its aims or its rationales, and the exercise, wherever possible, of pressure on their government to challenge it. Will Hays, head of the Motion Picture Producers and Distributors of America (MPPDA), expressed these views in no uncertain terms. He was a Republican and former cabinet officer who was finding his way under a new Democratic administration. Hays voiced the objections he had mentioned in a 1933 memorandum to the secretary of state, on the occasion of the proposed world economic conference. Denying that the quota was based on moral or cultural grounds – quoting British writers to the effect that Hollywood produced moral and wholesome pictures – Hays found the restrictions to be an artificial barrier to commerce, organized in a protectionist spirit by sectors of the trade and the Federation of British Industries. U.S. companies, he noted, had to finance British films instead of spending their money in the United States, where it could produce better films.

By the British plan trade has been forced into unnatural channels and the result has been a large reduction in the showing of good American films and the filling of the English quota with shoddy English films.[20]

He noted that British exhibitors were against the 1927 act. As the time for renewal of the act came closer, the efforts of the MPPDA to eviscerate it, and the length and strength of the arguments against it, grew formidable.

5.2. Planning for the renewal of the act

As in 1926–7, the British government wished to legislate for and with the film trade, rather than impose some scheme upon it. The government had ventured into the matter at least partly at the request of the trade,[21] had found voluntary agreement impossible, and so had legislated. If this had created any expectation that the trade would eliminate its internal differences and address the desirability of the renewal of the act on the basis of some consensus, then it was about to be disappointed.

As Hays had noted, despite (or because of) overfulfillment of the quotas, the Cinema Exhibitors Association (CEA) had pressed the Board of Trade to lower the exhibitors' quota. In November of 1934, R. D. Fennelly, a senior official of the Films Department at the board, noted in "The Present Position of the Film Industry,"[22] that quotas were being exceeded, and he thought this a sign that the act had achieved its aims. He also noted that British films were popular in the Dominions but that little money was to be earned in that direction. There had not been much penetration of the American market. He admitted that there were areas of Britain "where the public are unwilling to accept British films of any description. These areas are mostly in the East End of London and in certain areas of Glasgow." He deplored quota quickies, noted the continuing split between the exhibitors and the producers, and mentioned the suggestions that had been made for a quality test, possibly measurable by production cost. His suggestion was the appointment of a departmental committee to go into matters with the trade. Dickinson and Street found that the same renter–exhibitor split so often commented on manifested itself once more in the committee's report.[23] The Board of Trade, then headed by Walter Runciman, concluded that it had no alternative but another inquiry conducted independently of the trade. The resulting committee became known by the name of its chairman, Lord Moyne. The other members of the Moyne Committee were A. C. Cameron, J. S. Holmes MP, J. J. Mallon, Eleanor Plumer, and Sir Arnold Wilson.[24] They were appointed on 25 March 1936 and reported in November of that year. For the next two years there was intense activity in the trade, in Parliament, and in the diplomatic channels between London and Washington and between London and Ottawa, as the many interested parties sought a way to affect the final legislative outcome.

Events can be followed in Dickinson and Street's *Cinema and State* with some supplement, and with the perspectives added from the other two points of the North Atlantic triangle. Although Dickinson and Street summarize events well enough, there are problems with their culturalist interpretation, which are apparent in their summary:

The story of the evolution of the 1938 Film Act was very much the story of how the trade and the Americans tried to make sure that the Moyne proposals did not become law, or provide the basis for a wider, more imaginative films policy. (1985, p. 75)[25]

These historians regret the failure to implement the Moyne proposals or even a "wider, more imaginative films policy." From this viewpoint, the history becomes a story of dark forces (foreign, commercial, and philistine) arrayed against "imagination." "The trade" and "the Americans" are seen as the poles of an axis of resistance to the Moyne Report's manifestly enlightened ("imaginative") proposals. Since some elements of the trade thought quotas too high and not a good idea, and since the MPPDA had consistently opposed the protective quotas of 1927, Dickinson and Street's approach fails to do historical justice to the opposition of those groups. Criticism of and opposition to the Moyne proposals can be explained without a trade + Americans axis. The Moyne proposals failed to be implemented primarily because they were culturalist rather than commercial.

One of the ways in which the historian seeks historical distance is to try not to accept the categories the actors used – and that the historian also uses in reconstructing events – in the analysis of those events. On the contrary, the historian often tries to look at things differently. Dickinson and Street overlooked a major attempt to reconceptualize the role of the American film in 1930s Britain, Peter Stead's "Hollywood's Message for the World" (1981).[26] Stead's sharp-eyed view, which clarified my own groping thoughts, was that the government disingenuously used culturalist and patriotic rhetoric to legitimate giving protection to British producers. Its adversaries were the yahoos of the Left and the Right who shared an anti-Americanism, and a moderate Left that was trying to forge a British film culture patterned around

a national film institute, a network of film societies, a number of intellectual film journals, a whole tradition of documentary film-making and close links between those interested in film and educationalists, especially those engaged in adult education. . . . One is always struck by the optimism; the break-through was always just round the corner and any day the masses would opt for quality films. (Stead 1981, p. 27)

Obstinately, however, the masses preferred Hollywood films, films that some intellectuals feared would teach ordinary British people a different (and classless) language, make them less respectful, less religious, more footloose and ambitious, and less law-abiding.

Film and the rise of Hollywood provided . . . another chapter in the traditional story of how elites and intellectuals have regretted the social consequences of industrialisation and urbanisation. (Ibid., p. 30)

And, Stead might have added, democracy and equality are also among those things with which traditional elites have had trouble coming to terms. With a newly enfranchised mass electorate, Stead argues, the government knew better than to try to dictate audience taste. It instead was cool, opportunistic, and realistic in its response to culturalist anti-Americanism (ibid., p. 23).

Stead enables us to get a perspective on the events of the time different from that of any of the participants and also to get a perspective on other historians. It is clear that in Stead's categories, both Low and Dickinson and Street fall within the anti-Hollywood, optimistic, educationalist, leftist British film culture.[27] They show no signs of seeing that theirs is a partial angle of view, with obvious limitations. On the contrary, these three authors fail to alert the reader to their assumptions, perhaps because they find them natural and correct.

Using Stead's alternative perspective, let us trace Dickinson and Street's outline of what happened, supplemented by a reconsideration of British and American official records.[28] As in the 1920s, two aspects stand out in the 1930s: dissatisfaction with the effects of the domination of American imports, and a desire to secure a share of the U.S. domestic market so as to make competitive British films financially viable. The manner in which the government orchestrated the process of reconsidering the Cinematograph Films Act did not, it is plain to see, particularly address either aspect. Indeed, it seemed ready to legislate for this industry without any clear policy, other than reaching compromise provisions that would afford some protection. Only in the matter of the quality of British films did exports get considered, and then not thoroughly.

The Moyne inquiry was independent of the warring interests in the trade (and of the Board of Trade as well – an underremarked weakness), which in effect freed it from seriously considering the economic and political pressures coming from the public (cf. Fennelly's remarks and other evidence of U.K. public opinion) and from American firms. We might then see the endgame, from the publication of the White Paper (legislative proposals) in July 1938, to the final law, passed after more protracted parliamentary debate and intense transatlantic lobbying, as being a measure of the political will of small but well-placed elites to ensure public legislation that suited their own interests, regardless of whether it accorded with the wishes of the public. In agreeing to this, the government was conceding protection to a section of capital, but not on such a scale that it would inflame the mass electorate. The view of the security-minded that a wartime Ministry of Information would need a functioning and skilled film industry under British control was hidden from Low, Dickinson and Street, and Stead. This was neither a cultural nor a commercial imperative.

The Moyne Committee was lobbied by Sir Alexander Korda against allowing further control of the industry to foreigners (i.e., Americans); in other words, what looked like sheer nationalism was invoked (by a naturalized Hungarian), although, as noted, national security considerations may have been behind it. Klingender and Legg (1937) expressed a simple Communist "conspiracy" view of American machinations. But at least they understood that Britain was a sufficiently attractive foreign market to the United States that the U.S. industry was prepared to pursue any strategy that would help preserve its market share, including becoming participants in British firms, or setting up subsidiaries.

The Moyne Committee came up with the following major recommendations:

1. a more robust form of film financing – possibly a film bank;
2. higher quota levels for British films, beginning at 20 percent for renters and 15 percent for exhibitors and rising to 50 percent for each after ten years;
3. a quota for British short films;
4. a quality test for films to qualify as British under renters' quota, adjudicated by a commission independent of the trade;
5. an end to the automatically British status of Australian and Canadian films; and
6. a close watch on foreign ownership and control.

Intellectuals, especially those in Stead's "film culture," seem to have liked the Moyne Report – and they may have been the only ones who did. There was unanimous hostility in the trade to point 4. All sides considered that whether a film possessed entertainment and exhibition merit was better judged by experts (meaning people with knowledge of the business) than by lay persons. The trade was divided on the short-film proposal.

Following the publication of the report, the Board of Trade did not proceed immediately to a White Paper but instead once more solicited reactions from the trade, which was found to favor some quotas and to be divided on other matters. Simon Rowson, in a letter to the Board of Trade's Committee on Cinematograph Films, argued that the definition of British needed rectification – not to exclude others but to introduce some certainty, so that investors could know in advance whether a film would be classified as British.[29] In this committee's deliberations there was, as well, discussion of a letter to the *Times* of 16 June 1937 by the Labour peer Lord Strabolgi, which raised a wider matter: the distribution of British films in the United States. Strabolgi wanted the quota imports to be contingent on reciprocal treatment of British films in the United States. Although only a mild version of this idea went into the resultant Cinematograph Films Act of 1938, it became part of Board of Trade thinking and was much bandied about in the immediate postwar period.[30] At the time, however, Dr. Leslie Burgin, parliamentary secretary to the Board of Trade, minuted that he could not contemplate the government agreeing to such an idea when there was a general movement toward free trade.[31] R. D. Fennelly noted that:

the producers found the United States renters very difficult on the subject of reciprocity. The producers may recommend that this should be a *sine qua non,* but it seems doubtful whether they will be able to produce even the heads of any scheme much less a workable one.[32]

In general the British producers' interests were the most protectionist and aggressive. The general feel of Board of Trade minutes is that as an infant industry the film trade was best left alone. The producers, by contrast, saw it as in need of nurture, especially by a guaranteed market share. Whether either side seriously considered public preference in the matter is doubtful, given its absence from the files. The facts of the matter are in dispute among historians. Low (1971, chap. 8), Aldgate (1983), Dickinson and Street, and many others side with the official view that liking for U.S. films in the working class areas of London's East End and Glasgow were exceptions. Richards, myself, Stead, and Biery and Packer incline to think there was a decided public preference for U.S. films. Stead (1982, pp. 92–3) makes a convincing case for the preferability of American speech and accent to the West End voices of so many British thespians.

Anyway, the Board of Trade concluded that a cost test was more practicable than a quality test, and the idea of a minimum production cost of £15,000 per film was floated, with films in the £45,000–60,000 range counting for double quota credit. The Board of Trade wanted discretionary powers to vary the quota and the cost amount and to make exceptions. They plumped for 20-percent quotas for renters and 15-percent quotas for exhibitors, rising to 30 percent for renters and 25 percent for exhibitors over ten years. There was to be a quota for short films for the first time, but no cost test.

When these proposals were made into a White Paper, the cost amount was halved, and a reciprocity option was created under which a renter who paid more than £20,000 to acquire a British film for foreign distribution could count it against his quota obligation.

Other minor recommendations in the White Paper involved tightening up the existing restrictions on blind and advance booking; dropping the "scenario author" provision of the 1927 Act; stipulating that films made in the Dominions could qualify for renters' quota provided they passed the "cost test"; and allowing up to three unadvertised "try outs" of films before a trade show. (Dickinson and Street 1985, p. 93)

While not agreeing that it is the whole story, one must concede to Dickinson and Street that between the issuing of the White Paper in June 1937 and the passing of the act in March 1938 there was intensive lobbying by and on behalf of the MPPDA, by the renters in the United Kingdom, mostly dominated by U.S. firms; by British producers; and by British cinema interests. Exhibitors and American firms wanted no further squeeze on the supply of American films, and they wanted extra credit if American-backed superproductions were made instead of quota quickies. This, of course, also entailed the acquisition or creation of new subsidiary companies to produce films, own studios, and permit the importation of American stars. With the Soviet Union virtually closed as a market to American films, and Germany and Italy in the process of being closed, and with restrictions and quotas existing in most European countries, the outcome in the United Kingdom was bound to be hard-fought. Although we shall (in Part III) be looking at how the issues were viewed from the United States, it is important to stress here, as Dickinson and Street (1985) and Street (1985) have done, that there was a double international context that gave the U.S. interests some leverage with the British government. These contexts were the movement toward trade liberalization and the worsening international situation.

Trade liberalization had been a prime goal of Secretary of State Cordell Hull since he took office in 1933, soon after the Imperial preference policy had been created at Ottawa in 1932, itself partly an answer to the Hawley–Smoot tariffs of 1930.[33] As the international situation deteriorated in the 1930s, British statesmen looked to a trade agreement and other signs of Anglo–American cooperation as a counterweight to Germany. Thus the British government was renewing protectionist measures for films at a time when general U.S. pressure was for liberalization and when courting the goodwill of the United States was of the highest national significance.

5.3. The final battles over legislation, 1937–1938

We are fortunate that for two points of the North Atlantic triangle, at least, a number of historians have examined the emergence of the 1938 act. Principal among these are *The British Film Industry* (1952), Kottman (1968), Dickinson and Street (1985), and Street (1985). Furthermore, although each utilizes a different set of sources, their conclusions from the evidence are congruent, even if authorial point of view colors things differently.[34] In outline, the events of the final months are these. Legislation was published in October 1937 and scheduled for debate in November. The 1927 act expired on 31 March 1938, and this date thus served as the deadline, keeping events moving at a brisk clip. Given that the principle of protection – the quota – was conceded by all parties, discussion centered on details, specifically: quota levels; quota definitions (British, quality); quota extensions (to short films); quota credits (for expensive productions, and for acquisition of foreign distribution rights); quota administration (Should the act allow the Board of Trade some flexibility?); and the proposal for a Films Commission (or controlling body). Once the bill was before Parliament, the forces at work within Britain concentrated on seeking levels of quota obligation and terms of quota definition that best suited their interests. The Americans concentrated on those matters and on the maximizing of credit for the making of expensive films in Britain. Because British and U.S. firms, and British unions, all had M.P.'s who spoke for their interests, and because the issues had become no less emotional since 1927, the government had to proceed in a cautious and conciliatory manner.

A major effort was made by the Americans to get legislation postponed until the overall trade agreement had been negotiated. Their plan was to bring films under such a general liberalizing measure and then insist that British internal legislation be consistent with such a liberalized regime. It was, after all, fair to ask why Britain was legislating over a major U.S. export commodity while making preparations for wide-ranging trade liberalization talks. A compromise proposal that interim legislation merely continue the current provisions of the 1927 act for the time being was made. It was turned down for "administrative reasons" – the nature of which I have nowhere seen clarified.[35] It is true that much discussion and public inquiry had been proceeding on the assumption that fresh legislation was in view, and it might have seemed unconvincing, if not politically difficult, to announce that everything must go on hold pending the outcome of the trade talks. This could hardly avoid looking like capitulation to U.S. pressure, and, since U.S. domination of the British market was the matter at issue, such an impression would have been unfortunate.

By arguing that films were a cultural rather than a commercial matter, hence internal and not discriminatory, the case was made that the legislation could and should go ahead, since the trade talks could have no bearing. When Joseph Kennedy, the new U.S. ambassador to the Court of St. James, arrived on 1 March 1938, in the final stages of the legislative process, he took the view that the American film industry could live with the legislation. Indeed, he explicitly argued that although agreeing to it involved some concessions, that would build up a debt that could be cashed by the United States in the trade talks. He did not foresee what he was later to concede: that the British would successfully resist including motion pictures in the trade talks altogether.

One of the oddities of the official files, both U.S. and British, is that they reveal the relative isolation of Will Hays, allegedly the motion picture "czar." His memorandum opening the U.S. case struck the Foreign Office as so reasonable and convincing that they fretted about whether the Board of Trade could produce a convincing countercase.[36] Subsequently, Hays seems to have expanded his aim in an endeavor to dispute the very principle of the British legislation, urging that they not legislate at all, and, in the latter stages, proposing that the legislation enshrine quotas that declined toward zero, rather than rose toward 50 percent. So long as he could make common cause with Cordell Hull's peace-through-trade-liberalization policy, some of his demands were passed on by State Department officials. But his over ambition, his sometimes strident over statement, and his empty threat that his principals were toying with the idea of an anti-British publicity campaign seem to have boomeranged – not so much with the British as with those more serious-minded officials of the State Department who were always sensitive to the charge that they were instruments of Hollywood. Hays ended up quarreling with his own immensely skilled and experienced London representative Fay Allport and seems to have quieted down only in the face of the implacable authority of Kennedy. At all events, his final set of fourteen points were mostly not met and, had it not been for the new opportunities presented to Hollywood by the outbreak of war eighteen months later, the legislation might well have succeeded in its aims of enlarging the sector of the British market reserved for British films and stimulating a good deal of Hollywood production in Britain.[37] As it was, the latter development was postponed until the dual crises of the 1947–8 boycott and the renewal of the 1938 act occurred at almost the same time.

Let us proceed as follows. The proposed legislation was thoroughly debated in the Commons in November 1937 and February 1938, and in the Lords in March 1938. None of the historians mentioned has analyzed these debates closely. The debates reveal the issues and the disposition of forces amongst the political elite that were closely attended to by U.S. observers.

Oliver Stanley,[38] who had succeeded Walter Runciman as president of the Board of Trade, introduced the Second Reading and commented frankly that the 1927 act had been protectionist and yet had been passed by a free trade House of Commons. This protection was given because the products of the film industry were special; films were vehicles for cultural propaganda. He was making an attempt to weld together the arguments from commerce and culture.

Although foreign boots may give a man a corn, they cannot give him an idea, whereas a permanent and unrelieved diet of foreign films can give their audiences not only ideas but ideals, ideas and ideals which, whatever their comparative merits with our own, are at least alien to them.[39]

Stanley's phrasing points clearly to legislative control of the industry as a form of social control. "Foreign" here is of course, throughout, a code word for "American," so that, translated, what he was saying was that foreign ideas and ideals, whatever their comparative merits, were foreign. Overlooked was the obvious point that foreign ideas and ideals might substantially overlap with indigenous ones. Their not seeming at all "alien" may have endeared the ideas and ideals embodied in U.S. films to their worldwide audiences.

Moving through the bill, Stanley also commented on the Moyne Committee's ideas for a Films Commission and a quality test. The former, he said, was not acceptable to all branches of the trade; the latter, he said, was vulnerable to the argument that it would introduce an element of uncertainty into investment decisions, which would be discouraging. So a cost test, along with a special-case quality test, was to be used. He concluded by adverting again to the propaganda power of film. Although the long quotation that follows may strike the reader as puffed-up rhetoric (Stead [p. 21] calls it "disingenuous") and not altogether coherent, my own inclination is to take it seriously, both on its face and as an example of just how powerful films seemed and how important it was to have the means to control them, which only a domestic industry could guarantee. It is intriguing that it links the bill into the developing international situation (albeit a trifle obliquely), a factor that increasingly affected all Anglo–American relations.

I do not think I can exaggerate the importance of this Bill. This industry is no ordinary industry.... Today we in this country know that we are on our defence, and are doubly on our defence. We are on our defence as Westerners and as democrats. The decadence of the West is just as much the talk of the bazaars of the East as the decay of democracy is the stock leader of the newspapers of the dictators. Wherever in the world a film by its lack of taste or lack of character, by showing an exotic and eccentric minority as a national element, by showing the fantastic in the guise of the normal, gives colour to either of these beliefs, then it is weakening our defences. I do not want our defences to be made in Hollywood. I want the world to be able to see British films true to British life, accepting British standards and spreading British ideals. I believe that this Bill does give to the British producers their chance, and it will be our task, their task and the task of the British public to see that they make use of it.[40]

Consider what Stanley's peroration said. Films are important for projecting the nation in the lands of bazaars and of dictators. If those projections are self-damaging, that only confirms the suspicions of the democratic West held in both places. This form of defense – British life, standards, and ideals presented in British films – should not to be left to Hollywood. "Why not?" is implicitly, but obviously, answered.

Tom Williams,[41] for the Labour Opposition, announced that they would not oppose the Second Reading, even though they agreed that no one in the industry wanted just this bill. Much of Williams's time was devoted to a vigorous plea for a Films Commission to take over the supervision of the industry from the Board of Trade. The commission could then be in charge of a quality test. Harassed by Stanley, Williams could not name producers who favored the quality test, but he insisted he was right. Just how powerful the commission should be, in his model, was revealed when he commented critically on the evasions of the 1927 act.

If there were a commission whose job it was to examine this industry from top to bottom and to have their eyes on every movement in order to see that British control did not altogether fly over to America, or anywhere else, they would not wait for the next two months while an advisory committee was called together; they would act at once.[42]

Evasions of the 1927 act were thus blamed on Americans, who were seen as those needing control, yet the idea of a commission with "eyes everywhere" did not daunt this union stalwart. But we must also notice the agreement with Stanley that control must be retained in Britain. Whether Williams would also have agreed that films were a line of defense against the dictators is unclear.

G. R. Hall Caine,[43] a member of the Board of Trade's Cinematograph

Films Advisory Committee, complained that exhibitors delinquent on their quotas were excused, more often than not, because of insufficient supply of qualified films. If the cost test and the double-quota provisions reduced the supply still more, he felt that would be unfair. He made the obvious point that technological changes could be rapid in the film industry and a Films Commission would have be accorded considerable flexibility.

R. C. Morrison[44] refreshingly commented,

Having, for my sins, read the Debates of 10 years ago, I am amazed at the foolishness of the speeches of some of the so-called wise men of the House.... On all sides.... Ten years ago the representative of the Liberal party, Lord Runciman, described this Bill as Protection of the most brazen character, without excuse in art or trade. He was followed by the Leader of the Opposition... and the late Lord Snowden, in equally extravagant speeches, with very little attention to actual facts. The Debate of ten years ago has finally destroyed my faith in wise men who speak with imperfect knowledge of their subjects. The speeches were mainly directed to proving that the producers would make vast fortunes and that the exhibitors would be ruined. Actually producers have lost money and the circuits have done well.[45]

Among other matters he took up was the hope, expressed in that previous debate, that the potential for Britain to have an internationally successful film industry would be given a chance to realize itself by the provisions of the 1927 act. Whether such an industry would be more than nominally British and whether its products would be recognizably British was open to question:

There is a good deal of humbug talked about British films.... In 1933 British films were put on the map of America by a Hungarian who produced the film called *The Private Life of Henry VIII*. If you look through his list of British films you will have some difficulty in discovering a British point of view. In *Catherine the Great, Don Juan, Sanders of the River, The Scarlet Pimpernel, Moscow Nights*, and *Elephant Boy* there is nothing particularly, predominantly or outstandingly British, but these were the productions [with] which, through the genius of a Hungarian whom we discovered in our midst, we have put British films, we are told, on the map of America.

It is becoming more difficult to define an American or British picture. The only difference is that a film is either made in America or in Britain. I do not think that anybody in this House would tell me that when Gracie Fields makes a film in Hollywood it makes her an American, putting over American ideas.[46]

Morrison went on to speak of films on British subjects made in Hollywood being similar to films of British subjects made in Britain. The success of *The Private Life of Henry VIII* had induced investors to rush into film production, with disastrous results. Under the slogan "world production," he said, "Britain was going to produce films for the whole world." The result, however, was loss of money and loss of jobs.[47]

Geoffrey Le Mander,[48] a Liberal M.P. who had in 1930 endeavored to amend the 1927 act to raise the quota levels and create incentives for the "world center of production" idea, explicitly compared films to radio and the press, to illustrate the point that there should be the same attitude toward foreign ownership in all three cases. He also took it for granted that film was powerful propaganda, both as regards national prestige and as regards the promotion of goods. He argued that the center of U.S. power in the British film industry was the renters and compared them to the armaments industry. He predicted that there was a future risk of a boycott, as had happened in France. He suggested that U.S. protestations that they intended to do a great deal of production in Britain might not continue much after the bill was enacted.[49] He also touched on the aim of securing a market for British films in the United States. Ranging widely in the foreign field, he also queried the situation regarding the Dominions, suggesting that "the time has come to include in this Measure a provision that there must be reciprocity" – that is, that if a Canadian film is to count as British, then a British film should count as Canadian, were there ever to be preferential measures in Canada for Canadian films. Oddly, Mander did not mention Canada but Australia and India.[50]

Sir Adrian Baillie[51] admitted to having himself lost some money in production and noted that in the prospectus for Odeon Theatres there had been a promise that the company "would not in any shape or form, or in any circumstances, directly or indirectly, indulge in the production of British films."[52] Maj. James Milner[53] stressed the problem of U.S. control of the industry through renters, production, and increasingly through cinemas. "A very close watch indeed will have to be kept if the British film industry, such as it is, is not to come still more under the control of American interests." He referred to the "possibility" of Americans making films in Canada as a serious loophole, and he reiterated the demand for reciprocity from the Dominions, "especially bearing in mind the fact that the origin of the Bill was very largely a meeting of the Imperial Conference in 1926."[54]

Sir Arnold Wilson, a member of the Moyne Committee, mounted a vigorous defense of the proposals that the government had dropped. He articulated a passionate nationalism and laid the blame for many of the faults the bill sought to rectify on the Americans or their agents. He chided the Board of Trade for treating continued foreign domination of the film industry as inevitable. He warned of the possibility of using remote British possessions as places to make quota-qualifying films. His anti-Americanism surfaced. He deplored

not the contagion of Communism or Fascism, which good or bad, represents ideals not primarily selfish, but of the worship of money, and of violence, and the acceptance of the lowest motives as natural and inevitable.... Whatever people say in theory, it is very remarkable how nationalist they become. I want to see our films become more representative of national ideals and outlook, and to see every part of our land play its part in our films. I want to see less of the machine-made film.

He then quoted an unnamed "English film journal" as follows:

America has defeated national film production in every country of screen importance. She has stifled every national screen aspiration in a blanket of cosmopolitan vulgarity, as innocent of formative expression as of social integrity.[55]

Readers will perhaps not need to be told for what group "cosmopolitan" was the code word, nationalists often complaining of the frustration of their cultural aims by the internationalism of "rootless cosmopolitans."

Wilson seems to have rung a bell, because he was immediately followed by Reginald Sorensen,[56] who said that he

rather assumed that the chief function of the cinema in this country was to accomplish what I am sure will never be accomplished, or even attempted, in any other way – the annexation of this country by the United States of America. As it is . . . American finance is enthroned and is largely in control of the situation.[57]

Confessing that he personally disliked many American films, he particularly mentioned U.S. slang and accents as distasteful. These films were said to cause "mental dyspepsia" in the patriotic British public, on the one hand, and to be "merely an opiate" on the other. We see at work the typical contradictions brought about by the elitist confronting the fact that the public on whose behalf he wishes to make a call to arms displays just those sentiments that are to be resisted.

Much of the remainder of the debate harked back again and again to achievements of British short films and the inadequacies of British long films, the upshot being a plea to impose a higher quota of shorts initially. Vyvyan Adams,[58] a member of the Entertainment Panel of the British Film Institute, and hence undoubtedly articulating the views of Stead's "film culture," contrasted British films unfavorably with those of France and Germany, noting (in a perhaps guarded rebuff to earlier comments) that "since Germany went half mad and excluded all Jewish control and co-operation from its cinema industry, it is remarkable that no German film has been worth seeing."[59]

Despite the length of the debate and the importance attributed to the topic, the proceedings seem to have been rather low key. Internal evidence is that attendance was sparse and not much heat was generated. Undoubtedly this had to do with the decisions of the Opposition parties not to divide the House, merely to reason with the government for stronger provisions. We can take it, then, that there was broad bipartisan agreement on what the bill did, and disagreement mainly about whether it could or should do more. Those who thought the latter were not, however, prepared to oppose the bill in principle. The bill was referred to standing committee and did not come back to the floor of the House until February. Between these two debates there was a flurry of transatlantic diplomatic activity.

Preserved in the Foreign Office files at the Public Record Office is an alarmist account of the "sinister" monopolistic practices of the U.S. motion picture industry written in the British consulate in New York in October by Consul J. E. M. Carvell and transmitted by the British Embassy to London on 2 November 1937.[60] These eighteen foolscap pages are an indictment. The memorandum describes the U.S. majors as a "super-trust" and analyzes their tactics with independent exhibitors in the expectation they will utilize the same strategy and tactics in the British Empire market. A careful analysis was made of the MPPDA and its political influence. It was noted that Sol Rosenblatt, administrator of the National Recovery Act, had been a legal counsel of MPPDA companies and had drawn up a Code of Fair Trade Practices to the advantage of the MPPDA. That organization, some of its functions known only to Hays himself, generally focused on protection, coordination, intelligence, and propaganda for the industry. Its legal staff included some of the best brains in the country. Analyzing the Foreign Department of the MPPDA, the report noted:

This department employs the services of several persons who are skilled in the sphere of public relations and of whom some have had experience of the U.S. Foreign Services. These are sent abroad to lend their expert assistance to local branches of the M.P.P.D.A. whenever difficulties arise or whenever foreign governments are contemplating introducing legislation which may injure the interests of the American industry. These emissaries, having the entree to U.S. diplomatic missions, are often able to secure the timely backing of the U.S. diplomatic representatives, many of whom being political appointees, are very sensible of the political influence wielded by the industry and its sponsors. It may be mentioned in this connection that a Mr. J. M. Beck and a Mr. Fay W. Allport, who was formerly Commercial Attaché to the U.S. Embassy in Paris, were in London at the time when Lord Moyne's committee was taking evidence and cabled daily reports to New York.

Moves by major U.S. companies into the British cinema sector were described as a "menace." By reclassifying some earnings as royalties, the consul contended, U.S. firms evaded a substantial amount of U.K. income tax on their profits. The Kinematograph Renters Society (KRS) was described as a camouflaged branch of the MPPDA – camouflaged because an open subsidiary or branch in Britain, just as in Canada, Australia, India, and elsewhere, might have aroused criticism. Canada was described as a flagrant example of monopoly control. A strategy for gaining a headlock on Australian exhibition was described, and other colonies and Dominions were also covered.

There can, I think, be little doubt that some of this report was leaked to M.P.s hostile to U.S. interests in Britain to give them fuel for their allegations of ruthless and unscrupulous business practices. E. L. Mercier of the Department of Overseas Trade (DOT), in forwarding the despatch to the Board of Trade for comment, described it as alarmist and containing inaccuracies, such as on membership of the MPPDA and exclusion of British firms from the KRS, which he denied was a camouflaged branch of the MPPDA. In his response of 3 January 1938, Fennelly commented that the KRS was under U.S. domination, whereas exhibition was not. An anonymous hand wrote "a tainted source" where Mercier had referred to Allport as his source. Elsewhere the minute writers referred to the picture painted as "horrifying" and "distressing." After some delay the Board of Inland Revenue informed the DOT and the Foreign Office on 4 April 1938 that Consul Carvell had not stated the income tax situation correctly.

Nothing in the file discloses the source of Consul Carvell's observations, which could have stemmed from trade sources with contacts on both sides of the Atlantic, such as Korda – always lobbying for a British film industry, of which, naturally, he would be the kingpin, and at the same time cultivating the other side to see if there was a career to be had as a mogul in Hollywood – and possibly also from disenchanted officials in the U.S. government, well informed about the information being gathered at the Department of Justice, which was working up material for its antitrust suit against the major integrated film companies that was eventually publicly launched on 20 July 1938. However gathered, the information was deployed in a tendentious manner, since most of what was described was normal and entirely legal business practice, not unlike any other big business. The cries of indignation were those of mandarin officials out of touch with the market and the profit motive.

By late January and early February 1938, some newspapers were carrying stories of spreading unemployment in the film industry, as the time neared for existing legislation to lapse and successor legislation had not yet been passed.[61] (See Fig. 5.3 for a map showing studio locations.) As a result of the work in committee, the Dominions Office telegraphed the government of Canada and the other White Dominions on 21 February 1938, announcing that strong objection had been made against the continuance of the provision of the 1927 act whereby films produced in all parts of the Empire ranked for British quota.[62] The reasons given were lack of reciprocity, displacement of U.K. product, and that such films were a loophole for foreign organizations. In revised legislation to be moved in the House two days later, the government proposed that Dominion films not be eligible for renters' quota but that if they satisfied the general tests for British films they would be eligible for exhibitors' quota.[63] Were any Dominion to offer genuine reciprocity the situation would change.

None of our authors (not even Kottman) gives any attention to the effect of the proposed 1938 act on Canada. We need to recall the ambitious hopes entertained in official and business circles in Canada that they could gain some benefit from being technically British. It had been hoped that both Hollywood and Britain might set up subsidiaries in the Dominion, that Dominion businessmen themselves might launch an industry to produce films for the sector of the market reserved for British films. In fact all that had happened was that Hollywood had done a limited amount of quota

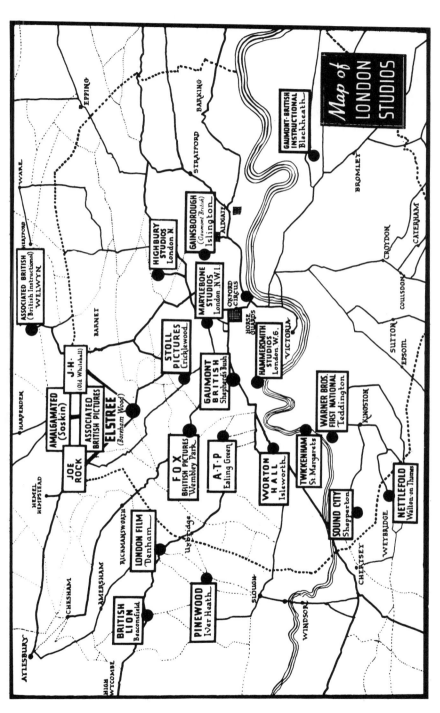

Figure 5.3. A Hollywood on the Thames? Map of the London studios that British legislation sought to protect, 1937. (*International Motion Picture Almanac, 1936-1937* [New York: Quigley, 1937]. By permission of Martin S. Quigley and Quigley Publishing Company, Inc.)

quickie shooting in Canada but did not even bother to ensure that those major productions set in Canada that were shot there met the U.K. quota qualifications. In the hostility to quota quickies, Canada became a victim for in effect allowing the Americans to exploit a loophole in the British law that gained U.K. film production and labor none of the advantages the 1927 act was designed to provide. As we saw in Part I, pressure from British Columbia resulted in the Canadian High Commission in London lobbying to stop the loophole being closed. The British response was that Canada was a principal culprit in undermining the intent of the 1927 act. The specific telegram to Canada stated:

You should know . . . that one of the main causes which has brought matters to a head is the fact that present system has led to production in British Columbia on behalf of United States interests of films of inferior quality solely for renters' quota in United Kingdom where owing to their qualifying as British films under 1927 Act they displace from renters' quota here corresponding number of home produced films. So far as our information goes these films have not been exhibited at all in Canada.[64]

The telegram went on to note that only if there was Dominion-wide reciprocity would the situation change, this offer being made in the full knowledge that such powers resided with the several Provinces. Foreign Office annotation displays satisfaction at seeing the U.S. film interests outwitted.[65]

When the bill was reported back from Standing Committee on 23 February 1938, it had been altered, and the changes had to be run through, debated, and agreed to before it could be read a third time and sent to the Lords. Nearly seven hours of debate were not enough, and the proceedings spilled over to more than three hours the following day. Many amendments went through without demur, and further changes were withdrawn under threat of dividing the House. Notable changes were the transmogrification of the Moyne Committee's Films Commissions idea, and the 1927 act's Advisory Committee, into a new compromise, the Cinematograph Films Council, a large body of twenty-one, with eleven nontrade members in the majority. A move to restore the commission idea was defeated by a vote of 201 to 140. In an embarrassing episode, the government presented an amendment that would allow expensive films produced by American companies in Great Britain to count for triple renters' quota. Dickinson and Street claimed that it was withdrawn because of the absence of Oliver Stanley through illness and a front bench crisis created by the resignation of Anthony Eden. The evidence does not bear this out. The amendment was withdrawn when members pointed out that it could reduce the total number of films available for rental and thus work a hardship on exhibitors unable to fulfill their quota.[66] Examples cited of expensive films produced or planned were *A Yank at Oxford, The Citadel,* and *Wings of the Morning.* Le Mander argued that the companies involved – MGM and Twentieth Century–Fox – would produce a smaller number of films, thus also reducing employment.

The parliamentary under secretary to the Board of Trade, Captain Euan Wallace,[67] who had charge of the government's case, was accused by Sir Adrian Baillie of "having a certain bias against British pictures,"[68] a charge he vigorously repudiated. Instead, Captain Wallace enunciated the following principle:

The film industry is, after all, the servant of the public, and the public, if they prefer to see American films, are entitled to see them. The only legitimate object of a Measure such as this is to rectify the position...and to give the industry a chance of competing on fair terms with its rivals.[69]

We see, then, an infant-industry argument, rather than a protectionist argument, at work.[70] The terms on which the British industry had to compete with the American were seen as not fair. It had a head start, it had access to a large domestic market, it was well financed. None of these quite amounts to unfairness, which is, one might suppose, why from time to time attempts were made to intimate that the Americans enhanced their natural advantage with sharp practice. Whether a plausible case was made that the practices objected to were unfair is questionable. A certain amount of block booking and blind booking continued, despite their illegality under the 1927 act, and we may recall that this was predicted because it was argued that it was not simple and unfair sharp practice but a form of advance planning that offered advantages to the exhibitor as well as the producer–distributor. This is not to deny that legitimate objection could be made to it, merely that there is more to be said. The fact that it continued informally by gentleman's agreement was also explained by some as the result of fear. Again, it could be at the same time that it was good business strategy in which both sides agreed to collude.

One other matter of interest came up at the Report stage, namely the exclusion of Dominion films from renters' quota. Despite the vigorous lobbying from British Columbia and the high commissioner's communications, no voice was raised in the House of Commons to defend the Canadian point of view. On the contrary, a certain mild excoriation of the use of the Empire to make quickies was indulged in.[71] Finally the bill was reported, read a third time, and sent to the Lords.

The Lords had only a brief debate on Second Reading. Interestingly, the debate was led for the government by Sir Philip Cunliffe-Lister (now Viscount Swinton), the author of the 1927 act. As before, he stressed the commercial rather than the cultural arguments, speaking of film's "enormous indirect value to trade"[72] Only in second place did he mention the influence of films in spreading the culture of the country in which they are made. Unlike Rachel Low, he considered his 1927 act a success, for it recreated the British film industry, which constantly overfulfilled its quotas, and the films received showing in the Empire.[73] Although he characterized the intention of the 1927 act as the production of good British films, he also suggested that a good British film was one a "sufficient number of British people will pay to go and see" (col. 992). This refreshing populism and espousal of the point of view of the filmgoer was not one that found much other expression in the speeches of either Lords or Commons.

Lord Strabolgi noted that the 1927 act had been opposed by the Opposition on free trade lines, something that he did not agree with because of the special cultural, educational, and commercial circumstances that made it "absolutely necessary to maintain a flourishing British industry" (col. 995). In passing he suggested that the arguments made in another place that had led to the triple-quota credit amendment were fallacious, since exhibitors had to devote a proportion of screen time to British films, not a certain number of films. Thus an expensive, triple-credit film might simply be shown for more weeks than a cheaper, single-credit film. He also pleaded for his colleagues to view the leaders of the U.S. film industry not as villains but simply as businessmen out to do the best they could. At this point one might long for a word about the consumer, but one would long in vain.

Lord Moyne, as might have been expected, made a rueful speech in which he intimated that the Films Commission idea might be revived in committee. But he also showed his elitism and confusion about popular taste. While arguing that it was not impossible to make good British films, he faced the fact that they might not command the audience. His solution was not Cunliffe-Lister's – namely, produce films British people will pay to go to see – but rather the education of public taste so that people would pay for films of British flavor, but producers must also "learn to turn out films in accordance with the consumers' taste" (cols. 1005–6). The confusion is manifest in these snobbish comments:

While and so far as this taste for spectacular films is maintained, no doubt the United States will keep this advantage. The United States is the home of mass production, founded on mass consumption and mass taste, and we are all familiar with the methods of sensational publicity upon which this system depends. (col. 1006)

His argument was that British films should pander to consumers' taste only insofar as those consumers could be weaned away from the spectacular and the sensational.

Most striking was Lord Moyne's view that this rectification of the taste of British filmgoers should be paid for in part by the U.S. film companies, because they extracted £6.5 million per annum from their business in the United Kingdom.

This renters' quota is admittedly a burden on the foreign producer.... Surely out of this very large sum it is not unreasonable that American producers, through their renters, should make a contribution to production here in England. (col. 1008)

Given that these earnings of U.S. firms were legitimate results of their business efforts, it is hard to see the reasonableness of their being asked to make a contribution to help their potential rivals. It is as though a winning runner with a long lead and in sight of a record time were being urged to slow down to let rivals close the gap somewhat. This is hardly the spirit of competition in either sport or business. Furthermore, Lord Moyne argued that this contribution the Americans could reasonably be asked to make to British production was instead of direct import duties. Since the 1927 act was drawn so as to be nondiscriminatory, and since the same was true for the drafters of the 1938 bill, in this he seems to have been out on his own particular limb. That may help to explain why the recommendations of his committee were not fully accepted by the government, although it does not explain why the government chose him to head the committee in the first place.

The interventions of Viscount Bridgeman and Lord Stonehaven[74] continued the pattern of attending to the interests of the producers and not the consumers. The latter spoke disparagingly of "the regrettable amount of films of foreign origin describing foreign life and foreign scenes that are shown here."[75] The former said bluntly,

We should, when considering this Bill, study first and foremost the interests of the producer because it is the producer alone who has the power to transform a large number of spasmodic and casual workers in the industry into permanent employees.[76]

When we consider that one of the most powerful cultural and educational arguments in favor of films has always been their power to depict vividly foreign peoples and foreign scenes, we become aware of the unconscious anti-Americanism at work. Of course, the United States was a large, foreign land, full of amazing physical scenes and with a form of society different from that of the United Kingdom. It would not be hard, then, to welcome the avid consumption of American films as serving to broaden the knowledge and outlook of British audiences. No one in Parliament, or in any official papers I have come across, still less in the predominantly left-leaning intellectual film press, articulated this point. Yet it was implicit in filmgoing, in fanship, and it was celebrated in the fan magazines that tried to make their readers familiar with both the real and the imaginary landscape of the United States.

The government's plans to move the bill through Parliament as a bipartisan measure ran into difficulty when the Commons induced the withdrawal of the triple-quota credit provision, thus displaying a good deal more interest in the technical details of the bill than had perhaps been expected. Meanwhile, assurances had been given to the United States that this sort of encouragement would be enacted, thus addressing one of their concerns. In the exchanges with Ambassador Kennedy, it was apparent that he regarded the bill as not especially damaging but that in return for the U.S. concession to it, concessions by Britain in the trade talks would be expected.[77] But a further snag developed in the Lords. Although Lord Strabolgi's attempt to reintroduce the Films Commission idea was defeated and the triple-quota credit provision was passed, Lord Moyne succeeded in raising the renters' and the exhibitors' quotas for British films. The government had reduced them for the first year of the new act in order to provide a period of adjustment to the new "antiquickie" provisions that might temporarily shrink the supply of films. Now that the bill had been amended in the Lords, it required reapproval by the Commons, and hence there was opportunity to overthrow this change and also the possibility that the Commons would not go along. Only by the use of a three-line whip (requiring mandatory attendance and voting by government M.P.'s) could such a result be hoped for, and this would abandon the pretense of bi-partisanship and might still not succeed were rumor to surface that the government was kowtowing to U.S. pressure.

In the Lords, on 14 March 1938, the triple-quota credit provision was introduced in a modified form. To be eligible for it, a film must exceed the cost test by five times rather than four, and renters were limited in the amount of their footage obligation they could fulfill with multiple-credit footage. It was presented as an incentive for U.S. firms to spend more lavishly on their U.K. productions; the same, of course, went for British firms, whose expensive films would be attractive to renters wanting British footage while at the same time aiming at a film quality that might permit sales in the United States. The defeat of the government in the raising of quotas seems to have been the persuasive handiwork of Lord Moyne, convinced that there was no reason to go easy in the first year.

In trying one last time to put a Films Commission into the legislation, Lord Strabolgi produced a new argument highly germane to our purposes. He pointed out that there was much talk of the divisions of interest within the trade in the United Kingdom, not only between its three sectors of production, renting, and exhibition but also within those sectors, between those with different national loyalties, integrated and nonintegrated firms, and by specialty. He contrasted this situation with that in the United States, where the industry was orchestrated by the Hays Organization, which

looks after the general interests of the industry and...imposes a kind of self-discipline on the industry. When the industry wants something from the Federal Government it is the Hays Organisation – Mr. Hays was a very distinguished Senator [sic] – which is received by the appropriate Department and puts the views of the industry.[78]

Before continuing with Lord Strabolgi's comments, it should be noted that they are an oversimplification. There were in the United States production companies outside the Hays Organization that were discontented with it; states rights distributors were outside of it; and the National Association of Theater Owners (the equivalent of the CEA) was also not part of it and sometimes adversarial in its relations to it. These matters will become clearer in Part III.

Lord Strabolgi continued,

This smaller and almost infant industry in England is not at all organised as the Americans are. You have no body in this country that can speak for the industry as the Hays Organisation does in the United States. . . . I hoped that this Commission would have been the people to negotiate across the water with the Hays Organisation and see that British cinematograph films which were worthy had fair treatment in the great United States market and also that the United States industry would co-operate in this country in helping our industry. That is what I hoped, but in any case some such body as this is needed.[79]

Cunliffe-Lister poured some scorn on this, as he was perhaps entitled to do. Nevertheless, Strabolgi was addressing a fundamental weakness of the British trade – its degree of division against itself – and a fundamental strength of the U.S. trade – its presentation of a more or less united front to its own government and to foreign governments. But in place of a voluntary and fundamentally political organization – the MPPDA was a lobby and a co-ordinating organization[80] – Strabolgi proposed what is now called a "quango" (quasi-autonomous nongovernmental organization), created by legislation, charged to harmonize trade interests that could not do it themselves. His model may well have been the Reichsfilmkammer of Germany, where corporatist models of industrial organization were being tried out.

British parliamentary practice requires that Lords amendments be agreed or not agreed to by the Commons, and then insisted upon or not insisted upon by the Lords. The national government had, however, a substantial majority of both houses and was prepared in the final stages, when it looked like the balance of Oliver Stanley's proposals would be upset, and when promises had been made to the United States, and when legitimate industry protestations had been voiced about the substantial defaults that would follow raised quotas, to impose a three-line whip. The whip was used to get agreement to the Lords' passing of the triple-quota credit, and disagreement with the Lords' alterations to the quotas. On the latter, Stanley argued partly that trade conditions made quota easement wise, and that trade decisions had been made on the basis of his White Paper and deserved to be fulfilled.[81] With a certain amount of grumbling and a higher quota for short films, the Lords agreed not to insist on their quota figures.

5.4. The final shape of the 1938 act

Thus, finally, after a protracted process of two years, the 1938 Cinematograph Films Act was put in place to govern the film industry in the United Kingdom for ten years. By 1948, the act provided that 30 percent of the rental and exhibition markets should be reserved for British films, so defined strictly by their labor content and their costing not less than two pounds per foot to produce. During this time it was also hoped that the multiple-quota credit and reciprocity credit provisions would encourage U.S. production on a lavish scale in Great Britain, providing work for British labor and personnel, retaining some U.S. earnings in the country, and, perhaps, encouraging some investment in studios and facilities. Obviously it was also hoped that such enhanced activity would stimulate British production to seek liaison with American firms in order to create films on a scale that would make them marketable in the United States.

Were these the "very different terms" Low claimed? Low (1985, pp. 49–53) expressed regret that the Films Commissions had been aborted and that the power of the American majors was unshaken. This latter view is difficult to understand. If, at the end of ten years, the 1938 act still envisaged 70 percent of the British market being in U.S. hands, what would it mean to talk of shaking U.S. power? Low's commitment, of course, was to the art of British cinema, of which she yearned to see more. Perhaps, like so many others, she connected its relative paucity with the power of the U.S. companies. The power of the American companies, however, had something to do with their supplying a product the public was willing to pay to see. Possibly, were their product totally prohibited, the public could have been induced to substitute British films – albeit on a reduced scale, since the very size of British cinema-attendance figures was not unconnected to the availability of the U.S. product. Absent such a draconian move, British films owed their existence to, indeed were in a certain way parasitic on, the exhibition industry created around the American product. Thus there was an art of British film, not despite the power of the U.S. majors, but because of it.

Dickinson and Street write that the new act "revealed the government's willingness to rely on American finance rather than try to reorganise the industry." They quote without adverse comment the annual report of the Association of Cine-Technicians (ACT), a left-wing union, that the act "was fundamentally unsound in that the basis . . . is not primarily concerned with the development of a flourishing British film industry independent of foreign control" (1985, p. 100). Again there seems to be some confused thinking. The ACT view turned on the word "flourishing." As long as "flourishing" meant film production to a standard set by the Americans and in hopes of success in the U.S. market, the goal was a long way off. Much British money having been lost in film production, it was quite sensible to try to involve U.S. money in large quantities. With money comes a certain amount of say-so. Yet a British film-industry capacity was maintained at all times during this period, when there was quiet behind-the-scenes preparation for war and for a Ministry of Information that would both control and make use of film. Both would be independent of foreign control, in the relevant sense. Dickinson and Street's reference to reorganizing the industry is not further spelled out. The organizational problems of the British film industry were hardly the issue addressed either by the new act or by the Moyne Committee, which had a narrower focus.

Street's assessment (1985) was that the U.S. industry lacked muscle in Britain, given the principle of protection already established by the 1927 act. She diagnosed a greater willingness to placate the Americans in the Foreign Office, given the place of the United States in their geopolitical concerns, than in the Board of Trade. She alluded to a "public opinion" concerned that U.S. interests had a hand in the 1938 act. True, some elements of the trade and the press made an outcry, which may have affected the mood of the Houses of Parliament. Yet the cinemagoing public, consuming U.S. films on a large scale, did not display any distress at U.S. lobbying over the new films bill.

Much of the discussion we have been reviewing was notable for its lack of attention to the mass of cinemagoers. Newly enfranchised on a large scale, not yet ready to vote against a paternalistic style of government, they were seldom attended to. A great deal of the argument was entirely internal to various of the ruling business and political elites from which the politicians and civil servants were largely drawn. All the members of these elites were in every respect quintessentially British. There was thus the usual irony in their fretting concern to defend British ideas, ideals, and atmosphere. The spread of these among the elites was apparently unproblematic, since they were able to talk about it and differentiate it so effortlessly. Somewhere out there, however, there seems to have been a great mass of gullible folk whose cultural inheritance was being undermined. We are not obliged to accept that way of construing matters.

Notes

1 Low's multivolume work began appearing in 1948; the earlier volumes were cowritten with the film critic Roger Manvell. There was thus a direct connection through him to the anti-Hollywood, elitist film culture that was constructed in Britain between the wars. (See Stead 1981 and Stead 1989, pp. 105ff.)

2 Discussion of the spread of sound films is in Gomery 1975, chap. 6.

3 This point was forcefully made by *The British Film Industry* 1952. Film studios were of course also specialized and purpose-built, yet that fact did not lead to horizontal integration in that sector. During World War II some British film studios were converted into aircraft factories and warehouses. See PRO, BT 64 61/17029/40, BT 64 95/7714/43, and BT 64 2178.

4 Although they were purpose-built, individual cinemas did have two uses to which they could be put in parallel with showing films: advertising and concession sales. The former was exploited much more extensively in British cinemas than American; the latter has at times been a principal generator of profit for cinemas.

5 Douglas Gomery argues that chaining cinemas was a conscious development of the retail policy of the chain store, which had been flourishing in the United States for some time before films came on the scene. See Gomery 1979.

6 For a succinct account of him, see Low 1985; for a family memoir, that by his nephew (Korda 1979) is useful.

7 Apparently the lessons drawn were principally two: that there was a formula for success in the United States and that the formula was to cash in on history. The first lesson was obviously correct, and there was some truth in the second, if one is to judge by the manner in which Hollywood itself was to exploit British and Empire history in its ventures into what Richards (1973) has called "The Cinema of Empire." Yet clearly there was more to it. None of Korda's later Imperial epics, such as *Sanders of the River* or *The Four Feathers,* had the kind of success in the United States enjoyed by *The Private Life of Henry VIII.* On film finance in the 1930s, see Street 1986.

8 *Film Daily Yearbook* for 1934 reports, as of 1 January 1934, 16,885, with 1,807 closed. Huettig cites a figure of 17,000 + in 1938 (1944, p. 75).

9 These figures are given in a *Saturday Evening Post* article, "England Challenges Hollywood," by Biery and Packer (1933), a copy of which is found in Public Record Office file FO 395 487. The article had been clipped by the British Library of Information in New York and passed on by the Foreign Office to the Department of Trade and to John Grierson at the General Post Office. It argued that the British needed money, know-how, and technical facilities. It pointed to the preferences of the British public for American films and their resistance to "Buy British" campaigns when it came to films. It noted the popularity of some British actors and actresses now become Hollywood stars and that this had happened to Herbert Marshall, even though the film that introduced him to American audiences had had a limited U.S. release. Angus Fletcher, of the British Library of Information in New York, commented that although the *Saturday Evening Post* was hostile to everything British, the article, by two staff writers, was reasonably fair.

10 See also a British comment, note 4 to Chapter 6 in the present volume.

11 Rowson is an intriguing but obscure figure. He has no *Who's Who* entry. During World War II he joined the Films Division of the Board of Trade.

12 The value of the pound fluctuated during the mid- to late 1930s, going as high as $5.00 in 1935 and down to just over $4.00 in 1940. A central figure is £1 = $4.50, hence the figure $27,750,000 given in the text.

13 Sir Robert Gilbert Vansittart (1881–1957), educated at Eton; joined Foreign Office (1902); rose to Permanent Under Secretary (1930–8). Sir Arthur Willert (1882–1973), educated at Eton and Balliol; worked on the *Times* (1906–20); joined Foreign Office (1921), head of the News section and press officer; resigned 1935; head of Ministry of Information for Southern Region (1939–45).

14 Memo, attached to Kearney to Willert, 22 April 1931, PRO, FO 395 452.

15 Kearney to Willert, 24 March 1931, PRO, FO 395 452.

16 Ibid. This, alas, was an analytic error. The secret of success in the film trade is the control of distribution. See Thompson 1985.

17 Ibid. I am insufficiently expert on the social nuances of this period to say for sure whether these cautious phrases referring to "type" and "repute" were coded anti-Semitism. The social acceptability at the time of anti-Semitic sentiments is perhaps apparent from their appearance in civil service minutes. Two I came across in the Foreign Office files are these. C. Duff commented, "The Gaumont–British is, like any other film company, essentially commercial. Indeed, it is known in the trade as Gaumont–Yiddish." Minute on Fletcher to Kenney, 20 September 1934, FO 395

517 P 2747. A paper in the same file (P 3343), Fletcher to Kenney, 16 November, 1934, described Gaumont–British representatives as being patronizing and boastful toward the Americans. J. G. Ward minuted (29 November 1934), "The racial origin of the Gaumont–British people is unlikely to have produced much modesty."
18 Willert to Tyrrell, 25 March 1931, PRO, FO 395 452.
19 Rowson 1935, p. 2. Page numbers are given hereafter in parentheses in text.
20 Hays to Secretary of State, 26 April 1933, NA, RG 59 1930–1939 550 S1 Agenda / 77.
21 A full analysis of why the British film legislation of 1927 and 1938 was under-taken at all is beyond the scope of this book, although hints are present in the House of Commons debates analyzed in §4.3. As we saw there, the legislation was spon-sored by the Conservative Party government and opposed by the Labour Party Opposition. Commercial and cultural arguments were bandied back and forth, while political matters were studiously ignored or circumlocuted. Judging by Hollins (1981), there was something else going on. Although his essay has a rather narrow focus, Hollins incidentally provides evidence that there was abroad among the Con-servative political elite the view that film was an important propaganda device with which to influence the large numbers of newly enfranchised voters. This elite had good links with the film trade, links that would have been of little value were the industry totally foreign controlled. One might thus be inclined to look, in such an analysis, for further evidence that behind the commercial and cultural arguments for film legislation stood some such view as that an important propaganda medium such as film or radio should not be permitted to fall completely under foreign control.
22 PRO, BT 64 99.
23 On the divisions in the trade, see also PRO, BT 64 89 / 6551 / 37.
24 A. C. Cameron, about whom details are hard to discover, was Secretary for Education of the City of Oxford. Acted as Joint Honorary Secretary for Commission on Educational and Cultural Film, financed by Carnegie Endowment, which pro-duced report, *The Film in National Life* (1932), recommending foundation of a British Film Institute. Later became Secretary of Central Council for School Broad-casting. (Sir) Joseph Stanley Holmes (1878–?), company director; National Liberal M.P. for Harwich. James Joseph Mallon (1875–1961), Warden of Toynbee Hall; later a governor of BBC. Eleanor Plumer (1885–1967), university lecturer; then warden of Mary Ward Settlement, of St. Andrews Hall, University of Reading; then principal of St. Anne's College, Oxford. Sir Arnold Talbot Wilson (1884–1940), soldier, author, and speaker on the Middle East; Conservative M.P. for Hitchin.
25 Given this thesis, it is curious that one of the authors, Street (1985), has covered somewhat the same ground elsewhere in an essay arguing that the Americans failed to achieve most of their aims regarding the 1938 legislation (1985).
26 Stead treated these ideas slightly differently in "The People and the Pictures" (1982).
27 A nice example of Low's views is this conclusion to an article (Low 1946–7) describing the sorts of audience research that had been done: "May one confess to a feeling of depression at the prospect of bigger and better schemes for pinpointing majority preference? Has ever an art been so hampered? However desirable scientific accuracy may be in the interests of sociology, it is to be feared that its enlistment in the cause of commercialism in the cinema can only delay the appearance of higher standards of artistic appreciation." Low's depression is understandable, given the

fact that earlier in the article she swallowed the claim that the British Institute of Public Opinion could "forecast with a satisfactory degree of accuracy whether such and such a film will be a box-office success."

28 Street (1985) is a much more historically balanced approach to the events of the late 1930s.

29 Rowson to Cinematograph Films Committee, 21 June 1937, PRO, BT 89 / 6551 / 37.

30 Strabolgi in fact published two letters to the *Times* close to one another. On 26 May 1937, he argued that the 1927 act had failed by producing quota quickies, by not opening up the American market to British films, and by provoking speculation and consequent financial losses. Given that the trade could once more not agree on revisions to the act, he urged that government policy give first consideration to "the national or public viewpoint. . . . Seeing that films are probably the most powerful cultural and propaganda factor in the world today, British policy should . . . aim at: (*a*) Increasing our prestige and influence throughout the world, and (*b*) increasing the usefulness of films as a medium for the education, enlightenment, and entertainment of our own people at home and throughout the Empire." What needed to be secured was a "fair deal in the markets of the world for our producers," utilizing "our enormous buying power" as a weapon if necessary. In turn this would stabilize the industry and encourage governments to develop and make available educational films. He assumed that unofficial soundings would be taken of those assembled in London for the Imperial Conference.

His follow-up letter of 16 June, in addition, backed a cost test of quality and a proviso for American concerns to get quota easement by purchasing British films for overseas distribution. His remark that such a scheme might be sympathetically received by "far-sighted leaders of the American film industry" strongly suggests that he was floating a trial balloon for those interests.

31 Burgin, minute, 26 May 1937, PRO,BT 89 / 6551 / 37.

32 Ibid.

33 The development of this policy is authoritatively summarized in Gardner 1956, pp. 12–22. Specialized studies include Allen 1957 and Schatz 1970–1.

34 *The British Film Industry* relied on published materials and tried to remain studiously detached. Kottman worked entirely from U.S. and Canadian primary materials and concluded that the flurry over films was insufficient to disturb the (different) political imperatives that were driving both the British and the Americans toward a trade agreement. Dickinson and Street seem to have been all set to be scandalized that Britain truckled to American demands but were compelled by the evidence to conclude that the Americans failed to gain most of their objectives. Street, *seul,* interlarding British and U.S. official papers, seems mainly to have been impressed by the agility of the Board of Trade's use of a cultural argument to defend the legislation while wholeheartedly pursuing policies that gave primary place to commercial considerations.

35 In introducing the bill in the Commons, the president of the Board of Trade, Oliver Stanley, mentioned that he knew how much the House objected to "legislation by reference." *Parliamentary Debates (Commons),* 4 November 1937, vol. 328, col. 1159.

36 Atherton to Troutbeck, 2 February 1937, conveying Hays's memorandum, and minutes of 5 February 1937 thereto; PRO, FO 371 20669.

37 The details of all this are recounted in Street 1985.

38 Oliver Stanley (1896–1950), lawyer and Conservative M.P.; president of the Board of Trade (1937–40).

39 *Parliamentary Debates (Commons)*, 4 November 1937, vol. 328, col. 1161.

40 Ibid., col. 1173.

41 Thomas Williams (1892–1966), prominent member of Cooperative Movement; Labour M.P. for Finsbury.

42 *Parliamentary Debates (Commons)*, 4 November 1937, vol. 328, col. 1183.

43 See Chapter 4, note 48.

44 Robert Craigmyle Morrison (1881–1953), first Baron; Labour M.P. for North Tottenham.

45 *Parliamentary Debates (Commons)*, 4 November 1937, vol. 328, cols. 1190–1.

46 Ibid., cols. 1192–3.

47 Ibid., cols. 1193–4.

48 (Sir) Geoffrey Le Mesurier Mander (1882–1962), company director; Liberal M.P. for Wolverhampton.

49 *Parliamentary Debates (Commons)*, 4 November 1937, vol. 328, cols. 1197–8.

50 Ibid., cols. 1199–1200. "A lot of very bad films, from our point of view, are produced in India and Australia."

51 (Sir) Adrian Baillie (1898–1947), Conservative M.P. for Tonbridge.

52 *Parliamentary Debates (Commons)*, 4 November 1937, vol. 328, col. 1204.

53 Baron James Milner (1889–1967), lawyer; Labour M.P. for Southeast Leeds.

54 *Parliamentary Debates (Commons)*, 4 November 1937, vol. 328, cols. 1208, 1213, and 1214, respectively.

55 Ibid., cols. 1230–1.

56 Reginald William (Baron) Sorensen, (1891–1971), Christian Socialist; Labour M.P. for West Leyton.

57 *Parliamentary Debates (Commons)*, 4 November 1937, vol. 328, col. 1233.

58 Samuel Vivian Terice Adams (1900–51), political author; Conservative M.P. for West Leeds.

59 *Parliamentary Debates (Commons)*, 4 November 1937, vol. 328, col. 1252.

60 PRO, FO 371 21530.

61 Clippings in PRO, LAB 8 76.

62 The CEA specifically lobbied to this effect: See their letter to Oliver Stanley of 17 December 1937, PRO, BT 64 91 / 6024 / 38.

63 PRO, FO 371 21530, Paper A 1342.

64 Telegram no. 38, 17 February 1938, to Acting United Kingdom High Commissioner in Canada, PRO, FO 371 21530 A 1342.

65 Ibid.

66 *Parliamentary Debates (Commons)*, 24 March 1938, vol. 332, cols. 432–5.

67 Capt. Euan Wallace (1892–1941); Unionist M.P. for Hornsey; held several junior ministerial posts.

68 *Parliamentary Debates (Commons)*, 24 March 1938, vol. 332, col. 470.

69 Ibid., col. 472.

70 Indeed, the solicitor general rejected a proposed amendment specifically on the grounds that it introduced an element of trade discrimination (ibid., col. 486).

71 *Parliamentary Debates (Commons)*, 24 March 1938, vol. 332, cols. 589–92.

72 *Parliamentary Debates (Lords)*, 3 March 1938, vol. 107, col. 987.

73 Ibid., col. 989. Citations given hereafter in text.

74 Robert Clive Bridgeman (1896–1982), Viscount Bridgeman; soldier and alderman. John Lawrence Baird (1874–1941), Lord Stonehaven; formerly diplomat, then M.P.; Chairman of Conservative Party Organization (1931–6).

75 *Parliamentary Debates (Lords)*, 3 March 1938, vol. 107, col. 1016.

76 Ibid., col. 1013.

77 Note on conversation of the U.S. Ambassador and the President of the Board of Trade, 15 March 1938, PRO, FO 371 21530, paper A 2080.

78 *Parliamentary Debates (Lords)*, 14 March 1938, vol. 108, col. 79.

79 Ibid., col. 80.

80 MPPDA functions are fully discussed in Moley 1945 and in Chapter 9 of the present volume.

81 *Times*, 29 March 1928.

CHAPTER 6

War and currency crisis, 1939–1945

Designed as a phased program lasting ten years, the results of the 1938 Cinematograph Films Act were to be fundamentally distorted and defeated by the depredations of World War II. Before the second quota year was completed the practicability of achieving the levels specified in the legislation was called into question by the demands of war: commandeering of studio space, restrictions on building, rationing and requisitioning of materials, controls on capital expenditure, controls on foreign exchange, and last but by no means least, conscription of manpower for the armed forces and essential industries. Despite such crushing disabilities the war was something of a boon to British films in transatlantic trade. Film production was officially encouraged and directed as an intrinsic part of the total war effort. Films assisted domestic morale and the projection of the national image abroad. The industry had a mission that, even if it was imposed, was readily accepted. Several of the major integrated U.S. film companies (especially Warners Bros. and MGM) were themselves fiercely anti-Nazi and hence sympathetic to Britain. Well before Pearl Harbor they put out various feelers to Britain through official and unofficial contacts.[1] The subject matter of the war itself provided a ready-made and appealing basis for film stories that were much more widely distributed in the United States and Canada than any previous British films had been. And this seemed to infuse a confidence in both creative and managerial personnel that promised to be sustained well beyond the cessation of hostilities. If ever there was a chance for the British film industry to become a serious player in the international film trade, World War II provided it. As it turned out, more than fifteen years were to pass after the end of the war before this happened, and its realization turned less on British confidence and creativity than on secular changes in the U.S. film industry that permitted the encroachment of non-American films into the American domestic market on a significant scale.

6.1. General issues

With the 1938 act in place and the American attempt to include the cultural matter of films on the agenda for the Anglo–American trade talks firmly

179

rebuffed,[2] things might have seemed all set for another decade of protection from the cold blasts of American competition, and hence another chance to get British production up to export standard. In retrospect the situation was much less promising. For one thing, the American industry had strong incentives to pursue the British market aggressively. With the German and Italian markets gradually being closed off[3] and a strict quota system in France, the English-speaking parts of the British Empire constituted a larger proportion of Hollywood's overseas commerce than they ever had before. Some slight evidence of this is the number of Hollywood films of the 1930s that were set in Britain or the British Empire, or that were filmed versions of classics of English literature, often deploying large casts of distinguished British expatriate actors and actresses. Given that it was sometimes said that there were areas of the United States where English accents were un-intelligible, there must have been countervailing box-office attractions that made such movies appear commercially viable.[4] Then, again, the new 1938 act had offered financial incentives to Hollywood to film such material in Britain itself. Low provides details of the results (1985, pp. 259–70); suffice it to mention here that she acknowledges that three MGM films made in Britain – *A Yank at Oxford, The Citadel,* and *Goodbye Mr. Chips* "were among the most successful and best remembered films made in Britain during the thirties" (p. 269).

The implications of this are a controversial matter. Low, as we saw in the Chapter 5, claimed they were profound. My own view is that less changed than meets the eye, lining up with the view of Lord Grantley (see §6.4). Thanks to the 1938 act, the Americans were no longer in the business of financing cheap British productions as a kind of tax on their U.K. operations. The provisions of the 1938 act diverted their interest to filmmaking in Britain on a much more lavish scale; whether the films came from their own British units or were contracted from British producers, it made sense to try to distribute them in the United States. The costs of reviving the British film industry, which was economically collapsed at the time the 1938 act was passed, were to be set by Hollywood standards.

Despite the disruptions caused by wartime conditions, certain structural features of the film industry remained intact and other tendencies in the structure were strengthened. What remained intact was the overall structure of the American motion picture industry overseas. Notoriously, it was vertically integrated at home, with a substantial degree of horizontal integration as well. Fox and MGM, for example, each held some shares in the other. The various prominent families, such as the Schencks, the Mayers, and the Selznicks, through descent and marriage, tied several of the companies together by other means, as well as providing bases for rivalry in certain cases – intrafamily rivalry that defied economic rationality. Abroad, even before the formation of the Motion Picture Export Association in 1945, the companies belonging to the Hays Organization had means of coordinating their actions in relation to countries thought to be recalcitrant. American majors supplied a product for which there was a substantial demand.

In an important development, on 20 July 1938 the U.S. Department of Justice filed a petition in equity in the U.S. District Court for the Southern District of New York State against the major motion picture companies, their associated and subsidiary companies, and numerous individuals connected with the industry. The petition alleged that the defendants jointly and severally had violated the Sherman Antitrust Act, in that they operated producer–exhibitor combines; that they divided the country into territories rather like spheres of interest, where they agreed not to compete; and that they tried to suppress independent theaters by discriminating against them in block booking, full-line forcing, the imposition of preferred playing time, and high rentals. The petition prayed that the court would among other things restrain the acquisition of further theaters; nullify the contracts, combinations, and conspiracies in restraint of trade; declare the integration of production and exhibition unlawful; enforce divestiture of theaters on the majors; and prevent collaboration between the studios by the loaning of stars or pooling of assets.[5]

The wheels of this case turned rather slowly. An amended and supplemental complaint was filed in 1940, and the first consent decrees were entered into immediately after, in which, in return for the petitioner not insisting upon divestment, the companies agreed to be bound by a system of trade practices not unlike the code of self-government developed under the National Recovery Act (see Nizer 1935). The case was reactivated in 1944 and carried to the Supreme Court. Eventually, beginning in 1948–9, the companies entered into consent decrees whereby they agreed to break up their vertically integrated structures by selling off theater chains.[6] British officials were heartened by this 1938 development, since it was their view that the closely integrated monopoly of the U.S. industry was a principal obstacle to the distribution of British films there. They could not know that the legal machine would take more than a dozen years to reach its result, and the consequent loosening up of the U.S. market a few years more (see Cassidy 1958). When all that did happen, British films finally found an entree to the American market, but in nothing like the manner or on the scale hoped for.

By contrast to the parlous and even bankrupt state of British film production in 1938, the American industry at the time was in relatively good health, and it grew stronger during the war. All the major companies had survived the Depression and were maintaining a steady supply of films to their integrated units. Using Securities and Exchange Commission figures, Rosten reports that with the exception of Universal and (in 1939) RKO, the major companies were solvent, with earnings steadily increasing in the late 1930s and ample profits, even if those from 1938–9 were substantially less than for the bonanza year 1937 (1941, pp. 376–7). Moreover, it was

Table 6.1. *Number of long films registered in Great Britain, 1939–46*

Year ending March 31	British	Foreign	Total
1939	103	535	638
1940	108	399	507
1941	65	400	465
1942	46	457	503
1943	62	454	516
1944	70	376	446
1945	67	377	444
1946	83	364	447

Source: *The British Film Industry* (1952), p. 82, derived from the Board of Trade statistics.

a time of technical advance in color film; in particular, the expensive process Technicolor® was increasingly favored for superproductions, and it was a time of considerable creativity that was not divorced from box-office success (see Schatz 1988; Flannery 1990). In 1937 Walt Disney had released his first feature-length animated film, *Snow White and the Seven Dwarfs*, Selznick released *Gone with the Wind* in 1939 – a film that was for many decades to hold the position of being the most successful ever, and a great British talent – Alfred Hitchcock – had been lured to Hollywood by the same Selznick. Nothing in the world matched the capacity of the Hollywood production machine to publicize and build anticipation for such films. Rosten reports some four hundred journalists reporting full-time from Hollywood to publications throughout the world (1941, p. 7).

So, as the production side of the British film industry struggled to revive its fortunes (not achieved by the outbreak of war, according to *The British Film Industry* [1952, p. 83]), it confronted a robust competitor needing to strengthen its position in the international market more than ever before. British cinemas, in turn, were hungry for American films. *The British Film Industry* suggests that a working figure of 600 new feature-length films per year was a minimum requirement to supply British cinemas. At the outbreak of war there had been approximately 4,800 cinemas, a figure that was officially determined to have fallen only to 4,415 by July 1941, amounting to some 4.2 million seats. In due course almost half of the existing film studio space in Britain was requisitioned for war purposes. Thus at a time when land, labor, and capital were short and subject to official control, there was little doubt that there would be a decline in the number of films it was possible for the British production industry to supply.

The actual parameters of that decline are shown in Table 6.1, where the figures in the column "Foreign" are virtually all American. Obviously enough, in 1942, when 46 British long films were completed, a strict enforcement of the 20 percent renters' quota would have permitted only 230 long films to be rented. Instead, easements of the quotas had to be made, at the same time as a substantial number of rereleases of older films was undertaken to keep the cinemas supplied. The cinema habit was such that it was felt that longer runs of films would merely spread the potential patronage out over longer periods, rather than increase the returns for any one film. This reasoning derived from figures such as those of Rowson (1936, p. 96), which indicated that on average cinemas were about one-third full. An interesting change in audience habits during the war was the increase in attendance, from an average of 19 million per week in 1939 to over 30 million per week in 1945. Gross box-office receipts nearly trebled (*The British Film Industry* 1952, pp. 82–3). However, increased entertainments tax and the excess profits tax soaked up much of this increased revenue into the Treasury.

What were the plans for the cinema in this new situation of total war in which government undertook to plan virtually everything? Notoriously, but also briefly, the government closed the cinemas immediately upon the outbreak of war. Whether it was done for economy or for fear of air raids, they were soon opened again. This hesitation was actually uncharacteristic. There is plenty of evidence that as war approached, well-placed civil servants had developed coherent ideas of the role of the cinema in total war. Although not by any means an essential industry whose personnel should be completely protected from the draft, it was far from being at the bottom of the priorities. The government intended to make considerable use of it, in three specific ways: to boost domestic morale; for propaganda in North America, and for political warfare.

In the matter of domestic morale, movies had two clear functions: One was as a channel of war information, for news of the fighting, and for government instructions, information, and propaganda. Films, both entertainment and official, were an integral part of the Ministry of Information's plans for the press and the mass media. It wished to ensure that films presented information and messages from the government and, reciprocally, to block information or attitudes disapproved by the government.[7] The other, slightly less directed, function was as a major form of mass entertainment and recreation. The war required long hours of work from a population that could not be rewarded with luxuries such as diversity of entertainment. With gas rationing and the closing and mining of many popular beaches, outdoor holidays and getaways were severely constrained. Movies, especially shamelessly escapist ones, thus became a valuable tool for managing the population – both those in the services and civilians – when it was in search of recreation.

The war information function ensured that there was a role for continued British domestic film production, both commercial and official, and both fictional and factual. The mass recreation function ensured that there was in addition a role for continued American imports. At a time when Britain was at war and the United States was not, and when domestic U.S. politics ensured that much of the war matériel Britain wished to obtain from the United States must be paid for in cash, which meant by liquidating dollar assets, the option of simply refusing to spend dollars for American films was always available to the government. This option seems not to have been seriously contemplated. In fact considerable sums were devoted to purchasing the Hollywood product, because of the role films were given to play among the mass of the population engaged in total war.

It seems to have been apparent to the British ruling elites of the interwar period that, were Britain to be drawn into a war with the dictators, the United Kingdom would do well to cultivate the United States, at least to secure a tilt toward a fellow democracy and, in the best-case scenario, open support. However, the United States had laws about the activity of foreign propagandists on its soil, and public attitudes toward the United Kingdom were a complex matter. Isolationist and neutralist forces, which were strong and popular, were suspicious of all foreign entanglements and pointed to World War I as a case where the United States had overridden its own better judgment and failed to clear up a European mess that was now as bad as ever. There were also substantial communities in the United States of Irish and of German descent who were anything but inclined to see their country support the British and French side. And, finally, overlapping with all of these, and even with some who sympathized with Britain otherwise, was the strong political and commercial opposition to European empires, principally the British. Britain had long been in the process of window-dressing the Empire as a Commonwealth of Nations, somehow held together not by force of possession but by "family ties" and "shared values," and indeed in some cases Britain's rule was justified as a "trusteeship" pending eventual self-government. However successful this campaign was for domestic consumption, it was not taken too seriously by antiimperialists in the United States. In addition to American political hostility to imperialism as such, the Ottawa tariffs of 1932 were regarded there as a clear indication that the British Empire was also a commercial conspiracy damaging to the interests of the United States.

The task of the British North American propaganda machine – the Foreign Office, the British Council, the British Library of Information in New York, the British Travel Council, and, eventually, the American Section of the Ministry of Information – was, Orwell-like, to counter these American attitudes while never being caught actually doing any propaganda (see Taylor 1981). The disposition of Hollywood studios to make films with British themes and starring British thespians, the disposition to make in Britain films that were subsequently distributed in the United States, and, of course, to a limited degree, the distribution of British films, fictional and factual, in the United States, were the main prongs of the British North American propaganda policy as regards films.

Finally, films were to be used in political warfare. Throughout the British Empire there were territories that were outside the battle zone (Palestine, the African colonies), those that were embattled (India, Egypt), and those that had been overrun (Malaya, Hong Kong, Singapore, Burma). In all of these, political warfare was carried out (whenever possible) through the press, pamphlets, broadcasts, and films. It was considered important that war news be presented in a manner that made it clear that the British would be back, and that fictional films which undermined the position of the ruling race should not be shown. Since independence movements were particularly strong in the East, political warfare considerations regarding films seem to have been especially sensitive there. Mountbatten's South East Asia Command headquarters, for example, made sure that the films prepared gave an account of the war that suited the aims of political warfare. All films shown in India were subject to censorship into which the military had major input.[8]

A sideshow here, or perhaps a merger of the American propaganda and political warfare issues, was the strong efforts made after Pearl Harbor to present the Far Eastern war as all part of the same world war and not, as some Americans were inclined to think it, a war in which a primary aim of the British, French, and Dutch was to reestablish their prewar empires, rather than simply to defeat the Japanese.[9] Parallel to this was the official belief that the Far Eastern war was eclipsed in the public mind by the campaigns in the Atlantic, the Middle East, and Europe. Once it became apparent that Germany would be defeated, efforts were made to increase awareness of fighting in the Far East in order to prepare the public for the strong possibility that the war there would last well beyond VE-Day (see Thorne 1978; Jarvie 1988b).

From all this we can see that the war greatly enhanced the international significance of film and sensitized a good many institutions and their personnel to its uses and dangers. It also created conditions for unparalleled cooperation between the two allies and film rivals, once Pearl Harbor had settled the issue of American attitudes toward the war. The subsequent sections of this chapter will look at the special agreements and restrictions placed on American films; the collaboration between the allies on films; British postwar planning for films, including their aims for the overseas sales of the commercial industry; and the execution of these plans during the reconquest of Europe.

6.2. The Anglo–American Agreements and lend–lease

Until lend–lease came to the rescue, the British government sought to curtail the remittance of dollars owed to American film companies whose product had found an audience in Britain, while also trying to avoid any significant drop in the number of films shipped. A clear narrative line can be extracted from the surviving British official files.

Soon after war was declared, the president of the Board of Trade indicated to cinema exhibitors that he was toying with the idea of restricting the amount of dollars the American companies would be permitted to remit to their principals in New York. The figure involved was subject to some dispute, since how much the companies earned from their British operations was confidential information. Sums of £5–10 million were discussed. The correct figure was probably closer to the lower estimate. It was by no means certain that the American companies would agree to continue to provide their full line of film product if remittances were curtailed, no matter what form the curtailment took. Overseas sales were a substantial part of profitability, and profitability had much to do with the companies' continuing success in raising loans to finance production. Explicit note was taken of this in 1940 when Board of Trade officials conferred with officers of the Cinema Exhibitors Association (CEA) and the Kinematograph Renters Society (KRS). Cinemas were currently forbidden to store more than 20,000 feet of film on the premises, and the KRS suggested a waiver on this amount. Films could then be stored in advance of showing and not be subject to interruptions of transportation. This would forward the aim of keeping cinemas open. Rupert Somervell[10] wrote that if "there should be a threat later in the year to withhold foreign films from this country, he might assure the President [of the Board of Trade] that the industry thought they could carry on and that it considered that it would be safe to 'call the bluff.' Mr. Smith [of the KRS] said that he considered that it would be and the other three concurred."[11]

Although, as Somervell's query makes clear, there was some sense of risk, in fact what the British government settled for was accepted by the American companies. British officials did not want to curtail the supply of American films, but rather to economize on the amount of dollar exchange spent on films, in order to divert some of it to the purchase of higher-priority items. Furthermore, at this stage at least (cf. Chapter 7), the idea was not to tax away the American companies' earnings in the sterling area but merely to prevent them being changed into dollars. Such an aim immediately created a second problem: Were the American companies to accumulate substantial credits in sterling, they might be tempted to purchase companies and property in the sterling area, something also not considered desirable.

Ambassador Joseph Kennedy called on the president of the Board of Trade to discuss the upcoming measures. He made a simple point: that the continuation of American film production in Britain depended upon U.S. companies receiving a remittance of a certain percentage of earnings. Loss of 75 percent of these would create the "necessity for a complete re-organisation of the American film industry."[12] Although he did not specify a figure, Kennedy left the impression that they should be left at least 50 percent of their earnings. However, his own preference was for Britain to specify a dollar figure that the United Kingdom was prepared to expend on American films. Kennedy's weight as both the ambassador of the country the British were assiduously cultivating and a former film executive with some sense of what the American companies truly needed seems to have made his ideas ones the British chose to accommodate. For example, in a preliminary meeting with representatives of the American companies, the Board of Trade toyed with the proposal that 50 percent of the earnings of films booked before the outbreak of war could be remitted but only 20 percent of subsequent earnings. The companies' representatives kept their counsel, merely indicating that "it would be difficult for them to maintain either the quality or the quantity of their film production in this country in war-time."[13]

Mr. Lever of the Prudential Assurance Company advised the Board of Trade that an American boycott was unlikely but a tactical interruption of supply was a possibility.[14] Either way, American finance was vital to British production and could be replaced only by a government film bank. Subsequently, the British made a second offer of 60 percent remittable from the first six months of war, 40 percent from the second six months, and abolition of the quota, provided the American companies guaranteed to spend £500,000 per annum on film production in the United Kingdom. Frozen sterling balances were to be kept in fixed-rate British-government securities.[15] Confronted with this, Kennedy came clean and named the figure of $17.5 million as the minimum. If Britain would go for that, he said he would try to get U.K. production restarted and guarantee the uninterrupted flow of films. Were the quota dropped, the same money could be spent on fewer, perhaps propaganda, films.[16] Less than three weeks later Kennedy was of the opinion that continued film production in Britain under wartime conditions was of doubtful practicability.

The eventual agreement of November 1939, lasting one year, was drafted by F. W. Allport and slightly modified by Board of Trade and Treasury officials. It conceded the $17.5 million minimum but retained the quota. This agreement finally gave historians some figures (Table 6.2).

Dated from November and only finalized in exchanges of letters in February 1940, the agreement permitted the companies by May of that year to remit $15.05 million of their $17.5 million. They were opting for a front-loading tactic, in which all their remittances were transferred early, rather than being spread out evenly over quarters or months. No doubt that had something to do with all remittances having been frozen during the period of negotiation and the companies' consequent need for cash flow. It may also have reflected a tactical decision by the companies to remit funds quickly

Table 6.2. *Dollar remittances of U.S. film companies, 1939–40*

Company	Amount to 27 April 1940	+ Amount to 25 May 1940
20th C.–Fox	$ 2,200,000	$ 706,000
Columbia	854,000	262,000
MGM	2,665,000	514,000
Paramount	1,752,000	362,000
RKO	1,395,000	485,000
United Artists	1,200,000	400,000
Warner Bros.	1,948,000	302,000
Totals	$12,014,000	$3,031,000

Source: PRO, BT 64 90/50054/40.

and then to press for more. If the latter was the case, they guessed incorrectly, because the total remittances permitted under the second agreement (1940–1) were reduced to $12.9 million.[17]

The British saw their concession of $17.5 million in the first agreement as temporary, granted partly because some contracts had been drawn before the war and American production planning had been made in ignorance of the drying up of British revenues. Apparently the intention always was to bring the amount remitted in the second agreement down toward the 25 percent originally entertained. However, when the Board of Trade approached Ambassador Kennedy to conduct the negotiations for the second agreement he indicated that he would not be prepared to recommend any drastic reduction to the companies, that he would not dissuade them from cutting imports were a drastic reduction imposed, and that he thought the negotiations should be concluded quickly. Somervell commented, "This gives us a good idea of the gentle and friendly spirit in which the negotiations are likely to proceed, and it seems to me that our first effort had better not err on the side of generosity."[18]

Simon Rowson, who had joined the Board of Trade as a film expert, wrote a paper entitled "The Problem of Film Remittances (1940–41)" that argued there was no way film production in Britain could absorb all the blocked American earnings unless U.K. costs were unacceptably inflated above U.S. averages. He noted that the film business was doing well, as signaled by the higher collections of entertainments tax. The American companies were also doing well in the domestic market, where, he calculated, their distribution receipts aggregated about $325 million, or about 2.75 times as much as was spent on motion picture production. The clear implication was that the U.S. companies were not, as Americans say, "hurting." Were they to distribute British pictures in the United States they could take £4 million at the box office. (To get this figure he made an unspecified assumption about the box-office potential of British films in the American market.)[19] In a Treasury proposal filed just after this, a figure of $5 million, later raised to $7 million, was postulated. Reasoning that the total take was in the region of $30 million, of which $10 million was spent on British production and then recouped in dollars from American release, $5 million was said to represent 25 percent of what the American companies might wish to remit. (This either assumes the total take to be net of U.K. costs, or these were simply forgotten.) If $7 million was conceded, the proposal went on, then the quid pro quo should be a promise that at least 75 percent of the total U.S. output of films would be shipped to Britain.

As negotiations dragged into September, Rowson wrote a minute mentioning that Ambassador Kennedy's position was that the United Kingdom needed American films. Rowson, by contrast, suggested that if there were a patriotic appeal the public would forego American films, especially if entertaining British pictures were substituted. Turning to a possible boycott by the Americans, he noted that there were current sums owed them that they would be hard pressed to collect and that there was a six-months supply of U.S. films in the country. At a maximum Britain could produce four or five pictures per week, whereas the demand was for ten to twelve. The film industry would have to be nationalized, and the Americans would realize that postwar trading conditions would not be any more favorable to them.

It is clear from this that Rowson, although now working in government, continued to be a partisan of the producer interests of the British film industry. He displayed sensitivity neither to public taste, which he cheerfully believed to be manipulable by patriotic appeal, nor to the higher politics of relations with the United States. A U.S. boycott would have been serious for Britain, not just for its effect on the cinemas and the public but also for Anglo–American relations. To alienate a major communications industry, and one with good relations to Roosevelt's administration, would need strong justification.

Naturally, the Americans argued that the loss of all other European markets had made Hollywood's position much worse than anticipated the year before, and so they were now less ready to accept the drastic reductions intimated then. "The industry has a great importance for the United States, politically and otherwise, and the Ambassador would have to stand out against any serious reduction in the amount of dollars which it might be allowed to earn on films exported to the British market."[20] Although this admission of the tough corner Hollywood found itself in encouraged British officials to think a boycott unlikely, they nevertheless realized that they would need ministerial permission, Foreign Office input, and possibly even Cabinet agreement were they to call any bluff that Ambassador Kennedy might try. No such attempt was made, for in the decisive meeting between the Chancellor of the Exchequer and Kennedy, the latter's insistence on $12 million carried the day. As Dickinson and Street note (1985, p. 128), the decisive argument seems to have been political. Rendell of the Treasury wrote apologetically to Somervell, "I need hardly say that I left the room in a rather shocked condition.... I can only apologise for putting you up to do our dirty work and then selling out over your head."[21] But that was not the end of it. Kennedy and the chancellor subsequently disputed over whether the sum agreed to applied to the seven original companies or to an augmented group of eight. Again the Treasury yielded, and another $1 million was found, "at the same time making it clear that we consider him [Allan Steyne] and his master to be dirty dogs."[22]

A truly complex situation confronts us. File minutes show that the Board of Trade's officials – Somervell, Rowson, and a Miss Kilroy – were themselves sometimes at odds on what board policy should be, and on the strategy and tactics of negotiation. We see from Rendell's letter that officials even of different departments might work out arrangements and then see them abandoned by their political masters. And we also see that the Americans were far from being easily talked out of their positions. Their decision to protect an export industry by having negotiations concerning it handled by the ambassador and his staff, rather than by the companies themselves, was clearly a shrewd use of the knowledge that there were things the British government wanted from the United States. Yet what the British achieved should not be overlooked. Without curtailing property rights, without nationalization, they withheld the legitimate earnings of foreign firms for many months, and did it without those firms seriously interrupting export shipments. As we saw earlier, both British and American production dropped during the war period, and revivals and reruns had to take up the slack. Whatever their deficiencies, the resulting film shows did not prevent a huge surge of cinemagoing in wartime.

By July 1941 the Treasury was becoming concerned at the size of the accumulated balances of blocked funds. The suggestion was made that an overall review of films policy was required, and that the American companies might be told that, as there was little likelihood of the discharge of their accumulated balances, they might want to be further involved in producing films in Britain.[23] The evidence suggests that the Americans were becoming restless at the situation, too, but that their thoughts were not turning to utilizing their monies to back production in Britain. Rather they were endeavoring to marshal the support of their government to press Britain to release more of the funds. Kennedy meanwhile had been replaced by John G. Winant,[24] who proposed that the renewal of the agreement be negotiated between the companies and Board of Trade officials, but that the question of the accumulated balances be subject to separate negotiations between the ambassador and the Chancellor of the Exchequer. Winant stressed the interest of Secretary of State Hull and President Roosevelt in these matters.[25]

Will Hays had been busy at the American end. He had a meeting with the British ambassador, Lord Halifax, in the spring, "made...for me by

Figure 6.1. Lord Halifax in Hollywood, 22 July 1941, shakes Louis B. Mayer's hand. *Left to right:* Will Hays, Y. Frank Freeman, Halifax, Eddie Mannix, Mayer, Hunt Stromberg. (Will H. Hays Papers, Indiana State Archives, Indianapolis, IN.)

the President," and another in July in Hollywood (see Fig. 6.1). Hays's view was that the Motion Picture Producers and Distributors of America (MPPDA) companies faced a financial emergency. They were having to finance productions that would be exported to Britain, without being able to count on the revenues from that territory. His calculations were rather different from those of Rowson. He argued that in the first two years of the agreements some $70 million was owed, while remittances of only some $31.7 million were allowed. This meant that $38–40 million was impounded. He noted that the Lend–Lease Act had eased the exchange conditions, and that the showing of American films in British cinemas earned the British government some $50 million in taxes.[26] Lord Halifax wrote to the Chancellor, Kingsley Wood, that the motion picture people "are doing a very good job of work in our cause; – so good, in fact, that I see they are to be hailed before a Senatorial Enquiry Committee!."[27] True, (some) American film companies were making anti-Nazi, anti-Japanese, and pro-British films. Whether this had to do with pro-British political sentiments and with revulsion against the Nazi persecution of Jews or whether it was a cynical ploy to squeeze more favorable terms out of the British is purely speculation. Prominent Hollywood companies had for several years been embedding such a political line in their films. Senator Nye and the isolationist and America First groups all accused Hollywood of taking sides and making propaganda to push America into war. Since this was an aim of high British policy, it was not in the British interest to alienate Hollywood.

The pressure had its effect, and by October the British Treasury was conceding that half of the blocked sterling could be transferred, and then the amount permitted under the current agreement was raised to $20 million. Summing it all up, Sir Arnold Overton wrote that Hollywood had got Roosevelt's ear,

and that he would wish in view of the help they have been giving to his administration to help them on his side. Consequently we felt that any attempt on our part to drive a bargain with the American film industry or to curtail their resources by administrative measures was doomed to failure since representations from the State Department would be certainly made and considerations of higher political importance would force us to give way to them.

In the circumstances we have felt that there was nothing for it but to mark time on major issues at any rate until the Americans had come into the war. That has now happened but I think it is still too early to start any definite action.[28]

When the time came for definite action, the British had learned to face the realities. Whereas previously they had required negotiations to be conducted in London, where the companies concerned were operating, in August of 1942 Rupert G. Somervell went to the United States to talk with company heads. This came about because in early June 1942 the U.S. government had forwarded and endorsed a claim of RKO to its blocked sterling on the grounds that company was about to go bankrupt. At that point the British Treasury, anxious to get rid of the deferred dollar liability that the accumulated balances represented, was ready to unblock all film sterling, provided the Americans granted some concessions in civil aviation. They were therefore inclined to concede the RKO claim as a favor to the U.S. government. Soon after, in early July, the British Embassy passed word that the other American companies were preparing to put in an application for the transfer of all the blocked sterling.[29]

Somervell pointed out the great value the blocked sterling balances had been to British domestic production, the standard of which they had raised substantially. "This had been made possible by the fact that the Americans had a direct incentive to buy the American rights of British films and to give them a proper showing in the U.S.A."[30]

Looking to the future the Treasury will wish to lessen the amount of dollars required by the American film companies by diverting as large a proportion as possible to the Exchequer, while the Board of Trade will wish to retain a substantial amount of the American film revenues in this country for assisting British film production.

This was an unabashedly predatory attitude toward the earnings of a foreign business. American companies were, in good faith, shipping merchandise to Britain and from it earning substantial sums. Because of the technical fact that the exchange of sterling for dollars was centralized through and controlled by the Bank of England, the British government had their hands on those earnings. Civil servants then began to presume that these private assets were legitimately to be "diverted" to the Treasury and "retained" in the country. One does not have to be a partisan of Hollywood to view such attitudes as astonishing. Given that no government, either Labour or Conservative, had ever decided to nationalize the film industry, that possibly, as Stead (1981) argued, they always curbed their concern about films and the pressure from domestic producers by deferring to the strong public demand for American films, what may have been developing in the minds of key civil servants at the Board of Trade and the Treasury was an utterly unrealistic attitude.[31] Preoccupation with sterling balances and high, even confiscatory, taxation lulled them into overlooking the twin facts of mass public opinion – to which politicians are always sensitive – and the wishes of a potent superpower ally.

The full significance of this letter by Somervell will become obvious in Chapter 7. Somervell and other key civil servants were in the best position to advise their political masters in 1947 that the U.S. film industry was unlikely to accept the Eady–Dalton attempt to maintain the same number of American films shown in the United Kingdom while appropriating 75 percent of the net to the British Treasury as an ad valorem duty. As we saw in Chapter 5, there was self-deception at work when civil servants advised both that the Americans would not boycott Britain because they needed the market too much, and that were they to boycott, the British film industry could step in and fill the breach. Neither prediction was fulfilled, illuminating the level of competence of British officials specializing in film matters. Or, given Somervell's vacillations, there was more nerve available for fighting the Americans than for boldly telling the Treasury it was out of touch.

At all events, the American film companies did apply jointly for the release of their blocked sterling and, interestingly, the Treasury agreed.[32] Somervell then argued that because this reduced the incentive to buy British films for distribution in the United States, some substitute scheme to protect the British film industry should be devised, in consultation with the producers. The suggestion was made that quota regulations be altered to favor the buying of British films for distribution in America rather than the distribution of British films in Britain. No whisper here of the cultural argument. Rather, in the privacy of interoffice communication it is clear that what was happening was exactly what Ramsay MacDonald had charged the 1927 act with being, and what the American companies had all along maintained – namely, that the legislation was being manipulated to protect a British industry from foreign competition, or, even more startling, an American industry was being singled out for special measures aimed at improving the fortunes of British films.

Britain had, in the years since the 1927 act, abandoned free trade, yet the United Kingdom was still committed to trading policies that were not discriminatory – that is, not directed against a single country. It is hard to reconcile the material in these Board of Trade files with a scrupulous attention to that international commitment. The scandal here (to which Dickinson and Street [1985] are apparently oblivious)[33] is that not only was a single country discriminated against – the United States – but also that one sector of British business was favored at the expense of another. The cinema exhibitors, who were almost entirely British but earned much of their living from showing American films, were discriminated against: Their conditions for doing business were worsened. Legislative and other measures were utilized to make American firms less ready to offer product than they would be in a free market, and parallel measures aimed to foist off on the cinema exhibitor a non-American product with the argument that the one was a substitute for the other. No systematic attempts were made to show that they were substitutes from the consumer's point of view.

The American firms had suggested that negotiations for the release of their sterling balances should take place in New York, and Somervell got permission to go over and handle them personally. The American companies had hired Wendell Wilkie to present their case. Once again they employed a distinguished lawyer and political figure, in this case one experienced in international affairs. The negotiations were smooth, and quick acceptance was offered by the companies. While Somervell was in New York he met Sidney Bernstein,[34] who was in the United States to promote the distribution of British government films. Bernstein proposed that Somervell use the lever of the blocked sterling to pressure the American companies to give Bernstein's films proper distribution.[35] Somervell's amenable attitude indicates that there was a presumption of the legitimacy of protectionism and discrimination.

6.3. Military and other cooperation

An aspect of wartime activities too specialized to be gone into fully here was cooperation among the three governments on film matters. The cooperation was both civilian and military, and it involved production, distribution, and exhibition. There was a good deal of sharing of film. The U.K. Ministry of Information, the U.S. Office of War Information, and the Canadian National Film Board looked at each other's films, sometimes distributed them, sometimes secured the original footage and reused it. Film people were brought into both civilian and military film production, distribution, and exhibition. Elaborate distribution and exhibition bureaucracies were created to deliver the latest commercial films, documentaries, and newsreels to the troops at home and abroad.[36]

The armed services of all three powers had photographic units that made films of much of the war activity, from battle to ceremonies and meetings.[37] Allied cooperation was thought to demand strict coordination of the release of this material, so that Canadian, British, and American troops and civilians would, for example, see newsreels of the Normandy landings at about the same time. Since there was elaborate military and governmental censorship, this meant a high degree of cooperation and coordination, much of it passing between London and Washington.

Film people from all branches of the industry thus learned to work together with their allies, and they developed some sense of each other's business savvy. Yet for all that, national loyalties seem to have predominated, with both British and American personnel looking after the interests of their own country's film prospects in the postwar world.

6.4. Postwar planning and British ambition

The ambition for a Hollywood on the Thames refused to go away. Every time the British industry climbed out of a slump and succeeded in getting one or more of its films distributed in the United States, the dollar signs danced before the eyes of the film producers and, of course, the Treasury. That an established industry in another country should be less than willing to share its domestic market with a foreign competitor is hardly surprising, although it was, surprisingly, rarely faced by those dreaming this dream. The period of intense Anglo–American cooperation initiated by Pearl Harbor and spilling over, as we have seen, into certain sectors of the film industry, coincided with something of a revival of the British film industry that went well beyond its success at its official mission. Perhaps the war itself, which touched the lives of the vast majority, harmonized sentiments and provided a ready-made subject that resonated not only in films that dealt with it overtly but also in others with no direct connection. An example would be Laurence Olivier's *Henry V* (Two Cities/Eagle Lion 1945), shot lavishly in Technicolor®, with locations in Eire (Rep. of Ireland), which was specially distributed in the United States to maximize its potential audience (see Knight 1953).

The production of such films and their success in the United States gave great encouragement to creators, critics, and businessmen in an industry where much of the game is guesswork.[38] From about the middle of the war until what we might think of as the final crisis for the film trade in 1949, British thinking and action about the international picture suffered from vaulting ambition. Although my way of framing it may betray a certain skepticism, this does not derive from any doubts about British capacity to make films of the requisite caliber and commercial potential. True, there was much to learn about the popular audience, particularly in America, and the capacity for sheer volume of production necessary to be self-sustaining was always in doubt. The skepticism comes rather from an attempt to appreciate the true economic conditions and the logic of the situation that they dictated.

First there was the entrenched dominance of the American industry in its own market and in all the more lucrative markets around the world. (A feature of this was that the American public, and many foreign publics too, associated film entertainment with U.S. films.) Second, this domination was maintained partly by American product being handled through subsidiaries under the control of New York – not by agents or third parties. Third, this entrenched situation was financed on a large and continuing scale that in a sense presupposed the huge internal market, as well as access to the largest capital market in the world, where a good deal of experience in the financing of motion pictures – a highly specialized activity – had been accumulated. Furthermore, any attempt to secure even a portion of this system by a competitor was naturally going to be resisted, since when the business was good it was very good indeed, and even when it was bad it was far from horrid. From time to time, for commercial or diplomatic reasons, it suited an American distributor to handle a British picture that might have some success. This was true more frequently during the war than ever before, but it did not change the overall structure of the situation. As emphasized several times already, only when this structure was altered in the 1950s did a Hollywood on the Thames become possible, and the structural alterations were not induced by British government measures nor by British pressure to penetrate the U.S. market: They were induced by the decline of the American industry under the internal domestic competition of television.

With all this in mind, we can now turn our attention to British thinking during the war about the prospects for the U.K. film industry as an international business in the postwar period. One group within the industry, represented mainly by the union Association of Cine-Technicians, advocated nationalization of the industry and continuing quotas, but a free flow of films and personnel.[39] The British Film Producers Association (BFPA) hoped to utilize the quota legislation to pry reciprocity out of the American industry, as well as to seize the Agfa process from a defeated Germany and use it as an alternative to Technicolor®.[40] In a minute written about postwar prospects, the ubiquitous Simon Rowson mused on the effects of color and television and predicted that within three years of demobilization the British industry could manufacture one hundred films per annum. Alexander Korda, meanwhile, who had spent part of the war in Hollywood and had financial interests in United Artists, suggested some form of partnership between the two industries, with the British industry partly financed from the earnings of American films in Britain. He correctly predicted that there would be a sudden drop at the box office after the war on account of reduced earnings and the availability of alternative entertainments.[41]

In July of 1943 the trade associations of many industries received a letter from the Board of Trade about the board's plans for reconstruction. Hugh Gaitskell,[42] then a civil servant at the board, wrote that the four reasons why reconstruction of the film industry was important were (1) the need for export earnings; (2) the developing world market; (3) the tendency of trade to follow the film; and (4) the general prestige value of motion pictures.[43] One clear conclusion that emerged from the responses was that the quotas would continue. The attitude toward the United States is indicated by a meeting that Gaitskell had with the president of the Board of Trade in September 1945 in which Gaitskell spoke of an ambition to capture one-tenth of the U.S. market.

Dickinson and Street (1985), in one of their longest chapters (7), endeavored to unravel the intricate series of discussions about films that took place during the war, when state finance of the British film industry and the possibility of a supreme controller of the industry were considered. The official files of the period are bulging with schemes, reports, and minutes. The internal troubles and remedies of the British industry are not our concern, but we may note that the commercial justification for such drastic intervention was always the El Dorado of export earnings in the U.S. market and a concomitant decrease in dependency on U.S. product. As I have stressed more than once, no evidence was produced that British films were substitutes for American films on a broad scale, either in the United States or the United Kingdom.

Official efforts to formulate policy after the 1938 act can be traced back to the report of Nigel Campbell's committee in 1941.[44] Its mandate was to look into the necessity of earnings dollars then and in the future; the propaganda value of British films throughout the world, and especially the Empire; and getting some order into the industry. In the report the problem of the poor entertainment quality of the average British film was noted. The industry was described as inefficient, extravagant, mismanaged, and exorbitant in distribution, rentals, and labor costs. Government licensing of directors and producers was suggested. A Films Commission was mooted to take over the Board of Trade's role. The report urged that American filmmakers be brought over to teach their techniques of management and cost control, while using up blocked funds. Two other proposals were that a bilateral agreement to increase U.S. distribution of British films should be negotiated, and that the double features be abolished to speed up the circulation of films and to reduce the necessity of importing second features.[45]

What is first to be noted about this report is that it did not add up to or derive from a policy for the film industry. To say that the industry was disorderly and costly, for example, says little enough, especially as much the same could be and was said about Hollywood. That it would be nice to earn dollars with British films was no doubt true, but the suggestion that bilateral negotiation with the Americans was the solution was not true. Conspicuously absent from the report was any consideration of audience satisfaction, of what the paying public wanted in Britain and in the United States, and what resources Britain had to supply those wants, and what machinery would be required to process those resources.

Apart from the fact that British audiences might favor American mass cultural materials, including stars, there were the obvious questions of whether Britain could produce musicals, westerns, horror films, and gangster films that would be acceptable audience substitutes for their American originals; and there was the further and even more difficult question of whether British creative and financial resources were sufficient to sustain efforts in that direction. A constant theme reiterated by industry outsiders to officials was that the occasional film (such as a "western" set in Australia) was no answer to the need for sustained output. Block booking and blind booking, we recall, grew partly from the producer-distributor's desire for security, and also partly from the exhibitor's. Neither party wished to be improvising at the last minute, since this exaggerated the inherent uncertainty and risk of the business. Thus any attempt at import substitutes for Hollywood material needed to guarantee continuity of supply. No sooner has the exhibitor counted his week's takings than he is worrying about whether next week's will be as good. If a product appears that the public likes – westerns, or a new star – the exhibitor wants to know that more will be forthcoming on a continuing basis. Furthermore, since public taste is fickle, he also wants producers and distributors to be making modest tests of new product to keep the audience interested and pleased.

Then there was the question of whether the aims were achievable. The entrenched position of the American industry was dual: There were the well-grooved and well-financed patterns of its business; and there was the carefully cultivated and placated audience. Hollywood certainly was not going to yield this territory easily, and the resources were there for a protracted struggle.

Politically the Campbell Report was also naïve in not making anything of the fact that it proposed taking away from the Board of Trade a piece of its turf. Bureaucrats seldom readily yield up territory. In this respect they are no different from businesses, including those in Hollywood. It would hardly stretch the powers of board officials to concoct some powerful arguments as to why an independent Films Commission was not a good idea. For one thing it would place the execution, and possibly also the formulation, of film policy outside the control of the executive, hence also beyond parliamentary accountability. Then there was the complexity. Given the intricate grid of connections between the Board of Trade, the Treasury, the Bank of England, and the Foreign Office, it would be hard to see that a new organization at one remove could simplify matters. It was also obvious that such a commission and other proposals in the report would scarcely find favor with the Americans.

It is scarcely surprising, then, that when the president of the Board of Trade asked his officials for their views on the report there was: (1) a delay (said to be due to preoccupation with negotiations for the renewal of the Anglo–American Agreement); and (2) a negative verdict. A. G. White, writing for the films division, said it was necessary to settle on a films policy before discussing the merits of the measures proposed. In commenting on double features, he made the sole reference to audience preferences, noting that if such programing patterns had been unpopular the companies would not have persisted with them. Dropping them would therefore be an unpopular measure.[46] Ambivalence was expressed about whether encouraging the Americans to produce in Britain would discourage rather than train the locals, and there was the question of American resistance to some of the ideas.

Ought we not, if possible, to contrive not to arouse the combative instincts of the American companies? And if we must have a trial of strength, would it not be well to postpone it until after the war?[47]

No surprise, then, that a joint scheme by the president of the Board of Trade and the Chancellor of the Exchequer, put to the Lord President's Council (which had primary responsibility for formulating domestic policy) was rejected for lack of specifics. During the search for these, doubts strengthened. Gaitskell commented,

In short, I feel that some of the aims which the Campbell Report has in view are doubtful, some can be achieved with a Films Commission, and some only by a Films Commission endowed with powers to which Parliament would very likely object.[48]

The upshot was a decision to withdraw the proposals and think further. Simon Rowson worked at the Board of Trade during the war, and he quarreled with White's somewhat skeptical attitude. Ensuring that the matter stayed alive, the Lord President's Council requested a report on the industry and stressed again the cultural argument, which was not the issue. They emphasized

the importance of ensuring that British films presented a more faithful picture of the life and character of the British people; and particular reference was made to the unfortunate impression which some British films had created abroad, particularly in India and in Colonial territories. The primary need was to see that the controlling influences in the industry were exercised by sound and public-spirited people.[49]

The sentiments expressed here boded ill for the direction and policy of a part of show business, a business whose values and personnel were far from being "sound" or "public spirited."[50] They strengthened the hand of J. Arthur Rank, the lay preacher and moralist film magnate, who often seemed to want to set a tone rather too high for the simple business of pleasing the public and making money. Gaitskell, in subsequently drafting some notes for films policy, ruled out nationalization and sought curbs on monopoly. (He did not connect the two). He also noted the need to foster independent production and improve sales abroad. Once more we have, in the thinking of a British official, not notes for a policy but a wish list, a wish list that changed little over the next nine years.

Between 1944 and 1946 the search for policy focused on the question of monopoly, as a result of a report entitled *Tendencies to Monopoly in the Cinematograph Film Industry* (1944), known familiarly as the Palache Report. The emergence of three circuits or chains in Britain, vertically integrated with two production and distribution groups, led to their being called before the Monopolies Commission, a statutory body with powers to investigate and report on public interest in the matter. Labour left-wingers such as Michael Foot seemed to have a visceral distrust of monopolies when they were in private hands. Much the same people, however, enthusiastically embraced the creation of publicly owned monopolies through nationalization. This reflects the two main objections to monopoly: that from concentration of power, which can be misused; and that from absence of competition, which can increase costs and lower efficiency. Our concern in this book is international trade, not domestic industry. The objection to monopoly from concentration of power has a cultural / political ring to it. Internationally this would mean that the projection of Britain abroad, and especially to the Empire, through films, was in too few hands, which, were they to be diffusing the wrong message, would not be checked by competition but only by direct intervention. The objection to monopoly from lack of competition is of course a commercial, not a cultural, objection. The idea is that a greater variety of product is delivered to the public at lower cost if no one can take monopoly profit. The value of competition internationally is the same as at home, with the proviso that if governments insert themselves into the business commercial firms find themselves at a disadvantage.

When it came to international trade neither the cultural argument nor the competition argument applied. No one pointed to the films of Rank or the Associated British Picture Corporation as culturally / ideologically deficient because of their monopolistic position, nor were their films thought unsuitable for international trade on account of their cost. The measure of these things was the U.S. film industry, and it was not known for the modesty of its expenditures – although it was known for its capacity to cut prices. More important, the U.S. film industry was itself oligopolistically and vertically organized, and this raised the obvious point that perhaps commercial success domestically and internationally was not unconnected to the development of such concentration. Insofar as it was a policy objective of the British film industry and those concerned with it in government to have a vigorous export trade, especially a dollar-earning one in the United States and Canada, it might well be thought that concentration of economic power was a prerequisite.

In written comments on the Palache Report, Lord Grantley made the point that the "keen and rich" Mr. Rank was largely responsible for the survival of British filmmaking during the war. "Let us wait until peace brings easier conditions before we harry temporary monopolistic tendencies." He went on to argue that

> You will not get British films into U.S.A. theatres by inter governmental negotiations. The industry is too complex and too dependent on direct popular support for any government to force the situation. The only way to ensure the increased presentation of British films in the U.S.A. is to buy control of a distribution and circuit owning company. Even if all films exported were smash hits, they would be crowded off the screens there by the major companies, who must get all the screen time they can to get the cost and profit on their own 100% owned negatives.[51]

These shrewd comments by an industry veteran with extensive experience in the film business were treated rather high-handedly by Gaitskell in his minute. Although Lord Grantley was a director of one of Rank's companies, Gaitskell wrote, his "general reputation was not one for any great intelligence or expertise on films"; still, it would be a good plan to "keep him on our side."[52] The "our side" does suggest that there was developing in the civil service a sense that they were becoming advocates of a policy or a design for the industry, one that might meet resistance from the trade; hence the cultivation of friends in that trade was important. Lord Grantley's hint that Rank's monopoly was a temporary tendency was no doubt disingenuous. That hardly warranted dismissal of his views as merely partisan or lacking intelligence. They were in fact largely correct. In particular we should note his stress on the issue of direct popular support as a constraint on the industry, one that neither commercial firms nor national governments could ignore. He showed how the logic of the situation would not change even were all British films smash hits. In that best-case scenario there would be the necessity of buying into the American distribution / exhibition system in order to command screen time. Only large British firms were wealthy enough to contemplate such moves. There was, then, a compelling argument for the concentration of economic power in the British film industry, so long as it nursed the ambition of making films on a scale that would realize substantial earnings in the United States.

This was not congruent with the cultural justifications, which usually saw pluralism as good for artistic endeavor, even if not for national purpose. These may explain why the Palache Report was a charter for independent production and the curbing of monopoly. The economic prosperity of the U.S. industry, at home and abroad, was not unconnected, however, to its oligopolistic character. The Palache Report argued that film was not just another commodity.

Already the screen has great influence both politically and culturally over the minds of the people. Its potentialities are vast, as a vehicle for the expression of national life, ideals and tradition, as a dramatic and artistic medium, and as an instrument for propaganda.[53]

Dickinson and Street (1985, p. 145) quote this passage and align themselves with the film culture that found such lines of thought agreeable. They fail to notice that when the report turned to cultural arguments it contradicted the interest in exports. In championing the independent producers Palache specifically expressed the view that they should make films that were not dominated by the desire to appeal to the foreign market.

Sometimes this conflict was overcome with the ingenious argument that the film that worked best abroad was the one steeped in its culture of origin, rather than the one that aimed at some international style. Certainly the British films that did well in the United States had been very British, and most attempts to imitate the American product had been flops. Yet this was evidence at the margin: the occasional film that did well abroad, or the occasional Continental film that did well in Britain. It did not follow that the great bulk of the film diet of the masses could become a mosaic of films steeped in all sorts of different styles of "national life, ideals and tradition." Indeed, the worldwide success of the American motion picture could be taken as demonstrating that the basic diet demanded by almost all filmgoers was American.

One piece of evidence of the mood and the confusions abroad in Britain on these matters, as thinking continued about films in the postwar world, was the 1944 debate in the House of Lords, which took place between the emergence of concern about monopoly and the appearance of the Palache Report. It was led by Lord Brabazon of Tara.[54] His stance was decidedly culturalist: Films were not mass-produced, he said, but an

expression of art, literature, imagination, and technical skill, and there is no reason at all why we should not be able to hold our own in this and to produce as good films as the Americans, or better.[55]

He went on to speak of Britain having a whip hand over the Americans when the remittances were frozen, yet he also conceded consumer sovereignty and that "people will have American films."[56] He made other points of interest: that a British distributor paid a higher percentage of takings for

American films than was paid in America itself; that the Hays Organization was a monopoly and should be within the purview of the monopolies inquiry; and that the Hays Organization gave the American industry one voice abroad, which the British industry lacked. Not all of these points were accurate, and certainly his assertion that "thirty per cent. of the net revenue of the film industry in America, the fifth biggest industry in that country, comes from this country" was simply incorrect. Floating the idea of a reciprocal quota, he wound up with the culturalist argument that

the time has come to see that this industry, so important for propaganda purposes, for the spread of prestige of this country, should grow in strength and vigour and take its share side by side with America as a great picture-producing country.[57]

In a fascinating maiden speech, Lord Grantley[58] said that Britain was lucky that British screens were dominated by American films and not by those of an enemy, commenting,

I frankly cannot see why we should persuade the Americans for love to stop trying to dominate the industry. I think that if we dominated any industry in this great Empire of ours we should try to stick to that domination.[59]

This financier also emphasized the cultural arguments from propaganda and education, but used them to criticize the 1938 act and its trade-dominated Advisory Council. He stressed that marketing was the key to success in the motion picture business and that marketing abroad could only be undertaken by large and well-financed, vertically integrated organizations. Thus he defended his colleague Rank.[60]

Lord Strabolgi bemoaned the American domination and stressed the necessity of gaining a share of the American market, "if we are to be able to produce the high quality films in this country without losing a great deal of money."[61] His view was that Britain would be in a strong position after the war, but his optimism might strike us now as naïve:

We shall have to bargain with America in a friendly way on other great matters, such as civil aviation and foreign trade; why not bargain with them, on the highest level, on this question of reasonable playing time for suitable British films? It has not been attempted in the past because we have been in a weak position in many ways, and not least diplomatically; but after the war we shall have immense prestige, and we should have a much more friendly feeling with America, as comrades in arms. I think, therefore, that reciprocity could be obtained by friendly arrangement.[62]

Lord Strabolgi was reflecting sentiments that we shall see pervaded the civil service, and he even signaled the desirability of an ad valorem tax.[63] What he was unaware of was the different way in which things were being viewed in the United States. Cordell Hull certainly did not envisage a regime of bilateral bargaining between Britain and the United States; the MPPDA companies were looking to the British abandoning their legislative protection and accepting competition in the market as structured; American film men in the services were planning an aggressive repossession of property and markets in occupied Europe.

The Earl of Selborne[64] also affirmed that there was nothing to prevent the United Kingdom turning out as many first-class films as any other country in the world, and he agreed that exports were essential. He saw the mission of British films as helping Americans understand the English, although he used that to endorse the idea of continuing the Ministry of Information's work after the war. So we see again and again the confusion of the cultural and the commercial. No one faced up to the possibility that even were American resistance overcome, the demands of the market would not ensure that internationally successful British films would be especially British. The commercial and the cultural aims were by no means mutually consistent.

6.5. The reconquest of Europe, 1944–1945

From the 1930s U.S. film companies had exported less and less to the Axis powers and the territories they occupied, and, after entry into the war, nothing at all. Some light can be thrown on the subsequent history of the Anglo–American film trade by considering what happened in Europe in the final months of the war. Anglo–American military plans for using films in Europe were fairly simple.[65] The Political Warfare Executive, which was part of SHAEF (Supreme Headquarters Allied Expeditionary Force), was, like its parent organization, Anglo–American in personnel. Its task was to show films to the populations of occupied countries and to do so as close behind the front lines as feasible, utilizing existing cinemas where possible and mobile projection units where not. The films they showed were a mixture of official films, newsreels prepared for the purpose, and selected feature films. All the occupied countries had governments in exile in London, and it was of course planned to hand over administration to them relatively expeditiously, and perhaps even before that to permit the return of normal civilian commerce and business, including films. Both of the allies had ambitious film industries, one aiming to reestablish and even improve its prewar position of dominance and prosperity, the other seeking to challenge that in all possible markets. Elements of the allied military forces were sympathetic to the aims of the industry of their own country, and some anticipated a return to that industry upon demobilization; other elements in the military were concerned to see Europe on its feet, not especially beholden to the United States, and to some extent meeting its own needs in such cultural/propaganda matters as film. This split mirrored one we shall find in the State Department. Meanwhile, the governments in exile anticipated postwar shortages of dollars even more acute than in the United Kingdom; were apprehensive about the reassertion of American dominance; and, in some cases, were concerned to bring about the instauration of a film industry of their own. The stage was set for a good deal of conflict over film.

In discussing their postwar moves, the British Ministry of Information acknowledged that an Anglo–American unit could not be relied upon to put the purely British point of view, "which under such circumstances we might for political reasons be very anxious to do."[66] So it was planned that the ministry move in its own personnel after the Psychological Warfare units moved out. The ministry expected to continue some of the activities of Psychological Warfare, such as mobile cinemas and publications, but to operate concurrently.

As in all Ministry of Information records, what remains in the public archives is scanty, forcing us to reconstruct a good deal. There is evidence of conflict with the Foreign Office over personnel, but almost nothing about policy.[67] From the American files one can infer a basic fact: The transition from occupation, to liberation, to the restoration of civilian government proceeded much more quickly than the planning bureaucrats seem to have envisaged. That is to say, the period when their schemes had free play because Allied armies were in charge of liberated areas was, with the exception of Germany, very brief indeed, weeks only, whereas Rowson had envisaged two or three months.[68] As we shall see when amplifying the story from the American point of view, far less was achieved in this interregnum period than seems to have been hoped for. Both countries thought they would have opportunity to enhance the position of their export film industry; neither seems in fact to have succeeded. Consider this statement by an official of the Board of Trade:

We think there is a sporting chance of establishing long term markets for British films in Europe, and since the making of a few extra prints will certainly not overtax the resources of the film industry . . . we certainly shall be able to supply the liberated countries without prejudice to the supply of British films to better markets. Moreover, our view in I.M.1. [Industries and Manufactures] – which is also the view of the D.o.T. [Department of Overseas Trade] – is that there is probably a good deal of truth in the slogan "Trade follows the film". A further consideration is that, the wider the market for British films, the better shall we be able to afford to make *good* films (which in our language does not mean films acclaimed by Mrs. C.A. Lejeune [influential critic of the quality Sunday newspaper *The Observer*], but films which will earn good money at the box office and have a sufficient popular appeal to get widely shown in the U.S.A., and so to earn dollars). . . . Finally, there is the political aspect: Br. films "project Britain". Notwithstanding, therefore, that in the short run there may be very little, or even no, net sterling gain, I still think that the British producers should be positively encouraged to push the export of British films to liberated Europe.[69]

However strongly the Board of Trade believed this, and whatever the Ministry of Information was up to, it was not well known. The Foreign Office wrote to the board early in 1944, wondering whether the board was acquainted with the situation which appears to be developing with regard to post-war films in liberated countries. It appears that the M.O.I. [Ministry of Information] are prepared to sacrifice the feature market entirely to our American friends leaving the British film market to provide the shorts. The Americans are grasping this opportunity with both hands, and for the last few months all their principal features have been titled and dubbed in readiness for continental showing.[70]

This ill-informed letter had the advantage for the historian that it elicited a long reply from Gaitskell, reviewing developments to date. He said that about a year previously, before the Americans had begun their preparations, the Ministry of Information had approached the British Film Producers Association for a number of films to show in liberated territories. The BFPA had enthusiastically agreed and submitted a list of films, which was reviewed by the Political Intelligence Department of the Foreign Office, which had been slow and arbitrary in its selections, leaving the BFPA rather bitter. A special company – the British Commonwealth Film Corporation – had been set up to handle matters between the BFPA and the ministry. The eager producers were even prepared to double the twelve films the ministry was financially responsible for with another thirteen for which the producers would be financially responsible, although handling would still be by the ministry.[71] The American companies, Gaitskell reported, were to do their own distribution, but the films had to be reviewed by the Office of War Information. He noted that in Italy the British would distribute twelve films, the Americans forty, and he argued that given the relative sizes of the industries this was hardly unsatisfactory.[72]

In concluding his letter Gaitskell emphasized an important point: that before the war the American companies all had distribution offices in the territories concerned, whereas the British companies did not. Hence this was a wholly new venture for Britain. Indeed the producer Michael Balcon had commented that in his view the original scheme had been aimed at establishing "British pictures in these new markets in preference to competing foreign product." His correspondent had bemoaned the fact that the Ministry of Information was concerned with propaganda, not with commerce.[73] During this time both the Dutch and the Czechoslovakian officials in London discussed their postwar film plans, the former floating the trial balloon of a government film-buying monopoly and asking whether Britain would object, the Czechoslovakians declaring that they "did not wish their market to become the close preserve of Hollywood."[74] While finding no grounds for objecting to state trading monopolies, provided they were non-discriminatory and temporary, Britain did object to the French government "showing unpleasant signs of preferring state trading for its own sake."[75]

Although Gaitskell may have thought the British had a jump on the Americans, this turned out not to be the case. Bernstein, who was moving around rather freely for the Ministry of Information, observed the Americans setting up effective organizations in a manner that bested the British:

The American companies (through the State Department and the Office of War Information) have arranged to send to Italy Mr. Reginald Armour, representing O.W.I., and a representative from the trade. These gentlemen will not only arrange for the establishment of an organisation (or organisations) to distribute U.S. films, but will also represent the U.S. Government, in negotiations with the Italian Government, regarding future legislation affecting film imports, quotas and distribution.[76]

Unfortunately it turned out that after the transfer from the Ministry of Information the BFPA had returned to the prewar practice of selling blocks of films to local businesses rather than following the American example of setting up their own distribution organization. There was also the complication that the Ministry of Information and Office of War Information had been working closely together, and it would be difficult for their personnel to represent BFPA with European governments.

At all events, whether from crossed wires, bureaucracy, or reluctance of British producers to commit to a wholehearted attack on the European market, it seems that Britain did not manage to steal a march on the Americans, who were well prepared and effectively organized. Unlike the British they had mainly to reactivate their prewar distribution network and feed films into it. They were ready to do this even while conditions were still unsettled, including the conditions under which, and the currency in which, payments would be made. (I pursue the story further in Chapters 12 and 13.) American actions were evidence that they took exports seriously and that this sense permeated the war machine and its personnel at least as much as it did on the British side. Although the U.S. film industry was not guided and controlled by federal legislation and government officialdom as the British film industry was, that did not preclude wide understanding among the Americans of the U.S. industry's goals and their value. Thus there was coherence and coordination, even though no locus of central policy or direction.

Lack of policy – or, at the least, apparent lack of policy – may explain the rather inconclusive House of Commons adjournment debate, late in 1945, about the importation of American films. Opened by Robert Boothby, a flamboyant and slightly maverick Tory M.P.,[77] it focused almost exclusively on the alleged £20 million per year that was being remitted to the United States to pay for film rentals. Because of the low footage tariff and the way in which tax liability was calculated, he thought these remittances excessive. Boothby mentioned with some surprise that there was no ad valorem duty on films[78]; in this he may have been preparing the ground for its eventual introduction. As will become clear in Chapter 7, it had originally been destined for the 1946 finance bill but was held over until the 1947 finance bill. Boothby expressed admiration for Humphrey Bogart but claimed that it was a case of "bacon before Bogart,"[79] a phrase that was capped by the secretary for overseas trade, replying for the government, when he championed "food before films."[80]

It was a cordial debate, with only Michael Foot injecting a note of controversy when he argued that the American industry acted like a monopoly in excluding British films.[81] As usual, however, if one searches for nuggets of rational argument they are hard to find. Both Earl Winterton,[82] an Odeon shareholder, and Walter Fletcher,[83] a small theater owner, expressed pious hopes for the production of more British films and stressed that delays in derequisitioning studio space were preventing British production from rising to the highest level. Boothby and others claimed to be sure that were decently made British films available the public would support them. Some confusion was displayed, however, since Boothby and others thought that lower budgets would be sufficient, while others thought higher budgets were necessary. Among the latter group was Capt. Richard Adams,[84] who told of British troops in Italy being so embarrassed by British films that they claimed they ought to be paid to watch them. He also said bluntly that a second-rate American film was preferable to a second-rate British film because the level of expenditure ensured a polished production and able acting.[85] Fletcher claimed Britain could not out-Hollywood Hollywood, and Boothby thought there was an appetite for short films.[86]

None of this speculation was backed by evidence, and when Communist M.P. Willie Gallacher[87] remonstrated that British films were unintelligible to Scotsmen and that there was no such thing as a British way of life, only middle-class caricatures on the screen, he seems not to have been taken as seriously as he deserved.[88] The government claimed that derequisitioning was proceeding apace and that plans for the industry were afoot. However, there was a cautionary note:

Progress towards this aim of producing more, and producing better, British films is not likely to be helped if we start by ruthlessly disregarding the interests of the American film producers. We must contemplate discussions with them. I must therefore be careful what I say, in advance of such discussions.[89]

This remark shows that there were counsels of moderation and good sense at work in government circles. Later events show that other counsellors got the upper hand. Hilary Marquand[90] wound up by saying that development of the final policy would have to await the occasion of the renewal of the Cinematograph Films Act.

Notes

1 "The U.S.A. is now keen to do mutual film propaganda with this country. We are having approaches made from various American interests"; Los Angeles consul to State Department, 17 March 1939, PRO, FO 395 637. It is difficult to know what weight to give to such reports of "feelers." Almost every other Foreign Office American Department file does, however, indicate great apprehension lest Britain be caught making propaganda in the United States – apparently for fear of arousing an anti-British backlash that could swamp the elements sympathetic to Britain's

cause who were being carefully cultivated. On foreign film propaganda in the United States, see Parker 1991.

2 See the file on the U.S.–U.K. trade negotiations of 1938, PRO, BT 64, 30 / 600 / 38.

3 PRO, FO 395 637, Paper P914 / 151 / 150.

4 "British films still find it very difficult to compete with American films in country places, and especially in the West, because British accents, whether genteel or dialect, are not easily understood. It is nevertheless gratifying to be able to report that the three most successful films showing in New York at present are British: *Pygmalion, The Lady Vanishes* and *The Beachcomber.*" British Library of Information (New York) to News Department, 18 January 1939, PRO, FO 395 637.

5 Some evidence of the interest taken in this case in Britain is the fact that the Department of Justice's press release and a complete copy of the petition, as reprinted in the *Motion Picture Herald,* are in PRO, FO 371 21530.

6 The full story is authoritatively narrated and analyzed in Conant 1960.

7 On official films, see Thorpe and Pronay 1980. Surprisingly, we have as yet no comprehensive study of the Ministry of Information in World War II.

8 See material on the 1944 dispute between Mountbatten and the viceroy of India (Wavell) over responsibility for censorship, IO, Information Dept. L / I / 1 / 735 SEAC censorship Stilwell–Mountbatten Dispute 1944.

9 See PRO, FO 371 46334B, Paper 1412. See also Thorne 1978 and Jarvie 1981a, 1985, and 1988b.

10 Rupert Churchill Somervell (1892–1969), educated at Eton and Magdalen College, Oxford: Served in 60th Rifles and RFC; civil servant, Ministry of Labour (1919–37); Board of Trade (1937); Under Secretary (1941); retired 1952 from Industries and Manufactures Department.

11 Minutes of meeting between Somervell, Pritchard, and Rowson, Board of Trade, with Mears (CEA) and Smith (KRS), 13 June 1940, PRO, BT 64 58 / 8906 / 40.

12 Meeting with U.S. Ambassador, 22 September 1939, PRO, BT 64 94 / 50054 / 41.

13 Ibid.

14 On the position of the Prudential Assurance Company in British film finance, see Street 1986.

15 Letter of 25 October 1939, PRO, BT 64 94 / 50054 / 41.

16 Meeting with U.S. Ambassador, 3 November 1939, ibid.

17 Press notice, 8 January 1941, PRO, BT 64 94 / 12908 / 41.

18 Somervell to Rendell (Treasury), 8 August 1940, PRO, BT 64 61 / 12979 / 40. This is the earliest of several official documents in which Somervell's tone can only be described as supercilious. That he became a central figure in Board of Trade dealings with the American film companies does not speak well of the selection and the training of civil servants. Eton, Oxford, and the army did not equip Somervell to match, still less to act superior toward, talent of the likes of Joseph Kennedy, Fay Allport, Don Bliss, Allan Dulles, and Paul Nitze, with all of whom he came into contact over film matters.

19 Rowson paper, 7 August 1940, PRO, BT 64 61 / 12979 / 40.

20 Note of conversation with Steyne (U.S. Embassy), 9 September 1940, ibid.

21 Rendell to Somervell, 23 October 1940, ibid.

22 Ibid.

23 Rendell (Treasury) to Somervell, 31 July 1941, and Minutes of Interdepartmental Meeting of Treasury and Board of Trade officials, 27 August 1941, ibid.

24 John Gilbert Winant (1889–1947), educated at St. Paul's School and Princeton; successively representative and Senator from, governor of, New Hampshire (1925–6, 1931–4); Chairman of the Social Security Board (1935–7); director of the International Labor Organization (ILO) Geneva (1939–41); London Embassy (1941–6); suicide, 3 November 1947. (Bellush 1968.)

25 Loc. cit., PRO, BT 64 61 / 12979 / 40.

26 Hays to Halifax, 24 July 1941, PRO, BT 64 94 / 12908 / 41.

27 Halifax to Wood, 15 September 1941, ibid. Halifax was alluding to the Wheeler–Clark investigation – *Hearings before a Subcommittee of the Committee on Interstate Commerce,* which are reproduced in part as Document 1 in Culbert 1990, vol. 2, Part I. See §12.3 of the present volume.

28 Overton to Wilson, 23 December 1941, PRO, BT 64 94 / 12908 / 41.

29 Waley to Somervell, 10 July 1942, ibid.

30 Somervell to Waley, 15 July 1942, ibid.

31 As an example of ambition becoming grandiose, consider the following remarks: "We want to see more and better British films made – and you may take it that that is the Government's attitude... to make pictures that will justify ranking the British film industry alongside the American." Somervell to Skinner, 1 March 1940, PRO, BT 64 58 / 4660 / 40.

32 Somervell minute, 24 July 1942, PRO, BT 64 94 / 12908 / 41.

33 As when, for example, they write of politics "discouraging the British government from taking a tough line with the American producers [error for "distributors"]" (1985, p. 123). They do not make clear what business the British government would have taking a tough line with companies wishing to collect earnings gained by legitimate means.

34 Lord Sidney Bernstein (1899–1991), built small chain of cinemas that he inherited into the major Granada circuit in Britain; introduced Saturday-morning children's shows; researched audience preferences; Founding member of Film Society; after war service with MoI and SHAEF, worked with Alfred Hitchcock on *Rope, Under Capricorn,* and *I Confess;* when commercial television began in 1955, his Granada station was very successful.

35 Somervell to Phillips, 27 August 1942, PRO, BT 64 94 / 12908 / 41.

36 Research in this area continues to be published at this writing. An excellent contemporary survey of the situation for the United States was *Movie Lot to Beachhead* (Editors of *Look* magazine, 1945); something similar for Britain was attempted as late as 1989 by Coultass. Chapter 12 of Jowett (1976) sketched an outline, which was filled in by Koppes and Black (1987). Thorpe and Pronay (1980) and Pronay and Spring (1982) contain useful essays, as do many other volumes and journals, such as the earlier work of Black and Koppes (1974); Black (1976); and Koppes and Black (1977). An important contribution is David Culbert's publication (+ fiche) of a substantial selection of declassified U.S. government records relating to film (Culbert 1990).

37 Indeed, Admiral Mountbatten had a crew solely to cover his own activities (see Jarvie 1988).

38 Uncertainty is shown to explain a great deal by Rosten 1941 and Powdermaker 1950.

39 PRO, BT 64 95 / 4934 / 43.

40 BFPA Report, 1 July 1944, ibid.

41 Korda to Waterhouse, 16 June 1943, ibid.

42 Hugh T. N. Gaitskell (1906–1963), educated at Winchester and New College, Oxford; university teacher; wartime civil servant; Labour M.P. elected (1945); Chancellor of the Exchequer (1950–1); leader of Labour Party Opposition (1955–63); represented middle-class Fabian trend in party; fought bitter battles with its left wing.

43 He thus put films in the category that later was almost wholly occupied by a flag-carrying national airline.

44 Sir Nigel Campbell (1878–1948), educated at Eton; a director of financial house of Helbert Wagg.

45 Report of 19 September 1941, PRO, BT 64 95 / 2974 / 42.

46 It might not be wholly inappropriate to insert a piece of personal evidence here. My career as a British cinemagoer began during World War II with visits, first to Disney films, and later to other films with my parents, aunts, and cousins. My recollection is that there were two kinds of double bills: those where the feature was supported by a western or some other manifestly B picture; and "double features." The double feature was popular with us all, since it filled up a whole evening or afternoon, gave us two chances of getting to see a good film for our money rather than one (we were easygoing about sitting through bad films), and (not to be forgotten in austerity Britain) the double bill meant up to 3½ hours of cozy warmth in a generally underheated country.

47 Notes by A. G. White, 4 March 1942, PRO, BT 64 95 / 2974 / 42.

48 Ibid.

49 Ibid., Lord President's Council minutes, 26 February 1943.

50 Peter Stead claims great explanatory power for viewing films as part and parcel of "show business," run by "showmen" (Stead 1989, chap. 1).

51 Grantley to Dalton, 16 October 1944, PRO, BT 64 96 / 4085 / 44.

52 Ibid., Gaitskell minute, 21 October 1944.

53 Quoted by Dickinson and Street, 1985, p. 145.

54 See Chapter 4, note 41.

55 Parliamentary Debates (Lords), 23 February 1944, vol. 130, col. 922.

56 Ibid., col. 926.

57 Ibid., col. 933.

58 Who, as Captain the Hon. Richard Norton, had been involved in film finance for some fifteen years; hilariously recounted in his memoirs, Silver Spoon (Grantley 1954). A lively character, his nickname was "The Wicked Uncle."

59 Parliamentary Debates (Lords), 23 February 1944, vol. 130, col. 937.

60 Ibid., col. 940.

61 Ibid., col. 944.

62 Ibid., col. 945.

63 Ibid., col. 946.

64 Roundell Cecil Palmer (1887–1971), Earl of Selborne: educated at Winchester and Oxford. Company director; Conservative M.P. for Newton, then Aldershot, (1910–40).

65 On Germany in particular, see the excellent Culbert 1985.

66 Routh to Grubb, 27 January 1944, PRO, FO 930 241.

67 PRO, FO 930 241.
68 Rowson, "British Feature Films for Liberated Territories," 29 September 1943, PRO, BT 64 141.
69 Memorandum by Welch, 16 March 1943, BT, 64 141.
70 W. T. Varley to Gaitskill [Gaitskell], 24 January 1944, PRO, BT 64 141. The final claim was an exaggeration.
71 A list of the films circulating in France, Belgium, and Italy was provided to the House of Commons a year later; see *Parliamentary Debates (Commons)*, 17 January 1945, vol. 407, cols. 185–91.
72 Gaitskell to Varley, 26 January 1944, PRO, BT 64 141.
73 Balcon to Hall, 26 October 1943, ibid.
74 Minutes of meetings 15 December 1943 and 10 March 1944, ibid.
75 Memo of 15 March 1944, ibid.
76 Bernstein to Rank, 3 May 1945, ibid.
77 Robert John Graham Boothby (1900–86). Created Baron, 1958. Educated at Eton and Magdalen College, Oxford. Unionist M.P. for East Aberdeenshire (1924–58).
78 *Parliamentary Debates (Commons)*, 16 November 1945, cols. 2538–9.
79 Ibid., col. 2541.
80 Ibid., col. 2566.
81 Ibid., cols. 2560–2.
82 Edward Turnour (1888–1962), Earl Winterton; educated at Eton and Oxford; journalist; Unionist M.P. for Horsham (1940–51).
83 Walter Fletcher (1892–1956), educated at Charterhouse and Lausanne University; Businessman; Conservative M.P. for Bury (1945–55).
84 Harold Richard Adams (1912–78), educated at Emanuel School and University of London; Labour M.P. for Tooting (1945–55).
85 *Parliamentary Debates (Commons)*, 16 November 1945, col. 2550.
86 Ibid., col. 2541.
87 William Gallacher (1881–1965), Socialist activist; Communist M.P. for Fife (1935–50).
88 *Parliamentary Debates (Commons)*, 16 November 1945, cols. 2564–5.
89 Ibid., col. 2567.
90 Hilary Adair Marquand (1901–72), like John Grierson, a Laura Spellman Rockefeller Fellow in the United States (1925–6); professor of economics; wartime civil servant; Labour M.P. for Cardiff, then Middlesborough (1945–61); held various ministerial posts.

Trial of strength: Hollywood's boycott of the
British market, 1947–1948

7.1. Overview

Markets that were heavily dependent on the supply of American films were
vulnerable to collective action by the suppliers. Will Hays recalled how
boycott was used successfully against France in 1928. (Hays 1955, pp. 402–
5). Several conditions had to exist for a boycott to be effective. There must
in fact be a boycott – that is, a solid united front among the American firms.
Alternative sources of supply (stockpile, reissues, other countries, increased
domestic production) must be inadequate, or unacceptable to the audience.
The level of perceived demand must stay high.

The longest and most completely successful boycott the American motion
picture industry ever carried out was against Great Britain over the autumn
and winter of 1947–8. Its two sides were ostensibly ill matched. It was a
boycott by private American companies, aimed at altering a British government policy. The policy restricted the percentage of distribution rentals
that American companies could convert into dollars. The British government, to avoid the accumulation of sterling indebtedness that the measures
of 1939–43 had entailed (see §6.2), had devised a scheme to divert the
rentals to the Treasury by means of an ad valorem customs duty.

The problem facing the American industry was to organize and maintain
a united front, while staving off the charge that their boycott was an illegal
monopoly action. The problem for the British government and film industry
was to find substitutes for American films (possibly even by diverting demand from films) or to get the Americans to accept a new trading situation.
Although the American front did develop weaknesses over the months, it
did not break, and although the question of the legality of the boycott was
moot, the wheels of the antitrust machinery could turn very slowly indeed,
long enough to make clear the unacceptability of the new trading situation
and for it to come home to the British that they had failed either to find
substitutes or to divert demand. When high policy considerations were

This chapter is a revised version of Jarvie 1986a.

invoked to press for an end to the dispute, British officials at the Treasury and Board of Trade had no effective counter.

When the British government imposed the 75-percent ad valorem duty on imported films on 6 August 1947, it was one of several measures aimed at reducing dollar outflow. Two days later the Motion Picture Export Association (MPEA) announced that its members (the eight major U.S. film distributors) would halt all shipments of new films to Britain. They complained that the duty was confiscatory and had been imposed without the Anglo–American talks customary in film matters. It took eight months of manoeuver and negotiation to end the boycott. In a "Memorandum of Agreement" dated 11 March 1948,[1] Britain agreed to repeal the duty and to permit film revenues of up to $17 million to be remitted to the United States annually, plus a sum equivalent to the dollar earnings of British films in the same year. Any unremittable film revenues were permitted to be spent only in specified ways within the sterling area, mainly in the film and leisure industries. In their turn, MPEA members agreed to resume shipment of new films to Britain.

The consequences of this episode are difficult to sort out.[2] Was the boycott a golden opportunity for the British film industry on which it failed to capitalize or that was snatched away just as it was about to do so? Was the outcome a victory for the U.S. film industry or a badly needed influx of American money into British film production? Above all, what can we learn from this episode about Britain's position in the international trade in films in the North Atlantic triangle?

To summarize the argument: the "Dalton Duty" was an anomalous measure, poorly thought out, inconsistent with Britain's film policy and trade policy.[3] It exposed deficiencies in government attempts to manage the British film industry. Imposed hastily and ad hoc, it did not soak up any dollars or raise any revenue, but it had the unintended consequence of encouraging the production of high-quality American films in British studios; this was the new beginning of a trend to American production in Europe ("runaway" production) that was part of the opening up of the U.S. domestic market to European-made films. Once the duty was in place its retention became a measure of Britain's capacity to act in its own interests against American interests. Its removal was an acknowledgment that the overriding common political interests between the two nations were such that it was imprudent for Britain to persist with actions that seriously annoyed such a powerful ally.

7.2. Trade policy and film

Since 1932, British trade policy had centered on Imperial preference. This was supplemented, in the postwar period, by bilateralism – meat deals with Argentina and the like (despite subsequent signature to the General Agreement on Tariffs and Trade [GATT]); by contrast, American trade policy was multilateralist and aimed, theoretically, at achieving free trade via GATT. Whatever the policy pursued, some argued that exceptional treatment should be accorded to the protection of what may be termed "cultural" commodities: books, plays, performances, educational materials. Were films such a cultural commodity? To American officials (and their Supreme Court) it seems that they were not;[4] British officials held that they were. On this disagreement turned the treatment eventually accorded to films in the General Agreement on Tariffs and Trade, concluded in March 1948.

The commercial importance of film expenditures to Britain was not great. Although Great Britain was Hollywood's most lucrative overseas market, motion pictures only ever accounted for 4 percent of British dollar expenditures. As we have seen, in pre-war justifications of the 1927 Cinematograph Films Act this cultural argument was used: The act was supposed to ensure the continued production of films of a distinctively "British" outlook. The following extract dates from 1938:

HM Government have never considered the position and influence of the United Kingdom film industry as primarily an industrial question, but rather as a cultural question; they feel it essential, as a matter of national policy, that cinema goers in the United Kingdom should be given an opportunity of seeing some proportion of films in which they can expect to have portrayed the manners and life of their own country.

Whether these attitudes were truly held, and if truly held strictly adhered to, or whether this was dissimulation, we shall later see.

By contrast, the U.S. government had no cultural or commercial policy for the film industry; there was no significant tariff on imports; and tendencies to monopoly were under constant surveillance and challenge. Of course the Motion Picture Association of America (formerly MPPDA) maintained that its products promoted American values, but many U.S. government officials were skeptical of these claims. If American companies discriminated against imported films, this had less to do with defense of American values than with the fact that the industry was fully geared to satisfy domestic demand. Imports would threaten commerce, not culture.

7.3. The situation in the U.S. and U.K. film industries in 1947

The year 1946 was high tide for the American film industry. In that year it sold more tickets and made more money than in any previous year. But almost immediately, as Table 7.1 shows, there was a drastic falling off. By mid-1947, little short of general panic was abroad in Hollywood. In such circumstances, naturally, all foreign markets – and especially the largest one, the United Kingdom – were matters of urgent concern. Meanwhile, a small number of British films had been shown with success in the United

Table 7.1. *U.S. motion picture admissions, average admission prices, and estimated attendance*

Years	Admissions incl. taxes ($ mill.)	Average price incl. taxes (cents)	Estimated annual attendance (mill.)	Estimated average weekly attendance (mill.)
1935	556	24.9	2,233	42.9
1939	659	26.5	2,487	47.8
1941	809	28.5	2,839	54.6
1945	1,450	39.8	3,643	70.1
1946	1,692	41.0	4,127	79.4
1947	1,594	42.9	3,716	71.5
1948	1,503	43.3	3,471	66.8
1949	1,445	44.5	3,247	62.4
1950	1,367	44.3	3,086	59.3
1951	1,299	44.9	2,893	55.6
1952	1,233	45.3	2,722	52.3
1953	1,172	47.5	2,467	47.4
1954	1,210	50.5	2,396	46.1
1955	1,217	53.1	2,292	44.1
1956	1,225	54.4	2,252	43.3
1957	1,116	56.9	1,961	37.7

Sources: Box-office receipts: U.S. Department of Commerce, *U.S. Income and Output, 1958*, p. 151, and *National Income Supplement to the Survey of Current Business, 1954*, pp. 206–8. Admissions prices derived from U.S. Department of Commerce data and from U.S. Bureau of Labor Statistics, *Admission Price Index*. Attendance from box-office receipts divided by admission prices.

States. This had stimulated J. Arthur Rank and others to revive the dream of a Hollywood on the Thames, turning out films that would earn dollars in America.[5] Rank had a distribution deal with Universal, facilitated by part ownership. On a 1947 visit to the United States, he cultivated the big-five companies with a view to more showings of British films. At the time, Hollywood treated Rank as a genuine threat (Wood 1952, p. 219). This may have had to do with what one senses was a lack of proportion in the way some Americans perceived Great Britain. If British elites, as Corelli Barnett (1972) and others have argued, were slow to recognize the decline of Britain's real economic and military power, there may have been a similar lag in American perceptions of that decline. The fact was that Britain did not possess a home market for films nearly large enough to sustain film production on the imagined scale and, furthermore, was in no position to raise the working capital necessary to finance it. Indeed, a good deal of British production finance depended on the proceeds of exhibiting American films (ibid., pp. 236–7).[6] In addition, the much-vaunted success of British films in the United States had in fact been quite modest and began rapidly to tail off as the war and its comradely sentiments receded.

7.4. The buildup to the duty

An ad valorem duty on imported films was seriously entertained as early as 1935 in the "Joint Report to the Chancellor of the Exchequer by the Board of Customs and Excise and the Board of Inland Revenue on the Taxation of Imported Cinematograph Film (3 March 1935)."[7] Assessing the value of films for duty purposes was identified as a problem, in addition to possible conflicts with treaty obligations.

It is important to ask why such a duty was considered. The commercial argument was protectionism: Taxing imported films was a way of reducing their price competitiveness with the domestic product. Such a construction of policy was always, as we have seen, publicly disavowed. Why protect the home product? Commercial and cultural reasons were advanced. There may in addition have been political considerations (such as propaganda and morale), but these were not disclosed. The commercial reasons given were to maintain employment (scarcely a problem in the full-employment postwar years); to maintain production capability (shown to be important by the war); and, possibly, to gain dollars from exports. There was also a cultural argument. Imported films imported a foreign culture; home-produced films reflected the home culture. Both belonged to mass culture, a phenomenon that elicited the paternalistic tendencies of ruling elites, as we have seen. Standards in home-produced films were thought to be too low, but at least they did not Americanize the population. Protectionism and cultural self-defense had been the two main reasons given for the 1927 act. An ad valorem duty, however, was a redistributive measure intended to prevent foreign film companies from retaining all the earnings of their films. It was designed to ensure that fewer sterling resources were spent for films. Any benefits to the home industry were indirect.

By the time the ad valorem duty was enacted in 1947, saving dollars was its sole official rationale. The earnings of American film companies during the war were as shown in Table 7.2. Remittances had been restricted between 1939 and 1942 in order to conserve dollars for "essentials" (§6.2). On release of the frozen funds in the latter year, when lend–lease came fully into operation, more than $100 million had been remitted home by the American film companies. The attractions of a duty, rather than a freeze, was obviously that massive future obligations would not accumulate.

The immediate origin of the legislation of 1947 seems to have been a 1944 interdepartmental meeting of officials held at the Treasury under instructions by the Chancellor of the Exchequer to fix a limit on the use of dollars for films. Presiding was Sir Wilfred Eady, joint second secretary of

Table 7.2. *Film remittances: United Kingdom to United States, 1935–46*

Year	Remittances (£/mill.)
1935–9 (avg.)	7.0
1939–40	4.8
1940–1	5.7
1941–2	8.5
1942–3	26.5
1943–4	15.6
1944–5	16.9
1945–6	18.1

Source: PRO, BT 64 204: Letters between A. G. White, Board of Trade, and Sir Henry French, British Film Producer's Association, 28 October, 6 and 19 November, 1946.

the Treasury; also present were Sir Archibald Carter, Mr. Mundy and Mr. Taylor (of Customs and Excise), Mr. Chambers (Inland Revenue), and Hugh Gaitskell (Board of Trade). In the course of the meeting five options were laid out:

1. a scheme to prevent U.S. earnings rising above a permitted amount;
2. a distribution quota, based on pre-war remittances;
3. a reduced quota legislated to override existing contracts;
4. all films in excess of the quota to be liable to duty;
5. a link between the quota and the amount of earnings of British films in the United States.

It was recorded that Customs preferred a tax on value but that the Treasury and the Board of Trade favored option 1.[8]

In his memorandum of the meeting, Gaitskell noted that the Chancellor had turned down the special-tax idea a month before and was seeking option 1. He also noted that the idea was to treat all revenues from films above the quota as excess profits, so that, with Excess Profits Tax at 100 percent, their earnings would go to Inland Revenue. Eady expressed strong opposition to any scheme that would involve blocked balances.[9]

Whatever the deeper roots of the scheme, a basic disposition of forces was discernible in this meeting. The politicians were looking for a way to spend fewer dollars on films, and the officials found that their various departments favored different options. For the next three years much paper passed back and forth as scheme after scheme was devised, revised, and abandoned. The Customs scheme, which looked so unpromising on paper, was nevertheless, duly modified, the one enacted (but never implemented) as the Dalton Duty.

Although four departments were represented at the meeting (even if, technically, both Inland Revenue and Customs were part of the Treasury), and although at least three others were subsequently drawn in – namely, the Bank of England (newly nationalized); the Lord President's Office (the supposed overlord of domestic policy); and the Foreign Office – the bulk of subsequent discussion was between the all-powerful Treasury and the lesser-ranked Board of Trade. Furthermore, they were departments with very different concerns, if we are to go by the documents preserved. Treasury officials saw films as something of a consumer luxury during a time when the watchword was austerity; something distastefully American; something anomalous in the scheme of taxation and tariffs. The Board of Trade had responsibility for, and an intimate acquaintance with, the film industry, a sense of the dependence of the British industry on American product and capital, and a tradition of close consultation with American interests.

Perhaps to write of the two departments in this undifferentiated way is already to oversimplify. Morgan (1984) argues persuasively that within the Treasury the problem was that the perspective of the Overseas Department was inadequate. Morgan was discussing the overall sterling crisis of 1947 and its (mis)handling, and he included the Chancellor of the Exchequer, Hugh Dalton,[10] in his indictment. With respect to films, collateral evidence of inadequacy can be seen partly in Eady's eagerness to tax the earnings of American companies, his officials' fond illusion that the American industry would settle for what it could get, and the slowness to abandon these suppositions in the face of events and to accept the necessity for a settlement. In this regard one suspects that political sympathies made little or no difference: Worsting the Americans was something with broad appeal. Complicating things at the Board of Trade, film matters were overseen by Rupert Somervell, who leaned toward Treasury views. The inadequacy of Board of Trade officials is perhaps revealed in their inconsistency: First they argued that the duty would create political trouble with the Americans; later they discounted that possibility. To what extent they felt it incumbent upon them (or prudent) to back up the Treasury's opinions is a matter for others to judge.

Initially, Board of Trade officials doubted the wisdom of the Customs' scheme. In a minute to Gaitskell's memorandum, G. L. S. Shackle, the economist, then a middle-level civil servant, suggested that an ad valorem duty could be justified during a period of exchange difficulty but at other times "it might prejudice Anglo–American relations generally in the economic and financial spheres."[11] (An unsigned memorandum of 19 June raised the "question of the amount and kind of retaliation to which we might expose ourselves from the Americans": For example, Britain's international insurance business might be subjected to retaliatory measures.[12])

By 6 June a Mr. Rendell wrote that the Chancellor now wanted to treat the issue as an exchange problem and that the duty had the advantage of not involving altering the quotas of the 1938 act. In July the experts at the Board of Trade met, and Somervell began to draft a scheme. When this was shown to Ernest Rowe-Dutton[13] at the Treasury, he exhibited a caution matching Shackle's replying that he did not want "to get committed to a proposal that will involve us in open warfare."[14] He was to change to a more aggressive line as discussion proceeded.

Such a harder line was first articulated by another Treasury official, Edward Beddington-Behrens. British films would never get a square deal in the United States without the cooperation of the American film industry, he reasoned. Such cooperation would never be forthcoming unless and until means were found of making it too expensive for the American companies to keep out British films. The American companies *were* vulnerable, he argued: By and large their domestic earnings no more than covered their costs, and their U.K. earnings accounted for the bulk of their profits. In order, therefore, to put over a satisfactory "reciprocity" deal, the British government must convince the American companies that steps would otherwise be taken to control their U.K. revenues to the extent of, say 50 percent. After five years, British films might be able to stand on their own feet: "We now incline to the view that our N[o]. 1 bogey for making the [American film] companies' flesh creep should be the threatened imposition of heavy United Kingdom Customs duties."[15] Gaitskell summed up: "The real issue will be a political one. How tough are we prepared to be with the Americans?"[16]

No action flowed from these May 1944–March 1945 discussions. In August 1945 the issue revived, following the end of lend–lease. Rowe-Dutton wrote to A. G. White at the Board of Trade that some dollars-saving scheme was now urgent. Four days later he asked for, in case of need, the procedure "for a total prohibition of the import of American (or indeed all) films."[17] White commented,

I cannot help thinking ... that it would be the greatest possible mistake to antagonise the American companies and dislocate the business of all the renters and the exhibitors by hurriedly clapping on an import prohibition which ... would have little immediate effect on the volume of remittances to be transferred to USA. [The scheme] would have to be discussed in an atmosphere of heated and bitter controversy, and against a background of formidable pressure from all the exhibitors and the filmgoing public for some immediate settlement, no matter what concessions to the Americans we might have to make in order to get it.[18]

In a further exchange, with Cockfield of Inland Revenue, the possibility was raised that the Americans "might retaliate for the quota by reducing their film exports to us to a trickle as this possibility is sure to occur to someone."[19]

The position at this stage was that the Treasury, the dominant department in the British civil service, had been charged by the Chancellor of the Exchequer with a specific task: reducing dollar expenditures. They consulted with officials at the Board of Trade. The idea of increasing exports appealed to the Treasury, since more dollars earned by British films would offset those used to pay for the import of American films. It is important to note these differing departmental estimates of how much freedom of action there was. Some Treasury officials urged the view that the American film industry *was* vulnerable. Their arguments were financial. Board of Trade officials argued in a manner suggesting that they did not know whether the American industry was financially vulnerable but that they did know that the British film industry was vulnerable. In both departments there was some trepidation about the international political implications, although surprisingly little checking was done with the Foreign Office.[20]

The scheme that had emerged from the initial discussions of 1944–5 was shot down. But soon after, the new Chancellor of the Exchequer (Hugh Dalton) wanted to find a way to reduce dollar expenditures on films by one-half (they stood at £15 million per annum) and to do so without blocking funds and despite the fact that British distributors' had on hand a six-months stockpile of imported films.[21] Hopes of alleviating the overall dollar shortage were pinned on the negotiations for an American loan, which commenced 13 September 1945. Dalton and Eady did a bit of contingency planning in case the loan did not go through. In case of failure the Treasury indicated that it would suggest that tobacco imports be cut 20 percent and rationing introduced, and that all film remittances be blocked while a scheme to reduce them by 50 percent was devised.[22]

More schemes were floated and reviewed in the winter of 1946–7, the Customs scheme for an ad valorem duty gaining ground as doubts about treaty obligations and the basis of valuation were resolved – the latter by the device of making valuation retroactive and collecting against an estimate on entry. There was tough talk of reminding the United States of the consequences of a sterling–dollar war; the dangers were noted of any government monopoly on film imports; and Eady acknowledged the close connections of the U.S. film industry with the State Department, noting that the industry "seems to be able to put pressure on Mr. Winant at will."[23]

Officials were urged to keep the discussions to themselves in order not to jeopardize the loan negotiations or passage of the loan by Congress.[24] One wonders how this affected Board of Trade officials, who had developed close and cordial relations with American consular and film industry representatives in London. Security was far from flawless. On 11 January 1946, Donald Nelson, president of the Society of Independent Motion Picture Producers, wrote from Hollywood to Will Clayton, under secretary of state, expressing worry at a rumor he had heard from Joseph Kennedy that "there wasn't the slightest question but that England would freeze the proceeds from distribution of American films and that it was just a matter of when."

Nelson asked Clayton to inquire into this, as he had understood it to be a condition of the British loan that there would be no freezing of funds. Four weeks later Clayton replied,

I find that the Department has had no indication of any intention on the part of the British Government to freeze the proceeds from the distribution of American films. It seems to me that such proceeds would be the result of "current transactions," in the sense used in the Anglo–American financial agreement, and therefore not subject to freezing.[25]

Clayton's wording was cautious, leaving it uncertain whether the department knew and would not say or whether it was truly in the dark.

The loan passed Congress on 15 July 1946. The dollar gap, for the moment, was closed. Films were not, however, to be left alone. The duty was prepared for inclusion in the 1946 finance bill but then dropped; one year later it was revived. A new reason to justify a duty appeared in a Treasury paper by E. J. Kahn noting that since 1934 successive Chancellors of the Exchequer "have asked officials to devise ways and means of reducing this burden on our balance of payments."[26] The five options of 1944 were reduced to three: (1) heavy import duties, (2) import licensing, and (3) promotion of British films.

What Kahn called a "burden" amounted to some 4 percent of British dollar expenditures. I doubt that this civil service view was shared by the general public, which felt entitled to its leisure expenditure on films and that other dollar-draining "burden," tobacco. Recognition of this may be implicit in the conspicuous absence from the reduced list of options of the total prohibition of film imports from nonsterling countries. Whatever their personal tastes in entertainment, officials were now working for a popularly elected government, in peacetime. The postwar period in Britain was often nicknamed "the Age of Austerity" and Labour's second Chancellor of the Exchequer, Sir Stafford Cripps, taken as emblematic of it. But that mood does not explain why British officials persistently sought to discriminate against the American companies supplying Britain with popular entertainment. Decades of files reveal no voice raised against the whole enterprise, no one arguing that officials well paid from taxes might have more regard for the interests of the taxpayers. We noted earlier Peter Stead's claim that the reason the British government confined its activities vis-à-vis Hollywood to rhetoric and protection for British producers was in order not to threaten the public's entertainment. If he is right, one wonders why politicians were encouraging civil service schemes to do so.

Indeed, given how often Sir Wilfred Eady's name crops up, one wonders whether much of the energy with which the topic was pursued derived from this one man's idée fixe. Concerned with some such scheme since his time at Customs many years before, Eady, as we shall see, was the last holdout in face of the clear necessity of giving in to the American boycott. Contrast this with the attitude of Shackle, who held that the scheme discouraged the Americans from making any concessions in bilateral and trade talks and inspired other countries to contemplate such moves. This exacerbated American feelings and did not augur well for the planned trade talks. In a revealing phrase, A. G. White of the Board of Trade noted that the options had been put up to Eady at Treasury, "so we shall hear more of this when Sir W. Eady has picked his fancy."[27] If that is what Sir Wilfred did, then a sharp lesson was coming from the experience of the MPEA boycott.

At the time films were an important form of public entertainment and, despite fluctuations in their economic fortunes, looked set to stay that way. But the dollar gap continued to be on the minds of Treasury officials. Rowe-Dutton noted,

We are now free from any inhibition imposed on us by the loan negotiations, and it had always been my idea that we could then tell the American film people that by hook or by crook film remittances from this country must be halved, either directly by taxation on imports or indirectly by an increase in the remittances for British films from the United States. I should have seen every advantage in opening up the battle before Eric Johnston comes to this country in the autumn, so that when he comes, the opportunity might be taken of clinching a deal.[28]

In response to the views of Rowe-Dutton and Kahn, White reminded them that the heavy-import-duty option had been an emergency measure, prepared in case the American loan had failed to pass. He suggested doing nothing prior to review of the quota legislation in 1948.[29] It is not hard to reconstruct the concerns that would make White want to ignore Rowe-Dutton's idea of dictating to the American companies. The framework of film policy in the United Kingdom was the 1938 Cinematograph Films Act, an intricate structure dependent on the cooperation of the British and American companies. A drastic new duty on imported films would upset whatever balance was thought to have been struck in the negotiations preceding the 1938 act.[30] Board of Trade letters once again warned of possible reprisals that would disrupt working arrangements and force piecemeal alterations of policy. The Treasury, having no responsibility for film policy, swept these considerations aside. Rowe-Dutton bluntly replied, "We cannot afford £18 million a year for American film royalties," and "it is implicit in all you say that films are sold on their merits. I shall take a great deal of persuading that this is a fact." A draft of a second letter, never sent, characterized many film imports as "trash," second features that the public merely put up with.[31] By this point the commercial and cultural arguments were inextricably intertwined in some minds. Board of Trade officials argued that

some of us were at one time attracted by the ingenious Inland Revenue scheme which gave birth to this file; but in the end we became afraid that, if this scheme was adopted, we might not get enough films.[32]

The Treasury was told that there was no desire to reduce the amount of films imported but simply to get the same amount for fewer dollars.[33] In due course almost the same phrase crossed the lips of representatives of the American industry, who were less than sanguine at the prospect. Stephen Holmes sharpened the Board of Trade's point of view: "In present circumstances, substantial film imports are considered to come within the range of essentials." Against other schemes circulating, he commented that they might result in fewer American films and/or in cinema prices going up. "I am afraid that I must say that just at this particular juncture we should view with alarm any violent battle with the United States' film interests with their very powerful lobby in that country, however privately benevolent our friends in the State and other Departments might be to our case."[34]

The issues finally reached the Cabinet at its prebudget meeting of 4 November 1946, when the expenditure of £17 million worth of dollars on films was queried. There was talk of reductions by increasing the production of British films. In response, the president of the Board of Trade, Sir Stafford Cripps, sent a lengthy note to Prime Minister Clement Attlee setting out the situation. It argued that domestic film production was on the rise because studio space and resources were being released from war use. Cripps optimistically asserted that the British public now preferred to see British films: "The Board of Trade are reliably informed that, striking a rough average between picture and picture, British first feature pictures are now out-grossing American first features in this market to the extent of no less than 20%." A marked improvement could be expected in 1948.[35]

Two other factors of high policy were relevant to political consideration of these matters: trade negotiations and the fuel crisis of 1947. Negotiations led by Britain and the United States were about to begin on issues of trade and tariffs, their upshot to be The International Trade Organization (ITO) and GATT. The United States wanted films included in these negotiations; the United Kingdom did not. Long-term questions of trade policy were at stake, as the United Kingdom sought to reconcile a theoretical commitment to multilateralism with an actual commitment to Imperial preference and bilateralism. Both sides were well aware that the issues raised domestic political passions (Gardner 1956, chap. 17). Speaking on the economic situation to the House of Commons, Cripps, as president of the Board of Trade, gave assurance that no hurried film policy would be implemented.[36] Whether the scheme eventually legislated seemed unhurried is another matter.

In addition to the deteriorating balance-of-payments situation and dollar shortage, the severe winter of 1946–7 resulted in an acute shortage of fuel. The Lord President's Office suggested the abolition of second features in order to save fuel, then suggested combining restrictions on imports with increased circulation of older films.[37] The Treasury countered that, rather than reducing the cake, the aim was to get a larger share for British producers. Sure that the demand by the masses for films would continue, they wanted to do nothing to damage the recovery of the British film industry. Besides, box-office receipts mopped up a lot of surplus purchasing power, from which the Treasury received a handsome rake-off.[38]

Murphy (1983) makes the intriguing suggestion that there was a third political factor at work: Palestine. Zionist groups in the United States were boycotting British products, including films. The possibility is that this formed a convenient excuse for the major companies, which numbered many supporters of Israel in their leadership, to underpromote and underbook British films. Certainly the receipts for British films in the United States were discouragingly low.

Thinking over the problems, Rowe-Dutton seems finally to have faced the implications of the backlog of imported but unreleased films, which he proposed to deal with by creating in effect a government import monopoly, permitting the licensing of imports through one company only.[39] Somervell quashed this by pointing out its incompatibility with the ITO principle of "national" treatment with respect to "internal" taxation.[40] It is interesting that it took a Board of Trade official to apprise a Treasury one of this, and also that the supposedly conservative mandarins of the Treasury produced a radically interventionist scheme.

The Lord President's Office, by contrast, commended Rowe-Dutton's idea as a good way to bring home to the Americans that dollar expenditures must be rational, even if the scheme were not actually implemented, in the end. Hollywood expected such a blow, and American awareness of Britain's problems made the time ripe.[41] This is one of the clearest indications that some officials foresaw the events that were to transpire and used draconian suggestions merely as a kind of bluff to impress their seriousness of purpose on U.S. film companies.

7.5. The decision is made

During April 1947 the scheme crystallized. By the fourteenth, Somervell conceded, despite his earlier warnings, that

unless all the American companies decide to act in concert and withhold a proportion of their films ... (a course which could hardly fail to do lasting harm to their goodwill[42]), the resultant shortage of films would certainly be embarrassing; but I hardly think it would bring us to our knees, and if we really cannot afford to pay for our "full ration" of celluloid ... the danger of shortage ought to be faced.[43]

There was, he granted, a risk of retaliation. A week later legal difficulties had not yet been overcome with respect to the definition of the films to which the scheme applied; fixing the responsibility for accounting; and ascertaining the amount of duty. A successful scheme could mean that quotas need not be renewed when the Cinematograph Films Act was renewed in 1948. Rowe-Dutton cautioned,

The "political" difficulties will arise from this barefaced attempt to confiscate a large part of the earnings of American film companies in the UK. We are in fact asking them to send in films and accept only (say) 50% of what they earn.[44]

On 28 April Rowe-Dutton reported that Eady now felt that the scheme for the duty should be drafted for the 1947 finance bill. In an eight-page note for the Chancellor, he reported that the Board of Trade did not think the United States would prohibit British films, because their earnings in the United States would help alleviate the dollar imbalance and reduce the duty on U.S. film shown in Britain. He also warned,

A more serious danger is that they might all combine and import no more films for exhibition in British cinemas. This, of course, would completely dislocate the circulation of films in this country. There should still be enough films (i.e., new British films and British and – probably – foreign re-issues) for most people still to be able to see, say, one picture a week...but...exhibitors would experience a sharp fall in their receipts, and if the boycott was prolonged, a large number of weaker exhibitors would almost certainly have to close down.... This...would almost certainly affect the takings of British films. Such a boycott would not be unprecedented, for there have recently been at least three or four cases when all the principal U.S. companies withheld their new films from particular European markets until the authorities of the countries concerned allowed the local distributors and exhibitors to offer more favorable terms than they had previously been willing to sanction. On the other hand, the companies could much less well afford to boycott our important market than, say, Holland or Scandinavia, and the Board of Trade are inclined to think that, rather than do that – especially at the present time, when they are believed already to be hard up for cash – the companies would still carry on and make the best of a bad job.[45]

All the ingredients for disaster show up in this note. Matters were not thought through. Assumptions about audience behavior were introduced a priori. The compliance of the American companies was predicted on the basis of speculation about their financial state without considering their financial resources, their sense of which cards they held, or consulting them as had been done in preparation for the 1927 and 1938 film acts and for the exchange agreements. Worst was the failure to think through the effect of interruptions to cash flow and of business uncertainty. British production was to continue and exhibition of reissues to flourish. There is no evidence that reissues were a substitute for the newest films. Reissues were primarily used as second features and for Sunday programs. It was hardly possible to extrapolate from this how well they would serve as substitutes for the latest Hollywood star vehicles.

On 5 May 1947 the principal civil servants involved met once more at the Treasury to give their considered judgment, which was in favor of the ad valorem duty. It was suggested that the Americans should be approached for discussion. Somervell saw "no useful purpose in talking to the Americans beforehand. The embassy in Washington would have to be notified just before the proposal was published."[46] So much for years of close consultation and cooperation between the Board of Trade and those good corporate citizens, the London representatives of the American companies.

An intriguing development on 20 May was that the Chancellor of Exchequer Dalton got cold feet. Rowe-Dutton wrote, "Although the Chancellor does not view our ideas with disfavour he feels he would not himself wish to take the initiative in the matter," so the president of the Board of Trade was asked to present the proposal to the cabinet.[47] Somervell responded, "If the Chancellor finds personal embarrassment in fathering the proposal himself (especially in view of what he said about films in the House, when he was referring to the Tobacco Duty) . . . "[48] Further tentativity was shown in that the cabinet agreed only to take powers, not yet to fix a rate of duty or to impose it.[49] This process began in the House of Commons in July, when Dalton added to his slogan "Food before Fags" the variant "Food before Films." Tom O'Brien,[50] of the National Association of Theatrical and Kine Employees (NATKE), asked if the Americans had been consulted, and Dalton replied somewhat loftily that that was not the way to govern. The slogan was further varied to "Food before Flicks."[51] A week later it had become "Grub before Grable." A split became evident among Labour M.P.'s, with O'Brien attacking the duty, as inviting retaliation, and it being defended by Benn Levy, M.P., an independent producer.[52] There were warnings of American reactions, and David Eccles suggested that Parliament was dealing with pinpricks when the overall dollar problem needed negotiating. Michael Foot[53] urged imposition of the duty at once. He castigated the "excessive tenderness of the Board of Trade towards the Rank film monopoly" and its efforts in the United States, suggesting that pursuit of that market would Americanize British films.[54]

7.6. The Americans learn of the duty

Eric Johnston, who had succeeded Hays as president of the MPPDA and had in 1945 split it into the Motion Picture Association of America (MPAA) and the Motion Picture Export Association (MPEA), planned a trip to London in May 1947. His business was the 1938 act, of which he wanted to secure an extension, rather than what was rumored as possible: a new act, which raised the quota to 50 percent. He proposed to offer a scheme that would improve the distribution of British pictures in the United States, as well as ways to foster coproduction in Britain.[55] The MPEA was assured by the Division of Commercial Policy in the State Department that the U.S. Ambassador to Britain, Lewis Douglas, had been instructed to begin informal discussion with appropriate British officials.[56] Before Johnston's trip began, the MPEA was informed by Fay Allport of the British enabling legislation permitting them to alter the tariff on motion pictures.[57] As the finance bill wended its way through Parliament, Don Bliss, the commercial attaché concerned with film matters at the U.S. Embassy in London, noted that the previous autumn the United Kingdom had pledged not to increase trade barriers until the trade negotiations in Geneva were concluded. Despite this undertaking, when tobacco was included on the U.S. request list for exempt items, the United Kingdom made "no offer" and did in fact increase the duty. The United Kingdom had also responded "no offer" on exposed film. He suspected that that tariff on films would also be raised.[58]

Allport reported to Johnston that he too expected the enabling powers to be used, because the £17 million remitted to the United States for films was becoming a national obsession.[59] Johnston went first to Geneva, where he met with the American trade negotiators. Article 15 of the draft charter for the trade agreement called for national treatment (i.e., treatment no less favorable than that accorded like products of national origin) in the application of all laws, regulations, and requirements. The United Kingdom demanded an exception for films. The United States reserved its position. The U.S. delegation felt that since the charter insisted on a nation's right to protect any industry, and since the film industry could be protected only by import duties or subsidies, the United States would have to agree to an exception to article 15 for movie quotas, which was the best way to protect films.[60] Bliss counseled Johnston to go to meet Dalton with an open mind to help and aim mainly at avoiding agreement to permanent measures for temporary problems.[61]

Johnston duly met the Chancellor on 23 July and suggested various alternatives.[62] The British Cinema Exhibitors Association (CEA) was against the duty and wrote to both the Chancellor and the Prime Minister predicting that the U.S. film industry would withdraw from the U.K. market.[63] J. Arthur Rank was also apprehensive. He had just returned from a visit to the United States, where he had endeavored to secure better American distribution for British pictures. Commenting to reporters, he expressed the view that an ad valorem duty might disincline the major American companies to push British films.[64]

Meantime, Johnston had consulted with his principals. He proposed maintaining the status quo on quotas and duties, blocking 25 percent of remittances for six months with a possible renewal for a further six. Blocked funds were to be spendable only in the United Kingdom, and all amounts were to be calculated at the exchange rate of the date of agreement. Allport thought Dalton might be under pressure to confiscate 50 percent or more and worried that the situation was deteriorating.

In the event, it was Cripps and not Dalton who met Allport on 5 August. Cripps put these points. The dollar shortage was acute; the Chancellor would announce new measures of dealing with it on the sixth at 3:30 P.M.

Johnston's blocking plan was out of consideration. Some ministers wanted to stop showing all foreign films immediately. Instead, there would be duties designed to reduce dollar outflow to one-quarter of the 1946–7 figures. This amount would be approximately equal to the earnings of British pictures in the United States. Any other plan must have the same result. Blocking was not the answer. In reply, Allport pointed to the stockpile of films; Cripps said that a special law could be passed to stop them circulating. Allport said the companies were not bound to bring in new films. Cripps said that that would not alter the situation. Allport said the duty would antagonize the United States, might lead to reprisals, and could be copied by other countries. Cripps repeated that the MPEA plan was no good: No repayment of blocked funds was possible before the American loan was repaid, and it was not due until the year 2000. Cripps said that if new films were delayed two or three months and a better plan came up, then . . . After the meeting Somervell told Allport privately that the government was under so much pressure politically that it had to act against films.[65]

7.7. Imposition of the duty

Under the enabling powers, a duty of 75 percent ad valorem was announced as "Additional Import Duties (No. 7) Order 1947." It was sometimes referred to as a 300-percent duty, but this was an artifact of its method of calculation. The value of the commodity for duty purposes was one-quarter of its gross value. The duty was then set at three times its dutiable value.

The situation remained an intricate one. In addition to the political and departmental complexities in the United Kingdom, the MPEA had five major companies to reconcile, and State Department officials were trying to act on three fronts at once. MPEA members quickly consulted and agreed to stop shipments to the United Kingdom. The State Department sought relief from the duty; to get films included in the GATT negotiations at Geneva; and more favorable treatment overall in the renewal of the Cinematograph Films Act. Don Bliss urged that the three issues be kept separate, not "linked."[66] There was also the acute dollar shortage created by convertibility. Making sterling convertible by 15 July had been a condition of the American loan, a condition the United Kingdom fulfilled:

The succeeding days brought a rude awakening. In the week beginning 20 July the dollar drain reached $106 million. The next week it was $126 million; the week after $127 million; in the week ending 16 August it was $183 million. In order to keep reserves steady at $2.5 billion, the Government had to make increasingly heavy drafts on the American Loan. By 16 August only $850 million remained. The loan at this rate would scarcely last another month (Gardner 1956, p. 312).

On 12 August Allen Dulles, of the firm of Sullivan Cromwell, the MPEA attorneys, initiated a series of attempts to lobby the State Department to send to Ambassador Douglas a brief arguing that the new duty was a violation of both the Double Taxation Agreement (part of the trade agreement of 1938) and the loan agreement of 1946. Robert Lovett of the State Department raised the question of the antitrust aspects of MPEA's boycott, expressed sympathy with the British plight, noted that other industries had also been hit, and concluded that some interdepartmental consideration was necessary. In a second discussion the same day Dulles allowed that some scheme might be devised that would use up blocked funds in the sterling area, so that the question of eventual conversion to dollars would not arise.[67]

As the British delegation to Washington to renegotiate convertibility was being assembled, the State Department asked the U.S. embassy in London whether the British delegation would include officials competent on film questions. The department did not want films on the agenda and inquired whether London agreed. The American industry was declared willing to work out a solution. The embassy replied that the U.K. delegation was briefed but not expert; while understanding the desire of the American industry to begin talks in Washington, the embassy suggested that, because of parallel quota matters, they should be concluded in London.[68]

In an 18 August summary of the situation, Bliss wrote that at the 23 July meeting between Bevin, Dalton, Douglas, and Johnston the British side had made it clear that a 75-percent reduction in remittances was necessary. The Americans countered with Johnston's offer of 25 percent blocked. The MPEA assumption was that the British were staking out a bargaining position, and they wanted to bring the matter up in intergovernmental financial discussions. Bliss wrote that the MPEA should deal directly with the British. Bliss's own view was that the duty was not a bargaining tactic but a panic measure popularly trading on anti-Americanism, anti-Hollywoodism, and the sense of crisis. Bliss wrote that Somervell privately agreed that the tax did not help the crisis, was a clumsy, long-term measure for a short-term problem, and would be replaced by something else.[69]

By 20 August the Justice Department had informed the State Department that the boycott did violate the antitrust laws, as would the British getting together with the MPEA. The Justice Department agreed, however, to go slow on taking action.[70] Soon after, British officials met in Washington with State and Commerce officials, and Eady met with Johnston and his advisers. Johnston's attempt to link a gentleman's agreement on sustaining the American companies' production in Britain to removal of the duty was resisted by Under Secretary Will Clayton.[71]

A month after the duty had been promulgated, then, the following was the disposition of forces. The British Treasury was convinced that the U.S. companies were vulnerable and that they would eventually rescind their boycott. The Board of Trade had muted its acute doubts, both about American resolve and about the effects on the British film industry of the boycott they had predicted, and made encouraging noises to the Treasury. In talking to American officials, however, they confessed to not liking the situation. Apart from the immediate effects, it possibly hampered their planning for films as a whole as they approached reconsideration of the 1938 act. On the other side of the Atlantic there was less urgency. Boycott, legal challenge, and diplomacy were simultaneously pursued. The MPEA sought constantly to prod the State Department into making a representation, possibly even delivering a note. But that department disliked any idea of linking the problem of the ad valorem duty to trade discussion in general. Furthermore, the Justice Department advised that they considered the boycott illegal.

The U.S. Treasury was asked to explore whether the duty violated treaties. They did not reply until 23 January 1948, when they opined it did not.[72] Records of twenty-three interdepartmental meetings can be found in the files, with MPAA officials and their lawyers often present. There was reluctance to take any hasty action, in view of the U.K. dollar problem. British ministers and officials maintained an adamant face of no concessions and committed almost nothing to paper in private indicating what they would settle for. They resolved to give the appearance of negotiating as long as the last installment of the loan had not been drawn, but that was all. A balanced appreciation of the situation was given by Bliss in a memorandum to the ambassador on 22 September 1947 (see Fig. 7.A in the appendix to this chapter). The U.K. duty was bilateralist, Bliss argued, reducing dollar outflow to the United Kingdom but also inflow from the United States. The Board of Trade had informed him that no consideration of film economics was involved in the duty, that they disliked it as awkward to administer while yet not stopping the outflow of dollars. However, Bliss reasoned, it would be politically difficult to change the duty at this point. The British government had to find a way to ensure that film earnings were surrendered or permanently neutralized. The duty's effects would be serious. Had the duty been operative in 1947, the worldwide profits of the seven major companies would have been only $10 million. To this prospect he added the note of the impending divorce of exhibition from distribution, as a result of federal antitrust action. Bliss advised the ambassador to tell Johnston to hunker down, for the time being, and, after the Marshall Plan had eased the dollar crisis, to insist on removal of the duty, even if this in effect meant that the U.S. Treasury was subsidizing film exports to the United Kingdom.[73]

7.8. Negotiations toward recision of the duty

The approach to a negotiated settlement of this dispute falls into two distinct phases. First officials tried to find a formula to rescind the duty while sustaining its principle – and this perhaps amounted to finding a formulation of what that principle was. Although the two sides rapidly approached such a point, the round of negotiations in December 1947 failed. There were only sporadic contacts in January. The second phase, which moved rapidly, commenced when the two governments took interest and pushed the parties together, and especially when the powerful British Foreign Secretary, Ernest Bevin, personally intervened.

August 1947–January 1948
During August and September the British government was getting conflicting advice. The CEA wrote directly to the Prime Minister, saying that the duty would extinguish the industry. The British Film Producers' Association (BFPA) dissociated themselves from the CEA and suggested that the members of the British group would step in and make up the lack of American films, although by 31 October they were becoming critical of the situation. The film unions were from the start highly critical of the duty and of the manner of its imposition, that is, without full consultation throughout the industry.[74] Meanwhile the Commonwealth Relations Office was confident that the American film industry was vulnerable; and Rowe-Dutton, at the Treasury, after a conversation with the president of the Federal Reserve Bank in New York, wrote that it made him "feel that we should harden our hearts when it comes to talking to the film companies."[75] There was a Commons debate in November, and Beverly Baxter, M.P., reminded the House how much Britain owed Hollywood from the war years. The political problem presented by these conflicting voices was compounded because others wanted even more drastic measures than the duty.[76]

Summarizing the situation once again in October, Bliss noted that pressure from American companies and British exhibitors was strong against his wait-and-see recommendation of the preceding month. Somervell informed him that the United Kingdom would be the greater loser in the long run and that the British and American industries should work out a solution, especially as American revenues might be on a downward slide and British revenues from the United States on the way up.[77] At another British interdepartmental meeting, Eady reiterated his opposition to blocked funds and said he was "not anxious to have very large sums of American money invested in film production in this country. The pressure of large amounts might inflate costs in the industry and press our British producers while destroying the national character of British films." In effect Eady's position was still to confiscate 50 percent of American film earnings: He would not have them blocked, he would not have them remitted, and he did not want them spent in the United Kingdom.[78]

On 7 November Allport met Eady, who affirmed his government's commitment to the duty. Allport said he convinced Eady that American film earnings were down and would now amount to $54 million if transferable, roughly one-third above the 1939 figure. Johnston's solution was a fixed sum freely transferable, plus whatever sum could be offset against British film earnings in the United States (an incentive to American companies to promote British films); the rest was to go into long-term sterling investments. Johnston refused to come over himself because the negotiations might fail.[79]

On the twenty-first the State Department sent a telegram to Ambassador Douglas authorizing him to convey to the British, when it was opportune, "earnest hope Dept. that problem ad valorem duty can be settled at an early date."[80]

In November Cripps had moved to the Exchequer, being replaced by thirty-one-year-old Harold Wilson as president of the Board of Trade.[81] This undoubtedly delayed further progress while both were being briefed. Eady opened the 17 December meeting by saying bluntly that previously suggested ideas were rejected. What the American film companies would be allowed to remit home was exactly what British films earned in dollars in the United States. Allport responded that he was leaving no room for discussion. Eady responded flexibly, but he reiterated that his real hope was to boost the dollar earnings of British films. Government policy was that imports must be matched by exports, and this policy would be maintained. (Tactlessly, Eady had formulated the principle of the duty as bilateralism. Such a formulation was hardly calculated to appease the Americans, whose dislike of bilateralism was no secret and was to be enshrined in GATT.) Allport pointed out the physical impossibility of 35–50 British films earning enough in the United States to offset the import of 350. Eady refused to look at the figures until the MPAA accepted the principle of the duty. Allport refused. No follow-up meeting was arranged.

In his memorandum reporting all this, Bliss commented that he thought Somervell and White at the Board of Trade were opposed to the duty and that it might have been imposed without consulting them (he was mistaken).

Also, it clearly has the approval of Sir Stafford Cripps, who regards it as only another case of austerity, fully justified in view of the exchange position...

We are now getting into a position where the personal dignity and prestige of Sir Stafford Cripps, as well as the British Government, are involved in a matter of principle. I think that Cripps is wrong in refusing to take into account the economics of the film trade and ignoring the principle established at Geneva. I doubt, however, that he will alter his view in the predictable future, and I am not even certain that amelioration of the dollar position through operation of the Marshall Plan will induce him to change his mind.[82]

Soon after the new year, the CEA met with Wilson to put a strong case for settlement. They pointed out that the supply of new films was almost exhausted, British production was uncertain, and that in three months there would only be reissues available. One of their most telling points was that no American imports would eventually mean no American money in British production. These points were conveyed to the Treasury, since the duty was their concern.[83] Harold Wilson was very much the energetic new boy, and he stuck to the official line on the duty – while preparing to set the quotas under the renewed Cinematograph Films Act as high as British producers could fill. But in view of the sudden settlement that followed, it is hard not to surmise that his own Board of Trade officials were trying to get the Treasury to back away from the duty.

January–March 1948

In a new-year review, Bliss noted that Allport was asking for official U.S. intervention: Even British officials were surprised that there had been none. The first response to Allport's request came from Ambassador Douglas, who was in Washington. On 2 February Douglas saw the British ambassador, Lord Inverchapel, and told him that he had had for some time the discretionary authority to raise the issue of the duty, had refrained from doing so, but now felt he must. He requested Inverchapel to receive Johnston and listen sympathetically. Douglas then instructed Waldemar J. Gallman, the chargé d'affaires in London, to raise the matter with Bevin in the following terms: The duty alienates goodwill; this could become permanent and express itself in hostility; Douglas wanted to discuss it with Bevin himself upon returning to London.[84] After seeing Johnston the British ambassador reported his understanding that Under Secretary Lovett and Ambassador Douglas did not want the matter to escalate to the level of intergovernmental discussion but rather to be settled. Johnston had warned that his "wildmen" colleagues wanted to mount an anti-British publicity campaign throughout the United States. President Truman was reported to have said that the duty could ruin the Havana Charter.[85] (Johnston and Allport left a sixteen-page memorandum with Inverchapel that he forwarded to London. The interstitial communications of British officialdom were such that it reached the Board of Trade only after the negotiations were completed.)

The second response was even higher up. In February Secretary of State George C. Marshall wrote to Douglas that he had talked to Frank McCarthy[86] and that although he did not know the merits of the case he thought the British duty arbitrary and unusual, and that Douglas should look into it in London.[87]

Despite such signs as a London *Daily Telegraph* editorial of 3 February that urged the government to settle the issue, the Foreign Office's request to the Treasury for a briefing for Bevin's meeting with Douglas called forth a hard line from Eady.[88]

Douglas met Bevin on 19 February and mentioned that the hostility of the film people might affect the passage of the Marshall Plan. In response Bevin arranged a secret meeting for Douglas with Chancellor of the Exchequer Cripps and Wilson. At this meeting Douglas was assured that the British were anxious to abandon the duty if a substitute could be found.

The Chancellor and the President of the Board of Trade then explained that one of our troubles had been the attitude of Mr. Johnston of the United States Film Industry, who had rather lectured us on this subject, and seemed to think that threats would induce us to remove the tax.[89]

Douglas, apparently sensing movement, cabled Johnston to come to London. On 2 March a decisive meeting was held, attended by Bevin, Cripps, Wilson, Eady, Woods, Johnston, Douglas, and Allen Dulles. "At the end of the meeting and the lunch which followed it, Bevin instructed Harold Wilson and Sir Wilfred Eady of the Treasury to meet with Johnston and Dulles with a determination to find a solution rather than a sceptical and negative approach."[90]

The same day Bevin received an impassioned letter from one of Labour's own M.P.s, Tom O'Brien, writing in his capacity as general secretary of NATKE, the film workers' union. He said that the film industry in Britain had never been at such a low ebb, with dismissals proceeding apace. He also argued that the public felt that they had had enough of austerity; to deprive them of the pleasure of cinemagoing was ill advised. His final argument was the general need for good Anglo–American relations.[91]

After Bevin's intervention and while Johnston was still in London, businesslike negotiations began. Allport sent Somervell a tentative outline of the arrangement the MPEA had in mind, thus indicating that Somervell's earlier rejection of consultation and Dalton's haughty view that that was not "the way to govern" had yielded to the fact that if the flow of films was to continue a scheme acceptable to the American companies must be found. There were twenty-seven points in Allport's memorandum, comprising a list of all the conceivable expenditures the American companies might want to make in the sterling area with their blocked funds. These consisted of either direct purchases or financial deals. The category of expenditure outside the film business was not separated, as it was to be in the final agreement. All normal business payments, from purchases of stories to executives' expenses and insurance, were included.[92]

A day later, on 5 February, an aide-memoire for the president of the Board of Trade on a possible settlement fixed on seven points. Of the U.S. companies' earnings in Britain, $12.5 million was to be convertible; $12 million was to be kept in the United Kingdom; and an unlimited amount could be converted against British films' earnings in the United States. If annual revenues were $50 million, this would give the United States half and the United Kingdom half. American companies were to resume normal film shipments, and any unremittable balance at the end of twelve months was to be ceded to the British government. While agreeing to a review after one year, the British could not foresee raising the amounts within five years.[93]

That day there appear to have been two meetings, one in which Johnston presented his ideas to a ministerial group and a working meeting with Wilson and his officials, Johnston bringing along Allen Dulles, J. Mulvey (of the Independents), Allport, O'Hara, and Bliss. The outline of a settlement was written up by the following day. Its main terms were that 25 percent of the average earnings of 1945–7 would be convertible – some $16 million – and this was to become a flat rate (raised to $17.5 million in the agreement). No ceiling on the amount of unremitted money spent in the sterling area would be imposed. No unspent balances would be ceded to the British government; rather, they were to be spent in permitted ways. In the agreement this became charities.

In the earlier meeting Johnston had stressed the American companies' willingness to produce films in Britain, provided they could keep the dollar earnings of such films. They also offered to push more British films in the United States; to make more of the United Kingdom as a tourist attraction (shades of the Canadian Cooperation Project); and even to set up a corporation to lend unspent remittances to other branches of commerce.[94]

Eady was not content and wrote to Sir John Woods that such measures as the transfer of Hollywood production to the United Kingdom or the buying of hotels were undesirable. He proposed that only $15 million be remittable and that $15 million remain in sterling, to be remitted against the earnings of British films in America; and the rest would go to the Treasury. Above all, he argued, the aim was to get the American companies to promote British films. Eady wrote this the very day the final details were being thrashed out. Not surprisingly, in a covering minute for Wilson, Somervell commented that Eady's suggestion ignored the American point of view.[95] Only strong State Department pressure transmitted through Bevin had made an agreement possible. In his minute of conversation with Johnston, Inverchapel had noted that direct pressure involving the European Recovery Program (ERP) had not been brought, but the suggestion of an anti-British publicity campaign had been taken as indirect pressure.[96]

A later incident was a test for the hypothesis that the settlement stemmed from Bevin's demand to clear away this minor irritation in Anglo–American relations so he could concentrate on ERP and European security. It was not long before Wilson proposed to raise substantially the quotas of the Cinematograph Films Act. This annoyed the Americans, and the assistant under secretary of state complained that the Foreign Office had not been informed, despite the delicacy of the situation with the ERP. At his suggestion Bevin signed a tough letter to Wilson in which he said that he would like to have been consulted and thought it unwise not to have consulted the Americans.

> This is a very delicate question in our relations with the United States.... With so much depending on the large questions on which we are in daily negotiation with the United States Government and, looking as we must do towards the development of our policy both in relation to security and to the European Recovery Programme, we need to take every care when dealing with less but highly explosive questions such as this.[97]

7.9. Conclusion and aftermath

Kenneth O. Morgan, a leading historian of the period, throws considerable light on the interdepartmental situation. He argues that the Overseas Department of the Treasury was inadequate and that Sir Wilfred Eady was out of his depth throughout the exchange and convertibility crisis. The Dalton Duty episode underlines this contention. As we have seen, Overseas Department officials were much given to speculating about American reactions and arguing about the strengths and weaknesses of the U.S. film industry and the possibilities for British films in the North American market.

Eady, in particular, pushed hard for his idea of absorbing American revenues by taxation and refused up to the very last to see the American point of view. Board of Trade officials sometimes concurred but mostly displayed a more down to earth appreciation of the genuine possibilities. Although both sets of officials were concerned with foreign relations, neither displayed much grasp. If anything, Board of Trade officials, used to working out matters in consultation with the Americans, showed more sensitivity, but not when they refused to stand up to the Treasury over acting first and informing afterward or when they let Wilson tell the cinema exhibitors to keep quiet about their difficulties for fear the American's hand would be strengthened. American officials were not badly informed. Indeed they stood in marked contrast to British officials, where diplomatic and analytic capabilities were concerned. Men of the caliber of Lewis Douglas, Eric Johnston, Fay Allport, Don Bliss, and Allen Dulles did their share of speculation about what the British were up to and how long they could hold out. But mainly they formulated aims based on economic and political reality, and this, naturally, gave them a better chance of success.

By March 1948 British film production was nearly at a halt, and American production in Britain was uncertain. Once the agreement was in place, millions of pounds were retained for spending in the United Kingdom. The result was a boom in American production in Britain.[98] The films produced in the following years testify to its effects, and some of the principal productions include

MGM: *Conspirator* (1949), *King Solomon's Mines* (1950), *The Miniver Story* (1950), *Quo Vadis* (1951), *Ivanhoe* (1952), *Time Bomb* (1952), *Mogambo* (1953)

Warner Bros.: *Under Capricorn* (1949), *The Hasty Heart* (1949), *Stage Fright* (1950), *Capt. Horatio Hornblower RN* (1951), *The Master of Ballantrae* (1953), *The Crimson Pirate* (1952)

Disney (for RKO): *Treasure Island* (1950), *The Story of Robin Hood and His Merrie Men* (1952), *The Sword and the Rose* (1952), *Rob Roy, the Highland Rogue* (1953)

Republic: *The Quiet Man* (1952)

Twentieth Century–Fox: *The Black Rose* (1950), *No Highway* (1951)

United Artists: *The African Queen* (1951), *The River* (1951), *Moulin Rouge* (1952), *Rough Shoot* (1952)

Selznick: *The Third Man* (1949)

The story of the duty and its withdrawal is a story of the British government coming to terms with cultural and commercial reality, a postwar process that covered many more important areas than film policy. At best the United Kingdom could afford a modest-sized domestic film industry that was dependent on substantial American support. At best a limited number of British prestige films could achieve limited American distribution. Only when the American industry developed severe structural problems did this change.

September 22, 1947

TO: The Ambassador

FROM: Don C. Bliss

SUBJECT: Film Financial Problem

In another memorandum I suggested the desirability
of a discussion with Eric Johnston during your visit to
Washington, and promised a statement for your use on
current aspects of the import duty on films. This is it.

Johnston replied to Clayton's letter of August 25
with a convincing explanation of the financial difficulties confronting the American film companies and stated
flatly that they did not intend to finance film production in UK from the 25% residue from the "Dalton duties",
nor did they intend to remit dollars for that purpose.
In a letter which Wilcox signed I told Johnston that we
would support that position and would undertake to negotiate an escape clause to the MPA commitment on film
production. We have now done this. At the same time I
pointed out that the American companies had other earnings in Britain, from films previously imported or which
they might produce here, and that these earnings might
be expected to continue "for a matter of months". (I
called attention to the weakness of a line of argument
which left these out of consideration and spoke only of
the 25% residue, especially when film imports have been
stopped and there is no such residue.) My thought was
that production might be financed from these "other
earnings" for a short period and argued that the companies might gamble on the possibility that we might
"between us" succeed, also "in a matter of months", in
arranging a satisfactory substitute for the import duty.
A telegram from Johnston to Wilcox in reply to this
reacted with enthusiasm to the idea that we had some
hope for the future, and that is why I feel that the
subject should be explored with Johnston while you are
in Washington.

So much for the background, and now we come to the
foreground, which does not present a pleasant aspect
just now, although I do have hopes for the future.

1. The problem is a dollar exchange problem, and
nothing else. It has nothing to do with film economics,
nor with the competitive aspects of the American film
trade in Great Britain. In dealing with dollar exchange
problems the technique favored by this Government is to
apply quantitative restrictions and to introduce domestic
rationing of limited available supplies. The economics
of the film trade are such that these standard techniques
are not applicable to film imports. The import duty
scheme introduced in August, therefore, was devised as
the nearest equivalent to a quantitative restriction,
and was announced as such - as intended to reduce the
burden of dollar remittances to 25% of its former level.
No attempt has been made to impose rationing on films,
and Board of Trade officials state that this is adminis-
tratively impracticable; otherwise they would be doing

that

Figure 7.A. Don C. Bliss to Ambassador Lewis Douglas, "Film Financial Problem,"
22 September 1947. (Washington National Records Center, Suitland, MD, RG 84,
Foreign Service Posts of the Department of State, London Embassy. Document 840.4
Films 9/22.)

that also. Furthermore, the figure of 25% was calculated to release film dollars to an extent approximating
the earnings of British films in the US. In other words,
bilateralism in its most vicious form. At Geneva and
elsewhere the US has consistently attacked quantitative
restrictions and bilateralism, and will surely continue
to do so in the future. In terms of basic economic policy,
we are in sharp disagreement with the UK on its approach
to the film remittance problem.

2. At Geneva, also, in developing the theory of
film economics which resulted in the concept of the screen
quota as expressed in Article 19 of the draft charter, our
main argument was that import duties represent an unsuitable device for the protection of national film industries.
Board of Trade officials responsible for films concur in
this view. Even though the new British import duty is not
a protective measure, it nevertheless constitutes a bad
example which other nations may take up for protective
reasons, to the disadvantage of both US and UK film exports. We must maintain consistently that the device of
import duties should not be applied to film imports, and
I am currently overlooking no opportunity to emphasize
that point in the Board of Trade.

3. The film import duty legislation bears all the
earmarks of a hastily-conceived measure, introduced in
an atmosphere of financial panic, partly for financial
and partly for political reasons. I understand from
Rupert Somervell (British Board of Trade) that literally
no consideration was given to film economics, and there
was no weighing of the inevitable consequences. Worst
of all, from the viewpoint of the civil servants, is the
fact that the measure goes into the situation backward.
Instead of operating, as an emergency measure should
operate, to effect an immediate stoppage of the dollar
outflow, this one postpones any effective check on remittances for as long as the American companies refuse
to ship films to Britain and can deliver new films from
their existing stocks. In time, of course, the supply of
new films will be exhausted, the returns from re-issues
will tend to shrink, and the volume of remittances will
dwindle. In the meantime there is no check on remittances,
although Cripps did threaten Allport, in his interview of
August 5, with "other measures", such as the cancellation
of existing registrations. However, there is no indication that such a drastic measure is in the wind, and I
should judge that it will not materialize in the present
situation of serious US efforts to meet Britain's dollar
crisis through the Marshall Plan.

4. Taking into account all the circumstances I am
not pessimistic as to the possibility of eventually in-
ducing the UK Government to abandon its import duty
scheme. Both Dalton and Cripps have intimated that they
are ready to consider alternative measures which would
have "the same effect". The civil servants in the Board
of Trade dislike the measure, regard it as awkward and

difficult

Figure 7.A. (*cont.*)

Appendix: "Film Financial Problem"

On September 1947, Don C. Bliss, the official in charge of film matters at
the U.S. embassy in London, sends U.S. Ambassador Lewis Douglas a robust
analysis of the situation during the boycott and counsels firmness in handling
the British. This document, entitled "Film Financial Problem," is reproduced
as Figure 7.A.

-3-

difficult to administer, and agree with the theoretical
argument against it in terms of film economics. However, they have intimated to me that the Government
would find it difficult to abandon the import duty after
all the publicity it received, and suggest that it would
have to be replaced by something equally spectacular,
simply for political reasons. As a current approach
they seem to be thinking along the line of a possible
downward revision of the rate, to a point where American
films could come in. They parrot the Cripps-Dalton view
that no film measure must result in the creation of deferred obligations and must require the "outright surrender" or permanent sterilization of any film earnings not
remitted in dollars. Against this line of thought I have
always argued strongly that the import duty measure should
be done away with altogether, and import duties never used
against films except for reasonable revenue purposes.

        5. The earnings of American film companies in the
UK, exceeding $60,000,000 annually at present, are of
great importance to them. Current action by the Department of Justice before the Supreme Court may result in
divorcing film production and exhibition in the US, and
the companies face heavy reductions in revenues if this
happens. According to a recent message from Johnston,
the Treasury and the State Departments recently made a
study for him which indicates that if the seven major
film companies had operated through 1947 under the terms
of the British import duty their net profits from world
production and distribution of American films after
corporate taxes would have totalled less than $10,000,000.
Note that this includes their earnings in the United States
as well as abroad. Actually, of course, their current
earnings are much greater, since they still include returns from exhibition, and the figures may be otherwise
specious. Nevertheless the result was a great shock to
Eric Johnston, and it certainly underlines heavily the
importance of their British operations to the American
film companies.

        6. From the British viewpoint, of course, they
simply cannot afford to remit $60,000,000 annually to the
US against films, and they will not be able to do so
until their economic strength is restored. Obviously the
American companies could not hold out until that development is realized - it will surely be a matter of years.
To my mind the only way out of this impasse is through
the hope extended by the Marshall Plan. In a matter of
months, we can hope, the situation will have clarified
to a point where it will be obvious that the British
dollar crisis has been surmounted. Then, and not until
then, can we discuss seriously the measures which should
replace the present import duty on films. My own feeling is that we should insist on a return to the status
quo ante in the light of US financial aid to Britain.
That will mean, of course, that the US Treasury will in
a measure be subsidizing the exports of films to the UK,
but that is exactly what has been going on for more than
a year and the same concept is applicable more or less
directly to all American exports to Great Britain. The

                                              American

Figure 7.A. (cont.)

-4-

American film companies would be well advised, if you can
give Johnston any hope that the Marshall Plan will be
realized, to stand pat on their present position and keep
quiet.' There is, of course, the question of whether
Marshall plan aid should be made the basis for continued
imports of such a product as films. It can be argued
with some cogency, however, that from the standpoint of
morale films are not as unessential as they might on first
thought seem.

7. When the situation breaks we should throw everything we have into a drive to get the import duty off the
books and to keep it off. Nor should we tolerate any
proposals to block sterling. I agree completely with
Dalton and Cripps on the undesirability of that. Legitimate protection of British film production is already
taken care of in the ITO Charter. The American companies
can be counted on to produce their share of films in the
United Kingdon. There is no reason why the British film
industry could not develop further, earn appreciable sums
of, dollars from exports, and go a long way toward covering the dollar drain from American films shown in UK.

DCB:ec

Figure 7.A. (*cont.*)

Notes

1 London, HMSO, May 1948, Cmd. 7421.

2 There is no mention whatsoever of the episode in the works of important historians of the period such as Gardner (1956), Bullock (1983), Milward (1984) or in the published memoirs of Clement Attlee, Dean Acheson, Hugh Dalton, or Will Hays. Morgan (1984) garbles it somewhat.

3 Although nicknamed "Dalton Duty," the duty might more appropriately be put to the credit (or otherwise) of Sir Wilfred Eady. The 1935 Joint Report (see §7.4 had concluded that the Ottawa suggestion of an ad valorem duty on films was unworkable because of the difficulty of setting a value on them. But Ernest Rowe-Dutton of the Treasury said that when Eady was at Customs in 1941 he had thought such a duty could be made to work. Rowe-Dutton to Sir Archibald Carter, 12 December 1945, PRO, BT 64 204.

4 In its 1915 decision refusing to extend to films the protections for free speech guaranteed by the First Amendment, the U.S. Supreme Court had held that "it cannot be put out of view that the exhibition of motion pictures is a business pure and simple, originated and conducted for profit, like other spectacles, not to be regarded, nor intended to be regarded by the Ohio constitution . . . as part of the press of the country or as organs of public opinion." (1915) 236 US 230, 244.

5 The result of Rank's 1945 trip to the United States "was to make him optimistic concerning the future; by the end of 1946, he said, his films would be making $15 million a year in America. . . . Before long, he said, Britain would be turning out pictures that would make more money in the American market than Hollywood" (Wood 1952, p. 218).

6 This and similar points are stressed by Murphy in his survey article (1983). See also Murphy (1989, chaps. 4, 11).

7 The report, of which I have been unable to locate a copy, owing to the thin (and thinned) holdings of Inland Revenue and Customs papers at the Public Record Office, was apparently a response to the suggestion for such a tax made at the Imperial Economic Conference of 1932 by a subcommittee (on film and radio) of the committee on Methods of Economic Cooperation, quoted in §3.2.

8 Minutes of meeting, 20 May 1944, PRO, BT 64 204. (Sir) Crawford Wilfred Griffin Eady (1890–1962), educated at Clifton School and Jesus College, Cambridge; Ministry of Labour (1917–38); Deputy Under Secretary, Home Office (1938); Chairman, Board of Customs and Excise (1940); Second Secretary, Treasury (1942–52).

9 Gaitskell memo of 20 May 1944, ibid.

10 Edward Hugh John Neale Dalton (1887–1967), educated at Eton and Cambridge; University lecturer; barrister; Labour M.P. for Bishop Auckland (1935–59); Chancellor of the Exchequer (1945–7); later held other ministerial posts.

11 Gaitskell memo of 20 May 1944, PRO, BT 64 204.

12 Whether this was shrewd anticipation or picking up on informal hints dropped by the Americans is hard to tell. Three years later British officials noted that Eric Johnston, Will Hays's successor, had suggested in speeches that the U.S. retaliate against U.K. shipping, insurance, and rubber to help dissuade the British government from discriminating against American films. See notes for Parliamentary Question dated 6 February 1947, PRO, BT 11 3687.

13 (Sir) Ernest Rowe-Dutton (1891–1965), entered civil service (1914); Treasury (1919); Third Secretary (1947): retired 1957.

14 Rowe-Dutton to Somervell, 6 November 1944, PRO, BT 64 204.

15 Beddington-Behrens to Somervell, 31 [sic] November [1944?], ibid.

16 Gaitskell to Rowe-Dutton, 30 March 1945, ibid.

17 Rowe-Dutton to White, 23 and 27 August 1945, PRO, BT 64 204.

18 White to Rowe-Dutton, 27 August 1945, ibid.

19 White to Cockfield, 7 September 1945, ibid.

20 Dickinson slightly oversimplifies the situation, as follows: "The British government was completely unprepared for the boycott. The civil servants who, during the war, had warned that government interference with the film trade might well provoke such a response, in 1947 advised that a boycott was unlikely. Because of the laissez-faire approach of the previous two years, the government lacked the administrative machinery to direct the industry. Faced with the fact of the boycott, the Board of Trade at last began to take steps to set up a film bank and in the meantime appealed to producers to use their resources to boost the output of British films" (1983, p. 85). Some foresaw the boycott, others shut their eyes to the possibility. The point about the absence of machinery is a valid one. It presupposes, however, that the duty was an act of film policy, when it was not.

21 Eady to Woods, 27 September 1945, PRO, BT 64 204.

22 The intricacies of negotiating and then legislating the loan are covered in Gardner 1956.

23 Eady to Dalton, 29 November 1945, PRO, BT 64 204.

24 Rowe-Dutton to Somervell, 7 February 1946, ibid.

25 Clayton to Nelson, 14 November 1946, NA, RG 59 841.4061 MP / 11–146, United Kingdom.

26 Paper by E. J. Kahn, 18 July 1946, PRO, T 231 446.

27 White minute of 2 October 1946, PRO, BT 11 3687.

28 Rowe-Dutton to Somervell, 18 July 1946, PRO, T 231 446.

29 White to Rowe-Dutton, 30 August 1946, ibid.

30 See Street 1985 and Chapter 5 of the present volume.

31 Rowe-Dutton to White, 2 September 1946, and draft of 4 September 1946, PRO, T 231 446.

32 Somervell memo, 4 September 1946, PRO, BT 64 204.

33 Holmes to Rowe-Dutton, 9 September 1946, ibid.

34 Holmes to Rowe-Dutton, 12 September 1946, ibid.

35 Cripps to Attlee, 20 November 1946, ibid.

36 *Parliamentary Debates (Commons)*, 10 March 1947, vol. 434, col. 976.

37 Nicholson to Clarke, 19 February 1947, PRO, BT 64 2283.

38 Rowe-Dutton to Nicholson, 24 February 1947, ibid.

39 Rowe-Dutton to Somervell, 4 March 1947, ibid. An unsigned comment on this letter said, "I should certainly think an *ad valorem* duty would annoy the Americans less than the Miranda suggestion of a monopoly company to take a rake-off."

40 Somervell memo, 18 March 1947, ibid.

41 Nicholson to Rowe-Dutton, 7 March 1947, ibid.

42 How did he manage to draw such a conclusion? Such minor matters are usually quickly forgotten, as was this one.

43 Somervell to Rowe-Dutton, 14 April 1947, PRO, BT 64 2283.

44 Note by Rowe-Dutton, 21 April 1947, ibid.

45 Rowe-Dutton draft note for the chancellor, 28 April 1947, ibid.

46 Minutes of meeting, 5 May 1947, ibid.

47 Rowe-Dutton to Somervell, 20 May 1947, ibid.

48 Somervell to Rowe-Dutton, 23 May 1947, ibid.

49 Dalton to Cripps, 18 June 1947, ibid.

50 (Sir) Tom O'Brien (1900–70), General secretary, NATKE (1932–70); Labour M.P. for Nottingham (1945–50).

51 *Parliamentary Debates (Commons)*, 2 July 1947, vol. 439, cols. 1448ff.

52 Benn Wolfe Levy (1900–73), educated at Repton and Oxford; Dramatist; Labour M.P. for Eton and Slough (1945–50).

53 Michael Foot (b. 1913), educated at Wadham College, Oxford; journalist and writer; Labour M.P. for Plymouth (1945–55), Welsh seats (1960 to date). Leader of Labour Party (1980–3); married to documentary film director Jill Craigie.

54 *Parliamentary Debates (Commons)*, 9 July 1947, vol. 439, cols. 2282ff. Foot had articulated a Catch–22 that is to be found elsewhere, namely, that getting British films into the international marketplace might internationalize (read "Americanize") them, thus vacating the principal cultural argument for protection.

55 Somervell argued, against this offer, that no fixed sum was guaranteed and that it increased the structural dependency of the British industry on the American. "There is some risk that reliance on the good will of the American companies might lead to British films being made with both eyes on the American market and losing their distinctive characteristics." Undated note by Somervell, PRO, BT 11 3687.

56 State Department to Douglas, 12 May 1947, NA, RG 59 841.4061 MP / 5–1247.

57 Canty to MPEA, 24 June 1947, ibid.

58 Bliss to Ambassador, 25 June 1947, WNRC, RG 84 840.6 Films (Confidential File).

59 Allport to Johnston, 10 July 1947, ibid.

60 Ibid.

61 Bliss to Ambassador, 24 July 1947, ibid.

62 British sources report him meeting the Chancellor (Rowe-Dutton to Taylor, 28 July 1947, PRO, BT 64 2283); U.S. sources report him also meeting the Foreign Secretary and the president of the Board of Trade (Bartlett to State Department, 13 August 1947, NA, RG 59 841.4061 MP / 8–1347).

63 CEA to Cripps, 19 July 1947 and 12 August 1947, PRO, BT 64 2283.

64 *Financial Times*, 26 July 1947. See also Wood 1952, p. 225. Some of the intricacies of Rank's position are outlined in Murphy 1983.

65 Report of Allport's talk with Sir Stafford Cripps, 5 August 1947, WNRC, RG 84 840.1–841.3 1947 (Confidential File).

66 Allport to Douglas, 1 August 1947, WNRC, RG 84 840.6 Films.

67 Memorandum of conversation, 12 August 1947, NA, RG 59 841.4061 MP / 8–1247.

68 State Department to London Embassy, 14 August 1947, and reply 15 August 1947, ibid.

69 Bliss to Harry Hawkins, 18 August 1947, WNRC, RG 84 840.6 1947 (Confidential File).

70 Bonesteel to Lovett, 20 August 1947, NA, RG 59 841.4061 MP / 8–2047.

71 Memoranda of conversation, 23 and 26 August 1947, ibid.

72 Lovett formally requested Treasury opinion on whether the duty violated the Double Taxation Convention of 1945 on 8 October. The original finding was that

it did not, but Treasury's legal department refused to initial a draft letter to that effect as it foreclosed the Department of State from arguing that the duty was a contravention of the *intent* of the Double Taxation Convention. "There is substantial force to an argument that the effect and purpose of the duty is to do indirectly something which the British Government, because of the convention, could not do directly." It took two further months of discussion before the original finding was confirmed in a formal letter to Marshall. See NA, RG 56 (Records of the Department of the Treasury, Office of the Secretary, General Correspondence), Great Britain, Tax on Motion Picture Films 1947.

73 Bliss to Ambassador, 22 September 1947, WNRC, RG 84 840.6 Films.

74 See the speech of Tom O'Brien, of the NATKE union, *Parliamentary Debates (Commons)*, 9 July 1947, vol. 439, cols. 2289ff.

75 Rowe-Dutton to Eady, 20 September, 1947, PRO, BT 64 2283.

76 See the remarks of Michael Foot and Mr. Scollan, *Parliamentary Debates (Commons)*, 9 July 1947, vol. 439, cols. 2300ff. and 2314.

77 Bliss memo for file, 13 October 1947, WNRC RG 84 840.1–841.3 1947 (Confidential File).

78 Minutes of meeting, 4 November 1947, PRO, BT 64 2283.

79 Bliss to State Department, 12 November 1947: "Eady stated that it is the 'considered decision' of the Government that this type of duty must remain in effect, and he is authorised to discuss only a possible revision of duty rates. (The principle involved is the Government's intention to absorb in taxation and thus permanently sterilize a fraction of film-earnings.) Allport informed him flatly, on the other hand, that no solution of the film problem would be acceptable to American interests which included maintenance of the ad valorem duty. . . . The imposition of the duty runs directly counter to the principles established at Geneva for the control of the motion picture trade through the use of permissible screen quotas." NA, RG 59 841.4061 MP / 11–1247 (Confidential File).

80 Lovett to Douglas, 21 November 1947, ibid.

81 Harold Wilson (b. 1916), Lord Wilson of Rievaulx (1983); educated at grammar school and Oxford; economics lecturer; Labour M.P. for Ormskirk, then Huyton (1945–83); many ministerial posts, including Prime Minister (1964–70, 1974–6).

82 Bliss to State Department, 23 December 1947, NA, RG 59 841.4061 MP / 12–2347.

83 Minutes of meeting, 7 January 1948, PRO, BT 64 2283.

84 Telegrams from State Department to London Embassy, 2 and 4 February 1948, WNRC, RG 84 840.6 Films.

85 Inverchapel to Secretary of State, 24 February 1948, and attached minute of meeting, 10 February 1948, PRO, FO 371 69014.

86 Frank McCarthy (b. 1912), spotted by Gen. George C. Marshall while still at the Virginia Military Institute; military instructor; press agent for the George Abbott agency (1935–9); recalled to active duty (1940); military secretary to Marshall (1941); secretary to the General Staff (January 1944); at war's end, became Assistant Secretary of State, but soon left to become Paris representative of the MPAA (1946–9); later an executive and producer at 20th C.–Fox (1949–62, 1965–72). Films include *Decision before Dawn* (1951), *A Guide for the Married Man* (1967), *Patton* (1970), and *MacArthur* (1977).

87 Marshall to Douglas, 11 February 1948, WNRC, RG 84 840.6 Films.

88 Minute by K. R. C. Pridham, 11 February 1948, PRO, FO 371 69014.
89 Bevin to Inverchapel, 20 February 1948, ibid.
90 Douglas to Lovett, 2 March 1948, NA, RG 59 841.4061 MP / 3–248.
91 O'Brien to Bevin, 2 March 1948, PRO, FO 371 69014.
92 Allport to Somervell, 4 March 1948, PRO, BT 64 2370.
93 Allport to Somervell, 5 March 1948, ibid.
94 Ibid.
95 Eady to Woods, 6 March 1948, PRO, BT 64 2370.
96 Inverchapel to Secretary of State, 24 February 1948, and attachments, PRO, FO 371 69014.
97 Bevin to Wilson, 2 July 1948, ibid. Wilson's reply of 8 July 1948 stiffly reminded Bevin of Wilson's statutory duty and, although he characterized American reaction as "a piece of gratuitous impertinence," Wilson offered to instruct his officials "to inform yours of any major change in this field so that they can where necessary inform (as distinct from consult) the U.S. Embassy of what we have decided and why we have reached our decisions."
98 Although there was some delay in releasing the full text of the agreement, Woodrow Wyatt informed the House of Commons that one film trade paper said twenty-three films were planned at a cost of $30 million. He was alarmed, believing that eight films per year would be quite enough. See *Parliamentary Debates (Commons)*, 30 April 1948, vol. 450, col. 863.

CHAPTER 8

Postwar measures: The boycott and its
aftermath, 1945–1950

8.1. Fond hopes

The historians Dickinson and Street (1985), write:

in the last years [of the post-war Labour government] – when, with Stafford Cripps
as Chancellor and Harold Wilson as President of the Board of Trade, it seems that
the politicians were moving towards a more determined policy of intervention –
there is evidence that their intentions were undermined by the civil servants.

The influence of the Board of Trade would, of course, have been very much
reduced if the government had taken the decision to treat the cinema more as an
aspect of culture and less as a branch of commerce. There was sufficient support
for such a decision outside the trade for it to be a realistic option.

Dickinson and Street take a standard view of the government during this
period as suffering from a failure of cultural nerve.

In my view the evidence favors explaining events of this period in Britain
as the result of a combination of ineptitude and inability to face the facts.
This is not at all inconsistent with the received view, but its emphasis is
different. The "facts" include the commercial rather than cultural nature
of the film industry and the impracticality of taxpayer financing of films for
the British audience on an adequate scale, not to speak of the scale dictated
by the ambition to make films that would sell internationally (i.e., in the
United States and Canada). Rather than a choice between commerce and
culture, there was only a choice between mass culture and elite culture.
France opted for a combination, subsidizing some films of broad appeal
(such as those starring Fernandel or Louis de Funès) and others aspiring to
cinematic art (such as the works by Clair, Cocteau, and Renoir). The former
aimed for domestic distribution, seizing opportunities for export as they
presented themselves (the Fernandel / Don Camillo series was coproduced
with Italian partners); the latter achieved overseas distribution on what
came to be called the "art-house" circuit, cinemas that showed films with
artistic pretensions. Italy had a similar policy. When, in the course of churn-
ing out their popular product for the domestic market, these countries came

across something that would sell well abroad (such as a film with racy content or featuring an emerging star), these were dubbed and sold to specialist distributors. No attempt was made to match Hollywood in scale and cost nor to tailor either mass appeal or art films for the North American market.[1]

The British, by contrast, continued to toy with the idea of becoming serious rivals to Hollywood, merely because the wherewithal could from time to time be raised to mount a production on a scale and to a level of professionalism that simulated Hollywood. Despite the clearly entrenched nature of the American motion picture industry in its domestic market; despite imperfect grasp of what North American audiences favored;[2] despite lack of stars known in North America; despite limited resources and an economic regime of austerity; despite all this, the dream remained alive. Millions were invested and lost in films some of which were culturally commendable, but none of which realized the hope of a permanent and assured position in the North American mass market. Whether or not there was what Dickinson and Street term "sufficient support" for a decision to treat films as culture is a moot point. The very concept of "culture" (meaning "the arts") was not one that British ruling elites at that time – Labour, Liberal, or Conservative – were accustomed to using at all, still less extending to films. The French used it more and did extend it to films, but that was not an argument calculated to cut any ice with British ruling circles or public opinion. Scottish lobbyists such as John Grierson and Lord Reith, who advocated an enhanced public service role for the film industry, did not make use of the concept.

My view inverts Dickinson and Street: British governments did *talk* culture but, despite that cultural rhetoric, consistently treated the film industry as an industry. They utilized cultural camouflage when extending protection to that industry, not because of the cultural value of film but in the hope of gaining commercial advantage for the pressure group of British producers and their backers and, indirectly, for the country as a whole, if they could penetrate the American market. The only noneconomic considerations were political, as we have seen. There was no change of direction under Cripps and Wilson; rather, more of the same, which, as Dickinson and Street correctly note, had bipartisan support. Hence the authors' hint of a civil service conspiracy to subvert Labour measures is questionable. They allude to "evidence" but do not cite it. That trade union proposals for the industry were brushed aside by the government is explicable without conspiracy. These proposals were self-serving (never addressing the problems of cost and efficiency), radically utopian, and expensive. The criticisms of interventionist schemes articulated by Hugh Gaitskell when he worked as a civil servant at the Board of Trade, or by Rupert Somervell, assistant secretary at the board, stand as valid on their own merits and do not need political explanation. My reading of the evidence, as discussed in chapter 6, is that so far as embracing radical or even draconian measures are concerned, there was plenty of support within the civil service, even in the supposedly arch-conservative department of the Treasury.

Dickinson and Street give evidential weight to proposals of trade unions and of committed communists (Ralph Bond, Frederic Mullally) without historical warrant. They criticize civil servants for proindustry bias and politicians such as Dalton, Cripps, and Wilson for being insufficiently socialist. Their approach is continuous with the "film culture" (as defined by Stead) of the period they cover. They intimate that real socialists would have nationalized the film industry. Dickinson and Street overlook the grave difficulties presented by any such move politically and internationally. The endless crises and ineptitude of the British film industry did not argue in favor of nationalization. However, one of the things that Clement Attlee's first administration did in fact do was to nationalize industries that were failing and in decline. This set back the structural readjustments of the British economy necessary to stay competitive. Nostalgic longing for more such nationalization is odd in a book published in 1985. Dickinson and Street themselves notice that, just as nationalization became an option (at the end of the 1940s), the film industry was about to decline, restructure, and yield its central position in mass entertainment to television. That process was painful, but at least most of the costs were born by private industry and capital, jobs were not endlessly featherbedded and protected, and tax-payer's money was not consumed trying to stave off the inevitable.

They also overlook relevant political evidence. Gaitskell, when he was a Board of Trade civil servant, suggested that Parliament would not accept nationalization, and his colleague A. G. White pointed out that the reason was the entertainment and propaganda potential of the film industry. Our close reading of the debates of 1927 and 1938 makes it clear that M.P.'s were highly suspicious of government control of the media of communication – a suspicion reluctantly suspended for the duration of the war. Nationalization of the film industry was not an agreed objective of the Labour Party, some of whose M.P.'s had opposed the Cinematographic Films Act. There is ample evidence that nationalization would not have passed the House of Commons, despite the large Labour majority. The film industry was not the coal, railway, or electricity industry – a commanding height of the economy. The bitter struggles over the acts of 1927 and 1938 in committee and in the House of Lords, and the concessions that the Conservative and National governments had to make, give credence to the judgment of officials, and of Dalton, Cripps, and Wilson, that nationalization was not contemplated.

8.2. The shape of British strategy

During and immediately after World War II, British export strategy for films was seriously disrupted by the acute shortage of dollars, needed during the war to pay for war material and after the war to pay for reconstruction.

The Anglo–American agreements between 1939 and 1942 that regulated dollar exchange for films had interfered with the fulfillment of the quotas of the 1938 Cinematograph Films Act. In the early part of the war it was an unrealistic policy to press the Americans to film in Britain itself, where half the studios were requisitioned and others were bombed out. After the war the dollar shortage continued and in some ways worsened, complicating thinking, especially in Whitehall, about the position of the British film industry at home and abroad. The 1927 and 1938 act, credited with saving the British film industry from extinction, was due for renewal in 1948. Higher quotas for British films were being bruited. However, because of the British public's well-entrenched taste for films made on the American scale, it was assumed that British films would have to compete directly. Thus, even apart from export ambition, British films would be expensive to produce. It followed that either they had to be exported – to recoup those costs – or sources of finance had to be found that could sustain steady, and possibly large, losses.

In the euphoric atmosphere created by the wartime alliance, the view had gained currency that there was a market in the United States for British films, provided the American distribution companies were cooperative. The strategy that emerged for pursuing that market was one of coproduction and coownership between British and American companies, arrangements that steered the films of the partners into each other's cinemas. Korda and Rank had both engineered American deals, and they were followed by the Associated British Picture Corporation (ABPC). Two obvious questions arose: What sort of films should the British make for export? And, how should those films be handled in the U.S. market? From these two derived a third question: What expectations were realistic?

Between 1944 and 1948, the strategy adopted was nicknamed "the prestige experiment" (*The British Film Industry* 1952, p. 96). "Prestige" films drew on British literary and theatrical classics and skills. General distribution of them turned out not to work in the United States; only showcasing and selective distribution would work. However, these films cost so much to produce that even healthy earnings by this latter method were insufficient, and flops (by either method) were disastrous. When the financial resources of Rank and British Lion proved unable to sustain their losses, the strategy changed. After 1948, as indicated at the end of Chapter 7, the retention of a large amount of film earnings in Britain in sterling gave the American film industry a strong incentive to make films there and British firms an incentive to cooperate with them and share in their success. The development was not immediate, for at the end of 1948 the British film production industry was once again in crisis and became the subject of an adjournment debate in Parliament.[3] But eventually there was a surge of American production in Britain as part of a postwar pattern of American film companies engaging in filmmaking all over Europe, especially in Britain, France, Italy, and, later, Spain.

The prestige experiment and the coproduction experiment were not explicitly formulated strategies on the part either of the British film industry or the British government. The Cinematograph Films Acts had aimed to protect British production from extinction by guaranteeing it a modest market share. Those acts had not laid down any other policy objectives for the British film industry with regard to the kind of films made, level of expenditure upon them, or the pursuit of exports. These were properly seen as concerns of the film trade, advised and guided by the Board of Trade. However the Board of Trade did not set any policy objectives, nor did the Cinematograph Films Council, and the trade organizations were split in multiple directions between exhibitors, producers, American renters, British renters, and trade unions. When the unions or the trade met in their councils, steering-policy agreements did not emerge, as the Board of Trade repeatedly found when undertaking consultations regarding reports or proposals. It might be said that the 1927 and 1938 acts embodied policy, or machinery for policy, at least domestically. Where they singularly failed, and where the machinery of the Board of Trade and the Cinematograph Films Council failed, was in formulating an economic foreign policy. Yet international trade was implicated in domestic film decisions, and exports had considerable impact upon profitability. To have a domestic films policy without a foreign one was to ignore vital variables in the policy equation.

So to describe the prestige experiment as a strategy is greatly to oversimplify, implying coherence and forethought where there may well have been none. Another way of describing the situation would be to say that 1945–50 saw in Britain a search for a film industry policy and the failure to come up with one, either by the industry or by the government, and, indeed, little evidence of the analytic thought that preparation of such a policy would require.

8.3. GATT and the 1948 act

As far as films were concerned, the American aim in the General Agreement on Tariffs and Trade (GATT) negotiations was to get countries to agree to remove all restrictions on free circulation. European countries short of dollar credits and aspiring to some film industry of their own were not greatly enamored of this American aim. Britain in particular was clear about one thing, as we have seen: that the protections afforded by the 1938 act would have to be continued indefinitely if British film production was to have any hope of surviving. Hence the aim was to except films from the general trade liberalization to the extent necessary to make British legislation immune to GATT challenge.[4] Film quotas were the only case of U.K. legislation inconsistent with the proposed agreement. Tactically the United Kingdom did not want to ask for films to be treated as an exceptional trade good, fearing that other countries would offer other goods as candidates for similar exceptional treatment; they feared to make a general exemption for film quotas lest that encourage other countries to put quotas in place that would be a bar to British films; and they hesitated to ask for exemption of present legislation, since that would tie hands as far as higher quotas went. Their best bet, it was thought, was to get films left out of GATT altogether.[5] When the Americans refused to go along with this, a series of negotiations took place, primarily in Geneva, with the Americans accepting British language about the legitimacy of quotas but the British accepting American insistence that quotas be of screen time only, not of distribution. Despite the opposition of the Cinema Exhibitors Association (CEA),[6] the British government agreed to drop the renters' quota in return for an explicit promise from Eric Johnston to continue American production in Britain.[7] Thus an important component of British film legislation for twenty years was abandoned as part of broad arrangements to govern the freeing of international trade.

Consequently, when the government's proposals for legislation to replace the expiring 1938 act were brought forward, the renters' quota was missing, but higher exhibition quotas were intimated (not stated). The new legislation did not contain a schedule of progressive increases of quota during the life of the act, but rather gave the Board of Trade power to set quotas from time to time subject to parliamentary approval. This gave the Board of Trade a substantially increased managerial role. It was during this period that an indiscretion forced the resignation of the Chancellor of the Exchequer, Hugh Dalton, who was replaced by the president of the Board of Trade, Sir Stafford Cripps, who in his turn was replaced at the Board by the junior minister, Harold Wilson. Wilson construed himself as something of a film fan[8] and made it clear, in, among other places, the papers that survive in the Public Record Office, that he wanted to develop a fully fledged and newly thought out film policy. By this time Board of Trade officials Somervell and White were highly experienced, and a great many schemes and options had been canvased over the years. Wilson, however, took office with the immediate need to finalize the plan for the new legislation, something that had a deadline all its own. He also came into office in the midst of the boycott crisis, although, as we have seen, the complexities and power plays of that episode seem not to have impressed him unduly. Could Wilson's ambitions produce a genuine policy in the matter of international trade in films?

Wilson's first major legislative appearance for the Board of Trade in the House of Commons was his role in shepherding through the new Cinematograph Films Act. Introducing the Second Reading of the bill, on 21 January 1948, he found it impossible not to refer extensively to the boycott that was then in force. His tone was not particularly belligerent, especially as the bill embodied the Geneva deal to abolish renters' quota in return for a promise of continued American production in Britain once trading conditions were normal. He hoped that he had given the House "some idea of the Government's policy for the industry" (col. 233), but this hope was forlorn. Apart from the quota, he took no definite stand on whether the state should own a studio, on how the film boycott was to be resolved, on the sources of film finance, and on the circuit monopolies. He announced an inquiry into the distribution and exhibition of films but would not specify what type of inquiry it would be. He also made two odd assertions – one about the audience, the other about the market.

What I am perfectly certain of is this, that if the cinema-going public had the choice today of seeing additional British or additional American films, they would demand a very much larger number of British films before their taste for them was glutted. (col. 219)

Wilson's confidence, as we know, did not derive from any evidence and was perhaps something a planner in charge of the industry should not have allowed himself to be "perfectly certain" about. The other odd assertion was that the British film industry "must in common prudence face the need for covering most of its costs by its proceeds in the home market" (col. 232). Wilson must have been one of the very few people who thought this was a recipe for films the British public would welcome with the same alacrity that they welcomed the Hollywood product. Perhaps Wilson was not yet fully conversant with his subject.

The continuing boycott meant that much of Wilson's speech was concerned with commerce rather than culture. In the subsequent debate this continued to be the case, commercial and structural issues overwhelming the cultural argument formerly stressed for protectionist legislation of this sort. The bill was not a partisan measure, so the Conservative spokesman (Oliver Lyttleton)[9] did not attack its very principle or seek to divide the House. Yet at this reading the bill, which was described by one member, Walter Scott-Elliot,[10] as sensible but not important and eclipsed by the prospect of the inquiry Wilson was setting up, was debated for more than eight hours (col. 290). It revealed more division within the ruling Labour Party than between the parties or within the Opposition Conservatives. Besides the Dalton Duty and the provisions of the bill itself, there was much discussion of the pros and cons of monopoly, whether private or nationalized, and of freedom of speech and creativity under such conditions, as well as of the problem of production costs. One of the more startling sub-dramas of the debate was the vehemence of Tom O'Brien's attack on his own Labour Party for their handling of the boycott dispute. O'Brien, who represented the union to which belonged "a section of the cinematograph industry workers, particularly those employed at cinemas, and the more simple technical jobs" (col. 252) was unequivocal:

It is no use burking the issue ... and talking about a great British film industry, and the production of British films, when there will very soon be no British film industry left to make films and no places left in which to show the films if they are made. (col. 243)

He went on to castigate the government for not consulting the Americans about the duty. He read a long statement from Eric Johnston about the American industry's readiness to compromise and insisted that things should never have reached a stage where one side or the other had to back down. In the course of his remarks he specifically entered a plea for the point of view of the public:

The most important factor in the entertainment industry is the audience, the people who pay to be entertained, and their voice must be heard. These 30 million people a week will be deprived soon of almost the sole remaining means of relaxation and amusement open to them in a world of gathering difficulties. (col. 244)

This was perhaps well said but a bit of an exaggeration. Radio, professional sports, the popular press, football pools, the pub, and countless other means of relaxation and entertainment were unaffected by the films boycott. Be that as it may, his was a lonely voice. Throughout the debate, speakers from both sides harped on the "we cannot afford the dollars" theme, yet in less than two months time the issue was settled and the dollars somehow found.

Three forms of possible government intervention were aired by speakers: government ownership of a film studio that could be rented to independent producers (O'Brien); government finance of films through a film bank; and government ownership of two cinema circuits (chains) to balance the two large privately owned ones (Joseph Mallalieu,[11] a left-wing Labour M.P.). The bill was bluntly declared "a producer's Bill" (col. 269) by Benn Levy, but in replying for the government the parliamentary secretary to the Board of Trade, John Belcher,[12] was cautious and noncommittal. Vigorous intervention by two Scottish members showed the first signs of sympathy for public taste and concern with whether it was properly catered to in the composition of the Cinematograph Films Council. Major McCallum[13] said that

the tastes, not only of the Highland people of Scotland, but of Scotland as a whole are entirely different from those of the English public. Films which go down well in England and Wales are complete "flops" in Scotland. Hon. Members who have had experience of some of the Glasgow cinemas will bear me out in that. (col. 251)

By constantly intervening on this theme it was kept before the House, and relevant changes were made in committee.

Among the more informed interventions was one by Dr. Stephen Taylor, Labour M.P. for Barnet, where both Elstree and Boreham Wood studios were located, and who was himself a member of the Cinematograph Films Council.[14] He outlined the ownership and activity of all the studios in his constituency and argued that American partners were inhibiting production in pursuit of the boycott. While dismissing most documentaries as boring, he castigated the film bookers for underestimating public taste when they refused to book a film such as *The Overlanders* because it had no stars (col. 259). Taylor argued that the Rank Organization's vertical integration (Fig. 8.1) was the correct commercial structure for reducing risk and matching supply and demand, but he then ended with a regret that films had not been from the first organized by a quango like the BBC. Natural monopolies should be under public control.

That House of Commons thinking on foreign trade was still primitive and had no grasp of the legacy of Cordell Hull was shown when a Liberal M.P., Edgar Granville,[15] demanded bilateral reciprocity with the United States on a film-for-film basis and threw into the pot the further suggestion that if the Americans received a British star they should reciprocate with an American star. "America must give our pictures a fair showing," he asserted, his whole tenor betraying the supposition that the U.S. administration or Congress was responsible. He even spoke of British stars being "sent" to Hollywood, apparently overlooking the fact that emigration from Britain was unrestricted and that hence no one individual and no organization was "sending" British talent to the United States: It was going of its own accord. What we see here is the embodiment of some of the problems. Granville showed no awareness of the new world trading order the United States was struggling to bring forth, no grasp of the weakness of Britain in relation to the United States, and no regard whatsoever for the interests of the public. More muddle between government and industry was displayed by Scott-Elliot, who argued that

the Americans could send us a good many more films for the same money owing to the fact that the British market is a considerably smaller market than the American market. (col. 292)

Winding up for the Opposition, Conservative M.P. Walter Fletcher,[16] former owner of a small chain of "flea-pit" cinemas, blithely stated that "the films we want to send to America are high-class films with great attractions which will make money for those who take them out there" (col. 320). It is especially odd to find a Tory talking in this way, and a former exhibitor to boot. Fletcher could be expected to know better than others that whether or not a film has great attractions or will make money cannot be decided by wishing. In the end, the box office is boss.

Benn Levy raised the question of whether nationalization could be reconciled with the freedom of a means of expression such as the film, which he compared to books and the press. Judging by scattered remarks elsewhere in the debate other members found this a problematic matter, and in winding up the debate the government spokesman offered, for example, to alter the legislation to ensure that the provisions in the bill designed to compel showing of six films per year produced independently of the large British and

American companies could not be misused by the government for party political or propaganda purposes.

Cyril Osborne,[17] for the Opposition, brought up Wilson's threat that if there was no settlement of the boycott "the cinema habits of the people of this country would have to be seriously altered" (col. 282).

I wonder if Members realise what would be the reaction of factory workers to the closing down of cinemas to that extent. I think it would be as serious, if not more serious, than if all the tobacconists shops were closed, or even the "pubs." If there is a breakdown involving the closing of our cinemas, there will be some very serious social consequences. (col. 282)

He was the lone voice to agree with Tom O'Brien that the problem of the dollars for films had been blown out of proportion.

An unexpected dose of democracy and good sense came from Victor Collins, M.P. for Taunton.[18] He spoke up most directly for the public, the persons who pay their 1s. 9d. But he also looked ahead and noted that there was an absence of film policy. In the ten years of the bill there could be as many differences in the position of the cinema as there had been in the previous ten years. He instanced television as a possible source of impact, much in the way films had impacted on the music hall. His views were not otherwise enlightened, and he certainly did not directly ask whether the bill was the sum total of policy.

Toward the end of the debate some cultural arguments were addressed, including films as cultural representation, as educator, and as influence. Walter Fletcher commented on the fact that the Empire had not been invoked at all. What the debate shows, by contrast with the two before it in 1938 and 1927, is the ready acceptance of protectionism and state intervention by almost all elected politicians, a closing of ranks in the face of American commercial pressure, and a singular forgetfulness about the new acute dependence on the United States and the formerly so important cultural arguments about films. Without those cultural justifications, which were never other than weak, there was no cogent reason why it should not have been left to international trade and the free market to supply whatever the British public evinced box-office demand for.

8.4. Making films for export

Criticism of Wilson for having no film policy within which to frame the 1948 Cinematograph Films Act needs to be moderated by noting that he was not responsible for the crisis created by the ad valorem tax, a measure not geared to any coherent film policy objectives, and that the renewal of the act came very soon after he became head of the Board of Trade. His initiatives intended to develop policy were not yet fulfilled. Once the various elements of his policy were announced and in place, however, we can see

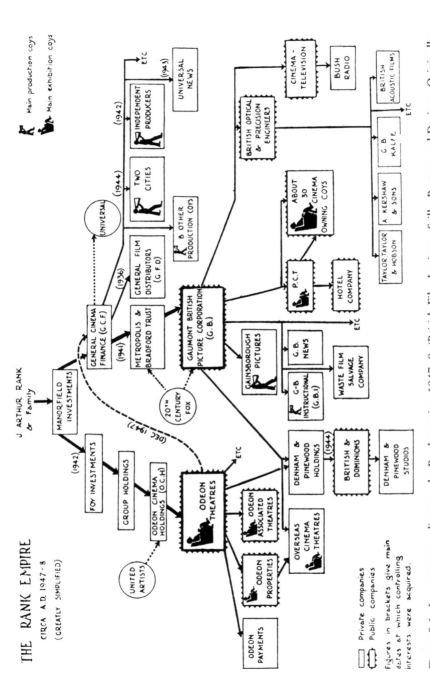

Figure 8.1. An attempt to diagram the Rank empire, 1947–8. (British Film Institute–Stills, Posters and Designs. Originally published in Alan Wood, *Mr. Rank*, London: Hodder & Stoughton, 1952. Used by permission of the Estate of Alan Wood.)

that they contained nothing coherent as far as economic foreign policy was concerned. Protecting the domestic industry and then stabilizing it and building it up were quite different from making it internationally competitive as regards offerings and price. My argument has been that no realistic assessment of the prospects and difficulties in this area ever took root, and hence all the various ideas and schemes and hopes did not add up to policy.

As the boycott crisis and the legislation were dealt with, it was becoming apparent that the prestige experiment was a catastrophic failure financially. Very expensive films had been produced that did not play particularly well either at home or in the United States. There were complaints about the British accents in *Moss Rose* from Grey, Georgia, to Scotia, California. Some attempts were made to give British films broad American release, and the feedback was hopeless: "British" became a kind of pejorative epithet among the public and exhibitors, as the following extracts from the *Motion Picture Herald* illustrate:[19]

I See a Dark Stranger: These English pictures are getting very poor. I would hate to think I had to play their pictures to make a living. Deborah Kerr will never reach the top if she has to play in pictures of this type. This is definitely a sour lemon – Greensboro, NC

Odd Man Out: I expected big things of this picture though I played it late. The college apparently enjoyed it, but the natives do not go much for this type of show. Acting very fine. *However, it will be appreciated only by a certain class of patrons,* consequently business was not above par – Middlebury, VT

Caesar and Cleopatra: This was a very poor picture. Technicolor was quite nice, the Patrons not only complained that the picture was boring but also that the seats were hard – Saskatchewan

A Matter of Life and Death: The newspapers gave this four stars. My customers gave it four bronx cheers. Colour, beautiful. *This type might be good for class houses, but they are poison to the guy with the average "thinker".* He sits and looks at the screen, gets up, smokes, sits again, kibitzes with his wife, who gets mad because she wants to sleep – Bridgeport, CT

The Rake's Progress: A very poor picture. Played this as a second feature, but it was a mistake. Patrons walked out on it. Plenty of complaints. It was as good as the usual English feature – Los Angeles, CA

Bedelia: Why must we be bothered with these English films? We apologise to our Patrons after each show – Inverness, MO

Bedelia: Who said that this rates with those made in Hollywood? It was terrible and so was business. They should introduce English stars in American films first – Riversville, WV

These comments agree very well with the complaints of Canadians that we came across in Part I, with the analyses of Grierson back in 1927, of members of the House of Commons speaking in both 1927 and 1938, with the views of Lord Grantley, and with the analysis of Richard Griffith.

Writing in the highbrow magazine *Sight and Sound,* Griffith (1949, 1950) carefully explained which British pictures had done well in the United States and precisely how that success had been engineered. Dumping the films into general release to every backwoods theater in the United States was counterproductive: it was costly and, when the film was unsuited to local tastes, it created negative word-of-mouth publicity for British films in general. Griffith quoted a New York showman as commenting, "When you're cultivating an export market, the only thing that matters is to give the market what it wants." Griffith argued that the creation by Sidney Bernstein and Thomas Baird of the Rota System in 1942, whereby the eight major American companies agreed to distribute one British feature film and two short films per year, gave some access and, in the special emotional conditions of wartime alliance, some success. The system ended when the war ended. By contrast, the failures of *The Life and Death of Colonel Blimp* (Archers 1943) and *Caesar and Cleopatra* (Rank 1945) began with the assumption of some $350,000 distribution and publicity costs each. An estimated seven thousand theater bookings were required merely to cover those. *Blimp* managed an estimated one thousand bookings and had to be heavily cut to fit programing constraints. *Caesar and Cleopatra* managed ten thousand bookings but was quickly killed by bad word-of-mouth publicity. *Henry V,* by contrast, succeeded by slowly building an audience through specialized and targeted distribution.

Griffith gave short shrift to the idea of a conspiracy to exclude British films or the theory that Rank was a mere puppet of U.S. firms. But, in much the same way as I am inclined to do, he gave considerable credence to the American public's apparent firm preference for the product of its own industry. This fact needed respect, because it followed that films were not perfect substitutes for each other and that a British film, even lavishly produced and with American names in the cast, was not necessarily thereby delivering the satisfactions the Americans audience expected. Short of delivering those satisfactions – that is, not Americanizing British pictures but getting right a formula for success that was unknown even to Hollywood – a much more ingenious and modest policy was required. Ingenious in that the interstices of the American market needed cultivation and that success on a large scale was not to be expected, and hence not to be built into initial production and distribution budgets. This analysis by Griffith made clear the crucial weakness of the British approaches to policy. Both the cultural and commercial arguments for a British film industry could readily be met by a modestly sized and modestly financed film production program. Provided such costs were kept down, whatever earnings could be taken in North America would be extra profit. Budgeting on the basis of expected North American earnings was imprudent, simply because, for all kinds of reasons, there was no way to tell whether the picture would be successful and hence what expectations were realistic. It is with these caveats in mind, I believe, that we should address the attempts at policy formation undertaken by Harold Wilson.

An intriguing document is a speech Wilson made on "Policy for British Films" to the annual meeting of the Association of Cinematograph and Allied Technicians on 11 April 1948 (Wilson 1948). This was, of course, a Labour minister addressing a trade union audience. The speech was a promissory note of inquiries Wilson pledged to make before formulating policy. He predicted the surge of American production in Britain that would come from the blocked sterling of the U.S. companies. He admitted British films were not really doing well in the United States (p. 8) and was looking for ways to give American distributors incentives to give them better promotion. He targeted high British production costs for inquiry and in effect warned the union that restrictive and other protective labor policies could no longer be justified (p. 12).

As the catastrophic end of the prestige experiment became apparent to all, Wilson registered his view of the situation:

The Government had already done what they reasonably could; first, by negotiation of the Anglo American Film Agreement; secondly, by setting up machinery for consultation through the National Film Production Council; thirdly, by investigating the studio situation through the Gater committee; and fourthly, by providing machinery for financial assistance to independent producers through the Film Finance Corporation. In addition, a thorough investigation of distribution problems was to be undertaken through the Distribution Committee. The Board of Trade did not, however, themselves produce films and they could not take any direct action to increase the present level of film production. Insofar as the present deficiency was due to the failure of American film companies to undertake production, it was obvious that the Board of Trade could not force American companies to produce films which they did not want to make here.[20]

Among all the many committees operating during Wilson's regime, there was not one that took a professional and informed look at the all-important North American market. There is not one document in the files that analyzes which British films succeeded in the United States and why. In the appointments to the various inquiries there was never an American adviser or even a member with extensive North American experience. It is hard to understand this. It is prudent, when trying to penetrate a market with one's goods, to have some understanding of what can be exploited in that market. The documents show politicians and officials simply speculating about North America and devising conspiracy stories of the reluctance of American firms to make room for British pictures. As to the trade, both Rank and Korda seem to have understood Grantley's point that buying into the American industry was the way to go. Ineptly, in 1941 Korda bought into United Artists, the one major company not vertically integrated, owning no theaters at all. Rank acquired an interest in Universal in 1937 and strengthened that in 1945. But, again, Universal was the smallest of the major producers and had few theaters compared to the big five. Griffith pointed out that Rank did not let his North American partner choose from his production program but preselected what was offered. Possibly desire to retain this kind of control explains why Rank did not consummate a deal with one of the big five, always assuming any of them was ready to do so. (As we shall see, Rank may have learned enough not to repeat this error in Canada.)

Wilson, we have seen (in Chapter 7), displayed a somewhat highhanded attitude, both toward the Americans themselves and toward his senior colleague Bevin's attempt to counsel moderation and consultation. The hauteur reminds one of Dalton's "that is not the way to govern" remark.[21] When Wilson met with the Cinema Exhibitors Association (CEA) in mid–1948, they wanted to argue the unrealism of the quota figures and the absence of guarantee that there would be ninety showable pictures available from British sources. In a letter nine months later to Lord President of the Council Herbert Morrison, Sir Alexander King of the CEA said of the quota figure, "It simply means, by law, we are compelled to show pictures that the public will not come to see. I am not saying all British films are bad but out of the first six months of this quota year, there were 20 that could be rated as poor and miserable efforts at entertainment."[22] Something of the kind had been put to Wilson at the face-to-face meeting, and the official record of Wilson's response read:

If it was true that the public preferred American films, then there would have to be a change in the public taste. This country could not in future afford as many dollars as had been spent in the past on American films.[23]

Wilson was consistent with the attitude he had been challenged to defend in the House of Commons. It was not a promising attitude in the senior government policymaker for the film industry. The argument from dollar shortage was neither exclusively cultural nor commercial: It was a mixture of both, with the addition of the political. There were of course dollars available for films, just as there were for tobacco, but the government was taking the position that it would set the priorities for their expenditure, rather than following the will of the public as expressed in demand. However, we have seen how Bevin's grasp of wider issues was something of a curb, and we have discussed Stead's contention that in the end governments were unwilling to deprive the public of entertainment that they desired. Thus, while these words of Wilson sound aggressive, little action was taken to put them into practice. The quotas were set high to placate the producers, but when the latter were unable to deliver on the necessary scale the quotas were reduced. Politics and commerce were the primary drivers of policy, rather than culture. But a policy that was geared to the assumption that the public would have to like the product was a curious one, and when there was the intention to manufacture that product at high cost and hope to cover some of that cost with sales abroad, one gets the dizzying sense that the policymakers were not dealing with the real world.

Apart from the aim to have a soundly based domestic film industry for both cultural and commercial reasons, it is hard to discern any definite aim in Wilson's ruminations. When fixing the first quota at 45 percent, he came much nearer to the British Film Producer Association (BFPA) figure of 50 percent than to the CEA figure of 25 percent. He had promised to set the quota "at the highest practicable level."[24] Yet all quotas were set in advance, so he had to work on the basis of the plans and promises of an industry notorious for its unreliability. He had set up a National Film Production Council, where all sections of the trade could meet under his chairmanship, and he also set up a revolving fund, the National Film Finance Corporation (NFFC), primarily to provide end money.[25] These were instruments of policy intended to give the industry coherence in organization and finance. Inquiries were made into studio space adequacy and into distribution, exhibition, and production costs. Yet a clear policy toward American imports and exports to the United States was never forthcoming. So far as one can see, if the BFPA had been able to escalate production to 75 percent of British needs, Wilson would have raised the quota that far, Bevin's warnings notwithstanding. Public taste was supposed to obey, not to command, in these matters. Yet the costs of filmmaking in Britain had escalated to a point beyond redemption at the British box office.

The BFPA brought forward a memorandum in 1949 showing that, from a box-office net of some £70 million, the gross receivable by the producers was £7.5 million. This would enable fifty films to be produced at £150,000 each. The ninety films planned for 1948–9 would therefore have to cost an average of £85,000 each.

Whatever economies may be made in the near future in the cost of production of films in this country it is certain that 90 films per annum cannot be made at an average cost of £85,000 each which will either satisfy the public or be able to stand up to American competition.[26]

It is not necessary to accept these figures to understand the general picture of the situation that they gave. The four thousand or so British cinemas were generating revenue for maybe twenty A-grade and twenty-five B-grade films per year, with no guarantee that if American films were excluded their earnings would flow to the British product. Thus, both for domestic and for export reasons the British film industry desperately needed either to retrench or to break into the U.S. market. Hindsight is cheap, of course, but one would have thought heavy backing to help Rank, Korda, and the Associated British Picture Corporation (ABPC) buy into American firms would have paid off, and also a more consistent encouragement to the Americans to produce films in Britain, as advocated by the CEA:

Table 8.1. *Distribution of Rank first-feature films in Canada*

Year	1944	1945	1946	1947	1948
No.	3	9	18	29	30

Source: John Davis to E.R. Ward, 8 February 1949, PRO, BT 64 2433.

We would like to see better relations with the American companies. We would like to see them taking a more active part in British production. They appear to us to be the only people with experience, money and a world wide distribution, remaining to whom one can look for 12–15 first class British films in a year thereby restoring a renters' quota. We should like to see them producing here and the "unit" plan withdrawn.[27]

The latter did come about – not, however, as an act of conscious policy but as fallout from the boycott and without the British producers having a hand in it. In fact, it is surprising how little Anglo–American coproduction there was at this period, when it was flourishing among Continental production companies.

8.5. Exporting to Canada and Europe

In the half-decade following the war, while the Imperial or, as it now was, Commonwealth ideal still flourished, the White Dominions continued to seem to hold out promise to the British film industry. Canada, despite its film trade being dominated by the United States, was collaborating with the British government in trying to foster Anglo–Canadian trade as a counterbalance to American domination and to deal with both the British and the Canadian shortage of American dollars. As we have earlier seen, the problem was some perceived public resistance to British films. In July 1948 Rank was able to report some progress in the Canadian market.

In Australia, in New Zealand, in South Africa, in every country where our product is shown consistently exhibitors are making money with British films. In Canada, in the last two years or so, where we have been able to give British films continuity of exhibition in our theatres the percentage of screen time has risen from approximately four per cent to 25 percent. And those theatres are taking no less money.[28]

The Rank organization had been making a sustained effort to penetrate the Canadian market (Table 8.1), first by buying into Nathanson's Odeon circuit and assuming control of it when Paul Nathanson fell ill. Revenue came to (Can) $239,103 for 1947 and (Can) $272,821 for 1948. These were apparently not final figures, because distribution in Canada took an estimated 2.5 years. Even more startling were poll results that showed a dramatic improvement in the image of British films in the eyes of the Canadian filmgoing public.

In a nation-wide poll conducted by [*Liberty Magazine*] ... the preference for British films was expressed by 32.1 per cent of those participating. This is a notable increase over the 25 per cent figures of the Gallup Poll report approximately a year ago – and a still greater improvement, of course, over the figure for four or five years ago, which was then about 3 per cent.[29]

As a supplement to these Rank figures, there were the efforts of Associated British–Pathé, which distributed three films in 1946 and eight in both 1947 and 1948, from which they realized some £18,363. It is not hard to put these figures in proportion. The combined Rank and AB-P totals were not sufficient to add £.5 million in three years to the roughly £7.5 million in one year we saw as typical earnings expectations at the domestic box office. The four thousand or so British cinemas were one-quarter of the American sixteen thousand or so, and the Canadian one thousand or so were one-quarter of the British. One can well see the glittering prize the American market had to represent.

The Rank strategy was multisided. While expanding the Odeon circuit, they continued to seek outlet with the Famous Players group. They avoided selling their films as British but tried to create a brand name in Rank to compare with MGM and other leading American producers. Spot booking in test markets was used, and films were frequently opened first in small towns away from the big cities. This was the slow strategy John Davis described, since it depended on the creation of a rolling word of mouth. Most significantly, measures were taken to select carefully those films that would be given Canadian distribution, and this was done by a Canadian committee, not by Rank's home office in London.[30]

Various schemes were floated by the industry to assist these overseas efforts. In the first place it requested a full-time consular trade officer for films. Then there was discussion of whether Canada could be encouraged to impose a British quota; whether Canadian politicians could be persuaded to make positive noises to counteract "the subtle impression which the officers of Famous Players are trying to convey, namely that the Canadian Government is not interested in the welfare of British pictures;"[31] and there were careful preparations to include films on the agenda of the trade promotion visit of the president of the Board of Trade to Canada in May 1949.

It might ... be practicable for the President himself to show a special interest in the market for British films in Canada and to take any opportunities which offer themselves for discussing the whole question with Canadian Ministers, since there can be no doubt that the expansion of our film trade there would help both sides. There can be no objection to mentioning the problem of the American-controlled circuit and the conviction of the British industry that matters would be helped if it were generally known that the Canadian Government were anxious that British films should be more widely shown if their merits made it likely that there would be a good public for them.[32]

Table 8.2. *Comparison of the takings of two feature films in Toronto, 1949*

	The Winslow Boy Shea's (2,386 seats)	Christopher Columbus Odeon (Carlton) (2,320 seats)
Wednesday		$ 2,500
Thursday		1,900
Friday	$1,041	2,200
Saturday	2,304	4,155
Monday	702	
Tuesday	676	
Totals	4,723	10,755

Source: Hanson to Jaratt, 26 October 1949, PRO, BT 64 2433.

The quota idea was, of course, bound to be rejected. Trade Commissioner Garner commented that "anything more than a mere suggestion would, I guess, be followed by an enquiry from the State Department, who never seem to be more than one step away from Hollywood."[33] There was no need to guess. The quota had been floated as a *ballon d'essai* in January with the predictable storm in New York and Hollywood.[34] Approaches to Famous Players were more successful, and a deal was concluded in late August of 1949 for them to show nineteen British features. This conforms with the view expressed by Nathanson when he was head of Famous Players that they were prepared to exhibit British films of good quality. The explanation, however, may have had more to do with the matters of the antitrust suit in the United States, the situation that had created the Canadian Co-operation Project, and the feeling therefore that this American subsidiary needed to show itself willing in order to be a good corporate citizen. Alas, Trade Commissioner J. Balcon reported that *Passport to Pimlico,* while drawing good crowds, was lost on young Canadians who had neither been to nor had any connection with England. He noted that British films in Toronto were earning the same reputation as French films in England. Since this was a reputation confined to the specialized and art-house circuit, it did not bode well for the kind of commercial advantage the British film industry wished to gain.[35] From the trade side, reports were equally disheartening. *The Winslow Boy* did mediocre business, mainly with older people, and seemed not to appeal to younger people. A comparison of its business with *Christopher Columbus* ("which received very bad reviews") was instructive (Table 8.2): The badly reviewed Technicolored epic, which imitated the Hollywood style, humiliatingly outdrew the quality British film. Among the films Famous Players were trying to promote were two Anna Neagle vehicles, although they were "not enthusiastic" about her drawing power. Several of the other films they were handling were clinkers on any scale of measurement. While I have not been able to obtain more evidence, the trend seemed to have already set in of great expectations being dashed – in this case not because of ineptitude in handling but rather, as in the 1920s, because of inadequacy of product. Arty or elite films were pitted against mass entertainment films with disastrous results. Carefully cultivated release patterns worked, but the returns were modest. Production uncertainty and contraction eventually meant fewer elite films to exploit carefully and the virtual disappearance of efforts in the mass entertainment bracket – at least for the international audience. Among the films that helped burn British fingers at this time were two attempts to ape the Hollywood musical: *London Town* and *Happy Go Lovely*.

In addition to this special push in Canada, we saw at the end of Chapter 6 that the British film industry endeavored to establish a strong presence on the Continent, especially in Western Europe. Conditions favorable to this were the occupation of many of these lands by the Anglo–American armed forces; the favorable image of British resistance to Germany, which was thought to have heartened all the occupied countries and warmed them toward Britain and things British; the hospitality extended to governments in exile in London during the war; and, as postwar conditions firmed up, the acute shortage of dollars everywhere. British films, when audiences were keen for any films, had the advantage to Western European governments of requiring sterling rather than dollars, although for several years some of these countries were short of sterling too. Conditions militating against British enterprise were the hard-currency shortage, the desire of several countries to restore a domestic film industry (on however modest a scale), and, in the eastern part of Europe, a preference for the films of the Russian ally.

Since almost all countries imposed exchange control, and since almost all countries blocked film earnings to one degree or another, figures have survived that show an extraordinary situation. At a time when the Rank Organization was expending money and ingenuity on the difficult Canadian market for meager rewards of less than £.5 million in three years, British films were building up massive credits on the Continent of more than £2 million, the great bulk of it in the Western Zones of occupied Germany, where Allied Control Commission policies effectively ensured a "captive audience" (Table 8.3). (See Pilgert 1953; Guback 1969, chap. 7.) These balances of £2.8 million had been accumulating since 1945, it should be remembered, and constituted about one-third of the net earnings in the domestic market in one year. Whether the Continental earnings themselves, even if remitted on a steady basis, would have been sufficient to make British films viable, in the absence of success in the United States, is doubtful. When the figures were revised at the end of 1949 there had been some settlement, and yet some £0.77 million was still outstanding.[36] The situation in the

Table 8.3. *Blocked balances in £ sterling*

	BCFC	Eagle–Lion	London Films	Pathé	Total
1949					
Japan	37,000				37,000
Holland	35,000				35,000
Poland		5,000			5,000
Austria	5,000	2,000		4,000	11,000
Germany	12,000	825,000		48,000	885,000
Czechoslovakia	14,000	10,000			24,000
Finland			8,000	1,000	9,000
Italy		13,000		5,000	18,000
France	2,000			5,000	7,000
Turkey				1,000	1,000
Indonesia		19,000			19,000
Totals	105,000	874,000	8,000	64,000	1,051,000
Estimated at end 1949					
Japan	70,000				70,000
Other terr.	50,000				50,000
Germany		1,975,000	134,000	100,000	2,209,000
Austria		2,000	34,000	10,000	46,000
Poland		8,000	14,000		22,000
Italy		80,000	80,000	16,000	176,000
Indonesia		37,000			37,000
Hungary			7,000		7,000
Yugoslavia			4,000		4,000
Greece			8,000		8,000
Denmark			5,000		5,000
Finland			10,000	1,000	11,000
France			120,000	5,000	125,000
Spain			34,000		34,000
Totals	£120,000	2,102,00	450,000	132,000	2,804,000

Source: French to Somervell, 28 March 1949, PRO, BT 64 4517.

British film industry was parlous indeed. In a possibly unguarded comment at the National Film Production Council, Sir Michael Balcon said that

the basic economic difficulties of the production industry had been obscured for a few years during and immediately following the war, because at that time there had been an illusion of prosperity. During the last two years or so, the position had deteriorated, partly because of falling box office receipts and partly because of the heavy increases in the cost of production. He could say that throughout his 30 years experience of film production (except for a short time during the war) producing films had never shown a profit in terms of the return received on money invested.

Table 8.4. *British film remittances (£) to the United States, 1946–51*

1946	1947	1948	1949	1950	1951
16,963,419	13,420,362	9,920,236	5,897,670	6,993,668	8,726,541

Source: *Parliamentary Debates (Commons)*, Written Answers, 6 March 1952, col. 7065, PRO, BT 64 4527.

Ealing Studios had, over their last 12 years of continuous production, shown a small loss and they had been able to keep going, partly because of the public spirited support of Stephen Courtauld, partly because their losses were cushioned by the distribution guarantee they held from the Rank Organisation.[37]

8.6. The end in the fifties

The Anglo–American Film Agreement, which settled the boycott in 1948, provided a framework for remitting $17 million per annum of blocked U.S. earnings, the rest to be expended in specific ways in the sterling area, including upon film production. The agreement was to last two years and needed renegotiation in 1950, for a year, and in 1951, for three years. Much had changed. The National Film Finance Corporation and the Eady–Levy scheme, which took a small amount from every admission and put it into a fund for British production, eased the financial instability of the British industry, rekindled the ambition for a Hollywood on the Thames. The presidency of the Board of Trade had passed from Harold Wilson to Sir Hartley Shawcross, and the long-time under secretary, R. G. Somervell, had retired in 1952. There was also a major change in the dollar position, as the European Recovery Plan and American purchases of raw materials in the sterling area for Korean War purposes rectified the shortage of dollars. Although the negotiators proceeded cautiously, reluctant to dismantle the protective machinery in case the situation worsened again, they came to think that the agreement provisions were effectively self-liquidating, since low British production (quotas set at 30 percent) and lowered box-office earnings meant that remittances plus permitted sterling uses were sufficient to reduce the accumulated balances.

From the American point of view the situation was different also. The war boom long over, Hollywood, as we have noted, was suffering from a grave downturn in domestic business that Eric Johnston claimed had led to losses of nearly $4 million in 1949. There had been a drastic slump in American film earnings in Britain as well, which were $68 million per annum before the agreement and would probably be down to $28–30 million in 1950 (Table 8.4).[38] In the second meeting the American companies complained that the film labor unions in the United States were directly lobbying the State Department to disapprove any continuation of the agreement that encouraged production overseas, with the threat of boycotting such pictures upon release in the United States. Somervell conceded that there was a physical limit to American production in Britain,[39] and the companies argued that their British productions did not do very well.[40] Fay Allport rather aggressively asked what the British officials were up to, and, when they would not state their objective, suggested that their aim was to divert almost all the American blocked funds into British production. Somervell, rather disingenuously, denied this.[41]

Johnston claimed that whereas receipts from Britain once had represented two-thirds of Hollywood's overseas earnings, this was no longer so, and the proportion was decreasing.[42] Wilson admitted that he would gain political advantage if the negotiations broke down, and he expressed this view of priorities: "I do not know – do not feel that films are a basic essential of life, and our people would always appreciate a break of that kind – or many of our people would."[43] While not quite on a collision course, the negotiations were both protracted and sticky, and once more the State Department was called in to push for final terms that were close to convertibility.

The decisive factor in these events has been the intervention of the American Ambassador on a footing completely different from that which he had taken up with the President and the Chancellor of the Exchequer on Mr. Johnston's first arrival of the 18th July, 1950.[44]

Basically, Board of Trade officials conceded, such agreements existed at the sufferance of the State Department. Thus, finally, an element of international political realism was introduced into British thinking about films, if rather late.

The U.S. Government thus becomes, as we have twice seen to our cost, the final arbitrator between H.M.G. [His Majesty's Government] and the U.S. film industry. The State Department on past form is fairly amenable to pressure from the film lobby and this pressure will not be made less effective by the fact that Eric Johnston now holds an important government post. Further, the American companies are at the moment more than usually hard up. In these circumstances I think that we cannot expect to retain the present Agreement with "possibly some smaller easement". In the past we have failed to take account of the weaknesses of our position and this has both wasted time and cost dollars, some of which we could probably have saved if we had been more forthcoming at the start. I hope we are not going to make the same mistakes a third time.[45]

By force of necessity, British film production was curtailed, as the extraordinary cost statistics of Table 8.5 indicated it simply had to be.

These colossal costs, sometimes far in excess of what Hollywood would have spent, had to be reduced, and some sort of drive was needed to improve poor foreign earnings. But even a flourishing and fully remittable level of

Table 8.5. *Production costs and earnings of selected British films*

Company	Title	Cost (£)	Box Office (£) U.K.	Box Office (£) Foreign
Ealing	*Hue and Cry*	104,222	96,812	n/a
	Frieda	168,435	227,017	n/a
	It Always Rains on Sunday	180,936	229,706	n/a
	Hue and Cry (reissue)		18,969	
	Saraband for Dead Lovers	371,205	87,338	n/a
	Scott of the Antarctic	371,588	214,223	n/a
	Passport to Pimlico	276,787	104,443	n/a
	Whisky Galore	128,715	n/a	n/a
	Kind Hearts and Coronets	224,853	n/a	n/a
	The Blue Lamp	142,304	n/a	n/a
APBC	*Brighton Rock*	n/a	366,496	5,561
	The Guinea Pig	252,418	415,692	9,065
	Queen of Spades	232,500	141,309	11,110
	Private Angelo	218,713	110,720	1,000
British Lion	*The Courtneys of Curzon Street*	315,810	238,731	16,154
	An Ideal Husband	506,600	149,559	57,078
	Anna Karenina	553,000	95,687	63,313
	Spring in Park Lane	238,000	280,193	57,512
	The Fallen Idol	397,568	150,533	192,770
	Bonnie Prince Charlie	760,000	94,327	n/a
	The Small Back Room	232,972	75,537	962

Sources: Ealing, PRO, BT 64 4491; ABPC, PRO, BT 64 4492 (UK and foreign figures are net); British Lion, PRO, BT 64 4493 (*Courtney's*, *Bonnie*, and *Small* foreign figures are non-USA; *Ideal* and *Anna* foreign figures are all USA; £36,000 of *Spring* is USA).

earnings in Europe would not make this industry profitable. Hard lessons had taken nearly three decades to learn, lessons that were part of getting used to a generally diminished British power and influence vis-á-vis the United States. In a weary moment, pouring cold water on the idea of a Development Council for the film industry, Somervell also signaled that the hardest lesson of all had been learned – the lesson of how little we all know:

If I thought I knew what the industry really needed, apart from the conversion to Christianity of its chief members, I should perhaps be more enthusiastic about the sort of body [a quango] that Sir Arnold Plant and Lord Reith would like to set up.[46]

Notes

1 It is instructive to note that the later Italian spectacle films (e.g., *Hercules Unchained*) featuring body builders, and the "spaghetti westerns," were created for domestic consumption and on modest budgets.

2 On the basis of one short trip to the United States, Rank decided that "film people here have not a very high opinion of the intelligence of American audiences. I have. If Shakespeare is done properly, as in the case of *Henry V*, they will like it." Quoted from Wood (1952, p. 218).

3 *Parliamentary Debates (Commons)*, 12 November 1948, vol. 457, cols. 1953–64.

4 See the documents in PRO, BT 64 2229.

5 White minute, 14 August 1946, PRO, BT 64 96 / 4085 / 44.

6 Harold Wilson, *Parliamentary Debates (Commons)*, 21 January 1948, vol. 446, cols. 221–2. Hereafter cited (in parentheses) in text by column number.

7 Johnston to Cripps, 10 October 1947, PRO, BT 64 96 / 4085 / 44.

8 Indeed, film critic. See his scathing remarks about getting tired of films about diseased minds in *Parliamentary Debates (Commons)*, 17 June 1948, vol. 452, col. 775.

9 Oliver Lyttleton (1893–1972) Viscount Chandos; educated at Eton and Cambridge; Unionist M.P. for Aldershot (1940–54); President of the Board of Trade (1940–1, 1945).

10 Walter Travers Scott-Elliot (1895–1977); educated at Eton. Coldstream Guards; company director; Labour M.P. for Accrington (1945–50); Ministry of Labour (1941–5); parliamentary private secretary to Secretary of State for War (1946–7).

11 (Sir) Joseph P. W. Mallalieu (1908–80); educated at Cheltenham and Oxford; newspaperman and author; Labour M.P. for Huddersfield, 1945–79; held several parliamentary private secretary posts.

12 John William Belcher (1905–64), railway unionist; Labour M.P. for Sowerby (1945–49); Parliamentary secretary to Board of Trade (1946–8).

13 Maj. (Sir) Duncan McCallum (1888–1958), educated at Christ's Hospital; Army. Conservative M.P. for Argyllshire (1940–58).

14 Dr. Stephen James Lake Taylor (1910–), Baron Taylor; Director of the MoI Social Survey during the war; elected Labour M.P. for Barnet (1945).

15 Edgar Louis Granville (b. 1899), Lord Granville of Eye; soldier. Liberal M.P. for Eye (1929–51).

16 See Chapter 6, note 81.

17 (Sir) Cyril Osborne (1898–1969). Conservative MP for Louth (1945–69).

18 Victor John Collins (1903–71); Viscount Stoneham; educated at Regent Street Polytechnic and University of London; businessman; Labour M.P. for Taunton (1945–50).

19 In a clipping to be found in PRO, BT 64 2366. Quoted by permission of Martin Quigley and the Quigley Publishing Co. Inc.

20 Wilson minute, 29 November 1948, PRO, BT 64 2372.

21 Notoriously, Sir Hartley Shawcross had said in the House of Commons on 2 April 1946, "We are the masters at the moment – and not only for the moment, but for a very long time to come." This is often misquoted.

22 King to Morrison, 25 March 1949, PRO, BT 64 4538.

23 Ibid., minutes of 19 July 1948.

24 Minutes of the National Film Production Council meeting, 21 December 1949, PRO, BT 64 2372.

25 End money is the element in a film-production loan package that is repaid last, and hence tends to be thought of as the money that makes completion of the picture possible. This is not quite correct, for end money should be kept distinct from something it sometimes overlaps with: the completion guarantee. The latter is a special, and especially risky, form of insurance against unexpected difficulties such as cost overruns and major illnesses. In most films it is never collected, but when collected it can be very large indeed. Howe (1972) says it is the riskiest of all forms of film finance.

26 Memorandum by Sir Henry French to NFPC, 4 November 1949, PRO, BT 64 2372.

27 King to Wilson, 21 March 1949, PRO, BT 64 4538.

28 Rank, speech to the CEA, 14 July 1948, PRO, BT 64 4538.

29 John Davis to E. R. Ward, 8 February 1949, PRO, BT 64 2433.

30 "Colonel Blimp Comes to Canada," *Canadian Business,* February 1949, in PRO, BT 64 2433, enclosed with Davis to Ward, 17 March 1949.

31 J. Earl Lawson to Board of Trade, 23 March 1949, ibid.

32 Brief for the Visit of the President of the Board of Trade to Canada, May, 1949, enclosed with Wack to Jopson, 6 May 1949, ibid.

33 Garner to Somervell, 28 July 1949, ibid.

34 "At a stage when there has been so marked an improvement in Canada's reserves of gold and dollars I consider that such discrimination against the United States especially in so volatile a field as films would be quite impossible. Moreover Hollywood has been very cooperative with the Canadian Government in connection with dollar saving programme [and] through Canadian Cooperative [*sic*] project of the Motion Picture Association of America agreed to have some films made in Canada." Telegram, Ottawa to Commonwealth Relations Office, 22 January 1949, PRO, BT 64 2433.

35 Balcon to Brewster, 1 September 1949, ibid.

36 FPA memorandum, 12 December 1949, PRO, BT 64 2372.

37 Minutes of the NFPC, 27 July 1949, ibid.

38 Anglo–American Film Talks Verbatim Reports, 15 May 1950, PRO, BT 64 4484.

39 Minutes of 17 May 1950, PRO, BT 64 4503.

40 A point made the following year in a story in the *Wall Street Journal* (18 April 1951), clipped at PRO, BT 64 4527.

41 Minutes of 17 May 1950, PRO, BT 64 4503. This even though Wilson had said as much in the House of Commons, *Parliamentary Debates (Commons),* 17 June 1948, vol. 452, col. 774.

42 Minutes of 18 May 1950, PRO, BT 64 4503.

43 Minutes of 23 May 1950, ibid.

44 Brewster minute of 2 August 1950, PRO, BT 64 4507.

45 Somervell to O'Donovan, 20 June 1951, PRO, BT 64 4527.

46 Somervell minute, 4 May 1950, PRO, BT 64 4520.

PART III

The U.S. motion picture industry and its overseas system

Private impulses, more than government policies, laid the basis for America's enormous global influence in the twentieth century, an influence based on advanced technology, surplus capital, and mass culture.

— Emily S. Rosenberg, *Selling the American Dream*

CHAPTER 9

The MPPDA and the beginnings of organization, 1920–1922

9.1. The story so far

One small country, Canada, went up against the film industry of its super-power neighbor and ended up as part of the domestic market, and a small part of it at that.[1] One medium-sized country, Great Britain, went up against the film industry of the United States and ended up understanding just what compromises power could impose when nations shared grand objectives to which film considerations had to be subordinated. Yet Britain did eventually become what Canada became much later, a site for extensive U.S. branch-plant operations. British exhibitors, distributors, and unions were happy about the availability of American films and the production of some of them in Britain; nationalists and members of the cultural elite were not.

My general theme has been that the domination of the international trade in films by the U.S. film industry was a result of entrepreneurship in the arena of supply. The U.S. industry delivered a popular product with more reliability, at lower cost, and with more presale publicity, than any of its rivals. In contrast to the Canadian and British industries, the American industry achieved a degree of vertical integration by 1923, linking production, distribution, and exhibition within single corporations. For governmental and international purposes this made the American motion picture industry coherent.

9.2. Thompson on American hegemony

Kristin Thompson's authoritative and scrupulous examination of the early situation in the American film export trade, *Exporting Entertainment* (1985), is based on the trade press and published official documents (such as the *Trade Bulletins* of the Department of Commerce). The story she tells is as follows. Before World War I, the growing world trade in motion pictures was dominated by French companies. By the end of that war, U.S. firms had usurped the position of the French, establishing themselves in a preeminent position that they have subsequently managed to maintain. After describing the weak trading position of the United States before 1914 and the penetration of the domestic market by European firms, she shows how the wartime shortage of films in belligerent countries gave the U.S. firms their opportunity. Partly assisted by the collection of economic intelligence begun by the new Department of Commerce (1910), U.S. firms moved rapidly into the virtual vacuum left by their rivals, especially in the far-flung markets of South America and Australia, which, Thompson argues, were strategically crucial. Success proved to be greatest where agent selling was discontinued and branch offices of home firms were opened in the foreign country. This tactic was followed by buying into the local distribution business. The greatest U.S. success was in Britain, where domestic production was virtually annihilated by the mid–1920s. Not perhaps incidentally, Britain was – and remained – the most lucrative overseas market for U.S. firms for at least the next forty years.

Thompson's claim that the big American push into foreign markets occurred in 1916 is confirmed by a printed general instruction from the State Department to U.S. consuls dated 15 December 1916:

The Department has already received from certain consular officers excellent reports concerning the market in their respective districts for motion picture films of American manufacture. These were brought to the attention of interested firms in the United States, which have expressed to the Department their practical value and have requested further information upon the market abroad for such products.

It is therefore desired that you report fully in triplicate (quadruplicate from Latin America) upon the market for American films and accessories in your district, with particular regard to the following points:

1. Number of theaters, size, price of admission, and character of films shown in same.
2. From what agencies these theaters obtain their supplies of films, and what they pay for the service, giving names of agencies and what make of films they handle...
3. Recommendations as to necessary improvements, particularly as applicable to American film manufacturers, not only of films but of accessories.
4. General information regarding the popularity of motion picture plays with respect to the class of patronage, etc.

Wilbur J. Carr[2]

The war broke out in August 1914, and this circular was dated twenty-eight months later, indicating in its opening line that soon after the formation of the National Association of the Motion Picture Industry (NAMPI) in 1916 the industry had mobilized the foreign service to collect economic intelligence for it and had fed back tips as to what sort of information would be most helpful.

Thompson endeavored to carry the story forward from these early days to the coming of sound but perhaps with rather less success, since she shifted from a relatively detached point of view to one sympathetic to European attempts to resist American domination. The Europeans tackled this task by seeking the strength of coproduction and by pressuring governments partially to close European markets to American motion pictures. Germany, Britain, and France all passed quota laws. Import substitution works only if domestic films are adequate substitutes for imports. Failed ventures in Canada and quota quickies in Britain were part of the result of British legislation. Protection more discriminating in its effects took a long time to devise, and by then the unique character of American films was more or less conceded.

Thompson laid down the basic argument that American success in the international trade in motion pictures was founded upon innovation in supply, particularly distribution. To confirm her account from a different source, I quote Clarence J. North, first chief of the Motion Picture Division in the Bureau of Foreign and Domestic Commerce, writing in 1927:

The motion pictures of practically all our larger companies covering perhaps 85 per cent of the total number of pictures that are sent abroad are distributed through the branch offices of the firms themselves. Such branch offices are known as film exchanges, and are located in the capitals and large commercial centres of practically every foreign country. Famous Players (distributing Paramount pictures) has over 125 foreign offices and Fox, Universal and Metro–Goldwyn–Mayer, have nearly as many. Now a film exchange in Paris, let us say, operates in exactly the same way as a film exchange in Boston. It is under the control of a branch manager who has a staff of salesmen probably four or five who cover a certain definite territory and who deal directly with the theatre owners. They sell pictures usually in blocks of from a dozen to four dozen, although it is possible for a theatre owner to take fewer at a higher price, however for each. The terms on which such pictures are sold is either a flat rental price which may vary from $5,000 down to $5.00 per day dependent on the class of theatre, the age of the picture, whether it is being shown for the first time and a number of other factors. If it is not sold on a flat rental basis then the theatres guarantee the exchange a certain amount for the picture and a certain percentage of the theatre receipts besides. The product of the larger companies is practically never sold outright.

In certain cases motion pictures are distributed through an exclusive agent, for example; the Jury interests represent Metro–Goldwyn–Mayer in England and the Gaumont Company represent them in Egypt. It sometimes happens that one American company will represent another in the foreign field, as in the case of Famous Players, which has been representing Metro–Goldwyn–Mayer in Australia. However, when an agent represents an American company abroad, his method of distributing pictures is exactly the same as if such pictures were distributed by the branch office of the firm, the sole difference being that such agency would either get a percentage of the profits on all the pictures so distributed or else a flat commission of some kind on each picture distributed.[3]

With one possible cavil, this is a comprehensive account. The cavil is, obviously, whether North's statement that theaters could avoid block booking simply by acceding to a higher price was other than theoretical. Judging by the complaints in and from country after country, it was widely felt that in practice block booking was rigidly imposed.

American films were, then, being handled by branches of the home distributor, often part of an integrated company that also made the films, and films were of course a differentiated product, not a case of "When you've seen one film, you've seen them all." In the development both of stars and of certain packaging genres such as the western and the slapstick comedy, the American film industry created an identifiable, even individualized, product. This itself had to go hand in hand with reliable supply and reasonable price. Thompson notes that American films were by no means the least expensive in those early days. In Britain more might have to be paid for an American first feature than for a British. Cost, however, was not an absolute. Cost was a relative matter, to be calculated in relation to the potential audience. An hour's worth of anonymous film that brought in an audience of 100 (n), for a cost of $10 ($x$), would be costing per customer

$$\frac{x = \$10}{n = 100} = \$0.10 \ (v)$$

Now clearly, if an hour of American film, which cost 50 percent more, brought in twice the audience, the cost per customer would be less:

$$\frac{x = \$15}{n = 200} = v = \$0.075$$

We might think of v as a cost value for the delivery of a certain number of paying customers to the cinema. If an American film – say a western or a comedy – could be relied on to generate consistently more clicks on the turnstile counter than films of comparable length from other sources, their distributors clearly held a comparative advantage that would not be wiped out were they to raise their prices somewhat above the competition.[4]

Reliable distribution covers at least two matters. One is the vexed problem we have seen time and again in Britain and Canada of assured delivery of the films themselves. A cinema owner or manager's main problem is to have some cans of film promptly delivered to his door on the day for which they have been promised, that is, the day after his advertised and contracted run of the previous film has ended and on the day for which his publicity has announced that the new film will begin. More generally, a cinema operator wanted to be able to book well in advance, so that strong and weak pictures could be balanced over a season, attractions could be arranged to suit the audience's seasonal expectations and cinemagoing patterns, a mix of the different kinds of product with proven appeal to differing audiences could be offered, and advertising campaigns could be planned. Companies that could offer product information in advance that would permit such planning and deliver reliably when the time came were attractive business partners.

The other aspect of reliability was a reliable supply of differentiated product. As a constituency was built up for comedies, westerns, stars, and spectacles, part of the reliability the exhibitor sought from the distributor was that the films promised for the future would fulfill expectations. A comedy star would not turn up in *Hamlet;* a gunslinger would not venture comedy; a spectacular would have more or at least equal spectacle and thrills to ones shown previously. This was an aspect of the organization of supply at which the American industry excelled.

9.3. Before the MPPDA

Among the official papers bearing on the motion picture industry that survive in U.S. archives, recurrent concerns are evident:

1. overseas restrictions on American films;
2. organization by foreign firms and governments to promote locally made films at home and abroad; and
3. disarray and lack of cooperation both among U.S. firms and between the U.S. motion picture industry and the federal government.

These concerns bear heavily on the origins of the Motion Picture Producers and Distributors of America (MPPDA).

Although the usual story is that it was anxiety about censorship initiatives at the federal level that galvanized the industry to create the MPPDA, I think the evidence will show that the three concerns just listed were the deeper cause, and that the MPPDA response to them had more to do with the success of the industry than did their handling of censorship matters.

Both Canada and the United Kingdom featured prominently in the concerns expressed in points 1 and 2. In Chapter 2 we had occasion to look at the incidents in Ontario in 1911–18 which suggested that Anglo–Canadian patriotism was being manipulated in order to place American motion picture firms at a business disadvantage. Later there were protests from the United States because only British subjects could get licenses to operate motion picture theaters in Ontario. Quota laws apparently mimicking those of the United Kingdom were subsequently enacted in several Canadian Provinces but not implemented. Canada's use of tariffs and taxation was carefully monitored by American officials, and eventually, in the 1940s, the Canadian Cooperation Project was invented to head off proposed postwar restrictions.

When, in 1915, an American film called *Hearts in Exile* (World Film Productions 1915) was banned by the British Board of Film Censors on the grounds that it was offensive to the Russian ally, Lewis J. Selznik angrily told the State Department, "The ban . . . means a considerable financial loss to American capital."[5] The State Department refused to protest, arguing that the ban was within the scope of British municipal law.[6] Eventually the department sent out a circular telegram instructing selected U.S. consular and diplomatic posts to send in reports regarding foreign censorship of films.[7] Diplomatic posts routinely report on all sorts of purely internal and domestic matters. The interest in film censorship, which looks so obviously a domestic concern, had, however, a commercial underlay. As in Québec, any form of strict censorship that functionally discriminated against American films was a restriction on trade, and disavowals could be taken as disingenuous. From 1920, the annual reports of the British Board of Film Censors were digested and sent to Washington, on the theory that British censorship discriminated against U.S. films.

More directly commercial lobbying first shows up in papers from 1918, when the American Chamber of Commerce office in London compiled a report on the importation of films into the United Kingdom and forwarded it to Washington as a lobbying document. The occasion of the lobby was to try to head off British restrictions on shipping space for motion pictures. Internal evidence suggests that the shortage of shipping space and the fire risk from motion pictures had been used to suggest restricting their shipment on grounds that they were nonessential goods. The memorandum proceeded to argue that the 90–95 percent share of the British motion picture market enjoyed by the U.S. industry made Britain "probably the most important Market in the world for American Film Companies." Interruption in supplies would close many "English Theatres." It would also damage the propaganda that American films made for "American . . . manners, customs, ideas and so forth," as well as American foreign trade. Commerce and culture were comingled.[8]

Other documents in the files of the Bureau of Foreign and Domestic Commerce indicate that the London commercial attaché's office was aware that attempts were being made by British trade interests to recapture some of the ground lost to the American film industry after 1916. It was noted in September 1918 that Lord Beaverbrook was a central figure in these maneuvers and that he took advantage of his strategic position as minister of information.

When the American Bureau of Information takes up matters with the British Ministry of Information they are directed to associations with men who are the competitors of the American representatives here and who will probably be included in Lord Beaverbrook's combination. You, no doubt, are familiar with the history of Lord Beaverbrook. He was a Canadian business man who had been financially successful in certain promotion ventures which had not been altogether approved in Canada. He came to the United Kingdom and went into politics. He is said to have made arrangements for the present Government and to be one of the leading, if not the leading, political factor in Great Britain at the present time. It is rumored that the present Government insisted upon his being made a peer, although the greatest opposition was created both in Canada and in the United Kingdom. Lord Beaverbrook's creation as a peer was no doubt the leading reason why Canada has taken such a strong position against the creation of hereditary titles in that Dominion.

Through his experience as a promoter, through his great political influence, as well as through his favorable position as Minister of Information, Lord Beaverbrook is undoubtedly in a unique position to start a movement for the domination of the British Film Industry. American interests, I think, are planning an amalgamation to meet this threatened movement.[9]

In England, early in 1919, the Cinema Exhibitors Association (CEA) held its annual meeting, attended, among others, by Lord Beaverbrook and at least eighteen M.P.'s. The principal complaints, as reported to Washington, were against the variability of local-authority licensing practices for cinemas, the entertainment tax, and the "threatened American invasion." T. P. O'Connor advised the British government to keep their hands off as regards censorship and foresaw the day when a cinema would be attached to every elementary school.[10]

American officials also took interest in an interview given to the *Times* by one H. M. Jenks, proprietor of Harma's British Photoplays. He had just returned from a visit to the United States. Jenks lamented the concession of so much of the British film trade to the Americans but noted that limited capital, stories in British films lacking universal appeal, and also the lack of combination and organization in the U.K. industry resulted in British concerns "unnecessarily competing against each other." He speculated that in the United States capital from liquor manufacturers was moving over to the cinema in anticipation of the Volstead Act. He noted that the size of the American domestic market ensured a basic return on outlay and hence that there were no significant overhead costs associated with overseas sales, including those booked far ahead. By contrast, British producers forced to book far ahead had to face heavy carrying costs. The next step of the American companies would be to raise rentals to prohibitive levels and take control of the cinemas as they became nonviable.

Jenks conceded that there was some public opposition to British-produced films but asked the industry to take advantage of the current of popular national feelings to overcome it.[11] Jenks thus explicitly linked national sentiment to commercial advantage.

To some of the British, things may have looked rosy in the American garden, but this is not necessarily how they were seen there. For example, officials at the Department of Commerce expressed some dissatisfaction with State Department consuls in Latin America for not reporting on the motion picture industry there and for failing to reply to the circular questionnaire.[12] Doubts were also in the air as to the effect of aggressive export drives on international good feeling. In a 1920 circular addressed to all diplomatic and consular officers on the subject of international trade competition, it was said that "trade competition is believed to be a frequent carrier of the germs of ill-feeling between the nationals of the United States and the nationals of other countries." To meliorate this it was urged that such competition should be put on the basis of friendliness, frankness, and fair dealing. In urging the filing of reports on commodities affected by ill feeling, on propaganda to create ill feeling against the United States, and on secret deals that injured U.S. interests, discretion was important in order not to create the impression that the United States was about to engage in a trade struggle with another country.

This delicacy of feeling was not perhaps universally shared. American officials thought that Canada and the United Kingdom were active in promoting exports. In 1919 Canada was specifically mentioned by Secretary of Commerce Redfield as having appropriated money for trade promotion using the motion picture.[13] Trade promotion using motion pictures is a very different matter from promoting the export of motion pictures – or is it? The House resolution that had led to Secretary Redfield's appearance read:

Resolved, that the Secretary of Commerce be requested to report upon the value of moving pictures as a means of commercial promotion at home and abroad.

The argument was consistently made that films were a flagship trade good, one that gave general promotion to other sorts of goods, sometimes directly and sometimes merely by publicizing material aspects of life in their country of production. After World War I, U.S. officials and legislators seemed well aware that other countries were energetically organizing to pursue foreign trade. The United Kingdom and Canada were both cited as having reorganized their trade ministries, which were described as well staffed and in pursuit of commercial intelligence.[14]

Much of this material is from American files that were generated as officials organized to persuade Congress to fund more aggressive activities and data collection by the Department of Commerce, a context that should not be forgotten in assessing reliability. The 1919 effort regarding motion pictures was aborted, however, because Secretary Redfield judged it unwise to place the $69,000 request before a cost-cutting Congress. In the ensuing Republican administration of Warren G. Harding, Herbert Hoover was the new secretary of commerce (and Will H. Hays the postmaster general), a position Hoover held until 1928, ample time during which to reshape the department. Hoover's years as secretary of commerce were for long a lost or neglected historical topic. The surge of revisionist scholarship beginning in the late 1950s, however, stimulated by the opening of his papers in 1963, has taken that era as a central topic of dispute. The issue of direct concern here is the argument that Hoover was a progressive, modern man, a disciple of scientific management and of responsibility and self-government by industry. His aim as secretary was to revitalize and stabilize the economy by steering a course between laissez-faire capitalism (the deficiencies of which he was well aware) and the menace of etatism. Awkwardly christened "corporatism," Hoover's policy was to use the Department of Commerce to assist his three stabilizing goals of waste elimination, the collection and dissemination of statistical data, and the expansion of foreign trade.[15]

Hoover's assistant for publicity, Christian A. Herter (who, more than thirty years later, became secretary of state) reopened the motion picture question in 1921. He wrote to William A. Brady – fight promoter, theatrical impresario, and, at that point, president of NAMPI – informing him that

in connection with the contemplated enlargement of some of the functions and investigations of the Bureau of Foreign and Domestic Commerce...we are considering the establishment of a small section devoted to the study of the motion picture industry in its relation to export and import problems, foreign film production, etc.

Mr. Hoover has asked me to inquire from you whether you know of any individual who has a real knowledge of the industry in this country, and who is at the same time familiar with the import and export problems which the industry has to face.[16]

F. H. Elliott, executive secretary of NAMPI, replied on Brady's behalf, asking for the salary proposed. Julius Klein, director of the Bureau of Foreign and Domestic Commerce, replied in clarification that the matter was at the study stage, which would need to be completed before a proposal was made in the next budget.

I may say that Mr. Hoover and I have discussed on several occasions the significance of motion picture exporting both as a straight commodity trade and as a powerful influence in behalf of American goods and habits of living. I hope you will assure the officials of your Association that we shall be more than pleased to have any indications from them as to how this branch of the government might be of service either through its Washington organization or through its trade commissioners and commercial attachés abroad.[17]

Incomplete as the record is, since Brady seems to have shared his ideas with Hoover face-to-face, these are signs in official Washington of awareness and of thought being given to government facilitation of foreign trade in motion pictures all the way up to a future and very business-minded President. Klein's warm words to NAMPI also prefigured what was to be at times a rather close relationship between Commerce officials concerned with motion pictures, and the trade organizations of the industry.

Early attempts at motion picture trade intelligence were of varying quality. The Research Division of the Bureau of Foreign and Domestic Commerce was sent a report on the film industries of France, Germany, Italy, and England, written by an assistant trade commissioner and found not satisfactory for the Senate by Leland Rex Robinson, Klein's assistant director. The report had declared these foreign industries to be puny compared to that of the United States, successfully importing few films. This was an illustration of how poor information could be when culled from trade sources and newspaper reports by someone with no special knowledge.[18]

By contrast, in 1921 the Foreign Commerce Department of the Chamber of Commerce of the United States published a "Report on the Department of Overseas Trade [DOT] and Governmental Foreign Trade Promotion

Work in Great Britain." Twenty-five pages long, the report is perhaps the best piece of historical intelligence on this British government department in existence. It is thorough, detailed, and analytic – accompanying its descriptive prose with effective organizational diagrams and flowcharts. Picking its way among the intricacies of Foreign Office and Board of Trade predecessors, trade commissioners, Imperial trade correspondents, and the like, the creation of the DOT under their joint auspices was outlined. Comparing DOT's activities to that of the Bureau of Foreign and Domestic Commerce, the report noted the confidentiality of much British commercial intelligence compared to the publication and general sale of such information in the United States. Sharp criticism was directed at the organization of the DOT, including its putting "the United States and the Philippines in the same group as Central Europe, Western Europe and Belgian Congo [which] is as mystifying as the crowded Eastern Section, which takes in the Balkans, Asia Minor, North Africa over to Tunis, and most of the Far East." An inordinate number of personnel concentrated on exhibitions and fairs.

A feature of the equipment and method of operation of the D.O.T. which at once attracts the attention of an American observer, is the comparative absence of labor-saving office equipment; another is the extreme care given to the recording of the arrival, whereabouts, and facts of each piece of incoming correspondence; and another, the time and pains spent on the drafting of replies to inquiries...

There is nothing in any country to compare with the size of the D.O.T., with its headquarters personnel running to a total of over 560 in 1921, and its 50 Commercial Diplomatic Officers stationed in 29 foreign countries.[19]

In assessing lessons for the United States, the author of the report argued that the four-year-old DOT had succeeded in meliorating some of the friction between the Board of Trade and the Foreign Office, achievements that could survive were it abolished and its functions distributed back to the two departments. Bringing the U.S. Commerce and State Departments "closer" would similarly improve effectiveness.[20]

So much, then, for the beginnings of the U.S. federal government's machinery for collecting and diffusing economic intelligence about motion pictures. We now look in detail at the organization of the motion picture industry itself. NAMPI was replaced in 1922 by the Motion Picture Producers and Distributors of America (MPPDA), a body that survives, under a variant name, to this day.

9.4. The formation of the MPPDA

Hays on the task of keeping the MPPDA together and going and progressing: "Many a night I got down on my knees, or I couldn't have gone on.... Over and over I felt as if I couldn't carry on."

Despite an official history (Moley 1945), despite the memoirs of its founding president, Hays (1955), the accessibility of his papers,[21] and the continuing existence of its successor organization the Motion Picture Association of America, Inc. (sometimes simply called the Motion Picture Association), the formation of the Motion Picture Producers and Distributors of America (MPPDA) is shrouded in mist. Or, to write in less metaphoric terms, such accounts of its formation as have been given by historians and others are not fully compatible with one another, tend to be fuzzy on the details, and sometimes may even be exercises in mystification. The body of received opinion is that NAMPI was ineffective in coping with the attacks on the motion picture industry being mounted by the Volstead Act forces through state and local authorities around the country and by the Federal Trade Commission. Hence a new and strengthened body was required, with a public figure to head it. Hays, a Protestant layman and political operative from Indiana, was paid a huge salary (estimates vary from $100,000 to $250,000) basically to act as a front man, a lightning rod, a promiser that things would be bettered. The organization of which he was put in charge was an industry lobby group that became a self-censorship body.

This account is problematic. Just why was the predecessor organization, NAMPI, so unsatisfactory that it could not be reformed but had to be replaced, when membership of the two bodies extensively overlapped? If censorship was the problem, why were all sorts of departments to deal with other matters set up? What made the motion picture industry chiefs approach Postmaster General Will H. Hays? How much was he paid, and what, really, was his job to be?

It is important, first, to place the whole matter in the context of the growth of corporatism – the growth, that is, of the organization of American industry into national corporations controlled from New York (and, to a lesser extent, other large cities), corporations that envisaged themselves as serving the U.S. consumer with their products and serving the United States in general with their overseas earnings. It followed that government and business should cooperate, since both sought to advance the interests of the citizens. Less as a matter of ideology than of practice, it also followed that there could and should be circulation of elites between business and government. Herbert Hoover was something of a high priest of the corporatist movement. The belief was that business was a moral pillar of the community: a case of work creating wealth, of community responsibility, and hence an example to all. Business needed strictly to regulate itself in its dealings, its financial probity, the demeanor and hence credit worthiness of its leaders, its support of charity and good works in the communities where it employed people and elsewhere, and all of this without monopoly, since corporatists believed that competition was one of the engines of virtue.[22]

A most visible expression of corporatism had been the formation of trade organizations in many industries.[23] These became the favored mechanism of communication and regulation between the U.S. government and business firms. Instead of innumerable individual firms seeking government help, the industry pooled its problems and needs and communicated them through the national trade organization. That organization could then be the conduit for government advice and regulation and also for the management of consumer, interindustry, and intraindustry problems. In order not to violate the monopoly laws, the trade organization could never be seen as directing or coordinating the business activities of its members. It always needed to be seen as no more than a conduit: for example, for overseas trade intelligence collected by the government. That this course was a tricky one to steer is shown by the fact that the MPPDA was cited as a defendant in the 1931 antitrust case in Canada (see §1.4) and by the Federal Trade Commission in a 1928 suit. The issue of whether to cite it again emerged in a 1938 Department of Justice suit (see §11.3).

NAMPI was an early attempt at a trade organization for the motion picture industry. But motion pictures were quite unlike coal, steel, or petroleum. For one thing, there was some vertical integration in the industry, even in 1921; for another, the manufacturers of films – the producers – were not the most powerful firms in the business. Scarcely any of the original companies that belonged to the Motion Pictures Patents Company trust (1908–18), for example, loomed large in the business by 1921.[24] In the motion picture trade, there were thousands upon thousands of cinema owners; quite a few distributors (including the smaller, or "states's rights" firms); and also quite a few production companies. It was becoming clear that a trade body with authority would need to be dominated by the small number of integrated producer–distributor firms, firms that were organized in some semblance of a modern corporate structure, regardless of whether they were in fact public corporations freely traded on the stock exchange.

My view is that it was less the immediate threat of censorship and federal legislation to regulate motion pictures that caused the decision to scrap NAMPI than NAMPI's inadequacy as spokesman and representative of the industry, as demonstrated by its response to these difficulties. The NAMPI model had been the employment of someone from the industry to be a kind of organizing secretary of the trade organization – a model typically followed in the United Kingdom. To remedy the deficiencies of that model, where the national body was manifestly a creature of the powerful firms and could exercise no influence or control over them, what seemed to be required was an organization staffed by persons familiar with politics, business, and law but not themselves former or present employees of the major members of the organization. And at the same time there was a need to structure the organization so that proper weight was given to those firms that carried it. This line of reasoning leads me to believe that it was for reasons of corporate business, more than for immediate political worries about censorship or federal legislation, that a new form of trade organization was undertaken. The difficulty was that no model from any other industry fit motion pictures, so something new had to be devised.

This still leaves us to explain why a completely new organization was begun, rather than a restructuring of the old. The answer is fairly simple.

By withdrawing their support from the old organization, the powerful members achieved their aim of reform without having to abide by the constitution of NAMPI. Without their participation NAMPI could not survive. Furthermore, a new organization prevented them being saddled with the staff of the previous body, which was dissolved.[25] And finally, in terms of public relations, by their new organization the movie magnates were endeavoring to signal to the world of trade and commerce, as much as to legislators and censors, that their industry was making a new start.

A trade organization something like those in other industries was badly needed by the movies. It was a business acutely conscious of the fact that it had originated as little more than a circus sideshow, was developed without reference to or support from the major sources of corporate and investment capital in the United States, and was owned and managed by men of quite a different stripe from the corporate barons who had built up huge corporations in other branches of American industry. The movie men were, almost without exception, from humble beginnings, not just financially but educationally and socially. A considerable proportion was first-generation American, and almost all had found their way into movies on an opportunistic basis, having begun life either in other trades or on the sidelines.[26] Their firms had begun by operating hand to mouth, having usually to generate their own capital, and hence had for long been held in private form, such as one-man ownership, family ownership, or partnerships. They had need of the major capital market because their continued success depended on degrees of expansion, consolidation, and takeover that transcended the resources available through self-finance.

One function of a trade organization was to make an industry coherent, to represent it on the map of corporate America. To accomplish this, it was important to have on board as pilot someone who understood that map, who had contacts in industry and government, and who was or could be persuaded of the worthiness of the cause of domesticating the motion picture industry into an accepted part of American business. The eventual choice was Will H. Hays.

Who was Hays? Although only in early middle age, Hays was already considered a master of two vital talents: management and public relations. It was the combination of these two talents that he had applied to the uphill task of organizing Harding's presidential election campaign of 1920. As a reward, he had been brought from the Republican National Committee to head the U.S. Post Office, a large department thought to be functioning poorly. Within a short time he was credited with having turned it completely around. Historians of that organization must be left to pronounce on whether credit went where credit was due, but Hays and many others certainly believed the credit was his, and his papers are replete with letters from postmasters and postal employees all over the United States praising his regime and wishing he had not left.

Hays was a "modern man," the kind of Republican progressive to whom

Figure 9.1. Will H. Hays and corporate executives of the motion picture business at a staged signing of his contract with the MPPDA. *Top row, left to right*: Winfield Sheehan, Myron Selznick, Rufus Cole, Courtland Smith (MPPDA secretary), William Fox, Samuel Goldwyn, J. J. Atkinson, Robert H. Cochrane; *Seated*: Lewis J. Selznick, Earl Hammons, J. W. Williams, Hays, Adolph Zukor, Marcus Loew, Carl Laemmle. (Will H. Hays Papers, Indiana State Archives, Indianapolis.)

censorship was anathema because he thought it totally misconceived the problem. The problem was to get more and more good films made, in order to crowd out the bad. In a word, Hays's optimism did not allow him to believe in Gresham's law. He thought that if the leaders of the industry were men of integrity and goodwill, their influence and example would generate movies that would entertain the public and lead it to reject inferior films.

It was to this man that the industry leaders made their approach in 1921. After taking his time to consider their offer and setting some stiff conditions, Hays accepted (Fig. 9.1). The full offer was made in the following terms:[27]

December 2, 1921

Dear Sir:

The undersigned producers and distributors of motion picture films realize the necessity for attaining and maintaining the highest possible standard of motion picture production in this country and are striving to have the industry accorded the consideration and dignity to which it is justly entitled, and proper representation before the people of this country so that its position, at all times, may be presented in an unbiased and unprejudiced manner.

We realize that in order to ensure that we will have proper contact with the general public and to retain its confidence, and in order to attain complete accord in our industry, that it will be necessary to obtain the services of one who has already, by his outstanding achievements, won the confidence of the people of this country, and who, by his ability as an organizer and executive, has won the confidence, admiration, and respect of the people in the motion picture industry. We feel that our industry requires further careful upbuilding and a constructive policy of progress.

It is our opinion that the necessary qualifications to assist us in our work are possessed by you and we shall consider it a great privilege if you will accept an invitation from us to become the active head of a national association of motion picture producers, and distributors of which the under-signed shall be members, and such additional membership as they shall be able to procure. The compensation which we are prepared to pay in the event of your acceptance is One hundred thousand Dollars a year under a commitment satisfactory to you for a period of three years.

We trust that you will consider this offer favorably and will induce the President of the United States to relieve you from your present high duties as a member of his cabinet.

Very respectfully,

Famous Players–Lasky Corporation By Adolph Zukor, Pres.	Pathé Exchange Inc. By [blank]	Triangle Distributing Corporation By L. Waters, President
Fox Film Corporation By William Fox	Realart Pictures Corporation By Morris Cohn	Universal Film Manufacturing Co. By Carl Laemmle, Pres.
Goldwyn Pictures Corporation By Samuel Goldwyn, Pres.	R-C. Pictures Corporation By Rufus S. Cole, President	Vitagraph Inc. By [blank] United Artists Corporation By Hiram Abrams Pres.[28]
Metro Pictures Corporation By W. E. Atkinson, Gen. Mgr.	Selznick Pictures Corporation By Lewis Selznick	

Apart from the reference in the opening sentence to the "highest possible standard of motion picture production," this letter addressed the issue of public relations for the industry, obtaining for it consideration, dignity, and confidence. Its careful phrasing seems designed to match the man to the job description. Careful upbuilding and a constructive policy of progress could well describe Hays's attitude to the Post Office and to industry. We know little of the exact terms that Hays imposed, other than that he sent his executive assistant, J. Courtland Smith, from Washington to New York with letters of introduction to each of the company heads,

with a view to possibly aiding in getting some of the things done that might consistently be done before March fifth. He has consented to do this for me and I know you will be glad to talk to him.[29]

Moley tells us that Hays's main concern before taking up his duties was to execute a large number of interlocking contracts between himself and each of the companies and between the companies themselves. (Moley 1945, pp. 36, 44–5). While "inservable," these presumably reassured Hays of the bona fides of the men who had approached him.

But perhaps the most fascinating aspect of the matter is that Hays was

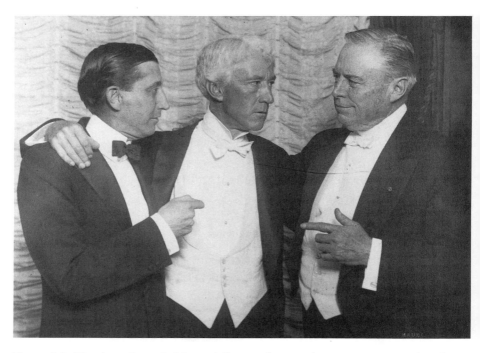

Figure 9.2. The three "czars": Hays of films, Judge Kenshaw Mountain Landis of baseball, and Augustus Thomas of the theater, probably at an autumn 1922 dinner for them (see Hays 1955, p. 362). (Will H. Hays Papers, Indiana State Archives, Indianapolis.)

hired before the proposed national association was formed. Hence he was involved in the design and launching of an entirely new body. There were essentially no models to copy. Hays always, and I think rightly, denied that he was the "czar" of motion pictures, the way Judge Landis was considered the czar of professional baseball. (Fig. 9.2 is an amusing photograph of Hays with Judge Landis and Augustus Thomas; they were often said to be the three czars, respectively, of motion pictures, baseball, and the theater; see Hays 1955, p. 362). When not being jovial, Hays made it clear that his job was nothing at all like that of the commissioner of baseball. The new organization was constrained from having any executive functions within the industry because of antitrust law and also because the company heads were not in need of someone to run their businesses for them. In the end, what Hays and the directors created was an organization that carried out some vital functions of coordination: It helped establish standard contracts; it enforced self-censorship; it served as a conduit for overseas business intelligence collected by the government; and it acted as the advocate and mouthpiece of the industry. The British and American slang word "mouthpiece" for both a spokesman and a gangster's lawyer fits well with the aim of the industry leaders to correct the bias and prejudice to which it, and they, had been subjected.[30]

Yet it is, I think, valid to stress that the desire for a movie spokesman had outdistanced any clear conception of what that job would amount to. Hays was a specialist in public relations, a consummate politician, and so was his Canadian opposite number Col. John Cooper. But one of the principal tasks that Hays faced, and his industry employers faced also, was that of inventing the parameters and functions of the job they had created. Hays was clear about this in his memoirs, but historians have not, I believe, been sensitive enough to it. Hays was improvising a job while trying to invent it – possibly for as long as the first decade of his tenure.[31]

Hays's memoirs report that he believed in the movies and believed in the probity of the leaders of the large companies who had approached him but was under no illusions either about other leaders and lesser lights or about the difficulty any head of a large organization had in ensuring that nothing done by any member of his organization would violate his wishes. If it needed to be, this was brought home during Hays's first visit to Hollywood in the July after his appointment (Figs. 9.3, 9.4) when he attended two welcoming events. There was a Cleaner Films Rally at the Hollywood Bowl, staged by his new employers, who gave their employees the day off in order that they might attend it. There was a star-studded banquet, at which the initial atmosphere was said to be frosty. The bosses may have seen the necessity of his presence, but the troops were highly ambivalent, and, had he appeared as the moral dictator or stuffed shirt they feared, were ready to oppose him as a threat to the commercial health of the commodity from which they derived their livelihood.

Two points are worth noting about the original by-laws of the MPPDA, as drawn up in March 1923. The first was that Hays had wanted a veto power over actions by the association and that this was deleted in proof. Hays was president and CEO and presumably could not be given orders, but he apparently was satisfied in other ways that he had enough control without the veto. This deletion was prudent, for it meant that when, in the early days of World War II, the directors of the MPPDA wanted to investigate his adequacy in the job, there was no question of his being able to veto the inquiry (§12.1). The other point is the specific disclaimer stating that "the Association has no jurisdiction or control over the internal affairs or business policies of its members."[32]

Clearly, then, just as Hays had no control over the internal affairs of the firms in the MPPDA, the association itself was not an owning or holding corporation either. The original corporate members were as follows:

Figure 9.3. Marshall Nielan, Hays, and Abraham Lehr at the Goldwyn Studios, July 1922. (Will H. Hays Papers, Indiana State Archives, Indianapolis, British Film Institute—Stills, Posters and Designs.)

Joseph M. Schenck Production Company
Select Pictures Corporation
Metro Pictures Corporation
Educational Film Exchanges, Inc.
Universal Film Exchanges, Inc.

Vitagraph, Inc.
Goldwyn Distributing Corporation
Fox Film Corporation
Famous Players–Lasky Corporation

Shortly thereafter seventeen more were elected:

Kenma Corporation
Talmadge Productions, Inc.
Buster Keaton Productions, Inc.
Warner Bros.
First National Pictures, Inc.
D. W. Griffith, Inc.
Eastman Kodak Company
Bray Productions, Inc.
Christies Film Company, Inc.

Distinctive Pictures Corporation
Principal Pictures Corporation
Preferred Pictures Corporation
Producers Distributing Corporation
Hal E. Roach Studios
Ritz Carlton Pictures, Inc.
Inspiration Pictures, Inc.
Kinogram Publishing Corporation

Figure 9.4. Lunch, probably at Schenck's United–Select studios, during Hays's first West Coast visit, July 1922. Norma Talmadge (or Colleen Moore?), the only woman present is "serving" Hays. Clockwise around the table from Talmadge are Rupert Hughes (obscured), Marshall Nielan, Hal Roach, Max Puett, Maurice Mackenzie (Hays's secretary), F. W. Beetson, Allen Holubar, Lawrence Boynton, Joseph Schenck, W. J. Bryan, Jr., David Selznick, and Abraham Lehr. (Will H. Hays Papers, Indiana State Archives, Indianapolis.)

Almost immediately three firms – Selznick's Select Pictures, Preferred Pictures, and Vitagraph – resigned, leaving a total of twenty-three. This membership elected a total of eighteen directors:

Albert H. T. Banhaf	David W. Griffith	Marcus Loew
Philip G. Bartlett	Will H. Hays	Saul E. Rogers
Rufus S. Cole	Siegfried F. Hartman	J. Robert Rubin
Benjamin P. DeWitt	Karl Kirchway	Lewis J. Selznick
William Fox	Harry G. Kosch	George A. Skinner
Frank J. Godsol[33]	Carl Laemmle	Adolph Zukor[34]

Shortly after the completion of the process of setting up the MPPDA, Hays wrote a lengthy letter to his old friend George Ade partly addressing the question of how the motion picture industry came to select him. He offered several reasons. It had obtained the services of the head of the biggest distributing organization in the United States, the U.S. Post Office. It had a man whose aim in life was to promote harmonizing. It had a man reputed to work twenty-four hours a day. It had a man reputed to be a great organizer. But, in the end, he admitted, "I just don't know."[35]

In trying to design a new sort of organization and make it effective, Hays said in his memoirs that he arranged to have ten departments. This does not quite square with the original by-laws, which set up six committees: Finance, Membership, Public Relations, Foreign Relations, Law, and Title. No doubt these were quickly modified and increased, but we see at once that there was no inkling of the future censorship section, the Production Code Administration. Attacks on the morals of the movies were the business of the Public Relations and Foreign Relations Committees; the rest were for internal matters (finance, membership) or for the specific concerns of legislation, contracts, or theft.

In his memoirs Hays wrote that he identified ten areas of problems for the industry when he took over:

1. internal disorders, such as bad trade practices and scandals;
2. censorship and other threatened restrictions;
3. a diplomatic crisis with Mexico over resistance to the portrayal of Mexicans in American films;
4. building a more perfect union in the industry, one that would be self-governing;
5. improving the quality of pictures quickly;
6. improving the demand, through organized public opinion;
7. securing the practical cooperation of educators;
8. helping distributors to overcome fraud and loss;
9. helping exhibitors to adjust contract problems; and
10. improving the quality of advertising. (Hays 1954, pp. 329–30)

The six committees of directors were faced with the ten problem areas, and the result was an organization that grew until it had ten departments, all under the direct executive control of Hays:

Public Relations (later Community Service)

Public Information

Foreign Relations (later International Department)

Legal Department

Theatre Service

Conservation (concerned with fire regulations)

Title Registration (established 1925)

Advertising Code Administration (established 1930)

Production Code Administration

Protective Department (legislative and political liaison)

Besides sending a representative to Mexico, suspending and then reinstating Roscoe Arbuckle as a film director, and organizing to defeat the Massachusetts censorship referendum, Hays in his first year was much concerned with the internal relations of the industry, especially that between his distributor members and their exhibitor clients. It was only in 1923, after he had overcome the teething problems and had tackled some urgent domestic matters and experienced some moments of despair, that he set out for his first foreign trip, to Europe. What he wrote about this may be a bit exaggerated, but it sets us up well for what was to come: "The organized industry plunged into the sphere of foreign relations...[and] it assumed responsibilities that have made it almost an adjunct of our State Department" (Hays 1955, pp. 333–4).

What Hays meant was that American films were a goodwill ambassador and a super salesman for the United States, its way of life, its values, and the goods it had to sell. Along with some seventy associations representing one hundred fifty thousand firms, the MPPDA in 1922 was about to join the corporatist capitalist movement that would try to curb "destructive" competition, engage in industry self-regulation, provide links between business and government, and vigorously seek overseas markets (Hogan 1977, p. 44). The U.S. government did not have a film policy and did not develop one throughout the period covered by this book. This partly accounts for the fact that from overseas it sometimes appeared as though MPPDA policy and behavior *was* U.S. policy and behavior. By his own account, Hays's reception in Europe and access to government leaders struck him as though he was a "quasi-government representative" (Hays 1955, p. 513). Technically he was the plenipotentiary from Hollywood (strictly, New York); to foreign governments he appeared at times to be the plenipotentiary from Washington.

The organization and its policies that he set out to develop, especially its economic foreign policies, were within the scope of a situation in the United State of no federal policy; no film quotas; nominal rather than protective tariffs on films and no subsidies; and, above all, no discourse employing cultural arguments about the role of films in sustaining the United States as a distinct entity. This large industry, with a significant international dimension, the products of which penetrated much of the world and indeed constituted for many citizens of the world their principal source of information about the United States, had grown up with little help, and, indeed, a certain amount of hindrance, from the federal government. This most visible evidence of American empire, coping with which loomed large (and looms still) on the cultural and commercial agendas of many countries, presented a deceptive face. Those promoting it abroad appeared to be backed by the U.S. government, yet when that government was approached with a foreign complaint it could truthfully respond that it had no direct control over, or responsibility for, Hollywood movies. At most the complaint could be passed on to the MPPDA, soon commonly known as the Hays Organization, with the request that it use its good offices to settle it.

In the matter of foreign complaints, Hays was forced to develop a foreign policy if foreign economic aims were to be advanced. But at first, all he could do was procrastinate. He could promise that the process of housecleaning was going on in the motion picture industry and constantly counsel the movie companies to be more careful. But since complaints derived from motion pictures already made and shown, the most that could be promised was better results in the future.

As he developed it, Hays's foreign policy was consciously ideological. In a 1938 speech Hays put it forcefully, in the course of listing the values represented and embodied in American motion pictures:

There is a special reason why America should have given birth and prosperous nurture to the motion picture and its world-wide entertainment. America in the very literal sense is truly the world-state. All races, creeds, all men are to be found here – working, sharing, and developing, side by side in more friendship among greater diversities of tribes and men than all the previous history of the world discloses. Our country represents the greatest single unity of races, people, and culture. Is it not possible that very quality enabled America to express itself by the creation and development of the motion pictures?

The screen owes much, indeed, to the country of its birth and development. It is distinctly the product of the America spirit – vision, initiative, enterprise and progress. It is of these precious values that I want to speak.[36]

This universalism strongly reinforced the commercialism, and vice versa. Hays was drawing on a long tradition of universalism in American thought and outlook, which can be traced back to the Pilgrim father John Winthrop's famous image of the city on the hill, America seen as a beacon to all the world. Winthrop in turn derived his imagery from the Gospel according to Saint Matthew, which says, "Ye are the light of the world. . . . Let your light shine before men, that they may see your good works" (Matt. 5:14–15). Consciously copying this image, Hays wrote in his memoirs:

At the end of fifty years' journeying the American Motion Picture Industry stood on a mountaintop from which the beacon of a silver screen was sending rays of light and color and joy into every corner of the earth. (Hays 1955, p. 508)

Thus we see Hays articulating in 1938 an economic foreign policy that he did not have in 1922 but that was fully formed by the early 1930s. His characterization of Hollywood's economic foreign policy as shining the light of entertainment and joy over the earth permitted a benign interpretation of American universalism, its products exported in a genuine conviction that the United States was a more perfect union among men than hitherto achieved. This was the reverse point of view to that of much of the outside world, and of course from that perspective his position seems insufferable and strongly ideological. When America was founded, its ideals were indeed derived from eighteenth-century European thought that yearned for the emancipation and enlightenment of all humanity. But since the eighteenth century, other countries had pursued those same ideals along paths different from the United States, and the cultural elites of those other countries were bound to resent intensely the hidden message of American films that American ideals, values, mores, are the best – especially as they would usually deem their own the best.

So, just as government officials could foster the foreign trade of the American film industry although there was in fact no government policy toward the film industry to guide and control them, so could the industry itself fulfill an ideological purpose while retaining what is now called "deniability." When foreign governments complained about Hollywood's behavior or output, State Department officials could disclaim all responsibility and even sympathize with the criticism. When the complaint was to the effect that a Hollywood film represented foreign nationals in an offensive light, State Department officials could explain that in a free country they had no control over such matters. They would willingly pass on the complaint and urge Hollywood to be less thoughtless, but that was the limit.

If the complaint was that American films were dominating foreign screens, or that American firms were buying up the film industry in another country, State Department officials could respond that the United States was an open market for films, with nominal tariff barriers and obstacles to capital acquisition. Hence if American firms and films were doing well abroad, while foreign firms and films were not matching that achievement in the United States, that presented a lesson in the free market. American companies must be giving the customers what they wanted, whereas foreign companies were not.

Foreign countries that were not wholly convinced that they were merely being bested, losing a fair game played on a level playing field, sometimes moved to intervene in ways that favored their domestic industry, arousing American indignation. This indignation came not only from the film trade but also from some federal officials, especially those in the Department of Commerce. Among the diplomats at the State Department, as we have already glimpsed, there were conflicting views. Since the United States was officially against restrictions on trade and commerce, representations against foreign restrictions on their films were in order from American diplomats. Yet to some of those diplomats, Hollywood was a vulgar industry, dominated by crass and venal individuals.

Hays's developing economic foreign policy perfectly complemented this situation, for it attended to the commercial argument and denied or ignored the cultural argument. The policy can be split into two planks:

1. no foreign impediment to American films;
2. no American impediment to foreign films.

In fulfillment of the first plank, quotas and tariffs were denounced on general grounds of principle; the same principle ensured that retaliation in kind was never threatened. Foreign cultural concerns that resulted in protective legislation were interpreted as ingenious ways to rationalize discrimination. The desire of foreign countries to have a film industry, however, was care-

Table 9.1. *Feature films produced in the United States, 1930–9*

Season	All cos.	Para-mount	Loew's	Fox	Warner Bros.	RKO	Columbia	Univer-sal	UA	All others
1930–1	510	58	43	48	69	32	27	22	13	198
1931–2	490	56	40	46	56	48	31	32	14	167
1932–3	510	51	37	41	53	45	36	28	16	203
1933–4	480	55	44	46	63	40	44	38	20	130
1934–5	520	44	42	40	51	40	39	39	19	206
1935–6	517	50	43	52	58	43	36	27	17	191
1936–7	535	41	40	52	58	39	38	40	19	208
1937–8	450	40	41	49	52	41	39	45	16	127
1938–9	526	58	51	56	54	49	54	45	18	141
Mean	504	50	42	48	57	42	38	35	17	176

Source: U.S. Senate, Temporary National Economic Committee, Investigation of Concentration of Economic Power, Monograph No. 43, *The Motion Picture Industry–A Pattern of Control* (Washington, D.C.: USGPO, 1941).

fully endorsed, and American companies ploughed back some of their foreign earnings to assist this aim. And all of this was orchestrated through an MPPDA machine that had representatives stationed overseas, good liaison with American foreign service counterparts in large markets, powerful commercial and political links with local people – in other words, good contacts for direct, face-to-face negotiations, with Hays convening the company heads in New York whenever necessary to provide rapid feedback and decisions by cable or phone. When all else failed the industry utilized the links it had built to Congress, the administration, and the Departments of State and of Commerce, to persuade foreign governments to cooperate with the MPPDA.

The second plank, despite being negative, was no less controversial. It is true that no moves were made by the industry to get high tariffs or quotas imposed upon films in the United States. But this did not make the country an open market. Throughout the interwar period, few foreign films were nationally distributed in the United States. Europeans interpreted this as an exclusionary policy, which to some degree it was – but by the industry, not by the government. U.S. firms tailored their aggregate film output to the large domestic market. The number of films they made was governed by two considerations: supply capacity and demand capacity. Studios seemed to have an upper limit. Nearly all of the major producers made between forty and sixty films per year (Table 9.1). Without going into the theory of administration, my guess is that financial and quality control were difficult at higher numbers.

Be that as it may, this production program by the big five, the little three, and the independents seldom resulted in less than an aggregate of five hundred films per year. This number was more than sufficient to supply all the screens of the nation and to allow for frequent program changes. The only gap in the system was that the five big vertically integrated companies produced only about three hundred of these pictures, not enough for their theaters to make three double-feature changes per week. Hence those companies relied for adequate supply of product first on each other, and second on smaller U.S. firms. Given this dependency, it is not surprising that much closer relations developed with domestic suppliers (including partial sharing of production costs) than with foreign ones.

The situation I am sketching, then, is of an economically withdrawn but politically powerful country that had within it a flourishing mass culture industry that was successfully penetrating markets around the world, to the chagrin of local interests. Yet the federal government of that country had no specific film policy, merely an overall policy of assistance to any American export industry threatened by foreign restrictions. It is far from clear that there was any strategy that would have avoided the general policy of Americanizing the world or could have checked the Americanization of the film industry. One can imagine localized success, as in the USSR. But resistance to American cultural penetration soon meant resisting the power of the American empire, resisting dollar imperialism; many tried, few succeeded.

Perhaps the forms of the mass media, their neutralizing of differences of social system, are not so much features of their American origin as they are of their origin (and function) in advanced industrial society.

I hesitate to argue that American universalist ideology was precisely the thing about so many Hollywood movies that the world liked. John Grierson, in an analysis of the popularity of Hollywood films written in 1927 (see Introduction, §B), was less cautious: He argued that their optimism and egalitarianism much enhanced the pleasure Hollywood narratives delivered.[37] Will Hays, in the speech quoted earlier, added to the list "vision, initiative, enterprise and progress." Indonesia's President Sukarno said that Hollywood in effect preached revolution because it showed a society in which ordinary people had houses with several rooms and possessed automobiles (quoted in McLuhan 1965, p. 294).

Sukarno made an important anthropological point. When a trade good enters a society from the outside, it is anthropologically naïve to suppose that it has the same cultural meaning in the recipient society as it has in the donor society. We have all heard the tales of European traveler's trading glass beads and trinkets to natives as usable goods. Yet those natives may well use the beads and trinkets for social purposes the trader does not grasp, merely thinking he has duped them. Even supposedly "useful" trade goods like weapons have to have their functions analyzed carefully. From the time of Captain Cook to Khaddafi and the Shah of Iran, advanced weaponry had been traded for social and cultural purposes that go well beyond the utile nature of the goods. We need to look, not only at what is done with the goods, but from whence they came and by whom they are used.

Notes

1 See Jarvie 1991 for a detailed discussion.

2 General Instruction No. 497, 15 December 1916, WNRC, RG 84 Post Records Consul-General, Paris, 1916–1935.

3 North to Boston District Office, 11 February 1927, NA, RG 151 BF&DC General Records 281 Motion Pictures General 1927.

4 Among the best treatments of film economics are Greenwald 1950 and Waterman 1978.

5 Selznick (World Film Corp.) to Secretary of State, 8 September 1915, NA, RG 59 841.4061 Films, Microfilm M580, Roll 98.

6 London Embassy to State Department, 8 September 1915, and State Department to London Embassy, 13 September 1915, NA, RG 59 841.4061 1910–1929, Microfilm M580, Roll 98.

7 Telegram of 26 March 1917, NA, RG 59 841.10 / 8a, ibid.

8 Kennedy to Cutler and enclosure, August 28 1918, NA, RG 151 281 United Kingdom, Motion Pictures, Box 1564.

9 Kennedy to Cutler, 23 September 1918, ibid.

10 *Morning Post,* 10 January 1919, attached to Kennedy to Cutler, 14 January 1919, ibid.

11 *Times,* 18 June 1919, attached to Brock to Cutler, 23 June 1919, ibid.

12 See the exchange of letters in 1920, NA, RG 151, 281, Motion Pictures General File 1918–1925.

13 Redfield testimony before the Committee on Interstate and Foreign Commerce, House of Representatives, 65th Congress, 3rd Session, House Resolution 571, 1 March 1919.

14 Material in NA, RG 151 141.1 Estimates, fiscal Motion Picture 1921, folder "Foreign Trade Promotion after the War."

15 See Hawley's essay "Herbert Hoover and Economic Stabilization, 1921–22," in Hawley, ed., 1981, pp. 43–79; see also Hawley 1981.

16 Herter to Brady, 10 August 1921, HHH, Commerce Papers, Motion Pictures.

17 Klein to Elliott, 30 August 1921, NA, RG 151, Bureau of Foreign and Domestic Commerce, General Records, 160.2 Specialties Divisions.

18 Robinson to Research Division, 28 September 1921, NA, RG 151, Bureau of Foreign and Domestic Commerce, General Records 281, General – Motion Pictures.

19 Report on the Department of Overseas Trade and Governmental Trade Promotion Work in Great Britain, November 1921, HHH, Commerce Papers, Great Britain, pp. 17–18.

20 Ibid., pp. 19–25.

21 The quotation that opens this section is from an index card of 24 February 1948 reporting Hays's comments on the difficulties of his job, Will H. Hays Papers, Indiana State Library, Indianapolis.

22 See, among others, Brandes 1962, Cuff 1977, Hawley 1973, Hawley 1974, Hawley 1981, Hawley 1981a, Hogan 1977, Hogan 1987, McConnell 1966, Seidel 1973, Weinstein 1968, Wiebe 1967, Joan Hoff Wilson 1975.

23 Hogan 1977 reports that by 1922 there were seventy trade organizations, representing some 150,000 firms (p. 41).

24 On the trust, see the special issue of *Film History*, vol. 1, no. 3, 1987.

25 Hawley 1981 says Brady was later involved in scandal. It is unclear if this possibility was a factor in 1921.

26 A lively journalistic account of their origins is sketched in Gabler 1988; see also French 1969, Zierold 1969, and, of course, Ramsaye 1926.

27 This text was photo reproduced in Ramsaye 1926, p. 816, and was miscalled a "round robin" by Moley 1945, p. 32.

28 Biographical File, Hays Papers. The copy at Indianapolis is a carbon flimsy without signatures and may not, therefore, be a true copy of the final letter of appointment, although it corresponds to that reproduced by Ramsaye. The failure to type in the names of signing officers for Pathé and Vitagraph is open to various interpretations. By the time Hays underwent the signing ceremony, nearly four months later (Fig. 9.1), Earl Hammons of Educational Films and J. D. Williams of First National had joined the lineup.

29 Hays letters of introduction for Smith, 20 January 1922, Correspondence Files, Hays Papers.

30 For this point I want to thank Marybelle Burch, formerly Indiana Archivist in charge of the Hays Papers.

31 In a 1990 paper presented to the Organization of American Historians in Washington, D.C., "Movies, Politics and Censorship: The Production Code Administration and Political Censorship of Film Content," Gregory Black independently argued that Hays spent much of the 1920s defining his job and getting a grip on his organization.

32 By-laws proof, 13 March 1922, Hays Papers.

33 On Godsol, see Lewis and Lewis 1988.

34 The names of these directors are printed in the by-laws proof of 13 March 1922 Hays Papers. The names of the corporate members are taken from a memorandum for the files by J. Courtland Smith, Hays's executive assistant, 22 March 1922, Hays Papers. There can be little doubt that if Select dropped out, Selznick soon ceased to be a director of MPPDA. The papers in the Hays collection do not chronicle this.

35 Hays to Ade, 28 March 1922, Hays Papers. Murphy (1969, pp. 46–7) stresses that in the Harding campaign Hays concentrated on publicity, finance, and party organizational matters and was not a top strategist.

36 Hays speech "What's Right with America," delivered to the Poor Richard Club, Philadelphia, 18 January 1938; HHH, Post-Presidential Papers, Hays file. Evidence in the Moley papers indicates that this speech was drafted, if not fully written, by Raymond Moley; see Moley to Hays, 3 January 1938, Raymond Moley Collection, HIA, Hays file.

37 Grierson at PRO, BT 64 86 / 5511 / 28.1. See Jarvie and Macmillan 1989.

CHAPTER 10

Machinery without policy, 1923–1932

This chapter shows how the newly reconstituted trade organization, the Motion Picture Producers and Distributors of America (MPPDA) developed working relations with the U.S. Department of Commerce. Within the Department of Commerce, in the Bureau of Foreign and Domestic Commerce (BF&DC), a strengthened Specialties Division added personnel who concentrated on motion pictures, a group that eventually grew into the Motion Picture Section. Machinery to collect economic and political intelligence was refined, and the State Department was drawn in to assist the effort, especially in face of the attempts of European governments to cap Hollywood's market share. Some attention is given to the main personalities, especially Hays, who developed their distinctive styles but had, in the judgment of some, considerable difficulty in formulating a clear and effective foreign policy for the motion pictures.

10.1. The developing government–MPPDA relationship

Contacts between the BF&DC and the former motion picture trade organization, the National Association of the Motion Picture Industry (NAMPI), had been cordial (§9.3). Indeed, government officials may have been somewhat in advance of the industry in their thinking. By 1923 the collection of economic intelligence on motion pictures by the government had been under way for more than a dozen years, even though coherent industry lobbying had been sparse. Senate Resolution 121, passed in 1921, had been directed at promotion of trade through motion pictures at home and abroad, not at the promotion of motion pictures as an export commodity. The year 1921 had been a slump year for the U.S. film industry, a fact that may have affected the formation of the MPPDA and enhanced interest in using the federal government to assist the industry, more than any social pressures for censoring motion picture content – strong though those were. Social pressures against motion pictures, seeking to license theaters, subject films to prior restraint, curb the oligopolistic practices of the industry, and often stemming from the same source as progressivism and prohibitionism – a militant Christianity – discouraged government assistance to the industry. But matters were not so simple. Will Hays was an abstemious Protestant layman of some national distinction, yet he apparently saw no conflict between those values and becoming deeply involved in the promotion of the industry.

Whether economic conditions, the rejuvenated trade organization, or both were responsible, the collection of materials by government gradually improved during the 1920s, first data on the domestic market and then on markets abroad. As late as October 1922 the director of the Census Bureau (another Commerce bureau) was complaining that simply getting facts and figures for the Census of Manufactures from the film industry was proving difficult (despite "the urgent request of the moving picture association"), due to the fact that "many companies are not greatly interested, and not only neglect to make reports, but seriously object to furnishing the figures."[1] Meanwhile, an article in the *Annalist* for 9 May 1921 had analyzed the motion picture business as a promising one for bankers to venture into, offering advice on how to discriminate good loan prospects from poor ones. Prominent among its points was the stress on distribution as "of far more importance commercially than production"; on the 16,000 or more theaters in the United States, compared to the 17,500 in the rest of the world combined; and on exports as having grown from $5 million per annum in 1912 to $12 million in 1920. The capacity of those 16,000 U.S. theaters to garner revenue was, of course, much greater than that of the 17,500 in the rest of the world put together. Nevertheless, the foreign market presented a clear opportunity for development, and the strategic stress was on distribution. Although the MPPDA had "Producers" in its name, it was in fact the trade organization of the major New York distributors. A separate organization for producers, the Association of Motion Picture Producers (AMPP), was organized in July 1924. Known informally as the "West Coast Association", because its headquarters was in Los Angeles, it was close to, but must not be confused with, the MPPDA (see Hays 1955, pp. 357–8). The latter organization was much concerned with harmonizing the domestic business practices of distribution and managing the distributor–exhibitor interface. It also was bound to be drawn into the export drive and to serve as a source of pressure, of demands, of coordination and mediation between government and industry.

Typical of the matters that would be brought to Hays's attention in the years to come was a letter from one Henry Howard, of the Grasselli Chemical Company of Cleveland, representing the Foreign Trade Committee of the Cleveland Chamber of Commerce, to the BF&DC. The head of the BF&DC was Herbert Hoover's right-hand man, Dr. Julius Klein (see Fig. 10.1).[2] Howard's letter asked Klein to investigate, in Latin America and the Far East, the rumor that "all the rotten films that cannot be exhibited in this country are sent to one or more of the foreign countries mentioned,

Figure 10.1. Corporate Progressives celebrate. Herbert Hoover and his bureau chiefs on the roof of the Commerce Building after his nomination for the Presidency, 15 June 1928. The man on Hoover's right is Julius Klein. (Herbert H. Hoover Presidential Library, West Branch, IA.)

and do great damage to the reputation of the United States and American business."[3] In a covering memorandum Klein commented, "From what I have seen in South American [South America] the highest quality American films, as well as the poor ones, are circulated there just as they are in this country.... Nevertheless ... you might send out ... half a dozen queries to a few of our offices."[4]

Klein took the opportunity, while dealing with the complaint, to comment:

We are becoming more and more interested in this matter of the trade promoting possibilities of American films. Commercial Attaché Arnold, who has just arrived here from China for a brief visit, tells me that our films are having a profound effect upon Chinese trade, in the main a very favorable one; so much so, in fact, that we are considering the appointment of a special trade commissioner in our China organisation for the purpose of getting advice as to the character and distribution of films for that area, especially with reference to the so-called educational pictures.[5]

Klein elaborated on these themes in a letter to Hays, acknowledging the latter's congratulations on an editorial Klein had written titled "Trade Follows the Motion Pictures."[6] He also skillfully suggested that Howard's interest was "that as a commercial nation we are not yet capitalising on all of the admirable openings created by the activities of your industry in foreign countries."

We have been giving considerable thought to this subject and our plans for the new fiscal year contemplate some special efforts toward making the pictures even more effective media in behalf of our trade in foreign countries.... I feel... that the commercial influence of our dramatic pictures is only beginning to be understood. I was particularly impressed by this fact during my service as Commercial Attaché at our embassy in Buenos Aires.[7]

Klein urged Hays "to command our organisation whenever we may be in a position to serve you."[8]

Perhaps because his plate was full, there is little evidence that in his first couple of years in office Hays gave special attention to the Commerce invitation. Throughout 1922 and 1923, his concentration would seem to have been on the domestic image of the motion picture industry, trying to paint it as a fount of probity and respectability, the local theater manager a solid member of the Chamber of Commerce and the Rotary Club. Yet

The producers of pictures are going to great lengths to cooperate with the Government in every way, of course. There are definite movements now in process of most far-reaching consequence, such as the promotion of international amity by the careful depicting of peoples to each other. The fact is, steps have been taken to make certain that every picture which is made here shall correctly portray American life, opportunities and aspirations to the world, and, too, that we correctly portray to America the life of other peoples. We are going to sell America to the world with American pictures.[9]

Hays requested that a State Department official be appointed to work with the MPPDA on polishing the image of U.S. films abroad. One W. Phillips got the job, but no records of his work survive.[10] It is somewhat surprising that Hays wrote so confidently about cleaning up a central complaint made against American motion pictures at home and abroad. But his final sentence shows how oblivious he was to a general concern that underlay many of the specific objections. Some of the items for sale in the selling of America – egalitarianism, capitalism, individualism – were highly objectionable to many of the regimes in whose territories the selling was to take place, good examples being Canada and the United Kingdom. Other items – vulgarity, national stereotyping, jingoism, the underside of American life – were objectionable to some domestic as well as many foreign elites.

10.2. Mobilization to cope with quotas in Europe

When Hays assumed the job of president of the MPPDA, he wrote in his memoirs (Hays 1955, pp. 329–30), he identified ten areas in which the trade had problems needing immediate attention (see §9.4). Only one of these, strenuous Mexican diplomatic objections to the stereotypical treatment of their nationals and their history in American films, involved foreign affairs. He did, however, organize an International Department (originally called Foreign Relations Department) to fight to keep the channels of foreign trade open. By 1924, developments abroad were beginning to loom larger on his agenda. It was during this year that his brother-in-law, F. L. Herron,[11] began to work as manager (later foreign manager) of the MPPDA.

As a Republican free trader, Hays set his face against the protectionist forces in the United States, whose efforts were to culminate in the Fordney–McCumber and Hawley–Smoot tariff acts of 1922 and 1930. The organized motion picture industry never, throughout the whole period covered by this book, strove for high tariffs or other restrictions on film imports. No doubt this stemmed less from virtue (although Hays's personal free trade convictions were genuine) than from the economic lock that the members of the MPPDA and the Independent Motion Picture Producers and Distributors of America (IMPPDA) had on their trade. Foreign firms were solely producers by this time, all domestic distribution in the U.S. being in the hands of American firms. As I have stressed, distribution is the economically strategic center of the industry, which takes the lion's share of what is left of the box-office dollar, after theater expenses and overheads are deducted. Thus the occasional foreign film that was successfully shown in the United States would return most of its dollars to the American distributors who handled it. Some commentators thought the vertically integrated major companies had a vested interest in excluding foreign product. On the contrary, no major integrated U.S. company produced enough films to supply its own cinemas – hence it was always in the market for supplementary product. Furthermore, a major strategy during the 1920s was for American firms to have foreign subsidiaries: There was thus actually an incentive to import and exploit certain foreign-made films.

But the analysis is running ahead of the narrative of events. Before questions of cultural sovereignty were raised, it was, as we have seen, the trade practices of the American motion picture industry abroad that had caused rumbles of discontent, especially the practices of block booking and blind booking. In the autumn of 1923, the British National Film League had been organized to resist such practices and to promote British films. It was not successful and by 1925 was declared defunct by the U.S. consul in Manchester.[12] In January 1924, Sir Oswald Stoll, of Stoll Theatres, was reported by the consul as arguing, in the company's annual report, that war

Figure 10.2. Hays greeted at Waterloo Station on his 1923 visit to London. (Will H. Hays Papers, Indiana State Archives, Indianapolis.)

debt repayments were making the public dislike American pictures. A penciled note added in the State Department's Division of European Affairs said:

Stoll is an important person in the theatrical and cinema world in Great Britain: his bitterness will accordingly be passed on. The English films are notoriously bad particularly the "comic" ones, which are obviously written by persons with an atypical English sense of humor. His remark therefore that the American films are "bad and indifferent" is somewhat ridiculous.[13]

Again in 1924, U.S. consular officials took note of newspaper editorials in the *Montreal Star* and the *Sydney Bulletin* deploring the American monopoly of the film industry in Canada and Australia, respectively, and urging that the British government financially assist the U.K. film industry to produce films that would serve to "weld the Empire more closely together."[14]

These rumblings were not disregarded. As early as 1923, Hays wrote, after his first trip to England (Fig. 10.2), he had suggested to some of the distributor members of MPPDA that their position abroad would be strengthened if they imported a few good foreign films. Looking back, he wrote:

The policy of our team was to support the American picture position in every practicable way: by making the best possible pictures; by maintaining free trade; by inviting cooperation from every quarter; by keeping well informed on foreign problems of all sorts; by seeking solutions in person, on the basis of mutual advantage; by drawing into the American art industry the talent of other nations in order to make it more truly international; and, finally, by a confident and resourceful sales policy. (Hays 1955, p. 509)

Perhaps the central plank here was the collection of information. If available well in advance, this gave the industry time to study what was happening abroad and calculate its reaction, including coordination with federal government agencies. It is, however, quite unclear from Hays's remarks whether he had a clear idea about the need to mobilize resistance. In a contemporary statement of policy, Herron said,

In regard to these attacks in the French papers, we feel the best thing to do in the matter is to quietly sit back and let them do all the talking and not answer. That has been the policy of the Association ever since it started, not only in its domestic problems, but its foreign ones. Controversies and arguments in newspapers never lead to any good end.

Foreign pictures shown in America have in most cases been financial failures. They don't seem to grasp the ideas that the American public demands in motion pictures.[15]

This complacent attitude did not last. The Hays representatives in Toronto, Colonel John Cooper, and in London, Fay Allport, engaged in vigorous exchanges in newspapers in the 1930s and after.

On 18 August 1924, the British publication *The Cinema* carried news of a conference to be held in London in October at which Stinnes Movie Enterprises hoped to organize concerted European and Scandinavian resistance to American movie imports. Although such a concerted "Film Europe" never materialized, it was precisely the sort of threat that worried the U.S. industry (see Lewis 1933, chap. 13). What transpired instead of the concerted effort was the enactment of quotas in the major markets of Germany (the *Kontingent* scheme), France (visas), and the United Kingdom (quotas), copied by many smaller countries. These systems of restriction were the principal impediment against which the Hays organization lobbied and that, as World War II drew to a close, they struggled to prevent reemerging in the postwar world.

A circular addressed to all commercial attachés and trade commissioners abroad by the Department of Commerce went out on 24 November 1924. It said,

One of the Bureau's most valuable contacts is the Motion Picture Producers and Distributors of America, Inc., of which Mr. Will H. Hays is President. We are particularly anxious that our services to this industry should be effective and that we should make a special point of keeping it posted on all developments affecting it throughout the world. This is desirable because of the great importance of the industry, as well as by reason of the high esteem and appreciation in which the Bureau and its efforts are held by this organization. Dr. Klein has personally expressed the wish that we should be alert to forward promptly all items likely to be of interest.

The motion picture producers [distributors] are vitally concerned with every phase of the local motion picture situation, such, for example, as the following: New laws or restrictions, actual or threatened; the activities of local producers; censorship regulations, particularly changes; combinations or re-alignments of film distributors or theatre owners; new theatre construction or consolidations; changes in the attitude of the public or the exhibitors toward American and foreign productions; any action threatened, either governmental or public, which would prove inimical to American pictures.

In reporting on these or any similar phases of the matter, timeliness is of the utmost importance. A short report on some significant development sent at once will be much more valuable than a more detailed one on the general situation at a later date. Do not hesitate to use the cable if the matter is of prime importance. More comprehensive reports going into all phases of the subject are also desirable whenever such can be furnished.

Sent under the signature of Warren L. Hoagland, chief of the Specialties Division, this circular indicated that a cozy relationship was developing between the BF&DC and the MPPDA. This was to be a continuing fact throughout our period, notable in the tone of much of correspondence of the eventual chiefs of the Motion Picture Division and its heirs, Clarence J. North[16] and Nathan D. Golden.[17] This was not, of course, the first circular to foreign service posts on motion pictures (see §9.2), but it was the first from the Department of Commerce. Its immediate importance for the scholar is that it initiated the flow of information that is to be found in the Department of Commerce records at the National Archives. This was a period when, under the impetus of Hoover's revamping of the department, it was expanding its own foreign service. Eventually this duplication of effort became a point at issue between the State and Commerce Departments and was resolved in favor of the former. Thus these two sets of circular instructions, of 1916 and 1924, were the bases of several later follow-up circular instructions that reiterated, updated, or respecified the kind of information needed.

Late in 1924 there was a correspondence between Herron and Klein, stimulated by Herron's claim that certain periodicals and newspapers had twisted consular and trade commissioner reports

in such a way that it does this industry a great deal of harm abroad. As you realize, any publicity sent out in this country relative to the tremendous amount of business that we are doing in certain foreign countries in motion pictures over the amount of their domestic business does not add particularly to the fostering of pleasant trade relations between this country and these other countries. Most of the reports of this sort that are put out are published by the individuals through pure ignorance of the material that they are dealing with.[18]

He requested that all material be centralized in Washington and that he be permitted to help sanitize it before release. He noted that Hays had presently met with the editors of the trade papers to explain the aims of the industry abroad and how to push the product without making it obnoxious to foreigners. In Great Britain, Herron reported, a to-do was in progress about the data-collecting activities of U.S. consuls, and a rumor was abroad that the United States, not satisfied with 90 percent of the British market, was shooting for 100 percent.

Klein was sympathetic, but in some difficulty. Material was already funneled through Washington by both the State and Commerce Departments. It was censored before release, and care was taken "to give out only information that will not be harmful to American interests." However, some of the information was not confidential, so, he thought, Hays's approach to the trade papers was probably the best solution.[19]

A different way of dealing with Herron's worries was to centralize motion picture intelligence within the BF&DC. This occurred on 23 March 1925, when Clarence J. North was brought back to the Specialties Division and took overall charge of motion picture work. His chief, Hoagland, left him to take the initiative and draw up plans "for closer cooperation with the motion picture industry and the maximum of service to it."[20] Many of the papers of the bureau for this period are missing, but traces of two concrete moves made by North do remain. They were an extensive questionnaire to the motion picture companies about the quantities, types, and values of pictures shown abroad, the number censored in whole or in part, and the amount of duty paid; and, more significant, the creation of a separate Motion Picture Division within the bureau. Neither the actual questionnaire nor the aggregated figures from the replies have survived, but this was certainly an ambitious attempt to lay down a statistical base on the foreign trade of the industry.[21] I suspect that if the response received was unsatisfactory, this was less because of company reticence than company inadequacy. Although the major motion picture corporations were medium-sized businesses, they were not run on the principles of scientific management. In the absence of such principles, it is questionable whether reliable data of the kind North requested could have been compiled by them. Indeed, it was only over the subsequent decade that it came to be realized that the compilation of accurate data was a vital weapon in the battle to protect the U.S. market share. The industry needed the MPPDA and its own government to go to bat against foreign governments, and those bodies needed to have in their hands lots of basic facts to show that there was mutual advantage in the position the U.S. industry was advocating.

The second initiative, creation of a separate Motion Picture Division in the BF&DC, required high-level support within the department and Congressional budgetary approval. Yet it went ahead quickly and was announced by Hoover as commencing on 1 July 1926. In the next twenty years, budget cutting sometimes led to its amalgamation with other divisions, followed by its reappearance in better times. On the basis of the incomplete records in the files, my guess is that its small staff was intact throughout the period but that they sometimes did other work and that some promotions were denied them.

Two considerations weighed heavily in these matters. The first was the great success of the American motion picture abroad. Although in dollar amount it was by no means a leading export industry, being a center of publicity and visibility it had a striking presence abroad. This enhanced the claim that films were a form of advertising for American goods, services, and life-style, and possibly even for America and Americanism. Cultural as well as commercial arguments were used to defend the U.S. market share.

The second consideration was that foreign governments were beginning to take cognizance of the market share held by U.S. firms. So far as we know, in the pre–World War I period, when the U.S. movie market was dominated by foreign firms and pictures, nothing was done by the federal legislature and authorities – indeed, taking such an interest might not have been thought appropriate, given the doubtful standing of the motion picture business among American industries. It could hardly have been a surprise to American corporations when the agitation of nationalist and business elites in foreign lands succeeded in galvanizing governments into action explicitly designed to reduce the American market share. The industry faced a bewildering maze of restrictions on its overseas trade: tariffs, import fees, censorship fees, visas, exhibiting fees, exchange controls, and, eventually, dubbing fees and quota or *Kontingent* restrictions. These were highly technical, highly political matters. It is not surprising, therefore, that the MPPDA eventually employed high-powered staff and consultants and found it convenient to work as closely as was permitted with the State Department.

Whether protectionist or whether sincerely concerned about national culture, foreign governments were regulating international trade in motion pictures in a manner that placed individual American firms at a severe disadvantage. Individual firms were, after all, without standing in any attempt to affect the trading policies of a foreign government. And even if they could find an ear to listen, they spoke only for themselves. Thus what the new situation demanded, once its reality and likely persistence had been acknowledged, was that U.S. firms have a single spokesman, who, where possible, had the backing of public opinion and of the U.S. government. This ideal situation was never in fact achieved. Although the U.S. film industry was not as chronically divided as the British, it did have divisions, most notably between the MPPDA and the IMPPDA, and between the MPPDA and the theater owners not controlled by the integrated companies.

Luckily these divisions seldom made much impact on foreign trade matters, where the sheer dominance of the MPPDA companies made the MPPDA the natural leading spokesman. Public backing of foreign operations was another matter. The inchoate masses, to be sure, were devoted movie fans. But they are excluded from public opinion, which is normally a euphemism for powerful elites, lobbies, pressure groups, and the press. Jowett (1976), Sklar (1976), and May (1980) have adequately documented the amount of such "public opinion" in the United States that was hostile to the content of motion pictures and the business practices of the industry.

All of these conflicting pressures had to be negotiated and renegotiated over the decades, especially as the motion picture business changed rather drastically and as the geopolitical position of the United States altered, altering thereby the definition of the major interests of the United States. To repeat, on sheer dollar scale U.S. motion pictures never earned a great deal as an export, so it was fortunate that the Hoover–Klein regime at Commerce and the subsequent Hull regime at State took a strong personal interest in fostering their welfare abroad. It is, in a way, remarkable testimony to its capacity for self-promotion and exaggeration of its own importance that the movie industry managed to continue to get favorable treatment out of its government throughout the period 1920–50.

10.3. The British legislation of 1927 as seen from the United States

On 23 June 1925, Alfred Nutting, of the U.S. consulate in London, cabled the State Department to pass on the complete text of the *Morning Post* letter of 20 June deploring the cultural influence of American films in the British Empire and the accompanying editorial (see §4.2). He noted that none of the signatories was connected with the industry and hazarded that "the movement on behalf of British films is undoubtedly gaining strength almost daily, and the subject will be a prominent one at the forthcoming Advertising Convention at Harrogate. The block-booking system, – a point of acute controversy a few years ago[22] – is largely responsible for the present agitation."[23]

By August, an American Major Solbert was in London trying to find out from the Board of Trade or, as it turned out, from the Federation of British Industry (FBI), what the British agitation portended. In a confidential briefing he was informed that feeling was so strong in Britain and the Empire that the U.S. market share would be reduced one way or another. A voluntary agreement with the American industry was preferred, in which some 10 percent of the films distributed in the United Kingdom was reserved for British pictures, which were in turn released in the United States. Cofinancing and even coproduction were also offered. The threat was that unless a voluntary agreement was made, the eventual solution would be legislation, and that might reserve, on the German model, as much as 20–25 percent of the market for British films. The acting commercial attaché noted,

Solbert tells me in confidence that Will Hays, and the more thinking of the American picture producers, realize that the virtual monopoly which American pictures have in the Cinema Theatres of the world is unhealthy, and that they want above all things to see good exhibitable British pictures produced, that they have no objection to British legislation which will, by the imposition of duties, aid in securing a market here for British productions, but that they do object most strenuously to legislation in this or other countries on the German contingent plan, which admits of all sorts of abuses, and in Germany has led to one Company securing an absolute monopoly on the motion picture business. He says that, with the influence which they wield in the American press, the American picture industry will, or at least may, start a vigorous anti-British campaign, if legislation of an undesirable type is enacted here.[24]

What transpired was a long series of maneuvers (detailed in Part II), as the Board of Trade endeavored to get unanimous endorsement by the British industry of a plan that would make legislation unnecessary. But the different interests of the exhibitors (who wanted to keep the public happy), the renters (who included the London branches of the major American companies), and the producers made such agreement impossible. Nothing in the American official files confirms Solbert's view that Hays and some of the major companies were genuinely interested in good British pictures being produced. "Genuineness" here might mean their willingness to entertain some kind of coproduction and cofinancing to assist British pictures to come up to what the Americans considered commercial par. American ventures abroad, first in Germany and then in Britain, were indeed a response to – not an attempt to preempt – the disliked legislation.

Indeed, in early 1926 Hays asked the State Department to file protests with countries passing "harmful legislation against one of America's greatest industries." He named Australia and Hungary and said legislation had only just been headed off in Austria, Czechoslovakia, France, England, and Holland. The departmental response was another circular, to all embassies and consulates, asking for reports on agitation against American films and on any government action, stating whether it was discriminatory and offering suggestions for overcoming its harmful effects. It ended, "You are authorized ... to take ... appropriate steps ... to protect the interests in question."[25] This major call for information produced a flood of replies from posts in fifty-eight countries and an indication of the scope of the economic intelligence-collecting effort made on behalf of the motion picture industry. The dispatches reported that in most markets American films were utterly dominant and wildly popular. Alas, the total market represented by the rest of the world was small.

Agitation of one kind or another *was* reported from London; officials in Ottawa reported no evidence of discrimination "other than in import duties." The dispatch continued, "There is, from time to time, sporadic criticism of American motion picture films and of the danger to Canada of permitting the United States to provide nearly all of the Canadian public's reading material and motion pictures. No official cognizance has, however, been taken of any of these statements." Officials of the Bureau of Motion Pictures in Canada, thought it unlikely there would be a quota system there. They thought British pictures needed to learn how to tell a story in film and improve their technique.[26] However, quota legislation introduced into the Ontario Provincial legislature on 16 March 1928 was withdrawn after an *Ottawa Citizen* editorial argued that it would provide protection for poor British films the public did not want.[27]

Although agitations against American films were both commercial (where there was a local industry) and cultural, neither tariffs against foreign films nor quotas on foreign films were in a technical sense discriminatory, since they applied equally to all foreign films. Yet American films overwhelmed the market and carried the burden, so in effect these measures were discriminatory. It was hard for the MPPDA or the U.S. government to devise a strategy. Some that were tried were to discourage loans to countries where the state had a financial interest in the industry, because that would mean that the funds could be used in part to finance pictures to compete with American pictures. The other strategy was to try "to build up a body of industrial opinion through the Chambers of Commerce in this country" recognizing the advertising value of American pictures and so extend passive support to the struggle of the U.S. film industry.[28]

Given that there was no technical discrimination, however, there was little for the government to protest about. The longer-term strategies of building up information, getting the industry better organized and coordinated, and securing a "trojan horse" position inside the quota barriers perhaps only gradually came into focus as making an accommodation possible. Thus the importance of the creation of the Motion Picture Division within the BF&DC, headed by North. Simultaneously it was proposed to appoint a trade commissioner to Europe who would concentrate on motion picture matters. North specifically asked Herron of the MPPDA to consult on the membership of an advisory committee to act as a general guide for the work of the new division.[29] Not surprisingly, North had already had to try to quash foreign rumors that Hays had received his MPPDA appointment with the connivance of the U.S. government.[30] When another politically prominent Protestant layman was appointed as the new secretary of the MPPDA – former governor of Maine Carl E. Milliken[31] – North learned of it by letter.[32]

Events in London were clearly the center of interest at this point, because Britain was the largest foreign market and influenced markets throughout the British Empire, which added up to a sizable proportion of foreign revenue (Table 10.1). Surprisingly, North, recently appointed, had at first, in 1925,

Table 10.1. *Markets for American films, 1925*

Market	% of America's foreign revenue	Ratio of American films to total (%)
United Kingdom	35	95
Germany	10	16
Australia–New Zealand	8	95
Scandinavia	6	85
Argentina	5	90
Canada	5	95
France	3	70
Japan	3	30
Brazil	3	75

Source: Lewis (1933), p. 397.

pooh-poohed the British agitation. Commenting on the House of Lords debate (§4.2), he wrote,

A number of acrimonious references were made to the lack of support which the British producer gets from exhibitors in his own country, these all evidently preferring to show pictures of American origin for the reason that they secure greater profits from such showings.

I do not imagine that this is more than talk and I do not think there is any danger of further action against the importation of American pictures.[33]

Such complacency was, of course, to receive a rude shock. While events dragged out for two years, as the British government tried hard to avoid imposing legislation on a divided British film industry, there was, all along, momentum to see that something was done. Another form of complacency was the view that the U.S. industry could, should it so wish, simply buy up the British industry.[34] The complacency could not, however, long survive the appointment of a special trade commissioner for the Department of Commerce assigned to Europe, specializing in motion pictures and commanded to find out what the true situation was. This officer, from 16 August 1926, was George R. Canty.[35] Klein gave him careful instructions to consider himself under the orders of permanent field officers. He was to undertake no investigation and to establish no contacts without previous consultation with the resident officer.[36] These bureaucratic restrictions were intended to avoid ruffling feathers and to ensure that turf rivalries did not impede the work. In his turn, North instructed Canty that developments in France were pivotal and that Canty was to attend the Motion Picture Congress there. He was then to proceed to London to find out whatever he could at the

Imperial Conference (see §2.3). He was also to tour through Berlin, Prague, Vienna, Budapest, and Rome, looking into the situation created wherever there was a *Kontingent*.[37]

In a long and detailed letter of instruction to Canty the following month, North indicated that there had been close consultation with Herron. Canty was told that they needed to know the best way to fight *Kontingent* systems in place and the best ground for fighting them off where they were threatened. Following this he was to compile information on the local film industry, especially any production plans that might prove competitive. Perhaps because of earlier complacency regarding British developments, Canty was based not in London but in Paris and was sent all over the place, rather than concentrating on the big market where there was no quota but where U.S. interests were certainly threatened. By January 1927, North seems to have forgotten his own blithe confidence that the agitation was mere talk and counseled Canty that he might soon be urgently needed in London:

There is no question but that the possibilities of film legislation in England are still uppermost in the minds of the trade. Between ourselves no one, except possibly Lowry and Herron doubts that there will not be some sort of film quota introduced when Parliament reassembles and it is of the highest importance to keep informed of just what is going on. By this I mean not only what may be officially given out but likewise whatever can be picked up through such channels as Mr. Tennyson of the FBI and Freedman and others high up in the industry there. . . . Be prepared to go over there at a moment's notice.[38]

North seems to have been gradually changing from a follower to a leader – or if not a leader, then a powerful cheering and coaching section. When Canty wrote suggesting utilizing the weapon of boycott against a threatened Czechoslovakian quota, North liked the idea in principle but predicted that the U.S. companies' ranks would break as soon as one of them saw an advantage. This lack of a solid united front explained, he thought, the continuance of the German *Kontingent* system.[39] The proposed British legislation was, he considered, a crucial case, for the additional reason that its progress was being watched in other countries before they made their moves – he specified Italy.[40] Yet the Hays Organization acted in a manner that fell short:

What you can accomplish to a considerable degree depends on the manner in which the various companies pull together both here and abroad. As I see it, at the present time there is comparatively little cooperation between the companies in Europe and considerable [*sic*] less over here. Furthermore, it seems to me that the start in cooperation must be made right in New York and then reflected to the men in charge of the offices in Europe. The Hays people should take the lead in this and so far I certainly don't think that they have. In other words, the thing first to be established if it can be done, is a definite policy on the part of the Hays foreign department. I am not sure that this could be done under any circumstances and least of all under the present regime but I have hopes that steps may be taken in that direction.[41]

One possible explanation of the complacency of the companies in the Hays Organization was their belief that they could evade the quota through a combination of British subsidiary firms and Empire-based firms, both making films that would qualify as British. The understanding within the BF&DC was that

If a film made in Canada would be included in the British quota, some American companies would be ready to go over to some place like Vancouver and set up a studio, partly in order to enjoy the British preferential rate, but primarily in order to increase the number of full American films that would be admitted into England.[42]

Perhaps they were in this more realistic than North, since he took their attitude to be defeatist. The correspondence reveals that their best intelligence was that the intention was to fix the quota at between 7.5 percent and 10 percent, neither figure a catastrophic inroad into market share. It is unclear whether they were aware before publication that the draft bill would contain a sliding scale that would raise the percentage over the life of the legislation. But even with these concessions, North's points that what happened in Britain could affect the policies of other nations, and that there should be some coordinated policy between the companies, were unanswered.

As 1927 moved on, his view of the MPPDA grew even more jaundiced:

Right now ... the Hays organisation seems to have lapsed from its former nervous state into one of almost complete apathy. That is to say they now claim they may as well take this course and beyond lodging an informal protest they apparently intend to do nothing further. ... I cannot help observing somewhat guardedly however, that the Hays people came in for a certain amount of underground criticism that their representative abroad [Edward C. Lowry, appointed 23 May 1927] should have returned to this country [the United States] just about the time that the film bill was introduced. Of course Herron laughs it off by saying after all there is nothing further which can now be done as the situation is out of hand. Unfortunately however, this follows close on claims made over a long period of time that said representative did not believe that there would be a quota, with the inference that his contacts were such that he could stave it off.[43]

A month later, North was even more specific about the MPPDA's deficiencies:

There is no question but that the American companies and the Hays organisation as well have never made even the faintest gesture towards compromise or have they indicated any particular willingness to show British films in this country.

This of course does not indicate any aversion to British films as such but they know that any British films they do show will probably mean a financial loss to them and they were not willing to sacrifice anything to keeping the British trade in good humor. I believe that if they had been willing to do so, they would never have had this quota row.[44]

If we take Hays and North at face value, each had urged the U.S. motion picture companies to take on some British films for American showing in order to offset their own overwhelming dominance of the British market. I doubt North's view that this would have preempted the quota row, which had more than one root cause. North himself vacillated on his explanation, for in another letter written at almost the same time he offered quite a different explanation of the British legislation: "The idea that children in England and the British Dominions are being affected psychologically by American films which extol everything American is one of the fundamental factors behind the British Films Bill."[45]

What can we conclude about policy, from the evidence so far presented? Basically, that despite the German legislation of more than two years before and the moves toward legislation in France, the MPPDA was unable to coordinate its member companies to forge a strong, determined, and united resistance to the British legislation, complete with compromise positions. Instead, disarray and distrust, together with misleading information, ensured that the British put in place a scheme that failed to achieve its objectives, that was easily evaded by the American companies, but that taught them a hard lesson about trading conditions in Europe. Whatever their philosophy of trade, whatever their statesmen preached, European governments were prepared to intervene to structure the motion picture market in ways considered favorable to sustaining at least some domestic industry. It might be going too far to say the British legislation marked a turning point, but clearly it was a major defeat for the MPPDA foreign department. They needed to reorganize and regroup. In one way they eventually took a leaf out of the book of the BF&DC by appointing a permanent European representative of the MPPDA, a kind of roving ambassador from the U.S. motion picture industry, an idea first floated in the autumn of 1927.[46]

10.4. In the wake of the British legislation

In attempting to characterize the feeling aroused in the U.S. film industry by the British legislation of 1927, North rejected a *Montréal Daily Star* editorial's conclusion that it was a feeling of great bitterness. He agreed that it could not be said that the American interests liked the 1927 Cinematograph Films Act, but it was a mistake to exaggerate their reactions.[47] At much the same time it was apparently beginning to sink in that preemptive work on films that might give offense or be subject to censorship abroad could save money. North requested that Canty try to arrange for regular reports on the reception in Europe of major American films, especially those with foreign settings. He also requested full information on how the censorship worked in each country. This material was to be used for briefing Col. Jason Joy, who was in charge of the Association of Motion Picture Producers (AMPP) in Los Angeles and who apparently convened monthly meetings of senior production executives to consider types of pictures in demand and the possible reception of pictures in production.

No doubt Canty filed frequent reports all through this period on the problems of the British legislation, as North's replies indicate. I have been unable to locate these in the National Archives – which may mean that the only survivors are those published in the various trade reports. This uncertainty is a pity, because one of the few reports that did survive sketched a fascinatingly confused situation in the American industry. Canty commended Fay Allport, trade commissioner in Berlin, for a "slick job" and a scientific report on the German situation that "was about the best service that the Bureau has rendered the film trade of America in its operations in Europe since I have been on the job." Without Allport's work there was no telling how far astray the American trade representatives in Berlin would have gone "in their frenzy." Canty commented on the despondency among the "American boys" in France because of the indefinite and flexible new French decree, effective 1 March. When Allport's work was quoted, Colonel Lowry, the MPPDA representative, claimed that it was his own work. Canty kept mum, but commented to North:

If I took exception to everytime he [Lowry] reached out for our accomplishments at these trade meetings, I would be in a constant state of turmoil with him, and my standing with his outfit would be still lower than it is now.

I am reporting this to you as another check against *his* absolute lack of co-operation; his dishonest practices at our expense.[48]

Thus at a crucial point, when France had imposed what North described as the worst restrictions in Europe, there was anger and mistrust between the bureau's senior and competent trade attaché and the MPPDA European representative. The French scheme issued visas for the import of foreign films only on condition that the company distributed French films abroad and, although the regulations were not fully spelled out, it was intimated that only seven foreign films would be given visas for each French production. This would have had the effect of a quota of 14–15 percent. A visit to Minister Edouard Herriot had produced vague and contradictory assurances that there would be a sincere attempt "not to apply the decree in any drastic way."[49]

Instead of taking the British legislation as the turning point, we might better think of the German, British, and French efforts as a sequence of ascending severity that eventually brought the U.S. industry face to face with the new reality in foreign trade. In coping with that reality, it hardly made sense for the industry to be divided against itself and for the trade organization to stand in rivalry to government officials charged with as-

Figure 10.3. MPPDA President Will Hays in Paris in 1928, posing with Edouard Herriot. The others are possibly Herrick, the American ambassador, and Hays's secretary Earl Bright. (Will H. Hays Papers, Indiana State Archives, Indianapolis.)

sisting them. Sitting at the center of webs for gathering economic intelligence, Canty and North might have seemed like rivals to those trying to justify the existence of the MPPDA – especially abroad. But these were misappreciations of the situation: Government and industry needed to work together in facing attempts to restructure the market for their films. The upshot in the French situation was that Hays himself went to France, in the spring of 1928 (Fig. 10.3), where he entered into direct talks with government ministers. As a result, the workings of the decree were modified, as he relates in his autobiography and in a letter to Hoover:

As you remember, in France last spring they passed a regulation providing that for every four films which we imported into France we had to buy and distribute one French film here. It was the first time in the history of business that any country had attempted by internal legislation to enforce exports. I went immediately to

France, and with the assistance of the Department of Commerce, the Department of State and the American Embassy there got it changed, as you know. They abandoned the principle of enforced exports and we agreed to the regulation that for every seven films which we imported we would buy one French film to be distributed by us in France or any place else or not distributed at all.[50]

The situation in the United States was complex. The MPPDA itself was by no means universally accepted as industry leader, either by the independents or the states' rights groups.[51] The Commerce and State Departments had different attitudes toward the trade in motion pictures; the latter, in particular, was capable of discriminating between the interests of commerce and the interests of the United States. And there was pressure from the myriad voluntary organizations of the period as well as from the councils of various churches, social workers, and social scientists, and local politicians. We shall see how the BF&DC led without seeming to do so until the MPPDA molded itself to its prescription.

To return once more to the British legislation as viewed from the United States: In Britain, anticipation of legislation had revived the flagging production industry and led to the flotation of a number of new companies, with capital estimated to total £7.2 million ($36 million), in August of 1928. Much of this activity was speculative and failed to take account of the fact that it was uncertain just how many motion pictures the quota legislation would command, because it was fixed as a percentage of what the American companies chose to import.[52] In a scathing analysis, the *Economist*, on 14 July 1928, summed up: "The Government called the tune, the public paid up, and the promoters went off with the profit of nearly £400,000, apart from what may accrue through the exercise of options on deferred shares."

The act caused a slump in American business because it outlawed block and advance booking; in the resulting buyer's market, prices for rentals dropped. But of course this situation was temporary; the new structure did settle down. Although the percentage quotas in the act were written in terms of footage, an estimate was made of the quota obligations of each major U.S. producer, as shown in Table 10.2. At the time when these figures were being compiled, it was estimated that, with double features, the British market consumed some 890 films per year, approximately half new, half reissues. British speculators were not alone in their optimistic attitudes, since Canty estimated that the growth of the market was such that by 1932 consumption would have reached 1,000 features per year. This would entail that by the time the act expired some 200 British films would be required, colossally more than the capacity of British studios. Thus the overproduction of the first years of the act would likely be followed by an acute shortfall. This could result in higher prices for British product. Efforts to penetrate the U.S. market having been to no avail, British firms were establishing arrangements with Continental firms. Without such foreign outlets British

Table 10.2. *Estimated quota obligations of the American majors, 1928*

Company	Approx. no. trade shown (1 Sept. 1927– 31 Oct. 1928)	Number of British films required				
		2d,3d years (10.5%)	4th year (12.5%)	5th year (15%)	6th,7th years (17.5%)	8th,9th years (20%)
Paramount	80	8	10	12	14	16
MGM	41	4	6	7	8	9
First National	69	7	9	11	12	14
Fox	51	5	7	8	9	11
Universal	74	8	10	12	13	15
United Artists	9	1	2	2	2	2
Warner Bros.	33	4	5	5	6	7
PDC	40	4	5	6	7	8
Est. total		41	54	63	71	82

Source: Canty to Bureau (Motion Picture Section), 30 August 1928, NA, RG 151 BF&DC General Records, 281–U.K. Motion Pictures.

films would not have enough invested in them to achieve the necessary quality. It was easy to foresee that quota quickies would result and that the American companies could reduce the quantity of films shipped.

Canty noted that, unlike in Germany, in Britain audience tastes definitely leaned toward films of American style and theme, whether made in Britain or not. This tended to place the U.S. and U.K. industries in direct competition, with no special cultural advantage for the domestic product. This vexed issue, namely whether the British public preferred British pictures, continues to divide historians because such evidence as there is can be interpreted differently.

The difficulties for the Motion Picture Division in dealing with the MPPDA come out sharply in the activities of Herron, the foreign manager. He submitted a memorandum to Dr. Klein on why the MPPDA opposed contingents and quotas, offering the following arguments (my summary):

1. Films cannot be foisted on the public.
2. The public wants to be entertained by good films.
3. Producers should foster those rather than nationalistic feelings.
4. Otherwise they will force uninteresting pictures on the public.
5. The quota act is the expression of a commercial conspiracy against America, engineered by a small group of people who saw a business opportunity in exploiting the political prejudices of the non–motion picture section of the public.
6. The claim is that quotas protect culture.
7. This implies an amazing lack of faith in each nation's culture.
8. Cultural protection should be left to the censors.
9. The American market is open.

10. Only films that cater to the audience will succeed.
11. American companies are on the lookout for such foreign films.[53]

Such a mixture of disingenuousness, paranoia, inconsistency (cf. points 1 and 4), and lack of political sense was aggravating to North. He thought that both Herron and Hays had not faced up to what was happening and were fully expecting the League of Nations Conference on the Abolition of Import and Export Prohibitions and Restrictions, held in Geneva in 1928, to do away with quotas. North, by contrast, was now clear that "such European countries as feel that they want to have film restriction are going to have it irrespective of the Geneva or any other conference."[54] He later reemphasized this view to Herron directly.[55]

In addition to wanting to din some international political realism into the MPPDA leaders (who may have been reflecting the views of their principals), North also wanted them to give credence to the cultural argument.

I honestly do think that the cultural argument is one which can honestly be advanced in good faith and which must be legitimately met. England, for example, I believe, was stampeded into their film legislation almost entirely through their patriotic societies who believed that English customs and tradition were in danger. (I am not overlooking the fact either in the case of England that the fact that she was losing trade through the influence of American films had a considerable amount to do with her adoption of legislation.)[56]

This is loosely written (it conflates the United Kingdom with "England") and overdrawn (viz., "stampeded" to describe a process that took years) no doubt. Its interest is that the chief of the Motion Picture Section was telling his European representative that cultural arguments were not to be dismissed as a smokescreen but to be seen as a legitimate concern that would have to be accommodated. Putting "the Hays officials in New York on the right track"[57] was clearly an uphill battle. Herron wrote to the State Department that

It looks more and more as if the conference to abolish trade barriers was organized and backed by these countries for just such trade barriers as seem to individually be directed at their own commerce, while they don't feel it should apply to barriers which affect our commercial relations.[58]

We saw that Herron considered censorship the legitimate weapon for cultural defense (point 8). Yet no sooner had Germany introduced a bill to ratify the Geneva Convention on Export and Import Restrictions, in February of 1929, than Herron seized on the fact that the Geneva agreement abolished restrictions and turned to censorship for cultural defense, to lobby the State Department to head off ratification by the United States. In a careful reply, Theodore Marriner, chief of the Division of Western European Affairs, revealed that "the entire question of foreign regulation of Motion Picture Imports is receiving the careful consideration of the Department, with a view to finding some means of alleviating the present burdensome conditions."[59] This important review, which was to lead to protests to the offending countries, revealed some of the tensions within the State Department concerning this boisterous industry.

North's view was that the best basis for a protest was the arbitrary and vague nature of some of the foreign legislation, which gave no assurance to foreign firms that laws and regulations would not suddenly be changed.[60] Simultaneous representations, it was proposed, should be made to France, Germany, Italy, Austria, Hungary, Spain, and Czechoslovakia.[61] On the way to a decision on this, the State Department files for February and March 1929 yield several fascinating memoranda from the Office of the Economic Adviser at the department, drafted by Horace Villard, three of which need detailed summary and analysis here, because representations to foreign governments on these sensitive matters were delayed until they had been circulated within the department.[62] The first memorandum argued that the success of foreign restrictions was largely facilitated by the disarray of the American companies, which prevented a united front and formulation of a common policy. Villard suggested the formation of a foreign arm of the MPPDA to study world markets and to regulate overseas distribution by means of internal agreements among the companies and external agreements with foreign countries. He also suggested a review board to pass upon the social, racial, and cultural suitability of a film for export to a particular country. His final idea was the development of a common policy with regard to overseas investment and on measures to be taken in face of arbitrary or unfair discrimination.

Before proceeding, we can note the internal evidence that Villard was not well acquainted with the MPPDA: It already had a foreign department. Another problem with his analysis was that prior restraint on exports for social, racial, or cultural reasons was as thorny an issue as ever divided the companies. Everyone, from foreign governments to self-appointed experts, wished to counsel Hollywood in these matters. Hays himself was offering assurances that internal company policing would do the trick. Except for the period of World War II, when military and Office of War Information (OWI) review did some filtering, for the whole of the period covered by the present study this was an area where the companies could never agree to submit themselves to outside review. Unmentioned in Villard's memorandum is a glaring problem with regard to its first and last proposals, for these would have involved coordination and market sharing. Such moves would have drawn the attention of the Anti-Trust Division of the Department of Justice, which was already scrutinizing the industry over the Standard Exhibition Contract. The formation of the Motion Picture Export Association (MPEA) in 1945 was facilitated only by an explicit waiver from the Department of Justice.

Villard returned to the subject twice, although both of his subsequent memoranda were dated 25 March 1929: One appeared in the open files; the other, marked "Strictly Confidential," was kept separate. Former Secretary of State Charles Hughes had declined to make simultaneous representations, but his successor's (Frank B. Kellog) advisers were urging (a) the scope and potential influence of motion pictures, and the leading role of the United States in trade in them; and (b)

a certain moral responsibility attached to the exhibition of films, especially in the case of less intelligent or untutored races. The type of films shown in the less sophisticated markets of the world is often detrimental not only to the prestige of the white race but to the reputation of Americans. Mr. Hughes is reported in the past to have deplored the impression thus created in the minds of foreigners as to the standard of morals prevalent in the United States.[63]

Which brings us to Villard's second memorandum of the same date, one much more clearly intended for internal use. It argued that no strong grounds existed for protesting restrictions on the importation of films "because of the semi-cultural qualities of motion pictures."[64] Furthermore, in no country were the restrictions such as to deprive the United States of its leading place in the market.

Under prevailing theories of international trade it is the inherent right of every nation to adopt whatever measures of a non-discriminatory nature it may consider essential for the protection of domestic industry. Inasmuch as the film restrictions in question apply equally to all countries and are internal measures designed primarily to stimulate home production, there is no legal ground here for complaint.[65]

Since trade follows the film, Villard argued, promoting motion picture exports would be in line with current commercial policies and would provide substantial support for foreign trade in general. The argument therefore should be that the restrictions injured an important American industry, set a precedent for other countries, were against the spirit of the Geneva conference, and were matched by no similar restrictions in the United States. (Villard here overlooked the fact that in 1928, at the second round of Geneva talks, France, Germany, and Italy had explicitly insisted on the right to regulate imported films.[66] Having laid the possible basis for protest, Villard then went on to argue against it and to counsel patience and self-help by the industry seeking foreign commercial arrangements.

As with North, Villard took the cultural objections to have considerable merit. Foreign countries were justified in protesting against the stereotyping of their nationals in American films:

Thus the French are resentful that their nationals are so often pictured as immoral, the Spaniards and Italians that they are so frequently villains, the English that they are snobs, etc. The sensitiveness of the Latin temperament to constant tactless allusions of this kind has found vigorous expression on several occasions in Spain, Brazil, Mexico, and Costa Rica. The latter country in fact has deemed it necessary to legislate against the exhibition of films which might give rise to demonstrations or outbursts of national feeling.[67]

Villard, however, as a senior officer of the State Department, was able to take a much wider view.

It is debatable whether the present widespread exhibition of American motion pictures is desirable from the viewpoint of the United States. It is obvious that a considerable proportion of the Hollywood product bases its entertainment appeal on cheap emotionalism, sensational or suggestive episodes, or over-emphasized scenes of wealth, fast living or immorality. . . . Of . . . importance from the viewpoint of American prestige is the questionable impression created in the minds of foreigners as to the ideals and standards prevailing in the United States. The many pictures of "wild west" shootings, the exaggerations of fashionable life (with such scenes as intoxication in a country claiming prohibition), and lately the "underworld" and "gangster" themes, certainly do not tend to establish a favorable conception of American manners and morals. That the standard of American films shown abroad is harmful to this country's reputation was pointed out by former Secretary Hughes, who deplored the "pernicious distortions among other peoples with respect to the way in which our people live and the prevalence here of vice and crime." Although false propaganda of this sort is of course entirely unconscious on the part of American producers, who are concerned only with the commercial aspects of the industry, it is largely responsible for spreading the notion that the United States if not peopled principally by bandits and bootleggers is at any rate the land where every one achieves financial or industrial success. There is the further tendency in the ostentatious depiction of riches and the attributes of wealth to make for unrest and dissatisfaction abroad, which in turn gives impetus to attempted immigration with resulting disillusion and resentment.[68]

This jaundiced picture of Hollywood's output would have been worthy of one of the British Foreign Office mandarins encountered in Part II. It is quoted at length to show that in the higher reaches of the permanent bureaucracy at the State Department there were officers who entertained genuine doubts as to whether it was in the national interest to foster and support the foreign success of the motion picture industry. Its products created a certain amount of static in the diplomatic air, and it unconsciously projected the United States abroad in a manner officials found far from desirable. Villard did not note that there were strongly positive aspects to this projection of the United States, of the sort we have seen argued by Grierson.

Concluding his analysis, Villard pointed to the considerable agitation in Europe over the alleged American commercial invasion in a number of fields and the possible exacerbation of this by vigorous actions against film restrictions. This counseled that any communication on the matter, though firm, "should not be too antagonistic in tone and . . . any mention of retaliation should be strictly avoided."[69]

The notes eventually delivered by the U.S. ambassadors to France, Germany, Italy, Hungary, Austria, Czechoslovakia, and Spain, under instructions dated 29 March 1929, went alike to countries with restrictions and to those contemplating them. They were couched in general terms of injury to an important American industry and did not indicate that the United States would feel compelled to retaliate. This, however, was only the first move in a protracted involvement of the State Department during 1929 in the struggle with France over its system of restrictions. With the expiry of the French regulations on 31 March and the failure to announce new ones, the major U.S. companies proceeded to boycott the French market, that is to say, to conclude no further deals. They continued, of course, to fulfill all their advance contracts. The whole summer was spent in various kinds of negotiations involving Harold Smith, the new Hays representative in Europe, Norman Armour of the State Department, the U.S. ambassador to France, and various others, including Canty. France is outside the immediate concern of this volume, but it was there that the State Department was sucked in deeper than ever before. The Hays Organization insisted on the view that since France only gave credence to high foreign officials, the negotiations had to be the responsibility of the State Department, with film company personnel attending as technical experts. Whether reluctantly or not, this role was accepted and played. Played once in France, it was played again whenever French regulations were under review. There was of course to be similar involvement in Germany, with whom there had been a successful 1930 conference on sound (Fig. 10.4), but the political situation there shortly became so ominous that nothing could be done.

As background to these foreign developments it is important to bear in mind the situation of the MPPDA and its component companies in the United States. As a powerful trade organization, it was subject to accusations of monopoly and of trade malpractice. These accusations from other bodies were joined by actual proceedings against member companies, instituted in 1928 by the Federal Trade Commission and the Anti-Trust Division of the Department of Justice. As self-appointed moral censor and guardian of the major companies, the MPPDA was subject to criticism whenever the motion picture product was not up to the standards some expected. Hays's prominence was such that he became a lightning rod for the accusations of moral insufficiency, rather than the individual moguls who controlled each company. Such organizations as the Federal Motion Picture Council in America, Inc., the National Council of Women, and the Citizen's League of Maryland for Better Motion Pictures attacked Hays personally as a disappointment.[70] Jowett (1976, pp. 171–80) has covered all this extensively and questions whether the public relations strategy of the Hays office had really worked:

After 1930 . . . Hays time was beginning to run out; for ten years he had managed to channel public opinion into fairly innocuous but constructive projects; eventually, however, the failure of the self-regulatory concept to bring about tangible results weakened many of the public relations connections that had been so carefully cultivated.[71]

Figure 10.4. Hays when MPPDA relations with Germany were cordial: The German–American Film Conference that created a sound patents cartel, Paris, June 1930 (with Dr. A. Plugge of Spitzberg). (Will H. Hays Papers, Indiana State Archives, Indianapolis.)

This leans a little too closely to Hays's own assessment, I fear. Before continuing, I add a jaundiced opinion not untypical of other ones in the files. There was a vitriolic attack on Hays in the trade paper *Film Spectator* in 1929 headed "Hays Is Done." The thesis of the article was that it was "stupid" of the film industry to keep Hays in his present position. Noting that the exhibitors were estranged because of MPPDA business methods, it went on to say that he had also antagonized the women's clubs by his trickery and deceit. "Thanks to his pious mantle of Presbyterianism, which concealed the politician beneath it, he managed to make the women's clubs believe he was almost as good as he said he was." A wedge between Hays and his employers was driven deeper:

When the motion picture producers first put Hays under contract it was their belief that along with him they were buying the entire Presbyterian church, and . . . he did nothing to prevent such an idea taking root. . . . He was a member of an administration which later was revealed as one of the most corrupt in the history of the United States.[72]

With a certain glee, the article recounted Hays's agonized and self-exculpatory testimony before Congress.

On 1 April 1930 a new Production Code (i.e., self-censorship rules) was issued to cover sound motion pictures, and the secretary of commerce, among others, was invited to endorse it. Counseling that critics thought it was window dressing and that hence it would be embarrassing were any government official to comment, North argued that the "new" code was merely a restatement of what did not work:

While it is being announced again ostensibly because of the revolution of the art through the use of sound, the real reason is I believe on account of the attacks made on the Hays organization recently by various types of reformers and more notably by the Federal Council of Churches in the columns of the *Churchman*. These attacks assert that the Hays organization is not living up to the principles set down in its code governing what should appear on the screen and is allowing producers to go beyond the bounds of decency in many films.[73]

All these harsh sentiments were echoed in 1930 by Professor Fred Eastman, of Chicago Theological Seminary, in his influential series in the *Christian Century*. Describing how Hays had put Mrs. Thomas G. Winter, former president of the General Federation of Women's Clubs and a vociferous critic of the movies, on the payroll of the MPPDA to promote better pictures, Eastman compared Hays to a dentist – who extracted the teeth of his critics (Eastman 1930d). None of this is intended to gloss over the deficiencies of Hays's regime but simply to draw attention to the rather embattled state of the MPPDA as it sought to carry out its mandate to represent the interests of its members at home and abroad. Not to be forgotten, in addition, was the passing of the Hawley–Smoot tariffs in 1930. Some foreign managers feared that they would provoke retaliation and that this would be directed against motion pictures because they were such a prominent target.[74]

Besides the personal attacks on Hays, there were drastic ideas floating about how to regulate the movies. We need only mention, since Jowett has covered this ground, that William Marston Seabury, a lawyer who had formerly worked in the industry as general counsel to the Motion Picture Board of Trade, had authored books in which he urged treating the movies as a public utility subject to some sort of federal regulation, on the lines of agriculture or broadcasting, which would outlaw restraint of trade yet regulate prices. Seabury was sufficiently unsure of the value of domestic regulation that he argued for a role for the League of Nations.[75] No doubt in hindsight it is easy to dismiss such schemes. At the time, there was no way of knowing whether they would ride forward as did Prohibition to impose the ideas of an organized minority on a passive majority.

In a minor key, perhaps, there were also events in Canada, where quotas were being legislated in several Provinces (see §3.2), and there were rumblings in the press and in Parliament about the absorption of Famous Players

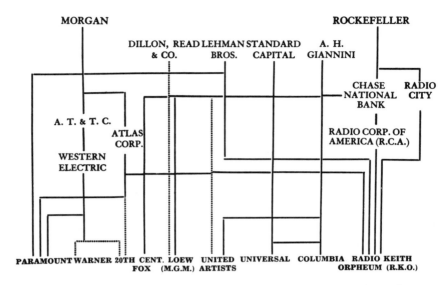

Figure 10.5. Direct financial control or backing, 1936. (F.D. Klingender and S. Legg, *Money Behind the Screen* [London: Lawrence and Wishart, 1937].)

Canadian Corporation by Famous Players Lasky. R. B. Bennett, then leader of the Opposition, said in the House of Commons (16 May 1930) that the merger should be investigated to determine the national interest, the rights of minority shareholders, and the possible application of the Anti-Combines Act. The minister of labor stated that the company was under investigation.[76]

Bedeviling virtually everything else was the transition to sound, which had been under way since the late 1920s. The process has been thoroughly detailed by several historians, who do not always agree with one another (Geduld 1975; Gomery 1975; Walker 1979; Cameron 1980; Thompson 1985, chap. 5). What is clear in a general way, though, is that the process of selecting a standard technology was itself protracted, involving not only false starts, such as synchronized disks, but also the settlement of all patent disputes around the system eventually adopted. Surprisingly little of this appears in the motion picture papers of the archives, yet we know that it was this transition that made the interdependence between the motion picture industry and major U.S. corporations such as AT&T and RCA an intimate one. F. D. Klingender and Stuart Legg, in *Money Behind the Screen* (a source that must be used with caution, since their outlook on the United States is that of the Comintern in the 1930s) provide a useful diagram vividly illustrating this (Fig. 10.5). Then again, as the technical systems settled down, the filmmaking and distributing strategies needed modification. For a while there was the possibility of both sound and silent versions; then there were the various ways to make English-language films accessible to non–English speakers: shoot several language versions on the same set with different players, dub the stars, add inter- or subtitles, and so on. And whatever strategy was adopted, there was the question of where the foreign version would be made and how to ensure that it would be compatible with equipment available in the cinema.

The fear in Hollywood and New York, naturally, was that whatever they did, their foreign versions would seem unnatural and that local film industries would suddenly have an advantage denied them in the silent era. North told Canty:

Practically every large company is putting money, sometimes a lot of money, into foreign language pictures. How are these being actually received? If not, why not? Are English, French and German pictures making greater headway now? If so, where and why? Are new legislative enactments or special trade agreements imminent? How are those in force now working out? Have any new censorship problems been raised by sound pictures and if so where and what kind? Is the wiring field any where near the saturation point? . . . Each company now has a much larger investment in the foreign field than he ever did in the old silent days and he wants to get it back plus a reasonable profit.[77]

It would be a considerable time before all this settled down, with Hollywood setting up foreign-language units abroad where those were required by legislation (as with dubbing in France after 1933) and making arrangements to produce other foreign versions domestically.[78]

When the conclusions of Canada's White Report (Chapter 1) were transmitted to North, he commented that the report revealed conditions that the Federal Trade Commissions had investigated domestically with the same culprit, Paramount.[79] He later noted that the agitation in Canada about the American film industry smacked of the agitation taking place in the United States itself—aside from the tendency to think that forced showing of more British films would alleviate matters.[80]

Perhaps we can end this chapter with a review of the situation as it stood on the eve of Franklin D. Roosevelt's inauguration, an event of little significance for the motion picture industry except insofar as new secretaries of state and of commerce would be appointed and that the recovery programs of the administration would have some effect on the movie business. Quotas were in place in Britain, and they had been legislated in some Provinces of Canada but were not enforced. The changeover to sound was fully consolidated, and the volume of the film trade had considerably diminished, despite the advent of the double feature in certain theaters. We remember that in 1928 Canty had predicted that the British market demand might grow to as much as one thousand feature films per annum. Figures supplied by North directly to the outgoing secretary of commerce in October 1932 showed the opposite trend (Table 10.3), and we can only speculate about the causes. For what they are worth, North's speculations were that the quota act would have done little good for Britain had films remained

Table 10.3. *Distribution of feature films in Britain, 1926–31*

	1926	1927	1928	1929	1930	1931
American	620	723	558	495	519	470
British	36	40	95	87	142	139

Source: North to Chapin, [?] October 1932, NA, RG 151 BF&DC General Records, 281–U.K. Motion Pictures.

silent but that the advent of sound reduced American production; the act gave an incentive for American companies to buy British pictures, because the companies did not then look with favor on overseas production ventures; and Britain

through the medium of the dialogue picture [sound film] has been able to capitalize on its fine stage traditions and each year since the passage of the quota law has been producing films in greater quantity and of a type which have been much more popular than before.[81]

Notes

1 Steward to Emmet, 24 October 1922, HHH, Commerce Papers – Motion Pictures.

2 Julius Klein (1886–1961), taught Latin American and Spanish history and economics at Harvard (1915–23); book *The Mesta* (1920) a classic; joined Department of Commerce (1917); director of the Bureau of Foreign and Domestic Commerce (1922–9); became assistant secretary of commerce, 1929–33; *Who's Who* describes as Protestant. There is an excellent sketch of Klein and his outlook in Seidel (1973, chap. 3).

3 Howard to Klein, 27 December 1922, NA, RG 151, Bureau of Foreign and Domestic Commerce, General Records 281, General – Motion Pictures (hereafter cited as NA, RG 151, BF&DC 281, plus file identification.

4 Klein to Morse, n.d., ibid.

5 Klein to Howard, 4 January 1923, ibid.

6 *Commerce Reports*, 22 January 1923.

7 Klein to Hays, 29 January 1923, NA, RG 151, BF&DC 281, General – Motion Pictures.

8 Ibid.

9 Hays to Keeley, 23 August 1924, NA, RG 151, BF&DC 281, General – Motion Pictures.

10 Hays to Hughes (Secretary of State), 8 July 1922, NA, RG 59 1910–1929, 811.4061 / 215–811.4061 / 527.

11 Frederick L. Herron (d. 1957), friend of Hays from Wabash College; U.S. diplomatic service before World War I; served in Thirteenth Engineers and First Division; after war on special service in Europe; head of the Foreign Department, MPPDA (1922–41). Hays's second wife was Herron's sister.

12 U.S. Consul in Manchester to State Department, 13 January 1925, NA, RG 59, Great Britain 1910–1929, 841.4054 / 3–841.407 / 1, Microfilm M580, Roll 98.

13 Dispatch of 2 January 1924, ibid.

14 Consul General at Montréal to State Department, 20 May 1924, NA, RG 59 842.4061 Motion Pictures, Canada, 1912–1929, Microfilm M1435, Roll 19.

15 Herron to Vice Consul Alfred D. Cameron, 5 December 1925, WNRC, RG 84 Post Records Consul General Paris, 1916–1935.

16 Clarence J. North's biographical details are unknown to this author.

17 Nathan D. Golden's biographical details are unknown to this author.

18 Herron to Klein, 20 December 1924, NA, RG 151, BF&DC 281, General – Motion Pictures.

19 Klein to Herron, 24 December 1924, ibid.

20 Hoagland to Herron, 23 March 1925, NA, RG 151, BF&DC 281, General – Motion Pictures, 1925.

21 Klein to Hays, 28 May 1925, ibid.

22 The reference is to agitation against block booking in 1921, reported in a despatch of 22 April 1921, NA, RG 59, Microfilm M580, Roll 98, Great Britain 841.4054 / 3–841.4071. The British National Film League was formed in November, with the elimination of blind and block booking as one of its main aims. For details, see Low (1971, chap. 3).

23 Nutting to State Department, 23 June 1925, NA, RG 59, State Decimal File, 841.4061 / 47, Microfilm M580, Roll 98.

24 Mowatt Mitchell to North, 1 August 1925, NA, RG 151, BF&DC 281, Motion Pictures – U.K.

25 Circular of 30 January 1926, NA, RG 59, 1910–1929, 800.4038 / 112–800.4061, Sound Motion Pictures.

26 Dispatch from Ottawa, 10 March 1926, ibid.

27 Dispatch from Ottawa, 29 March 1928, ibid.

28 North to Rochester Chamber of Commerce, 5 November 1925, NA, RG 151, BF&DC 281, General – Motion Pictures.

29 North to Herron, 24 June 1926, NA, RG 151, BF&DC General Records, 160.2 Specialties Division.

30 North, 16 February 1926, NA, RG 151, BF&DC 281, United Kingdom.

31 Carl Elias Milliken (1895–1963), studied successively at Bates College, Harvard University, Colby College, and University of Maine; lumberman; Baptist: governor of Maine (1917–21); Secretary of the MPPDA / MPAA (1926–47).

32 Herron to North, 8 February 1926, NA, RG 151, BF&DC 281, General – Motion Pictures.

33 North to Mowatt Mitchell, 15 May 1925, NA, RG 151, BF&DC 281, Motion Pictures – United Kingdom.

34 See Butler to North, 19 January 1926, ibid.

35 George Romuald Canty (1889–1968), born Cork, Eire (Rep. of Ireland); U.S. citizen; educated at Northeastern and Georgetown Universities; Secretary to a member of Congress; traveled for State Department; editor of trade magazine and reporter; entered BF&DC (7 July 1924); trade commissioner in Paris (1926–37), then went on leave; joined State Department 16 November 1943; Assistant Chief Telecommunications Division until 12 August 1944; Assistant Chief of Division of Commercial Policy, 24 April 1946.

36 Klein to Cooper, 17 August 1926, NA, RG 151, BF&DC 281, Motion Pictures – General, 1926.

37 North to Canty, 9 September 1926, ibid.

38 North to Canty, 12 January 1927, NA, RG 151, BF&DC 281, Motion Pictures – General, 1927.

39 Canty's boycott proposal is cited in North to Herron, 14 April 1927, NA, RG 151 BF&DC 281, Motion Pictures – General, 1927.

40 North to Isaacs, 20 May 1927, ibid.

41 North to Canty, 15 September 1927, ibid.

42 Chalmers, Division of Foreign Tariffs, to Secretary of Commerce, 24 February 1927, NA, RG 151 BF&DC 281, Motion Pictures – United Kingdom.

43 North to Canty, 14 April 1927, NA, RG 151, BF&DC 281, Motion Pictures – United Kingdom.

44 North to Cooper, 20 May 1927, ibid.

45 North to Montréal Office, 17 May 1927, NA, RG 151, BF&DC 281, Motion Pictures – Canada.

46 North to Canty, 15 September 1927, NA, RG 151, BF&DC 281, Motion Pictures – General.

47 North to Donnelly, 6 December 1927, NA, RG 151, BF&DC 281 – Canada Motion Pictures.

48 Canty to North, 14 March 1928, NA, RG 151, BF&DC 281, France Motion Pictures.

49 North to Klein, 14 March 1928, ibid.

50 Hays to Hoover, 1 May 1929, HHH, Presidential Individuals, Hays file. See Hays 1955, pp. 420ff., and Moley 1945, pp. 174ff.

51 The Independent Motion Picture Producers and Distributors of America was only one organization. Other letterheads showing up in the Archives belong to the Allied States Association of Motion Picture Exhibitors and the Unaffiliated Independent Motion Picture Exhibitors of America.

52 Canty to Bureau (Motion Picture Section), 30 August 1928, NA, RG 151, BF&DC 281, U.K. Motion Pictures.

53 Enclosed with Herron to Klein, 19 September 1928, NA, RG 151, BF&DC 281, France Motion Pictures.

54 North to Canty, 18 October 1928, NA, RG 151, BF&DC 281, Motion Pictures General.

55 North to Herron, 7 March 1929, ibid.

56 North to Canty, 18 October 1928, ibid.

57 Ibid.

58 Herron to Economic Adviser, 19 December 1928, NA, RG 59 1919–1929, 840.00 B / 4–840.4061 MP / 8.

59 Herron to Marriner, 18 February 1929, and Marriner to Herron, 23 February 1929, NA, RG 59 560 M 3 / 95.

60 North to Herron, 7 March 1929, NA, RG 151, BF&DC 281, General Motion Pictures.

61 Memorandum, Foreign Restrictions on U.S. Films, 25 March 1929, NA, RG 59 1910–1929, 800.4038 / 112–800.4061 Sound Pictures.

62 Memorandum from EDKLeC to Marriner et al., 21 February 1929, NA, RG 59, 862.4061, Microfilm M336, Roll 79, wrote of Villard preparing an "exhaustive"

memorandum on the whole issue. This is the second document of 25 March 1929, analyzed third in sequence in the paragraphs that follow.

63 Memorandum, "Foreign Restrictions on US Films," 25 March 1929, NA, RG 59 1910–1929 800.4038 / 112–800.4061 Sound Pictures.

64 Memorandum, "Foreign Restrictions on American Films," 25 March 1929, NA, RG 59 1940–1944 [sic] 800.4061 Motion Pictures / 4½.

65 Ibid.

66 Acting Secretary of State to Hays, 14 March 1930, NA, RG 59, 560.B23 / 12–560.M5/150, Treaties Division Files, Box 2705.

67 Memorandum, "Foreign Restrictions on American Films," 25 March 1929, NA, RG 59 1940–1944 [sic] 800.4061 Motion Pictures / 4½.

68 Ibid.

69 Ibid.

70 Federal Motion Picture Council in America, Inc., to Stimson, 6 December 1930, NA, RG 59 1930–1939, 811.4061.

71 Jowett 1976, p. 182. Jowett revisited this territory in a later essay (1990).

72 "Hays Is Done," Film Spectator, 21 September 1929, pp. 3–4. Film Spectator was an eccentric element of the trade press. Quotations on p. 3.

73 Memorandum by North, 29 March 1930, NA, Microfilm M838, Roll 10, Department of Commerce, Alphabetical File of the Secretary, Motion Pictures.

74 North to Kann, 16 June 1930, NA, RG 151, BF&DC 281, General – Motion Pictures, and North to Canty, 20 November 1930, ibid.

75 See Seabury 1926 and 1929. Seabury was involved in the origins of the Payne Fund Studies. (Cf. Vaughn 1990 and Jowett 1991).

76 Ottawa Consulate to State Department, 26 May 1930, NA, RG 59 1912–1929 842.4061 Motion Pictures Canada, Microfilm M1435, Roll 19.

77 North to Canty, 20 November 1930, NA, RG 151, BF&DC 281, General Motion Pictures.

78 Luis Buñuel (1983) offers some glimpses into this.

79 North to Ottawa, 13 July 1931, NA, RG 151, BF&DC 281, Canada Motion Pictures.

80 North to Meekins, 22 September 1931, NA, RG 151, BF&DC 281, Canada Motion Pictures.

81 North to Chapin, [?] October 1932, NA RG 151, BF&DC 281, U.K. Motion Pictures.

CHAPTER 11

The system in operation, 1933–1941

Between the inauguration of Franklin D. Roosevelt on 4 March 1933 and Pearl Harbor on 7 December 1941, the U.S. motion picture industry overcame organizational problems and bad economic conditions, only to face the serious challenges of the renewal of Britain's Cinematograph Films Act and the deterioration of business conditions elsewhere in Europe. The means, methods, policies, and personnel for coping with these crises compared favorably to their predecessors. Not only were foreign negotiations coordinated, but they were conducted without threats and with some attempt to position for the future. There were a couple of minor skirmishes when Canada tried to alter tariffs and income taxes on foreign movie operations, but these were handled by the U.S. companies in a prudent and unruffled manner. It had taken Will Hays more than ten years to get MPPDA member companies to agree on policy and on concerted action to implement it.[1]

Severe domestic difficulties beset the U.S. motion picture industry throughout this period. The absorption of the immense recapitalization costs of converting to sound, the long-lasting impact of the Depression, the bankruptcy and reorganization of five of the major companies, and the gradual approach of the largest antitrust suit ever filed against the motion picture industry were major punctuation marks in an era of great uncertainty. Box-office returns fluctuated widely from year to year, and public taste remained hard to fathom.

The move by the MPPDA that received histories always stress is the imposition of a newly stringent Production Code in 1934, a code that made the double entendres of the Marx Brothers and Mae West of only a year before unacceptable (see Vaughn 1990; Jowett 1990). It was under these rules that American films gained their reputation for emotional infantilism in the treatment of the relations between the sexes, but also, and in parallel, for indulging the depiction of emotional and physical violence. The pressure to impose these rules stemmed from a need to reduce market uncertainty. If motion pictures could become innocuous, then their marketability was guaranteed, even if box-office returns were not. However, it cannot be too

336

often stressed that domestic innocuousness by no means ensured overseas innocuousness. The caricaturing and stereotyping of foreigners, the ethnicity of villains, the decision to make films on themes unacceptable to the authorities or to vocal elites, ensured a stream of complaints against Hollywood films. Fortunately these were either from small markets (a special effort was made toward Latin America, since it was not small and grew in importance as war approached in Europe), or from central Europe, where fascist regimes were devising impediments to the free operation of Hollywood, which was not only a foreign, but also taken to be a Jewish, business. No doubt broad sentiment in the U.S. motion picture business was, like business sentiment generally, reflective of overall sentiment in the country. (Stromberg 1953). Yet extensive foreign operations and the large Jewish presence in the industry led to more rapid disillusionment than in other industries at the prospect of business as usual in fascist Europe. As other historians have chronicled, several major studios began to put out overtly antifascist and anti-Nazi movies, long before those sentiments could be said to be dominant among the American public.

In trying to impose a coherent narrative on these eight years, I have once more chosen to center on the struggle over British legislation. Thus section 11.1 concludes at the point (1936) where the U.S. industry begins to focus on proposals for the renewal of the Cinematograph Films Act. Section 11.2 concentrates on the successes and failures of U.S. lobbying surrounding that act and the immediately following Anglo–American trade talks of 1938. Section 11.3 traces the impact of the European lineup for war and the measures taken concerning motion pictures in the two years before the United States joined in that war. The important events of the three and one-half years of war itself will be taken up in Chapter 12.

11.1. Personnel and issues, 1933–1936

Roosevelt's inauguration on 4 March brought to an end a long period of Republican rule, and in particular the term of a president, Hoover, who, as secretary of commerce, had expanded and systematized the federal government's efforts to assist business overseas. It also raised an interesting question about Hays, whose connections were almost exclusively Republican. Struggling as he was to coordinate the MPPDA firms and get a concerted policy, the question arose whether he would deal effectively with officials of the new Democratic administration. He hand-wrote an encouraging note to Roosevelt in November 1934, referring to their meeting and their friendship.[2]

Among the inheritances from the Hoover years there was on the agenda an International Monetary and Economic Conference, eventually called for London in June 1933. Although its principal topic was currency stabilization and the gold standard, the new secretary of state, Cordell Hull, hoped to be able to get through a general lowering of tariff barriers. Thus it was that at the point where general discussions of the American proposals were going on in Washington, Hays began vigorously lobbying against the British quota legislation. In a some-what grandiose ten-page letter to Hull in 1933, he maintained that Hollywood had won its preeminent overseas position by fair means, providing nonparochial entertainment that simultaneously stimulated shopping.

The story of the American motion picture abroad is the story of an unending effort on the part of governments throughout the world to bar through artificial restrictions the American motion picture in the hope that the resultant starved entertainment demand in the respective countries will in some mysterious way assure the creation there of an industrial asset comparable to that possessed by the United States, which was the result of years of toil, creative effort, investment and self-discipline. Foreign governments have not accomplished their purpose but the quantity of American films shown abroad has been constantly reduced. The American industry has been faced with a progressive loss of income. The injury to American and World Trade is real and immediate. Of the total distribution of Motion Pictures outside of America, over 90% were formerly of American production. At present, only about 25% are American.[3]

I leave to the reader the task of spotting the fallacy in Hays's statistics, which made the picture look much more pathetic than it was. Consider that the letter went on to detail the schemes of several countries, to complain of the manner of their operation, to complain again that the 1927 Geneva talks had not outlawed quotas, to impress upon the secretary the earnestness of Hollywood's attempts at self-improvement, and that the author described films as agents for world peace, mental release, and international good will. Only twelve days later, with news that foreign countries were sending delegations to Washington preparatory to the world conference and that the British were to come first, Hays wrote again – another five, single-spaced pages solely detailing the grievances against Britain.[4]

But if that were all, there could be little truth to my suggestion that the situation was improving, that government–MPPDA cooperation was becoming more harmonious and effective, that the MPPDA was beginning to articulate and implement a coherent economic foreign policy, and that Hays and his men were beginning to have genuine power to negotiate and compromise with foreign governments. None of this was to be accomplished by barrages of paper, a good deal of rhetoric, and some, it must be said, oversimplified if not disingenuous arguments. Up to this point, Hays's communications with government officials had seldom talked turkey: that is to say, taken officials into the confidence of the industry in order to suggest on what terms it was realistically prepared to compromise. The issues were always presented as a battle between Saint George and the dragon, good and evil, free trade and protectionism, despite the efforts of North and

Canty (see Chap. 10) to explain that foreign countries had genuine concerns of various sorts, which, like it or not, they were going to legislate.

My guess is that Hays was aggressive on paper but that in private conversations he was more forthcoming, presumably in the same way as his principals in New York were in private forthcoming with him. I conclude this only because the amount of exasperation expressed with him and his organization lessens during this period, although stresses and strains show up during representations made during the working out of the terms of the renewal of the British Cinematograph Films Act in 1937–8.

Besides his brother-in-law Frederick Herron, who also produced lengthy memoranda to government agencies, the Hays Organization in 1933 appointed Fay Allport, former consul general in Berlin, lavishly praised by Canty, as MPPDA representative in Europe, based first in Paris and then in London. (On Allport, see Jarvie 1983.) Again showing striking longevity, Allport stayed in this post until 1957. Harold L. Smith, chairman of the American Chamber of Commerce in France, was technically the senior official, but Allport's ability seems to have made him the most effective person. He worked closely with the consular or commercial officers at foreign service posts who had responsibility for motion picture matters, in much the same way as Canty.

The political intricacies were that the MPPDA and its affiliates, the Association of Motion Picture Producers (AMPP) and the Motion Picture Theater Owners of America (MPTOA, representing the theater arms of the vertically integrated Big Five companies),[5] had their opponents within the industry, especially among the exhibitors. Thus these opponents were aggrieved when the Roosevelt administration took advice about its National Recovery Administration (NRA) Trade Practices Code primarily from political contributors and others affiliated with the Hays organization.[6] Apparently unaware of these connections, both Senator Joseph Robinson, the Senate majority leader, and Congressman Parker Corning of New York contacted the President to inform him that the movie industry was conducting a propaganda war against him. Robinson wrote,

I am advised that a subtle campaign is being started through the media of the motion pictures designed to render the Administration unpopular.... You will recall that Mr. Will Hayes [sic], former Chairman of the Republican National Committee, has been occupying for some years the position sometimes called the Dictator of the moving picture industry. It would be just about within his calibre to inaugurate a movement of this nature. If it is not counteracted injustice may result.[7]

Congressman Corning drew attention to the movie *Gold Diggers of 1933*, calling it "the most vicious bit of propaganda I have ever seen."[8] His innocence of propaganda was matched by his innocence of the Democratic sympathies of Warner Bros., which had produced the film, and even of the film itself, which dealt with theater people getting by in the Depression and had a song about the veterans of World War I, "Remember My Forgotten Man." Most audiences took the finale song, "We're in the Money," to be a reference to the New Deal and the NRA, the symbol of which was displayed at the end of the picture (and many pictures of the time).

Roosevelt does not seem to have bought the idea that the movie industry was against him. Movies were shown at the White House three or four times a week, made available gratis by the industry. In describing this arrangement, Steven Early, the President's press secretary, commented that

there is a perfectly satisfactory working arrangement now between the White House and the motion picture people, which includes Mr. New's office. New is Will Hays' representative in Washington and is head of the Washington office of the Motion Picture Producers and Distributors of America.... When any problem comes up, related to motion pictures, which can be dealt with directly we always do it with New's office. I am glad to say this office here has given most valuable service on three occasions lately.[9]

It is entirely possible that Early was referring only to mundane arrangements for showing films, but evidence turns up later to suggest that more was meant. For example, when in 1935 Democratic Party elder Colonel Edward M. House wrote to Roosevelt about the wisdom of a movement to replace Hays with a Democrat, Roosevelt replied that it was well to let sleeping dogs lie. "If this last is true, I agree with you that we should keep out of it."[10] When Joseph Kennedy was brought into the administration (Beschless 1980), Hays praised him in a letter to Raymond Moley, who showed it to Kennedy, who in turn wrote highly of Hays:

I am for him because I think he is getting a rotten deal. He saved the motion picture industry at least five times over the past ten years and his efforts were always for decency. He just couldn't be one hundred places at once to keep his eye on them. Another good fellow getting a rotten break.[11]

Hays in fact made fulsome pledges of loyalty to Roosevelt in the latter's third term. What Kennedy may have been referring to were attacks on Hays from within his own membership. Evidence of these was a *New York Times* story reporting Hollywood as outraged at Hays's spineless attitude toward overseas protests about U.S. films and at his failure to extract support from the State Department. Consideration was being given to a Washington lobby independent of Hays.[12]

But in truth, rotten deal or not, Hays was reaching an unassailable position, presiding over functioning machinery for handling the great challenge of the renewal of the Cinematograph Films Act. Of course there were difficulties, indecision, and misunderstandings, but he did not emerge weakened.

At the Department of Commerce, the Motion Picture Division, which had been created as a section of the Specialties Division in 1926 and elevated to division status in July 1929, was merged back into Specialties in July

1933 for purposes of economy. In 1936 Herron lobbied for its restoration as a separate division, a move that was made the following year.[13]

The gaps in the record make it difficult to determine whether there was explicit reorganization of the State Department as well. Much later evidence suggests that Cordell Hull took a personal interest in motion picture matters, and of course he advanced his fundamental policy view that increased international trade was the long-term solution to hostility among nations. The visibility of motion pictures, their propaganda for the United States and its civil society, their symbolic status as a trade good, warranted greater attention to this industry than its purely economic importance.

After 1926 Canada had direct diplomatic relations with Washington, so the tax incidents of the 1930s provide the first evidence of the machinery handling a matter in a small, but contiguous and valuable, market. In a general search for ways to increase government revenues during the Depression, the Canadian Federal government in 1933 imposed a withholding tax of 13 percent of rentals on foreign film distributors. When British firms requested that Commonwealth firms be exempted, the United States protested, and the compromise was to shift the calculation of the withholding tax from gross rentals to net revenues.[14] In April and May of 1936, a bill proposed on a nongovernmental initiative in the Nova Scotia legislature to tax and license distributing companies was headed off by direct State Department contacts with the premier of Nova Scotia and a united front among the major and the independent exhibitors.[15]

11.2. Challenging the renewal of the Cinematograph Films Act

The British Cinematograph Films Act was perhaps the major piece of anti-American film legislation in the world. It controlled access to Hollywood's largest overseas market, which yielded some $50 million in revenues between 1935 and 1939, which, after deducting $15 million in U.K. expenditures, resulted in remittances to New York of between $35–40 million. By contrast, in March 1939, net remittances from France were estimated at some $2 million.[16] The act had some success and established the principle that government intervention in motion picture matters was legitimate national policy. When the Moyne Report appeared in Britain in November 1936 (§5.2), it rang alarm bells in the MPPDA, because it recommended not just renewal but strengthening of the 1927 act, on the grounds that the basic economic advantages of the U.S. industry made its position of dominance unassailable by any other means.[17] Two particular points in the report that caught the attention of American officials were its attack on American firms buying up elements of the British domestic industry, which was said to be against the public interest, and the suggestion of a Films Commission to administer the act and in effect have overall supervision of the film industry. Fortunately for the U.S. interests, these proposals had plenty of domestic opposition, and it quickly became apparent that they would not succeed. Much of early 1937 was taken up with getting this clear. Notable was a telegram signed by Hull urging U.S. Ambassador Robert W. Bingham to oppose the Moyne recommendations.[18]

Yet in June there was evidence of problems within the State Department. In a letter to Herron, the chief of the Division of European Affairs had stressed that

it was up to the industry to present its views to the Board of Trade, leaving it up to the Embassy to support those views rather than present them.

Until this time, the American interests had been operating through the Kinematograph Renters Society, a British organization, and had expected the London embassy to present the American point of view to the British government. Instead, the embassy arranged for Allport to deal directly with officials at Britain's Board of Trade.[19] Allport, an experienced commercial diplomat, was to be a crucial mediator in obtaining agreement to the final settlement. In a conversation with one official, Fennelly, he shrewdly detected some differences within the Board of Trade, with higher officials seeing the final shape of the act as depending upon political considerations but lower-level officials hoping its final shape could be tailored to make its measures work as intended.[20]

Chapter 5 described in detail the process of renewal of the act, so at this point it is only necessary to highlight the issues and how discussion of them was perceived by American officials and representatives of the film trade. The original, printed memorandum of MPPDA response to the Moyne Report was a vigorous attack on the entire principle of quotas, with special vigor reserved for the Films Commission proposal. Since the Board of Trade was as appalled by some of the Moyne Report as was the American industry, the diplomatic note that Foreign Secretary Anthony Eden sent on 30 July 1937 stressed that the White Paper proposals were different.[21] However, an analysis of the White Paper by the U.S. Embassy for the ambassador, concluded that although the White Paper was an improvement upon the Moyne Report, especially in requiring fewer British-quota films (by the device of giving double-quota credit for expensive productions in Britain and quota credit for exporting British films to the United States) and imposing a minimum cost test for quota registration purposes, the proposals were still framed so as to give incentives for a large number of medium-cost (and, it was reasoned, mediocre) British films to be produced. Extending the principle of quota credit pro rata, the American companies felt, would give them an incentive to invest sufficient money in films made in Britain to make them salable abroad. To the Americans' relief, the White Paper did not impose a viewing test.[22]

After the November debate in the House of Commons (§5.3), Herron seems to have become fearful that a huge conspiracy against American interests was developing in Britain. He wrote to Culbertson, "Labor forces in England [sic], as usual, have been gathered together with the English producers and exhibitors and ganged up against our people so that it is most serious."[23] To Culbertson's chief in the Division of Western European Affairs he said, "Men who have lived here twenty years state that they have never run into such vicious anti-American feeling as is behind this whole fight."[24] The chairman of the House of Commons Standing Committee was reported as saying that if amendments were known to be American-backed they would be summarily rejected, in view of the committee's strongly anti-American and pro-British sentiments.[25]

Herron's panic seems to have been shared by Hays, who told Allport on the phone that he had seen the British ambassador (Sir Ronald Lindsay)[26] and told him that there would be no reciprocal trade agreement between their two countries unless the films bill was delayed or made satisfactory to the United States; Hays had also showed Lindsay the galley proofs of an anti-British publicity campaign some of his members wished to begin in the United States. Hays further told Allport that he was annoyed with Allport for not demanding greater concessions.

Allport was astonished at Hays' attitude because he has reported to Hays every step of his negotiations. He says he feels that in view of his conversations with [Sir William] Brown it will be very difficult for him now to alter his requests and make stiffer demands. It has been his feeling right along that if his suggested amendments were adopted the resulting bill would be on the whole not unreasonable. He professes not to know just what further concessions Mr. Hays wants.[27]

Obviously nonplussed by Hays's attitude, Allport tried to act consistently and, after many meetings and discussions, and while the bill was still before the Standing Committee, he boiled down the American demands, as he understood them, into five points:

1. Quota credit pro rata for expensive pictures produced or acquired from British firms for foreign distribution.
2. Elimination of minimum cost test.
3. Employment of American personnel on American-produced films in Britain without jeopardizing the films' quota status.
4. Relief from the renters' quota in the current year, owing to uncertainty and the low output of British studios.
5. Legislation not to be allowed to preempt upcoming reciprocity negotiations between the United Kingdom and the United States.[28]

He was told by Fennelly that the president of the Board of Trade, Oliver Stanley, would agree to the first three, refuse the fourth, and was prepared to listen on the final one. No reply has survived in the files to Allport's telegrams reporting these development to Hays in New York. Herschel Johnson, chargé d'affaires in London, seems to have been mediating between Allport and Hays, or, possibly, between the permanent officials of the

MPPDA and the principals of their member companies. Over the Christmas break Hull (or Assistant Secretary of State Francis B. Sayre) intervened and asked Hays to provide a clear statement of what the MPPDA would settle for. One can see the necessity. Unless State Department officials had reliable information of this sort, they could hardly negotiate effectively. And if Hays thought that Allport's stand was weak, then Allport could not be their source of guidance. At all events, the request produced a document that became jocularly known as "Hays' Fourteen Points." Paraphrased, these were as follows:

1. Number of films, not footage, to be the basis for quota counting; quota to decrease to zero during the life of the act.
2. Renters and exhibitors quotas to be equal.
3. Each quota film to be available for use by both renter and exhibitor.
4. The cost test to be determined on a cost-per-foot basis, with no viewing test.
5. Multiple credits to be given for labor costs, at about £1 per foot.
6. One quota credit to be given for each British nonquota film acquired for distribution in any one foreign country for not less than £10,000.
7. An extra credit to be given where a renter acquired a British film for world distribution that cost not less than £4 per foot on labor costs.
8. Quota credits to be freely transferable.
9. Four non-British technicians to be permitted above the 75-percent British labor stipulation.
10. The quota easement granted exhibitors until the expiration of the act to be extended to renters.
11. No Films Commission to be created; no body to be empowered to increase quotas, labor costs, or the minimum for foreign rights.
12. No quota for short films, or, if such a quota, equal for exhibitors and renters and without a quality test.
13. Liability for violations to be shared equally between exhibitors and renters.
14. Films wholly photographed in the British Dominions to count as British.[29]

Responding to an American note of 3 December, the United Kingdom reiterated the necessity of the legislation for cultural reasons but argued that, as drafted, the legislation went some way toward meeting the requests of the American renters. Furthermore, some of the provisions were flexible, which would safeguard against quotas at hardship level.[30] This was smooth but did not address the true American concern over "inflexible legislation," namely that the act was about to preempt an issue the United States wished to raise at the upcoming reciprocal trade talks. The State Department wanted the British to legislate "reasonably within our trade agreement demands" or, failing that, to pass interim legislation until the British delegation to the talks reached Washington and Ambassador Kennedy reached London.[31] Johnson dutifully reminded the British that on the eve of negotiations the proposed law "actually imposes additional restrictions on an important American commodity."[32] The same message was passed to Sir Ronald Lindsay in Washington, after he had explained that the legislative process could not be delayed: "It was difficult to see how it could help affecting our attitude toward concessions on certain important British exports to us."[33] At the same time, an influential State Department officer such as Francis Sayre wanted the department to keep its distance from the motion picture industry:

The position taken in this telegram [no. 55, 4 February 1939] commits the State Department to backing to a large degree the complaints of the moving picture industry. I do not have too great confidence in the leaders of the moving picture industry and would regret to see the State Department too thoroughly committed to battle for the claims of the industry.[34]

Meanwhile, Johnson and Allport had studied the fourteen points between themselves and with Sir William Brown, the latter conversation one they kept secret from the American industry (viz., Hays). Attention was drawn to the points that seemed against the whole principle of the legislation (such as points 1 and 8), and the political difficulties surrounding the bill were outlined:

it would be a mistake to underestimate the political influence of those groups whose interest in the films bill is based on their concern at the cultural influence of films. Many of these are individuals well known to the public who are both articulate and aggressive and not particularly interested in the purely trade aspect of the film problem.[35]

They were sensitive to the domestic politics of the legislation. Allport agreed to keep his participation secret from New York, and their cable stressed that any further approaches to the Foreign Office should avoid publicity if they were not to exacerbate Stanley's political problems. Confirming Allport's previous insight, the embassy concluded in February,

It has become quite apparent that the Board of Trade's views on the films matter are pretty much at variance with Stanley's and that in the latter's mind it has become a political question pure and simple.[36]

Despite these political problems, a note was sent to the Foreign Office complaining about the failure to delay legislation to await Kennedy's arrival and articulating formally Hays's Fourteen Points.[37] When Stanley brought forward his amendments, they covered several of the points. However, as we know, the House of Lords amended the bill in ways the government could not accept. Between that time and the bill's reversion to the Commons, Lord Strabolgi approached Allport, and Stanley approached newly arrived Ambassador Kennedy, to seek their help in preparing the final shape of the amendments. Summarizing what was achieved, Herschel Johnson calculated that seven of the Fourteen Points had not been met; four had been met in part (2, 6, 7, and 9); and three had been met in full (4, 5, and 8). It was possible that six of the points would be adjusted later. Weighing the value of the concessions, he argued that the triple-quota provision and the possibility of adjustment could benefit the American companies: "Some hold the opinion that their position is better than it was under the 1927 Act."[38]

This was not, apparently, the position of Hays – or at least of his principals. In an effort to get his (or their) way at the trade talks, if not in the Houses of Parliament, Hays directed another long memorandum to Hull in October. Recalling his Fourteen Points of 4 January, he claimed that only one had been accepted in its entirety, and three in part, "with modifications that materially impaired their value from the industry's standpoint." Apparently not having seen Johnson's assessment, which presumably was prepared in consultation with Kennedy and Allport, Hays declared:

At the time that the Act was passed, it was recognised both by the State Department and the motion picture industry that the British authorities had failed to give adequate consideration to the recommendations that had been placed before them on behalf of the American motion picture industry and, further, that the provisions of the Act, as passed, were highly detrimental to the interests of the industry.[39]

Highly detrimental, or better than the 1927 act? These positions are not contradictory and had much to do with Hays's implacable opposition to the very principles of the British legislation and his inclusion of their self-liquidation among his Fourteen Points. In his own summary of point 1, he had a second paragraph stating that the quota for the first year of the act should be 10 percent, or at most 12.5 percent, and should decrease in each successive year until completely eliminated. That this point was not conceded came as no surprise to Allport, Johnson, or Kennedy, all of whom seem to have found Hays intransigent.

Hays went on to chronicle the British refusal to include motion pictures in the trade talks and their adamant refusal to conclude a separate agreement about the treatment of motion pictures at special talks with the ambassador. (The exchanges between Hull and Kennedy on these matters show that Kennedy's view was that the legislation was too new and too tightly drawn to make such approaches fruitful.) Hays argued that the new act would require the expenditure of $85 million over its ten years on the production of films in Britain, monies that would have to come out of the annual remittances of $25 million. He described it as a 33-percent levy. Such was the need of foreign revenue, and such was the gearing up of manufacturing plants in the United States that

if the British Films Act is thus allowed to operate through its term in its present form, it will inevitably bring about such a dislocation in American production as may eventually destroy the present position the American industry has earned throughout the world by the quality of its production and the efforts of its management.

He ended with a vague threat of "other steps to persuade the British Government."[40]

This document is evidence that although matters were much improved in government–MPPDA relations, so that business could be transacted (with Kennedy and Allport being invited to help amend a British act of Parliament), a bullying and unreasonable attitude was still abroad in the industry. Fortunately, the memorandum was directed to Hull and not to the press. But given the heroic efforts made by State Department officials and by Hays's own man in London, based on the Fourteen Points extracted from Hays only with difficulty, the general tenor of the piece – that the American industry was being badly treated and that the efforts had not been good enough – was hardly calculated to win friends. Hays's memorandum was sent on to London, where, after two months of delay, Herschel Johnson wrote to tell the State Department just what he thought of it. He found it an interesting example of special pleading. He claimed that the MPPDA knew that the Fourteen Points could not be met in full by the British government; they knew the trade talks would collapse if the United States insisted on pressing their demands;[41] they knew the 1927 act had to be replaced by legislation that corrected its abuses and deficiencies:

The 14 Recommendations were not based on any just appreciation of the practical possibilities in Great Britain. It may be said that the producers' [i.e., the MPPDA] motive in presenting them was to ask for the maximum possible in the hope of thereby improving their bargaining position.

While conceding that the State Department had not succeeded in getting the British government to draft its legislation in accordance with the Fourteen Points, Johnson suggested comparing the act with the original bill.

It will be found that many of the most objectionable features of the proposed legislation were eliminated or softened in their effect in the Act (e.g., the elimination of the "viewing test" requirement, inclusion of "reciprocity" clause, etc.).

To the able representative in London of the Motion Picture Producers and Distributors of America, Inc., is due a large part of the credit for persuading the Board of Trade to make its attitude more reasonable; the State Department and its London representatives, however, were in constant consultation with Mr. Allport at each stage in the development of the legislation and they supported Mr. Allport's aims with the British authorities in every practicable way.

American motion picture interests in Great Britain were not wholly dissatisfied with the Act as finally passed, and in the final analysis it is these interests which have to operate under its provisions.

And to conclude, he enlisted Kennedy as sharing this view.[42]

Before passing to the final years covered in this chapter, we need to make sense of Hays's behavior. One gets the distinct impression that Hays protested so loudly to please his bosses; a more effective approach would have been to educate his bosses in the facts of international relations and the domestic politics of Britain (Fig. 11.1). U.S. motion picture companies wanted, after all, to go on doing their lucrative business in Britain and the Empire. From the mid-1920s it had been apparent that in British countries

Figure 11.1. Hays in Hollywood, 6 June 1938. *Top row, left to right*: George Schaeffer, Sydney Kent, Abraham Blumberg, Albert Warner; *bottom row, left to right*: Barney Balaban, Harry Cohn, Nicholas Schenck, Hays, and Leo Spitz. (Will H. Hays Papers, Indiana State Archives, Indianapolis.)

and many others the regime under which they would be permitted to do so was not the kind of regime under which they operated at home. Hence the responsible approach was to concentrate on minimizing what they found the worst features of the proposed regime and not to give the impression of trying to force a sovereign nation to act other than it wanted. In all cases their best arguments, which got the biggest concessions, were the ones in which they showed that British proposals would defeat their own aims and followed that up by proposing substitutes.

11.3. The approach of war

Hays's prognostications look even more absurd in hindsight. Within months of the passing of the Cinematograph Films Act of 1938, the overseas operations of the American motion picture industry were curtailed far more

Figure 11.2. Lobbying in Washington, probably 1941. *Left to right*: Albert Warner, Nicholas Schenck, Hays, George Schaeffer, and Joseph Hazen, meeting with Harry Hopkins. (Will H. Hays Papers, Indiana State Archives, Indianapolis.)

drastically than they ever had been before. The totalitarian nations of Germany and Italy exhibited increasing hostility to the free operations of U.S. film companies, which began to reduce their activities in those markets, and with the outbreak of war and the German occupation of much of Europe, film shipments virtually ceased, and revenues owing were virtually uncollectable.[43] Nevertheless, the war years were to prove immensely profitable to Hollywood.

Before we come to those years, however, we need to look at what for the United States continued to be prewar years, and what for Europe were the gathering storm and the first, disastrous, years of war: 1939–41. At home the U.S. film industry was under pressure, for in 1938 the Anti-Trust Division of the Justice Department had filed suit to force a dismantling of the vertical integration of companies that owned theaters and also managed production and distribution. This certainly was the most severe government challenge the industry had yet faced. By approaching Secretary of Commerce Harry L. Hopkins, the MPPDA found a way out (Fig. 11.2).[44] Commerce undertook to investigate the film industry and to suggest a restructuring that would, it was hoped, satisfy the Department of Justice. Another challenge was the accusation made by some legislators that the movies were making war propaganda.[45] This showed an interesting division, with Hays concocting elaborate memoranda to disprove the charge, and major figures in the industry, such as Darryl Zanuck, Walter Wanger, and Jack Warner, admitting the practice and wanting to intensify it.

The worsening European situation seems to have sobered down the MPPDA in foreign relations. For example, when the Canadian government proposed to remove a 60-percent exemption on nonresident dividends and royalties, raising the tax from a 2-percent effective rate to a full 5 percent, Colonel Cooper called on the U.S. commercial attaché to reassure him that in his view the increase would not go through.[46] After the budget speech of 25 April, which announced the increase, Cooper and John Michel, of the New York office of the MPPDA, lobbied Dr. Clark, deputy minister of finance, but came away with the impression that there would be no change. Calculating that the tax would amount to about $45,000, it was deemed not to warrant further action. Consul Peterson at Ottawa concluded that it was not a discriminatory move but represented "an effort on the part of the Government to increase its revenues."[47] Nevertheless the MPPDA asked for a formal or informal approach by the legation to protest. Asked for comment and recommendations, Consul Peterson argued that since Michel's lobbying was on record, a legation protest would not be productive.

A second reason for declining to make a protest is that if the Canadian government should make an objective investigation of taxation on film remittances it might conceivably be decided that payments in respect of film rights comprise royalties since title in the films themselves always remains with the producer and to a certain extent the transaction lines up with the ordinary interpretation of "royalty." The tax on royalties generally is 12.5 per cent although at present film remittances are specifically exempted from the 12.5 per cent levy under sub section 7 of Section 27 of the Income War Tax Act.[48]

Thus, although the instinct of the MPPDA was to protest directly and through their government, they were flexible as to whether formal or informal approaches were used, and the State Department decided to ask officials on the spot the wisdom of such a move before ordering it. Nothing in the archives indicates that the MPPDA continued to press the issue.

To jump ahead a little: In 1941, when the Canadian government had prohibited the import of nonessential articles, thus completely excluding many American firms from the Canadian market, it was proposed to hike the 5 percent tax to 15 percent. When the MPPDA proposed that the U.S. government protest, they were discouraged on the grounds that Canada was a "found" market anyway and that what they did earn was freely remittable, which was not the case in many countries. Industry representatives lobbied Ottawa directly and succeeded in having the tax proposal dropped to 10 percent, at which point the State Department concluded that no official protest should be made.

Meanwhile, in the United Kingdom, as the first anniversary of the 1938 act approached, so did the point where the Films Advisory Council would be called on to advise the Board of Trade on the workings of the act and the setting of quota and other figures for upcoming years. Remarkably, a newspaper campaign began in which the precipitate drop of British production from over two hundred to under one hundred films per year was bemoaned and suggestions were made that the U.S. firms had lived up to the letter, but not the spirit, of the legislation.[49] Shortly afterward, in May, with rearmament in full swing, it was reported that the British were contemplating an excise tax on films, something vigorously opposed by the British film trade. It was calculated that the tax would yield £764,385, of which £416,782 would fall on U.S. companies.[50]

Naturally, Hays proposed that Ambassador Kennedy officially protest, but he declined, on the grounds that a high-powered British delegation was forming a united front to lobby against the tax and that an American initiative might split the front. Besides, Kennedy reasoned, if the U.K. government intended to finance rearmament in part by severely crippling the British film industry, Hollywood had no serious complaint, since a possible source of competition was eliminated thereby. Kennedy's wizardry or insight must have seemed amply confirmed when the proposed tax was withdrawn on 21 June.[51]

As soon as war broke out in Europe, it became apparent that many aspects of foreign trade and currency exchange in Britain would be subject to government control, including those affecting the film industry. We can now retrace the course of events as the Americans reacted to and tried to shape them, focusing our attention on the relations between the MPPDA and the State Department in the period when the hope of business as usual was becoming forlorn. In the immediate aftermath of the declaration of war by Britain, Kennedy telegraphed that it was unclear how many cinemas would be permitted to reopen and that the United Kingdom was contemplating suspending the quota, licensing imports, and controlling foreign exchange.[52] In his first conference with Oliver Stanley he was informed that remittances to $5 million might be permitted. Kennedy asked just how the people of Britain were going to be entertained and suggested another meeting when plans were less vague and indefinite.[53] Allport went to see Somervell and urged that American interests be consulted prior to any action.[54] Kennedy was told in confidence that what Stanley had in mind was 50 percent of the remittances on films already in the country and $5 million a year thereafter. "As I see it this is very close to destruction for the American film industry and I should think a catastrophe for the theaters in England."[55]

A new note was struck, however, when it transpired that Hays and the heads of the various companies were studying the problem in the hope of coming up with a scheme "acceptable to the British Government and still sufficient to safeguard the present and future needs of the industry."[56] While awaiting this material, Kennedy sent a cable that is of great interest. Aware that the United States took more than $30 million per year out of Britain, and estimating that as three times the entire profit of the whole industry, Kennedy argued that complying with the British demands would destroy the American industry. It followed, he thought, that "we have got to be very tough." This would be possible because the needs of British morale made American films as important as war materials. So he suggested informing the British that "unless they pay for them, they cannot have the pictures." In addition, American production in Britain would proceed, provided the U.S. companies could take out all their money and have guarantees of staff and some way of proceeding during air raids and other difficulties. He also noted that since

the English have knowledge of the telegrams which arrive from the companies, they are in quite a good position to know what the American head offices are thinking. Therefore, I would suggest that the proposition of Mr. Hays be transmitted to me in the confidential code and then before it is handed over I can give my opinion on it, but the English will just laugh at me if it is once sent through to the offices here.[57]

The tough line was new from Kennedy, who had hitherto been rather conciliatory toward the British. His predictions of the collapse of the U.S. industry were rather hyperbolic. The attitude of "No money, no movies" might have seemed as shortsighted as he claimed any British confiscation of American movies in the United Kingdom would be. If Britain was doomed, as some evidence suggests Kennedy was beginning to think,[58] short sight was to be recommended – on both sides.

The passage quoted has both historical and historiographical significance. Its historical significance is that it provides direct evidence that the Americans were aware that the British monitored all cable traffic, and that some Americans did not trust the monitoring authorities not to inform interested British government departments of the (commercial) intelligence so gathered.[59] Although such monitoring is known for a fact to historians, it is not usually officially admitted to by the British government, in common with general British practice on intelligence and security matters.[60] Additional historical significance of the Kennedy telegram is that it shows the State Department as close enough to the motion picture industry to consider using its confidential codes for the transmission of commercial messages. Evidence scattered elsewhere suggests that the industry was charged for the privilege, but it is the very extension of it that I wish to stress. (One can imagine the reaction at the Foreign Office to the suggestion that its coded traffic be used as a conduit by the J. Arthur Rank Organisation.) The historiographical significance is that from this point on a great deal of internal communication of the Hays Organization is copied in the records of the State Department, marked for transmission to or from Hays. This is a windfall for historians of a kind of material totally missing in the Canadian and British archives.

In the event, "the minimum position which the industry feels it can accept" on remittances was $17.5 million, that is, half of what was remitted in normal years, even though, with box-office returns down by 50 percent, the MPPDA thought their total earnings in the current year would be in the region of $10 million. This was to prove a gross (and possibly a deliberately misleading) underestimate. The coded cable requested that the information be passed on to the London offices of the MPPDA firms. The suggestion was made that Stanley would do well "not to cause adverse repercussions in circles which are now most cooperative with British interests."[61] This realistic proposal moved things along quickly – although Stanley's first reaction to the figure of $17.5 million was, according to Kennedy, to blanch[62] – so that a draft text was in the United States before the end of the month, and Hays sent along his final notes for terms on 3 November.[63] Dickinson and Street (1985), usually fiercely nationalistic and anti-American, concede the possible wisdom of the final terms of $17.5 million, since an assault on the profits of a highly visible industry with a strong anti-Nazi and pro-British record might not have increased sympathy and understanding.

Although the industry was not unanimous, its tendencies were obvious, and Hays was out of step. For example, in a letter he typed personally to Roosevelt he congratulated him "on the progress of right purposes as indicated by the vote on the Neutrality Resolution." This was in the course of lobbying to have the Justice Department agree to be satisfied with the recommendations of the Commerce Department regarding the industry.[64] In his reply Roosevelt held out no such hope.

If the study now being made in the Department of Commerce should result in an economically desirable solution of the problems of the motion picture industry, it is conceivable that such a solution might furnish a basis for settlement of the pending equity suit. But the Attorney General tells me that unless or until a settlement is proposed which the Department of Justice believes is in the public interest, he would not be warranted in delaying or otherwise altering the normal course of litigation involving the film industry. I concur in the view of the Attorney General on this point.[65]

As we shall see, Hays's views on neutrality were as different from those of Roosevelt as were his views on the antitrust suit.

At all events, the agreement was completed by 18 November, with a secret pledge by Oliver Stanley to replace the quota on 1 April with one of two schemes: either the substitution by the American companies of production-loan equivalents for their quota obligations, or the purchase of British films to the same level of expenditure.[66] The MPPDA praise for this agreement was fulsome. Herron wrote of the "magnificent terms" that had

Table 11.1. *Quota year 1938–9, feature films*

Company	Spent	Obligation
Warner Bros.–First National	£205,000	£126,000
United Artists	250,000	50,000
20th C.–Fox	414,937	121,000
RKO Radio Pictures	176,000	100,000
Columbia	115,000	85,000
MGM	420,000	132,000
Paramount (approx.)	250,000	136,000
Total	£1,830,937	£750,000
Est. (1939–40)	£2.6 mill.	£1 mill.

Source: Dispatch No. 4216, London Embassy to State Department, 22 December 1939, NA, RG 59 1930–1939 841.4061 Motion Pictures/218.

been obtained by the ambassador ("much more than I thought could possibly be reached in my most optimistic moments") and extended the companies' thanks for splendid and efficient cooperation.[67] It is entirely possible that the praise had less to do with the amount of $17.5 million than with the promise to substitute a monetary obligation for the quota obligation. Because triple-credit pictures cost five to six times the amount of single-credit films, actual expenditures at the time were more than double statutory obligations, as we see in Table 11.1. If we assume that these figures, compiled in London for the confidential information of the State Department, are approximately correct, the attractiveness of requiring merely the money equivalent of the quota obligation becomes apparent. However, I draw attention to the overlooked fact that U.S. firms were investing substantially more in their British quota pictures than they were legally obliged to do, and that this cannot but have benefited the British industry.

Throughout 1940 and 1941, the overseas position of the U.S. film industry worsened, despite the technical neutrality of the United States. The Axis powers did not permit the circulation of American films in the areas they controlled, which began to encompass a good deal of western Europe and of Asia. This in itself may have increased the realism of the MPPDA and hence its willingness to be forthcoming with the State Department and to effect better working relationships. What can be tracked in these two years are the discussions and plans surrounding the reworking of the remittance agreement, the discussion over frozen balances, and the position of the motion picture industry on the foreign policy question of the day: neutrality.

The Control Committee for the remittance agreement with Britain consisted of Allport, Somervell, and T. K. Bewley of the Treasury. The committee received monthly statements of the amounts remitted within fourteen days of the end of the month. A list of permitted transactions was drawn up, and a retroactive system arranged so that if a transfer was found in violation a restoration payment could be made. Thus a close working relationship existed between British officials and a key officer of the MPPDA. In one way or another, such relationships would continue for the next dozen years. They naturally created, on the U.S. side, some expectation of consultation and fair treatment.

When the "monetary quota" variation on the Cinematograph Films Act was legislated, the Americans were delighted: It permitted them to make half the number of films for almost half the cost, although all would be of at least double-credit quality. It was described as "the most constructive step taken since the Films Act, 1927."[68] Analyzing the situation of the exchange agreement, as the time of its renewal approached, it was argued that the British needed American films more than Hollywood needed the British market. Yet the evidence was that Hollywood had not reorganized to cut its production-expenditure cloth to fit its smaller overseas market, that the British knew this, and that their need was primarily for entertainment and morale. Thus, if Hollywood was prepared to be tough, perhaps they could once more get 50-percent remittances.[69] There was, of course, the point that the British had indicated that the second year of agreement would involve a reduction from the $17.5 million of the first year.

The British opened negotiations aggressively by proposing a figure of $5 million, called "fantastic and unrealistic" by Alan Steyne, then overseeing film matters at the U.S. Embassy in London. He reiterated Kennedy's argument that it was not tenderness toward Hollywood that made the embassy "go to bat" but the widespread ramifications of the British proposals throughout the American economic structure and the resulting great potential harm. He offered visions of this powerful publicity and morale machine being dealt a death blow for a few million dollars. Somervell replied that the British thought they could get by with fewer films, shorter hours, closing many theaters, abandoning double features, and reissuing old pictures.[70] Kennedy telegraphed to Washington that he would not negotiate, suggesting a boycott of the British market after 28 October and that any agreement eventually reached have a clause outlawing a rumored Films Control Commission with dictatorial powers over the industry.[71]

It is hard to avoid the inference that this pressure, plus Kennedy's high political standing in British eyes, led to concessions. In the end $12.5 million, a figure signaled the preceding year, was agreed to after Kennedy had personally negotiated with Kingsley Wood and Horace Wilson (§6.2).

Meanwhile, in November, a consent decree settled the first phase of the antitrust suit.[72] But the industry was in trouble, not only with the administration, but with Congress as well. The high visibility of the industry was a standing temptation to publicity-seeking Congressmen to place it prominently on any list of institutions to be investigated. Before Pearl Harbor, one of the issues being investigated was conformity to the Neutrality Act.

In January 1941 Hays wrote a long reply to the isolationist senator Burton K. Wheeler stating that "the established policy of the organized motion picture industry ... most emphatically is NOT to carry on a 'violent propaganda ... to incite the American people to war.' "[73] Hays also sent a copy of the correspondence to Roosevelt, who thanked him and teasingly asked, "Why do you say at the end of your letter to Wheeler 'With kindest personal regards'!"[74] Shortly afterward, Roosevelt endorsed Hays's reappointment:

It was good to talk with you the other day though I did not have a chance to tell you that I personally would be made very happy if you could go on in your present work. You are the kind of Czar that nobody could call "a Dictator" because you are fair-minded and do not use a whip but still get things done for the general good.[75]

Hays was delighted and revealed that he had just signed another five-year contract.[76] In June he pledged that his "complete loyalty is at your command in this crisis in our national affairs."[77] That same month Roosevelt addressed the Academy Awards dinner by direct line, making more remarks that suggest he wished to orchestrate the mass media. He said that the dictators did not like American films because of the values they represented, and he explicitly enlisted the industry:

I do not minimize the importance of the motion picture industry as the most popular medium of mass entertainment. But tonight I want to place the chief emphasis on the service you can render in promoting solidarity among all the peoples of the Americas.[78]

The following day Frank Capra, vice president of the Motion Picture Academy, telegrammed his congratulations on the speech and assured Roosevelt of the cooperation of the industry.[79]

Even before the Lend–Lease Act had been signed on 11 March 1941, Hays fired off a bumper memorandum of nineteen legal-sized pages (plus eleven pages of appendixes and the whole text of H.R. 1776, the Lend–Lease legislation). He argued that the bill would so improve the United Kingdom's dollar exchange situation that simple equity and economic necessity both required that the industry should receive sufficient remittances to maintain its essential service. To push this view Hays went to Washington for an interview with Hull, then with the president, and then with the British ambassador and his financial counsellor Pinsent. With the British Hays stressed the President's interest and that the matter would be taken up via diplomatic channels.[80] In a conversation with Under Secretary of State Sumner Welles, Hays argued for downplaying the propaganda value of motion pictures "because of the political capital that would be made by those groups opposing the policies of the two governments." Instead of classifying films as an essential war need, informal approaches to the British were best.[81] In his interview with Sir Gerald Campbell,[82] Assistant Secretary of State Breckenridge Long indicated that the motion picture industry would use some of the released funds to engage in work for the United States in South America. The memorandum of Long's conversation says the total of the blocked funds was some $26 million, but a copy of the memorandum presented to Campbell showed the cumulated sum to be closer to $32 million.[83] Later, Hays suggested withholding $36 million from the $250 million payment the United States was giving Britain for the right to establish bases in the West Indies. Long countered that paying MPPDA out of U.S. government funds for films delivered to England was "out of the question." He also noted that since the British were still obligated to pay, in dollars, out of their own funds for all articles for which they had contracted prior to 1 January 1941, their exchange position was not much easier.[84]

By June, the generally accepted estimate of blocked remittances was $36 million. The office of the adviser on international economic affairs in the State Department reviewed the situation and concluded that the geopolitical argument of the need to counter German propaganda in South America with American films, and the British requirement that Hollywood continue to provide full and customary service of films to Britain, supported the case for full remittances. However, in invoking the clause in the exchange agreement which stated that any improvement in the foreign exchange position of the United Kingdom would be taken into account, there was little doubt that the British would regard films as just one more element in their current negotiations around lend–lease.[85] Despite these various maneuvers, nothing transpired. We need to notice, at this point, that the State Department was becoming a little protective of the MPPDA. The coordinator of Latin American affairs, Nelson Rockefeller, had appointed Jock Whitney to take charge of film matters. This created an organizational anomaly, because Whitney had direct access to film producers from his own contacts. This meant a connection between the U.S. government and Hollywood that by-passed the MPPDA. The result was "a considerable amount of concern on the part of Hays and his group." While

it is perfectly clear that . . . the Hays organization is willing to give surface cooperation to the Whitney group, neither Hays nor his organization intends to weaken their position with the motion picture producers. . . . Under the circumstances, I strongly recommend that every possible effort be made by the Department to avoid any action that would appear to discriminate against the Hays organization. Quite frankly, I believe that we can steer a perfectly realistic middle course and, in fact, act as a leavener in attaining full and friendly collaboration between Hays and Jock Whitney.[86]

Much was of course to change six months down the road when the United States entered the war and created a number of links between its government and the motion picture industry that were not mediated through the MPPDA. I have in mind organizations such as the Office of War Information, the War Department's Bureau of Public Relations, and the Army's Psychological Warfare units.[87]

Hays continued to press wherever he could, because, one must assume, there was pressure on him from the company executives. "Management of the Companies is being criticized by stockholders for continuing to send pictures without recovering some reasonable proportion of that territory's part of the production costs." His immediate aim was to persuade Roosevelt to have Harry Hopkins call the matter to the attention of the British government during his forthcoming mission. Roosevelt refused, because of "the nature of Harry Hopkins' visit to London." He counseled further use of the usual channels of the State Department and the British ambassador.[88] Shortly afterward, Cordell Hull put all his weight behind the issue with the British ambassador, Lord Halifax.

I set forth every possible fact and viewpoint that would be calculated to impress the British from their own standpoint, as well as the merits of the proposal and request of the moving picture companies. The Ambassador seemed far more impressed than during the three times I urged this matter on him heretofore. He promised unequivocally and repeatedly that when he goes to London next week he will do his very best about a reasonable settlement. He said that he agreed fully with everything I said.[89]

There were, of course, two issues tangled up, at this late point. One was the next renewal of the exchange control agreement and the amounts therein; the other was the transfer of the blocked balances. The London embassy was told to handle them separately.[90]

Adding to the complications for Hays and the MPPDA was that he had not calmed the isolationists in Congress, who intended to hold hearings to see if the movie industry was in violation of the Neutrality Act. Lowell Mellett wrote to Roosevelt to alert him that "the best men in the Industry" – that is, Wanger, Zanuck, Freeman – were prepared officially to go into the hearings proclaiming they were doing everything they could "to make America conscious of the national peril." But Hays wanted to be the sole spokesman of the industry, and his aim would be to show that motion pictures were not being used for defense propaganda. Mellett counseled Roosevelt not to see Hays until after the hearings, because that might suggest that Hays was expressing the President's views, and that in turn might cause the weak members of the industry to pull their punches.[91] In the event, the hearings were aborted by Pearl Harbor (see Moley 1945, chap. 10).

Hays's difficulties were not soon to be lightened. The London embassy gathered that the British were far from ready to concede the transfer of blocked funds. Indeed, there was talk of persuading Hollywood to build a British Hollywood with those funds and of asking the Americans to be content with restricted dollar remittances for the foreseeable future, including the immediate postwar period. Although the companies had shown good profits in the two preceding years, indications were that unless $20 million in remittances was permitted annually they would have trouble in breaking even.[92] The British concluded that the U.S. industry would have to make the necessary internal adjustments and possibly curtail the number of films it shipped to the United Kingdom. Were the companies to accept these premises, the new agreement would have similar terms to the one expiring. However, the blocked balances were not to be allowed to grow but were to be invested in British production. It was intended to increase the amount of screen time devoted to British films and to enforce single-feature programs.[93]

Hull found this "quite an unsatisfactory basis for a solution of the problem." He emphasized the enormous efforts the American government was making under lend–lease and stressed that he and the "highest officers of the American Government" expected an adequate and fair settlement. He offered to lend the money against British-held securities and asked that Lord Halifax be reminded of their recent conversation.[94] This effort eventually resulted in a somewhat conciliatory letter from Kingsley Wood, Chancellor of the Exchequer, which suggested detailed negotiations with the industry.[95] Of course, by this point the embassy and the State Department were so deeply involved that their being excluded from negotiations was out of the question. There were also higher policy matters – "inter-governmental discussions, the nature of which the film companies cannot be informed" – which made it seem the Hopkins mission should handle the negotiations, at least to begin with. On analyzing the letter they found that it veiled all the proposals so far rumored, saying, for example, that the British did not wish to use the exchange difficulties to force the American companies to produce in the United Kingdom while nevertheless suggesting that film production in Britain should be built up to "represent more closely the relative importance of the United Kingdom within the aggregate market for English-speaking pictures."[96]

An agreement was eventually reached that raised remittances to $20 million, precisely the figure that Steyne had accepted as necessary if the industry as a whole was to break even.[97] It deserves to be said how the British proposals looked from the American angle. Responsible officials conceded the British dollar exchange difficulties. There was no argument there. But they also wondered whether the British were not trying to get their hands on monies earned by U.S. firms to build up British production. Mired in the middle of a terrible war, some British officials continued to think that Britain was entitled to produce a larger proportion of the films for the English-speaking markets of the world than they had ever before. It is hard to know on what possible theory of international trade a nation could demand for itself a greater share of a market that it had invested little in, produced little for, and in which it had never been able to sell its product on anything remotely like the required scale. Similarly, on what theory of international trade was a government entitled to treat the export earnings of the industry of another nation as funds somehow misappropriated or diverted, and hence ripe to be sequestered and used to build up their own competing industry? These issues are the heart of the matter, for a combination of communism among the unions and intellectuals and etatism in elements of the civil service, as well as naked financial opportunism among those who were in the film business, were entertaining such schemes. Instead of treating movies like oil – namely, as a foreign good much in demand in Britain and hence costing a certain amount of foreign exchange – it was convolutedly reasoned that American movies were successful not because of the economic advantages they enjoyed and the preference schedules of the public but rather because of American sharp practice in depriving British entrepreneurs of a rightful share.

This feature of British thinking about films, often hypocritically denied in official statements, continued to bedevil relations with the United States until the 1950s.[98]

Notes

1 That the MPPDA was an integral as well as an integrating agency of the motion picture business was forcefully proclaimed when it was named a codefendant in the major antitrust suit known as U.S. *v.* Paramount Pictures, et al., launched in 1938 and continued in various forms until the 1950s. In a memorandum defending the naming of the Hays Organization as party to the suit, Paul Williams, special assistant to the attorney general, who drafted and framed the complaint, argued that the MPPDA was a central agency through which many of the activities of the membership were conducted and a medium for conferring on matters of mutual interest. The standard exhibition contract, the credit committees, the clearance arrangements, and the boards of trade had all been organized and created by the Hays Organization. It represented the industry before committees of Congress and state legislatures and acted as a "central defense committee" in all legal proceedings in which its members were involved, whether it was a party or not, causing one or more of its attorneys to attend trial. Finally, the Production Code Administration was entirely the creature of the MPPDA and had extended its control to all producers and exhibitors of motion pictures, whether members or not. This was a mechanism arbitrarily to restrain and prevent interstate commerce. Williams to Attorney General Arnold, 15 July 1938, NA, RG 60, Department of Justice, Anti-Trust Division, 60–6–0, Part II, Box 88. In the same file is a memorandum from Thurman Arnold, 7 February 1939, making the decision to segregate the MPPDA from the complaint and to seek authorization for a separate one. The reasoning was that introducing the censorship issue into an otherwise commercial case might confuse the issue and prevent a successful resolution.

2 Hays to Roosevelt, 7 November 1934, FDR, President's Personal File, Will Hays, no. 1945.

3 Hays to Hull, 14 April 1933, NA, RG 59 1930–1939 550 S 1 Agenda.

4 This heavy-handed and verbose lobbying tactic was characteristic of Hays. The drumbeat of his rhetoric and the reiteration of his arguments are in innumerable memoranda, some typed, others actually printed, to be found in the files of the State and Commerce Departments, the Committee on Reciprocity Information, the Temporary National Economic Committee, the Justice Department, the National Recovery Administration, and the personal files of Presidents.

5 See Lewis 1933 (pp. 299–302).

6 Myers to Early, 10 December 1933. There is a privately printed pamphlet denouncing both – The "Hays Office" and the N.R.A., by A. B. Momand of Shawnee, Oklahoma – in the Hays file at the Herbert Hoover Presidential Library. Four years later the Allied States Association of Motion Picture Exhibitors submitted to the House Committee on the Judiciary a "Petition for Relief from Contracts, Combinations, Conspiracies and Monopolies in the Motion Picture Industry," a document that may have contributed to the antitrust suit that was launched the following year. See NA, RG 144 TNEC Motion Pictures P 12, Industry File.

7 Robinson to Early, 24 March 1933, FDR, President's Official File, OF 73 Motion Pictures 1933 Jan.–June.

8 Corning to Early, 14 June 1933, ibid.

9 Early to Nancy Cook, 6 May 1933, ibid.

10 Roosevelt to House, 20 March 1935, in Roosevelt and Lash 1950 (p. 467).

11 Hays to Moley, 8 July 1934, and Kennedy to Moley, 17 July 1934, HIA, Raymond Moley Papers, Joseph Kennedy file.

12 This article ("Revolt in the West," New York Times, 24 November 1935, Arts Section, p. 4), not indexed under Hays in the New York Times Index, is a rather odd piece of "inspired" reporting. Under a Hollywood dateline, initialed D.W.C., it purports to report a sense of outrage and embitterment in Hollywood against the "spineless" attitude of Hays toward foreign protests against American films and threatened embargoes. The Hays office cannot, it is said, be relied upon; the American Chamber of Commerce does not recognize the MPPDA; and so a delegation should go to Cordell Hull to make stringent demands. All comments are said to be off the record, but the one name mentioned is that of Irving Thalberg, who complained that he might not be able to make Musa Dagh, about the Armenian massacres, because of Turkish protests. The idea of a West Coast delegation to Hull was structurally incoherent. It is unclear whether this story was a warning to Hays, a real attempt to see that his contract was not renewed that autumn, or a rumbling of discontent by independent producers against the pressure of the integrated majors, through the MPPDA, to accept its advice about subject matter. The attitudes of the State Department are considered throughout this chapter. That the MPPDA, through its Production Code, in a sense oppressed nonmembers was argued within the Department of Justice (see note 1 in this chapter).

13 Memorandum from Engle to Kerlin, 27 March 1935, and attached correspondence, NA, RG 40 General Records of the Department of Commerce, Office of the Secretary, General Correspondence 70801/230 Motion Picture Division, BF&DC and Acting Secretary of Commerce to Herron, 4 June 1935, NA, RG 151, BF&DC, General Records, 160.2 Specialties Division.

14 Ottawa Embassy to State Department, 13 April 1933, NA, RG 59 1930–1939 842.321/21–842.4065/40 Canada; and 1 May 1933, 23 August 1933, 842.5123 MP.

15 1 May 1933, ibid.
16 Paris Embassy to State Department, [?] March 1939, WNRC, RG 84 Paris Embassy 840.6, Films.
17 Hays Memorandum, 4 January 1937, NA, RG 59 1930–1939 841.4061 MP.
18 Hull to Ambassador, 16 March 1937, ibid.
19 Dunn to Herron, 22 June 1937, NA, RG 59 1930–1939, 841.4061/MP.
20 Allport memorandum, 10 August 1937, ibid.
21 Eden to Bingham, 30 July 1937, WNRC, RG 84 London Embassy General Records, vol. 18, 840.6.
22 Confidential Memorandum, 3 August 1937, NA, RG 59 1930–1939, 841.4061 / MP.
23 Herron to Culbertson, 17 November 1937, ibid.
24 Herron to Dunn, 18 November 1937, ibid.
25 Dispatch to State Department, 19 November 1937, ibid.
26 Sir Ronald's competence in this field was revealed to the Americans when he was reported in a conversation to have held that "British taste was on a higher plane than the general average of quality exhibited in this country." This provoked the marginal comment, "Perhaps, but look at the box-office receipts!" Memo of conversation, 10 December 1937, ibid.
27 Herschel Johnson to State Department, 13 December 1937, ibid. Hays later denied to Sayre that he had said there would be no trade agreement conversations unless the British legislation was suspended. Memorandum of conversation, 15 December 1938, ibid.
28 London Embassy to State Department, and enclosure, 20 December 1937, ibid.
29 Hull to London Embassy, 12 January 1938, summarizing memorandum by Hays under letter of 4 January 1938, ibid.
30 Johnson to State Department, 13 January 1938, ibid.
31 State Department to London Embassy, 31 January 1938, ibid.
32 Johnson to State Department, 8 February 1938, ibid.
33 State Department to London Embassy, 10 February 1938, reporting a conversation between Sir Ronald Lindsay and Pierrepoint Moffat, 9 February 1938, both ibid.
34 Sayre to Secretary of State, 1 February 1939, ibid.
35 Johnson to State Department, 18 January 1938, ibid.
36 London Embassy to State Department 12 February 1938, ibid.
37 State Department to London Embassy, signed by Hull, 15 February 1938, ibid.
38 Johnson to Secretary of State, 4 April 1938, ibid.
39 Hays to Hull, 20 October 1938, ibid.
40 Ibid.
41 A full account of these trade talks is given by Arthur Schatz 1970–1.
42 Johnson to Secretary of State, 4 January 1939, NA, RG 59 1930–1939 841.4061.
43 See the 1940 reports from Berlin in NA, RG 59 1940–49 840.4061 Europe, MP.
44 H. M. Warner to Hopkins, 6 March 1939, FDR, Hopkins Papers, Box 117, Motion Pictures. See also Warner to Roosevelt, 5 September 1939, FDR, President's Official File, OF, Box 4, Motion Pictures 1939, and the correspondence attached. Warner increased the pressure of his plea, having just returned from trying to prepare his European operations for war.

45 See Hays's exchange with Senator Wheeler, 13 and 14 January 1941, attached to Hays to Moley, 17 January 1941, Moley Papers, HIA, Hays file.
46 Peterson to Chargé, 7 March 1939, NA, RG 151, BF&DC 281, Canada Motion Pictures.
47 Peterson to Chargé, 10 May 1939, ibid.
48 Peterson to Chargé, 29 May 1939, ibid.
49 London Embassy to State Department, 23 January 1939, NA RG 59 1930–1939 841.4061 Motion Pictures / 153.
50 London Embassy to State Department, 10 May 1939, ibid.
51 Kennedy to State Department, 13 June 1939 and 21 June 1939, ibid.
52 Kennedy to State Department, 12 September 1939, ibid.
53 Kennedy to State Department, 22 September 1939, ibid.
54 Allport Memorandum of Conversation, 4 October 1939, ibid.
55 Kennedy to State Department, 9 October 1939, ibid.
56 Hull to London Embassy, 12 October 1939, ibid.
57 Kennedy to State Department, 13 October 1939, ibid., as well as in WNRC, RG 84, American Embassy, London, General Records, 840.6 1939.
58 A clipping from the *Boston Transcript* of 26 November 1940 reports Kennedy making off-the-record remarks to Hollywood people about the United Kingdom being finished and his not going back there; FDR, President's Official File, OF 3060 Kennedy.
59 Having read all the papers to do with films in this period that I could identify in the Public Record Office, I must report never to have seen a single hint that Board of Trade officials, for example, had foreknowledge of American proposals based on cable intercepts. This either speaks well for the discretion of all concerned and for the weeding process or must suggest that not all that was intercepted was passed on. Given that diligent historians have unearthed much more sensitive intelligence material from marginalia and similar material in the PRO, the latter hypothesis is the one I favor.
60 For example, Philip Taylor, one of the authorities on these matters, describes the routing of all commercial cable traffic through a single point but does not cite an official source confirming this (see Taylor 1988, pp. 163–4).
61 State Department to London Embassy, 16 October 1939, nos. 1232–3, NA, RG 59 1930–1939 841.4061 MP. These cables are signed "Hull," but the initials beneath are those of Assistant Secretary of State G(eorge S.) M(essersmith).
62 Kennedy to State Department, 2 November 1939, ibid.
63 Hays to Keating 3 November 1939, ibid.
64 Hays to Roosevelt, ([?] November 1939), FDR, President's Personal File 1945, Will H. Hays 1934–1941.
65 Roosevelt to Hays, 20 November 1939, ibid.
66 Kennedy to State Department, 18 November 1939, NA, RG 59 1930–1939, 841.4061 Motion Pictures / 205.
67 Herron to Messersmith, 27 November 1939, ibid.
68 Steyne to Ambassador, 30 April 1940, WNRC, RG 84 London Embassy 840.6 Films.
69 Steyne to Ambassador, 15 July 1940, ibid.
70 Steyne to Ambassador, 8 October 1940, ibid.
71 Kennedy to State Department, 8 October 1940, NA, RG 59 1940–1945 841.4061 Motion Pictures / 251.

72 Warner to Roosevelt, 25 November 1940, FDR, President's Official File, OF 73, Box 4, Motion Pictures 1940. The acting director of the Bureau of Foreign and Domestic Commerce wrote, "The Consent Decree accepted by the motion picture industry on November 20, 1940, eliminates the blind selling principles of H.R. 135 (Section 1-B), as motion picture distributors commencing September 1, 1941, must trade show within exchange districts all films prior to their release. The Consent Decree also modifies compulsory block booking (Section A) and no longer forces the purchase of the complete line. Under the consent decree no distributor shall offer for license or license more than five features in a single group. Exhibitors under the consent decree may if they so desire buy individual films and are privileged to see the films prior to their release.

It is therefore believed that the new reforms instituted by the Consent Decree should be given a fair chance of operation and that the present legislation is unnecessary since some of its features are taken care of under the Consent Decree." Memorandum to the Secretary, 25 January 1941, NA, RG 151, BF&DC 281, Motion Pictures General.

73 Hays to Wheeler, 14 January 1941, copied in Hays to Moley, 17 January 1941, HIA, Moley Papers, Hays file.

74 Roosevelt to Hays, 22 January 1941, FDR, President's Personal File 1945, Will H. Hays 1934–1941.

75 Roosevelt to Hays, 7 February 1941, ibid.

76 Hays to Roosevelt, 14 February 1941, ibid.

77 Hays to Roosevelt, undated; Roosevelt to Hays, 5 June 1941, FDR, President's Personal File, Will H. Hays 1945.

78 Roosevelt speech of 27 February 1941, FDR, President's Official File, OF 73 Motion Pictures, Box 5, Folder 1941 Jan–Aug.

79 Telegram, Capra to Roosevelt, 28 February 1941, ibid.

80 Burke to Welles, 19 March 1941, NA, RG 59 1940–1945 841.4061 Motion Pictures / 279.

81 Memorandum, 26 March 1941, ibid.

82 Sir Gerald Campbell (1879–1964), educated at Repton and Trinity College, Cambridge; consular officer, U.K. High Commissioner, Ottawa (1938–41); Minister at British Embassy, Washington, DC (1941–5); Director General of British Information Service, New York (1941–2).

83 Memorandum of Conversation, Sir Gerald Campbell and Mr. Long, 2 April 1941, ibid.

84 Memorandum of Conversation, Mr. Will Hays and Mr. Long, 14 April 1941, ibid.

85 Livesey to Long, 4 June 1941, ibid.

86 Memorandum, 3 July 1941, NA, RG 59 1940–1945 841.4061 Motion Pictures / 388.

87 For some of this, see Koppes and Black 1987; and Steele 1985, chap. 6.

88 Hays to Roosevelt, 24 July 1941, and Roosevelt to Hays, 29 July 1941, FDR, President's Personal File, Will H. Hays 1934–1941.

89 Memorandum by Hull, 13 August 1941, NA, RG 59 1940–1945 841.4061 Motion Pictures / 192.

90 Steyne to Ambassador, 2 September 1941, WNRC, RG 84 London Embassy 1941 840.6 Films.

91 Mellett to Roosevelt, 27 August 1941, FDR, President's Official File, OF 73, Motion Pictures 1941 January–April.

92 Steyne to Francis Colt de Wolf, 29 August 1941, WNRC, RG 84 London Embassy 1941 840.6 Films.

93 Winant to State Department, 11 September 1941, ibid.

94 Hull to London Embassy, 12 September 1941, ibid.

95 Wood to Winant, 25 September 1941, ibid.

96 Steyne to Ambassador, 25 September 1941, ibid.

97 Golden to W. Ray Johnston [Monogram Pictures], 2 December 1941, NA, RG 151, BF&DC 281, Motion Pictures – UK folder 1939–1942.

98 A principal culprit may have been Simon Rowson, who, since the time of his rather balanced analyses for the *Journal of the Royal Statistical Society,* had become more nationalist and had latterly joined the Board of Trade as an adviser on films. (Although as Rowson 1933 shows the nationalism had deep roots.) A propos of Rowson's participation in a conversation between Steyne, Somervell, and Archibald (British managing director of United Artists, substituting for Allport), Steyne commented, "It is obvious that Mr. Rowson feels he must earn his £600 a year and he is therefore likely to exercise a considerable nuisance value in suggesting complicated formulas for the American companies, and in general throwing sand in the gears." Memorandum of Conversation, 16 January 1940, ibid.

CHAPTER 12

Protecting the system in wartime, 1942–1945

World War II saw no hiatus in the international trade in films. Film exports from the United States to Canada proceeded without interruption, and although films sent by sea must sometimes have gone down among the immense losses of shipping tonnage to U-boats, this is never referred to in the archives, and a steady enough supply of new American films continued to reach the United Kingdom, as well as Australia and New Zealand and any neutral country that permitted them, especially the markets of South America – which were a target of opportunity for the United States. The U.K. film industry also flourished, despite the requisitioning of studios, rationing, conscription, and controls on capital investment. Fewer films were made than in peacetime, but it is widely agreed that their creativity and relevance were remarkable, and some at least went down well with both domestic and overseas audiences. That some wartime British pictures were liked in the United States raised once more the vexed question of whether, when the countries were no longer pooling their resources to fight common enemies, when Hollywood no longer felt a special obligation to give British films some exposure to American audiences, British films could find a secure and regular transatlantic audience. Could British films make that permanent breakthrough into the North American market that would provide a stable basis for high-cost and competitive operations?

There was also a reciprocal question asked by the American industry. Could, after their valiant war service in keeping up the supply of entertainment films and wholeheartedly cooperating with the U.K. government on its film projects, U.S. film companies use Allied gratitude for victory, the total alteration of the politics of Europe, once and for all to get rid of the trade barriers to U.S. films?

This chapter will not proceed wholly chronologically. Section 12.1 pursues the story of the continuing struggle with the British over dollar remittances and the quota. Section 12.2 overlaps in considering the separate theme of postwar planning for the motion picture industry within the military and on the MPPDA–State Department axis. Section 12.3 looks at the

Figure 12.1. Changing of the guard, 1945: Sixty-six-year-old Hays, after twenty-three years as head of the MPPDA, poses with his successor, Eric Johnston. (Will H. Hays Papers, Indiana State Archives, Indianapolis.)

way certain events between June 1944 and VJ-Day in August 1945 impacted on planning for the future of motion picture exports.

The entry of the United States into the war in late 1941 seemed a logical place to begin this chapter, since it so fundamentally altered the character of the political relations between the three North Atlantic triangle nations, and the same logic seemed to dictate ending the chapter when victory began the process of transforming those political relations once more. The death of Roosevelt, in April 1945, and the new Truman administration could have been used to end the chapter, except that there was continuity in film policies and much else between these two Presidents. Another choice might have been the resignation of Will Hays (despite his five-year contract, signed in 1941) and his replacement by Eric Johnston[1] in September 1945 (Fig. 12.1). This event, which also saw the creation of the Motion Picture Export Association (MPEA), is as significant as anything can be for the story Part III seeks to tell. If some of the strengths and weaknesses of the U.S. motion picture industry came, as I have argued, from their recruitment of high-caliber personnel who stayed a long time on the job, then the occasions of changeover to new personnel deserve the closest examination. Still, these three events occurred close together, and the end of the war can suffice as an adequate point to turn to the postwar world. Furthermore, immediately following the capitulation of the enemy a drastic policy consequence – the end of Lend–Lease – threw many calculations off.

12.1. Exports and payments in wartime

In Chapter 11 we saw how British officials worried away at the issue of dollar remittances from Britain. That the two countries were, after Pearl Harbor, cobelligerents; that lend–lease had made dollar credits available to Britain for the purchase of vital matériel; that the British ambassador, Lord Halifax, and the secretary of state, Cordell Hull, had direct discussions about motion pictures; that Roosevelt had expressed sympathetic interest in the industry's concerns: These facts should not mislead us into thinking that British resolve to hold out would crumble. In fact, full dollar settlement was not conceded until well into 1943. What clearly could no longer transpire was any attempt by the U.S. companies to withhold films from the British market. From now on, the requests for dollar transfers proceeded without threat.

However, in February 1942 Allport and Alan Steyne of the U.S. Embassy in London once more suggested to the Board of Trade that the quota be reduced. In his letter of refusal Rupert Somervell of the board noted that there was shortage of local product and hence no reason to use powers to reduce American obligations.[2] Returning to the exchange issue, Hays filed another memorandum (of eighteen legal-sized pages, plus several appendixes) with the Treasury and the State Departments in May. In this he laid stress on the motion pictures as a factor in maintaining civilian morale and as functioning to spread news of the American way of life. Motion pictures accomplished both ends only when and to the extent that they entertained people, unlike the subsidized products of the totalitarian countries. Hence the U.S. motion picture industry was anxious to continue to supply Britain with its full line of pictures. But world revenues to the U.S. industry had fallen by 30 percent on account of the war. The companies were prepared for economies and lower profits but not to make inferior or unsalable merchandize. The impounded funds were needed if proper pictures were to be supplied to the British Empire, "if we are to provide our troops, our Latin–American neighbors, our government agencies and our home front."[3] The one new idea was to suggest that since the United States would be spending huge sums for military purposes in the United Kingdom, it should be able to use blocked sterling to reimburse the motion picture business at home.

Anticipating the objection that other holders of blocked sterling would make the same request, Hays's memorandum argued that the movie totals were current accruals from the war and would be reinvested in more war-effort movies.[4] He made a special plea concerning the allegedly grave financial situation of RKO. Breckenridge Long, on Hull's instructions, conferred with the U.S. Treasury, saying the motion picture producers had rendered the United States a great service in tying the public into the war effort and presenting that effort to the people. He also affirmed that they had done necessary and important work in Britain.[5] Secretary of the Treasury Henry Morgenthau, by contrast, said he understood why the State Department had operated on behalf of the motion picture industry before but that in the present matter he felt unable to separate the industry from other American interests that had large balances blocked in England. He referred to the attitude of the State Department as favoritism toward the motion picture industry and said that it was for the secretary of state to take the matter up through diplomatic channels.[6]

In declaring Hays's new idea with regard to the blocked balances a Treasury matter, the State Department seems to have blundered. Secretary Morgenthau was clearly unimpressed by Hays's elaborate arguments and hence unwilling to help unblock the sterling. Furthermore, he used the occasion to intimate that the State Department was favoring the motion picture industry, something in which his department was not going to join.

Looking ahead, the State Department's Division of European Affairs pointed to the undesirability of accumulated blocked balances: They would become a drain on sterling after the war, when the U.S. government was more or less committed to maintaining the position of sterling. This pointed to the desirability of the transfer of balances being freely permitted. However, it was specifically held that there was no special case to be made for the motion picture industry. The maintenance of sterling through Lend–Lease in effect meant that the United States was financing its exports to sterling countries.

The greater the volume of imports (including movies) from this country into Australia the greater the volume of dollars which we will sooner or later have to provide to Australia. In other words the American Government and tax-payer will be paying for motion pictures which may be sent to Australia. . . . This would suggest . . . that we exercise some direct voice in determining what commodities should be exported and in what quantities.[7]

Almost as good as his word, Hays wrote to Roosevelt, enclosing two "brief" memoranda and asking for consideration. Referred to Hull, there was in the latter's letter to Roosevelt no disclosure of divided views in the State Department or between State and Treasury; it was merely noted that Hays's scheme would require the concurrence of the British Treasury and the American Treasury. The latter was reported as studying the matter without yet having reached any definite conclusion.[8] It is difficult to know whether Roosevelt had any hand in the fact that over the summer the logjam was broken and the intention to free up the remittances was eventually voiced by the British.[9] In September, when Somervell was in Washington to discuss lowering the quota to one film per company purchased at £20,000, rather than one film per 100,000 feet, Hull summarized their discussions on frozen funds with Sir Frederick Phillips and reported that it was his expectation that the frozen funds would be released.[10]

In a letter to Allport of 23 October 1942, the British Treasury did indeed agree to the transfer of all blocked film rentals accumulated in the first three years of the agreement. This move was coupled with a lowering of the monetary quota in order to require each American company to make one film and then to spend the rest of its obligation on acquiring the rights to British films. This reduced the pressure on limited facilities and simultaneously created further incentive for British producers to undertake more ambitious projects and for U.S. companies to acquire the films and release them in the United States. The successful negotiation of these matters strengthened the position of Hays and the MPPDA in the eyes of what seems to have been by this time a rather skeptical group of industry leaders, who, in the face of the wholesale new demands of war, were subjecting MPPDA and its activities to a stern cost–benefit analysis.

In 1935 and 1938 there had been signs of dissatisfaction with Hays. This came to a head in 1941 among high executives of the major companies. Shortly after Pearl Harbor, the member companies of both the MPPDA and the Association of Motion Picture Producers (AMPP) created an extraordinary "Committee of Six" or "East–West Committee," with an unlimited mandate "to analyse various problems of the industry and make such recommendations as they see fit." The six comprised three powerful executives from the board of directors of the MPPDA in New York (Austin C. Keough, J. Robert Rubin, and Joseph H. Hazen) and three more from its West Coast affiliate the AMPP (Herbert Freston, Mendel Silberberg, and Maurice Benjamin). Darryl F. Zanuck described them as the six "top attorneys" of the industry with whom he had worked in "securing Willkie for the Senate Investigation."[11]

The reason for setting up this committee was the feeling that the Hays Organization had been doing a poor job of public relations, especially in Washington. Zanuck wrote of "Pettijohn's fraud when he waved a letter which he claimed proved his personal contact with President Roosevelt."

I told them in no uncertain terms that that Administration had been friendly to the motion picture industry because the Administration appreciates the fine constructive work of the Industry and not because Hays or Pettijohn or anybody else has an inside track with the President or with you. I told them, as a matter of fact, that what had been done for the Industry was done in spite of our feeble representation in Washington and not because of it.[12]

Two particular public relations disasters were obviously the very fact of the Wheeler–Clark investigation itself (§ 11.3), which a more effective public relations organization might have headed off or neutered early on. The other was what Zanuck refers to as the Browne–Bioff scandal, which stemmed from the unionization of Hollywood (see Ross 1941, chap. 9). The press had exposed violent and corrupt labor racketeering in Hollywood during the 1930s. Both George E. Browne and William Bioff were sent to jail. Joseph M. Schenck, head of Twentieth Century–Fox, was in turn convicted of perjury in the matter of a one hundred thousand dollar payoff to the racketeers and was also sent to federal prison, for one year plus one day. Schenck, it so happens, was a director of the MPPDA. The acute embarrassment caused the industry has been analyzed by historians with different central interests; suffice it to say that neither the racketeering nor the jailing of Schenck, a leading light of the MPPDA, is so much as mentioned in Hays's memoirs.

In addition to rearranging and streamlining the MPPDA organizational chart and indicating that the post and duties of every single employee was to be scrutinized, the Committee of Six asked C. C. Pettijohn to resign and replaced him in Washington with J. C. Bryson from the West Coast; they stipulated that Hays was to secure an executive assistant; and they demanded that

the Hays office be so organized as to permit General Hays to be free of detail and routine so as to reserve his time and energies for the study and establishment of important policies and for the handling of matters of unusual significance or great importance.[13]

Hays at this point was in his sixties, and we may take this committee and the embarrassments that precipitated it as evidence that he was losing his grip. His new executive assistant, C. F. Coe, referred to the inquiries of the Committee of Six as the MPPDA's own personal Pearl Harbor. The MPPDA, too, had survived. On the face of it, that was remarkable. There was government censorship by several bodies, there was less foreign trade to handle, and the dependence of the industry on government permissions and control of materials meant that there was less for the MPPDA to do. Somehow, the War Activities Committee and the Public Relations Committee of the motion picture industry became affiliated to the MPPDA, rather than separate means of pulling it apart. This brings out what is perhaps obvious, that however well the U.S. motion picture industry seemed to work when the view was from Ottawa or London, looked at close up at home, it was riven with internal difficulties, uncertain, and often on the verge of chaos. The "present regime," about which the State Department had expressed such grave doubts when it came to formulating and carrying out an economic foreign policy, was still in place, still struggling to formulate and to carry out a coherent policy.

By this time Hays's personal position (as opposed to the position of his creature, the MPPDA), must have been strong, for I decode Bryson's remedies as consisting partly of "kicking him upstairs" – restricting him to "elevated" duties, requiring that he have an executive assistant to handle everyday matters, and shaking up the organization of the body he had created from scratch. Industry leaders were obviously reluctant to dispense with him so soon after re-signing him in 1941; this may partly have been because of possible political difficulties, partly because in certain matters he was seen as effective. Besides which, by this point the industry was treating itself as having been recruited into the war effort, with "General" Hays at its head. Such leadership was agreeable to Roosevelt, who urged Hays to stay on, much as he had in 1935,[14] and when, in May 1944, he was first told the news that Hays was to be succeeded by Eric Johnston, a Republican, and that hence the war machine would be handed over to the Republican Party, he told Early, "Will you speak to me about this but do something about it in the meantime."[15] It is not clear what, if anything, Early did, but Johnston did not succeed Hays until September 1945.

12.2. Postwar planning

As we have seen in Part II, the British began their postwar planning soon after war broke out. Whereas the United States kept well informed of this process as it developed in Britain, the reverse was not true. The British industry was, of course, "penetrated" by the London branches of the major United States distributors, run by a mixture of British and American personnel. Even so, the task of penetration was made easier by the fact that motion pictures were an issue of public policy in Britain but not in the United States. Thus the Americans soon heard that the Board of Trade was reluctant to set up a Royal Commission on the film industry and was content to let the Cinematograph Films Council make its own investigation. All such developments were assiduously reported to Washington and given their own interpretation there. One general way in which to contextualize postwar planning is to refer to the passage in Hays's memoirs where he discusses the 1930 negotiations with Germany over the film trade and patents.

> The business philosophy of the Germans was sharply different from ours. Repeatedly they made it clear that agreements must be "on a basis which would not jeopardize our position." More than once they came back to the thesis that "the conference must find some way to assure us of a fair share of the business in the non-exclusive territories." The Americans, on the other hand, being already strong in the field and aggressive in selling, were willing to leave the result to their own efforts without seeking any such guarantees.
>
> The thinking of the Americans was based chiefly on the two concepts of free trade and open competition (Hays 1955, p. 422).

There is no need to accept these sentiments at face value, especially given the evidence already brought out in this book. Many elements of American business were very ready to seek market restriction when they felt truly threatened (although their official philosophy was free trade). But there is also no reason to deny that Hays in this passage does manage to articulate a fundamental way of seeing things that governed the thought of many American businessmen and officials dealing with movies. The cultural reasoning behind some European demands they claimed not to be able to understand. An etatist or mercantilist business philosophy, on the other hand they understood but did not philosophically endorse. Allowing for the greater sensitivity and subtlety of some officials, especially in the State Department, the common reaction was to decode all European postwar planning for a cultural revival of their film industries as one or another maneuver to take a market share by "unfair" – that is, governmental – means; to deprive the Americans of a market they had earned; and to divert monies, where demand for American films was strong, to subsidize the "cultural" effort to have an indigenous film industry. One other aim they detected in Britain, but not in other countries, was that of challenging Hollywood in its domestic market and utilizing the monies diverted by market control and diversion to finance that challenge.

No doubt it is impossible to fix any date when postwar thinking and planning began on the American side. We also ought to divide the subject for analytic purposes into several separate problems. There was a special and technical problem that would arise immediately after the liberation of occupied countries by Allied armies. Whether Allied or belligerent, the population would be a captive audience for movies that could offer instruction, information, and, of course, entertainment. There was the question of what to show and what not to show. The task of commissioning films and of selecting from those already made for showing in the immediate aftermath of liberation was one for the psychological warfare specialists at headquarters in London and Washington, and dispersed through the different war theater commands.[16] As to what not to show: German and other Axis movies were thought to be in circulation in territories under German control, and a policy was needed to deal with that situation. Necessary equipment, electrical power, and a supply of suitable films were to be brought in by military units. It was assumed that most showings would be free.

A second phase very early came into focus, too: When the wave of battle had passed, there would be a period of military government, then a restoration of an interim civilian government, pending constitutional and electoral decisions. This would be the period when stocks of films available locally would have been "screened" for suitability and when basic equipment and utilities had been restored. The role of American film companies in that period raised the questions of the reacquisition of copyright and other properties abandoned or seized at the commencement of hostilities; the recommencement of the businesses of distribution, exhibition, and importation; assembling of personnel, expatriate and local; and the selection of films for display in such a delicate time and after such a long interval. It was decided that first military and then local currency could be accumulated, but remittances were a problem.

Once stable national regimes were in place, a third phase was entered when the question of the treatment to be expected and negotiated for American motion pictures was to be faced with the new regimes (see Table 13.1). As we saw, throughout the 1930s virtually all European governments had regulated the import of films from the United States. The MPPDA and its member companies intensely disliked these restrictions, and it was their aim to see that they were not reimposed.

Clearly the period immediately after liberation, under military and then interim civilian rule, when in many countries large numbers of U.S. forces would be present, was a window of opportunity, for in that period U.S. personnel would have considerable say in the motion picture fare offered and the legislative arrangements regulating it. Once in place, such arrangements might survive after the full restoration of constitutional and democratic government. These continental European developments were common to the thinking of the two large powers in the North Atlantic triangle, because the British also had ambitions concerning film exports, and by and large also wished to oppose state monopolies and tightly restrictive legislation. The British, however, were more confused in their aims. One of the lines they looked to was bilateral arrangements favoring the British industry in a particular country. The snag here was the higher-level policy decision that had already been made to pursue a freer and nondiscriminatory framework for international trade.

As is obvious, two large policy designs were involved. One was the Atlantic Charter, which spelled out the general political values of the Allies and, hence, set the general terms of the sorts of regimes that would be permitted to succeed German occupation (many already in place in shadow form in London). The other was the conviction, of Cordell Hull and others, that the international trading system had to be reformed, as a long-term policy to ensure stable peace (Gardner 1956, pp. 12–22). Part of this policy was the specific aim of a general movement toward freer trade (Maier 1977). Both these grand designs were to be pursued in a postwar Europe in which, it was becoming apparent, the United States would be the major player. It followed that it was more important than ever for the U.S. motion picture industry to cultivate close relations with, and a sympathetic attitude from, the federal government and its organs. The changed trading system would be negotiated between governments, and any concerned industry needed to let its government know its situation. Of course this meant the State and Commerce Departments but also the military, the machine that would have the power to open the window of opportunity in the areas it would control. Both Britain and the United States had motion picture people in uniform or attached to the military in the relevant units concerned with information, propaganda, and psychological warfare.

During the late 1930s and early 1940s it became increasingly apparent that the State Department, rather than the Commerce Department, was the primary target of cultivation by the MPPDA.[17] Economic intelligence was a far less problematic matter than orchestrating the full majesty of the newly powerful United States in behalf of its loyal and selfless motion picture industry.[18] The industry felt it had cooperated with alacrity in government schemes to regulate and censor films at home and abroad, to assist in the making of special types of films, to make the latest features available to troops around the world without charge, and, through its War Activities Committee and bond-selling campaigns, had generally acted as good corporate citizens. The industry hoped to spend the credit thus built up on avoiding the restoration of the restrictive prewar trading situation in motion pictures.

Facing them were, of course, their critics. Much has already been said about those within the ranks of government officials. Outside government, things were also far from ideal. Despite years of efforts by Hays, the industry and its leaders did not yet have an image of probity and responsibility:

Some of the pioneers who deserve the accolade for accomplishment are generally considered over-fed, over-dressed and over-paid gents who spend their enormous bonuses at race tracks, throw only crumbs to their stockholders, and commit orgies of extravagance, waste and ineptitude.[19]

There were political critics of the kind behind the Wheeler–Clark investigations; there were religious forces unreconciled to the morality of the movies shown and of the industry as they saw it; there were undercurrents of anti-Semitism; there were charges of profiteering, made against almost all war industries; and more.

Inasmuch as the industry is going to need friends in the not too near future, because these requests for draft deferments and easy commissions that are falling to picture folk are hitting a mighty sour note in the public's mind and heart. I KNOW BECAUSE I'M ON THE RECEIVING END OF HUNDREDS OF LETTERS EVERY WEEK.[20]

The writer, the columnist Jimmy Fidler, was trying to curry his way back into favor with the industry he had given hostile testimony against at the Wheeler–Clark hearings. This is no reason to discount his assertion that specific aspects of Hollywood behavior were bad publicity and did not help the industry to get the best treatment.

Films, as well as the behavior of the film community, were subject to attack. The scandal about *Mission to Moscow* (Warner Bros. 1943) centered on a film that was plausibly accused of presenting the Soviet Union in a favorable light.[21] It was also the stalking horse for an equally troubling charge: that in playing up to the government's wish for such films, the film industry was playing up to Roosevelt, who some of his detractors thought to be little less than an American Mussolini. One Walter H. Brooks wrote to Hays,

Through no fault of yours nor of the industry as a whole, there has been the appearance of evil, i.e. the apparent over-willingness on the part of a few to make the film industry seem to be a New Deal agency. Instead of the appearance of patriotic cooperation, film industry has created the appearance of submission to Moscow and Washington. Racial characteristics of Harry Warner or others who relish the sound of "Me and the President" have given a wrong impression. It is not to be wondered that political enemies take advantage.[22]

It was impossible, I think, for the motion picture industry to traverse these shoals and reefs on the way to good public relations without suffering some damage. The issue was rather one of damage control, keeping the vessel in the best possible shape.

Sometime before 21 October 1943, the MPPDA began serious discussions with the State Department, seeking its cooperation in maintaining overseas markets. The inevitable Hays memorandum – always the spoor in the archives that allow us to trace these meetings – was carefully couched to stress that the motion picture business was not your run-of-the mill export business. For one thing, 40 percent of the product was exported. For another, commercial success stemmed from artistic worth. Thus the supremacy of American motion pictures had been earned on merit, not inherited. Motion pictures were the most international of commodities, by virtue of their traffic in universal human emotions. Yet they were also the product of a large domestic industry whose spending linked it with many other industries and tax-collecting agencies, and it was a useful instrument for fostering goodwill south of the border. Takings from the foreign market financed the extra quality of the films that the domestic market enjoyed. Resistance to subsidy, to restrictions and discrimination, and "the right of our government to delivery of our message on the American Way of Life" all argued for the movies' foreign fate being an entirely proper concern of the government.

This memorandum is provided, therefore, as a plea to our government to apply its wisdom, experience and sanctions to the end that home-produced motion pictures may continue to present the nation's intrinsic *and extrinsic* values to the peoples of the world without crippling limitations inspired through foreign governments.

Such presentation, inherently, is delivered to the hearts and souls of men while receptivity is as elemental as seeing and hearing, laughing and crying, loving and struggling. The impression is not superficial, it is indelible. As a national asset it must be preserved for all home industries and continuing American freedom at home and abroad.[23]

The present-day reader can well imagine that, as we shall later see, this rather flowery style of presenting the MPPDA case was ill designed to melt the stonier or more cynical hearts within the State Department. The problems of the way in which motion pictures were seen by these groups, and the kind of damage they and their associated trade practices could do to broader U.S. interests with foreign countries, were simply not being addressed. The harsh truth was that the motion picture business was a rather small industry, however noisy and however much the secretary of state might wish to indulge them. They had a record of causing a good deal of irritation in international relations, while nevertheless building up an unshakable position of world domination. This kind of attack at the top did not succeed, I suspect, in advancing the aims of the industry far. However, those aims were substantially advanced by other methods.

Meanwhile, to continue at high policy levels: In advance of the settlement of overall policy (the Berle memorandum, to be discussed shortly), Hull wired the American ambassador to Britain, John G. Winant, in January 1944:

As you know, there is at present in Great Britain a serious agitation against the predominance of American films in British market and there is reason to believe that the American motion picture industry may be confronted with serious difficulties which will require close cooperation between the Hays organization, the Department and the Embassy with a view to effecting solutions satisfactory both to the American and British interests involved. In the circumstances, we believe it would be very helpful if you could designate an officer in the Embassy of the same calibre and experience as Alan Steyne to be responsible for all motion picture questions referred to the Embassy. Will you kindly let us know if you agree with this proposal and inform us of the name of the officer you have designated for the purpose indicated.[24]

Winant agreed and appointed Avery S. Peterson, who had handled film matters in a previous posting at Ottawa.[25]

With the immensely experienced Allport working in New York prior to his return to London in early 1945, and a senior State Department official designated to specialize in motion picture matters at the London embassy, and with, in Washington, Francis Colt de Wolf, chief of the Telecommunications Division of the State Department, having handled motion picture matters for the preceding five years,[26] working together with George Canty, who had been the Commerce Department's roving European representative concerned with motion pictures from 1926 to 1937, and who was by this time assistant chief of the Division of Commercial Policy at the State Department, both the MPPDA and the government had positioned themselves in advance to bring their best talent to bear on the anticipated difficulties. This was evidently part of the discussions with the MPPDA, because Hays explicitly addressed the issue of the quality of personnel and the structuring of the State Department to handle motion pictures in a letter to Hull's successor Edward R. Stettinius,[27] written immediately after de Wolf and Canty had lunched with senior MPPDA directors in New York.[28]

Clearly also as a result of the Hays Organization's requests, the State Department set the machinery in motion for a new circular letter laying down policy in the forthcoming postwar period. A memorandum was drafted, entitled "American Motion Pictures in the Postwar World," and circulated for comment in January of 1944. As before, much the most critical and interesting comment on the draft came from the Division of Economic

Studies, the successor to the Office of the Economic Adviser. Adviser Leroy D. Stinebower wrote that although agreeing with most of the instruction, he had found a disturbing undertone. He instanced the phrase "an intensification of effort by the Department and industry to insure maximum protection and facilities for the industry in the post-war period" as excessively positive and aggressive. A broad and powerful context was deployed against such a posture:

It is certainly pertinent to recall that many of the restrictions and discriminations of the past decade to which the instruction refers, were in no small part a product of our unwillingness or inability to take a sufficient volume of goods and services to make possible the transmission of payment to the United States for the goods and services which the world desired to obtain from this country. Among those payments to the United States were the very lush royalties on motion pictures.

Motion pictures are undoubtedly in a special category among American exports. The cultural and propaganda value of this production can not be overlooked. Would it not be possible, without sacrificing our interest in these latter values, to make this instruction a more objective request for a survey of the situation prevailing abroad and less of the opening gun of a new "exports without imports" campaign?[29]

Stettinius's special assistant endorsed Stinebower's memorandum as "containing an important point." As a result the drafter, de Wolf, who had informed Long that the draft "had been very carefully considered and discussed with representatives of the Hays Organization," revised it. But when it was passed for final approval to A. A. Berle, who was to be the signatory, he cut four sentences right out that had emphasized the value of American motion pictures as propaganda for democracy, and the need of foreign revenues if they were to retain their high quality and persuasiveness. To give readers the chance to decide for themselves what to make of this document, I reproduce it entire as Figure 12.2. In its modified and polished form, the instruction was long on background but restrained on required action. It reiterated the need for keeping advised of local actions that would burden American films, and it requested feedback on what sort of movies best entertain and best persuade local audiences. The overall aim was bluntly stated as "to remove existing obstacles to the distribution of American films wherever possible and to prevent any extension of such barriers in the future."[30]

Hays had, then, achieved his goal of lining up the State Department officially behind the motion picture industry on account of the value of its products in international relations. Internal dissent might continue to be

Figure 12.2 *(facing)*. "American Motion Pictures in the Postwar World." A basic State Department policy document governing efforts to assist the American motion picture business overseas after the cessation of hostilities. (National Archives, Washington D.C., RG 59, General Records of the Department of State, 1940–1944, Document 800.4061 Motion Pictures/409A.)

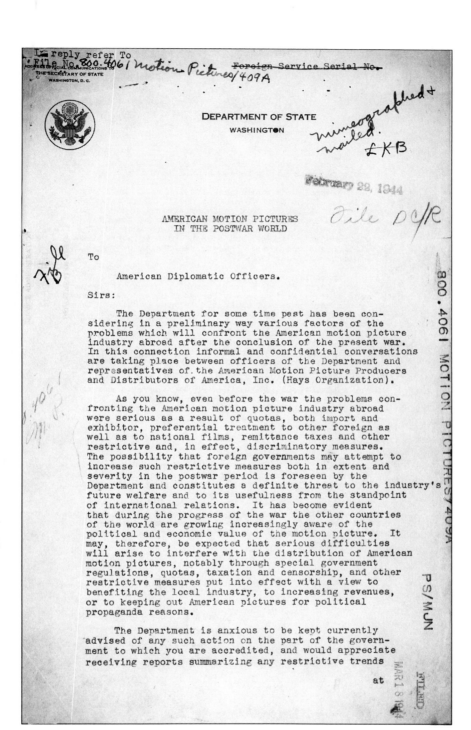

In reply refer To

File No. 800.4061 *Motion Pictures*/409A ~~Foreign Service Serial No.~~

ADDRESS OFFICIAL COMMUNICATIONS TO
THE SECRETARY OF STATE
WASHINGTON, D. C.

DEPARTMENT OF STATE

WASHINGTON

mimeographed + mailed.

£ K B

February 28, 1944

File DC/R

AMERICAN MOTION PICTURES
IN THE POSTWAR WORLD

To

　　American Diplomatic Officers.

Sirs:

　　The Department for some time past has been considering in a preliminary way various factors of the
problems which will confront the American motion picture
industry abroad after the conclusion of the present war.
In this connection informal and confidential conversations
are taking place between officers of the Department and
representatives of the American Motion Picture Producers
and Distributors of America, Inc. (Hays Organization).

　　As you know, even before the war the problems confronting the American motion picture industry abroad
were serious as a result of quotas, both import and
exhibitor, preferential treatment to other foreign as
well as to national films, remittance taxes and other
restrictive and, in effect, discriminatory measures.
The possibility that foreign governments may attempt to
increase such restrictive measures both in extent and
severity in the postwar period is foreseen by the
Department and constitutes a definite threat to the industry's
future welfare and to its usefulness from the standpoint
of international relations. It has become evident
that during the progress of the war the other countries
of the world are growing increasingly aware of the
political and economic value of the motion picture. It
may, therefore, be expected that serious difficulties
will arise to interfere with the distribution of American
motion pictures, notably through special government
regulations, quotas, taxation and censorship, and other
restrictive measures put into effect with a view to
benefiting the local industry, to increasing revenues,
or to keeping out American pictures for political
propaganda reasons.

　　The Department is anxious to be kept currently
advised of any such action on the part of the government to which you are accredited, and would appreciate
receiving reports summarizing any restrictive trends

at

800.4061 MOTION PICTURES/409A

PS/MJN

MAR 18 1944

FILED

Figure 12.2.

at present in effect, or which are contemplated, which would place an undue burden on American pictures.

Secondly, it would be helpful also to have your opinion of the type of picture that is most acceptable to local audiences from an entertainment standpoint and most effective from the standpoint of the broader considerations already mentioned. Reference to specific pictures which already have been shown in your jurisdiction and which you consider beneficial or detrimental would be appreciated.

In connection with these two considerations of picture content and restriction of imports, the Department would like to present for your consideration certain of the more outstanding factors of the problem. In many important ways the international distribution of American motion pictures presents a unique problem different from that of other American industries.

In the first place motion pictures, in addition to constituting one of our principal export commodities, can have an important intellectual value. The right kind of film can present a picture of this nation, its culture, its institutions, its method of dealing with social problems, and its people, which may be invaluable from the political, cultural and commercial point of view. On the other hand, the wrong kind of picture may have the opposite effect.

Thirdly, the American motion picture industry is dependent in a most important way on its foreign receipts to maintain the quality of its product. The importance of this fact is apparent when it is realized that these foreign receipts in normal times represent approximately forty percent of its total revenue.

Fourthly - and this is an important consideration - American motion pictures act as salesmen for American products, salesmen that are readily welcomed by their public.

You

Figure 12.2. (*cont.*)

380

3

You are, of course, generally familiar with the
considerations outlined above and with the many additional
advantages that accrue from the foreign distribution of
American films. The Department feels, however, that it
is particularly important at this time that you should
fully understand the value of the American motion picture
to the national welfare and the importance that the government attaches to the unrestricted distribution of
American motion pictures abroad, especially in the postwar period. The Department desires to cooperate fully in
the protection of the American motion picture industry
abroad. It expects in return that the industry will
cooperate wholeheatedly with this Government with a view
to insuring that the pictures distributed abroad will
reflect credit on the good name and reputation of this
country and its institutions. It is for this latter
reason that the Department is requesting your comments
and suggestions concerning the pictures themselves.

The program that the Department has in view is a
long range one designed to remove existing obstacles to
the distribution of American films wherever possible and
to prevent any extension of such barriers in the future.

Consequently, while suggesting certain factors to
be considered, the Department does not want you to feel
limited by these suggestions. In order that your comments
may be of maximum value the Department should be in a
position to turn them over to the American motion picture
industry, but should you wish to transmit any comments
or information of a confidential nature which you do
not desire to be forwarded, the Department will, of
course, respect your wishes in the matter.

Very truly yours,

For the Secretary of State:

Embassy or Legation File No. 840.6.
GRC
TD:FdeW:DMO
HGK

Figure 12.2. (*cont.*)

381

expressed, but the public posture of the department all the way up to the secretary, and the tone of communications with foreign posts, was just what the MPPDA desired. Hays's memorandum may have been florid, but some at least of its elevated sentiments were capable of being consistently maintained. Spyros Skouras, president of Twentieth Century–Fox, wrote to de Wolf after the January luncheon enclosing a list of all the prewar restrictions on U.S. films in continental Europe. He expressed the view that

the State Department can aid the motion picture industry immeasurably in helping it act as a spearhead abroad, pointing the way to a truer and higher sense of life. Through the medium of the motion picture, American ideas and ideals can be disseminated throughout the world. The minds of the people can become diffused [sic] with what is kind, honest and free. This is the most important thing that must be done to wipe out the opposite propaganda of hatred and brutality.[31]

In his reply de Wolf said he found this "most heartening."[32]

Even before the Berle memorandum was sent out, the newly appointed Peterson analyzed for the ambassador the situation as it was developing in Great Britain. The call for an investigation of monopoly in the British film trade was interpreted as a straightforward thrust at the Americans. "The proponents of the investigation foresee that American films may monopolize the British market and it is this phase which the Sub-Committee [of the Cinematograph Films Council, chaired by Albert Palache – hence, eventually, the 'Palache Report' (§6.4)] is to investigate." Described by Sam Eckman (managing director of MGM in London, who was acting for the MPPDA during Allport's absence in the United States), as the ringleader and most embittered was Michael Balcon,[33] who charged that no British films had been purchased for distribution in the United States since frozen currency was released. In response, Eckman urged that every means be sought to give some distribution to British films in the United States.[34] As it happened, the Rank monopoly, not the obsessions of Michael Balcon, was to be the principal concern of the monopoly inquiry.

At the end of his analysis Peterson noted Eckman's fears that collaboration between the Office of War Information (OWI) and the Ministry of Information on the distribution of forty selected films in post-war Europe "might impair the future American film position in Europe,"[35] which brings us to those very matters. The short interregnum when SHAEF would be the effective government was the window of opportunity for American films. The OWI and the MoI had selected films suitable for showing by the authorities, with an arrangement to collect revenues. A full exploration of this planning in all its intricate military depth is out of place in this volume, but it is useful to consider the following OWI document, "Film policy toward Germany: Guidance for selection of British and American motion pictures for showing under occupation":

The question of when to re-open German cinemas, and under what auspices, is to be determined by G-5 / SHAEF and PWD / SHAEF. The coice [sic] of motion pictures to be shown in German cinemas upon their reopening is subject to policies laid down by the British and American governments through their informational and propaganda agencies. It is not the policy of these governments to entertain or divert the German people after their defeat. Why then show any motion pictures at all? The answer is that in addition to the desire which SHAEF may have of using film showings as a means of winning civilian acquiescence or cooperation, the Allied governments have declared their intention of reorienting and reeducating the German mind out of its enslavement to Nazi and militarist doctrine. The choosing of films for showing in occupied Germany is therefore to be carried out as an act of political warfare – warfare against an idea, against a legacy of ten or more years of Nazi thinking and practice, which a German defeat will automatically wipe out.[36]

The paper went on to give, as values to be found in the films selected, the attractive variety and decency of democratic life, the contrast between freedom and regimentation, the appeal of peaceful effort against warlike effort, recognition of the courage and humanity of the Allied populations, and recognition of flourishing culture in the Allied countries contrasted to the inferior efforts in Germany under the Nazis. Positive guidelines for the entertainment films selected were professional polish, everyday situations, acknowledgment of shortcomings, dramatizations of resistance to ignorance or reaction, and aspects of the war with which Germans might be unfamiliar. Negative guidelines counseled avoiding the depiction of great wealth or of waste, avoiding blatant or complacent nationalism, racial or cultural prejudice, excessive criticism of British or American institutions, portrayal of predatory enterprises such as gangsterism or exploitative capitalism, and inaccurate portraits of Germany or ridicule of Germans. Among films recommended were *I Married a Witch, Here Comes Mr. Jordan, Stagecoach, Tawny Pipit* (with minor excisions), and *Dumbo*. Several titles were accompanied by summary-rationales:

A Man to Remember: The story of an American small-town physician who refuses to cater to the complacency of the town's most substantial citizens, and who, by his moral example and his selfless fight against disease, emerges as the hero of the community.

San Demetrio: A war picture on a subject unfamiliar to the Germans. Portrays plain men going about their dangerous daily work in the Merchant Navy, and avoids flag-waving. Outstanding screen technique.

Quiet Wedding: A portrait of British life at its best, showing also the ability of the English to laugh at themselves.

Dr. Ehrlich's Magic Bullet: A German doctor, while hounded by bureaucratic reaction and professional jealousy, carries on a lifelong pursuit of scientific truth and emerges with medicines to cure great scourges of mankind. A tribute to German scientific leadership of another day, faultlessly presented in a setting of the old Empire.[37]

The clear impression given by this and other documentation is that the Allies were preparing for what they expected would be an encounter with a brainwashed and mentally enslaved population unaware of the ways of life and values of their conquerors. Films were to be part of an overall campaign to pry them loose from that enslavement, the policy of "reeducation" (see Pilgert 1953; Pronay and Wilson, 1985). Some, of course, were skeptical of the ability of propaganda to do all this, but one can see prudence counseling that no risk of omission should be taken. Thus there is sometimes the hint that audiences in occupied countries, having been subjected to years of German propaganda, might also be partly brainwashed and in need of correction. Hence the careful selection of films for screening to them, too.

As the *Wall Street Journal* had it, "American movies have gone into Continental battlefields right behind the landing barges and have been distributed to foreign populations along with food and DDT louse killer."[38] American military personnel assisted firms in retrieving their property, and OWI readily handed over operations and films to those firms as its mandate expired.[39] The Americans were well informed about the film plans of governments in exile in London. Movie people in the armed services kept civilians informed:

The French are planning all kinds of restrictions on the importation of films, which means, of course, principally against American films, and I am very much afraid that unless someone from the Hays organization as well as a Film Attaché for the American Embassy is sent over rapidly that they will try to push through their nefarious plans and beat us to it.
    Being in PWD [Psychological Warfare Division] I cannot fight with them as my job is to keep on good terms with them.[40]

It is clear from this that reestablishment of the movie trade was something elements of the American military and political authorities were eager to facilitate. The same was true of some British, especially Sidney Bernstein, who had worked in the MoI and then in PWD-SHAEF. His pugnacious partisanship for British films had probably alerted Robert Riskin and L. W. Kastner to a potential rivalry, since he was a senior motion picture executive in Britain.[41] He was reported to be preparing to sue the seven major American companies for conspiring to destroy his business.[42]

Meanwhile, in Parliament, it was announced that the Rank Organization had agreed to limit its theater acquisitions. The following day (23 February 1944) there was a debate on monopoly in the film industry in the House of Lords (§6.4), the contents of which were carefully transmitted by the London embassy to Washington, emphasizing the places where hostility to American interests was expressed. Lords Brabazon and Strabolgi were singled out as hostile to American ownership in British firms, American domination of the market, and American closure of their own market to British films.[43] Politically, the American analysts decided there was not much support for the criticism, other than the widespread impression that the vertically integrated companies in the United States would not tolerate the competition involved in screening British films.[44]

And if we are impressed by the Americans' misinterpretation of what the British were up to, we can see that the reverse process was going on as well. What has here been described as postwar planning to remove obstacles to free trade in films could be and was interpreted much more strongly in certain trade circles in the United Kingdom as an American assault on the postwar market, not merely facilitated but coordinated and planned by the Department of State. The British trade paper *Kinematograph Weekly*, of 30 March 1944, led with a story about a grand scheme to provide the American film industry with a worldwide organization, with a specialized representative in all leading countries. A leading exponent was said to be George Canty. To further the ends of the industry, it was said that OWI had requested an increase from forty to one hundred features for screening in liberated territories.

Reported back to Washington,[45] this information was responded to in no uncertain terms:

FOR YOUR INFORMATION NO-ONE IN THE DEPT HAS HAD ANYTHING TO DO WITH THE SUBJECT MATTER OF YOUR 14766 OF MARCH 30, 1944. THIS IS ENTIRELY AN INDUSTRY MATTER.[46]

The documents allow us to see how it was possible to misread government–industry relations in this way. The MPPDA certainly intended to mount a major campaign to regain its lost foreign markets, with well-placed military officers planning to move in immediately behind the fighting to resuscitate the former structure of business. Enhancement of the Foreign Department of the MPPDA into a full-fledged subsidiary, the Motion Picture Export Association, was also being planned. And during the rebuilding in Europe the industry intended to have more than one European representative, since the foreign managers were convinced that they needed full-time help to deal with the government attitudes and policies they anticipated. With all this in mind they had been assiduously lobbying the State Department to throw its weight behind their efforts. Some officers in that department, as formerly there had been within the Commerce Department, seemed eager to comply; others were hostile. To the observer it might have looked, after the circulation of "American Motion Pictures in the Postwar World," as though the support was unqualified. But we know that the economic advice the department was getting drew attention to the simple fact that foreign countries had to find some means of paying for any successful American export drive. There was also continuing concern as to whether the American way of life as advertised in the movies was quite the image of the United States that the department would wish projected abroad. And there were, it goes without saying, wider political contexts.

In seeking to establish democratic regimes in formerly occupied territories, the United States was well aware that it scarcely served that aim immediately to dictate to or push around fledgling regimes as they sought political autonomy and cultural identity. Some of the immediate business the United States would have with such regimes was of geopolitical significance, and hence not to be sacrificed to the interests of a noisy but small export industry.

Canty and de Wolf, it is true, had met with motion picture executives, but their press release was a long way from the coordinated government–industry effort reported in *Kinematograph Weekly*. Hays and his men, it is also true, had found sympathetic ears in the State Department, all the way from the former secretary down. But that department was structured to ensure that divers aspects of proposed moves were considered before action was taken. What was also true, but underplayed in the *Kinematograph Weekly* story, was the newfound pride of the British film industry, its wartime successes on American screens, which fueled the long-standing ambition to counter American domination of the British market by penetrating deeply the American domestic market. Rank, Korda, Balcon, and Bernstein all certainly shared this ambition.

To these gentlemen and to some of the observers of the scene, there had to be a conspiracy. Britain had writers, actors, and filmmakers who felt they were professional. This was proved by the way they flourished when recruited to Hollywood. Why, then, did their home product not get shown in the United States? They were no more inclined to believe the evidence of public distaste and even hostility than was the American industry to acknowledge the depth of offense that some of its films caused abroad. Each tended to reinterpret events as the machinations of local business interests intent on controlling the trade. Both British and Americans overestimated the degree to which there was coordinated action by the other.

In a review of the developing situation in the United Kingdom, the U.S. Embassy predicted that the Palache Committee, were it to make the case that "through monopolistic tendencies importers of American films tend to restrict production opportunities for British films," could provide the basis for postwar restrictive legislation regarding imported films. The report also concluded there was slight possibility of the elimination of the quota system that reserved screen time for U.K. films and promoted British production. Yet the effort to rebuild the U.K. industry and to seek overseas markets would not indicate a rapid escalation of quota percentages. More likely was the development of a "reciprocity" argument regarding films, in order to justify expenditure on them of scarce "hard currency." The overall picture was said to be one in which any change would come gradually, if only because of public taste, and that opportunity would be "available to the

American industry to adopt whatever counter measures or protective devices ... seem to be appropriate."[47]

It appears that, beyond the Berle memorandum, the MPPDA wanted to ask the State Department to cooperate in the project of "an attempt to remove existing obstacles to the foreign distribution of American films wherever possible." Thus Carl E. Milliken sent a new twenty-five–page "Memorandum Relative to the Economic and Political Importance of the Distribution of American Motion Pictures Abroad and the Restrictions Now Imposed on Such Trade by Foreign Governments." His request was that this form the basis of discussion with the State Department's Division of Commercial Policy – where Canty was housed. The address to the level of policy clearly did not portend a series of individualized representations in foreign capitals, but was much more an effort to add motion pictures to Cordell Hull's effort to liberalize international trade after the war. After a historical survey – a sketched analysis of the motion picture economics of the United States, stressing their dependence on foreign revenues – the memorandum argued forcefully that rental payments were not taxable royalties, and that all restrictive legislation was, in effect, discriminatory. Although such legislation was nominally drafted to cover all imported or foreign films, since the United States usually had from 50–90 percent of the British market, the law was in effect directed primarily, and sometimes exclusively, against American films.

Specifically, Milliken sought

a greater degree of protection ... for American films in the commercial treaties, trade agreements, tax conventions and other agreements that the United States Government may conclude with the governments of foreign countries.

There followed a detailed inventory of the various restrictive measures in force "and those which were in force in Axis and Axis-occupied countries."[48] Oddly, since Milliken's survey was thorough, but arranged by type of restriction, two months later Allport supplied Canty with the same information, only arranged by country. With the two documents, one could see either (for example) all the countries that applied special taxes to imported movies or (for example) all the different restrictions imposed on foreign movies in France. The countries were grouped into Axis; Axis-occupied; other belligerents; and neutrals. The latter three were subdivided between countries with trade agreements with the United States and countries without such agreements. Save for fiscal restrictions, which was held over for a later communication, Allport noted that the material was a nearly complete survey.[49]

With some dismay the American companies watched the return of a protectionist attitude toward films in the provisional governments of Italy, France, Belgium, and Holland and mounted efforts to try to head off action. But the biggest European apple was, of course, Britain, where the Palache

Report had been completed and transmitted to New York for analysis. In a twelve-page summary and commentary on it signed by Milliken, it was surprising how many of its recommendations were declared either matters of domestic policy or notional (e.g., quota increases) in present circumstances. What Milliken's letter fastened on and attacked was the proposal for a films tribunal (Films commission) with the power to arbitrate disputes; enforce separate booking; draft new laws to alter the cinema circuit system; ensure a square deal for independent producers; prevent cinema acquisitions; allocate studio space; favor medium-cost pictures rather than "highly speculative luxury products"; and impose standard contracts. There was an irony, Milliken noted:

The Films Council's Committee was appointed to investigate tendencies to monopolies in the cinematographic industry, with a view to eliminating them if found. It now proposes, however, by means of an all-powerful commission of control, to set up a monopoly over the industry more far reaching and destructive than any monopoly that could have arisen within the film industry itself.

This central feature of the report

would subject American and British companies alike to a bureaucratic straitjacket that would undoubtedly succeed in crushing the industry into submission to the views of the Tribunal, but would crush out the fundamental artistic and economic vitality of the industry in so doing.

It also ran counter to the State Department's proclaimed policy of removing all artificial barriers to international trade, since the new body and its framework legislation would immeasurably increase the number and severity of the restrictions placed on the American film trade in Britain.[50]

Milliken's letter was a kind of alert to the State Department to watch the progress of the report's recommendations, but not a request for intergovernmental action.[51] Milliken's arguments were commercial: resistance to subjecting an established form of international trade to more, rather than fewer, restrictions. Dickinson and Street acknowledge that the reasoning of the Palache Committee, by contrast, was cultural, reflecting "the importance attached to national culture, the value of the independent producer, the twin dangers of American and British monopoly" (1985, p. 146). The actual words of the Palache Report were, however:

A cinematograph film represents something more than a mere commodity to be bartered against others. Already the screen has great influence both politically and culturally over the minds of the people. Its potentialities are vast, as a vehicle for the expression of national life, ideals and tradition, as a dramatic and artistic medium, and as an instrument for propaganda.[52]

The language and phrasing are unmistakably from the British side, but the sentiments expressed could be echoes of those in the overwritten memoranda of Hays and Coe. Once the importance of the prosperity of the film trade was asserted and the "Trade follows the film" argument deployed, the State Department was usually fed the sociopolitical idea of the film's value as an instrument of policy, fostering images of democracy, progress, and the American way.

Both sides tended to discount each other's cultural protestations – at the time and in historical perspective. The MPPDA, as we have seen and will continue to see, took British cultural arguments – on the occasions when the Board of Trade and the Foreign Office resorted to them – to be a smokescreen for those British interests who wanted to reserve some part of the lucrative film market for themselves. British officials and British historians alike evinced great suspicion of American arguments about the free flow of ideas and information as an essential ideal of the postwar world order, seeing it as a rationalization to secure and even extend already existing American economic advantage.

12.3. Resumption of European operations

There was no clear-cut point at which postwar planning became mixed up with postwar action, because the rolling back of the German occupation of the European mainland began in June 1944 and was not completed until May 1945. However, during the autumn of 1944, with the end of the war in sight, the British began to implement their ideas about the postwar structure of the industry, and the Americans began their response. So we now turn to those final months of the war. Perhaps the cardinal point to keep in mind is the rapidity with which events developed. France was invaded on 6 June 1944, Paris was taken on 25 August, and Brussels on 3 September. Subsequently progress slowed, but that autumn civil administration was taking over in large areas of Italy, France, and Belgium, and, among other things, attending to film matters. It thus became strategically important to have a firm U.S. policy in dealings with Britain, a victorious power, a large film market in itself and its Empire, and the coliberator of conquered Europe. This would, so to speak, set an example of relations between the two strongest military powers and provide an object lesson and perhaps some leverage on other, smaller, countries.

The long-term issue in Britain was, of course, the operation of the Cinematograph Films Act of 1938, the quota provisions of which had been frozen since 1942 at a distributor's quota of 20 percent. In April 1945 the statutory percentage was to be 27.5 percent unless the executive order was renewed. Allport asked the State Department to find out the Board of Trade's intentions and, should they intend to allow the statute to take effect, to protest that this would work a hardship, since the physical difficulties of production in Britain would make fulfillment of even 20 percent difficult.[53] Hays wrote that this kind of communication between the industry and the State Department was "working smoothly and satisfactorily," engendering hope that the problem of full and continued access to foreign markets would be assured. There remained, he pointed out, the problem of remission of revenues earned in those markets. He warned that the British were contemplating reimposing the restrictions removed in 1942–3, and he found one new argument: "From an economic and political standpoint, the international balance of payments is disturbed by the progressive accumulation of earned but untransferred funds, which become a liability to debtor and creditor nation alike."[54]

Pursuing contacts at all levels, Hays spoke with and wrote memorandums to Secretary Stettinius to bring to his attention the broad range of areas of postwar concern:

restrictive legislation;

dollar exchange;

Committee on Postwar Programs;

Committee on Freedom of Information;

multilateral trade agreement;

other treaties and trade agreements;

International Information Division;

double taxation agreements; and

the coordinating role and space problems of the Telecommunications Division.

Stettinius's reply was cordial and cooperative.[55] The machinery was working smoothly, and the only question was effectiveness. The machinery was working so smoothly that Milliken even consulted the State Department as to whether the MPPDA should retain the services of an international lawyer and whether a New York–based or a Washington-based person was preferable.[56]

Although Avery S. Peterson had been placed in charge of motion picture matters at the London embassy in 1944, it was not long before his reports were being written by Don Bliss, who eventually became the motion picture specialist in London for the next five years.[57] This able and talented American civil servant was as crucial a factor in the ensuing years as Allport (see Jarvie 1983). Although the machinery of communication between industry and government was good and worked well, the problems of postwar policy had not been resolved. The State Department was agreeable to assisting the MPPDA and its members within reason but did not consider the more aggressive and expansionist aims of the MPPDA to be realistic or reasonable in the developing context, a context in which the economic crisis and the political dangers were so severe that eventually, in response, the Marshall Plan came into being (see Hogan 1987; Milward 1984). Nothing on this scale was anticipated in the discussion we have been reviewing; that is to say, it was not apparent to the planners of the MPPDA that the economic well-being of postwar Europe would become both the responsibility and the charge of the United States. In such a context the motion picture could at best play a limited part, and certainly its trade could not expect unlimited freedom of action. Some of these considerations concerned British officials, who thought their actions would be shielded by U.S. officials. They somewhat overplayed the hand.

Allport's September inquiry about British quota plans had been met with the assertion that no decision had been made. Subsequently the footage quota was indeed set at 25 percent in 1945–6, rising to 29 percent and 33 percent in the subsequent years. These figures were well below the statute, which provided for 37.90 percent, 42.85 percent, and 42.85 percent, respectively. The Americans' main interest, however, was in the monetary quota. When it was announced, in the House of Commons, that the Board of Trade intended to modify the terms of the monetary quota by increasing the £1 per foot labor-cost requirement to 30s., to take account of inflation, the Americans became quite upset and asked for the proposed order to be withdrawn to allow time for discussions. The Americans maintained that the Board of Trade was wrong not to have consulted them, and they also argued that the labor-cost rate was fixed until the Cinematograph Films Act expired in 1948. The embassy was able to document this understanding from their files, but the British officials maintained that this was a misunderstanding, for they would not have intended to grant that.

It is our hope that the Board of Trade may decide to drop its proposal in view of our opposition. In the course of the discussions it was clear that neither Mr. Gaitskell nor Mr. White had studied their own files carefully, and that they were in fact unaware of some of the commitments, expressed or implied, which had been made by the Board of Trade in the course of the original discussion in 1940. On the other hand, they may decide to defend their position, in which case it may be necessary to arrange further discussions at a higher level, perhaps between the Ambassador and the President of the Board of Trade.[58]

This sharp reminder to the Board of Trade that the Americans were alert, and that British policy affecting a predominantly American business could hardly be made without reasonable consultation and discussion, seems to have helped. Bliss subsequently reported an amicable atmosphere in which consultation with the Americans was agreed to and direct talks between Somervell and Allport were planned. In informal discussion with White, Bliss reported the difficulty the American firms were having in meeting current quota obligations. White's response was that the situation was rapidly improving and production capacity increasing.[59]

The Americans knew their argument was juridical and that the British point of view was more realistic in face of the rise in labor costs. Bliss and Allport concluded that it would be best to accept the British decision and seek other modifications to compensate. One sticking point was whether the British were obliged to consult.

Apparently Somervell's reasonable and cooperative attitude is considerably modified in the Board of Trade and we are beginning to suspect that he had received definite orders from above – perhaps even from Dalton – to maintain a stiffer attitude toward American claims. In a telephone conversation yesterday ... [h]e could not agree that the Board of Trade is obliged to consult or seek concurrence of either the Embassy or the American companies. ... All of his current tactics involve a reluctance to put his attitude in writing.[60]

Yet to the surprise of the Americans the final exchange of letters showed a conciliatory attitude on the part of the Board of Trade, "possibly because of internal stresses within that organization."[61] The question of principle was set aside, but some of the American demands were conceded, while the Americans agreed not to protest the 50-percent increase in the £1 per foot labor cost.

As the end of the European war approached, Nathan Golden, still in charge of film matters at the Commerce Department's Bureau of Foreign and Domestic Commerce, made a trip to Europe to assess the situation.

The motion picture situation in Europe never has been more complicated than at present, what with growing nationalistic tendencies and the improvement of competitive product, British particularly; and I think that it will take two or three years before our position will be crystallized in this area.

Under consideration was a State Department proposal for a motion picture adviser for Europe. At present, Golden remarked,

officers unfamiliar with the trade's requirements ... are handling American film problems and also ... insufficient information is being submitted for our background purposes.

While professing indifference as to whether the officer came from Commerce or State, Golden confirmed that "an officer with a diplomatic designation surely would make a better impression than one known simply as an 'Attaché'. ... I would prefer to have an experienced career commercial officer designated for the position, one who from past experience with motion picture reporting would know at once the needs both of the Bureau and the State Department."[62] Golden's reference (in the first quotation) to "Europe" is to be taken to refer, I think, to continental Europe, since the personnel in Britain were highly qualified and clearly not suffering from the deficiencies he noted. The news from Britain continued to be good, in that the Palache Report was decisively shelved: No new legislation was passed until the Cinematograph Films Act was renewed in 1948; no action was taken on controversial proposals; and a trade committee was assigned to take care of the uncontroversial proposals."[63]

Behind the scenes, however, the MPPDA was gearing up to press again against quotas. The accumulated exhibitor defaults on their quota obligations by June 1945 emboldened Allport to write that he was preparing a case for the State Department to suggest that the British abandon the quota, "in the joint interest of the British and American film industry." The basic argument was to be that Britain, as a film-exporting country, could not "afford to maintain isolationist quota legislation that only serves to invite reprisals against British films abroad."[64]

Noted with interest was a kite-flying article under the signature of J. Arthur Rank targeting American remittances as "unbalanced" and needing to be compensated by distribution of British films in the United States.[65] By now Canty had been shifted over to be assistant chief of the Telecommunications Division of the State Department, to handle commercial motion picture questions. To correct for the lack of effective continuity or correlation in the department's policy, Telecommunications initiated fortnightly consultations between it and representatives of the industry. Additionally, weekly meetings were held with the chief of the Motion Picture Unit of the Bureau of Foreign and Domestic Commerce. Canty had in effect become the motion picture adviser.[66]

Two days after the Japanese signed the surrender on 2 September 1945, President Truman, fulfilling the pledges given to an always balky Congress, halted lend–lease shipments. Britain and Canada were suddenly forced to find dollar credits for American goods. All the machinery and diplomacy and planning assumptions that had been developed around films in the preceding three years were upset. Suddenly motion pictures were back in the position of being a possible victim of acute national economic difficulties, the prevailing situation for the remainder of the 1940s.

Notes

1 Eric Johnston (1895–1963), educated at University of Washington; U.S. Marine Corps (1917–22); Director, U.S. Chamber of Commerce (1934–41), president (1942–6); President MPAA (1945–63); Special Ambassador to the Middle East, 1953.

2 Steyne to Somervell, 3 February 1942, and Somervell to Steyne, 19 February 1942, WNRC, RG 84 London Embassy 1942 840.6 Films.

3 Hays, Memorandum, attached to Hays to Long, 12 May 1942, NA, RG 59 1940–1944 841.4061 Motion Pictures / 409.

4 Ibid. These new ideas are heavily underlined in pencil.

5 Long, Memorandum of Conversation, 19 May 1942, ibid.

6 Long, Memorandum, 19 May 1942, ibid.

7 Memorandum, 18 June 1942, NA, RG 59 1940–1944, 811.4061 Motion Pictures / 734.

8 Hays to Roosevelt, 4 July 1942, Hull to McIntyre (Secretary to the Presi-

dent), 23 July 1942, FDR, President's Personal File no. 1945, Will H. Hays 1942–1945.

9 Steele (1985, p. 210, note 47) accepts Zanuck's account.

10 Hull for Hays to Allport, 25 September 1942, WNRC, RG 84 London Embassy, 1942, 840.6.

11 Zanuck to Early, 28 November 1941, FDR, Early Papers, Z "Misc.," Zanuck actually listed W. C. Michel of Twentieth Century–Fox, who must have later been replaced by J. Robert Rubin.

12 Ibid. C. C. Pettijohn, an old crony of Hays from Indiana, was general counsel to the MPPDA.

13 Confidential Memorandum, 19 February 1942, Hays Papers. This is in fact the committee's report.

14 Roosevelt to Hays, 22 January and 7 February 1941, Hays to Roosevelt 14 February 1941, FDR, President's Personal File, no. 1945, Will H. Hays.

15 Roosevelt to Early, 13 May 1944, FDR, Official File 73 Motion Pictures.

16 See Office of Strategic Services to Golden, 12 September 1942, requesting whatever information was available on film activity in Allied and neutral countries to improve "our film export policy from the standpoint of cultural relations (psychological warfare)." NA, RG 151, BF2DC 281, General – Motion Pictures.

17 Seidelman (of Universal) to Hays, 3 January 1944, Hays Papers: "I do hope that the cooperation with the State Department will be cemented further in the months to come as we shall certainly need their help in the post war planning."

18 The Commerce Department's economic intelligence program had changed its function rather than faded out. The Motion Picture Questionnaire sent out on 5 January 1943 was explicitly redesigned in cooperation with the Psychological Division of the Office of Strategic Services. See Golden to Geist, 16 December 1942, enclosed with Acheson to American Diplomatic and Consular Officers, 5 January 1943, Diplomatic Serial No. 3649, NA, RG 59 1940–1944 800.4061 Motion Pictures / 159A.

19 Report by Roy Norr on MPPDA public relations planning for 1941–2, 11 February 1942, Hays Papers.

20 Fidler to Hays, 10 March 1943, Hays Papers.

21 See Culbert 1980; see also memorandum, Norr to Coe, 27 May 1943, Hays Papers.

22 Brooks to Hays, 4 September 1943, Hays Papers.

23 Hays to Hull, 21 October 1943, NA, RG 59, 800.4061 Motion Pictures / 332. This was submitted at the period when Hays's executive assistant was Coe, who drafted most documents. The paragraphs quoted are fine examples of the style Mortimer Adler declared he disliked, and termed "Florid Staccato."

24 Hull to Winant, 11 January 1944, WNRC, RG 84, London Embassy, 1944, Confidential File, 840.6 Films.

25 Winant to State Department, 29 January 1944, NA, RG 59 841.4061 Motion Pictures / 469.

26 Hays to Stettinius, 17 January 1944, NA, RG 59, 111.673 / 15.

27 Ibid.

28 State Department press release, 13 January 1944, Hays Papers: "They discussed the importance of freedom of expression everywhere in the world. This is regarded as one of the basic factors in the maintenance of future peace. Mr. de Wolf em-

phasized to the picture executives their responsibility to exercise the greatest care in the fair picturization of all other nations and their institutions and the fair presentation of the United States and its people to the world."

29 Memorandum, 11 January 1944, NA, RG 59 800.4061 Motion Pictures / 408.

30 A. A. Berle, "American Motion Pictures in the Postwar World," 22 February 1944, NA, RG 59 800.4061 Motion Pictures / 409A.

31 Skouras to de Wolf, 1 February 1944, NA, RG 59 800.4061 Motion Pictures / 398.

32 De Wolf to Skouras, 5 February 1944, ibid.

33 Eckman to State Department for MPPDA, 9 January 1944, WNRC, RG 84 London Embassy, Confidential File 1944, 840.6 Films.

34 Peterson to Ambassador, 16 February 1944, ibid.

35 Ibid.

36 21 July 1944, NA RG 208 OWI, Records of the Historian – Overseas Branch, OB Motion Picture Bureau Aug.–Sept. 1944.

37 OWI London, Film Policy Toward Germany, etc., NA, RG 208 Records of the Historian Overseas Branch; Box 2, OB Motion Picture Bureau: Aug–Sept 1944.

38 "*Movie Diplomacy* Propaganda Value of Films Perils Hollywood's Rich Markets abroad; Foreign Governments Favor Home Product – Britain Trains Cinema Envoys but U.S. Is Well Entrenched," *Wall Street Journal,* 16 August 1944.

39 Some of the intricacies and confusion of the situation as it developed are deducible from Riskin to Barrett, 12 August 1944, NA, RG 208 OWI Records of the Historian Overseas Branch, Box 2, OB Motion Picture Bureau 1942–45. Riskin laid great emphasis on the films as pieces of commercial property to be used by the military and OWI for psychological purposes but then to be handed over to agents of their owners.

40 L. W. Kastner (PWD-SHAEF) to Robert Riskin (OWI-NY), 28 October 1944, NA, RG 208 OWI Records of the Historian, Overseas Branch, Box 2, Overseas Branch Motion Picture Bureau Oct–Dec 1944. This letter, which describes the situation in Paris in detail, and others in the series give one a sense of déja vu. This is because Kastner had been Paris manager for Columbia, and Riskin the screenwriter of several Capra films. Two buddies from Columbia, then, now constituted themselves as advance men for the MPPDA in newly liberated Europe.

41 See Moorehead's account (1984, chap. 7). The credit grabbing of this authorized story can be judged by the doubtless imaginary scene (pp. 132–3) where Bernstein tells Louis B. Mayer to his face that MGM had never done a damned thing for the British. He was referring to the studio that made a specialty of films of the Empire, of British literary classics, and had recently released *Goodbye Mr. Chips, Waterloo Bridge, The Mortal Storm, Escape,* and *Nazi Agent.*

42 London Embassy to State Department, 22 April 1944, WNRC, RG 84 London Embassy, 1944, Confidential File, 840.6 Films.

43 London Embassy to State Department, 26 February 1944, ibid.

44 London Embassy to State Department, 1 March 1944, ibid.

45 London Embassy to State Department, 30 March 1944, NA, RG 59 1940–1944 800.4061 Motion Pictures / 429.

46 State Department to London Embassy, 26 April 1944, ibid.

47 London Embassy to State Department, 14 April 1944, NA, RG 59 1940–1944 841.4061 Motion Pictures / 505.

48 Milliken to de Wolf plus enclosure, 23 May 1944, NA, RG 59 1940–1944 800.4061 Motion Pictures.

49 Allport to Canty, 14 July 1944, ibid.

50 Milliken to de Wolf, 14 September 1944, NA, RG 59 1940–1944 841.4061 Motion Pictures / 9–1444.

51 Dickinson and Street (1985) give the report a generally sympathetic interpretation. In the course of this they admit that "the report could not be expected to receive much support from the industry which it had so severely criticised. Since its recommendations were primarily intended to help a group, the independent producers, who as yet hardly existed, there was no major interest group among the employers ready to speak for it" (p. 147). Indeed, there was only one group in the industry that spoke up for the report, and that was the militantly left-wing union, the Association of Cine-Technicians. The union run by Labour M.P. Tom O'Brien, the National Association of Theatrical and Kine Employees (NATKE), made no representation on the issue. Dickinson and Street nevertheless say that the Board of Trade discounted "the views of labour." Only the views of the vociferous communist leadership of one union were discounted.

52 *Tendencies to Monopoly in the Cinematograph Industry* (Palache Report, 1944, p. 6).

53 Allport to de Wolf, 29 September 1944, State Department to London Embassy, 11 October 1944, WNRC, RG 84 London Embassy Confidential File 1944 840.6 Films.

54 Hays to Hull, 12 October 1944, NA, RG 59 1940–1944 800.4061 Motion Pictures.

55 Hays to Stettinius, 28 October 1944, and Stettinius to Hays, 24 November 1944, ibid.

56 Memorandum of Conversation between Milliken, Canty, and Fowler of Commercial Policy, 11 December 1944, ibid.

57 His succession was mentioned in Milliken to de Wolf, 15 March 1945, NA, RG 59 1945–1949 841.4061 Motion Pictures / 3–1545. Don Carroll Bliss (1897–1978), educated at Dartmouth; career foreign service officer; at U.S. Embassy, London (1941–9), rising from commercial attaché to Consul General; later U.S. Ambassador to Ethiopia.

58 Bliss to State Department, 16 February 1945 NA, RG 59 1945–1949 841.4061 Motion Pictures / 2–1645.

59 Bliss to State Department, 27 February 1945, ibid.

60 Bliss for the files, 14 March 1945, WNRC, RG 84 London Embassy 1945 840.6 Films.

61 Bliss to State Department, 21 March 1945, ibid.

62 Golden to Van Blarcom, 1 April 1945, NA, RG 151, Bureau of Foreign and Domestic Commerce, General Records, 281, Motion Pictures General 1944–1950.

63 Bliss to State Department, 18 May 1945, NA, RG 59 1945–1949 841.4061 Motion Pictures / 5–1845.

64 London Embassy to State Department, enclosing Allport letter, 5 June 1945, ibid. (Confidential File).

65 Rank, "The Contribution of British Films to International Understanding," *Imperial Review and Empire Mail,* 31 May 1945.
66 Memorandum, Canty to de Wolf, 4 August 1945, NA, RG 59 1945–1949 800.4061 MP / 8–445.

CHAPTER 13

Adapting the system to peace, 1945–1950

The U.S. motion picture industry endeavored to adapt its system of managing international economic relations to the conditions of peacetime, but it is doubtful if complete success was ever achieved before radical structural change overtook the industry not long after the war. In 1947 the industry suffered two calamities: a drastic falloff at the box office, and consequent unemployment; and a hostile investigation of its possible Communist proclivities by the House Committee on Un-American Activities. In 1948 judgment was handed down in the major antitrust case against Paramount et al. (in effect, the major integrated companies of the MPAA), beginning the chain of events that led to their divesting themselves of their theater holdings (see Conant 1960 and Waterman 1978 and the later literature cited in Waterman). And, not long after, television began to make serious inroads. The completion of the coast-to-coast microwave network and the escalating sales of television sets created a whole new home-centered pattern of leisure-time activities. Hollywood plunged into its worst economic crisis ever, one that displaced it as the major mass medium (see Stuart 1960). In movies of the early and mid–1950s there were sometimes slighting references to television, and the industry convulsed through gimmick "solutions" such as 3-D, Cinerama®, Todd–AO®, CinemaScope®, VistaVision®, and Panavision®. The lost audience did not come back, but neither did the industry fade into oblivion.

The episodes to be revisited in this chapter are the American attempts to quieten opposition to their motion pictures in Canada and the protracted struggle over the structuring of the British market, over remittances, and over the commercial fate of the British film industry, including its efforts to develop Canada as a kind of wedge into the dollar area. Beyond the trees of suspicion, confusion, and overreaction in the American view, I hope the reader will glimpse the forest of an acute sense of the disposition of power and the ability to think far ahead.

13.1. Reacting to British developments

As noted, in planning for the postwar world, the MPPDA and its officers fully anticipated trouble. It was not long in coming. What was the American point of view on the "dollar crisis" of 1947, the ad valorem tax on imported films, the MPEA boycott and its resolution (Chapter 7)?

The U.S. motion picture industry kept particular watch on J. Arthur Rank, who had visited the United States to explore the market for British films and who had bought into Universal, which then proceeded to seek State Department support for the allocation of scarce building materials in order to erect special exchanges in the United States to handle British films. Paul Nitze, then deputy director of the State Department's Office of International Trade Policy, commented that "the [State] Dept. favored wider distribution of British films in U.S."[1] Another example was the reaction to a report in the trade press[2] that the Rank interests in Britain were seeking a link with a large French firm, Gaumont. Phil Reisman, a vice president at RKO in New York, wrote to Golden,

It certainly verifies all of the things which we have been telling you that these people have easy access not only to France but to the rest of the Continent and are devoting their time currently to getting this set for the post-war period. It is quite obvious that if they can tie up enough theatres in these important situations that it will mean the eventual elimination of a great many American films, and although the commercial aspect is very important I think the propaganda value for our country is even more important and some day we are going to have to explain all this.[3]

Propaganda, then, was an issue alive and well, and as troublesome as ever. For example, with the windup of the Office of War Information (OWI), the creation in its place of the U.S. Information Service (USIS), and the incorporation of that body into the State Department, a delicate situation was created in which a major department, long the object of Congressional suspicion, gained control of the government's overseas propaganda machinery yet had to avoid the charge of political bias. The leading film companies had previously been accused of being extensions of the New Deal and / or war propagandists, so the efforts of the State Department to assist the motion picture export trade were by no means presumed politically innocent. In mid-1946, Secretary of State Dean Acheson had specifically to direct cultural officers not to involve themselves in motion picture matters but to leave that to economic officers, except where residual OWI films or the reporting of local reactions was concerned.[4]

In Parliament, on 6 November 1945, Robert Boothby, a maverick Opposition M.P., asked Chancellor of the Exchequer Hugh Dalton why dollars were being expended for "second rate American films" in present conditions. He signaled his intention to raise the matter later during the adjournment debate (see §8.3).[5] Against this background, Allport and Bliss had a relaxed evening conference with Somervell, newly restored to supervision of motion picture matters at the Board of Trade. The two main issues discussed were the renters' quota and the dollar problem. Allport argued for the abolition of the renters' quota, on the grounds that it was no longer necessary because American firms saw commercial advantage in making films in Britain.

Somervell listened to this argument with close attention, and it seemed to me that he was impressed, although naturally he did not commit himself. I have a feeling that this viewpoint may influence Board of Trade planning in this connection.

On the dollar problem, Somervell indicated that contingency plans were being thought out and that certainly films would be restricted before, say, cotton. He also said there should be no return to freezing funds, since such postponed obligations had proved irksome. Finally,

He feels that if necessity arises to restrict imports of American films it would be desirable to organize a preliminary exchange of views before action is taken.[6]

This last point was of considerable importance to the Americans. Not only did it mean they would have time to prepare; it also gave them the opportunity to ensure that any scheme was workable and equitable. Their representations over the 1938 act and their input to the Kennedy negotiations of 1939 had been valuable and constructive. It is unfortunate that soon after his resumption of responsibility for films Somervell gave this reassurance, only to fail to fulfill it in 1947 (see §7.5).

When Boothby did bring up the matter again in Parliament, as promised, the government's line was that they were releasing studio space quickly, permitting the import of new capital equipment, and that the prospects were bright, but that the quota would not be greatly altered before the expiration of the 1938 act.[7] The very raising of these matters in the House aroused anxiety in the American industry. At their prompting, Canty approached the Office of Financial Development and Policy to see whether in the "present negotiations with the British" (toward the Anglo–American Financial Agreement, or American Loan, signed 6 December 1945) some way could be found to protect the future position of the industry. He was told

of the plan to put future current [i.e. noncapital] transactions on a convertible currency basis and of the commitment which we hoped to secure which would prevent the use of exchange control to limit British imports [of American films].

He was also told that if the present negotiations did not go through, little could be done to prevent curtailment of British importation of American pictures.[8]

The loan was, however, negotiated and, after protracted debate, ratified by the legislatures of the United States and Great Britain.[9] The acute dollar crisis was for the moment forestalled. Thus the next development in Britain was legislation: the proposals of the Palache Report and the planning for the renewal of the Cinematograph Films Act of 1938. A general watch was being kept throughout the liberated and occupied areas by American officials, as is indicated by the wording of a State Department circular to certain posts in December of 1945:

> In order to permit appreciation of the foregoing situation in the liberated countries of Europe, the report should describe the trade trends manifested since the liberation, especially as they have influenced the importation and distribution of American feature films; whether any restrictions are operating against the American film trade that were non-existent during the prewar period, and especially whether they have carried over from the period of the Axis occupation or influence, or have been established since the liberation; and also it should transmit any available information concerning the status of American-company revenues from their film-distribution activities, differentiating, if possible, between prewar and current account.[10]

The president of the Board of Trade, Sir Stafford Cripps, announced in the House of Commons on 18 March 1946 that comprehensive legislation to replace the Cinematograph Films Act of 1938 was planned; that it would provide more permanent measures to deal with the growth of the cinema circuits (chains); that the Palache proposal of a tribunal would "impede" the ordinary progress of the industry and so would not be adopted; and that an independent board would be established to formulate a voluntary plan whereby the circuits would allocate playing time to independently produced British films.

In an analysis of this statement for the Motion Picture Association of America (MPAA), Allport fastened on the last point, which, he maintained,

1. sanctioned and encouraged the diversion of circuit screen time from American to British films;
2. increased the exhibitors' quota for the three circuits beyond the provision of the Cinematograph Films Act of 1938; and
3. enabled British films to obtain screen time on a basis other than that of strict box-office value.

Commenting on the first point, Allport noted that the Rank circuit in particular had for some time been giving preferred and extended playing time to British films, although there was no evidence that this was sanctioned by the government. Now such preference appeared to be government policy. As to the second point, it portended, he held, a shift in emphasis toward the exhibitors' quota as the main legislative instrument. The final point was largely theoretical, since independent films already were shown and there were few independent producers. It was simply a matter worth watching.[11]

Between these two announcements Allport had a second exploratory talk with Somervell, this time accompanied by Avery Peterson of the London embassy. Somervell hinted that the Treasury might be toying with the idea of a tax on outgoing film remittances but did not offer any definite information. Given that similar schemes had been under active consideration and drafting since 1944 (see §7.4), he was certainly being economical with the truth. He emphasized the need for sustaining film entertainment, even though it was his personal opinion that there were presently too many films on the market. As to the disappointment at the lack of success of British films in the United States, Somervell was inclined to favor the option of concentrating British exports on the Empire and the Continent. Allport noted that this conflicted with official statements that stressed exports to the United States in order to earn dollars. Although insisting that there would be legislation, Somervell let it be known that he favored dropping the renters' quota. The problem that seemed to worry him was that American production for British audiences would compete for studio space and talent with British production, and that expansion of facilities for American production could run into political problems.

As a final shot, Allport pressed arguments against legislation, claiming that British actions tended to set a pattern for restrictive legislation in other countries, and that as a result British as well as American exports could suffer. He suggested that some form of Anglo–American film treaty could be the answer, to establish the basic conditions for film exchange between the two countries. Although agreeing that the idea had merit, Somervell thought the British industry was some years from being on a footing to bargain with the American industry.[12] Apparently Allport hoped he was getting candor from Somervell, that two high officials were thinking aloud together to develop a working understanding of each other's point of view.

In a later memorandum for MPPDA head Eric Johnston, Allport went so far as to describe what was going on as a "national crusade" in support of British films, carried on in Parliament, the government, the press, radio, and the public at large.

The British public now praises rather than criticises British films. Their preference is reflected in the increasing popularity of British films. The movement is nationwide and is an expression of nationalism in the first instance, the economic consideration being important but secondary. It conditions the entire future outlook of the American film trade here.

Our companies consider it imperative to counteract this movement by all proper means, particularly by protective publicity. Hence the unanimous desire to establish an effective publicity or public relations unit here at the earliest possible moment.

There was also the question of British films in the United States.

The actual amount of British film revenue from the United States is not known. It has been variously estimated at from $3 million to $6 million annually. A dollar income from the United States for British films of, say, $10 million annually should provide excellent insurance against undue interference with American operations in Great Britain. It is a reasonable premium considering the amount of our stake in the British market.[13]

It was Allport's conviction that American films had no ready substitute, and that deprivation of them would plunge the British film trade into an economic slump. A slump would hurt those directly relying on the industry for employment and profit and would also reduce Treasury receipts from the entertainment tax. This last argument should appeal to the British government. By an (apparently) innocent mistake Allport had secured figures for the entertainment tax collected from cinema admissions, which showed that the Treasury was making more from American films than the American companies were, given that 85 percent of box-office revenues were generated by American films.[14]

As discussion of the renewal of the films act moved forward and the various sectors of the British film trade made their views known, the problems within the Kinematograph Renters Society (KRS) became acute. Because the renters of British films were irreconcilably divided from the renters of American films, the KRS could not develop a common position. Instead, those members affiliated with the MPAA endeavored under its auspices to prepare something suitable.[15] Since the Cinema Exhibitors Association (CEA) had proposed lowering their quota obligation because of shortage of British product, and the British Film Producers Association had recommended ending the renters' quota, it was clear that some changes of advantage to the American firms were likely and needed backing.

In section 7.9, I indicated that after the resolution of the ad valorem duty crisis and the boycott, some of the frozen monies were diverted into increased production in Britain. It is important to make the qualification that plans for this preceded those events. In particular, Warner Bros., even before their prewar studio was rebuilt, indicated that, in a joint venture with Associated British Picture Corporation (ABPC), they planned to make six major features for world distribution in Britain in 1947–8. These pictures would utilize American players, producers, and directors, and they would earn dollars for ABPC in proportion to the amount invested.[16]

It is possible that in imposing the ad valorem duty the British blundered, since in May 1947 Johnston planned a trip to London to offer "to increase substantially British film revenues from the United States," partly by increased distribution of British pictures there and partly by increased British–American film production. In return for this, he would propose a films act of only one year as a trial period, any extension for a longer period to not "encompass new quota provisions which would worsen the American motion picture position in Great Britain." The State Department instructed Ambassador Lewis Douglas that it was much interested in this entire question and hoped that an opportunity would be found to present these views before British authorities took any action that would affect the American industry.[17] This candy apple should, in a way, have been enough: Whereas in 1946 the earnings of British films in the United States were estimated at $3 million, in 1947 they were expected to be closer to $10 million.[18] Some further substantial increase in that figure would have eased the dollar problem and also satisfied the British Film Producers Association (BFPA).

Whether because of lack of trust or because of political complexities, this offer, if it ever was made, was not accepted. At all events, after 1948 it became moot, as the major U.S. companies faced the prospect of divesting themselves of their theaters and therefore hardly found themselves in a position to guarantee box-office receipts to British films. Johnston's trip became dominated by the ad valorem issue and the boycott. Hence when the draft of the films was laid before Parliament it was a continuation of the 1938 act, for ten years. As we know, the bill abolished the renters' quota and altered the exhibitors' quota to distinguish between first features and the rest of the program. Quotas were to be fixed by the Cinematograph Films Council. Small theaters were relieved of quota obligations; large circuits had enhanced quota obligations.

The competence of British officialdom as compared to American officialdom comes into question when one notes that the new films bill provided for quota periods of six months, although Article 19 of the Geneva draft charter for an International Trade Organization of the United Nations (ITO) and for the General Agreement on Tariffs and Trade (GATT), had allowed quotas only "over a specified period of not less than one year." The phrasing had been adopted because of a general conviction that distributors should have a reasonable period of stabilized conditions in which to operate. The story is taken up by Don Bliss:

When I directed White's attention to the inconsistency . . . with the Geneva undertaking White was taken completely aback and I received a distinct impression that the point had been overlooked. However, it was too late to change the text of the bill and he undertook to make it clear in a public statement that there was no intention of abrogating the principle established at Geneva.

As a matter of record, therefore, the Department's attention is directed to *Hansard* for Wednesday, January 21, Column 227. The President of the Board of Trade, in discussing the Cinematograph Films Bill, stated – "Clause 2 of the new bill now provides for a completely flexible quota structure, subject only to the limitation provided for in our international agreement concluded at Geneva, that the quota percentages must not be altered at intervals of less than a year."[19]

Another reflection on the general competence on the British side is an analysis of the actual state of the British film industry from the point of view of large international companies. Utilizing only Board of Trade figures, Allport calculated that, in the four quota years ending 31 March 1948, of Britain's feature film supply 70.5 percent were American, 7.6 percent were other foreign, and 21.9 percent were British. He also found that, of the American films registered, 70.8 percent were registered by the eight MPAA companies and 29.2 percent by other companies. Moreover, of the British films registered, 57.7 percent were over 4,000 feet in length, and 42.3 percent were between 3,000 and 4,000 feet in length. Allport commented,

Consequently, although British studios supplied 21.9% of the total number of feature films registered, as indicated, nearly half of these were "featurettes" – under 4,000 feet in length, classed as features merely by virtue of the provisions of the 1938 Quota Act. If these features had been classed as short subjects, British feature film production would have constituted 13.9% of the total supply.

Allport also analyzed the figures for the ten-year period ending 31 March 1948, seeking to identify the British films that, by the cost test, constituted serious entries into the international market.

I regard the Triple and Double credit feature film categories as representing the total supply of British features suitable for foreign distribution, i.e., for the international market. You will note that production under these two categories combined totalled 296 features during the ten year period, an average of 29 features annually, and constituted 35 percent of the total British feature film production during that period.[20]

Unless sources of finance for the British industry drastically improved, these figures made it clear that at most, if Johnston's initiative had gone through the American industry would have had available to distribute thirty to fifty British features per year. Given the improvement in British films, given the addition of American stars and talent to some, this might not have proved an onerous way to buy economic peace. Without fully demonstrating that there was any true intention to carry out such a scheme, this evidence at least makes it clear that it would not have been unacceptably risky and expensive for the Americans.

13.2. Trade policy and Canadian "cooperation"

The draft charter for the ITO included the provision that nations should seek "the reduction of tariffs and other trade barriers and . . . the elimination of all forms of discriminatory treatment in international commerce." Thus it is no surprise that when the Committee for Reciprocity Information, charged with collecting information on the trade behavior of other countries toward the United States, called for submissions prior to its hearings, the MPAA decided on a vigorous response to help influence the government's position in Geneva.

Sidney Schreiber, general attorney of the MPAA, submitted a twenty-four–page statement to the committee on 19 December 1946. The arguments were by this time fully familiar; here they were simply deployed in a manner that focused on the issue of reciprocity. Although the Geneva negotiations had been entirely economic in character, the MPAA could not forbear making some cultural and even political points. To this end they quoted sources that were, for the purpose, impeccable. The eighth report of the House Special Committee on Postwar Economic Policy and Planning (79th Congress, First Session) had proclaimed that the export of our best means of spreading American ideas as well as distributing American goods in nations desiring and in need of them, namely, the books, magazines, papers, and movies of this country, should be freely promoted (p. 13).[21]

Also invoked was a Congressional resolution and an Inter-American Conference affirmation of the importance of freedom of the press and information flow. Emphasizing that the United States placed no barriers on the importation of motion pictures, the statement argued that foreign governments that wished to stimulate a domestic film industry could do so "without barring access to our motion pictures."[22]

The document then listed the various impediments to which different countries had subjected American motion pictures. On import duties the point was made that it was important that such charges be levied evenly and not on those forms of film, such as positive film and color film, in which the United States specialized. Quotas were deplored, because their aim was always the exclusion of American pictures, regardless of how neutrally they were worded. Import licenses, exchange-control restrictions, and government film monopolies were also listed as discriminatory devices, along with remittance taxes (as in Canada).

After Johnston's appearance before the Committee for Reciprocity Information on 6 February 1947, the MPAA surveyed its members and submitted a Supplementary Statement on 27 February 1947. This was a formidable, fifty-three-page, printed document that repeated and supplemented the previous submission; it became something of a classic, or basic position paper, for the MPAA. Three countries singled out for special discussion were the United Kingdom, the Netherlands, and Norway. The United Kingdom, naturally, was included because of its size as a market, because of the quota legislation, and because of the example it set other countries. Norway and the Netherlands both had film trade organizations so unified, strong, and hostile that dealing with them was compared to dealing with government control.[23]

Although the American market was free and open and American films were dominant because of quality, the Supplementary Statement maintained that this dominance "coupled with important political aspects of the industry have caused it to become especially susceptible to attack and regulation in foreign countries." The Supplementary Statement confronted head-on the accusation that the openness of the American market was more apparent than real by pointing to the numerous British films that had been successfully distributed in the United States and to the vigorous antitrust actions to which the industry had been subjected.

Turning to the technical questions of the proposed trade agreement, the Supplementary Statement pointed out that standard provisions such as "most favored nation" treatment, or treatment not less favorable than that accorded like products of national origin, did not protect motion pictures from discrimination in countries where hardly any other imports and no domestic production existed. It followed that provisions specifically applying to films needed to be included in the upcoming agreement. The association submitted sixteen draft clauses that would outlaw all the most obnoxious practices, although admitting that this ideal could not be fully realized (p. 12).

There followed a country-by-country review. Canada was declared the outstanding foreign market, after the United Kingdom. Receipts from Canada averaged about 10 percent of all receipts from abroad (p. 21). Canada's remittance tax on film royalties, and the preferential tariff rate on films extended to British, French, Polish, and Ukrainian films, were decried. The United Kingdom was declared by far the most important foreign market for U.S. films, "being virtually as important as all of the other countries of the world and considerably more important than all of the other seventeen countries with which trade negotiations are to be undertaken" (p. 44).

In a separate submission to the Office of International Trade Policy at the State Department, the International (formerly Foreign) Division of the MPAA estimated that whereas U.S. firms would produce in 1947 about four hundred films suitable for international distribution at an approximate cost of $400 million, the British industry would produce forty-five films. It was emphasized that several wartime British films had grossed more than their production costs in the United States alone, particularly *Henry V, In Which We Serve* (Two Cities 1942), and *Caesar and Cleopatra*. Ten other British films were scheduled for wide distribution in the United States and could be expected to gross a total of $20 million.[24] Carefully not stated was the difference between what these films grossed and the revenues that would eventually find their way back to their British production companies. Recall that the Paris representative of the MPAA had estimated British remittances in 1947 at $10 million (see §13.1). Had the grosses translated into net, *Caesar and Cleopatra* would not have ended up one of the biggest British money losers ever.

A useful chart showing the formidable array of barriers American films faced in 1947 is presented in Table 13.1.

In June, in a telegram to the Geneva delegation, the State Department gave details of the package Johnston was devising:

Five U.S. exhibitor producers about to guarantee Rank $10 million gross screen time 1947. Other U.S. theaters to guarantee Rank $2 million. Other U.K. producers to be guaranteed $3 million U.S. screen time. Total guarantees $15 million compares with $3–5 million grossed U.S. 1946 by U.K. distributors. If possible obtain Department will communicate you re Blumberg arrangement.[25]

It is quite unclear by whom, and when, this offer was made and whether it was serious – that is to say, committed to paper, with robust guarantees. Still, it is evidence that British films were not out of the question for distribution in the United States, and that, even if distribution of them involved something of a loss, U.S. distributors preferred this to the British domestic legislation.

As preparations in Geneva went forward, there was some talk of attempting to discuss the British legislation there in order to request concessions. In a careful analysis, Bliss noted that the films act was a domestic regulation, and that in the draft of Article 15 there was reference only to bilateral negotiations, not to multilateral negotiations. He further held that if the United States demanded greater concessions from the British regarding both Commonwealth preferences and internal film regulations, "we might obtain either" but "the possibility of obtaining both may be questioned." Bliss reviewed the British situation and discounted the possibility of an emergency measure on film remittances, thought there was some chance of the renters' quota being abandoned, and argued for some reining in of MPAA demands:

On the proposal [by the MPAA] for a progressive reduction of the present rate, I have no hope at all that we could get this. The British philosophy in film matters since 1927 has been to reserve a constantly increasing share of the home market for British films, and in the present political atmosphere of vociferous attack on both the Rank "monopoly" and the "Americans" I see little prospect that the traditional attitude will be reversed. This is an approach which should be postponed for a considerable period, and at least until the current enthusiasm for expansion has waned.[26]

Bliss returned to the subject of screen quotas a few days later in a second memorandum to Winthrop G. Brown of the U.S. delegation at Geneva, in which he argued that since the United States admitted the principle that every nation has a right to protect its domestic industries and even insisted on that right, it must in logic accept that screen quotas were the only effective means of offering such protection to the unusual commercial commodity of film. Films were peculiar in having no significant value for tariff purposes upon entry to a country, their value only becoming apparent when screened. The position of the United States should therefore not be against screen quotas but rather to insist that screen quotas be governed by the same principles as applied to import tariffs. "In other words, discriminations should be outlawed, preferences should be eliminated, and revisions of screen-quotas should be open to negotiation in precisely the same manner as tariffs." Pursuing this line of thought, Bliss concluded that the MPAA suggestion that U.S. negotiators seek either a freeze on the British quota or a freeze followed by a progressive reduction be eliminated.

We see here an interesting case of a middle-level American official not only reining in the MPAA but arguing his country into a reasonable logic and consistency in its trade posture. Bliss had argued the trade delegation into allowing screen quotas as the equivalent of tariffs for the protection of a domestic film industry – subject to the same constraints as tariffs. One

Table 13.1. *Trade barriers (#) confronting the U.S. motion picture industry in 1947*

Country	Trade agreement with U.S.A.	Special taxes	Import duties	Tariff prefs.	Quotas	Exchange control restricts.	Gov't monop./ state trading	Discrim. compet. situation	Peculiar mktg. or other
Australia	None	#	#	#	#			#	#
Belgium–Luxembourg	1935	#	#						#
Brazil	1935	#	#		#			#	#
Canada	1935/38/40	#	#	#					
Chile	None		#			#		#	
China	None	#	#		#	#			
Cuba	1934	#	#						
Czechoslovakia	1938–9	#	#	#	#		#	#	#
France	1936–46		#		#	#		#	#
India	None		#	#	#			#	#
Lebanon	None		#			#			
Netherlands	1936		#		#	#	#	#	#
New Zealand	None	#			#	#		#	#
Norway	None	#	#			#	#	#	#
Union of South Africa	None	#	#						
USSR	None		#	#	#	#	#	#	#
United Kingdom	1939		#	#	#	#		#	#

Source: Based on NA, Bliss to Brown, 4 June 1947, RG 43, International Trade Files/Motion Pictures.

effect of this would be to permit the British exhibitors' quota, although to subject it to scrutiny from the angle of discrimination and to subject it to negotiation for reduction.

In a newly proposed article, this idea was enshrined and all other measures were banned.[27] This new draft became known as Article 15-B. Originally it had been phrased so as to outlaw quotas that had the result of discrimination or preference. Again, on reflection Bliss felt this was unrealistic. Within Britain itself the Rank circuits overfulfilled the quota, but more than one thousand small cinemas defaulted, without prosecution, because they simply could not obtain enough British films for weekly or biweekly changes of program. The British pointed out that screen time was not uniform earning time, because much depended on the type of theater and district, and that they intended to ensure quotas in the most lucrative earning areas. This Bliss found not unreasonable, and not really avoidable. Whether the films American companies produced in Britain would be classified as British for quota purposes was left to a gentleman's agreement, and a Somervell proposal to impose British film quotas in overseas colonies was found unacceptable by the Americans.[28] As a trade-off they suggested freezing U.K. screen quotas at 25 percent for the life of the trade agreement.[29]

To reassure the British that dropping the renters' quota would not mean an end to U.S. financing of film production in Britain, the Motion Picture Export Association (MPEA) telegraphed that responsible officers of RKO, Paramount, Twentieth Century–Fox, Warner Bros., Loew's, and Columbia had committed themselves to continuing to produce important feature films in the United Kingdom as in past years, provided the Dalton Duty was removed and that the conditions affecting production remained stable.[30]

In a summary of the negotiation process for Johnston, Will Clayton, assistant secretary of state for economic affairs, noted that the draft brought to Geneva had contained "no provisions which would protect the motion picture industry from the multiplicity of restrictions and discriminations" that had been hampering its foreign trade. However, Clayton said of the newly approved article (Article 19, by now) that

by omitting reference to any permissible device other than domestic screen quotas the Charter outlaws all other existing or potential measures which discriminate against American films, of which a formidable list was presented in your Association brief outlining the industry's difficulties in the 17 countries negotiating at Geneva.[31]

The text, as finally approved in Geneva, read as follows:

Article 19
Special Provisions Relating to Cinematograph Films

1. If any Member establishes or maintains internal quantitative regulations relating to exposed cinematograph films, such regulations shall take the form of screen quotas which shall conform to the following conditions and requirements:

(a) Screen quotas may require the exhibition of cinematograph films of national origin during a specified minimum proportion of the total screen time actually utilized over a specified period of not less than one year in the commercial exhibition of all films of whatever origin and shall be computed on the basis of screen time per theater per year or the equivalent thereof.

(b) With the exception of screen time reserved for films of national origin under a screen quota, no screen time, including screen time released by administrative action from minimum time reserved for films of national origin, shall formally or in effect be allocated among sources of supply.

(c) Notwithstanding the provisions of sub-paragraph (b) above, Members may maintain screen quotas conforming to the conditions of sub-paragraph (a) which reserve a minimum proportion of screen time for films of a national origin other than that of the Member imposing such screen quotas; Provided, that no such minimum proportion of screen time shall be increased above the level in effect on April 10, 1947.

(d) Screen quotas shall be subject to negotiation for their limitation, liberalization or elimination in the manner provided for in respect of tariffs and preferences under Article 17.[32]

Although the anger of the MPEA member companies about the Dalton Duty was understandable, they were fortunate to have the services of officials of the caliber of Bliss, who had established trust that he kept their interests uppermost. Bliss's astute handling of the matter comes into sharper focus in his memorandum for the record. The first reaction of some of the countries convening to negotiate the ITO charter was that films involved cultural considerations that set them apart from other commodities entering into international trade. Some argued that films should be excluded entirely from the trade discussions. Bliss comments,

Against this background our subsequent negotiations had to be conducted carefully in order to avoid raising the cultural issue, and we were lucky to escape it.

When Czechoslovakia, France, the Netherlands, and the United Kingdom entered provisional reservations,

we offered no arguments against these, lest a prolongation of debate invite a burst of oratory from delegations influenced by cultural considerations, and the Chairman's gavel fell.

He continues, "Our most important and most intricate negotiations were, naturally, those with the United Kingdom." At first the British opposed including films in the draft charter; then they conceded at the New York preparatory meeting that they were negotiable, but that was the limit they would go.

High-level action, in the form of a telephone call from Clayton to Cripps, broke down British resistance, and ... Somervell ... was brought to Geneva to negotiate with us.

The result, Bliss argued, was substantial gain for the United States.

Although we did not obtain everything we wanted from the film negotiations, and had to concede on a number of points, everything we have obtained is almost clear gain to the United States. It is true that in laying down rules for international conduct in the film trade we have circumscribed our own freedom to some extent, but the American motion picture industry has neither sought nor desired to reserve to the United States the right to invoke restrictions or discriminations against foreign films...

Too much publicity should not be given to the specific advantages obtained by the United States in this negotiation, and none at all should be given to the limitations which the Charter places on other countries with respect to film regulations. The Report of the Second Session will be studied carefully by all the Governments meeting at Havana in November. Many of them will observe that Article 19 requires them to modify existing practices and estops them from future action along lines which they may favor.

We shall not be completely safe until Article 19 has been finally and definitively adopted at Havana.[33]

Not all snags were, however, removed by Bliss's assurances. The MPEA was digging in its heels about the Dalton Duty, as a condition for its promise of continued production in the United Kingdom. The State Department believed that the sharp impact of the British ad valorem duty on the overseas trade of MPAA companies would prevent their leaders from agreeing to the concession. It did not help that Johnston was in the hospital.[34] Clair Wilcox, director of the State Department's Office of International Trade, signed a letter arguing that the companies would do well to gamble on the Dalton Duty being temporary, likely to be replaced within a matter of months by some measure that would block sterling until the dollar crisis was resolved. The U.K. delegation gave formal notice that if their reservation was not accepted by the United States in one or two weeks they would insist on reverting to the New York draft. "That would be a disaster, since it would leave all countries free to discriminate against films." A further pressure was the GATT negotiations. "We are now trying to write the film provisions into the General Agreement on Tariffs and Trade," which had a 7 October deadline.[35]

It transpired, once Johnston was back at work, that the MPAA companies were mainly concerned that the ad valorem duty took away much of the money they intended to dedicate to production, and that to commit themselves to make pictures in Britain if 75 percent of their earnings was to be taken in tax was out of the question. Bliss realized that this issue could be resolved by careful wording, since it was more a question of timing than anything else. He wrote directly to Somervell, urging him to assist in finding the right verbal formula, in order not to lose what he characterized as the great and permanent value of the charter negotiated at Geneva.[36] In addition to seeking some wording that would satisfy both sides, the presentation of it to Johnston was taken over directly under the signature of the U.S. Ambassador to Britain, Lewis Douglas. The ingenious wording agreed upon with the Board of Trade qualified the promise of production. American companies would be obligated to produce films in Britain, the document said,

provided that this undertaking shall be binding on any particular company only when such company is importing a significant number of new feature films from the United States.

Douglas's letter noted that the formula "assumes that the American companies will not be marketing films in the United Kingdom as long as the existing import duties are in force." He expressed the earnest hope that the MPEA would accept, thus allowing the Board of Trade to rescind a pledge they had given to the British exhibitors' association to maintain the renters' quota in order to ensure adequate film supplies.[37] There must have been an audible sigh of relief in the London embassy when Johnston cabled his acceptance on 27 September.[38]

Although the Dalton Duty episode, the Geneva talks, and the renewal of the films act overlapped in time, it is clear that American officials kept them quite separate and opposed attempts at linkage by the MPAA/MPEA. Strategic concessions on international agreements or in alteration of legislation were not to be traded against tactical maneuvers aimed at modifying a strictly local measure. Furthermore, general questions of film policy were to be separated from local emergencies in unrelated matters such as foreign exchange. This long-term thinking was a strength of the American side. Given the American view that the ad valorem tax was hasty, temporary, ineffective, and hence largely a response to domestic political pressures, there remains the question of why it took almost eight months to come to a meeting of minds on its removal, especially since all the elements of the deal that was finally accepted in February and March were already clear in November–December. Here I would differ from the broad political interpretation given by Bliss and his colleagues, namely, that the anti-American hysteria that was focused on films had to be placated. The fulminations of backbench M.P.'s and newspapers would have been easy for the Labour government to deflect, given its large Parliamentary majority, had it tried to do so decisively. A factor mentioned in the American records at the time, but that came to seem decisive on later reflection, was the succession to the presidency of the Board of Trade of the ambitious, intellectual, and left-wing minister Harold Wilson (Fig. 13.1). Films interested him a great deal, and many inquiries and schemes concerning them were generated while he was in charge. His left-wing credentials (he was a "Bevanite" – named after their leader, Aneurin Bevan) help us to understand his "get tough with the Americans" attitude (well dissected by Pelling, 1956).

Before we turn to the Cinematograph Films Act of 1948 and its first

Figure 13.1. *Left to right*: Howard Thomas, producer in chief for Pathé Films; F. J. Hopwood, managing director of Shell Petroleum; Harold Wilson, newly appointed president of the Board of Trade; and J. Arthur Rank. (British Film Institute–Stills Posters and Designs.)

years of operation under Wilson's Board of Trade, we also need to look at the American view of the Canadian Cooperation Project. At Geneva, the Americans had requested that the Canadians remove the small preference their footage tariff on films gave to the United Kingdom, and they also requested elimination of the remittance tax on motion picture profits.[39] Neither was expected to be granted, but neither involved very large sums of money. Of more immediate concern was the possibility of measures modeled on those of the United Kingdom to deal with an acute shortage of U.S. dollar credits at a time of need and reluctance to use them for "luxuries" such as motion pictures. An interesting twist to Canadian relations with and to Hollywood and its wares was the fact that Canada was inadvertently a site for a major early episode of the cold war. I allude to the Gouzenko case, the defection of a Soviet Embassy official to Canada in 1946, which eventually exposed the existence of an active and hostile Soviet spy network in Canada and Britain, raising questions about the United States. It also exposed, to Canada's embarrassment, the penetration of Canadian public life by persons whose Communist convictions influenced them to assist the spying effort. The case was subject to investigation by a powerful Royal Commission, and its findings cast some shadow on the National Film Board (NFB). Darryl F. Zanuck decided to base a semidocumentary feature film on the case (*The Iron Curtain* 20th C.–Fox 1948) and film the external scenes in and around Ottawa.

That filming is of interest to our present concerns in two ways. First, the Canadian reaction, as reported by the U.S. Embassy in Ottawa, was that

the movie is not going to help international relations at this critical point and that it is particularly unfortunate that Hollywood should seek to make money out of a very deplorable incident in Canadian history.

Second, a small but noisy minority with Communist sympathies took the view that

the people of Ottawa don't want this motion picture[,] directed as it is against Russia. We refuse to become victims of Hollywood's lying propaganda.[40]

This particular kind of positioning of Hollywood as a lying cold war–monger and a profiteer from a small country's embarrassment was not expressed by any influential bodies or persons during the U.K. discussion during this period. How much weight we should give it in Canada is difficult to say, yet we recall the filtering provision in the Canadian Cooperation Project to avoid Canada expending dollars on meretricious movies. Obviously movies exploiting national embarrassment or containing lying propaganda would count as meretricious expenditure.

Although J. Arthur Rank, Harold Wilson, and some of the politicians in Ontario and British Columbia thought there was a special affinity in Canada for Britain and things British (including films), as we have seen the quota laws favoring British films were passed in Canada but never invoked. To American observers, Canada and its film market continued for all practical purposes to be an extension of the United States (Jarvie 1990). Thus the evident eagerness of the MPAA to find palliative solutions to Canadian concerns, to flatter Canadian pride, and generally to offer recognition that Canada was distinct. The MPAA tried to come up with calculations of ways that dollars had been saved by the Canadian Cooperation Project. The NFB concentrated on film activities that Grierson thought would not bring it into competition with Hollywood, yet that would still utilize the medium for national purposes. Thus scattered in their programs of American films, Canadians received an allocation of NFB material. This did not create the problem that any attempt to deprive Canadians of American entertainment films or to divert their interest toward, say, British entertainment films, would have done. For despite the rhetoric and posturings of the elite, substantial sectors of Canadian public opinion dissociated themselves from any special affinity for Britain and things British and saw the consumption of materials from Hollywood as more compatible with their nationalist aspirations.

At all events, with the Canadian Cooperation Project in place, Canada continued to present a rosy market prospect to Hollywood. Of a nearly $80 million box-office gross in 1947, approximately six-sevenths remained in Canada; only $12 million was remitted to the United States. Some $5 million was spent that year on new theater construction, of which the existing stock was 1,693 theaters, located in 1,071 different Canadian cities, with an aggregate seating capacity of 874,094. In many towns and cities, motion pictures were stated to be the sole source of entertainment provided. This allowed the United States to argue that its movies were an essential cultural service, and this was reflected, perhaps, in a stable pattern of demand.

In summing up the achievements of the Canadian Cooperation Project, the U.S. Embassy in Ottawa listed:

an 82-percent increase in newsreel sequences featuring Canada;

release of 12 one- and two-reel tourist or travelogue subjects about Canada to 10,000–14,000 U.S. cinemas;

Nine features released in 1948 with Canadian sequences, 2 actually shot in Canada; and

tourist spending by U.S. citizens in Canada up 10.4 percent despite a drop in U.S. domestic tourism.[41]

Alas, the absence of critical comment in the files gives us few clues to how U.S. officials viewed these claims.

13.3. British schemes and Hollywood crisis, 1948–1951

One interesting reaction to British pressure to produce films in Britain and the Canadian Cooperation Project's encouraging of location shooting in Canada was trade union anger in the United States. For example, in February 1949 the *Hollywood Reporter* carried an item on a resolution of the Hollywood AFL (American Federation of Labor) Film Council requesting the U.S. government to wipe out trade barriers that forced American companies to produce abroad and, failing that, to ban the exhibition in the United States of American films made overseas. Any such action would, of course, have completely disrupted the Canadian Cooperation Project as well as standing arrangements with Britain.[42]

With the new films act in place, the first dispute with the United States arose over Wilson's refusal to appoint any representatives of the London branches of American firms to the Cinematograph Films Council, which, among other things, advised the Board of Trade on quota levels. Previously, American representatives had not been excluded.

Our expulsion from the Films Council means that we are now excluded from all of the numerous Committees and Commissions that the Government has formed or is forming in aid of British films despite the fact that our Companies are an important segment of British film production and supply the majority of films shown in Great Britain.

Thus wrote Allport, who attributed to the United Kingdom a policy of dropping an iron curtain between British and American film interests with the ultimate object of excluding the latter from the British market as rapidly as could be done without detriment to British interests.[43] Wilson's argument had been that with the end of the renters' quota there was no point in having distributors on the council. The American response was that the exhibitors' quota was of great interest to distributors, who should therefore have a chance to be heard in quota decisions.

Allport was firmly convinced that there was an orchestrated campaign in Britain to slander the American film industry in the press, among the critics, on the radio, and in Parliament. There were nationalist elements, political elements, and the intention to serve the interests of the independent producers.[44] He interpreted Wilson's refusal to appoint an American company representative as an unfriendly gesture.[45] Johnston responded by asking the embassy to intervene, which they did.

What the British posture portended was more specific than the Americans had expected: a rise in the exhibitors' quota, to 45 percent for first-feature films and 25 percent for supporting films, announced 11 June 1948. U.S. ambassador Douglas signed the information telegram sent to the State Department, which went on to suggest that the net effect of the raises was to limit severely the possibilities of American films' earnings in the United Kingdom.

We feel strongly that British are undermining essential basis of recent film agreement and their whole approach is contrary to spirit of that agreement.

We propose to protest to Wilson and perhaps on higher level. Would appreciate your comments.[46]

In an analysis of Wilson's actions after the quota announcement, Allport revealed that the exhibitors on the Cinematograph Films Council had voted unanimously against the measure and that it was rushed through on a narrow majority. The votes of one or two distributors, and perhaps their arguments, could have reversed matters. It therefore looked as though the Board of Trade had predetermined the quota levels and had made appointments to the council to ensure a majority.[47]

On 21 June, Johnston wrote for the MPPDA to Secretary of State George C. Marshall, requesting an embassy protest and an immediate call for negotiations. The department's response was that concern had been expressed to the British and that the call for negotiations was being studied.[48] At the London end, Allport stepped up his argument of bad faith on the British part. In a ten-point indictment he endeavored to convince Ambassador Douglas that a concerted campaign was under way. Furthermore, the Board of Trade had permitted a booking merger of the Gaumont–British and Odeon circuits, with the effect that two MPAA companies were immediately excluded from playing time on the new combined circuit and four others were subject to arbitrary dictatorship about which films they could show, on what terms and for how long, regardless of box-office strength. Wilson's view of the agreement as a short "breathing space" Allport interpreted as preparation time "to drive the American film industry from the British market."[49]

This was not mere hotheadedness on Allport's part. In a memorandum to the ambassador on 29 June 1948, Bliss, a loyal and hard-working American official, not lacking in a sympathetic appreciation of British problems and aims, mentioned that the ITO inclusion of exhibitor quotas as the proper method for protecting a domestic film industry was developed after extensive discussions with Somervell. Despite (and, indeed, he might have added, during) these discussions, the ad valorem duty was imposed, although it effectively constituted a second method of protection. It was replaced by the more equitable arrangements of the Anglo–American Film Agreement, but that was still another method of protection. Moreover, the newly set exhibitors' quota, at 45 percent, was an excessive increase on a normal market share of 20 percent, signaling aggressive intent.

One or the other of these barriers should be enough to protect British interests adequately.

In addition to these considerations we have your own personal feeling that the spirit of the film agreement has been seriously infringed by the series of actions which have followed its conclusion. To my mind the most important of these is the imposition of the high exhibitor quota; in addition we have the long list of measures and attitudes set forth by Allport in his memorandum.

I might add that the whole atmosphere at the moment is one of acute hostility, in which the British authorities have in effect declared war against the American film industry, with the American film industry responding in kind. Eric Johnston will doubtless tell you today of the results of his meeting yesterday with film executives in New York. At that meeting they were considering the question of whether or not to denounce the film agreement and resume their embargo of the British market.[50]

Despite extensive discussion with Somervell, which he thought had brought about a meeting of minds, Bliss concluded that the British had a hidden agenda, hidden in that it was not disclosed at Geneva or during the Anglo-American talks leading to the agreement. Given that Foreign Secretary Bevin genuinely wanted peace over films, given that Somervell was a professional civil servant, more moderate than some of his Treasury colleagues but disinclined to oppose them in their aggressive attitudes toward the American film industry, the author of the hidden agenda has once more to be Wilson, possibly with the support of Chancellor of the Exchequer Cripps. All of Wilson's political credentials suggest he would listen to the anti-American complaints of left-wing writers and trade unionists that over thirty years later so beguiled the historians Dickinson and Street.

The Americans were hurting and were looking around for a way to react. A protest had been lodged. Negotiations, however, implied a quid pro quo that the United States was not in a position to offer.[51] On a deeper analysis of the new quota proposals, Allport suggested that it was an "exceptionally adroit and carefully thought out device."

The first-feature market is the industry's principal source of revenue. From 80 to 90 per cent of the revenues of the American distributing companies in Great Britain are derived from their first-feature showings. Under the new quota, the first-feature business passes progressively from American to British films, by statutory compulsion, regardless of whether the British films shown as first features are actually first, second or third features in quality.

The purpose, in short, is to enable every British feature film, regardless of quality, to be shown as a first feature.

The excess of American first features would thus be diverted and offered as second features, in which position they would earn less revenue, although their appearance on the double bill might well be responsible for attracting the audience from which the nominal first feature would benefit. This was possible because the definition of first feature in the act was that feature for which the exhibitor paid the larger amount. Allport said the scheme was spearheaded by Wilson and Rank.[52] Rank, in discussions, had been described as cordial but fundamentally unfriendly to American interests. Given the determination of the Treasury to curb American film remittances, perhaps there was a scheme to achieve a lowering of American remittances below the permitted amount by means of a progressive diversion at the box office, as argued by Allport. It did not in the end succeed, of course, because the number and quality of British films – in terms of audience satisfaction as measured by willingness to pay – was no more satisfactory to the domestic cinemagoers than they proved to be to U.S. cinemagoers.

In the long term, two developments in film culture were required before the British dream could be realized in any form. One was the opening up of the somewhat parochial tastes of the giant U.S. domestic audience (see Jarvie 1978, chap. 3): if you like, a touch of Europe; the other was British recognition that to reach the mass audience a heavy touch of Hollywood was necessary. Whether or not the success of Hollywood popular culture was a result of its universalist populism, as Grierson held (see Jarvie 1989), or the result of Hollywood brainwashing the rest of the world into taking pleasure only from its hegemonic codes; the medium was American,[53] and a compromise with that fact was necessary for commercial success. British ambition was an issue: The aspiration to make films that were British in outlook, which would play (and recover their costs) in the American market. Had Britain been content, like France, with a heavily subsidized national industry mixing art films and popular movies, only a handful of which expected a modest distribution in the United States, the story would have been different.

Bliss could see no alternative to another protest. Besides two sorts of restriction on American films, the conduct of the Rank cinema monopoly constituted an effective third. Limitations on opportunities for American production in Britain, combined with the progressive diversion of revenues through the high first-feature quota, abrogated an understanding built into the Anglo–American Film Agreement. And all of this was done without the prior consultation and discussion of previous years, indeed, "rushed through in almost indecent haste, without consultation and without warning. The general tone is unfriendly."[54] He followed this with a somewhat defensive memorandum in which he explained that Somervell had always made it clear that the British intended to reserve some of the lucrative first-feature market for their own films. Bliss had gathered that this implied "a degree of protection for a domestic film industry just about sufficient to protect its legitimate market needs, or a little more," but the new quotas were "a gross perversion" of this idea.[55]

After a further meeting he reported back that Somervell genuinely believed that British production could fill a 40-percent quota; Somervell acknowledged that the Films Council vote on quota levels had been split between 25 percent advocated by the exhibitors and 50 percent advocated by the producers, the final figure therefore being a creation of the Board of Trade. Somervell admitted that the quota was rushed through because of his own misunderstanding of the parliamentary timetable. Bliss counseled the American companies, which he thought tended to exaggerate the problems, to live with the system for a year before taking any action. At most the ambassador might look to the British for a conciliatory move, such as a Films Council appointment.

Douglas telegraphed that hints from the Foreign Office of doubts about Wilson's policies, which were personally formulated and implemented by him, pointed to high-level political representations between Douglas and Bevin to secure modification and overruling of Wilson. The press of business was such that a meeting time was hard to foresee, so a beginning consisting of Bliss meeting Sir Roger Makins was suggested.[56] At the meeting Makins was joined by Somervell, and the British handed over an aide-mémoire of the technical legal basis for their actions, while the United States proffered an aide-mémoire of complaint for the same date. "Ambassador hopes follow up personal discussion with Bevin."[57]

At this precise point the State Department was alerted to an Exchange Control Act problem, namely, whether all the permitted uses of sterling spelled out in the Anglo–American Film Agreement needed prior authorization by the Bank of England or not. Allport, pointing to the absence of the issue in negotiations, took the position that the international agreement superseded the legislation. The Bank of England held that legislation took precedence. Technically, of course, the Bank of England was correct. The issue was whether, since competent officials had negotiated the agreement, it was not already in blanket conformity with the act. After some discussion it was promised that the circular letter of the Bank of England would be somewhat revised to soothe feelings.[58]

Interestingly, when Johnston and his aide Joyce O'Hara arrived in London, they explicitly asked that high-level political maneuvering be stopped while they concentrated on Rank, the greater threat. Johnston was reported to have told Rank that he could have either peace or war but could not expect to close the British market and still have access to the American. As a counter to the British quota, the new U.S. strategy was to offer complete American programs to exhibitors and not to permit the mixing of British and American films in the same program – although Universal, linked to Rank, and the American independents, did not go along.[59]

Once more, as over the issue with the Bank of England, the embassy had to be drawn in, and there was an exchange of letters between Somervell and Bliss, the latter trying to narrow areas of disagreement by using existing machinery and by suggesting that the last word should not lie with Wilson but with an impartial tribunal.[60] Bliss had predicted in early September that the ambassador could forget about films for two or three months, but not much longer.[61] Judging by the official record, he was pessimistic. There was a lull until March 1949, when Senator Knowland of California told the Senate about the 45-percent British quota and called it rank discrimination, contrary to the spirit of the European Cooperation Administration (ECA) and contrary to the spirit of reciprocity. It did not meliorate his concern that his statement was made on the day that the news ticker carried the Board of Trade announcement of a reduction in the quota from 45 percent to 40 percent.[62]

Following closely on this, Johnston wrote to Under Secretary of State James Webb to ask that negotiations be undertaken to eliminate entirely or substantially reduce the quota.[63] Naturally the British rebuffed the resulting inquiry, since they considered themselves free of obligation. Apparently the very general commitments to trade liberalization incorporated in several international agreements were to be set aside because of straitened circumstances. Some American officials were by no means unappreciative of British measures to reduce dependence on the United States. However, the small decrease in the quota, perhaps because more was expected, "created a new furor in the industry and aggressive criticism from both California Senators."[64] Of course the underlying cause of the furor was not the British action, which was, after all, a reduction. The cause of the furor, to use the hyperbolic language of the resolution passed unanimously by the Motion Picture Industry Council on 6 April 1949, was "the greatest unemployment in the history of Hollywood," which was somehow "in large part due to discriminatory trade barriers set up by the British government."[65] The Motion Picture Industry Council, cochaired by Cecil B. De Mille and Ronald Reagan, was the American equivalent of the British Film Industry Council and had as members the Hollywood AFL Film Council, the Independent Office Workers, the MPPA, the Screen Actors Guild, the Screen Directors Guild, the Screen Writers Guild, and the Society of Motion Picture Art Directors. It urged the Department of State to undertake negotiations to eliminate the quotas. It sent a delegation consisting of Ronald Reagan and Roy Brewer to see President Truman.

The Screen Actors Guild, of which Reagan[66] was president, took a militant line, suggesting adding a clause to any war recovery program permitting withholding aid from any country that impeded the free exchange of ideas by placing restrictions on the press, motion pictures, or periodicals. Truman's assistant John R. Steelman drafted a letter to explain that the British restrictions hardly served as "a serious impediment to the exchange of ideas between the United States and Great Britain." Moreover, basic foreign policy objectives could be encumbered by the "misuse of our great economic power to interfere with what other governments may consider elementary prerogatives of sovereignty." This letter was not sent.[67] Acheson met with a delegation of California Congressmen to discuss the British action that had been taken.[68]

Bliss had at this point counseled against protesting, because the U.S. industry's scheme of unit selling had been in place only six months and to protest so soon might signal American weakness. He believed Johnston agreed but that company presidents or AFL unions might jump the gun. The Anglo–American Film Advisory Council discussions that had been called and held in Washington had established a good atmosphere, but the concrete results, if any, were unknown.[69]

While the results of the second round of these talks in June were awaited, the political furor continued, with Senators Knowland and Downey threatening to repeal the reciprocal trade agreement act[70] and De Mille suggesting that the undisclosed British motive was "Trade follows the film."[71] Ambassador Douglas offered the new interpretation that after the agreement was concluded

there was a change of policy, along basic lines to which the whole government became deeply committed as a result of internal developments in the UK.[72]

The official papers begin to peter out at this point; however, we are fortunate that among them are two masterly reports by Don Bliss (which must have been among the last he submitted in that position) that consider the overall situation as of 5 July 1949 and update it to 10 November 1949. It is appropriate to conclude our attempts to understand the American angle on film trade in the North Atlantic triangle with an analysis of them.

Bliss's review opened by arguing that the acute dollar shortage, likely to extend well beyond the end of any renewed agreement in early 1952, decided the Board of Trade to

build up a British film industry as quickly as possible, regardless of cost, whether in strained Anglo–American relations or in sterling subsidies. To this end Harold Wilson and his colleagues at the Board of Trade decided to give British films the protection of a very high quota and to give British film production Government financial assistance if necessary. Only through such an autarchic policy, they felt, could the British bargaining position be improved to a point where American pressures could be resisted...

I am convinced that this is the true basis of the British film policy, and Harold Wilson has confirmed to me that such considerations motivated the Board of Trade. ...Its maintenance subsequently received the approval of the entire Cabinet.

British film policy, therefore, has a foundation on motives considerably more basic than the competitive considerations which American film interests believe to be dominant.

There were competitive considerations, Bliss argued, especially regarding Rank, who had hoped to enter the American market and thought his liberal attitude would facilitate that. The American boycott had reversed him, because he had lost money heavily and saw the British industry as intolerably vulnerable.

Different models of the film industry were held by the two sides bargaining the agreement that ended the boycott. The Americans saw the British industry continuing as before, with some growth. Wilson saw a potential of operating at a level to serve basic British policy, a level he intended to achieve by artificial stimuli as fast as possible. The Americans defined "first feature" rather narrowly as an outstanding public attraction. The British defined it more broadly. So whereas the Americans thought Britain capable of only thirty first features per year, the British were thinking in terms of ninety. BFPA lobbying for a high quota began only after the agreement was negotiated.

The London Unit Plan, the U.S. companies' scheme to permit booking of American films only as whole programs, was agreed to by six major companies, came into effect 1 October 1948, and had been a great success, forcing the revival of old British films for quota purposes. These were not strong box-office attractions. It was a weapon for the American side to use in future bargaining. Initial discussions of the Anglo–American Film Council were a disappointment, because the two sides could not reach accommodation. The Americans wanted better treatment by the circuits; the British wanted access to the American market and an end to the Unit Plan. On the former the Americans could not give any guarantees because of possible antitrust action – which may explain why Johnston's earlier plan for increased imports may have had to be abandoned. Bliss wrote,

In any case the points at issue represent in effect a private fight between the Rank film monopoly and the American film companies operating as a group. This is only indirectly a matter of concern to Governments, and a solution of this controversy were better left to the respective film industries to negotiate out between themselves.

On the question of the position to be taken by the U.S. government, the situation was anomalous, since the government had no film policies or responsibilities to trade off as concessions in reciprocity negotiations. The public relations approach in effect threatened the British with reductions in American financial aid unless they satisfied the demands of the U.S. motion picture industry.

The British are not receptive to pressures of this kind, and in fact we have overworked them in connection with ECA. Rupert Somervell remarked not long ago that Eric Johnston had visited London twice "clad in a complete suit of blackmail", once in connection with the British Loan, another time in connection with ECA.

Article 4 of GATT did not envisage the British policy but did not outlaw it. The British had some grounds for their feeling that their films were denied access to the American market. And the global balance of payments problem was far bigger than the motion picture situation.

Bliss's conclusion was that the issue was essentially political. The bold and risky policy of trying to double the capacity of the British film industry in a year or two was a function of

The rather brash personality of Harold Wilson, who is complacent about his "positive" approach to the film problem, and has committed himself so deeply in public and in private that he cannot retreat. I would not expect any change in attitude as long as he is President of the Board of Trade.

He owed his position to Cripps, was unpopular with his own party, and might not survive in a coalition. Thus the evolution of the British political situation might solve the problem; if not, Bliss believed Wilson had two years to find out if his gamble would fail.[73]

Events took an unexpected turn in 1949 when Rank reported a second year of heavy losses and his backers refused to finance further production. This meant that by the following year there was the possibility of massive exhibitor defaults on meeting the quota. Yet press and unions were concentrating on reducing the entertainments tax and refinancing the National Film Finance Corporation (NFFC). The Board of Trade was pinning its hopes on the Portal Report and the Plant Report. Johnston was prepared to offer, in negotiations for renewal of the Film Agreement, a reduction in dollar remittances, a guarantee of fifteen Anglo–American films made in British studios in return for a relaxation in the uses of blocked sterling.

Although expecting a lower quota, Johnston was keeping mum, in hopes that the deteriorating situation would do the job for him. So, after all the aggravation, the system was settling down again:

Eric is apparently prepared to play along with this British situation on a long term basis, in the hope that eventually the dollar position will improve to a point where remittances will be freely transferable. He thinks that he can carry the presidents of the companies on this policy.[74]

Later, rather than sooner, this was what transpired.

Notes

1 Nitze minute, 19 September 1946, NA, RG 59 1945–1949 841.4061 MP / 9–1946.

2 *The Cinema,* 19 February 1945.

3 Reisman to Golden, 6 February 1945, NA, RG 151, BF&DC 281, Motion Pictures – U.K.

4 Acheson circular of 7 May 1945, WNRC, RG 84 Ottawa Embassy 1945 840.6 MP.

5 London Embassy to State Department, 6 November 1945, NA, RG 59 1945–1949 841.4061 Motion Pictures / 11–645.

6 Bliss to State Department, 16 November 1945, ibid.

7 London Embassy to State Department, 16 November 1945, ibid.

8 Office Memorandum, Luthringer to Collado and Clayton, 23 November 1945, ibid.

9 For a full description, see Gardner 1956.

10 Circular to certain posts, 12 December 1945, NA, RG 59 1945–1949 800.4061 MP.

11 The "Cripps Plan," 19 March 1946, attached to Peterson to State Department, 20 March 1946, WNRC, RG 84 1946 840.6 Films. When the selection-board membership was announced on 9 October, it consisted of Lord Drogheda, Mr. David Bowes-Lyon, Mrs. Alan Cameron (Elizabeth Bowen), Mr. Charles Dukes, Mrs. Max Nicholson, Mr. R. C. G. Somervell, Mr. John Davis (Odeon Theatres), Mr. D. J. Goodblatte (ABPC), Mr. Mark Ostrer (GB), and Mr. A. G. White (Secretary) (report in *Times,* 9 October 1946).

12 Enclosure with Bliss to State Department, 18 June, 1946, NA, RG 59 1945–1949 841.4061 MP / 6–1846.

13 Bliss to State Department, "Motion Picture Situation," No. 2207 and attachments, 23 October 1946, NA, RG 59 1945–1949 841.4061 MP / 10–2346.

14 Bliss to State Department, ibid.

15 Peterson to State Department 27 January, 1947, ibid.

16 Gallman to State Department, 30 January 1947, ibid.

17 State Department to Ambassador, 21 May 1947, WNRC, RG 84 London Embassy 1947 840.6 Films.

18 Frank McCarthy to Clair Wilcox, 29 May 1947, NA, RG 59 1945–1949 841.4061 MP, Confidential File.

19 Bliss to State Department, 4 February 1948, NA, RG 59 1945–1949 841.4061 MP / 2–448.

20 Allport to Bliss, 12 April 1948, WNRC, RG 84 London Embassy 1948 840.6 Films.

21 This and the quotation from the draft charter are taken from Memorandum of Information and Views in Relation to Announced Multilateral Trade Treaty Negotiations, p. 5, attached to Schreiber to Committee for Reciprocity Information, 19 December 1946, NA, RG 364 Office of the Special Trade Representative for Trade Negotiations, General Correspondence, Trade Negotiations 1947, Schedule 15, Motion Picture Association.

22 Memorandum of Information, p. 8.

23 Supplementary Statement to the Committee for Reciprocity Information Submitted by the Motion Picture Association of America, Inc., p. 3, 27 February 1947, NA, RG 364 Office of the Special Trade Representative for Trade Negotiations, General Correspondence, Trade Negotiations 1947, Schedule 15, Motion Picture Association. Pages hereafter given in text.

24 Mayer to Wilcox, 28 March 1947, NA, RG 364 Office of the Special Trade Representative for Trade Negotiations, General Correspondence, Trade Negotiations 1947, Schedule 15, Motion Picture Association.

25 Washington to Geneva, 12 June 1947, NA, RG 43 International Trade Files, Motion Pictures.

26 Bliss to Brown, 12 June 1947, ibid.

27 Bliss to Ambassador, 24 July 1947, ibid.

28 Bliss to Brown, 12 August 1947, ibid.

29 Bliss to Hawkins, 18 August 1947, ibid.

30 State Department to Geneva, 22 August 1947, NA, RG 43 International Trade Files, Motion Pictures.

31 Clayton to Johnston, 25 August 1947, WNRC, RG 84 London Embassy 1947 840.6 Films.

32 Ibid.

33 Bliss to Brown, 27 August 1947, ibid.

34 State Department to Geneva, 12 September 1947, NA, RG 43 International Trade Files, Motion Pictures.

35 Wilcox to Johnston, 12 September 1947, ibid.

36 Bliss to Somervell, 12 September 1947, ibid.

37 Douglas to Johnston, 20 September 1947, NA, RG 43 International Trade Files, Motion Pictures. In his memorandum to the ambassador of 22 September 1947 (WNRC, RG 84 London Embassy 1947 840.6 Films), Bliss said explicitly that he wrote the letters signed by Wilcox and Douglas.

38 Johnston to London Embassy, 27 September 1947, ibid.

39 U.S. request of 19 May 1947, NA, RG 43 International Trade Files, ITO: Subject File, Motion Pictures.

40 Ottawa Embassy to State Department, 9 December 1947, NA, RG 59 1945–1949 842.4061 MP / 12–947.

41 Ottawa to State Department, 4 April 1949, NA, RG 59 842.4061 Motion Pictures / 4–449.

42 Ottawa to State Department, 1 March 1949, ibid.

43 Allport to Bliss, 2 June 1948, WNRC, RG 84 London Embassy 1948 840.6 Films.

44 Allport to Douglas, 4 June 1948, ibid.

45 Allport to Wilson, 7 June 1948, NA, RG 59 1945–1949 841.4061 MP / 6–748.
46 Douglas to State Department, 16 June 1948, ibid.
47 Allport to Bliss, 15 June 1948, WNRC, RG 84 London Embassy 1948 840.6 Films.
48 Johnston to Marshall, 21 June 1948, and Beale to Johnston, 30 June 1948, NA, RG 59 1945–1949 841.4061 MP / 6–2148.
49 Allport to Douglas, 23 June 1948, WNRC, RG 84 London Embassy 1948 840.6 Films.
50 Bliss to Ambassador, 29 June 1948, ibid.
51 State Department to London Embassy, 29 June 1948, NA, RG 59 1945–1949 841.4061 MP / 6–2948.
52 Allport to Bliss, 2 July 1948, WNRC, RG 84 London Embassy 1948 840.6 Films.
53 To use the phrase of Tunstall 1977.
54 Bliss to Ambassador, 7 July 1948, WNRC RG 84 London Embassy 1948 840.6 Films.
55 Bliss to Ambassador, 7 July 1948, ibid.
56 Douglas to State Department, 31 July 1948, NA, RG 59 1945–1949 841.4061 MP / 7–3148. Sir Roger Makins (b. 1904), created Baron Sherfield (1964); educated at Winchester and Christ Church College, Oxford; diplomat; Deputy Under Secretary of State, Foreign Office (1948–52).
57 Douglas to State Department, 13 August 1948, ibid.
58 Allport to Embassy [Bliss?], 23 August 1948, WNRC, RG 84 London Embassy 1948 840.6 Films.
59 Bliss to Brown, 30 August 1948, ibid.; Bliss to State Department, 24 August 1948, NA, RG 59 1945–1949 841.4061 MP / 8–2448.
60 Bliss to Somervell, 29 November 1948, ibid.
61 Bliss to Ambassador, 2 September 1948, ibid.
62 Knowland to Secretary of State Dean Acheson, 24 March 1949, NA, RG 59 1945–1949 841.4061 MP / 3–2449.
63 Johnston to Webb, 31 March 1949, ibid.
64 Attachment to Gay to Humelsine, 5 April 1949, ibid.
65 Resolution text attached to DeMille to Steelman, 14 April 1949, HST, Official File, Motion Pictures.
66 An amusing sidelight on Reagan as SAG president, in view of his subsequent career, is an anonymous letter someone wrote to Truman denouncing Reagan, Brewer, and Walsh as union busters, Republicans, and red-baiters. It describes Reagan as a leading conspirator in ousting the CSU union from the studios. Although pretending to be neutral, Reagan spoke against CSU, charging that they were Communists trying to wreck the movie industry. "The true character of this politically ambitious, publicity-seeking person was brought out recently by his wife, Jane Wyman, when she divorced him." Letter of 6 April 1949, HST, Official File, Motion Pictures.
67 Attachments to MSB[elcher] to [RP]A[ndrews], 14 June 1949, HST, Official File, Motion Pictures.
68 Memorandum of Conversation, 15 April 1949, NA, RG 59 1945–1949 841.4061 MP / 4–1549.
69 London to State Department, 26 April 1949, ibid.

70 Knowland and Downey to Acheson, 26 May 1949, ibid.
71 DeMille to Acheson, 27 May 1949, ibid.
72 Douglas to State Department, 4 June 1949, ibid.
73 Bliss to State Department, 5 July 1949, ibid.
74 Bliss to State Department, 10 November 1949, ibid.

Epilogue

Why then did American films dominate the screens of Canada and Great Britain between roughly 1920 to 1950? The short answer is that American films were an authentic mass media product in a way none of their rivals were, and that American business and government assistance promoted and marketed them so effectively that competition was crushed. This book has concentrated on a narrowly drawn question. The issues dealt with throw some light on broader questions concerning mass media, popular culture, and the dominant position of America and its materials.

The emergence of a mass media culture is a decisive new factor in the situation. The mass media of communication and entertainment stem from a rather specific set of historical circumstances: They could not emerge until mechanical and (later) electronic technology had made possible the servicing of vast numbers of customers at a small incremental cost (newspapers at a few pennies or cents, movie seats at only slightly more than that, radio and television ostensibly free). The mass media are thus emblematic of advanced industrial society, a social form for which they serve most useful functions. The characteristic routinization and homogeneity of skills and work patterns in industrial society are reproduced and endorsed by the media, which also serve as recreation. Moviegoing as a social practice, for example, conformed to the demands of the industrial workday and industrial shifts, being an activity that took a short time, was available long hours, and was governed by the clock and the calendar. The content of movie entertainment, too, while inviting a docile and socially acceptable reception in the movie house, could offer stories displaying a wide range of response to industrial life: escape, rebellion, success, subversion. The mass media, thus seen, are one of the institutions that respond to what Max Weber called the "disenchantment" of the modern world. They partially reenchant the world.

That an American-dominated industry in turn dominated this aspect of the process of reenchantment ensured that some at least of what we associate with the modern world would be linked to American institutions, values, traditions, and general outlook. This has infuriated and frustrated nationalists of many other countries ever since it became apparent. At various places in the book I hint that it was not accidental that the First New Nation[1] should be the one to perform that role. Modernity, after all, entails social transformations of all kinds. Such transformations can be modeled on many things, including America, a nation made from theory and ideals. If that nation strikes some as attractive, emulation of it (at least in part) makes sense. Its movies, by and large, presented an attractive picture, one not made less attractive by apparently frank and unsparing self-criticism. That very self-criticism, which seemed part of a process of correction, contrasted favorably with the self-portraits of other nations in their mass media.

Since we are not yet one hundred years into the era of mass media, it is no surprise that neither historical consensus nor ease of handling the topic is yet notable among historians. The mass media are, simultaneously, large and powerful commercial institutions and cultural intangibles. Whether and to what degree they are a separate causal factor in the shaping of modern life and society is likely to be debated forever.

The commercial institutions and processes of the movie market, however, we can come to grips with. Business is a form of risk taking under uncertainty. Some businesses are riskier than others. Public entertainment is among the riskiest of all large businesses, because it is a luxury, and because public taste is fickle. The rational businessman aims to reduce risk by reducing uncertainty. Any actions that will manage demand – that is, make films less of a luxury and make selection of them less subject to fickle whim – are bound to be attractive. Among the techniques developed within the motion picture business to manage demand were the star system, the genre system, and the systematic marketing of picturegoing as a habit or routine. Perhaps the technique least noticed but most important was what might be called "product spread," the technique of probing changing trends in demand by marketing a range of product that covers all the known bases: established stars, new faces, films without stars, films within genre, films beyond genre, films that expand, vary, or blend genres. There are sophisticated films, artless films, violent films, sentimental films. The function of spread is to offer the public a wide range of choice, while being prepared to concentrate production on any line of product that catches on. Some of the films in the spread are bound (or even indirectly intended) to be loss leaders. The advantage is that the industry is not caught making only films of a kind in which the public has no interest.

And there was the vertical and horizontal company integration, tending to oligopoly, to exploit the managed demand. These arrangements were pursued abroad as well as at home.

This system of product spread was not perfect, as witness the periodic slumps that punctuated the booms in film revenues, which had little to do with general business conditions. In the slump of 1946–7, for example, there may have been a structural change in the audience that no variation of ingredients would have preempted.

These techniques of demand management were and are costly. Films without stars, without publicity, not spread over the range of possible public preference, were much cheaper. Small studios in Hollywood that made only westerns or serials were low-budget operations, serving as a model for the British company Hammer, which specialized in horror films in the 1950s.

All the below-the-line costs of company organization were increased by above-the-line costs, or expenditures visible on the screen. Hollywood escalated budgets generally, and "production values" in particular, to polish and glamorize the product. But this escalation also functioned to inhibit competitors, who needed access to cash flow on a comparable scale.

What was the response of the competition? As if Hollywood's financial might were not enough, by the 1920s Hollywood was a world center for talent. It attracted acting talent from all over the world and, in addition, scouted out talent to bring back. It scouted vaudeville, the legitimate stage, radio, and other countries' films. It sought talent everywhere. No other industry seems to have been able to match it competitively. Possible stars in Germany, France, Italy, Britain, and Scandinavia were lured to Hollywood, then internationalized. When we think of Garbo, Dietrich, Sonja Henie, Shirley Temple, Anna May Wong, Dolores Del Rio, Errol Flynn, Peter Lorre, Sir C. Aubrey Smith, and Basil Rathbone, we get an idea of the vast reach of its talent search. Even Maurice Chevalier and Gracie Fields worked in Hollywood, two stars closely identified with their native lands.

That the system was American controlled was contingent. If, *per impossibile*, the Sony Company had bought into Hollywood in the 1930s rather than the 1980s, they would not have flooded the world with Japanese films and stars. On the contrary, on the good business principle of "If it ain't broke, don't fix it," both then and now one would expect the owners to let the system go on doing what, over the medium and long term, it seemed to do so well: make good profits in a risky field of business endeavor.

If the impact of films on the public is difficult to discern, the impact of business success in the mass media is easy to discern. Films, radio, popular music, and television have all followed the same pattern of directing at the audience a spread of product with marked formal and structural similarities but that encompasses a wide diversity of content. This strategy of product spread is expensive, since much of what is made will not succeed, but it also reduces the risk of the industry failing to grasp a new trend or fashion among the public. The techniques of product development and marketing used in the movie business also allow a certain amount of shaping and directing of public taste. Hollywood created stars out of whole cloth, the way the music industry sometimes creates hits or even performing groups out of whole cloth. But it is dangerous to minimize the ultimate autonomy of the public, since cases abound of attempts to sell it on fads or fashions that it literally did not buy.

Behind much of the story told in this book is the enigma of the public. It was and is an enigma to those who try to guess what it will take to; it remains an enigma to historians who find only fragmentary clues in what was seen and how it was interpreted, and hence about what it meant. The worldwide success of Pickford, Chaplin, and Fairbanks (Schickel 1973), of slapstick comedy and innocent adventures, was not manufactured or manipulated by the American film industry: It was discovered. It went on being discovered. The early years of Walt Disney were a struggle, but he is remembered as the man who gave the world a set of now universally known cartoon characters. There has been much speculation about why Chaplin, for example, delighted audiences as far away as China. Similar questions could be asked about Mickey Mouse. Although I would admit it is a trifle vague, my preferred explanation of these phenomena is to say that they were discovered in the film market in the United States, being brought to the surface by the working of intense market pressures upon the product-spread situation. Since the U.S. film industry endeavored to market overseas everything it produced – presumably on the grounds of, "who were the producers to judge whether foreign publics would like it" – the films' success at home was matched in some cases by success abroad.

It is difficult to think of anything quite like this in history. World-historical personalities, in Hegel's scheme of things, are influential beyond their immediate arena of war or power politics. Whether Chaplin was a world-historical personality is a matter for discussion (Maland 1989); if he was, the kind of influence he had was quite different from that of Julius Caesar or Napoleon. Here is where the work of this book remains open. It is hard enough to bring economic, political, and diplomatic history to bear on films, and films to bear on those subjects. But when we realize that the film variable itself is still poorly understood, we see how much work remains to be done if we are to make sense of how the world has been altered by the arrival and spread of the mass media. Only a small part of that question pertains to the particular fact that those media were, and are, dominated by the products of the United States.

Note

1 Seymour Martin Lipset's phrase (see Lipset 1963).

References

Primary sources

The following is a list of archives where the primary materials used in this work were found.

Canada

AO	Ontario Archives, Toronto
CFA	Canadian Film Archives, Ottawa
NYPL	North York Public Library Archives, North York
PA	Public Archives, now National Archives, Ottawa

United Kingdom

BFI	British Film Institute, London
IO	India Office Library, London
IWM	Imperial War Museum, London
PRO	Public Record Office, Kew, London (Record Groups: CAB, CO, BT, FO, INF, LAB, T, WO)

United States

AAMPAS	American Academy of Motion Picture Arts and Sciences, Beverly Hills, CA
FDR	Franklin D. Roosevelt Memorial Library, Hyde Park, NY
HHH	Herbert H. Hoover Presidential Library, West Branch, IO
HIA	Hoover Institution Archives, Stanford, CA
HST	Harry S. Truman Library, Independence, MO
ISA	Indiana State Archives, Indianapolis, IN
NA	National Archives, Washington, DC (Record Groups: RG 9, 43, 56, 59, 60, 84, 144, 151, 208, 353, 364)
USC	Doheny Memorial Library, University of Southern California, Los Angeles, CA
UCLA	University of California at Los Angeles, CA
WSH	United Artists Collection, Wisconsin State Historical Society, Madison, WI
WNRC	Washington National Record Center, Suitland, MD

Secondary sources

Aitken, H. G. J. 1959. *The American economic impact on Canada*. Durham, NC, Duke University Press.

Aitken, Ian. 1989. "John Grierson, idealism and the inter-war period." *Historical Journal of Film, Radio and Television* 9:247–58.

Aldgate, Tony. 1983. Comedy, class and containment: The British domestic cinema of the 1930s. In *British cinema history,* ed. James Curran and Vincent Porter, pp. 257–71. London, Weidenfeld & Nicolson.

Allen, William R. 1957. Cordell Hull and the defense of the Trade Agreements Programme, 1934–1940. In Alexander De Conde, *Isolation and security.* pp. 107–32. Durham, NC, Duke University Press.

Annett, Douglas. 1948. *British preference in Canadian commercial policy.* Toronto, Ryerson Press.

Backhouse, Charles. 1974. *Canadian Government Motion Picture Bureau, 1917–1941.* Ottawa, Canadian Film Institute.

Ball, John B. 1934. *Canadian anti-trust legislation.* Baltimore, Williams & Wilkins.

Barnett, Corelli. 1972. *The collapse of British power.* London, Eyre Methuen.

Bellush, Bernard. 1968. *He walked alone: A biography of John Gilbert Wynant.* The Hague, Mouton.

—. 1975. *The failure of the NRA.* New York, Norton.

Berton, Pierre. 1975. *Hollywood's Canada.* Toronto, McClelland & Stewart.

Beschless, Michael. 1980. *Kennedy and Roosevelt.* New York, Norton.

Betts, R. F. 1985. *Uncertain dimensions: Western overseas empires in the twentieth century.* Minneapolis, University of Minnesota Press.

Biery, Ruth, and Eleanor Packer. 1933. England challenges Hollywood. *Saturday Evening Post* 206 (29 July):12–13, 74–5.

Black, Gregory D. 1976. Keys of the kingdom: Entertainment and propaganda. *South Atlantic Quarterly* 75:434–46.

Black, Gregory D., and Clayton R. Koppes. 1974. OWI goes to the movies: The Bureau of Intelligence's critique of Hollywood, 1942–1943. *Prologue* 6:44–59.

Bladen, V. W. 1932. Notes on the reports of public inquiries into combines in Canada, 1888–1932. *Contributions to Canadian Economics* 5:61–76.

Bond, Ralph. 1946. *Monopoly the future of British films.* London, Association of Cine-Technicians.

Brandes, Joseph. 1962. *Herbert Hoover and economic diplomacy: Department of Commerce policy, 1918–1928.* Pittsburgh, University of Pittsburgh Press.

Briggs, Asa. 1961. *The birth of broadcasting.* London, Oxford University Press.

Brimelow, Peter. 1986. *The patriot game.* Toronto, Key Porter Books.

The British film industry. 1952. London, Political and Economic Planning.

Brown, Geoff. 1978. Which way to the way ahead? Britain's years of reconstruction. *Sight and Sound* 47:242–7.

Bullock, Alan. 1983. *Ernest Bevin Foreign Secretary, 1945–1951.* New York, Norton.

Buñuel, Luis. 1983. *My last sigh.* New York, Knopf.

Cameron, Evan William, ed. 1980. *Sound and the cinema.* Pleasantville, NY, Redgrave.

Canada, Ministry of Labour, and Combines Investigation Branch. 1931. *Investigation into an alleged combine in the motion picture industry.* Ottawa, Acland.

Canadian Encyclopaedia. 1988. Edmonton, Hurtig.

Cassady, Ralph, Jr. 1958. Impact of the Paramount decision on motion picture distribution and price making. *Southern California Law Review* 31:150–80.

Collingwood, R. G. 1939. *An autobiography*. Oxford, Oxford University Press.

Collins, Richard. 1990. *Culture, communication and national identity: The case of Canadian television*. Toronto, University of Toronto Press.

Conant, Michael. 1960. *Antitrust in the motion picture industry*. Berkeley and Los Angeles, University of California Press.

Constantine, Stephen. 1986. "Bringing the empire alive": The Empire Marketing Board and imperial propaganda, 1926–33. In *Imperialism and popular culture*, ed. John Mackenzie, pp. 192–231. Manchester, Manchester University Press.

Costigliola, Frank C. 1977. Anglo-American financial rivalry in the 1920s. *Journal of Economic History* 37:911–34.

Coultass, Clive. 1989. *Images for battle: British film and the Second World War, 1939–1945*. London, Associated University Presses.

Cuff, Robert. 1977. Herbert Hoover: The ideology of voluntarism. *Journal of American History* 64:358–72.

—. 1978. An organizational perspective on the military-industrial complex. *Business History Review* 52:250–72.

Culbert, David. 1985. American film policy in the re-education of Germany after 1945. In *The political re-education of Germany and her allies after World War II*, ed. Nicholas Pronay and Keith Wilson, pp. 173–202. London, Croom Helm.

Culbert, David, ed. 1980. *Mission to Moscow*. Madison, University of Wisconsin Press.

—. 1990. *Film and propaganda in America: A documentary history*. Westport, CT, Greenwood Press.

Curran, James, and Vincent Porter, eds. 1983. *British cinema history*. London, Weidenfeld & Nicolson.

Denny, Ludwell. 1930. *America conquers Britain: A record of economic war*. New York, Knopf.

Dickinson, Margaret. 1983. The state and the consolidation of monopoly. In *British cinema history*, ed. James Curran and Vincent Porter, pp. 74–95. London, Weidenfeld & Nicolson.

Dickinson, Margaret, and Sarah Street. 1985. *Cinema and state: The Film Industry and the British Government, 1927–1984*. London, British Film Institute.

Drummond, Ian M. 1977. *British economic policy and the Empire, 1919–1939*. London, Allen & Unwin.

Easterbrook, W. T., and M. H. Watkins, 1967. *Approaches to Canadian economic history*. Toronto, McLelland & Stewart.

Eastman, Fred. 1930a. Ambassadors of ill will. *Christian Century* 47 (29 January):144–7.

—. 1930b. The menace of the movies. *Christian Century* 47 (15 January):75–8.

—. 1930c. Our children and the movies. *Christian Century* 47 (22 January):110–12.

—. 1930d. What's to be done with the movies? *Christian Century* 47 (12 February):302–4.

—. 1930e. Who controls the movies? *Christian Century* 47 (5 February):173–5.

Eberts, Jake, and Terry Ilott. 1990. *My indecision is final: The rise and fall of Goldcrest Films*. London, Faber.

Evans, Gary. 1984. *John Grierson and the National Film Board*. Toronto, University of Toronto Press.

Flannery, Tom. 1990. *1939, the year in movies*. Jefferson, NC, McFarland.

Fowke, V. C. 1952. The national policy – old and new. *Canadian Journal of Economics and Political Science* 18:271–86; cited from reprint in Easterbrook and Watkins, pp. 237–58.

French, Philip. 1969. *The movie moguls*. London, Weidenfeld & Nicolson.

Gabler, Neal. 1988. *An empire of their own: How the Jews invented Hollywood*. New York, Doubleday.

Gardner, Richard N. 1956. *Sterling–dollar diplomacy*. Oxford, Oxford University Press.

Geduld, Harry M. 1975. *The birth of the talkies*. Bloomington, Indiana University Press.

Gomery, Douglas. 1975. The coming of sound to the American cinema: A history of the transformation of an industry. Ph.D. diss. University of Wisconsin.

—. 1979. The movies become big business: Publix Theatres and the chain store strategy. *Cinema Journal* 18:26–40.

Granatstein, J. L. 1982. *The Ottawa men: The civil service mandarins, 1935–1957*. Toronto, Oxford University Press.

Grantley, Lord. 1954. *Silver spoon*. London, Hutchinson.

Greenwald, William Irving. 1950. The motion picture industry: An economic study of the history and practices of a business. Ph.D. diss. New York University. UMI no. 73–22061.

Griffith, Richard. 1949. Where are the dollars? Part 1: *Sight and Sound* 19 (December):33–4.

—. 1950. Where are the dollars? Part 2: *Sight and Sound* 19 (January 1950):39–40.

Guback, Thomas H. 1969. *The international film industry: Western Europe and America since 1945*. Bloomington, Indiana University Press.

Halliwell, Leslie. 1985. *Seats in all parts*. London, Granada.

Harcourt, Peter. 1989. A moving target: Federal film policy within a global culture. *Transactions of the Royal Society of Canada*, ser. 5, 4:169–79.

Hawley, Ellis W. 1973. Herbert Hoover and American corporatism, 1929–1933. In *The Hoover presidency: A reappraisal*, ed. Martin L. Fausold and George T. Mazuzan, pp. 3–33. Albany, SUNY Press.

—. 1974. Herbert Hoover, the Commerce secretariat and the vision of an "Associative State." *Journal of American History* 61:116–40.

—. 1981. Three facets of Hooverian associationalism: Lumber, aviation, and movies, 1921–1930. In *Regulation in perspective*, ed. Thomas K. McCraw, pp. 95–123. Cambridge, MA, Harvard University Press.

Hawley, Ellis W., ed. 1981. *Herbert Hoover as secretary of commerce: Studies in New Era thought and practice*. Iowa City, University of Iowa Press.

Hays, Will H. 1955. *The autobiography of Will H. Hays*. New York, Doubleday.

Hogan, Michael J. 1977. *Informal entente: The private structure of cooperation in Anglo–American economic diplomacy, 1918–1928*. Columbia, MO, University of Missouri Press.

—. 1987. *The Marshall Plan*. Cambridge, Cambridge University Press.

Hollins, T. J. 1981. The conservative party and film propaganda between the wars. *English Historical Review* 96:359–69.

Hook, Sidney. 1987. *Out of step*. New York, Carrol & Gref.

Howe, A. H. 1972. Bankers and movie makers. In *The movie business: American film industry practice,* ed. A. William Bluem and Jason E. Squire, pp. 57–67. New York, Hastings House.

Huettig, Mae D. 1944. *Economic control of the motion picture industry.* Philadelphia, University of Pennsylvania Press.

Jarvie, I. C. 1972. *Concepts and society.* London, Routledge.

—. 1976. Nationalism and the social sciences. *Canadian Journal of Sociology* 1:515–28.

—. 1978. Seeing through movies. *Philosophy of the Social Sciences* 8:374–97.

—. 1981a. Fanning the flames: Anti-Americanism and *Objective Burma. Historical Journal of Film, Radio and Television* 1:117–37.

—. 1981b. Social perception and social change. *Journal for the Theory of Social Behaviour* 11:223–40.

—. 1982. The social experience of movies. In *Film / Culture: Explorations of Cinema in Its Social Context,* ed. Thomas, Sari, 247–68. Metuchen, NJ, Scarecrow.

—. 1983. International film trade: Hollywood and the British market, 1945. *Historical Journal of Film, Radio and Television* 3:161–9.

—. 1985. Suppressing controversial films: From *Objective Burma* to *Monty Python's Life of Brian.* In *Current research in film,* vol. 5: *Audiences, economics and law,* ed. Bruce Austin, pp. 181–96. Norwood, NJ, Ablex.

—. 1986a. British trade policy *versus* Hollywood, 1947–1948: "Food before flicks?" *Historical Journal of Film, Radio and Television* 6:19–41.

—. 1986b. Explorations in the social career of movies: Business and religion. In *Thinking about society: Theory and practice,* pp. 368–89. Dordrecht, Reidel.

—. 1988a. Dollars and ideology: Will Hays' economic foreign policy, 1922–1945. *Film and History* 2(Sept./Oct.):207–21.

—. 1988b. The Burma campaign on film: *Objective Burma* (1945), *The Stilwell Road* (1945) and *Burma Victory* (1945). *Historical Journal of Film, Radio and Television* 8:55–73.

—. 1991. The Canadian film market as part of the United States domestic market between the wars. In *Current Research in Film,* vol. 5: *Audiences, economics and law,* ed. Bruce Austin, pp. 147–60. Norwood, NJ, Ablex.

Jarvie, Ian, and Robert Macmillan. 1989. John Grierson on Hollywood's success, 1927. *Historical Journal of Film, Radio and Television* 9:309–26.

Jones, Stephen G. 1987. *The British Labour movement and film, 1918–1939.* London, Routledge.

Jowett, Garth S. 1976. *Film: The democratic art.* Boston, Little, Brown.

—. 1990. Moral responsibility and commercial entertainment: Social control in the United States film industry, 1907–1968. *Historical Journal of Film, Radio and Television* 10:3–31.

—. In press. Social science as a weapon: The origins of the Payne Fund Studies, 1926–1929. *Communication.*

Klein, Julius. 1920. *The mesta, a study in Spanish economic history, 1273–1836.* Cambridge, MA, Harvard University Press.

Klingender, F. D., and Stuart Legg. 1937. *Money behind the screen.* London, Lawrence & Wishart.

Knight, Arthur. 1953. The reluctant audience. *Sight and Sound* 22:191ff.

Koppes, Clayton, and Gregory Black. 1977. What to show the world: The Office of War Information and Hollywood, 1942–1945. *Journal of American History* 64:87–105.

—. 1987. *Hollywood goes to war*. New York, Free Press.

Korda, Michael. 1979. *Charmed lives*. New York, Random House.

Kottman, Richard N. 1968. *Reciprocity and the North Atlantic triangle, 1932–1938*. Ithaca, Cornell University Press.

Lasky, Jesse L. 1957. *I blow my own horn*. London, Gollancz.

LeMahieu, D. L. 1988. *A culture for democracy, mass communication and the cultivated mind in Britain between the wars*. Oxford, Oxford University Press.

Lewis, Howard T. 1933. *The motion picture industry*. New York, Van Nostrand.

Lewis, Kevin, and Arnold Lewis. 1988. Include me out: Samuel Goldwyn and Joe Godsol. *Film and History* 2:133–53.

Lipset, Seymour Martin. 1963. *The first new nation*. New York, Basic Books.

—. 1990. *Continental divide: The values and institutions of the United States and Canada*. London, Routledge.

Look Magazine, editors of. 1945. *Movie lot to beachhead*. New York, Doubleday.

Louis, William Roger. 1977. *Imperialism at bay, 1941–1945: The United States and the decolonization of the British Empire*. Oxford, Oxford University Press.

Low, Rachel. 1946–7. Audience research. *Sight and Sound* 15:150–1.

—. 1971. *The history of the British film, 1918–1929*. London, Allen & Unwin.

—. 1979. *Documentary and educational films of the 1930s*. London, Allen & Unwin.

—. 1985. *Film making in 1930s Britain*. London, Allen & Unwin.

McConnell, Grant. 1966. *Private power and American democracy*. New York, Vintage.

Mackenzie, John, ed. 1986. *Imperialism and popular culture*. Manchester, Manchester University Press.

McKercher, B. J. C. 1984. *The second Baldwin government and the United States, 1924–1929: Attitudes and diplomacy*. Cambridge, Cambridge University Press.

McLuhan, Marshall. 1966. *Understanding media: The extensions of man*. 2d ed. New York, New American Library, Signet. Originally published 1964.

Magder, Ted. 1989. From no films to Telefilm: Feature films and the Canadian state. *Transactions of the Royal Society of Canada*, 5th ser. 4:205–20.

Maier, Charles S. 1977. The politics of productivity: Foundations of American international economic policy after World War II. *International Organization* 31:607–33.

Maland, Charles J. 1989. *Chaplin and American culture: The evolution of a star image*. Princeton, Princeton University Press.

May, Lary. 1980. *Screening out the past: The birth of mass culture and the motion picture industry*. New York, Oxford University Press.

Milward, Alan S. 1984. *The reconstruction of Western Europe, 1945–1951*. London, Methuen.

Moley, Raymond. 1945. *The Hays office*. Indianapolis, Bobbs-Merrill.

Moorehead, Caroline. 1984. *Sidney Bernstein: A biography*. London, Cape.

Morgan, Kenneth O. 1984. *Labour in power, 1945–1951*. Oxford, Clarendon Press.

Morris, Peter. 1978. *Embattled shadows: A history of Canadian cinema, 1895–1939*. Montréal, McGill–Queens University Press.

—. 1986. Backwards to the future: John Grierson's film policy for Canada. In

Flashback, people and institutions in Canadian film history, ed. Gene Walz, pp. 17–35. Montréal, Mediatexte.

—. 1989. "Praxis into process": John Grierson and the National Film Board of Canada. *Historical Journal of Film, Radio and Television* 9:269–82.

Mullally, Frederic. 1946. *Films an alternative to Rank.* London, Socialist Book Centre.

Murphy, Robert. 1983. Rank's attempt on the American market, 1944–1949. In *British cinema history,* ed. James Curran and Vincent Porter, pp. 164–78. London, Weidenfeld & Nicolson.

—. 1989. *Realism and tinsel: Cinema and society in Britain, 1939–48.* London, Routledge.

Murphy, Robert K. 1969. *The Harding era.* Minneapolis, University of Minnesota Press.

Ninkovich, Frank. 1981. *The diplomacy of ideas: United States foreign policy and cultural relations, 1938–1950.* Cambridge, Cambridge University Press.

Nizer, Louis. 1935. *New courts of industry: Self-regulation under the Motion Picture Code, including an analysis of the code.* New York, Longacre Press.

Palache Report. 1944. See *Tendencies to monopoly in the cinematograph film industry.*

Parker, Richard. 1991. The guise of the propagandist: Governmental classification of foreign film. In *Contemporary research in film, vol. 5: Audiences, economics and law,* ed. Bruce Austin, pp. 135–46. Norwood, NJ: Ablex.

Pelling, Henry. 1956. *America and the British Left from Bright to Bevan.* London, Adam & Charles Black.

Pendakur, Manjunath. 1990. *Canadian dreams and American capital.* Toronto, Garamond Press.

Pilgert, Henry P. 1953. *Press, radio and film in West Germany, 1945–1953.* Bad Godesberg–Mehlem, HICOG (US).

Powdermarker, Hortense. 1950. *Hollywood, the dream factory.* Boston, Little, Brown.

Pronay, Nicholas. 1980. Introduction. In *British official films in the Second World War,* ed. Frances Thorpe and Nicholas Pronay, pp. 1–56. Oxford, Clio.

—. 1982. The political censorship of films in Britain between the wars. In *Propaganda, politics and film, 1918–1945,* ed. Nicholas Pronay and D. W. Spring, pp. 98–125. London, Macmillan.

—. 1989. John Grierson and the documentary – sixty years on. *Historical Journal of Film, Radio and Television* 9:227–46.

Pronay, Nicholas, and D. W. Spring, eds. 1982. *Propaganda, politics and film, 1918–1945.* London, Macmillan.

Pronay, Nicholas, and Keith Wilson, eds. 1985. *The political re-education of Germany and her allies.* London, Croom Helm.

Ramsaye, Terry. 1926. *A million and one nights.* New York, Simon & Schuster.

Reeves, Nicholas. 1986. *Official British film propaganda during the First World War.* London, Croom Helm.

Reynolds, David. 1982. *The creation of the Anglo-American alliance, 1937–1941, a study in competitive cooperation.* Greensboro, University of North Carolina Press.

Richards, Jeffrey. 1973. *Visions of yesterday.* London, Routledge.

—. 1981. The British Board of Film Censors and content control in the 1930s: Images of Britain. *Historical Journal of Film, Radio and Television* 1:95–116.

—. 1982. The British Board of Film Censors and content control in the 1930s: Foreign affairs. *Historical Journal of Film, Radio and Television* 2:39–48.

—. 1984. *The age of the dream palace: Cinema and society in Britain, 1930–1939*. London, Routledge.

—. 1986. Boy's own Empire: Feature films and imperialism in the 1930s. In *Imperialism and popular culture,* ed. John Mackenzie, pp. 140–64. Manchester, Manchester University Press.

Roosevelt, Elliott, and Joseph Lash, eds. 1950. *F.D.R.: His personal letters, 1928–1945*. New York, Duell, Sloan & Pearce.

Rosenberg, Emily S. 1982. *Selling the American dream*. New York, Hill & Wang.

Ross, Murray. 1941. *Stars and strikes: Unionization of Hollywood*. New York, Columbia University Press.

Rosten, Leo C. 1941. *Hollywood: The movie colony, the movie makers*. New York, Harcourt Brace.

Rowson, Simon. 1933. British influence through films. Address to the Royal Empire Society, 20 March 1933. London(?), privately printed.

—. 1934. The value of remittances abroad for cinematograph films. *Journal of the Royal Statistical Society* 97:633–40.

—. 1935. *The future of the films act*. [London], privately printed.

—. 1936. A statistical summary of the cinema industry in Great Britain in 1934. *Journal of the Royal Statistical Society* 99:67–129.

Schatz, Arthur. 1970–1. The Anglo–American trade agreement and Cordell Hull's search for peace, 1936–1938. *Journal of American History* 57:85–103.

Schatz, Thomas. 1988. *The genius of the system*. New York, Pantheon.

Schickel, Richard. 1973. *His picture in the papers: A speculation on celebrity in America based on the life of Douglas Fairbanks, Sr*. New York, Charterhouse.

Seabury, William Marston. 1926. *The public and the motion picture industry*. New York, Macmillan.

—. 1929. *Motion picture problems*. New York, Avondale.

Seidel, Robert N. 1973. Progressive Pan-Americanism: development and United States policy toward South America, 1906–1931. Ph.D. diss. Cornell University.

Sellar, W. C., and R. J. Yeatman. 1931. *1066 and all that*. New York, Dutton.

Sharp, Dennis. 1969. *Picture palace*. London, Praeger.

Sklar, Robert. 1975. *Movie-made America: A social history of American movies*. New York, Random House.

Slide, Anthony. 1986. *The American film industry: A historical dictionary*. Westport, CT, Greenwood Press.

Stead, Peter. 1981. Hollywood's message for the world: The British response in the 1930s. *Historical Journal of Film, Radio and Television* 1:18–32.

—. 1982. The people and the pictures. The British working class and film in the 1930s. In *Propaganda, Politics and Film, 1918–1945,* ed. Nicholas Pronay and D. W. Spring, pp. 77–97. London, Macmillan.

—. 1988. The people as stars: Feature films as national expression. In *Britain and the cinema in the Second World War,* ed. Philip M. Taylor, pp. 62–83. London, Macmillan.

—. 1989. *Film and the working class*. London, Routledge & Kegan Paul.

Steele, Richard W. 1985. *Propaganda in an open society: The Roosevelt administration and the media, 1933–1941*. Westport, CT, Greenwood press.

Strabolgi, Lord. [Joseph Montague Kenworthy]. 1933. *Sailors, statesmen – and others*. London, Rich & Cowan.

Street, Sarah. 1985. The Hays Office and the defence of the British market in the 1930s. *Historical Journal of Film, Radio and Television* 5:37–55.

—. 1986. Alexander Korda, Prudential Assurance and British film finance in the 1930s. *Historical Journal of Film, Radio and Television* 6:161–79.

Stromberg, Roland M. 1953. American business and the approach of war. *Journal of Economic History* 13:58–78.

Stuart, Fredric. 1960. The effects of television on the motion picture and radio industries. Ph.D. diss. Columbia University. University Micro-films.

Sussex, Elizabeth. 1975. *The rise and fall of British documentary*. Berkeley and Los Angeles, University of California Press.

Swann, Paul. 1989. *The British documentary film movement, 1926–1946*. Cambridge, Cambridge University Press.

Swinton, Viscount. 1948. *I remember*. London, Hutchinson.

Taylor, Philip M. 1981. *The projection of Britain, British overseas publicity and propaganda, 1919–1939*. Cambridge, Cambridge University Press.

—. 1988. Censorship in Britain in the Second World War: An overview. In *Too mighty to be free: Censorship and the press in Britain and the Netherlands*, ed. Uit Overdruk, pp. 157–77. Zuitphen, De Walburg Pers.

Tendencies to monopoly in the cinematograph film industry: Report of a committee appointed by the Cinematograph Films Council; chairman: Albert Palache. 1944. London, HMSO.

Thompson, Kristin. 1985. *Exporting entertainment*. London, British Film Institute.

Thorne, Christopher. 1978. *Allies of a kind: The United States, Britain and the war against Japan, 1941–1945*. Oxford, Oxford University Press.

Thorpe, Frances, and Nicholas Pronay. 1980. *British official films in the Second World War*. Oxford, Clio.

Tunstall, Jeremy. 1977. *The media are American*. London, Constable.

Vaughn, Stephen. 1990. Morality and entertainment: The origins of the motion picture production code. *Journal of American History* 77:39–65.

Walker, Alexander. 1979. *The shattered silents*. New York, Morrow.

Waterman, David. 1978. *Economic essays on the theatrical motion picture industry*. Studies in Industry Economics, No. 101, Department of Economics, Stanford University.

Watt, D. C. 1965. *Personalities and policies*. Notre Dame, University of Notre Dame Press.

—. 1984a. Britain, the United States and the opening of the Cold War. In *The foreign policy of the British Labour governments, 1945–1951*, ed. Ritchie Ovendale, pp. 43–60. Leicester, Leicester University Press.

—. 1984b. *Succeeding John Bull: America in Britain's place, 1900–1975*. Cambridge, Cambridge University Press.

Weinstein, James. 1968. *The corporate ideal in the liberal state, 1900–1918*. Boston, Beacon.

White Report. 1931. See Canada, Ministry of Labour, and Combines Investigation Branch.

Wiebe, Robert H. 1967. *The search for order, 1877–1920*. New York, Hill & Wang.

Wilson, Harold. 1948. *A policy for British films*. London, Association of Cine-Technicians.

Wilson, Joan Hoff. 1975. *Herbert Hoover: Forgotten progressive*. Boston, Little, Brown.

Winkler, Alan M. 1978. *The politics of propaganda: The OWI, 1942–1945*. New Haven, Yale University Press.

Wood, Alan. 1952. *Mr. Rank: A study of J. Arthur Rank and British films*. London, Hodder & Stoughton.

Zierold, Norman. 1969. *The moguls*. New York, Coward-McCann.

Filmography

African Queen, The, dir. John Huston, prod. Sam Spiegel (Horizon Romulus / United Artists, GB, 1951)

All Quiet on the Western Front, dir. Lewis Milestone, prod. Carl Laemmle, Jr. (Universal, USA, 1931)

Anna Karenina, dir. Julien Duvivier, prod. Alexander Korda (London Films, GB, 1947)

Bank Holiday (U.S. title: *Three on a Weekend*), dir. Carol Reed, prod. Edward Black (Gainsborough, GB, 1938)

Beachcomber, The (U.K. title: *Vessel of Wrath*), dir. & prod. Erich Pommer (Mayflower, GB, 1938)

Bedelia, dir. Lance Comfort, prod. Isadore Goldsmith (John Corfield, GB, 1946)

Birth of a Nation, dir. D. W. Griffith, & prod. D. W. Griffith & Harry E. Aitken (Epoch, USA, 1915)

Black Rose, The, dir. Henry Hathaway, prod. Louis D. Lighton (20th C.–Fox, USA, 1950)

Blue Lamp, The, dir. Basil Dearden, prod. Michael Relph (Ealing, GB, 1949)

Bonnie Prince Charlie, dir. Anthony Kimmins, prod. Edward Black (London Films / British Lion, GB, 1948)

Brighton Rock, dir. John Boulting, prod. Roy Boutling & John Boulting (The Boultings / Associated British, GB, 1947)

Cabinet of Dr. Caligari, The, dir. Robert Wiene, prod. Erich Pommer (Decla-Bioscop, Germany, 1919)

Caesar and Cleopatra, dir. & prod. Gabriel Pascal (Rank, GB, 1945)

Canadian, The, dir. William Beaudine, prod. Adolph Zukor and Jesse L. Lasky, Jr. (Famous Players–Lasky, USA, 1926)

Capt. Horatio Hornblower RN, dir. & prod. Raoul Walsh (Warner Bros., GB, 1951)

Casablanca, dir. Michael Curtiz, prod. Hal B. Wallis (Warner Bros., USA, 1942)

Catherine the Great, dir. Paul Czinner, prod. Alexander Korda (London Films, GB, 1934)

Cavalcade, dir. Frank Lloyd, prod. Winfield Sheehan (20th C.–Fox, USA, 1932)

Champagne, dir. Alfred Hitchcock (British International Pictures, GB, 1928)

Chinese Bungalow, The, dir. & prod. George King (British Lion, GB, 1949)

Christopher Columbus, dir. David MacDonald, prod. Sidney Box (Gainsborough / Rank, GB, 1949)

Citadel, The, dir. King Vidor, prod. Victor Saville (MGM, GB, 1938)

Claudia, dir. Edmund Goulding, prod. William Perlberg (20th C.–Fox, USA, 1943)

Clive of India, dir. Richard Boleslawski, prod. Darryl F. Zanuck (20th C.–Fox, USA, 1934)

Coney Island, dir. Walter Lang, prod. William Perlberg (20th C.–Fox, USA, 1943)

Conspirator, dir. Victor Saville, prod. Arthur Hornblower, Jr. (MGM, GB, 1949)

Corvette K–225 (U.K. title: *The Nelson Touch*), dir. Richard Rosson, prod. Howard Hawks (Universal, USA, 1943)

Courtneys of Curzon Street, The, (U.S. title: *The Courtney Affair*), dir. & prod. Herbert Wilcox (Herbert Wilcox / British Lion, GB, 1947)

Crimson Pirate, The, dir. Robert Siodmak, prod. Harold Hecht (Warner Bros., USA, 1952)

David Copperfield, dir. George Cukor, prod. David O. Selznick (MGM, USA, 1934)

Dr. Ehrlich's Magic Bullet, dir. William Dieterle, prod. Wolfgang Reinhardt (Warner Bros., USA, 1940)

Don Camillo's Last Round, dir. Carmine Gallone (Rizzoli Films, Italy, 1955)

Dumbo, dir. Ben Sharpsteen, prod. Walt Disney (Disney, USA, 1941)

Elephant Boy, dir. Robert Flaherty & Zoltan Korda, prod. Alexander Korda (London Films, GB, 1937)

Escape, dir. Mervyn Le Roy, prod. Lawrence Weingarten (MGM, USA, 1940)

Fallen Idol, The (U.S. title: *The Lost Illusion*), dir. & prod. Carol Reed (London Films / British Lion, GB, 1948)

Flag Lieutenant, The, dir. Henry Edwards, prod. Herbert Wilcox (British and Dominions, GB, 1933)

49th Parallel, The (U.S. title: *The Invaders*), dir. Michael Powell, prod. John Sutro (Ortus / GFD, GB, 1941)

Four Feathers, The, dir. & prod. Alexander Korda, Irving Asher (London Films, GB, 1939)

Frieda, dir. Basil Dearden, prod. Michael Relph (Ealing, GB, 1947)

Gold Diggers of 1933, dir. Mervyn Le Roy, prod. Robert Lord (Warner Bros., USA, 1933)

Gone with the Wind, dir. Victor Fleming (+ George Cukor, Sam Wood), prod. David O. Selznick (MGM, USA, 1939)

Goodbye Mr. Chips, dir. Sam Wood, prod. Michael Balcon (MGM, GB, 1939)

Guinea Pig, The (U.S. title: *The Outsider*), dir. Roy Boulting, prod. John Boulting & Roy Boulting (Pilgrim, GB, 1948)

Happy Go Lovely, dir. H. Bruce Humberstone, prod. Marcel Hellman (Associated British, GB, 1951)

Hasty Heart, The, dir. & prod. Vincent Sherman (Associated British, GB [Warner Bros. in North America], 1949)

Hearts in Exile, dir. James Young (World Film Productions, USA, 1915)

Heaven Can Wait, dir. & prod. Ernst Lubitsch (20th C.–Fox, USA, 1943)

Hello Frisco, Hello, dir. H. Bruce Humberstone, prod. Milton Sperling (20th C.–Fox, USA, 1943)

Henry V, dir. Laurence Olivier, prod. Laurence Olivier & Dallas Bower (Two Cities / Eagle–Lion, GB, 1945)

Hercules Unchained, dir. Pietro Francisi, prod. Bruno Vailati (Lux / Galatea, Italy, 1959)

Here Comes Mr. Jordan, dir. Alexander Hall, prod. Everett Riskin (Columbia, USA, 1941)

Hindle Wakes, dir. & prod. Maurice Elvey (Gaumont–British, GB, 1927)

Hitler's Children, dir. Edward Dmytryk, prod. Edward A. Golden (RKO, USA, 1943)

Hue and Cry, dir. Charles Crichton, prod. Henry Cornelius (Ealing, GB, 1946)

Ideal Husband, An, dir. & prod. Alexander Korda (London Films / British Lion, 1947)

I Married a Witch, dir. & prod. René Clair (United Artists, USA, 1942)

India Speaks, prod. Walter Futter (Walter Futter / RKO, USA, 1933)

Intolerance, dir. & prod. D. W. Griffith (Wark Productions, USA, 1916)

In Which We Serve, dir. Noël Coward & David Lean, prod. Noël Coward (Two Cities / Rank, GB, 1942)

Iron Curtain, The, dir. William Wellman, prod. Sol C. Siegel (20th C.–Fox, USA, 1948)

I See a Dark Stranger (U.S. title: *The Adventuress*), dir. & prod. Frank Launder & Sidney Gilliat (Individual / GFD, GB, 1945)

It Always Rains on Sunday, dir. Robert Hamer, prod. Henry Cornelius (Ealing, GB, 1947)

Ivanhoe, dir. Richard Thorpe, prod. Pandro S. Berman (MGM, GB, 1952)

Kind Hearts and Coronets, dir. Robert Hamer, prod. Michael Relph (Ealing, GB, 1949)

King Solomon's Mines, dir. Compton Bennett & Andrew Marton, prod. Sam Zimbalist (MGM, USA, 1950)

Lady Vanishes, The, dir. Alfred Hitchcock, prod. Edward Black (Gainsborough / Gaumont–British, GB, 1938)

Lassie Come Home, dir. Fred M. Wilcox, prod. Samuel Marx (MGM, USA, 1943)

Life and Death of Colonel Blimp, The (U.S. title: *Colonel Blimp*), dir. & prod. Michael Powell & Emeric Pressburger (Archers / GFD, GB, 1943)

Little World of Don Camillo, The, dir. Julien Duvivier, prod. Giuseppe Amato (Rizzoli–Amato–Francinex, France–Italy, 1952)

Lives of a Bengal Lancer, The, dir. Henry Hathaway, prod. Louis D. Lighton (Paramount, USA, 1934)

Lodger, The, dir. Alfred Hitchcock, prod. Michael Balcon (Gainsborough, GB, 1926)

London Town (U.S. title: *My Heart Goes Crazy*), dir. & prod. Wesley Ruggles (Eagle–Lion / GFD, GB, 1946)

Madame Curie, dir. Mervyn Le Roy, prod. Sidney Franklin (MGM, USA, 1944)

Mademoiselle from Armentières, dir. Maurice Elvey (Gaumont, GB, 1926)

Man to Remember, A, dir. Garson Kanin, prod. Robert Riskin (RKO, USA, 1938)

Master of Ballantrae, The, dir. William Keighley (Warner Bros., GB, 1953)

Matter of Life and Death, A (U.S. title: *Stairway to Heaven*), dir. & prod. Michael Powell & Emeric Pressburger (Archers / GFD, GB, 1946)

Miniver Story, The, dir. H. C. Potter, prod. Sidney Franklin (MGM, GB, 1950)

Mission to Moscow, dir. Michael Curtiz, prod. Robert Buckner (Warner Bros., USA, 1943)

Mogambo, dir. John Ford, prod. Sam Zimbalist (MGM, GB, 1953)

Mons, prod. Walter Summers (British Instructional Films, GB, 1926)

Mortal Storm, The, dir. Frank Borzage, prod. Sidney Franklin (MGM, USA, 1940)

Moscow Nights (U.S. title: *I Stand Condemned*), dir. Anthony Asquith, prod. Alexander Korda (London Films, GB, 1935)

Moss Rose, dir. Gregory Ratoff, prod. Gene Markey (20th C.–Fox, USA, 1947)

Moulin Rouge, dir. John Huston, prod. Jack Clayton (Romulus / United Artists, GB, 1952)

My Friend Flicka, dir. Harold Schuster, prod. Ralph Dietrich (20th C.–Fox, USA, 1943)

Nazi Agent, dir. Jules Dassin, prod. Irving Asher (MGM, USA, 1942)

No Highway (U.S. title: *No Highway in the Sky*), dir. Henry Koster, prod. Louis D. Lighton (20th C.–Fox, GB, 1951)

No Time for Love, dir. & prod. Mitchell Leisen (Paramount, USA, 1943)

Odd Man Out (U.S. title: *Gang War*), dir. & prod. Carol Reed (Two Cities / GFD, GB, 1946)

Overlanders, The, dir. Harry Watt, prod. Ralph Short (Ealing, Australia, 1946)

Palaver, dir. Geoffrey Barkas (British Instructional Films, GB, 1926)

Passport to Pimlico, dir. Henry Cornelius, prod. E. V. H. Emmett (Ealing, GB, 1949)

Peter Pan, dir. Herbert Brenon, prod. Herbert Brenon, Adolph Zukor, & Jesse Lasky, Jr. (Famous Players–Lasky, USA, 1925)

Private Angelo, dir. & prod. Peter Ustinov (Pilgrim, GB, 1949)

Private Life of Don Juan, The, dir. & prod. Alexander Korda (London Films, GB, 1934)

Private Life of Henry VIII, The, dir. & prod. Alexander Korda (London Films, GB, 1933)

Pygmalion, dir. Leslie Howard & Anthony Asquith, prod. Gabriel Pascal (Pascal Film Productions, GB, 1938)

Queen of Spades, dir. Thorold Dickinson, prod. Anatole de Grunewald (World Screen Plays / Associated British, GB, 1948)

Quiet Man, The, dir. John Ford, prod. John Ford & Merian C. Cooper (Argosy / Republic, USA, 1952)

Quiet Wedding, dir. Anthony Asquith, prod. Paul Soskin (Paramount, GB, 1940)

Quo Vadis, dir. Mervyn Le Roy, prod. Sam Zimbalist (MGM, USA, 1951)

Rake's Progress, The (U.S. title: *The Notorious Gentleman*), dir. & prod. Frank Launder & Sidney Gilliat (Individual / GFD, GB, 1945)

Random Harvest, dir. Mervyn Le Roy, prod. Sidney Franklin (MGM, USA, 1942)

Return of Don Camillo, The, dir. Julien Duvivier (Rizzoli–Francinex, France–Italy, 1953)

River, The, dir. Jean Renoir, prod. Kenneth McEldowney, Kalyan Gupta, & Jean Renoir (Oriental International Film / United Artists, India, 1951)

Rob Roy, the Highland Rogue, dir. Harold French, prod. Perce Pearce (Disney / RKO, GB, 1953)

Rome Express, dir. Walter Forde, prod. Michael Balcon (Gaumont, GB, 1932)

Rough Shoot (U.S. title: *Shoot First*), dir. Robert Parrish, prod. Raymond Stross (Stross / United Artists, GB, 1952)

San Demetrio London, dir. Charles Frend, prod. Robert Hamer (Ealing, GB, 1943)

Sanders of the River, dir. Zoltan Korda, prod. Alexander Korda (London Films, GB, 1935)

Saraband for Dead Lovers, dir. Basil Dearden, prod. Michael Relph (Ealing, GB, 1948)

Scarlet Pimpernel, The, dir. Harold Young, prod. Alexander Korda (London Films, GB, 1934)

Scott of the Antarctic, dir. Charles Frend, prod. Sidney Cole (Ealing, GB, 1948)

Second to None, dir. Jack Raymond (Britannia, GB, 1926)

Small Back Room, The (U.S. title: *Hour of Glory*), dir. & prod. Michael Powell & Emeric Pressburger (Archers–London Films, GB, 1949)

Snow White and the Seven Dwarfs, dir. Walt Disney & David Hand, prod. Walt Disney (Disney / RKO, USA, 1937)

Spring in Park Lane, dir. & prod. Herbert Wilcox (Herbert Wilcox / British Lion, GB, 1948)

Stagecoach, dir. John Ford, prod. Walter Wanger & John Ford (Walter Wanger Productions / United Artists, USA, 1939)

Stage Door Canteen, dir. Frank Borzage, prod. Barnett Brisken (Sol Lesser, USA, 1943)

Stage Fright, dir. & prod. Alfred Hitchcock (Warner Bros.–Associated British, GB, 1950)

Standing Room Only, dir. Sidney Lanfield, prod. Paul Jones (Paramount, USA, 1944)

Story of Robin Hood and His Merrie Men, The, dir. Ken Annakin, prod. Perce Pearce (Disney / RKO, GB, 1952)

Sweet Rosie O'Grady, dir. Irving Cummings, prod. William Perlberg (20th C.–Fox, USA, 1943)

Sword and the Rose, The, dir. Ken Annakin, prod. Perce Pearce (Disney / RKO, GB, 1952)

Tawny Pipit, dir. & prod. Bernard Miles (Two Cities / GFD, GB, 1944)

Third Man The, dir. Carol Reed, prod. David O. Selznick & Hugh Perceval (Selznick International / British Lion, GB, 1949)

This Is the Army, dir. Michael Curtiz, prod. Jack L. Warner & Hal B. Wallis (Warner Bros., USA, 1943)

Thousands Cheer, dir. George Sidney, prod. Joe Pasternak (MGM, USA, 1943)

Time Bomb (U.S. title: *Terror on a Train*), dir. Ted Tetzlaff, prod. Richard Goldstone (MGM, GB, 1952)

Treasure Island, dir. Byron Haskin, prod. Perce Pearce (Disney / RKO, GB, 1950)

Triumph of the Rat, The, dir. Graham Cutts, prod. Michael Balcon & Carlyle Blackwell (Gainsborough, GB, 1926)

Under Capricorn, dir. Alfred Hitchcock, prod. Alfred Hitchcock & Sidney Bernstein (Transatlantic, GB, 1949)

Uninvited, The, dir. Lewis Allen, prod. Charles Brackett (Paramount, USA, 1944)

Waterloo Bridge, dir. Mervyn Le Roy, prod. Sidney Franklin (MGM, USA, 1940)

Whisky Galore (U.S. title: *Tight Little Island*), dir. Alexander Mackendrick, prod. Monja Danischewsky (Ealing, GB, 1948)

Wings of the Morning, dir. Harold D. Schuster, prod. Robert T. Kane (20th C.–Fox, GB, 1937)

Winslow Boy, The, dir. Anthony Asquith, prod. Anatole de Grunewald (London Films / British Lion, GB, 1948)

Woman to Woman, dir. Graham Cutts, prod. Michael Balcon (Balcon–Saville–Freeman, GB, 1923)

Yank at Oxford, A, dir. Jack Conway, prod. Michael Balcon (MGM, GB, 1938)

Yankee Doodle Dandy, dir. Michael Curtiz, prod. Hal B. Wallis & William Cagney (Warner Bros., USA, 1942)

Index of names

f = the individual appears in a photograph
n = the reference is in a note
q = the source is quoted

Index of subjects

n = the reference is in a note
q = the source is quoted
t = a term is defined